PERU

RYAN DUBÉ

PERU

PACIFIC OCEAN

PERU

CHILE

BOLIVIA

Lake Titicaca

0   100 km
0   100 mi

Casma
Huaraz
Paramonga
Barranca
Huacho
RN Lachay
Sayán
Huaral
Callao
LIMA
MARCAHUASI
PACHACAMAC
INCAWASI
Chincha
Pisco
Reserva Nacional Paracas
Ica
TAMBO COLORADO
HUAYTARA
Nasca
San Juan
Chala
Punta de Lobos
Camaná
Mollendo
Ilo
Moquegua
Tacna
Arequipa
RN Salinas y Aguada Blanca
Desaguadero
Puno
Huancané
Juliaca
Santa Lucía
PUCARA
Ayaviri
Sicuani
RAQCHI
TIPON
CUSCO
Pisac
OLLANTAYTAMBO
MACHU PICCHU
ESPIRITU PAMPA
CHOQUEQUIRAO
Abancay
Quillabamba
Koshireni
Santa Rosa
Ayacucho
Huancayo
Tarma
La Merced
Satipo
Atalaya
Cerro de Pasco
Pozuzo
Huánuco
Huaraz
CHAVIN DE HUANTAR
Reserva Nacional de Junín
Lago de Junín
Parque Nacional de Yanachaga
Puerto Inca
Parque Nacional Otishi
Parque Nacional Alto Purús
Parque Nacional Manu
Boca Manu
Río Alto Madre de Dios
Parque Nacional Tambopata
RN Nacional Bahuaja Sonene
Puerto Maldonado
Iñapari
Assis Brasil
Macusani
Cotahuasi
Reserva Paisajística Sub Cuenca del Cotahuasi
Suyctambo
Santo Tomás
Alca
Chivay
Reserva Nacional Pampa Galeras
Aplao
Chuquibamba
TORO MUERTO
Tambillo
Cotahuasi
Huancayo

Contents

The Spaniards' first assumptions about Peru, when they sailed down its coast in 1528, involved barren beaches and savage cannibals. It was not until they journeyed through deserts and river valleys, up and over snowy passes, and into the altiplano, or high plains, that they realized the importance of the Inca. This empire, the New World's most advanced, had temples and highways rivaling those of Renaissance Europe along with an abundance of what the Spaniards most wanted: gold. In Cusco, the Inca capital, the Spaniards found four-inch-thick temple walls, shields, vases, and even hand plows—all made of gold.

Today, Cusco remains the primary draw for travelers to Peru. People come to wander the cobblestone streets, marvel at the Spanish churches built atop massive Inca walls, eat alpaca steaks and sweet corn, and party until dawn at the city's nightclubs. In the nearby cloud forest, reachable only by train or trek, is one of the world's greatest wonders: Machu Picchu, a city of stone carved into a towering rainforest ridge.

Yet Cusco and Machu Picchu are just the beginning of what Peru offers. There are at least a dozen archaeological sites around Peru that rival the historical

Clockwise from top left: Catedral de Lima on Plaza Mayor; hammock on a balcony in the Amazon rainforest near Iquitos; macaw; sand dunes near Lago Huacachina; climbing Huayna Picchu; dancers on Lake Titicaca's Isla Taquile.

significance of Machu Picchu. The ancient and enigmatic Nasca Lines are etched into the desert. There are perfect breaks to surf along the northern coast; snow-covered mountains to climb; freeze-dried-potato soup to eat in stone huts with Quechua families; and miles of Amazon River to float with nothing more than a hammock and a bunch of bananas.

But perhaps the most impressive experience in Peru is meeting its people, who continue to maintain the depth of their culture and unique identity today.

Clockwise from top left: llama at Machu Picchu; Larcomar shopping mall in Lima; textiles for sale in southern Peru; purple corn and limes, used to make a drink called *chicha morada*.

10 TOP EXPERIENCES

1 **Machu Picchu:** The fabled lost city is the Inca's most famous achievement (page 110).

2 **Cusco:** Inca and Spanish colonial culture clash in this fascinating city (page 138).

3 **Inca Ruins in the Sacred Valley:** The temples, fortresses, and terracing of Pisac (page 85) and Ollantaytambo (pictured, page 102) are second only to Machu Picchu in terms of beauty.

4 **Indigenous Culture:** Immerse yourself in vibrant local culture. Take in a folklore festival and stay with a family at Lake Titicaca (pictured, pages 223 and 232) or meet artisans in the Mantaro Valley (page 348) and Ayacucho (page 359).

5 Trekking in the Andes:

Spectacular treks abound in Peru. Make a pilgrimage to Machu Picchu on the Inca Trail (pictured, pages 22 and 115) or explore the snowcapped Cordillera Blanca (page 385).

>>>

6 Wildlife: Marvel

at Peru's rich biodiversity, from giant otters and pink river dolphins in the Amazon (page 249) to Humboldt penguins and sea lions along the Paracas coastline (pictured, page 309).

<<<

7 Rainforest Eco-Lodges: Spend

a few unforgettable days at one of the myriad eco-lodges deep inside the Amazon rainforest (pages 253 and 258).

>>>

8 Lake Titicaca: The beauty of the sapphire lake (page 232) is breathtaking. There's no better way to see it than by sea kayak (page 225).

<<<

9 Peruvian Cuisine: Lima has emerged as Latin America's culinary hub, showcasing dishes with an extraordinary range of flavors and ingredients (page 62).

>>>

10 Nasca Lines: There are certain mysteries, like huge "astronauts" and hummingbirds etched onto the desert plain, that remain beyond belief (page 326).

<<<

Planning Your Trip

Where to Go

Lima

Traditionally avoided by travelers because of its gray weather and grimy downtown, Lima is making a roaring comeback. On the **Plaza Mayor,** upscale restaurants and cafés now neighbor the country's most important colonial *catedral* and the presidential and archbishop's palaces. The outlying districts of **San Isidro** and **Miraflores** offer the greatest range of lodging, bars, and Peruvian cuisine. Bohemian **Barranco** is the nightlife district and favored backpackers' den.

The Sacred Valley

Begin your trip to the Cusco area with the Sacred Valley, which the Inca considered paradise for its fertile earth. Up and down the valley, the Inca built a string of their most sacred sites, including temples and fortresses in **Pisac** and **Ollantaytambo.** This charming valley is a destination in its own right with a great range of lodging and restaurants, day hikes, horseback rides, mountain biking, and more.

Machu Picchu

The Sacred Valley is cut by the **Río Urubamba,** which rushes toward the most famous achievement of the Inca: Machu Picchu. The fabled lost city is a breathtaking citadel arranged along a rainforest-covered ridge. Hiking either the **Salcantay route** or the **Inca Trail,** a paved stone highway that culminates in a bird's-eye view of the ruins, is a memorable way to arrive. The train ride in and out also affords incredible views of the area's scenery.

Cusco

After visiting the Sacred Valley and Machu Picchu, travelers are acclimatized to Cusco's high altitude. They are also primed for Cusco's complex culture, which remains today an antagonistic mixture of Inca and Spanish cultures. The Spanish erected more than a dozen **baroque churches** atop flawless Inca walls. Cusco must-visits are the artisan barrio of **San Blas,** the fortress of **Sacsayhuamán,** and the Inca sun temple **Coricancha.**

Lake Titicaca and Canyon Country

The highlight of a visit to **Lake Titicaca,** the world's highest navigable lake, is an overnight with a family on islands where villagers cultivate potatoes and quinoa on rock terraces. **Arequipa,** near Peru's southern coast, is a sophisticated colonial city known for its European feel, world-renowned cuisine, and 16th-century convents and churches built of *sillar,* a sparkling white volcanic stone. Stone villages dot the rim of nearby **Colca Canyon,** where **Cruz del Cóndor** guarantees spotting the world's largest flying bird.

The Amazon

If you fly above the Amazon, you will see clouds and an endless emerald blanket of vegetation, interrupted only by the muddy squiggles of

If You Have . . .

- **ONE WEEK:** Visit the Sacred Valley, Cusco, and Machu Picchu.

- **TWO WEEKS:** Visit all of the above but extend your time in the Sacred Valley to hike, mountain bike, and go horseback riding. Add a hike along the Inca Trail or the Salcantay trek to Machu Picchu, or experience the Amazon around Puerto Maldonado or the Manu Biosphere Reserve.

- **THREE WEEKS:** Add an overland adventure from the Moche, Sicán, and Sipán archaeological monuments of Peru's northern coast up into the Chachapoya cloud forest. This remote corner of Peru is rich in exotic birds, lost cities such as Kuélap, and off-the-beaten-path treks.

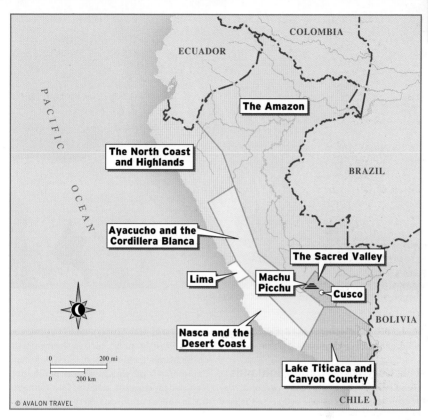

rainforest rivers. Here travel is by motorized dugout canoe, which is one of the best ways to see toucans, tanagers, and other rainforest birds. Near **Iquitos** it is common to see pink river dolphins and lily pads the size of dinner tables. Around **Puerto Maldonado** or **Parque Nacional Manu,** you have a good chance of seeing giant otters and other Amazon megafauna.

Nasca and the Desert Coast

Dug into the landscape 1,000 years ago and preserved by the arid climate, the unexplained **Nasca Lines** form hummingbirds, whales, and trapezoids. Nearby is the **Ica desert,** an unexplored area of sand dunes and an astounding variety of marine fossils. On the way to Lima, stop at the **Reserva Nacional de Paracas,** a coastal reserve for sea lions, 200 bird species, and the endangered Humboldt penguin. Farther on is **Chincha,** the center of Afro-Peruvian culture.

Ayacucho and the Cordillera Blanca

Nowhere is Peru's colonial past more palpable than **Ayacucho.** The most stunning city of Peru's Andes, Ayacucho has a gorgeous *cathedral* and two dozen other colonial churches and is surrounded by ruins from the pre-Inca Huari culture. Farther north trekkers who make it over Punta Unión, a pass at 4,750 meters in the **Cordillera Blanca,** rub their eyes in disbelief when they first see **Alpamayo.** It is but one of dozens of majestic snow giants that spring from Peru's high grasslands to form a spectacular

the postcard-perfect peak of Alpamayo in the Cordillera Blanca

tumble of broken glaciers, jagged peaks, and emerald lakes such as **Lagunas Llanganuco.**

The North Coast and Highlands

Huaca de la Luna, an adobe pyramid, was built by the ancient Moche people and is now surrounded by the colonial city of **Trujillo.** The cultures that succeeded the Moche left a string of impressive cities on the north coast, including **Chan Chan,** near Trujillo, and **Túcume** and **Batán Grande,** near Chiclayo. In the northern highlands, the gorgeous countryside around **Cajamarca** is rife with Inca paths, or **Qhapaq Ñan,** and the enigmatic canals of **Cumbemayo.** Up in the cloud forests farther inland, the **Chachapoya** people built a series of stone cities. The crowning achievement was **Kuélap,** a fortress perched on a limestone cliff.

When to Go

High season for visiting Peru is in the South American winter, **June-August,** when dry sunny weather opens up over the mountains and the Amazon. Prices for lodging tend to go up during these months, and hot spots like Machu Picchu can be crowded. Especially crowded times are **Inti Raymi,** the June 24 sun festival in Cusco, and **Fiestas Patrias,** the national Peruvian holiday at the end of July.

The bulk of the **rainy season** is **December-April,** when trekking and other outdoor activities are hampered by muddy paths and soggy skies. To avoid crowds, we heartily recommend squeezing your trip in between the rainy season and the high tourist months. **April-May** and **September-November** are **excellent times** to visit Peru. The weather is usually fine and prices for lodging tend to be lower.

There are some dry spots in the country, however, even during the wettest months, which make for **year-round options.** Peru's largest rainforest city, **Iquitos,** is far enough down the Amazon basin to have a less-pronounced wet season. Clouds move in most afternoons throughout the year, drop a load of water, and then shuffle away again to reveal sun. Peru's **desert coast** can also be visited year-round because hardly any rain falls here. Ironically, the sunniest months on the coast, December-March, are the wettest in the highlands. The weather is especially bright and sunny on Peru's extreme north coast, where surfers congregate for the white-sand beaches and huge seasonal breaks.

Before You Go

Vaccinations

Most travelers to Peru do get the vaccinations recommended by the U.S. Centers for Disease Control and Prevention (www.cdc.gov), which include **hepatitis A** and **B** and **typhoid** for the Andean areas, and **yellow fever** and **malaria** for certain rainforest areas.

Passports and Visas

Citizens of the United States, Canada, United Kingdom, South Africa, New Zealand, and Australia and residents of any other European or Latin American country do not require visas to enter Peru as tourists at the present time. Visitors entering the country can get anything from 30 to 180 days stamped into both a **passport** and an **embarkation card** that travelers must keep until they exit the country. If you require more than 30 days, be ready to support your argument by explaining your travel plans and showing your return ticket. **Extensions** can be arranged at Peru's immigration offices in Lima, Arequipa, Cusco, Iquitos, Puno, and Trujillo for US$21.

Transportation

Most travelers arrive in Peru by **plane,** and all international flights to Peru arrive in **Lima.** Travel to Cusco or the rainforest is an additional plane ride. Because of flight schedules, most travelers end up spending a night or a day in Lima either coming or going. We recommend travelers spend at least a day in Lima, preferably on the way home, to take in this amazing city. Peru's new intercity **buses,** with luxurious onboard service, are a great option for domestic travel.

The Best of Peru

This 14-day tour is the classic backpacker route that includes many of Peru's top attractions. The trip involves a journey through a nature reserve and sand dunes on the country's desert coast, a visit to the islands of Lake Titicaca, a hike through Cusco and Machu Picchu, and a dab of Lima's colonial center. While it is a good example of what Peru has to offer, it still leaves out a lot.

If you have extra time, add on a weeklong trip in the north, which has fascinating pre-Inca ruins, excellent hiking, and sandy beaches. Or spend a few more days in the Peruvian Amazon, which is teeming with wildlife and is home to unique indigenous cultures. Getting around is accomplished via a straightforward combination of planes, trains, buses, and *combis*.

Day 1

From **Lima** take a bus to **Pisco** (3 hours) and a short *combi* ride to the beach town of **Paracas,** where you can enjoy the sunset over the Pacific.

Day 2

Explore **Reserva Nacional de Paracas** and the **Islas Ballestas.** Watch sea lions and endangered Humboldt penguins and picnic on a wilderness beach. In the evening, take a bus to Ica (1 hour) and then a short taxi ride to **Lago Huacachina,** where you'll spend one night.

Day 3

Sandboard on the dunes above Lago Huacachina and then tour a **pisco bodega.** After a late lunch, take a bus to **Nasca** (2 hours).

Day 4

Enjoy a morning overflight of the **Nasca Lines.** Afterward, take the bus to **Arequipa** (6.5 hours), where you'll check in for a two-night stay.

Day 5

Tour sophisticated Arequipa, a sparkling white city best known for the 17th-century **Monasterio de Santa Catalina.**

Reserva Nacional de Paracas

Community Tourism

Community tourism, where travelers go beyond mere sightseeing and engage with local communities in a meaningful way, is a fast-growing global movement with many forms in Peru. The best community tourism operators have built long-term relationships that benefit communities in concrete ways, such as improving the quality of local schools or health clinics. Here are some great opportunities for homestays, volunteering, and cultural immersion in Peru, broken down by region.

CUSCO AND THE SACRED VALLEY

Peru's most reputable trekking agencies have forged long-term bonds with Andean communities and offer cultural treks and other well-designed, off-the-beaten-path experiences. These agencies include **Peruvian Andean Treks** (www.andeantreks.com) and **ExplorAndes** (www.explorandes.com). In Ollantaytambo, an NGO we recommend is **Awamaki** (www.awamaki.org), which helps weavers in the highlands community of Patacancha recover ancient weaving techniques and bring their weavings to overseas markets. Awamaki can set up a range of volunteer placements and homestays in both Ollantaytambo and Patacancha.

trekking in the Andes

THE AMAZON

There are many community travel opportunities in Puerto Maldonado and Manu, where most agencies and lodges have built relationships with local communities. In Puerto Maldonado, **Rainforest Expeditions** operates the gorgeous **Posada Amazonas** lodge in conjunction with the mestizo Ese Eja community of Infierno. The award-winning lodge is designed to offer guests an intimate experience with Ese Eja culture.

HUARAZ AND THE CORDILLERA BLANCA

We highly recommend **Responsible Travel Peru** (www.responsibletravelperu.com), which can arrange homestays and work experiences in Vicos and other communities around Huaraz. Another option in Huaraz is **Andean Alliance** (www.thelazydoginn.com), a nonprofit run by the Canadian owners of the Lazy Dog Inn. They can match your skills with local work projects and also set up homestays.

Day 6

Take a flight or bus trip from Arequipa to **Puno** (7 hours by bus).

Day 7

Explore **Lake Titicaca** with a day tour of **Islas Amantaní** and **Islas Uros.** Return to Puno for the night, or consider a stay with a family on Islas Amantaní.

Day 8

Continue onward to **Cusco.** From Puno you can fly, take a direct nonstop train, or ride a tour bus that allows you to see the ruins along the way (9 hours). Upon arrival, grab a 1.5-hour taxi or *combi* ride from Cusco to **Ollantaytambo,** a living Inca village in the heart of Peru's **Sacred Valley.**

Days 9-10

Recharge in the lush surroundings of the Sacred Valley. Options include touring Ollantaytambo's old Inca city and the **Temple of the Sun,** rafting the **Río Urubamba,** and going horseback riding or day hiking on one of the area's many **Inca trails.** On the second day, walk or mountain bike from the Inca ruins of **Moray** down a steep valley past the **Salineras,** or salt mines, and back to Ollantaytambo.

Day 11

Take an early morning train to **Machu Picchu** from the Sacred Valley. Spend a full day at Machu Picchu, then hop on the afternoon train-and-bus combination back to Cusco.

Days 12-13

Tour the Cusco area, where you will have two days to appreciate the churches, the artisanal neighborhood of **San Blas,** and the fortress of **Sacsayhuamán.**

Day 14

From Cusco, catch a morning flight to **Lima**'s airport, where you can leave your bags, and then take a quick look at the city center and enjoy a gourmet dinner in **Miraflores.** Then hop a red-eye for home.

Trekking to Machu Picchu

Most travelers to Peru think there is just one option for trekking to Machu Picchu—the four-day Inca Trail hike—but now there are at least four ways to hike to the Inca citadel. The following treks are the best ways to make a pilgrimage to the lost city of the Inca.

When to Go

The traditional **trekking season** in Peru is **May-August,** but the **best weather** is **June** and **July.** Avoid the last week in July, when Peru's hotels are often booked solid for the Fiestas Patrias (Independence Day) celebration around July 28. On the Inca Trail, you will encounter fewer people during the months of April, May, September, and October. These **"shoulder months"** are the **best times to trek** in Peru, as they are outside both the **rainiest months (November-March)** and the busiest tourist months (June-August). April and May, and even March if you don't mind an occasional rainstorm, are especially scenic because the rainy season has just ended and the highlands are lush and green.

Acclimatization

Plan for at least **3-4 days** to acclimatize before heading out on a trek anywhere in Andean Peru. The Inca Trail has two passes of approximately 4,000 meters, and you will tackle these far better if you are physically ready to do so.

Acclimatize by **sleeping low** and **hiking high.** A great way to acclimatize in the Cusco area is to spend your first few days in the Sacred Valley and then hike up out of the valley floor from places like Pisac, Urubamba, and Ollantaytambo.

Inca Trail

Peru is one of the world's top trekking destinations, and the Inca Trail is Peru's number one trek. Beginning in the high Andes with views of sparkling glaciers, the Inca Trail passes a dozen major Inca ruins before plunging into the cloud forest toward Machu Picchu.

PLANNING FOR THE INCA TRAIL

The Inca Trail is the only trek in Peru where all trekkers must hike with a **licensed guide** and where there is a **limit of 500 people per day.** These rules are a result of the Inca Trail's popularity and the impact that tens of thousands of trekkers have had on its stone trail and the surrounding ecosystem. For the Inca Trail, your only option is to sign up with a licensed agency—and **sign up early,** as the Inca Trail fills up **six months or more** ahead of time.

As a result of these new rules, **Inca Trail prices** have increased from as low as US$90 in 2000 to a minimum of US$500 today. Local agencies no longer offer last-minute Inca Trail trips; bookings are now done almost exclusively online because the trail's licensed operators have to confirm all reservations several months in advance. To check the official departure availability, visit the website www.machupicchu.gob. pe. If a date you want is already booked, it's still worth checking with agencies, as they often have cancellations.

FOUR-DAY INCA TRAIL

This hike, which threads two 4,000-meter passes on the way from the high Andes to the cloud forest, has become a signature experience for arriving at Machu Picchu. The first and third days contain moderate hikes, while the second day is the toughest and the fourth day is a short hike to Machu Picchu followed by the full ruins tour.

TWO-DAY INCA TRAIL

If camping is not for you, or you are short on time, try the abbreviated version of the Inca Trail.

Trekkers start farther down the trail in order to take in the final set of spectacular ruins at Wiñay Wayna and enter Machu Picchu at dawn and through the Sun Gate. You spend your first day hiking the Inca Trail and seeing ruins and your first night sleeping in a hotel in Aguas Calientes, at the base of Machu Picchu. The second day is spent exploring Machu Picchu.

Other Treks
PLANNING FOR OTHER TREKS

Any other trek in Peru, including the Salcantay alternative route to Machu Picchu, has a couple of planning options. The easiest, and most expensive, is to sign up with a reputable **agency** and let it take care of all the details. But you can also custom-design a trip and then hire an agency to take care of logistics such as transport, food, lodging, porters, cooks, and certified guides. If you can find a reliable **trekking or climbing guide,** available for US$80-110 per day, he or she can organize all these details for you for an extra fee. Or you can do it all on your own, which is complicated to negotiate properly but possible if you speak Spanish and are experienced at trekking.

Inca Trail

FIVE-DAY SALCANTAY TREK

While the trek past sacred **Nevado Salcantay,** a 6,000-meter-plus peak, does not contain the stone paths and ruins of the Inca Trail, this five-day trek offers a wilderness experience and spectacular views of the surrounding snow-covered peaks. It's also far less expensive than the Inca Trail, and trekkers are free to travel independently (unlike on the Inca Trail, where all hikers must sign up with a licensed agency). The trek is longer and higher than the Inca Trail, but new sustainable eco-lodges have been built along the Salcantay route to allow trekkers to travel fast and light and stay in relative comfort.

INCA JUNGLE TRAIL

This multi-activity option is a good choice for backpackers on a budget. What it lacks in Inca ruins it makes up for with wonderful cloud forest scenery. The route enters Machu Picchu from the high mountains and cloud forests on its downstream side. Participants are first transported to the Abra Málaga (4,300 meters), a high pass into the rainforest, for a stunning mountain bike descent from the alpine zone to lush cloud forest nearly 3,000 meters below. From here, trekkers camp and then head out the second day on a cloud forest trek to Santa Teresa, a riverside village. On the third day, hikers head up the Río Urubamba to Aguas Calientes.

Trekking Logistics
AGENCIES AND GUIDES

The motto **"you get what you pay for"** is especially true when it comes to hiring a trekking agency or guide. If you skimp on an agency, you can be guaranteed the agency will either skimp on you (poor food, no bathroom tent), the porters (low wages, no health care), or the environment (pit latrines, no regard for Leave No Trace principles). Go with an established, well-recommended agency. See pages 60, 115, 161, 167, and 502 for more information about tour companies.

ON YOUR OWN

Because of the altitude, most groups end up hiring a **porter** (mule driver) who carries loads on donkeys or llamas. It's hard to enjoy the scenery while hiking with a full pack at Peru's altitudes, no matter how fit you are. There are other reasons to hire a porter: It is a great cultural experience, helps the local economy, and makes your trip safer—porters often know the routes as well (or better) than a mountain guide, provide evacuation support, and can serve as camp guards.

Porters will expect you to pay their wages the day that they return to the main town, usually the day after the end of your trek. This means that for a four-day trek, you will pay the porter five days of wages.

Groups usually hire a **cook,** too. Peru's cooks pack in fruit, vegetables, sacks of rice, and often a live chicken or two.

Pay the people you hire fairly and treat them with respect. You are their employer, so you are ultimately responsible for their health and safety. These are some standard **daily wages:** US$10 for a porter and US$8 for every mule, US$15 for camp guardian, US$25 for a porter, and US$25-30 for a cook. Also, you are expected to provide shelter and food for your cook and porters.

If you are on your own, you will have to negotiate the **entry and grazing fees** that Andean communities increasingly charge trekking groups that pass through their lands. The fees change rapidly and, in general, are relatively minor. Grazing fees are generally around US$2-5 per horse. Inquire with an agency about fees ahead of time.

MAPS AND GEAR

The best place to get maps is the **South American Explorers Club** (www.saexplorers.org) in Cusco (Pardo 847, tel. 084/24-5484, www.saexplorers.org) or in the Miraflores neighborhood of Lima (Enrique Palacios 956, tel. 01/444-2150).

Most people who are trekking or climbing on their own bring all their own **gear,** but high-quality equipment can be rented for affordable prices in Cusco and Huaraz. Email agencies ahead of time for reservations and prices.

Best Eco-Lodges

The top tier of Peru's eco-lodges, both in the Andes and the Amazon, have a well-developed philosophy and strategy for caring for the environment and providing an organic, natural experience for guests. These lodges also typically train and hire local people, serve organic food produced by local communities, and provide eco-friendly services such as natural spa treatments and healing ceremonies. Here are some of our favorite eco-lodges in Peru:

- **Los Horcones de Túcume** (page 421) is in the backyard of the 26 massive pyramids of Túcume, one of Peru's most sacred healing centers outside the northern Peruvian city of Chiclayo. This rural lodge, built according to the building techniques of the ancient Moche culture, features rooms made of adobe and algaroba beams, which open up to covered terraces and views of the surrounding fields. The food here is as organic as it gets, and Don Víctor, a reputed shaman in the area, lives nearby the lodge and works with visitors on request.

- **Reserva Amazónica** (page 263) is the brainchild of leading Peruvian eco-pioneers José and Denise Koechlin, who also own the similarly eco-minded and elegant **Inkaterra Machu Picchu Pueblo Hotel** (page 136) at the base of Machu Picchu. Reserva Amazónica offers 41 private wooden bungalows, organic food, canopy walks, visits to local communities supported by the lodge, and its own line of organic shampoo and conditioner. Both lodges have extraordinary on-staff nature guides and other resources to explore and understand the surrounding environment.

- **Tahuayo Lodge** (page 299), a four-hour boat ride from Iquitos, is next door to the world-class Amazon biodiversity of the Tamshiyacu Tahuayo communal reserve. Founded by U.S. naturalist Paul Beaver, Tahuayo Lodge has been featured in *Outside* magazine and other publications for its off-the-beaten-path rainforest adventures. This lodge, with 15 wooden rooms, a hammock hall, and a laboratory-library complex, has access to both dry and flooded forest as well as a zip line that sends guest soaring 35 meters above the rainforest floor.

Peru's tropical sun is intense, so bring strong **sunscreen, a sun hat, sunglasses with UV protection,** and a **long-sleeved shirt.** Most trekkers use **trekking poles** for descending the scree slopes and steep trails. The weather is cold, but extreme storms are rare in the dry months from May to September. Bringing plenty of layers, including waterproof ones, is essential. On most Peru treks, **sleeping bags** rated for -18°C and thermal long underwear or fleece pants are fine.

Pretty much all supplies, with the exception of freeze-dried **food,** are available in markets in Cusco. You'll find pasta, powdered soup, cheese, powdered milk, beef jerky, dried fruit, and more.

White gas (*bencina blanca*) is sold at hardware stores along Calle Plateros in Cusco and at numerous places in Huaraz and Caraz. Get a shop recommendation from an agency or gear store to ensure you find the highest-quality gas, and fire up your **stove** before you go to make sure everything works. Remember that airlines sometimes reject travelers with camp stoves and fuel bottles that have been previously used. It's best to travel with a new stove and bottles, if at all possible.

HAZARDS AND PRECAUTIONS

While the vast majority of trekkers to the Cusco and Huaraz areas never encounter any safety threats, the more popular trekking areas have seen an increase in **theft.** If you leave your camp for a day hike, make sure to leave behind a camp guardian, such as a porter. Minimize the impact by bringing the **minimum of valuables** and only enough **cash** for the duration of your trek.

The main hazards of trekking in Peru, however, are straightforward: **sun, altitude,** and **cold.** If you protect yourself from the sun, acclimatize properly, and have the right gear, you will have a great time.

From the Inca to the Amazon

Because both **Cusco** and **Machu Picchu** are near the **Amazon,** we have designed this trip to encompass all three experiences. This trip, which can be done in less than 10 days, takes you to Peru's most important cultural ruins and allows you to see highlands, cloud forest, and rainforest. We recommend five days on your own to explore Cusco and the Sacred Valley and then a three-day stay in the Amazon rainforest with the lodge of your choice in the Puerto Maldonado area. If you'd like to extend your time in the Amazon, consider a seven-day rainforest tour in Manu.

Depending on your interests or travel dates, you might want to consider modifications to this itinerary. Between October and April, when the rainforest near Puerto Maldonado is rainy and many of its lodges are closed, fly from Lima to **Iquitos** instead and visit the **Reserva Nacional Pacaya Samiria.** Pacaya Samiria, like **Manu Biosphere Reserve,** is a huge tract of virgin rainforest where you have excellent chances of seeing a wide range of wildlife. Rains in the lowland Amazon of northern Peru are spread more evenly throughout the year.

Keep in mind that human development around Iquitos and Puerto Maldonado has had an impact on the rainforest within a one- or two-hour boat ride, and rainforest trips in these regions present less biodiversity than if you travel a bit farther in. An option in the Puerto Maldonado region that offers a chance to see biodiversity similar to that of Manu and Pacaya Samiria is the **Tambopata Research Center,** a seven-hour boat ride from Puerto Maldonado.

Day 1

Arrive in **Lima** and catch an early morning connecting flight to **Cusco.** In Cusco, take a taxi to **Ollantaytambo,** a living Inca village in the **Sacred Valley,** where you can rest and acclimatize.

Days 2-3

Tour the Sacred Valley, with stops at the Ollantaytambo **Temple of the Sun** and the market and ruins of **Pisac.** On day two, explore the village of **Chinchero** before hiking or mountain biking from the enigmatic circular Inca terraces at **Moray** past the crystallized salt mines known as **Salineras** and back to Ollantaytambo.

Day 4

Take the early morning train to **Machu Picchu** and spend the day touring the ruins and birdwatching in the cloud forest. Return on the afternoon train-and-bus combination to **Cusco,** where you will spend two nights.

Day 5

Experience Cusco's unique combination of Inca ruins, colonial architecture and museums, markets, and cafés.

Day 6

In the morning, start a 10-hour bus trip on the Inter-Oceanic highway, leaving behind Cusco and the high Andes as you descend into the Amazon to the town of **Puerto Maldonado.** Or to save time, grab an afternoon flight (30 minutes) to Puerto Maldonado.

Days 7-10

Make reservations with the jungle lodge of your choice and head out on a three- or four-night stay in the heart of the **Amazon rainforest,** where there is a huge range of wildlife, including giant otters, monkeys, and large mammals like tapirs. Hike through the rainforest with a guide, fish for *pirañas*, observe macaws on salt-licks, or explore the rainforest canopy by climbing a lookout tower 30 meters above the forest floor. Part of your last day will include a boat trip back to Puerto Maldonado, where you'll fly back to Lima and catch your return flight home.

market at Pisac in the Sacred Valley

Manu Biosphere Reserve

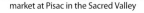

Getting Off the Tourist Track

This odyssey through Peru's **northern highlands** and **Amazon** is for those who want to get off the beaten path to experience an awesome cross-section of Peru's geography.

If you have a few extra days, there are several exciting side trips you could tack on to the base trip to fill out your travels. Consider starting in either **Trujillo** or **Chiclayo.** These cities are close to an array of pre-Inca ruins and their corresponding museums. The most ambitious idea is to fly to Chiclayo first to visit **Museo Tumbas Reales de Sipán** and **Túcume.** Then take a three-hour bus ride to visit Trujillo, along with the ruins of **Huaca de la Luna** and **Chan Chan.** From there you would head to Cajamarca and follow the trip described here.

However, if you want to spend extra time in virgin rainforest, you should explore the **Reserva Nacional Pacaya Samiria.** Get off the Yurimaguas-Iquitos cargo boat in the middle of the first night at the town of Lagunas. From here,

you can head out with a dugout canoe and a guide for a week of camping in the reserve.

Day 1

Arrive in **Lima** and then fly to **Cajamarca.** Cajamarca offers baroque churches, the carved aqueducts at **Cumbemayo,** and a stunning pastoral setting.

Day 2

After a morning visit to Cumbemayo, begin the rough overland journey to the cloud forest of the **Chachapoya region.** The first leg of the trip involves an afternoon bus from Cajamarca to the charming country town of **Celendín** (4 hours). There you will spend the night before heading to Leymebamba in the morning.

Day 3

Take a bus to **Leymebamba.** This is a spectacular eight-hour journey down and up the

Peru is the New World's cradle of civilization and has enough archaeological sites for a lifetime of study. From the birth of Peru's first city-states five millennia ago to the spectacular conquest of the Inca five centuries ago, Peru's history is well documented via a series of ruins, artifacts, legends, and written chronicles.

Nearly all visitors to Peru see Machu Picchu and Cusco, but here are some history and archaeology suggestions, broken down by region, for those who want to explore farther afield. Specialty operators like **Far Horizons Archaeological and Cultural Trips** arrange tours to these places with archaeologist guides and a series of exclusive lectures.

El Brujo

THE SACRED VALLEY

In **Ollantaytambo,** visit the **Temple of the Sun** or take the daylong hike to the **Inti Punku,** or Sun Gate. This sacred stone portal features spectacular views of the Sacred Valley and its snow-covered peaks.

Other archaeological must-sees in the Sacred Valley include the fortress and sun temple at **Pisac,** Inca walls at **Chinchero,** and the concentric agricultural terraces at **Moray.**

MACHU PICCHU

Once at Machu Picchu, hike farther afield to the **Inca bridge,** on the edge of the Machu Picchu complex, and the **Temple of the Moon,** a beautifully sculpted cave. Note that Temple of the Moon is done together with an ascent of **Huayna Picchu,** the peak above Machu Picchu. Arrive early to visit these sites, which close after the daily quota of visitors is reached.

CUSCO

In the Cusco area, do not miss the spectacular hike from **Q'enqo** to the fortress of **Sacsayhuamán.** We also recommend a half-day tour from Cusco to see pre-Inca ruins at **Pikillacta,** the Inca ruins at **Tipón,** and the magnificent Spanish colonial church at **Andahuaylillas.**

NASCA

See the **Nasca Lines** (giant renderings of monkeys, spiders, and other water-related symbols dug into the desert floor by pre-Inca people) by air.

Check out the elaborate aqueducts and other waterways that allowed the Nasca to transport water from miles away under the desert floor. Spiral staircases, which descend into the underground aqueducts, can be explored on foot.

LIMA

For an introduction to Peru's archaeology, visit the **Museo Nacional de Arqueología. Pachacámac,** an adobe ceremonial center 31 kilometers south of Lima, functioned as a temple and oracle for at least 1,000 years before it was desecrated by the Spanish.

THE NORTH COAST

Peru's pre-Inca cultures included the **Moche, Chimú,** and **Sicán,** which all flourished in the coastal valleys of Peru's north coast. These societies built giant adobe pyramids, which today are vast, eroding mud hills. They also left behind a variety of artifacts and gold treasures.

In **Trujillo,** view the Moche murals at the **Huaca de la Luna,** the expansive Chimú citadel of **Chan Chan,** and the city's well-preserved colonial mansions. Outside Trujillo, visit the Moche site of **El Brujo.**

In and around **Chiclayo,** view the impressive gold and silverwork in the **Lords of Sipán** exhibit at the **Museo Tumbas Reales de Sipán,** the Sicán pyramids of **Batán Grande,** and the new multimedia **Museo Sicán.**

Marañón Canyon, which is deeper than Arizona's Grand Canyon and ranges from high-altitude grasslands to the subtropical valley floor. Overnight in a hotel near Leymebamba's quiet central plaza.

Day 4

Explore Leymebamba with a visit to the Museo Leymebamba and a hike to the lost city of La Congona. That afternoon, take a *colectivo* down the Utcubamba Valley to Chillo or Tingo (1.5 hours). Plan on a two-night stay at one of the charming country lodges at the foot of Kuélap.

Day 5

Hike to the Chachapoya citadel of Kuélap or take the new gondola.

Day 6

Take a *colectivo* to Pedro Ruiz (1 hour) to get back to paved highway, and hop on a bus for Tarapoto (8 hours).

Day 7

Relax in Tarapoto by visiting Laguna Sauce or hiking to the local waterfalls. Spend another night in Tarapoto.

Day 8

The most adventurous part of this trip begins with an early-morning *colectivo* ride over the muddy, potholed road to Yurimaguas (6-8 hours). That afternoon, board a cargo boat down the Río Huallaga for a 36-hour ride to Iquitos.

Day 9

Rest up on the boat by swinging on a hammock, eating bananas, and watching the Amazon float by.

Day 10

Disembark in Iquitos in the morning or beforehand for a visit to the Amazon lodge of your choice, such as Tahuayo Lodge or Explorama Lodge.

Days 11-12

Rise early both days to catch sight of hoatzins and river otters at their early morning feeding. In the afternoon, wander the terra firma in search of tiny frogs or fish for *pirañas*.

Day 13

Return to Iquitos for a celebratory dinner—or keep floating on into Brazil.

Day 14

Fly to Lima and return home.

Two Days in Lima

Whether you're coming to Peru for the Inca ruins or the Amazon rainforest, there is a good chance that you'll spend some time in Lima. While the Peruvian capital has developed a bad reputation over the years, it has made a comeback as a modern megacity known for its colonial history, delicious cuisine, and excellent nightlife. There are endless ways to explore Lima, but here are a few suggestions.

Day 1

Head to central Lima, which is jammed full of interesting colonial houses, churches, and museums. After visiting the **Plaza Mayor,** do a tour of the **Casa de Aliaga,** a half block from the plaza. Afterward, check out the **Santo Domingo** church, and then walk upriver along Ancash to Desamparados. Look inside Lima's old train station and then head a few doors down to the **Museo de Sitio Bodega y Quadra.** Continue down Ancash and you'll reach **San Francisco,** the 16th-century convent best known for its catacombs, a public cemetery.

After a tour of San Francisco, walk back toward the Plaza Mayor, stopping at the historic **El Cordano** for a quick drink. Back on the Plaza Mayor, stroll down the commercialized **Jirón de la Unión,** which was once an aristocratic boulevard. Walk six or so blocks to Plaza San Martín, passing the **La Merced** church. At Plaza San Martín you'll find a statue honoring Argentine liberator José San Martín as well as the Grand Hotel Bolívar.

By this point you're probably thinking of lunch. Grab a taxi and head to Miraflores and the elegant **Huaca Pucllana** restaurant, next to the ancient adobe and clay pyramid of the same name. Or ask the driver to take you to the **Museo Larco** in Pueblo Libre. At Larco, pay your entrance fee and head to the excellent restaurant in the back. After lunch, admire the museum's collection of textiles and ceramics.

Indigenous performers in traditional Peruvian dress dance in Lima's Plaza Mayor.

Whether it's climbing ice, rock, or mountains, surfing point breaks, mountain biking, sandboarding, trekking, kayaking, or rafting, Peru has it. From the snowcapped Cordillera Blanca and the sand dunes in the Ica desert to the brilliant green waters of Lake Titicaca and the rivers of the Amazon, Peru has something for every adrenaline junkie.

CUSCO AND THE SACRED VALLEY

- **Kayak** and **raft** on the **Río Apurímac.**

- **Paraglide** off the rim of the Sacred Valley with Wayra, an outfitter near Urubamba.

- Take a **horseback ride** to **Maras** and **Moray.**

- **Rock climb** outside Cusco at the **Via Ferrata,** a system of ropes on a 300-meter rock face.

- **Trek** around **Ausangate.**

- **Climb** the highly technical glaciers and peaks of the **Cordillera Vilcanota.**

- **Mountain bike** in the high plains around **Paucartambo,** through cloud forests, and into the **Manu basin.**

LAKE TITICACA AND CANYON COUNTRY

- **Sea kayak** across **Lake Titicaca,** the world's highest navigable lake.

- **Trek, mountain bike, hike,** and **raft** in the **Colca and Cotahuasi Canyons,** twice the depth of the Grand Canyon.

- Break the 6,000-meter mark by climbing the snow-covered **Volcán Chachani** outside **Arequipa.**

THE AMAZON

- **Raft** and **kayak** down the **Río Tambopata,**

a 10-day journey from the high Andes to the Amazon.

- Ride a **zip line** through the rainforest canopy at the **Tahuayo Lodge** near **Iquitos.**

- **Mountain bike** from the **high Andes** into the **Manu basin.**

NASCA AND THE DESERT COAST

- **Sandboard** down 100-meter sand dunes at **Lago Huacachina.**

- **Trek** through the **Ica desert** in search of fossils, mummies, and wilderness beaches.

LIMA

- **Paraglide** along the seaside bluffs of **Miraflores,** the coastal suburb of Lima.

- Hit **world-class breaks** at **Punta Rocas** and **Punta Hermosa.**

- Ride Peruvian *paso* **horses** near Mamacona, on excursions around the ceremonial center of **Pachacámac.**

- Explore the **Pacific Ocean** between Ancón and Cerro Azul aboard a **sea kayak.**

AYACUCHO AND THE CORDILLERA BLANCA

- **Climb** perfect granite fissures and summit out on **Huascarán,** Latin America's second-highest peak.

- **Kayak** and **raft** the **Río Santa.**

- **Mountain bike** the **Cordillera Negra.**

- **Trek** past **Alpamayo,** voted the world's most beautiful mountain.

THE NORTH COAST

- **Surf** the pipeline at **Cabo Blanco** and the breaks at **Máncora.**

the Puente de los Suspiros in Lima's Barranco district

In the evening, find out what all the fuss is about Peruvian cuisine. Put on some long pants and head out to one of Lima's top restaurants, like **Astrid y Gastón, Central,** or **Rafael.** After an unforgettable meal, finish the day off with some live music. If you're in the mood for a show of Peruvian folkloric dance, go to **Brisas del Titicaca.** If you want jazz, try **Jazz Zone.**

Day 2

You're second day in Lima starts with a stroll along the **Miraflores** *malecón,* the elegant promenade overlooking the Pacific Ocean. Enjoy the green parks perched on top of the seaside cliffs. If you're feeling more active, rent a bicycle on the *malecón* or head down to the rocky beaches and try your hand at surfing. After, walk a few blocks to **Parque Kennedy,** where artists display their paintings during the weekends. Next, grab a taxi for the short ride to the **Museo de la Nación,** a large museum that provides a good layout of Peru's archaeological history.

Grab an early lunch and beat the lines. Try ceviche at **Punto Azul,** which also serves heaping plates of other seafood, or **Pescados Capitales.** After your meal, take a cab to **Barranco,** Lima's bohemian district. Get off at its main plaza and wander its streets lined with beautiful old mansions. Walk over to the romantic **Puente de los Suspiros** (Bridge of Sighs). A short walk on the cobblestone pathway underneath the bridge will take you to the sea. Back on Barranco's main streets, check out one of the many shops selling sophisticated handicrafts. Before sunset, grab a seat on the second-floor balcony of **La Posada del Mirador,** order a pisco sour, and watch the sun slip behind the Pacific. At night, stay in Barranco. For a rowdy night among locals, go to a *peña.* For some live rock, go to **La Noche.** If you want something more laid back, try **La Posada del Angel II** for good *trova* music.

Lima

Look for ★ to find recommended sights, activities, dining, and lodging.

Highlights

★ **Catedral de Lima:** At the center of Lima's rebirth is a refurbished main square and this 16th-century cathedral, with elegantly carved choir stalls and a huge painting gallery (page 39).

★ **Casa de Aliaga:** This colonial mansion in the heart of Lima's old town is in pristine condition, offering a fascinating glimpse into the opulent days of the viceroyalty (page 39).

★ **San Francisco:** This 16th-century convent has a brightly decorated patio and painting gallery above and labyrinthine catacombs below (page 43).

★ **Museo Metropolitano de Lima:** Travel through Lima's history via 3-D movies and an earthquake simulator (page 44).

★ **Circuito Mágico del Agua:** The biggest water fountain complex in the world has 13 interactive fountains and a light and laser show (page 44).

★ **Museo Larco:** With a huge collection of gold, textiles, and more than 40,000 ceramics, this museum offers a complete survey of Peru's archaeological treasures (page 45).

★ **Museo Nacional de Arqueología, Antropología e Historia:** The best way to wrap your mind around Peru's complex succession of ancient cultures is by visiting this compact and concise museum (page 45).

★ **Miraflores *Malecón*:** Enjoy the scenic view from the 10-kilometer-long seaside walkway on top of cliffs overlooking the Pacific (page 46).

★ **Bosque El Olivar:** Stroll among more than 1,500 olive trees in this 450-year-old park (page 47).

Lima is an extraordinary city, the maximum expression of Peru's cultural diversity—and chaos.

While nearly all international flights land at this gateway, Peru's biggest city is certainly not the biggest attraction for most foreign tourists, who often pass through without even stopping. Lima's drawbacks are clear to see—there is too much traffic, as expected in a city of nine million people, almost a third of Peru's population. Furthermore, overcast, foggy days all too often give the city a gray, depressing appearance. However, scratch the surface and Lima has plenty to offer. As the former seat of the Spanish viceroyalty, its historic center is filled with colonial churches, ancestral homes, and museums—more than enough to keep you busy for a day at least. And the sightseeing will help you work up an appetite for some of the best cuisine in South America—from mouthwatering ceviche and breaded shrimp in Miraflores and Barranco to spicy noodles in Barrio Chino (Chinatown) or a cup of purple pudding (*mazamorra morada*) along the riverside promenade of the historic center.

At night, Lima really comes into its own. As well as a huge selection of restaurants, the nightlife is the best in Peru, and a pisco sour (or two) is obligatory. Bars, clubs, and local music venues, called *peñas,* explode most nights with dance and the rhythms of *cumbia,* salsa, Afro-Peruvian pop, and a dozen forms of creole music. Limeños themselves are what make the city so diverse—an exotic cocktail blending coast, sierra, and jungle with African, Asian, and European.

Lima's oceanside location is another plus. Although it's often too cool for sunbathing, it's easy to escape the city smog by wandering down to the fashionable districts of Miraflores and Barranco for some fresh air, and there are good beaches just half an hour south of the city.

Do yourself a favor and see Lima at the end of your trip, not at the beginning. That way you have a better chance of understanding what you see and won't become overwhelmed in the process.

PLANNING YOUR TIME

Depending on your interests, Lima can be seen in a day's dash or several days to take in most of the museums, churches, and surrounding sights. Peru travelers tend to enjoy

Previous: Plaza de Armas, also known as Plaza Mayor; view of Miraflores. **Above:** horse-drawn carriage in downtown Lima.

Lima

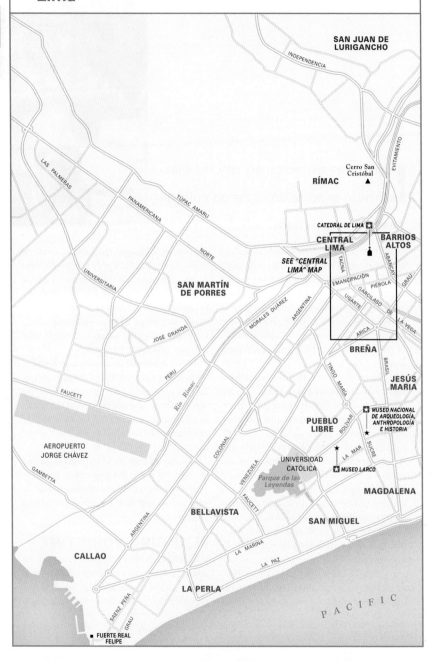

SAN JUAN DE LURIGANCHO

INDEPENDENCIA

Cerro San Cristóbal ▲

RÍMAC

LAS PALMERAS

PANAMERICANA

TÚPAC AMARU

NORTE

UNIVERSITARIA

CATEDRAL DE LIMA ✚

CENTRAL LIMA

BARRIOS ALTOS

SEE "CENTRAL LIMA" MAP

SAN MARTÍN DE PORRES

TACNA

ABANCAY

GRAU

EMANCIPACIÓN

PIÉROLA

GARCILASO DE LA VEGA

UGARTE

ARGENTINA

MORALES DUÁREZ

JOSÉ GRANDA

ARICA

BREÑA

BRASIL

PERU

TINGO MARÍA

JESÚS MARIA

FAUCETT

Río Rímac

MUSEO NACIONAL DE ARQUEOLOGÍA, ANTHROPOLOGÍA E HISTORIA

PUEBLO LIBRE

BOLIVAR

AEROPUERTO JORGE CHÁVEZ

GAMBETTA

COLONIAL

LA MAR

SUCRE

UNIVERSIDAD CATÓLICA

MUSEO LARCO

VENEZUELA

Parque de las Leyendas

MAGDALENA

FAUCETT

ARGENTINA

BELLAVISTA

SAN MIGUEL

CALLAO

LA MARINA

LA PAZ

LA PERLA

SAENZ PEÑA

GRAU

FUERTE REAL FELIPE

PACIFIC

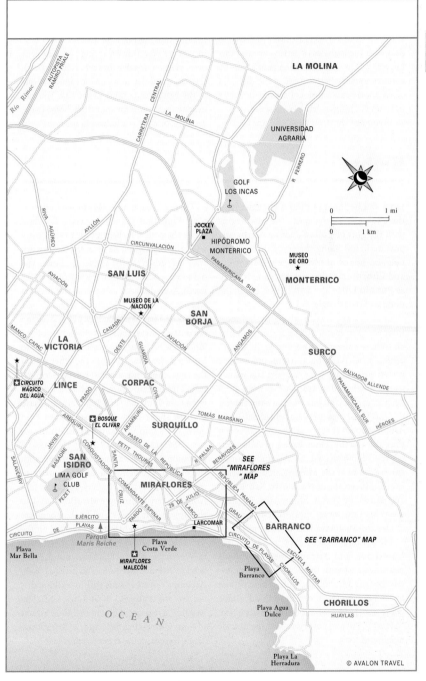

LA MOLINA

UNIVERSIDAD
AGRARIA

AUTOPISTA RAMIRO PRIALE

Río Rímac

CARRETERA CENTRAL

LA MOLINA

R FERRERO

GOLF
LOS INCAS

RIVA AGÜERO

AYLLÓN

CIRCUNVALACIÓN

JOCKEY
PLAZA

HIPÓDROMO
MONTERRICO

PANAMERICANA SUR

MUSEO
DE ORO
★

MONTERRICO

AVIACIÓN

SAN LUIS

MANCO CAPAC

MUSEO DE LA
NACIÓN
★

SAN
BORJA

CANADA

LA
VICTORIA

OESTE

GUARDIA

AVIACIÓN

ANGAMOS

SURCO

SALVADOR ALLENDE

★
CIRCUITO
MÁGICO
DEL AGUA

LINCE

PRADO

CORPAC

CIVIL

PANAMERICANA SUR

HÉROES

TOMÁS MARSANO

AREQUIPA

★ BOSQUE
EL OLIVAR

ARAMBURÚ

SURQUILLO

JAVIER

BASADRE

PETIT THOUARS

PASEO DE LA REPÚBLICA

R PALMA

BENAVIDES

SEE
"MIRAFLORES
" MAP

CONQUISTADORES

SAN
ISIDRO

SANTA

PEZET

LIMA GOLF
CLUB

SALAVERRY

COMANDANTE ESPINAR

CRUZ

MIRAFLORES

28 DE JULIO

LARCO

REPÚBLICA PANAMÁ

GRAU

EJÉRCITO

PARDO

LARCOMAR
■

BARRANCO

SEE "BARRANCO" MAP

CIRCUITO

DE

PLAYAS

CIRCUITO DE PLAYAS

ESCUELA MILITAR

Parque
Maris Reiche

★
Playa
Costa Verde

Playa
Mar Bella

★
MIRAFLORES
MALECÓN

CHORILLOS

Playa
Barranco

CHORILLOS

O C E A N

Playa Agua
Dulce

HUAYLAS

Playa La
Herradura

0 _____ 1 mi
0 _____ 1 km

© AVALON TRAVEL

Lima more at the end of a trip than at the beginning. After visiting Puno, Cusco, and other Peruvian cities, travelers are more prepared to deal with the logistics of getting around this huge city. They have also seen enough of the country to make better sense of the vast, and often poorly explained, collections in Peru's museums. Things start making sense.

If you are short on time and are visiting Cusco, one headache-free option is to fly from Cusco to Lima early in the morning and spend the day touring Lima on an organized tour (if you are planning on seeing Lima on your own, plan on one day for just acclimatizing). Various good day tours include lunch at one of the better restaurants in the city. You can head to the airport for your flight home in the evening, or early the following morning.

Sights

Lima can be thought of as a triangle, with the city center at the apex. The base begins with the port of **Callao** and the nearby airport and runs along the coast through the neighborhoods of **Miraflores, Barranco,** and **Chorillos.** Other neighborhoods, such as **Pueblo Libre** and **San Isidro,** are in the middle of the triangle.

Lima is jam-packed with sights, but most interesting to many people are the colonial churches, convents, and homes in Lima's center, which is safe but warrants precautions nonetheless: Leave your passport and money in the hotel, and guard your camera. Also keep an eye on your bag when at a restaurant.

Lima's best museums are spread out, set in neighborhoods that are sandwiched between the coast and the center. Excellent collections of pre-Columbian gold, textiles, and ceramics can be found at the Museo Larco in Pueblo Libre, Museo de la Nación in San Borja, and Museo de Oro in Monterrico. English-speaking and sometimes French-speaking guides are usually available at these museums.

Most Lima visitors stay in San Isidro, Miraflores, and Barranco, neighborhoods near the coast with the best selection of hotels, restaurants, and nightlife. There is little to see here, however, except for giant adobe platforms that were built by the Lima culture (AD 200-700) and now rise above the upscale neighborhoods.

There are so many sights to see in downtown Lima that you would need a few days to see them all. The best idea is to start early with the big sights, be selective, and work your way down the list as energy allows. The old town is bordered by the Río Rímac to the north, Avenida Tacna to the west, and Avenida Abancay to the east. The center of Lima is perfectly safe, but it is a good idea not to stray too far outside these main streets—except for a lunchtime foray to Chinatown or a taxi ride to Museo de los Descalzos, on the other side of the river. Mornings are best reserved for visits to Lima's main churches, which are mostly open 8am-1pm and 5pm-8pm daily and have English-speaking guides who request a tip only. Taxis into the center from Miraflores cost US$5 (30 minutes). For public transportation, there are a couple of options, with the best choice being the **Metropolitano,** the rapid bus system. Its buses run straight from Barranco through Miraflores and to the downtown center and back. There are several stations in Miraflores located on the Vía Expresa (20 minutes, www.metropolitano.com.pe, US$1). The other option is to head to Avenida Arequipa and catch a "Todo Arequipa" bus that runs within walking distance of the center (40-60 minutes, US$0.50). Avenida Arequipa is one of the main streets in Lima connecting the center to Miraflores. These buses run the entire avenue.

CENTRAL LIMA AND PUEBLO LIBRE

★ Catedral de Lima

Start on the **Plaza de Armas** (or **Plaza Mayor**), which is graced with a bronze fountain from 1650 and flanked on one side by the **Catedral,** built in the late 16th century. It contains the carved wooden sepulcher of Francisco Pizarro, who was murdered in 1541 by a mob of Almagristas, a rival political faction. As you enter, the first chapel on the right is dedicated to Saint John the Baptist and contains a carving of Jesus that is considered to be among the most beautiful in the Americas. But the highlights of the cathedral are the choir stalls carved in the early 17th century by Pedro Noguera and the **museum** (9am-5pm Mon.-Fri., 10am-1pm Sat., 1pm-5pm Sun., US$3.50). Paintings here include a 1724 work by Alonso de la Cueva that portrays the faces of the 13 Inca rulers alongside a lineup of Spanish kings from Carlos V to Felipe V.

Also on the Plaza Mayor are the magnificent **Palacio Arzobispal de Lima** (9am-5pm Mon.-Fri., 10am-1pm Sat., 1pm-5pm Sun., US$8 palace only, US$12 cathedral and palace combined), the Archbishop's Palace, which contains an impressive museum of religious art, and, on the corner, the **Casa del Oidor.** This 16th-century house has Lima's signature wooden balconies on the outside, with carvings inspired by Moorish designs and wood slats from behind which women viewed the activity on the square. Next door is the **Palacio del Gobierno,** the president's palace, which forms the other side of the Plaza Mayor and was built by the Spanish on top of the home of Taulichusco, the ruler of the Rímac Valley at that time. It was at this spot that liberator José de San Martín proclaimed the symbolic independence of Peru on July 28, 1821. There is an interesting changing of the guard (noon Mon.-Sat.) and a changing of the flag (5:45pm Mon.-Sat.).

★ Casa de Aliaga

A half-block from the Plaza Mayor down Unión is **Casa de Aliaga** (Unión 224, tel. 01/427-7736, www.casadealiaga.com, 9am-5pm daily, US$10), which was built in 1535 and is the oldest home on the continent still family-owned, after 17 generations. It is one of the best-preserved colonial homes in Peru, with a series of salons representing decor from the 16th, 17th, and 18th centuries. The land for the home was first deeded to Jerónimo de Aliaga, one of the 13 men who remained with Francisco Pizarro during his grueling

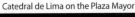

Catedral de Lima on the Plaza Mayor

Central Lima

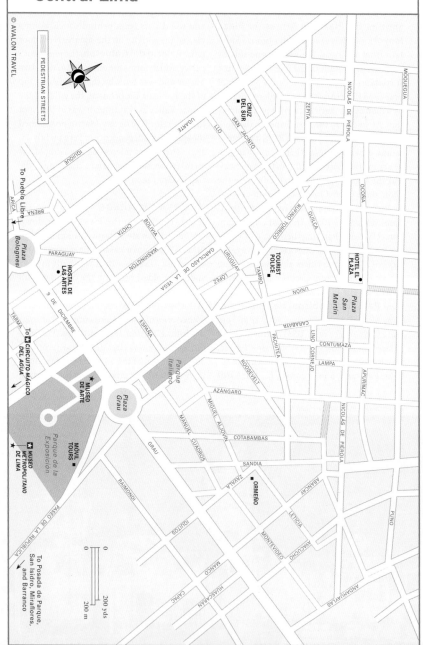

© AVALON TRAVEL

PEDESTRIAN STREETS

To Pueblo Libre

To CIRCUITO MÁGICO DEL AGUA

To Posada de Parque, San Isidro, Miraflores, and Barranco

0   200 yds
0   200 m

CRUZ DEL SUR

HOTEL EL PLAZA

TOURIST POLICE

Plaza San Martin

Plaza Bolognesi

HOSTAL DE LAS ARTES

MUSEO DE ARTE

MOVIL TOURS

MUSEO METROPOLITANO DE LIMA

ORMEÑO

Plaza Grau

Parque Italiano

Parque de la Exposición

MOQUEGUA
NICOLAS DE PIEROLA
ZEPITA
OCOÑA
QUILCA
RUFINO TORRICO
IQUIQUE
ARICA
BREÑA
PARAGUAY
9 DE DICIEMBRE
TARMA
UGARTE
LLO
SAN JACINTO
CHOTA
BOLIVIA
WASHINGTON
ESPAÑA
GARCILASO DE LA VEGA
LÓPEZ
URUGUAY
TAMBO
UNION
CARABAYA
PACHITEA
LINO CORNEJO
CONTUMAZA
LAMPA
APURIMAC
NICOLAS DE PIEROLA
ROOSEVELT
AZÁNGARO
MIGUEL ALJOVIN
COTABAMBAS
SANDIA
ZAVALA
ABANCAY
LETICIA
PUNO
GRAU
MANUEL CUADROS
RAIMONDI
IQUITOS
MANCO
CAPAC
HUASCARAN
MONTEVIDEO
AYACUCHO
ANDAHUAYLAS

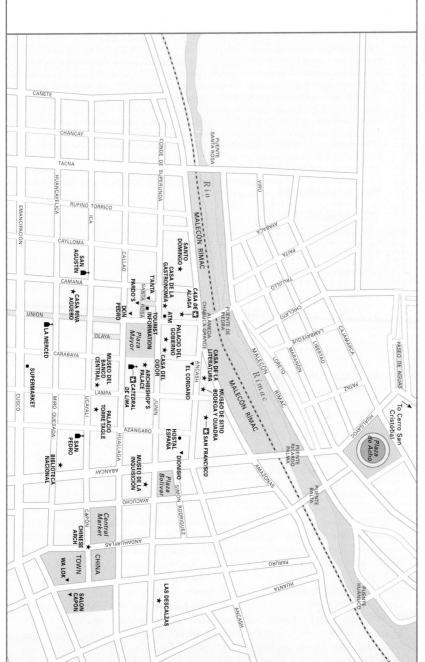

CAÑETE

CHANCAY

TACNA

HUANCAVELICA

RUFINO TORRICO

CAYLLOMA

EMANCIPACIÓN

CONDE DE SUPERUNDA

ICA

CALLAO

CAMANÁ

UNIÓN

OLAYA

CARABAYA

LAMPA

UCAYALI

CUSCO

MIRÓ QUESADA

CAPÓN

ANDAHUAYLAS

PARURO

PUENTE SANTA ROSA

Río

MALECÓN RIMAC

VIRÚ

ARABACA

PAITA

TRUJILLO

CHICLAYO

LAMBAYEQUE

LIBERTAD

CAJAMARCA

MARAÑÓN

LORETO

PATAZ

PASEO DE AGUAS

HUALGAYOC

SANTO DOMINGO ★

CASA DE LA GASTRONOMÍA ★

TANTA ▼
PARDO'S ▼

SANTA ROSA

DON PEDRO ▼

CASA DE ALIAGA

CASA DE LA LITERATURA ★

PALACIO DEL GOBIERNO ★

ATM ■

TOURIST INFORMATION

Plaza Mayor ★

CASA DEL OIDOR ★

ARCHBISHOP'S PALACE ★

CATEDRAL DE LIMA ✚

MUSEO DEL BANCO CENTRAL ★

PALACIO TORRE TAGLE ★

MUSEO DE LA INQUISICIÓN ★

SAN PEDRO ✚

BIBLIOTECA NACIONAL ■

CHABUCA GRANDE

ALAMEDA CHABUCA GRANDE

PUENTE DE PIEDRA

ANCASH

EL CORDANO ▼

JUNÍN

HOSTAL ESPAÑA ●

DIONISIO ▼

Plaza Bolívar

SIMÓN RODRÍGUEZ

AYACUCHO

CASA DE LA LITERATURA ★

MUSEO DE SITIO BODEGA Y QUADRA ★

SAN FRANCISCO ✚

AMAZONAS

MALECÓN RIMAC

MALECÓN RIMAC

R í m a c

PUENTE RICARDO PALMA

PUENTE BALTA

HUÁNTA

ANCASH

PUENTE HUÁNUCO

To Cerro San Cristóbal

Plaza de Acho

SAN AGUSTÍN ★

CASA RIVA AGÜERO ★

LA MERCED ✚

SUPERMARKET ■

AZÁNGARO

HUALLAGA

ABANCAY

Central Market

CHINESE ARCH

CHINA

TOWN

WA LOK ▼

SALÓN CAPÓN ▼

LAS DESCALZAS ★

Colonial vs. Republican Homes

The differences between colonial (1534-1822) and republican (1820-1900) homes are clear in theory but muddled in practice. Most of Peru's old homes were built in colonial times by Spaniards who received prized plots on or near the Plaza de Armas. These houses, passed down from generation to generation, were often restored in the 19th or early 20th century with republican elements. So most houses, or *casonas,* are somewhat of a blend. But all share in common the basic Spanish layout: a tunnel-like entry, or *zaguán,* leads into a central courtyard, or *traspatio.* The rooms are built with high ceilings and a second-story wood balcony around the courtyard. The homes of the wealthy have stone columns, instead of wood, and additional patios.

During the nearly three centuries of the Peruvian viceroyalty, homes went from the solid fortified construction of medieval times to the more intricate decorations of the baroque, which were often based on Mudejar, or Arabic, patterns brought from Spain. After independence, however, homes demonstrate neoclassic elegance and the more confident use of colors favored in the New World, such as bright blues, greens, and yellows.

COLONIAL HOMES

- *Traspatios* paved with *canto rodado* (river stones)

- Sparse interiors

- Heavy brown and green colors

- Simple ceilings, often made of plaster, cane, and tile

- Baroque or rococo decorations with Mudejar patterns

- Forged iron windows with intricate lace patterns

- *Celosia* balconies where women could observe but not be observed

REPUBLICAN HOMES

- *Traspatios* paved with polished stone slabs

- Elegant interior decorations and furniture

- Light yellow, white, and blue colors

- Elaborate, often carved, wooden ceilings

- Neoclassic decorations with ornate columns

exploration of Peru's coast in 1527. You can visit on your own, but in-house guides speak Spanish only. For English-speaking tours, try **Lima Tours** (tel. 01/619-6900).

Santo Domingo and Lima Riverfront

Near the Plaza Mayor is **Santo Domingo,** on the corner of Camaná and Conde de Superunda. This church was built in 1537 by the Dominicans and was remodeled in neoclassical style in the 19th century. At the end of the right nave is the Retablo de las Reliquias (Altar of the Relics), with the skulls of the three Peruvian Dominicans to have reached sainthood. From left to right, they are San Martín de Porras, Santa Rosa, and San Juan Macias. Next door is the attached **convent** (8:30am-5:30pm daily, US$2.50), with carved balconies around a patio, fountains covered with Seville tiles, and a library with colossal 17th-century choir books. This convent was the first location of the Americas' first university, **San Marcos,** and the balcony where students read their theses can still be seen in the Sala Capitular. The convent is open until 5:30pm, but get there by 4:30pm if you want to catch the last tour.

To the west of the presidential palace is the **Casa de la Gastronomía Peruana** (176 Conde de Superunda, tel. 01/426-7264, 9am-5pm Tues.-Sun., US$1), a museum celebrating Peruvian cuisine.

Alameda Chabuca Granda is a riverfront public space, within a block of the Plaza Mayor. The space, used by musicians and artists, is generally safe to walk around until 9pm, when the security guards go home.

Across the Río Rímac, the Rímac neighborhood was populated by mestizos and other people of mixed race during colonial times. The large hill on the other side is **Cerro San Cristóbal.** Walk upriver along Ancash to Desamparados, Lima's beautiful old train station that has been converted into the **Casa de la Literatura Peruana** (Ancash 207, tel. 01/426-2573, www.casadelaliteratura.gob.pe, 10:30am-8pm Tues.-Sun., free), a museum that charts the history of Peruvian literature in a series of well-organized rooms. There is also a small library.

Museo de Sitio Bodega y Quadra

A couple doors down from the Casa de la Literatura is the **Museo de Sitio Bodega y Quadra** (Ancash 213, tel. 01/738-2163 or 01/428-1644, 10am-6pm Tues.-Sun., US$3), which shows the restored home of the Bodega y Quadra family, featuring contrasting architecture from the colonial and republican eras and illustrating what life was like during these periods. The city spent years excavating and restoring the lower portion of the house, which highlights colonial-era floors and structures. The 18th-century house was the home of Juan Francisco de la Bodega y Quadra, a Spanish naval officer who explored Canada's Pacific coast.

★ San Francisco

San Francisco (Ancash and Lampa, 9:30am-5:30pm daily, US$2.50, US$1.50 students) is a 16th-century convent featuring a patio lined with centuries-old *azulejos* (Seville tiles) and roofed with *machimbrado,* perfectly fitted puzzle pieces of Nicaraguan mahogany. There are frescoes from the life of Saint Francis of Assisi, a 1656 painting of the Last Supper with the disciples eating guinea pig and drinking from gold Inca cups, and a series of paintings from Peter Paul Rubens's workshop depicting the passion of Christ. But the highlight is the catacombs, or public cemetery, where slaves, servants, and others without money were buried until 1821. The underground labyrinth is a series of wells, some 20 meters deep, where bodies were stacked and covered with lime to reduce odor and disease. After the flesh decomposed, the bones were stacked elsewhere.

Museo de la Inquisición

Impressive **Plaza Bolívar** is flanked by Peru's grand congress building and graced with a bronze statue in honor of liberator Simón Bolívar. On the far side of the plaza is the interesting **Museo de la Inquisición** (tel. 01/311-7777, ext. 5160, www.congreso.gob. pe/museo.htm, 9am-5pm daily, free), which served as the headquarters of the Spanish Inquisition from 1570 until it was abolished in 1820. The museum explains the harsh and bizarre punishments that the church doled out for crimes ranging from heresy and blasphemy to seduction and reading banned books.

Historic Downtown

The 16th-century **San Pedro** (Azángaro and Ucayali, hours vary, free) has a drab mannerist facade but has one of the most spectacular church interiors in Peru. Huge white arching ceilings lead to a magnificent altar covered in gold leaf and designed by Matías Maestro, who is credited for bringing the neoclassic style to Peru. At the end of the right nave, ask permission to see the mind-blowing sacristy, decorated with tiles and graced with a magnificent painting of the coronation of the Virgin Mary by Peru's most famous painter, Bernardo Bitti. Painted on the ceiling boards above are scenes from the life of San Ignacio. If you come in the morning, it is possible to ask permission to see the cloisters and two interior chapels as well.

Palacio Torre Tagle (Ucayali 363) is a mansion built in 1735 that is, like Casa de Aliaga, in pristine condition. Visits can be arranged by popping into the Ministry of Foreign Affairs next door at Ucayali 318. At the **Museo del Banco Central** (tel. 01/613-2000, 10am-4:30pm Mon.-Fri., 10am-1pm Sun., free), the ground floor holds a colonial money exhibit, one flight up is a 19th- and 20th-century painting gallery, and the basement shines with pre-Columbian ceramics and textiles (including a range of intriguing Chanca pieces). The paintings include a good selection of watercolors from Pancho Fierro (1807-1879), paintings from 20th-century artist Enrique Polanco, and etchings by Cajamarca's indigenous artist José Sabogal (1888-1956).

The church of **San Agustín** (Ica and Camaná, hours vary, free) has an 18th-century baroque facade that is one of the most intricate in the Americas and looks almost as if it were carved from wood, not stone. **Casa Riva Agüero** (Camaná 459, tel. 01/626-6600, 10am-8pm Mon.-Fri., US$7, US$1.75 museum only), an 18th-century home with all original furniture, has an interesting museum of colonial handicrafts as well as ceramics and textiles from the Lima culture.

Another interesting church is **La Merced** (Unión and Miró Quesada, hours vary, free), which was built in 1754 and holds a baroque *retablo* carved by San Pedro de Nolasco.

Parque de la Exposición

If you are taking a taxi from San Isidro or Miraflores into the center, you will travel along a sunken freeway known as the **Vía Expresa** (also nicknamed "El Zanjón," or The Ditch). The freeway emerges on ground level and passes along a series of public parks

before entering old town. One of these is the **Parque de la Exposición,** which was built in the 19th century and is still thriving today. The park is ringed with a high fence and is best entered at the corner of 28 de Julio and Garcilaso de la Vega. In addition to a couple of top-notch museums, the park has an artificial lake full of goldfish, gardens with lounging turkeys, and the **Kusi Kusi Puppet Theater** (basement of the German-style gingerbread house, tel. 01/477-4249, US$4, US$2.50 children), which has Sunday performances.

MUSEO DE ARTE

Also in the park is the **Museo de Arte** (Paseo Colón 125, Parque de la Exposición, tel. 01/204-0000, www.mali.pe, 10am-7pm Tues.-Fri., 10am-5pm Sat., 10am-7pm Sun., US$10 adults, US$5 students), which houses the best range of Peruvian paintings in the country, an espresso bar, and a cinema. The museum contains colonial furniture, some pre-Columbian ceramics, and a huge collection of paintings from the viceroyalty to the present.

★ MUSEO METROPOLITANO DE LIMA

The **Museo Metropolitano de Lima** (corner of 28 de Julio and Garcilaso de la Vega, Parque de la Exposición, tel. 01/433-7122, 10am-7pm Tues.-Sun., US$4) provides a virtual tour of Lima's history, complete with 3-D movies and an earthquake simulator. After seeing several museums and churches, this is a good way to bring all that history together. If you don't speak Spanish, it is best to bring a translator.

★ Circuito Mágico del Agua

The **Circuito Mágico del Agua** (Petit Thouars Esquina with Jr. Madre de Dios, tel. 01/331-0353, www.parquedelareserva.com.pe, 3pm-10:30pm Tues.-Sun., US$2, free under age 4 and over age 65) is popular among locals. It has 13 interactive fountains and a light and laser show. The place is said to be the biggest fountain complex in the world, within the eight-hectare **Parque de la Reserva,** which was built in 1929 to honor reservists that defended Lima from Chilean armies during the 19th century War of the Pacific. Among the park's gardens you'll find Italian-inspired archways and a statue to honor independence fighter Antonio José de Sucre. The yellow house in the middle of the park was designed by José Sabogal, the father of Peru's indigenist art movement.

★ Museo Larco

The charming neighborhood of **Pueblo Libre** is just south of central Lima and has a more relaxed, small-town vibe. Its best-known sight is the **Museo Larco** (Bolívar 1515, tel. 01/461-1312, www.museolarco.org, 9am-10pm daily, US$11), which rivals the Museo de Oro in terms of gold pieces and has far more ceramics and textiles. Founded in 1926 in an 18th-century mansion built atop a pre-Hispanic ruin, this museum has more than 40,000 ceramics and 5,000 pieces of gold and textiles. There are huge Mochica earrings and funerary masks, a Paracas textile with a world-record 398 threads per inch, and a jewelry vault filled with gold and silver objects. A back storage room holds thousands of pre-Hispanic ceramic vessels, including a Moche erotic collection that will cause even the most liberated to blush. There is an excellent on-site restaurant, and it is easy to reach by bus from Miraflores. Catch a bus at Avenida Arequipa that says "Todo Bolívar" and get off at the 15th block.

★ Museo Nacional de Arqueología, Antropología e Historia

A 15-minute walk from Museo Larco is Pueblo Libre's laid-back Plaza Bolívar and the **Museo Nacional de Arqueología, Antropología e Historia** (MNAAHP, Plaza Bolívar s/n, Pueblo Libre, tel. 01/321-5630, http://mnaahp. cultura.pe, 8:45am-4pm Mon.-Sat., 8:45am-3:30pm Sun., US$5 includes tour). Although smaller than the Museo de la Nación, this museum presents a clearer, certainly more condensed, view of Peruvian history, and linked with the Museo Larco, it makes for a complete day in central Lima. Exhibits include Moche ceramics, Paracas tapestries, Chimú gold, and scale models for understanding the hard-to-see Chavín and Huari sites.

The museum's most important piece is the Estela Raimondi, a giant stone obelisk that once graced one of Peru's first ceremonial centers, Chavín de Huantár (1300-200 BC), near present-day Huaraz. It is carved with snakes,

Circuito Mágico del Agua

pumas, and the first appearance of the Dios de los Báculos (Staff-Bearing God), which would reappear, in different incarnations, throughout Peru's ancient history. The tour includes a walk through the adjacent colonial home where independence leaders José de San Martín and Simón Bolívar stayed.

Around the corner is the 16th-century **Iglesia Magdalena** (San Martín and Vivanco), which has attractive carved altars and a gold painting of Señor de los Tremblores (Lord of the Earthquakes). An excellent restaurant, café, and pisco-tasting bodega, all steeped in tradition, are down the street.

SAN ISIDRO AND MIRAFLORES
★ **Miraflores** *Malecón*

Lima's coast offers great views of the Pacific, and the best place to visit the parks on top of the cliffs overlooking the blue ocean is along the Miraflores *malecón*. A recommended walk is to start at the Parque Maria Reiche, near the border with San Isidro to the north of Miraflores. From there, follow the path south, back into Miraflores. There are beautiful parks that offer excellent views, a small restaurant that is good for a drink, and a lighthouse. There are also playgrounds for children. If you go far enough, you'll eventually hit the Larcomar shopping center before reaching Barranco.

Lugar de la Memoria

To dig deeper into Peru's tragic history during the 1980s and 1990s, the recently opened museum **Lugar de la Memoria** (Bajada San Martín 151, Miraflores, tel. 01/719-2065, www.lum.cultura.pe, 10am-6pm Tues.-Sun., free) was built overlooking the Pacific with funds donated by the German government. It has permanent and rotating exhibitions on Peru's internal conflict.

Pyramids

What appears to be a clay hill plunked down in the middle of Miraflores is actually a huge adobe pyramid from the Lima culture, which built a dozen major structures in and around what is now Lima between AD 200 and 700. **Huaca Pucllana** (General Bolognesi 800, Miraflores, tel. 01/617-7148, www.huacapucllanamiraflores.pe, 9am-5pm Wed.-Mon., US$4) has a small but excellent museum that includes ceramics, textiles, reconstructed tombs, and artifacts from this culture that depended almost entirely on the sea for survival. A recently discovered pot shows a man carrying a shark on his back—proof that these people somehow hunted 450-kilogram sharks. No free wandering is allowed, but guides lead tours every 30 minutes around the ceremonial plazas and a few inner rooms. This is a good option if you cannot see the larger Pachacámac, 31 kilometers south of Lima. There is an upscale and delicious restaurant on-site that serves Peruvian cuisine with a modern twist.

A similar, though completely restored, stepped pyramid in San Isidro is **Huaca Huallamarca** (Nicólas de Piérola 201, tel. 01/222-4124, 9am-5pm daily, US$3.50), which offers a chance to understand what these temples once looked like. From the top, there is an interesting view over Lima's most upscale district.

Museo Amano

Museo Amano (Retiro 160, tel. 01/441-2909, www.museoamano.org, 10am-5pm Tues.-Sun., by appointment Mon.) has a small but interesting collection of 200 pre-Columbian ceramics, including a Nasca piece with a scene of human sacrifice, along with a range of textiles, which are the museum's specialty.

Museo Enrico Poli

The **Museo Enrico Poli** (Lord Cochrane 466, tel. 01/422-2437 or 01/440-7100, 9am-4pm, by appointment only, US$12) is one of Lima's more intriguing private collections, with a huge range of textiles, gold and silver objects, and other artifacts. The owner, Enrico Poli, gives the tours personally and speaks Spanish only. Agencies often visit here with their own interpreters.

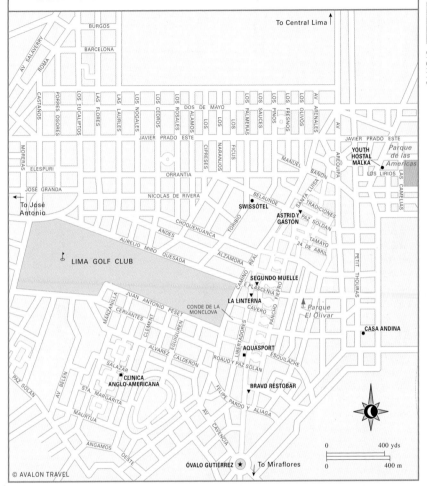

San Isidro

To Central Lima

BURGOS

BARCELONA

AV. SALAVERRY

ROMA

CASTAÑOS

PORRES OSORES

LOS EUCALIPTOS

LAS FLORES

LOS LAURELES

LAS NOGALES

LOS CEDROS

LOS ROSALES

DOS DE MAYO

LOS ALAMOS

JAVIER PRADO ESTE

LOS

LOS

LOS

LOS PALMERAS

LOS SAUCES

LOS PINOS

LOS FRESNOS

LOS OLIVOS

AV. ARENALES

AV.

JAVIER PRADO ESTE

Parque de las Americas

MORERAS

ELESPURI

JOSÉ GRANDA

To José Antonio

CIPRESES

NARANJOS

FICUS

ORRANTIA

NICOLAS DE RIVERA

CHOQUEHUANCA

ANDES

AURELIO MIRO QUESADA

BELAUNDE

SWISSÔTEL

MANUEL

SANTA TRADICIONES

SANTA LUISA

BAÑON

AREQUIPA

YOUTH HOSTAL MALKA

LOS LIRIOS

LAS CAMELIAS

ASTRID Y GASTON

PAZ SOLDAN

TAMAYO

24 DE ABRIL

PETIT THOURAS

LIMA GOLF CLUB

ALZAMORA

TORIBIO

REAL

SEGUNDO MUELLE

CAMINO

DE PLASCENIA

LA LINTERNA

CAVERO

PANCHO FIERRO

Parque El Olivar

JUAN ANTONIO PESET

MANZANILLA

CERVANTES

CLEMENT

EGUIGUREN

CONDE DE LA MONCLOVA

LIBERTADORES

AQUASPORT

CASA ANDINA

ALVAREZ CALDERON

ROAUD Y PAZ SOLAN

ESQUILACHE

SALAZAR

CLINICA ANGLO-AMERICANA

STA. MARGARITA

AV. BELEN

PAZ SOLAN

FELIPE PARDO Y ALIAGA

BRAVO RESTOBAR

MAURTUA

ANGAMOS OESTE

AV. CAVENCIA

ÓVALO GUTIÉRREZ ★

To Miraflores

To José Antonio

© AVALON TRAVEL

0   400 yds
0   400 m

ChocoMuseo

Chocolate lovers rejoice. The **ChocoMuseo** (Berlin 375, tel. 01/445-9708, www.chocomuseo.com, 11am-8:30pm Sun.-Thurs., 11am-9:30pm Fri.-Sat.), three blocks from Parque Kennedy, has hands-on workshops on how chocolate is made. Participants in the Beans to Bar class will get some theory about the cacao tree and harvesting before getting their hands dirty by roasting cacao beans and molding their own chocolate bars.

There is also a two-hour workshop (US$27.50 adults, US$19.50 children) where you can make truffles.

★ Bosque El Olivar

Tucked away in a residential area of San Isidro is **Bosque El Olivar**, one of the city's nicest green spaces with a history dating back more than 450 years. The 23-hectare park is home to some 1,500 olive trees that can be traced to saplings first brought to

Miraflores

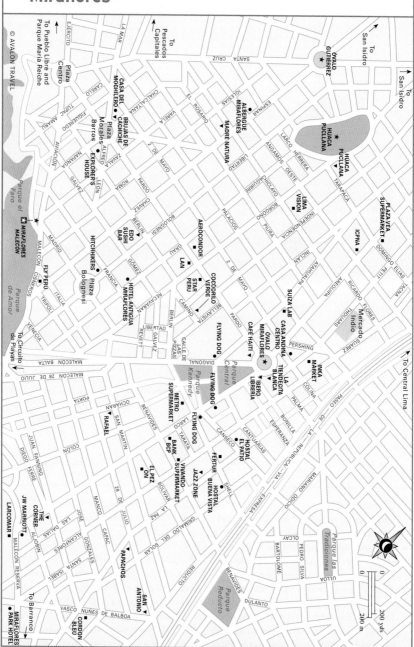

© AVALON TRAVEL

To Pescados
Capitales

To Pueblo Libre and
Parque María Reiche

To San Isidro

To San Isidro

ÓVALO
GUTIERREZ

SANTA CRUZ

HUACA
PUCLLANA

HUACA
PUCLLANA

ALBERGUE
MIRAFLORES

MADRE NATURA

CASA DEL
MOCHILERO

BRUJAS DE
CACHICHE

Plaza
Morales
Barros

EXPLORER'S
HOUSE

LIMA
VISION

PLAZA VEA
SUPERMARKET

ICPNA

EJERCITO

Plaza
Centro

MIRAFLORES
MALECÓN

FLY PERU

HITCHHIKERS

Plaza
Bolognesi

EDO
SUSHI
BAR

AEROCONDOR

LAN

STAR
PERU

HOTEL ANTIGUA
MIRAFLORES

COCODRILO
VERDE

SUIZA LAB

CASA ANDINA
CENTRO

ÓVALO
MIRAFLORES

CAFÉ HAITÍ

IBERO
LIBRERIA

LA
TIENDECITA
BLANCA

INKA
MARKET

Mercado
Indio

Parque el
Faro

Parque
de Amor

To Circuito
de Playas

FLYING DOG

FLYING DOG

Parque
Central

Parque
Kennedy

METRO
SUPERMARKET

FLYING DOG

LARCO

BANK
BCP

VIVANDO
SUPERMARKET

JAZZ ZONE

EL PEZ
ON

RAFAEL

FERTUR

HOSTAL
EL PATIO

HOSTAL
BUENA VISTA

To Central Lima

THE
CORNER

JW MARRIOTT

LARCOMAR

PAPACHOS

SAN
ANTONIO

CORDON
BLEU

MIRAFLORES
PARK HOTEL

To Barranco

Parque las
Tradiciones

Parque
Reducto

0   200 yds

0   200 m

Lima by Spaniards in 1560. This is a good spot to go to take a break from the city's rush. San Isidro's **municipal library** (República 420, tel. 01/513-9000) is located in the park. There are often plays in the theater in the same building.

BARRANCO

In the bohemian neighborhood of Barranco, **Museo Pedro de Osma** (San Pedro de Osma 423, tel. 01/467-0141, www.museopedrodeosma.org, 10am-6pm Tues.-Sun., US$7) holds an exquisite private collection of colonial art and furniture; the building is one of Barranco's oldest mansions and is worth a visit just for that reason. The **Museo de Arte Contemporáneo** (Grau 1511, tel. 01/514-6800, www.maclima.pe, 10am-6pm Tues.-Sun., US$3) has a nice selection of contemporary paintings from international and Peruvian artists, as well as modernist sculptures located on its terrace.

EASTERN LIMA
Museo de Oro

Monterrico, an upscale suburb in eastern Lima that is often sunny when the rest of the city is covered in fog, is known for its **Museo de Oro** (Molina 1110, Monterrico, tel. 01/345-1271, www.museoroperu.com.pe, 10:30am-6pm daily, US$12). This fabulous collection of gold pieces was one of Lima's must-see attractions until 2001, when a scandal broke alleging that many of the prize pieces were fakes. Newspapers pointed the finger at the sons of museum founder Miguel Mujica Gallo, accusing them of selling the originals and replacing them with imitations. The family countered, saying false pieces were bought by mistake, and that Mujica Gallo died of sadness in the process. Only true gold pieces are on display now, but the museum continues to suffer from a credibility problem. Gold pieces include spectacular funerary masks, exquisite figurines, and crowns studded with turquoise. It is a huge potpourri of gold, with little explanation in English, bought over decades from tomb raiders who work over Moche,

Nasca, Sicán, and Chimú sites. Other objects of interest include a Nasca poncho made of parrot feathers and a Moche skull that was fitted, postmortem, with purple quartz teeth. Almost as impressive is the **Arms Museum** upstairs, a terrifying assemblage of thousands of weapons, ranging from samurai swords to Hitler paraphernalia.

Museo de la Nación

Peru's largest museum, and cheaper to see than the private collections, is **Museo de la Nación** (Javier Prado Este 2465, tel. 01/476-9873, 9am-5pm Tues.-Sun., US$4, US$3 students), in the east Lima suburb of San Borja. Though criticized for its rambling organization, this museum, located in the same building as the Ministry of Culture, has a great chronological layout, making it perhaps Lima's most understandable and educational museum. There are three levels of exhibits showcasing Peru's entire archaeological history, from Chavín stone carvings and Paracas weavings all the way to the Inca. There are good models of Machu Picchu, the Nasca Lines, and the Lords of Sipán tomb excavated near Chiclayo in 1987, one of the great finds of Latin American archaeology. On the sixth floor is a chilling photo exhibit called *Yuyanapaq,* which means "to remember" in Quechua. The exhibit documents Peru's internal conflict between Shining Path rebels and state security forces that claimed almost 70,000 lives in the 1980s and 1990s. The government plans to move the museum when construction is finished at a new building outside Lima in Pachacámac.

OUTSIDE LIMA
Pachacámac

This extensive complex of adobe pyramids, 31 kilometers south of Lima in the Lurín Valley, was the leading pilgrimage center on the central coast and home to the most feared and respected oracle in the Andes. The name of Pachacámac in Quechua translates to "Lord of the World." Both the Huari and local Inca empires respected the oracle, adding to its

Barranco

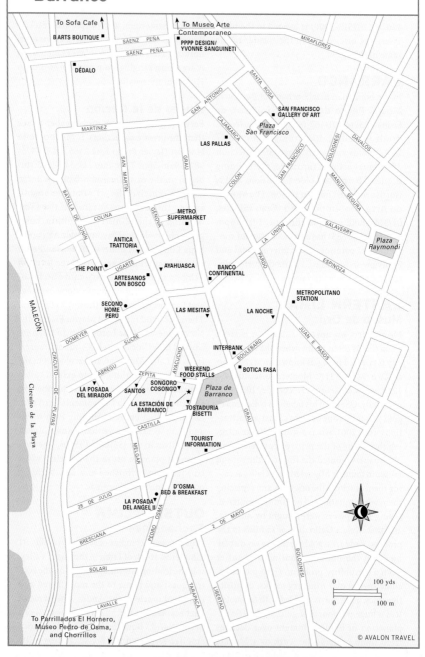

To Sofa Cafe

B ARTS BOUTIQUE

SÁENZ PEÑA
SÁENZ PEÑA

To Museo Arte
Contemporaneo

PPPP DESIGN/
YVONNE SANGUINETI

MIRAFLORES

DÉDALO

SAN ANTONIO

SANTA ROSA

SAN FRANCISCO
GALLERY OF ART

BOLOGNESI

DÁVALOS

MARTINEZ

CAJAMARCA

Plaza
San Francisco

LAS PALLAS

GRAU

COLÓN

SAN FRANCISCO

MANUEL SEGURA

SAN MARTIN

SALAVERRY

Plaza
Raymondi

BATALLA DE JUNÍN

COLINA

GENOVA

METRO
SUPERMARKET

LA UNIÓN

ANTICA
TRATTORIA

PARDO

ESPINOZA

THE POINT

UGARTE

AYAHUASCA

BANCO
CONTINENTAL

ARTESANOS
DON BOSCO

METROPOLITANO
STATION

SECOND
HOME
PERÚ

LAS MESITAS

LA NOCHE

MALECÓN

DOMEYER

SUCRE

JUAN E. PASOS

CIRCUITO DE PLAYAS

ABREGU

AYACUCHO

INTERBANK

BOULEBARD

Circuito de la Playa

ZEPITA

WEEKEND
FOOD STALLS

BOTICA FASA

LA POSADA
DEL MIRADOR

SANTOS

SONGORO
COSONGO

Plaza de
Barranco

LA ESTACIÓN DE
BARRANCO

TOSTADURIA
BISETTI

GRAU

CASTILLA

MELGAR

TOURIST
INFORMATION

D'OSMA
BED & BREAKFAST

28 DE JULIO

LA POSADA
DEL ANGEL II

PEDRO OSMA

2 DE MAYO

BRESCIANA

BOLOGNESI

SOLARI

TARAPACA

LIBERTAD

0   100 yds

0   100 m

To Parrillados El Hornero,
Museo Pedro de Osma,
and Chorrillos

© AVALON TRAVEL

prestige with additional buildings and consulting it for important decisions.

During his imprisonment at Cajamarca, the Inca Atahualpa complained bitterly because the oracle had falsely predicted he would be victorious against the Spaniards. But Hernando Pizarro was so intrigued by Atahualpa's reports of gold at the oracle that he and a troop of Spanish soldiers rode here from Cajamarca in three weeks. Pushing aside the priests, Pizarro strode to the upmost level of the stepped pyramid. He describes a cane-and-mud house at the top, with a door strangely decorated with turquoise, crystals, and corals. Inside the dark space was a roughly shaped wooden idol. "Seeing the filth and mockery of the idol," Pizarro wrote, "we went out to ask why they thought highly of something so dirty and ugly."

What can be seen today is the idol itself (probably a replica) in the on-site museum and excavations of the main temples and huge pyramids, which have revealed ramps and entranceways. From the top of the Temple of the Sun there is an impressive view of Lima's well-organized shantytown, Villa El Salvador, and the Pacific Coast. The Palacio de Las Mamacuña, the enclosure for holy women built by the Inca, can be seen with a guide only (US$6 for an English-speaking tour of the entire site). On the way to the ruins, you will pass **Reserva Pantanos de Villa** at Km 18 on the Panamericana Sur. There is a surprisingly diverse range of ducks and other migratory aquatic birds here that lures bird-watchers.

The easiest way to see the Pachacámac ruins and the corresponding **museum** is with an agency tour from Lima. Buses marked "Pachacámac" leave from Montevideo and Ayacucho in central Lima and can be picked up at the Primavera Bridge along the Panamericana Sur (US$4 taxi ride to the bridge from Miraflores). Ask to be dropped off at *las ruinas,* as the town of Pachacámac is farther along.

Pachacámac ruins, outside Lima

Entertainment and Events

NIGHTLIFE

Central Lima

There are a few night options in the center of Lima, and you should take a taxi to and from each one. On the Plaza San Martín is **El Estadio Fútbol Club** (Nicolás de Piérola 926, tel. 01/428-8866, www.estadio.com.pe, 1pm-11pm Mon.-Thurs., 1pm-3am Fri.-Sat., noon-3pm Sun.), a soccer lover's paradise bedecked with *fútbol* paraphernalia.

One of the largest and best *peñas* in Lima is **Brisas del Titicaca** (Tarapacá 168, previously Wakulski, near block 1 of Brasil and Plaza Bolognesi, tel. 01/715-6960, www.brisasdeltiticaca.com, Tues.-Sat., cover US$18). Foreigners come on Thursday nights for an extraordinary exhibition of dance and music from around Peru (9:30pm-1:30am Thurs.). Those who want to see the same dances, and dance a lot themselves, should come 10pm-2:30am weekend nights, when mainly Peruvians party. This is a safe neighborhood and is an easy taxi ride from Miraflores.

San Isidro

If you have come to Avenida Conquistadores for dinner, there are a few nightlife options that also serve light dinners along this strip. A popular choice is **Bravo Restobar** (Conquistadores 1005, tel. 01/221-5700, www.bravorestobar.com, 12:30pm-1am Mon.-Thurs., 12:30pm-2am Fri.-Sat., US$15-20), a swanky wine bar that fills with Lima's hip 30-something crowd. It has a good selection of pisco cocktails.

Miraflores

The nightlife in Miraflores is more spread out and harder to find than in the neighboring district of Barranco. And that is precisely why many a traveler ends up at **Calle de las Pizzas** (The Street of the Pizzas), a seedy row of pizza-and-sangria joints right in front of Parque Kennedy. But there are many other options.

If you're looking for live music, head to **Jazz Zone** (La Paz 656, tel. 01/241-8139, www.jazzzoneperu.com, cover US$8-12) for some of the best local music in town. Music normally gets going at around 10pm. Sit back and enjoy with a pisco sour. It also does stand-up comedy.

For cocktails and music, swing around to Calle Francisco de Paula Camino to **Cocodrilo Verde** (Francisco de Paula Camino 226, tel. 01/242-7583, www.cocodriloverde.com, 9pm-midnight Tues.-Wed., 9pm-12:30am Thurs., 9pm-2am Fri.-Sat., cover US$5-15). Next door, **Open Tapas Bar** (Francisco de Paula Camino 280, cell tel. 989-168-074, 8pm-1am Tues.-Thurs., 8pm-2am Fri.-Sat., US$10-15) is a new option with good food, drinks, and mix of music. On the same street is **Bizarro** (Francisco de Paula Camino 22, tel. 01/446-3508, www.bizarrobar.com, 9pm-3am Tues., 9pm-5am Wed.-Sun.), an upscale dance club.

A popular winter drink sold by street vendors in Peru is the herbal-based *emoliente*, with a history dating to colonial Lima. Now there is a place that serves *emolientes* with Peru's national drink, pisco—a block from Parque Kennedy, **La Emolientería** (Oscar Benavides 598, tel. 01/446-3431, noon-1am Sun.-Thurs., noon-3am Fri.-Sat., US$10) is a brightly lit *restobar*. On a chilly night, try an *emoliente* with pisco to warm up. **Huaringas** (Bolognesi 460, tel. 01/466-6536, www.brujasdecachiche.com.pe, noon-4:30pm and 7pm-midnight Mon.-Sat., 12:30pm-4:30pm Sun.) is rumored to have the best pisco sours in town.

For years, Peruvians had few options for beer, but now artisanal brewers are popping up. **BarBarian** (Manuel Bonilla 108, tel. 01/497-5978, noon-1am Sun.-Thurs., noon-3am Fri.-Sat.) is a busy pub popular with Peruvians just off Parque Kennedy. It has a long selection of cold brews. Another great option nearby is **Nuevo Mundo Draft Bar**

Gay and Lesbian Lima

Though smaller than in other Latin American capitals, Lima's gay scene is growing, with a few great new discos and bars. There are a number of websites on gay Peru, but the best and most up-to-date information is **GayCities** (www.lima.gaycities.com). This site, written in English, has travel tips, a chat room, links, and an opinionated listing of gay and lesbian bars, discos, saunas, cruising spots, and even retirement options. Other sites include **Peru Es Gay** (www.peruesgay. com) and **Gay Peru** (www.gayperu.com).

Gay and lesbian discos do not start swinging until 1am and continue until the wee hours of the morning. Entry is typically free on weekday nights and goes up after midnight on weekends. Miraflores's hippest, classiest gay and lesbian disco is **Legendaris** (Berlin 363, www.gayperu.com/ legendaris, 11pm-late Wed.-Sun., US$4.50 before midnight, US$6 after), which has extravagant decor, a great sound system, and room for 350. The flamboyant **Downtown Vale Todo** (Pasaje Los Pinos 160, Miraflores, tel. 01/444-6436, www.peruesgay.com/downtownvaletodo, 10:30pm-late Wed.-Sun., US$4 Fri.-Sat.) is still open despite some citizens' efforts to shut it down. This disco attracts a younger crowd, with drag queen performances and a cruising bar on an upper deck.

One of the only options in central Lima is **Sagitario** (Wilson 869, tel. 01/424-4383, www.gayperu.com/sagitariodisco, daily, free except after midnight on weekends), one of Lima's original gay-only bars. The neighborhood is sketchy at night, so travel by taxi. **Avenida 13** (Manuel Segura 270, off block 15 of Arequipa, tel. 01/265-3694) is a gay and lesbian dance club that is women-only on Friday.

Gay-friendly hotels include **Hostal de las Artes** in the center, **Hostel Domeyer** in Barranco, and **Aparthotel San Martín** in Miraflores. Other options can be found at **Purple Roofs** (www.purpleroofs.com).

(Larco 421, tel. 01/249-5268, noon-1am Sun.-Thurs., noon-3am Fri.-Sat.). It offers tours of its plant and workshops on preparing beer at home.

There is always something happening at **Larcomar** (Malecón de la Reserva 610, tel. 01/625-4343, www.larcomar.com), the oceanfront mall at the end of Avenida Larco. Even those who dislike malls are impressed with this public space, buried in the cliff side and overlooking the Pacific. **Aura** (Larcomar 236, tel. 01/242-5516, www.aura.com.pe, 10:30pm-7am Thurs., 2:30am-7am Fri., 10:30pm-7am Sat., cover varies), an expensive disco popular with locals in their early 20s, is here.

Barranco

The most happening neighborhood for nightlife any day of the week is Barranco. There are several spots close to Barranco's main plaza, including a number of bars and dance clubs on the Sanchez Carrión walkway. The best spot on the boulevard is **La Noche** (Bolognesi 307, tel. 01/247-1012, www.lanoche.com.pe,

7pm-3am Mon.-Sat., US$6-9), which has good live music. Tables are set on different levels to look down on a range of performances.

Located in a historic mansion, **Ayahuasca** (San Martín 130, cell tel. 981-024-126, www.ayahuascarestobar.com, 8pm-3am Mon.-Sat., US$10-15) is as much fun for its drinks as it is for its decor. Ayahuasca's interior is inspired by Amazonian shamanism and bright Andean designs while maintaining the villa's late-19th-century feel. Serving an excellent selection of pisco-based cocktails, it also has a good menu of appetizers and main dishes.

Overlooking Barranco's romantic Puente de los Suspiros (Bridge of Sighs) is the popular **Santos** (Zepita 203, tel. 01/247-4609, 5pm-late daily), with a long slender patio that fills up on weekends. With a view overlooking the Pacific, **La Posada del Mirador** (Ermita 104, tel. 01/256-1796, noon-midnight daily) is a good place to have a pisco sour at sunset.

Barra 55 (28 de Julio 206, 7:30pm-midnight Tues.-Thurs., 7:30pm-2:30am Fri.-Sat.) is one of the hottest new bars in Lima, with great gin cocktails and tapas. For a cold artisanal beer in a casual environment, try **Brewpub Wicks** (Pedro de Osma 201-A, www.brewpubwicks.com, 4pm-1am Mon.-Thurs., 3pm-3am Fri.-Sat., noon-10pm Sun.). On the same street is **La Posada del Angel II** (Pedro de Osma 218, tel. 01/251-3778, 7pm-late daily), with excellent *trova* music. There are two other locations down the street, each with baroque decor and a large angel statue in the entrance.

Barranco is full of *peñas* (live *criollo* music clubs) that make for a rowdy night out among locals. **La Candelaría** (Bolognesi 292, tel. 01/247-2941, www.lacandelariaperu.com, 9pm-2am Fri.-Sun., US$15) is a comfortable *peña* where spectators do not stay seated for long. With a slightly older crowd, **La Estación de Barranco** (Pedro de Osma 112, tel. 01/247-0344, www.laestaciondebarranco.com, 7pm-2am daily, no cover) is a nice place to hear *música criolla* in the digs of an old train station. The hippest, but still authentic, *peña* is **Peña del Carajo** (Catalino Miranda 158, tel. 01/247-7023, www.delcarajo.com.pe, 10pm-4am Fri.-Sat., no cover).

PERFORMING ARTS

For the most up-to-date listing of cultural events, pick up the monthly *Lima Cultura: Agenda Cultural* (www.limacultura.pe), which is available free in most museums and cultural centers, or view its website. *El Comercio* (www.elcomercioperu.pe) newspaper also has complete listings.

Lima's performing arts scene got a big boost with the opening of the **Gran Teatro Nacional** (Javier Prado Este 2225, San Borja, tel. 01/715-3659, prices vary). Located beside the Museo de la Nación and Peru's national library, this is a multipurpose theater that has concerts by Peru's National Symphony Orchestra and Peruvian folk musicals. There are also operas, ballets, and international jazz. Renowned Peruvian tenor Juan Diego Flórez has performed here a few times. Showtimes vary, so your best bet is to pick up the bimonthly program at the theater or visit

Teleticket, located in the Wong and Metro supermarkets. Another option for performing arts is **Teatro Segura** (Huancavelica 265, central Lima, tel. 01/426-7189), one of the oldest theater houses in Latin America.

Theater productions, always in Spanish, can be seen at **Centro Cultural de España** (Natalio Sánchez 181, Sta. Beatriz, tel. 01/330-0412, www.ccelima.org), **Centro Cultural PUCP** (Camino Real 1075, San Isidro, tel. 01/616-1616, http://cultural.pucp.edu.pe), **Teatro Canout** (Petit Thouars 4550, Miraflores, tel. 01/593-7654, www.teatrocanout.com.pe), **Teatro Marsano** (General Suárez 409, Miraflores), **Teatro La Plaza Usil** (Larcomar, tel. 01/620-6400, www.teatroplaza.com), **Alianza Francesa** (Arequipa 4595, tel. 01/241-7014, www.alianzafrancesalima.edu.pe), and **Teatro Británico** (Bellavista 531, Miraflores, tel. 01/447-1135, www.britanico.edu.pe), which occasionally has plays in English. Tickets are normally purchased at the box office for only US$8-12.

Other frequent cultural events, such as films, concerts, and expositions, are held at the **Instituto Cultural Peruano Norteamericano** (tel. 01/706-7000, www.icpna.edu.pe), with a location in central Lima (Cusco 446) and Miraflores (Angamos Oeste 106); and the **Centro Cultural Ricardo Palma** (Larco 770, Miraflores, tel. 01/446-3959).

SPECTATOR SPORTS

Lima is a great place to catch a **soccer game,** either at the recently remodeled Estadio Nacional along the Vía Expresa and 28 de Julio or at the Estadio Monumental Lolo Fernández in the Molina neighborhood. Games happen mostly on Wednesday, Saturday, and Sunday, and prices and locations are published two days beforehand in the newspaper. The two biggest teams in Lima are Alianza Lima and Club Universitario, called simply "La U." Tickets run US$5-9 and can usually be bought the same day for nonchampionship matches. Tickets are bought at the stadium, and at TeleTicket counters in the Wong and

Metro supermarkets. The cheap tickets, in the far ends of the stadium, can get rowdy, especially during games between rival Lima teams.

Bullfighting takes place at the Plaza de Acho (Hualgayoc 332, tel. 01/481-1467) near the center of Lima from late October to the first week of December. It's a centuries-old tradition that coincides with Lima's biggest festival, El Señor de los Milagros. Tickets for the Sunday afternoon events range US$30-100 for a two-hour contest featuring world-class bullfighters from Spain and Peru. Tickets are sold at TeleTicket counters in the Wong and Metro supermarkets.

Cockfights, traditionally part of *criollo* culture, are weekend events at various *peñas* and popular in the working-class neighborhoods on the outskirts of Lima. **Horse races** can be seen at the **Jockey Club of Peru** (El Derby s/n, puerta 3, Hipódromo de Monterrico, tel. 01/610-3000, www.jcp.org.pe). To watch American football or European soccer, head to **The Corner Sports Bar and Grill** (Larco 1207, tel. 01/444-0220, 11am-3am daily).

FESTIVALS

Lima's biggest festival is **El Señor de los Milagros** (The Lord of Miracles), which draws as many as 500,000 people on its main days, October 18 and 28; the festival is accompanied by bullfights at Plaza de Acho. The processions begin in central Lima at **Iglesia Las Nazarenas** (Tacna and Huancavelica), which was built atop a wall where an African slave painted an image of Christ in the 17th century. The wall was the only thing left standing after a 1755 earthquake, prompting this annual festival in October, the month when Lima's worst earthquakes have traditionally struck. To this day a brotherhood of priests of mainly African descent care for the image, which some anthropologists say is related to the pre-Hispanic cult of Pachacámac.

Other good festivals include **Lima's anniversary** (Jan. 18), the **Feast of Santa Rosa de Lima** (Aug. 30), and **Día de la Canción Criolla** (Creole Music Day, Oct. 31), when *peñas* hold a variety of concerts around the city.

Peruvian *paso* horse competitions are held in the Lurín Valley south of Lima and are highly recommended. These include the Peruvian Paso Horse Competition in February, a national competition in Mamacona in April, and the Amancaes competition, also in Mamacona, in July.

Shopping

Lima is the clearinghouse for handicrafts produced in places like Huancayo and Ayacucho, and they are sold with a considerable markup. There is a huge range of goods, from cheap tourist-oriented items to those sold in boutique shops, but bargaining is always an option. Several American-style malls have been built in Lima, most notably the cliff-side Larcomar at the end of Avenida Larco and under the Parque Salazar.

HANDICRAFTS

In **Pueblo Libre,** an excellent crafts markets with a cause is **La Casa de la Mujer Artesana Manuela Ramos** (Juan Pablo Fernandini 1550, 15th block of Brasil, Pueblo Libre, tel. 01/423-8840, www.casadelamujer-artesana.com, 9am-5pm Mon.-Fri.). Proceeds from this market benefit women's programs across Peru.

The largest crafts markets are in **Miraflores,** in blocks 52 and 54 of Petit Thouars. Market after market is filled with alpaca clothing, silver jewelry, ceramics, and textiles from all over the country. **Mercado Indio** (Petit Thouars 5245, 10am-6pm daily) and **Indian Market** (Petit Thouars 5321, 9am-8pm daily) are the best of the lot, with nicely presented stalls and wide selections. Nearby is a **Manos Peruanas** (Plaza

Artesanal, Petit Thouars 5411, tel. 01/242-9726, 10:30am-7:30pm daily), with a contemporary line of handcrafted silver earrings, necklaces, and bracelets. Other huge, cheap crafts markets are **Feria Artesanal** (Av. Marina, Pueblo Libre, 10am-6pm daily) on the way to the airport—every taxi knows it—or in central Lima across from Iglesia Santo Domingo, at the intersection of Camaná and Superunda.

In **Parque Kennedy,** you can find rows of Peruvian artists selling their paintings of Lima's colonial past and traditional life in the Andes. The artists are normally out on the weekends. Crafts are also normally sold in the parquet, sometimes by indigenous men and women traveling from Cusco and other Andean towns.

Miraflores's other main shopping strips are in the area next to Parque Kennedy that includes the streets La Paz, Schell, and Diez Canseco. The reasonably priced **Hecho a Mano** (Diez Canseco 298, 10am-5pm Mon.-Sat.) has a high-quality selection of crafts from all parts of Peru, especially Ayacucho. Another plaza at Diez Canseco 380 is filled with jewelry shops, and a wide selection of baby alpaca sweaters can be found at Diez Canseco 378.

For a more upmarket shopping experience, visit the hugely popular **Larcomar** (Malecón de la Reserva 610, tel. 01/625-4343, www.larcomar.com, 11am-10pm daily), an elegant open-air mall dug under Miraflores's Parque Salazar and perched over the ocean. Upscale alpaca clothing stores, the finest of which is **Kuna** (www.alpaca111.com), as well as cafés, a sushi restaurant, bars, a disco, and a 12-screen cinema, are just a few of the businesses here. An excellent place for high-quality jewelry and silver decorations is **Ilaria** (tel. 01/242-8084, www.ilariainternational.com), located on the second level.

The most sophisticated range of handicrafts in Lima can be found in **Barranco.** The high-end gallery **Las Pallas** (Cajamarca 212, tel. 01/477-4629, 10am-7pm Mon.-Sat.) has exquisite Amazon textiles, tapestries, and

Talk with artists and peruse their work in Parque Kennedy.

carved gourds from Huancayo, as well as colonial ceramics from Cusco; prices run US$30-800. Another good option for high-end crafts and art is **Dédalo** (Sáenz Pena 295, Barranco, tel. 01/477-0562, 11am-9pm Tues.-Sun.).

Artesanos Don Bosco (San Martín 135, Barranco, tel. 01/713-1344, www.artesanosdonbosco.pe, 10:30am-7pm Tues.-Sun.) was started in the 1970s by a Catholic priest in the Andean town of Chacas, near Huaraz. The initiative aimed to give young people working skills to escape poverty through artisanal crafts. Today, the organization has expanded, with offices in the United States, Cusco, and Barranco. High-end work is on display and includes contemporary furniture, ceramics, blown glass, weavings, and stone sculptures. For Ayacucho crafts, try **Museo-Galería Popular de Ayacucho** (Pedro de Osma 116, tel. 01/247-0599).

Sáenz Peña is the street for contemporary art. There are numerous galleries with artwork that is mostly modern and includes paintings, photography, and sculpture. Check out **Lucía** de la Puente Galería de Arte (Sáenz Peña 206, tel. 01/477-9740, www.gluciadelapuente. com, 11am-8pm Mon.-Fri., 3pm-8pm Sat.), in a large old mansion; PPPP Design (Grau 810, tel. 01/247-7976, www.ppppdesign.com, 10am-6:30pm Mon.-Fri., 10am-4pm Sat.); or Yvonne Sanguineti (Grau 810, tel. 01/247-2999, 11am-8pm Mon.-Sat.).

OPEN-AIR MARKET

There are several busy open-air markets in Lima where you can find stands full of fresh produce, meats, and seafood. These markets are still bursting with shoppers, even though large modern grocery stores have sprung up across the capital. One of the reasons is that they are often cheaper, while another is perhaps the personal relationships that store owners form with their clients. The best market to visit is the Mercado 1 (Av. Paseo de la República, 6:30am-9pm daily), in the Surquillo neighborhood, located right across the bridge from Miraflores on Ricardo Palma and the Vía Expresa. Many of Peru's top chefs are known to shop here.

CAMPING EQUIPMENT

If you need to buy outdoor gear, you will pay a premium in Peru, and your only options are Lima, Huaraz, and Cusco. Varying qualities of white gas, or *bencina blanca,* can be bought at hardware stores across Peru, so test your stove before you depart. Gas canisters are available only at specialty outdoor stores.

Miraflores has several camping stores: Alpamayo (Larco 345, tel. 01/445-1671, www.alpamayoexploracion.pe, 9am-1pm and 2:30pm-7pm Mon.-Fri., 9am-1pm Sat.) sells tents, backpacks, sleeping mats, boots, rock shoes, climbing gear, water filters, MSR stoves, and more. Similar items are found at Camping Center (Benavides 1620 Miraflores, tel. 01/242-1779, www.camping-peru.com, 10am-7pm Mon.-Fri., 10am-1pm Sat.). Todo Camping E.I.R.L. (Angamos Oeste 350, Miraflores, tel. 01/242-1318, 10am-8pm Mon.-Fri.) also sells more technical equipment like crampons and higher-end fuel stoves.

BOOKSTORES

The best bookstore in central Lima is El Virrey (Paseo los Escribanos 115, tel. 01/427-5080, www.elvirrey.com, 10am-9pm Mon.-Sat.). If you are looking for specialty books in science, history, or sociology, this is the place to find them. The store also has a new location in Miraflores (Bolognesi 510, Miraflores, tel. 01/444-4141, 9am-8:30pm Mon.-Sat., 11am-7pm Sun.).

Additionally, there are several bookstores, or *librerías,* in Miraflores with good English and other foreign-language sections. Despite its humble door, SBS (Angamos Oeste 301, tel. 01/206-4900, www.sbs.com.pe, 9am-7pm Mon.-Fri., 9am-noon Sat.) has the best collection of English-language guidebooks. Its storefront on Parque Kennedy goes by the name Ibero Librería (Larco 199, tel. 01/206-4900, 10am-8pm daily) and has an excellent selection of English-language books as well as helpful staff.

Recreation

BIKING

One way to see Lima is on a bicycle, either in a tour or setting out on your own. **Bike Tours of Lima** (Bolívar 150, Miraflores, tel. 01/445-3172, www.biketoursoflima.com) leads day excursions around Lima's bay area and through the colonial center. **Peru Bike** (Punta Sal D7, Surco, tel. 01/260-8225, www.perubike.com) also does city tours as well as mountain biking trips just outside Lima in the Pachacámac valley, and multiday tours in other parts of Peru. You can also rent a bike for a few hours from **Mirabici,** a municipal program that has a stand just outside the Larcomar shopping center in Miraflores. **BiciCentro** (Av. San Luis 2906, tel. 01/475-2645), in San Borja, is good for repairs and services.

BIRD-WATCHING

With an early start, there are several doable bird-watching day trips from Lima. **Pantanos de Villa** is a 396-hectare protected marsh within Lima's city limits. Here, you can see over 130 coastal marsh species, and the area is accessible by public transportation. For guaranteed sightings of the Humboldt penguin, your best option is the **Pucusana** fishing village. Public transportation also covers this route.

The updated edition of *Birds of Peru,* which has a forward by Peru's first environment minister, Antonio Brack, is an excellent bird-watching guide. The website of **PromPeru** (www.perubirdingroutes.com) is also chock-full of good information. To make your trip more efficient and learn more, you'll probably want to contact a guide. Princeton-trained biologist Thomas Valqui's company, **Gran Perú** (tel. 01/344-1701, www.granperu.com), leads a variety of scheduled tours and can also coordinate day trips and private trips. Swedish ornithologist Gunnar Engblom's agency, **Kolibri Expeditions** (tel. 01/273-7246, www.kolibriexpeditions.com), offers regular day expeditions in the Lima area.

HORSEBACK RIDING

Check out **Cabalgatas** (cell tel. 975-349-004, www.cabalgatas.com.pe, from US$45), an option for riding Peruvian *paso* horses near Mamacona, the town where the *paso* horse competitions are held each year. They lead interesting excursions around the ceremonial center of Pachacámac.

PARAGLIDING

First-time visitors to Miraflores, promenading the *malecón,* are sometimes surprised to find a paraglider just meters above their heads, zipping back and forth along the oceanfront bluffs. Although the thrill is short-lived, paragliding does offer an excellent alternative viewpoint of Lima. One recommended operator is **Peru Fly** (Jorge Chávez 658, Miraflores, cell tel. 993-086-795, www.perufly.com), which organizes flights in Lima and Paracas and also offers six-day basic-training courses.

SCUBA DIVING

There are no coral reefs on Peru's Pacific coast, but agencies do offer interesting dives. **AguaSport** (Conquistadores 805, San Isidro, tel. 01/221-1548, www.aquasportperu.com) rents all equipment for snorkeling and scuba diving. Standard scuba day trips from Lima include a 30-meter wall dive at Pucusana, an 18-meter dive to a nearby sunken ship, or diving with sea lions at Islas Palomino off Lima. Two dives are US$95, or US$55 if you have your own equipment. This agency rents a range of aquatic and off-road equipment.

SEA KAYAKING

For those who like to get out on the water but aren't surfers, there's always sea kayaking. **Peru Sea Kayaking** (San Borja Norte 1241-201, San Borja cell tel. 997-899-752, www.peruseakayaking.com, from US$70 pp) is a professionally run operation, with new equipment, that takes passengers out on the Pacific anywhere between Ancón and Cerro Azul.

SURFING

For surfers, you don't need to go far to catch a wave. In Miraflores you'll find dozens of surfers in the waters at the Makaha and Waikiki beaches, which are good for beginners. The bigger breaks are at La Herradura in Chorrillos and at Punta Hermosa and Punta Rocas. If you head instead to the beaches north or south of Lima, and you will find some of them untouched. Keep an eye out for opportunities to surf at **San Gallán,** one of Peru's few right point breaks in the Paracas National Reserve; **Pepinos** and **Cerro Azul,** near the mouth of the Cañete river valley; and **Playa Grande,** north of Lima, which is a challenging hollow point break for expert surfers. Good sources of surfing information include **Perú Azul** (www.peruazul.com).

For surfing classes, call Rocio Larrañaga at **Surf School** (tel. 01/264-5100), who will pick you up at your hotel and lend you a wetsuit and board. Also recommended is Carlos Cabanillas at **Eternal Wave Peru**

(cell tel. 945-119-998, www.eternalwaveperu. com), which has the Surfer's House for lodging. If you're just looking to rent, **Centro Comercial** (Caminos del Inca Tienda 158, Surco, tel. 01/372-5106) has both surfboards and skateboards. **Big Head** (Larcomar, Malecón de la Reserva 610, tel. 01/717-3145) sells new surfboards and body boards along with wetsuits. One of the better surf shops in Peru is **Focus** (Las Palmeras Block C, Playa Arica, Panamericana Sur, Km 41, tel. 01/430-0444). The staff is knowledgeable about local surfing spots, rents boards at a good price, and even has a few hostel rooms.

COOKING

For those familiar with Lima's culinary delights, it should come as no surprise that it hosts a cooking school licensed by **Cordon Bleu** (Nuñez de Balboa 530, Miraflores, tel. 01/617-8300, www.cordonbleuperu.edu.pe, prices vary by course). The various classes include short-term seminars on Peruvian food, international food, and even desserts. Another option is the hotel and restaurant management school **Cenfotur** (Pedro Martinto 320, Barranco, tel. 01/319-8000, www.cenfotur.com), whose workshop classes also feature cocktail making and

surfers off Lima's coast

wine-tasting. At either of these institutions you will have to make special arrangements for English-speaking classes.

TOUR AGENCIES AND GUIDES

Do not get hustled by agency reps at Lima's airport or bus stations. They will arrange travel packages that tend to be as expensive, or more expensive, than doing it on your own.

Sightseeing Agencies

A favorite travel agency in Lima is **Fertur Peru** (www.fertur-travel.com, 9am-7pm Mon.-Fri., 9am-1pm Sat.), run by the enterprising Siduith Ferrer, with offices in central Lima at the Plaza Mayor (Junín 211, tel. 01/427-2626) and Miraflores (Schell 485, tel. 01/242-1900). Fertur can buy a variety of bus and plane tickets for you and set up tours around Lima and trips to all of Peru's other attractions, including Cusco, Machu Picchu, and the Nasca Lines.

Peru's most reputable agency, in business for decades, is **Lima Tours** (Jirón de la Unión 1040, tel. 01/619-6900, www.limatours.com.pe), with offices in central Lima. Its city tours provide access to some of Lima's colonial mansions, including the pristine 17th-century mansion Casa de Aliaga. Because the company works with large international groups, it is best to make contact before arriving in Lima.

Run by an American-Peruvian couple, **Magical Cuzco Tours** (U.S. tel. 866/411-4622, www.magicalcuzcotours.com) offers several expeditions in Lima, including a half-day culinary tour and full-day visit to the nearby Caral and Pachacámac ruins. It can also help organize specialty tours to other parts of Peru.

Condor Travel (Armando Blondet 249, San Isidro, tel. 01/615-3000) offers a day tour of colonial and contemporary Lima, as well as visits to other attractions like Machu Picchu, Cusco, the Sacred Valley, and the Nasca Lines. **InkaNatura** (Manuel Bañón 461, San Isidro, tel. 01/440-2022, www.inkanatura.com) also offers tours to Machu Picchu, Cusco, and the Sacred Valley.

A good agency for booking flights and other logistics is **Nuevo Mundo** (28 de Julio 1120, tel. 01/626-9393), with its office in Miraflores.

Many of the recommended agencies sell tours run by **Lima Vision** (Chiclayo 444, Miraflores, tel. 01/447-7710, www.limavision.com, 24 hours daily), the city's standard pool service, which offers three- to four-hour daily tours of Lima's center (US$30), Museo Larco (US$40), Pachacámac (US$40), and Museo de Oro (US$50). Whether you buy from Lima Vision or from an agency, the cost is the same. All of Peru's main agencies are based in Lima.

Specialized Agencies

For those who can't make it to Paracas, **Ecocruceros** (Arequipa 4960, tel. 01/226-8530, www.ecocruceros.com) offers half-day boat tours from the port of Callao to see sea lions at the Islas Palomino.

Keteka (www.keteka.com) is a fascinating new agency started by two former Peace Corps volunteers. Using their network of connections, they offer a number of off-the-beaten path tours in Latin America. In Lima, Keteka offers a food tour, taking in the city's world-class cuisine and busy local markets. It also organizes a culture tour, with opportunities to see the Peruvian *paso* horse, the smoothest in the world, and the coastal *marinera* dance, finished off by some wine-tasting.

Food

Peruvian cuisine has an extraordinary range of flavors and ingredients, and nowhere is that more evident than in Lima. The range of high-quality restaurants is extraordinary. The best lunch deal is always the fixed-price *menú,* which typically includes three well-prepared courses. Upscale restaurants tack on a 10 percent service charge and an 18 percent value-added tax.

The center has good budget eateries, including some of the best *chifa* (Chinese-Peruvian food) in town. San Isidro and Miraflores have the most interesting and refined restaurants, where dozens of Cordon Bleu-trained chefs busily cater to their refined Lima clientele.

CENTRAL LIMA AND PUEBLO LIBRE

Other than the cluster of restaurants around Pasaje Nicolás de Ribera El Viejo and Pasaje Santa Rosa, central Lima's dining options are spread out. That said, it is worth taking a cab to some of them, especially the classics in Pueblo Libre.

Ceviche

Patrons of **Chez Wong** (Enrique León García 114, La Victoria, tel. 01/470-6217, noon-5pm Mon.-Sat., US$25) won't find a sign advertising the restaurant outside. But diners flock to this restaurant for one thing and one thing only: one of the best ceviches in Lima, if not all of Peru. The restaurant is literally the home of iconoclastic chef Javier Wong, considered by many to be a culinary master. Wong has maintained a loyal cultlike following at his small no-frills restaurant, where he prepares ceviche in front of his guests. No menus are available, so if you're looking for anything other than ceviche, this is not the place for you. Call ahead, as reservations are a must.

Peruvian

If you are staying in Pueblo Libre or visiting the Museo Larco, eat lunch in the neighborhood. **El Bolivariano** (Pasaje Santa Rosa 291, tel. 01/261-9565, www.elbolivariano.com, 10am-10pm daily, US$12) is a time-honored Lima restaurant in an elegant republican-style home, visited mainly by Peruvians. The menu includes Peruvian classics such as *seco de cabrito* (stewed goat). The Sunday buffet is a good opportunity to sample several Peruvian dishes. On Friday and Saturday night, the restaurant turns into a popular bar.

OK, it is a chain, but **Pardo's** (Pasaje Santa Rosa 153, tel. 01/427-8123, www.pardos-chicken.com.pe, noon-11pm daily, US$10) still serves the best spit-roasted chicken, with affordable lunch menus and open-air tables right off the Plaza Mayor. It also serves *anticuchos,* brochettes, and *chicharrones.*

In the same pedestrian walkway, **T'anta** (Pasaje Nicolás de Rivera el Viejo 142-148, tel. 01/428-3115, 9am-10pm Mon.-Sat., 9am-6pm Sun., US$7-14), a Gaston Acurio restaurant, serves up refined plates of Peruvian favorites *lomo saltado* and *recoto relleno* as well as creative inventions like *ají de gallina* ravioli.

Right on the Plaza Mayor, **Don Pedro** (Unión and Callao, tel. 01/713-9292, 8am-11pm Mon.-Fri., 8am-6pm Sun., US$8-14) is part of the age-old Union Club. It has a very good-value set menu and an elegant atmosphere. It specializes in a fusion of Peruvian and international styles with a wide of range of steak, chicken, and fish.

Near Iglesia de San Francisco is **Dionisio** (Ancash 454, tel. 01/427-5681, US$6-12). With the cozy atmosphere of a cellar, it is first and foremost a wine bar, but it also serves a wide range of traditional Peruvian dishes, such as *chuleta, bistec,* and ceviche.

Peruvian Cuisine

Peruvian food has won international attention for its rich diversity and flavor. Here are just a few of the Peruvian specialties. Keep in mind that some—like the raw seafood dish ceviche—is best on the coast, where the fish is fresh, rather than the highlands. The first dishes are served at almost all Peruvian restaurants, while the second group, including ceviche, *cuy,* and alpaca, are more regional.

Causa limeña is a creamy potato dish that often includes chicken or seafood, along with avocado and other vegetables in the middle. *Lomo saltado* is a beef stir-fry served with french fries and rice. *Ají de gallina* is a chicken stew in a hot and creamy yellow sauce, often served with potatoes and an egg. *Papa rellena* are stuffed potatoes with meat. *Tallarin verde,* a green Peruvian spaghetti pesto, is a great option for pasta. *Pollo a la brasa*—flavorful rotisserie chicken with a heaping side of french fries—is also a favorite among Peruvians.

In Cusco, many restaurants serve *cuy,* or guinea pig, as well as **alpaca** steaks. Another specialty in the highlands is *pachamanca,* where chicken, lamb, beef and other meats and vegetables are cooked in an oven in the ground. Wait until you get back to Lima for **ceviche.**

For drinks, the most popular is the **pisco sour,** the cocktail made from the grape brandy pisco. Another great pisco drink is the **Chilcano,** a mix of pisco and ginger ale. Also worth a try is **Inca Kola,** a yellow, bubble gum-tasting soft drink that competes with Coca-Cola in Peru. While in Cusco, also be sure to have a hot cup of **coca tea** in the morning and evening to warm up and help with altitude sickness.

LIMA'S TOP RESTAURANTS

Make a reservation at one of Lima's top restaurants and find out why the city has emerged as Latin America's culinary hub. These restaurants creatively interpret classic Peruvian dishes using local ingredients, giving you a taste of the cuisine that's both authentic and unusual.

- Astrid y Gastón Casa Moreyra (page 63)

- Central (page 64)

- Rafael (page 64)

- El Mercado (page 64)

- Huaca Pucllana (page 64)

Chifa

The influence of Chinese immigration to Peru is perhaps most evident in the popularity of Chinese-Peruvian cuisine, known as *chifa.* When in central Lima, do not miss the opportunity to sample *chifa* at one of the largest Chinatowns in South America. There are at least a dozen places spread along the town's two main streets, Capón and Paruro. The best known in Lima's Chinatown is **Wa Lok** (Paruro 878, tel. 01/427-2750, 9am-11pm Mon.-Sat., 9am-10pm Sun., US$12-17), serving more than 20 types of dim sum. A less-expensive good alternative with a more elegant dining room is **Salon Capon** (Paruro 819, tel. 01/426-9286, 9am-10pm daily, US$8-10), serving peking duck and *langostinos Szechuan* (sautéed shrimps with *ají* pepper). Both have lovely display cases of after-lunch desserts.

Cafés, Bakeries, and Ice Cream

Antigua Taberna Queirolo (San Martín 1090, tel. 01/460-0441, www.antiguatabernaqueirolo.com, 10am-10pm daily, US$8) is a charming Spanish-style café, open since 1880. This is a good place to come in the afternoon or evenings to sample pisco, made in the winery next door. Queirolo is famous for its *chilcano,* a mix of pisco and ginger ale with a touch of lime juice. Customers normally order a bottle of pisco and a liter of ginger ale, and then mix their own drinks. There is a slim menu that includes salted ham sandwiches, tamales, and *papa relleno* (stuffed potatoes).

Nearby, the cozy **Mezzanine Café Gourmet** (San Martin 484, Magdalena, tel. 01/262-7549, www.mezzaninecafegourmet. com, 1pm-11pm daily, US$4-9) is a few blocks from Magdalena's market and stands out for its food, drinks, and atmosphere. Popular with locals, it has a surprisingly large menu, with pizzas, salads, sandwiches, and Peruvian classics. Its coffee is some of the best in Lima, and its chocolate cake and *lúcuma* ice cream delicious. At night, there is wine, beer, cocktails, and sometimes live music.

Opening onto the lawns of the Museo Larco is the tasteful **Café del Museo** (Bolívar 1515, tel. 01/462-4757, www.museolarco.org, 9am-10pm daily, US$15). Pablo Lazarte leads the small kitchen and sends out delicious plates of tender lamb, steamed sea bass, and shrimp *causa.*

Across the street from the presidential palace is historic **El Cordano** (Ancash 202, tel. 01/427-0181, 8am-8pm daily, US$10), a century-old establishment that was a favored haunt of writers and intellectuals. Though its facade is a bit tattered, this is an excellent place to come for a pisco sour and one of its famous ham sandwiches.

SAN ISIDRO

San Isidro's restaurant and nightlife scene lives mostly on the Avenida de los Conquistadores, where you will find some of Lima's newest and most upscale restaurants.

Peruvian

The lunch-only **Segundo Muelle** (Conquistadores 490, tel. 01/717-9998, www. segundomuelle.com, noon-5pm daily, US$10-15) successfully combines pastas with seafood and tasty ceviche. Try the ravioli stuffed with crabmeat or lasagna with shrimp and artichoke.

San Isidro's classic Peruvian restaurant, with over 35 years in the business, is **José Antonio** (Bernardo Monteagudo 200, tel. 01/264-0188, www.joseantonio.com.pe, 12:30pm-4:30pm and 7:30pm-midnight daily, US$14-17). Said to have the best *lomo saltado* in town, the restaurant also offers *ají de gallina* and *causa* with *camarones.* Afterward, try *picarones,* a doughnut-like dessert.

Peruvian Fusion and Fine Dining

No restaurant has done more to put Peruvian cuisine on the map than ★ **Astrid y Gastón Casa Moreyra** (Casa Hacienda Moreyra, Av. Paz Soldán 290, San Isidro, tel. 01/242-5387, www.astridygaston.com, 12:30pm-3pm and 7pm-11pm Mon.-Sat., US$35-40), inspiring a generation of chefs by instilling pride in local ingredients while promoting creativity. Located in a refurbished colonial hacienda, this adventurous gourmet restaurant is the labor of love of a Peruvian-German couple, Gastón Acurio and Astrid Gutsche. For a starter, try the peking guinea pig, along with an *aguaymanto* sour, made with pisco and tangy *aguaymanto* juice. Save room for dessert.

One of the newest options is **Félix Brasserie** (Santo Toribio 173, cell tel. 982-521-454, 12:30pm-3pm and 7:30pm-11pm Mon.-Sat., US$30), which opened in 2016. Owned by celebrity chef Rafael Osterling, it gets good reviews for its seafood dishes and terrace.

Pizza

A really good pizza place is **La Linterna** (Libertadores 311, tel. 01/440-3636, 12:30pm-4pm and 6:30pm-11:30pm Mon.-Thurs., 12:30pm-4pm and 6:30am-12:30am Fri.-Sat., 12:30pm-4pm and 6:30pm-11pm Sun., US$10). Go for any of the thin-crust pizzas, or try *tallarines verdes* (spaghetti in spinach pesto), a Peruvian comfort food.

MIRAFLORES

Even if you are on a limited budget, splurging on one of Miraflores's top restaurants will be a memorable experience you will not regret.

Ceviche

You will not regret the cab ride to **Pescados Capitales** (La Mar 1337, tel. 01/421-8808, 12:30pm-5pm Tues.-Sun., US$15), a witty play on words (*pescados* means "fish" but rhymes with *pecados,* or "sins") that makes sense when you see the menu. Each dish is named for a virtue or a sin; Diligence will bring you a ceviche of tuna and *conchas negras,* while Patience will bring you a ceviche of shrimps with curry and mango chutney.

At a more affordable price, but also highly recommended, is **Punto Azul** (San Martín 395, tel. 01/445-8078, 11am-4pm Sun.-Wed., 11am-4pm and 7pm-midnight Thurs.-Sat., US$10-12). In addition to ceviche, it serves other delicious dishes from the sea, like *arroz con mariscos* (rice with seafood). One plate is enough for two, but arrive early because after 1:30pm you'll have to wait to get a seat. If you don't feel like waiting, walk a block over to **El Pez On** (San Martin 537, tel. 01/713-0863, www.elpez-on.com, noon-5pm daily, US$10-12), where the ceviche and cold drinks are just as delicious.

Peruvian

Long overshadowed by dishes from the coast and the Andes, Amazonian cuisine is just starting to make headway into Lima's restaurant scene. At the forefront of this movement is **Amaz** (La Paz 1079, tel. 01/221-9393, 12:30pm-11:30pm Mon.-Thurs., 12:30pm-midnight Fri.-Sat., 12:30pm-4:30pm Sun., US$30), where Malabar's Pedro Miguel Schiaffino serves up a variety of flavors and plates inspired by the Peruvian rainforest. The menu includes Amazonian staples like *tacacho con cecina* (roasted green plantains with dried pork) and more exotic options likes *churros pishpirones* (giant Amazonian snails).

For a buffet of *comida criolla,* try **Brujas de Cachiche** (Bolognesi 472, tel. 01/447-1133, www.brujasdecachiche.com.pe, noon-midnight Mon.-Sat., noon-4pm Sun., US$25-40). The buffet (Tues.-Sun.) includes a tour de force of centuries of indigenous Peruvian cooking.

Peruvian Fusion and Fine Dining

Virgilio Martínez's ★ **Central** (Santa Isabel 376, tel. 01/242-8515, www.central-restaurante.com.pe, 1:30pm-3:30pm and 8pm-11:30pm Mon.-Wed., 1:30pm-3:30pm and 8pm-midnight Thurs.-Fri., 8pm-midnight Sat., US$30-40) isn't just considered one of Peru's best restaurants, but one of the world's. In 2016 it was ranked the fourth-best worldwide by S. Pellegrino's closely watched World's 50 Best Restaurants. A former executive chef at Astrid y Gastón, Martínez is known for traveling Peru's high Andes and Amazon rainforest in search of little-known ingredients to garnish dishes like roasted grouper. Top it off with a coca leaf sour.

Another top contender is ★ **Rafael** (San Martín 300, tel. 01/242-4149, www.rafaelosterling.com, 1pm-3:30pm and 8pm-midnight Mon.-Fri., 8pm-midnight Sat., US$30), the creation of Rafael Osterling, located in a turn-of-the-20th-century house. Rafael cites his mother's home-cooked meals and his globe-trotting as inspirations for his fusion of Peruvian and international dishes. Try his *arroz con pato* (rice with duck slowly cooked in dark beer and onion relish). Osterling's other top-rated restaurant is ★ **El Mercado** (Hipolito Unanue 203, tel. 01/221-1322, noon-5pm Tues.-Sun., US$30), a great place for ceviche.

The elegant ★ **Huaca Pucllana** (General Borgoño block 8, tel. 01/445-4042, www.resthuacapucllana.com, noon-4pm and 7pm-midnight daily, US$25) has a magical feel when the ruins of the same name, only six meters away, are lit up at night. Guests sit at linen-covered tables on an open-air patio next to the ruins and enjoy dishes such as rabbit stewed in red wine and grilled lamb chops.

Sushi

With a culture of ceviche, it isn't surprising that Lima has latched on to sushi. Located at Larcomar mall, **Makoto** (Malecón de la Reserva 610, tel. 01/444-5030, www.makotosushibar.com, 12:30pm-midnight Mon.-Thurs., 12:30pm-1am Fri.-Sat., 12:30pm-11pm Sun., US$20) is an excellent, though touristy, sushi restaurant with high prices. **Edo Sushi Bar** (Berlin 601, tel. 01/434-4545, www.edosushibar.com, 12:30pm-3:30pm and 7pm-11pm Mon.-Sat., 1pm-4pm Sun., US$15) is a cool but sometimes crowded restaurant for authentic sushi located a few doors down from the Canadian embassy.

Burgers

Papacho's (La Paz 1045, tel. 01/253-6460, www.papachos.com, 12:30pm-midnight daily, US$10-15) probably has the best burgers in Peru. Try one with a side of sweet potato fries or onion rings and a Chilcano or artisanal beer to wash it down. It also has excellent comfort food, like mac and cheese, and delicious chocolaty desserts. There is also a location in the Larcomar mall.

Vegetarian

When you walk through a health food store to get to the restaurant, you know lunch will be balanced and nutritious. **Madre Natura** (Chiclayo 815, tel. 01/445-2522, 8am-9pm Mon.-Sat., US$6) is all that and is well-priced. Sit down for a soy-based hamburger, and leave with wheat bread in hand.

Cafés, Bakeries, and Ice Cream

One of Lima's classic cafés is surely **Haiti** (Diagonal 160, tel. 01/445-0539, 7am-2am Sun.-Thurs., 7am-3am Fri.-Sat., US$10), in operation for more than half a century on Parque Kennedy. Indoor and sidewalk tables are overflowing with Peruvians day and night. Haiti is less known for its food than its intellectual conversation, good coffee, and pisco sours. Right across the street is **La Tiendecita Blanca** (Larco 111, tel. 01/445-9797, 7am-midnight daily, US$14), an elegant Swiss-style café and deli that has been in business since 1937. Anything you eat here will be excellent.

For a quick sandwich on Parque Kennedy, go to **La Lucha** (Benavides 308, tel. 01/241-5953, www.lalucha.com.pe, 6am-1am Sun.-Thurs., 6am-3am Fri.-Sat., US$4). A recommended sandwich is the *chicharron* (fried pork with sweet potato). It has another location literally across the street on Pasaje Champagnat.

San Antonio (Vasco Núñez de Balboa 762, tel. 01/626-1303, 7am-10:45pm daily) is a bakery, café, and deli with 36 gourmet sandwiches (including smoked salmon and Italian salami), huge salads with organic lettuce, and an extensive dessert case with an out-of-this-world *tortaleta de lúcuma.*

Markets

Plaza Vea (Arequipa 4651, 8am-10pm daily), **Metro** (Schell 250, 24 hours daily), **Wong** (Bajada Balta 626, 8am-11pm daily), and the upscale **Vivanda** (Benavides 495, 24 hours) have large selections of international and domestic foods.

BARRANCO AND THE SOUTH

Slow-paced Barranco has a number of romantic eateries and cafés, and on the weekend, outdoor food stalls fill a walkway near the central plaza.

Peruvian

Songoro Cosongo (Ayacucho 281, tel. 01/247-4730, www.songorocosongo.com, 12:30pm-close daily, US$10-12) has been serving up Peruvian specialties for three generations. Dishes include *ají de gallina, anticuchos, sudado de pescado,* and *chicharron de pescado.*

With bow tie-clad waiters and an old piano, **Las Mesitas** (Grau 341, tel. 01/477-4199, noon-11pm daily, US$5-7) has an old-timey feel. For those on a budget, this is a great place to sample Peruvian food, including *humitas,* tamales, *sopa criolla, ocopa arequipeña,* and *lomo saltado.*

For a steak and red wine fix, ★ **Parrillados El Hornero** (Malecón Grau 983, tel. 01/251-8109, noon-midnight Mon.-Sat., noon-6pm Sun., US$8-10), in Chorrillos, is a must. The second-floor tables have impressive ocean views, and the grilled provolone and Argentine baby beef will do for your palate what it won't do for your cholesterol.

Peruvian Fusion and Fine Dining

Compared to Miraflores or San Isidro, fine dining options are more limited in Barranco, but there are a few exceptions, like **Amor Amar** (Jirón García y García 175, tel. 01/615-9595, 12:30pm-4pm and 8pm-11:30pm Mon.-Sat., 12:30pm-4:30pm Sun., US$15-25). The restaurant has a good menu of seafood specialties, like *tiraditos* and grilled octopus. Other options include risottos, duck, lamb, and beef. Cocktails are well done, and the varied wine list is pretty impressive.

Burgers

You probably didn't come to Lima to eat hamburgers, but if you just need a burger fix, one of the best places in all of Lima is **Twist** (Grau 384, tel. 01/252-9228, noon-11pm Tues.-Sat., noon-5pm Sun., US$10). The mouthwatering options include an alpaca burger or a Barranco burger, which includes *anticucho* sauce and chili peppers.

Pizza

The best pizzas are at **Antica Trattoria** (San Martín 201, tel. 01/247-3443, noon-midnight daily, US$10-15), a charming Italian eatery with stucco walls, exposed beams, and rustic furniture. The lasagna is excellent, as is the array of homemade pastas.

Cafés, Bakeries, and Ice Cream

Tostaduria Bisetti (Pedro de Osma 116, tel. 01/713-9566, 8am-11pm daily) is a great café located right across from Barranco's main plaza. Not only does it serve outstanding locally sourced organic coffee, it also roasts its beans in-house and has a "coffee laboratory" in the back. Its comfortable sofas, black-and-white photos on the walls, and hardwood floors make it a great place to sit back and relax. If you're lucky, there may be live music when you arrive.

Sofa Café (San Martín 480, tel. 01/719-4384, 8:15am-midnight Sun.-Thurs., 8:15am-1am Fri.-Sat.) is farther away from Barranco's plaza but offers a good menu that includes specialty coffees, cold Peruvian drinks like *chicha morada,* and sandwiches and desserts like tiramisu mousse. There are also good waffles and pancakes all day. Another good option if you want to relax for a bit is to grab a coffee at the open-air patio of **Dédalo,** the artisanal shop.

Markets

The large modern supermarket **Metro** (Grau 513, 9am-10:30pm daily) is within walking distance of all Barranco hotels.

Accommodations

There's no shortage of places to stay in Lima, whether you're looking for a five-star luxury hotel overlooking the Pacific or a backpacker hostel close to the action. If you're in town on business, San Isidro's financial district offers several high-end choices. In Barranco, you'll be in Lima's artsy center with a bohemian vibe and walking distance to a good selection of restaurants, bars, and *peñas*. Staying in Lima's colonial center is convenient if you want to be close to many of the city's churches and museums and don't mind the noise. A short taxi ride from Lima's downtown is the neighborhood of Breña. But overall, the best option is Miraflores, where you'll be walking distance to excellent restaurants and entertainment, charming parks lined with artists selling their work, and the city's magnificent oceanfront boardwalk.

CENTRAL LIMA AND PUEBLO LIBRE
US$10-25

A good budget option in downtown Lima is **Hostal España** (Azángaro 105, tel. 01/428-5546 or 01/427-9196, www.hotelespanaperu.com, US$7 dorm, US$20 s, US$22 d with private bath). This backpacker classic is a labyrinth of tight halls and patios, decorated with hanging ivy, marble busts, and reproductions of colonial paintings. The rooms are small and basic with clean, shared baths and hot water. Despite its location, the hostel manages to disconnect itself from the hustle and be a peaceful escape. With a charming upstairs restaurant and neighboring Internet café, this place fills up quickly; make reservations early.

US$25-50

Right on Plaza San Martín, **Hotel El Plaza** (Av. Nicolas de Pierola, tel. 01/424-5860, US$38 s, US$43 d) has well-appointed rooms with cable TV, fans, private bath, and breakfast included. Be aware that, at such good prices, it fills up fast.

SAN ISIDRO
US$10-25

The bulk of San Isidro's hotels are oriented toward high-class business travelers, but there is one great exception to this rule. **Youth Hostal Malka** (Los Lirios 165, San Isidro, tel. 01/442-0162, www.youthhostelperu.com, US$12 dorm, US$36 d) is a rare find and has its own rock-climbing wall. This converted home has simple clean rooms, Internet access, laundry service, and a grassy yard with a table-tennis table. The hostel is a block from a park, and a supermarket and a few restaurants are down the street. Rooms with private baths are US$5 more.

Over US$150

Sandwiched between the Camino Real Mall and a glassy office park, ★ **Swissôtel** (Via Central 150, San Isidro, tel. 01/421-4400, U.S. tel. 800/637-9477, www.swissotel-lima.com, US$299 s or d, with breakfast) is one of Peru's leading business hotels. All rooms have king beds, down comforters, large baths with tubs, and wireless Internet. Each floor has its own security card. You have your choice of food: Swiss, Italian, or Peruvian. An elegant swimming pool surrounded by a grassy lawn, a tennis court, a whirlpool tub, a sauna, and a gym make for a relaxing afternoon. It recently expanded with new rooms and a luxury spa.

Located in the heart of San Isidro's financial district, the **Westin Libertador** (Las Begonias 450, tel. 01/201-5000, www.libertador.com.pe, US$300 s or d, with breakfast) is the newest luxury hotel in Lima. This massive 301-room skyscraper includes two restaurants, a bar-lounge, a luxury spa, a heated indoor swimming pool, and Lima's top conference facility, which has hosted events by leading groups like the World Economic Forum.

MIRAFLORES

Along with San Isidro, Miraflores is one of Lima's upscale districts. The shopping and restaurants are top-notch, and you're only a ten-minute cab ride to nightlife action in Barranco.

US$10-25

A great place for budget travelers is **Explorer's House** (Alfredo León 158, tel. 01/241-5002, www.explorershouselima.com, US$8 dorm, US$18 s or d, with breakfast). The house-cum-hostel has a common kitchen and a TV room with a video library. The communal baths are clean, and laundry is US$1 per kilogram. The friendly owners, María Jesús and Víctor, give guests a remembrance gift on departure!

Casa del Mochilero (Cesareo Chacaltana 130A, 2nd Fl., tel. 01/444-9089, juan_kalua@ hotmail.com, US$5 pp dorm with shared bath, US$14 s) is a clean and plain backpackers' hangout, about 10 minutes' walk from Parque Kennedy, with bunk rooms, shared baths, and a group kitchen.

It doesn't get more secure than at **Hitchhikers** (Bolognesi 400, tel. 01/242-3008, www.hhikersperu.com, US$15 dorm, US$26 s, US$28 d, with breakfast), an old house tucked away behind fortresslike walls. There's no scrimping on space here: Shared rooms have tall ceilings, the communal kitchen has two rooms, and there's even a huge parking area that doubles as a table-tennis arena.

The cheerful ★ **Flying Dog Hostels** (Diez Canseco 117, tel. 01/242-7145; Lima 457, tel. 01/444-5753; Martir Olaya 280, tel. 01/447-0673; www.flyingdogperu.com, US$12 dorm, US$29 d, with breakfast) have become an institution in central Miraflores, and there are locations in other parts of Peru as well. The three Lima locations are all within a stone's throw of Parque Kennedy, and all guests eat breakfast at outdoor cafés on the park. The layout of each hostel is more or less the same:

tight dormitory rooms, a few private rooms, sitting areas, clean baths, and lots of hot water. If you make a reservation, be sure you know for which Flying Dog venue you've made it. They also have options for longer stays.

US$25-50

A great midrange option in Miraflores is **Hostal Buena Vista** (Schell and Grimaldo de Solar, tel. 01/447-3178, www.hostalbuenavista. com, US$45 s, US$55 d), a beautiful house with elegantly furnished rooms set in a small garden.

The charming **Hostal El Patio** (Diez Canseco 341, tel. 01/444-2107, www.hostalel-patio.net, US$45 s, US$56 d, with breakfast) is a memorable colonial home overflowing with plants and flowers and cheerfully painted walls. Large rooms have either tiled floors or carpet as well as homey furnishings and large windows. Ask for a mini suite for an additional US$5—you'll get your money's worth with a kitchenette. Rooms are interspersed with terraces, which are great places for reading or sunbathing.

US$50-100

A highly recommended place to stay while in Lima is the charming ★ **Hotel Antigua Miraflores** (Grau 350, tel. 01/241-6166, www. antiguamiraflores.com, US$98 s, US$113 d, with breakfast). This turn-of-the-20th-century mansion has all the comforts of a fine hotel and the warmth of a bed-and-breakfast. The rooms are large, cozy, and handsomely decorated with hand-carved furniture, local art, and warm colors. Plus the remodeled baths have big tubs. There are plush couches in the downstairs sitting room, and six types of breakfast are served in a sunny black-and-white-tiled café. Suites are also available, with kitchens and whirlpool tubs.

Across the street from the handicrafts-haven Inka Market, the upscale **Casa Andina Centro** (Petit Thouars 5444, tel. 01/213-9739, www.casa-andina.com, US$80 s, US$90 d, with breakfast) puts you in the middle of the action, but without the hustle. Rooms have everything for comfort: modern baths, firm beds, down comforters, cable TV, mini fridges, air-conditioning, and Internet access in the lobby.

Over US$150

Most of the five-star hotels are in San Isidro, but there are a few gems in Miraflores, including the **Miraflores Park Hotel** (Malecón de la Reserva 1035, tel. 01/610-4000, www.mirapark.com, from US$300 s or d). This elegant glass high-rise, located on an old park overlooking the ocean, offers the best in service, comfort, and views in Lima. The grand marble entry is decorated with antique furnishings that are complemented by modern art. The luxurious rooms offer ocean views, elegant furnishings, cable TV with DVD players, fax machines, and wireless Internet. Other amenities include a video library, massages (US$90), a swimming pool, and a squash court.

The oceanfront **JW Marriott** (Malecón de la Reserva 615, tel. 01/217-7000, www.marriotthotels.com, US$157 s or d) occupies prime real estate overlooking the Pacific Ocean and just across the street from the deluxe full-service Larcomar mall. The rooms live up to five-star Marriott quality and are nearly silent despite the busy street below. For the best view, ask for a room on one of the upper floors with an ocean view. Perks include glass-enclosed bars and restaurants, a casino, a pool, and a tennis court. A Starbucks is on the ground floor.

BARRANCO
US$10-25

The Point (Malecón Junín 300, tel. 01/247-7997, www.thepointhostels.com, US$10-12 dorm, US$30 s or d, with breakfast) is a backpacker option with everything a traveler needs: Wi-Fi, long-distance calling, a sitting room with cable TV, nice bunk beds with shared baths, cheap lunches, a pool table, surfing lessons, a book exchange, a travel agency, a grassy lawn, and an outdoor bar. This 11-room restored 19th-century house is just paces away from Barranco's best bars

and sweeping ocean views. There are frequent barbecues and nightly outings to nearby bars, which give guests a discount.

US$50-100

D'Osma Bed & Breakfast (Pedro de Osma 240, tel. 01/251-4178, www.deosma.com, US$49 s, US$55 d, with breakfast) is a great option if you are looking for a tranquil, family-oriented environment.

US$100-150

★ **Second Home Peru** (Domeyer 366, tel. 01/247-5522, www.secondhomeperu.com, US$125 s, US$140 d, with breakfast) is inside the home of Víctor Delfin, a prominent Peruvian painter and sculptor, and his works fill the first floor of the house as well as the five elegant guest rooms. Lilian Delfin, his daughter, is a welcoming and helpful host who will lead you on a morning visit to Víctor's studio. A swim in the cool pool overlooking the ocean from a cliff, with a lion fountain spouting above, is a must. The high ceilings, crisp white linens, and designer baths make any visitor to Second Home feel simultaneously at ease and refined. All rooms have a cable Internet connection. A night in this hotel should not be missed.

Over US$150

Far and away the most exclusive option in Barranco, and by far the most expensive, **B Arts Boutique** (San Martín 301, tel. 01/206-0800, www.hotelb.pe, from US$300 s or d) is a former presidential seaside retreat built in 1914. The ornate facade, Italian marble, and wood columns are accompanied by all of the modern amenities. Guest areas include a cozy library and a rooftop patio overlooking the Pacific. The hotel's restaurant has a menu that was prepared by Oscar Velarde, the owner of Lima's acclaimed La Gloria restaurant. Oh, and the hotel is also connected to the **Lucia de la Puente Art Gallery** (www.gluciadelapuente.com), which means that guests can enjoy private viewings. Even if you don't have the cash to spring for a night, if you like historical buildings, this could be worth a quick visit anyway.

AT THE AIRPORT
Over US$150

Inside the airport is the four-star **Costa del Sol-Ramada** (Av. Elmer Faucett s/n, Aeropuerto Internacional Jorge Chávez, tel. 01/711-2000, www.costadelsolperu.com, US$275 s/d with buffet breakfast included), which has a good restaurant, a sushi bar, and plenty of facilities. The hotel is in the airport compound, right across the taxi lanes from baggage claim.

Information and Services

VISITOR INFORMATION

Free maps and visitor information are available at **Iperú** (Jorge Chávez Airport, main hall, tel. 01/574-8000, www.peru.travel, 24 hours daily). There are other branches in San Isidro (Jorge Basadre 610, tel. 01/421-1627, 9am-6pm Mon.-Fri.) and Miraflores (Larcomar, tel. 01/445-9400, 11am-2pm and 3pm-8pm daily).

In Barranco, **Intej** (San Martín 240, tel. 01/247-3230, www.intej.org, 9am-1pm and 2pm-6:30pm Mon.-Fri., 9am-1pm Sat.) is the Lima base for all student travel organizations. Student travel cards can be acquired here with a letter on the appropriate school stationery, and student flights can be changed.

MAPS

For hard-to-find topo maps, head to Surquillo and the **Instituto Geográfico Nacional** (Aramburu 1190, tel. 01/475-9960, www.ign.gob.pe, 8:30am-4:45pm Mon.-Fri.), which also sells digital, geological, and departmental maps.

POLICE AND FIRE

Through **Iperú's** 24-hour stand (tel. 01/574-8000) in the main hall of the airport, you can report tourism-related crimes. The headquarters of the **national police** (Pezet y Miel 1894, www.pnp.gob.pe) are in Lince, and the **tourist police** (Moore 268, Magdalena, tel. 01/460-0849, dipoltur@hotmail.com) have an office in Magdalena. Dialing 105 also reaches police from a private phone. You can also call neighborhood security, called Serenazgo. For central Lima dial 01/318-5050, for Miraflores dial 01/313-3773, for San Isidro dial 01/319-0450, and for Barranco dial 01/719-2055. For the fire department, dial 116 or 01/421-2620.

IMMIGRATION OFFICE

Lima's **Migraciones** (immigration office, España 734, Breña, tel. 01/200-1000, 8am-1pm Mon.-Fri.) is near the center. Arrive early and with US$20 if you want to receive a new visa the same day.

HEALTH CARE

Lima has Peru's best hospitals, and it is easy, and quite inexpensive, to get parasite tests and yellow fever or tetanus shots.

Perhaps the easiest option, if you need a doctor, is to call **Doctor Más-Sanna** (tel. 01/626-8888, ext. 0 for emergencies, ext. 1 to make an appointment), a company that, for US$45, will send an English-speaking doctor to your hotel to check on you and write a prescription. You can even pay with a credit card if you notify them while setting up the visit.

If you prefer a clinic, all of the places listed here have English-speaking doctors. In central Lima, the **Clínica International** (Washington 1471, 7:30am-9pm Mon.-Fri., 7:30am-5pm Sat.) will see walk-in patients for about US$30. Doctor's visits cost around US$30.

The best (and most expensive) medical care in Peru is in San Isidro at the **Clínica Anglo-Americana** (Alfredo Salazar, block 3 s/n, tel. 01/616-8900, www.angloamericana.com.pe,

9am-9pm daily), which charges US$90 for a doctor's visit.

In Miraflores, a high-quality option is **Clínica Good Hope** (Malecón Balta 956, tel. 01/610-7300, www.goodhope.org.pe, 9am-midnight daily), which charges about US$60 for a doctor's visit. For lab testing and shots, **Suiza Lab** (Angamos Oeste 300, tel. 01/612-6666, www.suizalab.com,7am-6pm Sat., 7am-1pm Sun.) is very professional, clean, and reasonably priced. For dental problems, try the English-speaking **Dr. Flavio Vásquez** (Paseo de la República 6010, Suite 903, Miraflores, tel. 01/445-2586 or 997/88-7977, emergencies 24 hours daily).

Pharmacies

Pharmacies are common in Lima, and most of them are willing to deliver to your hotel. Near central Lima, the **Metro supermarket** (Venezuela and Alfonso Ugarte) in Breña has a good pharmacy. In San Isidro, try **Inkafarma** (Camino Real 1301, tel. 01/314-2020, www.inkafarma.com.pe), which also has several locations in Miraflores. Other options in Miraflores include **Farmacias 24 Horas** (Pardo and Comandante Espinar, Miraflores, tel. 01/444-0568, 24 hours daily) and **Boticas Fasa** (Larco 747, tel. 01/619-0000, www.boticasfasa.com.pe, 24-hour delivery).

BANKS AND MONEY EXCHANGE

For those just arriving in Peru, there are two exchange houses inside the Lima airport that change travelers checks for a 2.5 percent commission. In general, the best place to cash travelers checks is at any Banco de Crédito, which charges the lowest commission—1.8 percent. ATMs are ubiquitous across Lima and most of Peru. Almost all work with Visa, MasterCard, and Cirrus, and Interbank's Global Net and Banco de Crédito even handle American Express. Take care when getting money at night; it's a good idea to have a taxi waiting and to go with a friend.

Money-exchange businesses (*casas de cambio*) offer slightly better rates than banks and are mercifully free of the hour-long lines that snake inside most banks. There are a few exchange businesses on Larco in Miraflores and on Ocoña in central Lima. Be careful changing money with people on the street, even if they do have the requisite badge and bright-colored vest. Safe places for changing money on the street are Parque Kennedy or Pardo and Comandante Espinar in Miraflores.

Here is an alphabetical listing of banks and money changers by neighborhood. Banks are generally open 9am-6pm Monday-Friday and 9am-12:30pm Saturday. All banks are closed on Sunday.

In central Lima, there's **Banco Continental** (Abancay 260-262, tel. 01/595-0000), **Banco de Crédito** (Venezuela 1202, tel. 01/311-9898), **Interbank** (Jr. de la Unión 600), **Scotiabank** (Camaná 623-627, tel. 01/211-6000).

San Isidro, Lima's financial district, has a **Banco Continental** (Camino Real 355 second floor), **Banco de Crédito** (Jorge Basadre 301), an **Interbank** (Jorge Basadre 391-395), **Scotiabank** (Carnaval y Moreyra 282), and **Western Union** (Petit Thouars 3595, tel. 01/422-0014).

Miraflores's banks are generally clustered around the Parque Kennedy: **Banco Continental** (Pardo 791-795); **Banco de Crédito** (Av. Larco 611); **Interbank** (Larco 690); **Scotiabank** (Av. Diagonal 176); and **Western Union** (Larco 826, tel. 01/459-5368).

Barranco's selection of financial institutions are **Banco Continental** (Grau 414), **Banco de Crédito** (José M. Eguren 599, Ex-Grau), **Interbank** (Grau 300), and **Scotiabank** (Grau 422).

COMMUNICATIONS

Peru's national postal service (www.serpost.com.pe) has several offices in Lima; and you can find a **post office** (Camana 790, tel. 01/426-1780, 8am-7pm Mon.-Fri., 8am-4pm Sat.) in central Lima. The **Miraflores post office** (Petit Thouars 5201, tel. 01/445-0697, 8am-9pm Mon.-Sat., 9am-2pm Sun.) has slightly different hours. There are also courier services from **FedEx** (tel. 01/517-1600) and **DHL** (Santa Cruz 462, Miraflores, tel. 01/440-7934, ext. 4180253).

High-speed Internet access is ubiquitous in Lima. In central Lima, try **Internet** (Pasaje Santa Rosa 165, Center, 7:30am-2pm daily, US$0.75 per hour). Recommended places in Miraflores are **Alf.net** (Manuel Bonilla 126), **Refugio Internet** (Larco 1185), and the helpful and cheap **Via Planet** (Diez Canseco 339). These places do Internet calls as well.

For domestic calls, buy a 147 card and dial at Telefónica booths. If you plan to be here for a while, you can buy a cheap prepaid cell phone. For international calls, most Internet cafés have booths, but Skype or Whatsapp normally work just as well.

NEWSPAPERS

Lima's largest newspapers are *El Comercio* (www.elcomercioperu.pe) and *La República* (www.larepublica.com.pe), the latter which publishes a column by Mario Vargas Llosa. A popular weekly magazine for news, humor and cultural information is *Caretas*. *Poder* has articles by one of Peru's best investigative journalists, Ricardo Uceda. *Etiqueta Negra* (www.etiquetanegra.com.pe) is a literary and social commentary magazine, and *Bocón* (www.elbocon.pe) is the soccer paper. The best free sources of English-language news are *Peruvian Times* (www.peruviantimes.com) and *Peru This Week* (www.peruthisweek.com).

International newspapers are available from Miraflores street vendors in front of Café Haiti by Parque Kennedy.

LANGUAGE SCHOOLS

There are many Spanish schools in Lima, although getting away from all the English speakers is a challenge. A favorite school is **El Sol** (Grimaldo de Solar 469, Miraflores, tel. 01/242-7763, www.idiomasperu.com), which has several programs for travelers at the basic level and for those that are more fluent. The school offers students cooking and dancing classes, city walks, volunteer opportunities,

conversation workshops, and family homestays. A week of El Sol's intensive program (20 hours per week) is US$293; semi-intensive (10 hours per week) is US$156. You can brush up on your Spanish before your trip and keep up with your studies afterward with El Sol's **Web Spanish** (www.webspanish.com), which provides one-on-one Spanish classes online.

Also in Miraflores is **Hispana** (San Martín 377, tel. 01/446-3045, www.hispanaidiomas.com), which offers classes one-on-one and in small groups. A 20-hour week of the intensive study program in a small group runs US$240. It offers homestays with a Peruvian family and also has a student residence.

In San Isidro, language schools include the **Instituto de Idiomas** (Camino Real 1037, tel. 01/626-6500, www.idiomas.pucp.edu.pe), which charges US$130 for 36 hours of lessons. The institute is part of Peru's top university, the **Pontificia Universidad Católica del Perú**. You can also hire a private tutor. For one-on-one lessons, some recommended private tutors are **Lourdes Galvez** (tel. 01/435-3910, US$8 per hour) and **Alex Boris** (tel. 01/423-0697, US$8 per hour).

FILM AND CAMERAS

Lima's best film-developing and camera-repair shop is **Taller de Fotografía Profesional** (Benavides 1171, tel. 01/628-5915, 9am-7pm Mon.-Fri., 9:30am-1pm Sun.). Other top-quality developing with one-day service is available from **Laboratorio Color Profesional** (Benavides 1171, tel. 01/214-8430, 9am-7pm Mon.-Fri., 9:30am-1pm Sat.). A cheaper option is **Kodak Express** (Larco 1005, Miraflores, tel. 01/241-6515; Las Begonias 1370, San Isidro, tel. 01/441-2800; Grau 675, Barranco; 9am-9pm Mon.-Sat.). For digital camera technical glitches, contact **Jorge Li Pun** (General Silva 496, Miraflores, tel. 01/447-7302, 10:30am-8pm Mon.-Fri.).

LAUNDRY

In Breña try **Lavandería KIO** (España 481, tel. 01/332-9035, 9am-8pm Mon.-Sat.). In San Isidro, **Lava Center** (Víctor Maurtua 140, tel. 01/440-3600, 10am-6pm Mon.-Sat.) is reliable. Recommended places in Miraflores are **Servirap** (Schell 601, Miraflores, tel. 01/241-0759, 8am-9pm Mon.-Sat., 10am-6pm Sun.), which offers drop-off and self-service, and **Lavandería Cool Wash** (Diez Canseco 347,

Miraflores, tel. 01/242-3882, 8:30am-7:30pm Mon.-Sat.).

LUGGAGE STORAGE

Besides your hotel, you can also store bags at the airport (US$8 per day).

Getting There and Around

AIR

Lima's international airport is **Jorge Chávez** (LIM, tel. 01/511-6055, www.lap.com.pe), 16 kilometers west of the city center at Callao.

The leading domestic airline, with international flights as well, is **LATAM** (Pardo 513, Miraflores, tel. 01/213-8200, www.lan.com). It flies to all major Peruvian airports, including Trujillo, Chiclayo, Tumbes, Arequipa, Cusco, Puerto Maldonado, and Juliaca. LATAM charges non-Peruvian residents a separate, much more expensive fare for domestic flights than it does local residents. If you are not a Peruvian resident and you purchase the cheaper fare online, you will likely be charged the extra when you check in at the airport.

Other airlines for domestic flights are **StarPerú** (Pardo 485, Miraflores, tel. 01/242-7720, www.starperu.com.pe) and **Taca** (Pardo 811, Miraflores, www.taca.com), which also has international flights. There are also **Peruvian Airlines** (Pardo 495, Miraflores, tel. 01/715-6122, www.peruvian.pe), with flights to Cusco, Iquitos and Arequipa, and **LC Perú** (Pablo Carriquirry 857, San Isidro, tel. 01/204-1313, www.lcperu.com), recommended for flights to smaller cities like Cajamarca, Huaraz, and Ayacucho.

All of the international airlines that fly to Peru also have offices in Lima, including **Aerolíneas Argentinas** (Dean Valdivia 243, Of. 301, San Isidro, tel. 01/513-6565, www.aerolineas.com.ar), **Aeroméxico** (Pardo y Aliaga 699, Of. 501-C, San Isidro, tel. 01/705-1111, www.aeromexico.com), **Air Canada** (Italia 389, Of. 101, Miraflores, tel. 0800/52-073, www.aircanada.com), **American Airlines** (Basadre 265, San Isidro, tel. 01/211-7000, www.aa.com.pe), **United Airlines** (Víctor Andrés Belaúnde 147, Of. 101, San Isidro, tel. 01/712-9230, www.united.com), **Copa Airlines** (Los Halcones 105, San Isidro, tel. 01/610-0808, www.copaair.com), and **Delta Air Lines** (Víctor Andrés Belaúnde 147, Torre Real 3, San Isidro, tel. 01/211-9211, www.delta.com).

BUS

Highways in Peru have improved immensely over the last decade, making in-country bus travel not only cheap but efficient. Still, if you have the option, don't take night buses, as they are more prone to accidents, especially when traveling in the Andes. From Lima, buses head to every major city in Peru except water-locked Iquitos. Unfortunately, there is no main bus station in Lima. Instead, companies have their own terminals in the center and sometimes also on Javier Prado or Paseo de la República near San Isidro. If you can, take a bus from one of the terminals on Javier Prado. The area is closer to Miraflores, San Isidro, and Barranco, and safer than some of the neighborhoods around the central terminals. Take a taxi to and from the terminal, and keep a hand on all your belongings.

The two classic and reputable bus companies in Lima are Cruz del Sur and Ormeño. Móvil Tours and Oltursa, however, both get consistently strong reviews. **Cruz del Sur** (tel. 01/311-5050, www.cruzdelsur.com.pe), the best and most recommended bus company in Peru, has a terminal in the center (Quilca 531) and near San Isidro (Javier Prado Este

1100). Although it does not go as many places as Ormeño, Cruz del Sur's Cruzero is the most comprehensive bus service in Peru. Best of all, tickets can be bought instantly online, from any agency in Lima, or at the TeleTicket counters at Wong and Metro supermarkets (in Miraflores there is a Wong at Óvalo Gutierrez and a Metro at Schell 250, near Parque Kennedy). Spanish speakers can even call the Cruz del Sur call center (tel. 01/311-5050, have your passport number ready) and have their tickets delivered free of charge. Payment is in cash upon receipt of tickets. Buses leave first from the central Lima terminal and pick up passengers 30 minutes later at the Javier Prado terminal. For complete route information, see the company's website.

Ormeño (tel. 01/427-5679, www.grupo-ormeno.com.pe) also has a terminal in the center (Carlos Zavala 177) and an international terminal near San Isidro (Javier Prado Este 1059, La Victoria, tel. 01/472-1710). Ormeño has better coverage and is slightly cheaper than Cruz del Sur. To buy an Ormeño ticket, visit a terminal, go through an agency (the agency will get the tickets a few hours later), or call the Spanish-only call center (tel. 01/472-5000). Again, have your passport number when calling and cash in hand when the ticket is delivered.

The recommended **Móvil Tours** (Paseo de la República 749, La Victoria, tel. 01/523-2385, www.moviltours.com.pe) has a station near San Isidro and runs mainly to the northern cities, including Huaraz, Chachapoyas, and Chiclayo; fares are about the same as Ormeño.

The local favorite, **Oltursa** (Av. Aramburu 1160, Surquillo, tel. 01/708-5000, www.oltursa.pe), runs primarily a coastal route both north and south of Lima, along with routes to Arequipa and Chiclayo. The company comes highly recommended for its service (some claim that it's better than Cruz del Sur), and advance reservations can be made by telephone or online. You can buy your ticket by phone or at the **Tu Entrada** stands in Plaza Vea or Vivanda grocery stores. Tickets can also be delivered.

Phone reservations do not work well at the other companies; the best bet is to buy tickets at the terminal.

Expreso Wari (Luna Pizarro 34, La Victoria, tel. 01/330-3518) goes to Nasca, Ayacucho, and Cusco. **Flores** (tel. 01/332-1212, www.floreshnos.pe) has the best coverage of the small bus companies, lower fares, and a terminal in both central Lima (Montevideo 523) and near San Isidro (Paseo de la República 627, La Victoria). It has cheap buses for Arequipa, Cajamarca, Chiclayo, Nasca, Piura, Puno, Tacna, Trujillo, and Tumbes. **Soyuz** (México 333, tel. 01/205-2370, www.soyuzonline.com.pe) has good frequency on the south coast.

Companies whose travelers report frequent delays, breakdowns, or other problems include **Tepsa** and **Civa.** Recommended international companies are Ormeño and **Caracol** (Brasil 487, tel. 01/431-1400, www.perucaracol.com), which receives the best reviews and covers the entire continent. It partners with Cruz del Sur, so you can buy tickets from either company's terminals. Among other places, Caracol travels to Santiago, Chile; Santa Cruz and La Paz, Bolivia; Asunción, Paraguay; Córdoba and Buenos Aires, Argentina; Montevideo, Uruguay; São Paulo and Rio de Janeiro, Brazil; and Quito and Guayaquil, Ecuador.

Ormeño (Javier Prado Este 1059, tel. 01/472-1710) no longer travels to Brazil but runs buses to Bogotá, Colombia; Santiago, Chile; Buenos Aires, Argentina; and Guayaquil, Ecuador.

TRAIN

Between late March and early November, a passenger train still departs on Friday from Lima's antique Desamparados train station downtown. After climbing the steep valley above Lima it crests the Andes at a breathtaking 4,751 meters and continues to Huancayo. Trains return from Huancayo to Lima on Sunday evening, making for an interesting weekend outing. Tickets can be bought at the offices of **Ferrocarril Central Andino** (José Galvez Barrenchea 566, 5th Fl., San Isidro, tel.

01/226-6363, www.ferrocarrilcentral.com.pe) or from **Tu Entrada** (tel. 01/618-3838, www.tuentrada.com.pe).

LOCAL TRANSPORTATION
Taxi

If you want to make a spare buck in Lima, buy a taxi sticker from the market for US$0.50, plop it on your windshield, and start picking up passengers. Understandably, the vast majority of taxis in Lima are unofficial and unregulated, and assaults on passengers picked up at the airport occur occasionally.

If you have a cell phone, download the app for **Easy Taxi** (www.easytaxi.com/pe) or Uber to get a ride. If you prefer to call a registered taxi company, recommended companies include **Taxi Lima** (tel. 01/213-5050, 24 hours daily), **Taxi Miraflores** (tel. 01/477-1743, 24 hours daily), and **Taxi Móvil** (tel. 01/422-6890, San Isidro, 24 hours daily). To and from the airport, **Taxi Green** (tel. 01/484-4001) is recommended. Registered taxi companies generally cost an additional 30-50 percent.

If you feel comfortable, and have a smidgen of Spanish, stand on the street until a safe-looking registered taxi passes by. These should be painted yellow and have the taxi sign on the hood of the car and a registration sticker on the windshield or a line of square boxes along the side of the vehicle. Older taxi drivers tend to be safer than young ones. Of course, avoid old cars with tinted windows and broken door handles. Bargain before you get in a taxi or you will get fleeced. Fares from the airport to Miraflores should be US$15-20, from the airport to the center about US$15, from Miraflores to the center about US$6, and Miraflores to Barranco about US$4. Prices go up during rush hour and at night. Taxis can also be rented by the hour for US$12 (registered taxi) or US$8 (street taxi).

Bus

In 2010, Lima got its first rapid transit system, called **El Metropolitano** (www.metropolitano.com.pe). Metropolitano buses run a 30-kilometer line from the seaside neighborhood of Chorrillos through Barranco, Miraflores, and San Isidro to central Lima and beyond. This is the best public transportation to and from central Lima: It's faster, safer, and better on the environment. Fares are about US$0.75 and are paid using a reusable prepaid electronic card that can be bought at any station. There are five stations in Miraflores (28 de Julio, Benavides, Ricardo Palma, Angamos, and Domingo Orué), three in San Isidro (Aramburú, Canaval y Moreyra, and Javier Prado), and four in Barranco (Estadio Unión, Bulevar, Balta, and Plaza de Flores). There are several stations in the center, including the Estadio Nacional, located on the outskirts of downtown just outside the soccer stadium and close to Parque de la Exposición, as well as the Estación Central Grau and Jirón de la Unión. There is an express lane and another lane where the buses stop at each station. Visit the website for a map of the route and stations.

Traveling to other parts of Lima are the notorious *combi*, or minivan-type buses, and other, larger buses. These beat-up vehicles race through Lima's main streets crammed full of passengers and blaring anything from 1980s pop songs to *cumbia* or salsa. Managing these buses is a two-person job: one person is behind the wheel and the other has their head out the window yelling to onlookers where the bus is going and collecting fares from passengers. You can also tell the buses route by the sticker on the front windshield. Fares start at about US$0.30 and increase depending on the distance. To get off simply say *"baja"* ("getting off") or *"esquina"* ("at the corner").

Car Rental

The major rental car agencies are **Hertz** (Pasaje Tello 215, Miraflores, tel. 01/445-5716, www.hertz.com.pe), **Budget** (Larco 998, Miraflores, tel. 01/444-4546, airport tel. 01/517-1880, www.budgetperu.com), and **Avis** (28 de Julio 587, Miraflores, tel. 01/444-0450, airport tel. 01/517-1847, www.avis.com.pe).

Lima Bus Schedule

The following is a thumbnail of bus trip duration and prices to and from Lima with a range from economical to luxury service. At the bottom end, buses stop frequently, are crowded, and lack restrooms. The top-end buses are decked out with reclining semi-beds, clean restrooms, onboard food and beverage service, video, and a second story with great views. Prices increase 50 percent around holidays, including Christmas, Easter, and the July 28 Fiestas Patrias weekend.

City	Price	Time
Arequipa	US$20-50	13-15 hours
Ayacucho	US$20-35	9-10 hours
Cajamarca	US$25-48	14 hours
Chachapoyas	US$20-50	22 hours
Chanchamayo	US$10-27	8 hours
Chiclayo	US$19-40	12 hours
Cusco	US$30-50	21 hours
Huancayo	US$17-30	7 hours
Huaraz	US$15-26	8 hours
Máncora	US$28-60	16-17 hours
Nasca	US$15-40	8 hours
Pisco	US$13-28	4 hours
Piura	US$25-50	15-16 hours
Puno	US$34-60	21-24 hours
Tacna	US$37-60	18-20 hours (Chilean border)
Trujillo	US$20-42	8 hours
Tumbes	US$30-60	18 hours (Ecuadoran border)

Private Car

Private drivers can also be hired for the hour, day, or for a trip like the Nasca Lines. Many travelers who are only in Lima for a single day would greatly benefit from a driver who recommends museums and restaurants and then drops them off at the airport in the evening. A highly recommended driver is **José Salinas Casanova** (cell tel. 999-190-336, casanovacab@hotmail.com, US$14 per hour), based at the Hotel Antigua Miraflores. **Marcelino Cardena** (cell tel. 989-840-284, US$14 per hour) is also based at the Antigua Miraflores.

Southern Beaches

During Lima's summer months the beaches just south of the city are a popular weekend destination for students, office workers, families, and world-class surfers. Though they can be crowded, this is a good place to go if you need a beach fix, and it's much closer than taking a 20-hour bus trip to Peru's northern beaches.

Popular beach towns just south of Lima are Punta Hermosa and San Bartolo. You will find sandy beaches, world-class surfing waves, protected beaches for safe swimming, rocking nightlife, a few good hostels, and lots of *cebicherías*. The only time to visit these beaches is during the summer months, from mid-December to the end of April—skies are cloudy during the rest of the year. Make reservations well in advance, especially January to mid-March, when surfers from around the world flock here along with Peruvian students on summer break. The best time to go is Sunday-Thursday nights, when beaches are empty and hotel prices are often 30 percent lower than the weekend rates.

There are other options besides Punta Hermosa and San Bartolo. **Santa María,** at Km 48 of the Panamericana, is an upscale beach with a control point that admits only residents and respectable-looking daytrippers, though there are few or no lodging options. **Pucusana** is a picturesque fishing town at Km 58 of the Panamericana. **Puerto Viejo,** at Km 72 of the Panamericana, is a long beach good for beginning surfers—including a left point break that ranges 1-2 meters. **Leon Dormido** (Sleeping Lion) at Km 80 has a calm beach that is often crowded. The best parties are at **Asia,** at Km 97, which becomes an explosion of discos, condos, private clubs, and even car dealerships in the summer. Teenagers here for the parties pack the beach and the discos at night. Near Asia's beaches, and close to shore, there are several islands with great sea kayaking and possibilities to see Humboldt penguins and sea lions. Finally, **Cerro Azul,** at Km 128, is a forgotten port, with a small fishing community and a pleasant beach with both pipeline and beginner waves for all levels of surfers.

PUNTA HERMOSA

Thirty minutes south of Lima at Km 40 on the Panamericana, Punta Hermosa is a big-time surfing destination with a great range of beaches and services. It is here that **Pico Alto,** the largest wave in South America, forms in May and reaches heights up to 12 meters. The town itself is on a rocky peninsula, called La Isla, which is surrounded by seven beaches. From north to south, these are El Silencio, Caballeros, Señoritas, Pico Alto, Playa Norte, La Isla, and Kontiki. When covered in rocks and not sand June-November, Playa Norte is a good place to get away from the crowds, along with Kontiki. But wherever you stay in Punta Hermosa, these beaches are no more than 30 minutes' walk away.

Entertainment and Events

Every May or June, during the first big swell of the year, Punta Hermosa comes alive with Peru's annual big-wave competition. There is no fixed date for the competition, and it is usually organized within a week or two—check out **Buoyweather** (www.buoyweather.com, a paid site) or **Stormsurf** (www.stormsurf.com, free) for the right ocean conditions, or check **Perú Azul** (www.peruazul.com), the country's premier surfing website.

Recreation

Punta Hermosa has several places to rent a board and a wetsuit, get an instructor, and **surf** a variety of waves from gentle to suicidal. The best beginner beaches in Punta Hermosa are Caballeros, Pacharacas, and La Isla. Taxis and surfing camps can arrange transportation to beginner beaches farther south, such as Puerto Viejo and Cerro Azul.

The honest and straightforward **Marco León Villarán** (tel. 01/230-8351, www.peruadventure.com), who runs a bed-and-breakfast in town, can arrange a variety of fabulous adventures in the area. His main passion is **spearfishing**, and if you have the snorkel, fins, and mask he can lead you to just about any fish you have ever dreamed of seeing—or spearing—including 1.2-meter yellowtail or gigantic flounder near Punta Hermosa.

Marco is also a professional bone-and-fossil hunter who knows Peru's desert coastline very well—from the fossil-rich deserts of Ica to the pristine and remote surfing beaches north of Chiclayo. He owns a reliable 4WD van and is an excellent, affordable, and trustworthy option for getting into remote areas of the Ica desert.

Food and Accommodations

Punta Hermosa's better places are in La Planicie, a quiet neighborhood to the north of town that offers a nice respite from the rowdy surfer scene in town, a 10-minute walk away. A good restaurant and Internet access are here, along with Señoritas and Caballeros beaches. There are more hotels and nightlife, and the monster Pico Alto wave itself, near the center of Punta Hermosa—along with crowds of rowdy Brazilian and Argentinean surfers who are in town to test their mettle on waves that have made Punta Hermosa known as the Hawaii of South America.

If you're in the mood for seafood, **Cevicheria Manuel A Su Servicio** (Mz. V, Lote 10, Ampliación Santa Cruz, tel. 01/230-8060, 10:45am-8:30pm daily, US$10) gets good reviews for its ceviche. Try **La Casa de Gloria** (N. 1, la Planicie, tel. 01/230-8066, US$8) for home-cooked meals, sandwiches, and desserts, and **Don Nico** (Calle Cabo Blanco Mz. R, Lote 17, cell tel. 953-334-000, US$10) for juicy hamburgers and steaks in a relaxed ambiance.

On second thought, ditch the restaurants. Hungry beachgoers are instead going to **La Curva** (Caleta doc 218, noon-10pm Tues.-Sun.), a food truck court with some excellent meals. Some of the many options include **El Gringo,** serving hamburgers; **Pepe Winger,** serving hot wings; **Urbano,** with gourmet sandwiches and ceviche; **Hattori,** for sushi; **Octavio,** for succulent chicken and piping-hot fries; and **Dragon de Chi-Fan,** for *chifa*. Many of these trucks are also often in Lima; look them up online to find their location.

In the Planicie neighborhood, long-time Punta Hermosa resident Marco León Villarán offers something for everyone at the **Peru Adventure Lodge** (Block Ñ, Lote 1, La Planicie, tel. 01/230-8351, www.peruadventure.com, US$25 pp). His rooms are quiet, large, and comfortable, with tons of hot water and two Labrador retrievers who can lick you awake every morning for a bit extra. He and his wife, Gloria, prepare excellent meals. The family rents out boards and also organizes surf and fossil tours all along the Peruvian coast.

In Punta Hermosa, another camp is run by Oscar Morante, a surf guide who leads trips all around Peru for several international surfing agencies. His **Pico Alto International Surf Camp** (Block L, Lote 14, tel. 01/230-7297, www.picoalto.com.pe) is well worth it.

Getting There and Around

Probably the easiest way to get to Punta Hermosa from Lima is to hire a taxi (US$18) or arrange a pickup through your hotel. **Flavio Solaria** (tel. 01/230-7578, srtsurfcamp@yahoo.com) picks up groups from the Lima airport for US$30. Buses from Lima for Mala—which stop outside Punta Hermosa, San Bartolo, and Santa María—pick up passengers at the circle, or *trébol*, where Avenida Javier Prado intersects with the Panamericana in Monterrico. These buses, called Maleños, take 45 minutes to reach Punta Hermosa and charge US$1.50.

Three-wheeled *motocars* abound in

Punta Hermosa and are an option for getting between La Planicie and the town center (US$0.50).

SAN BARTOLO

Farther down the Panamericana, past an exclusive area of homes perched on a seaside cliff and an exclusive beach club known as La Quebrada, lies the laid-back beach town of San Bartolo. The town itself is perched on a bluff above an attractive horseshoe-shaped beach, lined with hotels, condos, and a *malecón,* known as Playa Norte. San Bartolo is less of a surfer party spot than the center of Punta Hermosa, with Peñascal, a right reef break that gets as high as four meters on the south end of the Playa Norte. There are gentler waves and a good place for swimming on the north end of Playa Norte, along with a few nice beachfront hotels. After entering from Km 48 of the Panamericana, the main drag into town is Avenida San Bartolo.

Food and Accommodations

Most of the eating options—except for the spit-roasted chicken at Mar Pacífico 495—revolve around seafood. There's a line of restaurants down Mar Pacífico. **El Rincón de Chelulo** (Mar Pacífico s/n, tel. 01/430-7170, noon-11pm Mon.-Sat.) wins out for a greater variety of fish and shellfish, unbelievable friendly service, and a larger US$5 lunch menu. These restaurants are in front of the plaza where the town's market opens up every morning. This square also has a few ice cream shops and pizzerias, open in summer only.

Prices in San Bartolo double on weekend nights, so if you are planning a budget trip, make sure to visit during weekdays. Prices listed are for weekdays.

Great service and plush surroundings can be found at **Sol y Mar** (Malecón 930, tel. 01/430-7096, www.solymarperu.com US$30 s, US$48 d), with white leather couches, huge tiled rooms, great baths, cable TV, fridges, full kitchens in a few rooms, and terraces with great ocean-view rooms. The other nice place on Playa Norte is **La Posada del Mirador** (Malecón 105, tel. 01/430-7822, US$30 s, US$40 d, with breakfast), with furnished apartments.

Hostal 110 (San Martín Norte 110, tel. 01/430-7559, www.hostal110sb.com, US$60) has six small but clean rooms, each with a mini fridge and a TV, overlooking the bay. The hotel, which has two swimming pools, also has two-bedroom apartments (US$230 per week) that it rents by the week. For small groups, this is a much better and cheaper option.

Getting There and Around

Probably the easiest way to get to San Bartolo from Lima is to hire a taxi (US$20) or take the Cruz del Sur bus, which stops at the town entrance. Local buses from Lima for Mala—which stop outside Punta Hermosa, San Bartolo, and Santa María—pick up passengers at the circle, or *trébol,* where Avenida Javier Prado intersects with the Panamericana in Barranco. These buses take 50 minutes to reach San Bartolo and charge US$1.50.

The Sacred Valley

Gazing upon this astonishing valley, it's no surprise that the Inca considered it sacred—an earthly reflection of the Milky Way galaxy.

While stargazers can debate the intricacies of Inca astronomy, what is beyond doubt is the fertility of the Sacred Valley. As Cusco was considered the navel of the world by the Inca, the Sacred Valley was the breadbasket and the Río Urubamba that flows through it the lifeblood. The valley's warm climate and sunbaked red granite hills have always been ideal for agriculture, and this region continues to keep Cusco well fed with myriad varieties of vegetables and grains.

The Sacred Valley runs roughly from Pisac to Ollantaytambo and beyond to Piscacucho before plunging toward the cloud forests around Machu Picchu and the jungle farther on. The climate is perfect: warmer than the chilly, thin air of Cusco and, crucially, below 3,000 meters, so altitude sickness is less of a factor. Inca palaces, fortresses, and sun temples dot this valley, along with charming Andean villages that produce and sell some of the country's finest handicrafts. Along with Machu Picchu and Cusco, the Sacred Valley is at the top of Peru's must-see list.

Two of the most interesting destinations in the Sacred Valley are the Inca villages of Pisac and Ollantaytambo. Pisac has always been well known for its daily handicrafts market, which gets busy on Sunday, Tuesday, and Thursday. But the market is not what it used to be, and the important Inca ruins in the hills above town are arguably a bigger draw. These ruins offer an interesting window into Inca life because they combine religious, civilian, and military architecture in a single location.

Ollantaytambo is Peru's best example of a living Inca village, where people still reside in graceful Inca homes and use the same waterways used by their ancestors 500 years ago. Ollantaytambo's sun temple towers above town and contains Inca stonework as impressive as that found in Cusco and Machu Picchu, and it is the second-most impressive Inca site in Peru.

Most Inca architecture, especially in the Sacred Valley, was built with the movements of the sun and stars in mind. The

Previous: storehouse in Ollantaytambo; view of the fertile Sacred Valley. **Above:** doorway at the Pisac ruins.

Look for ★ to find recommended
sights, activities, dining, and lodging.

Highlights

★ **Pisac Ruins:** What's unique about Pisac's Inca ruins, apart from their extraordinary beauty, is their range. Here you will find not only religious architecture, but also residential, agricultural, and military structures (page 85).

★ **Moray and Salineras:** This six-hour downhill hike is a gorgeous introduction to the Sacred Valley. Start at Moray, a complex of concentric agricultural terraces, and then head downhill past Salineras, a centuries-old salt mine that is still in operation (page 98).

★ **Ollantaytambo Temple:** Second in importance only to Machu Picchu, Ollantaytambo includes some of the Inca's best stonework, including a series of ceremonial baths, elegant trapezoidal doorways, and a sun temple that faces the rising sun (page 102).

★ **Inca Granaries (Pinkuylluna):** This moderate, 1.5-hour hike offers a spectacular view of Ollantaytambo, its gleaming sun temple, and interesting grain storehouses, known in Quechua as *colcas* (page 104).

© AVALON TRAVEL

The Sacred Valley

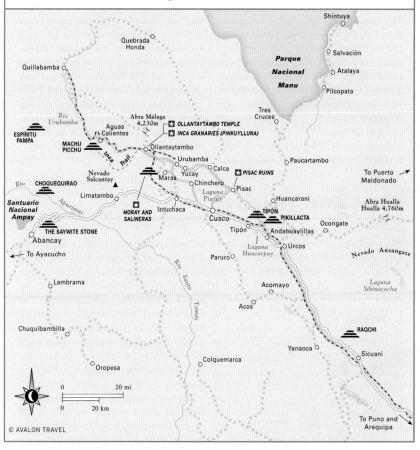

Shintuya

Salvación

Atalaya

Pilcopata

Parque Nacional Manu

Tres Cruces

Quebrada Honda

Quillabamba

Río Urubamba

Abra Málaga 4,230m

ESPÍRITU PAMPA

Aguas Calientes

MACHU PICCHU

Inca Trail

OLLANTAYTAMBO TEMPLE

INCA GRANARIES (PINKUYLLUNA)

Ollantaytambo

Urubamba

Calca

Paucartambo

To Puerto Maldonado

Nevado Salcantay

CHOQUEQUIRAO

Río

Apurímac

Limatambo

Maras

Yucay

Chinchero

Laguna Piuray

Pisac

PISAC RUINS

Huancarani

Abra Hualla Hualla 4,760m

Santuario Nacional Ampay

MORAY AND SALINERAS

Izcuchaca

Cusco

TIPÓN

PIKILLACTA

Ocongate

Nevado Ausangate

THE SAYWITE STONE

Abancay

Tipón

Andahuaylillas

Laguna Huacarpay

Urcos

To Ayacucho

Paruro

Lambrama

Río Santo

Río Tomás

Acomayo

Laguna Sibinacocha

Chuquibambilla

Acos

RAQCHI

Yanaoca

Sicuani

Oropesa

Colquemarca

0 20 mi

0 20 km

© AVALON TRAVEL

To Puno and Arequipa

temple-fortresses of Pisac and Ollantaytambo both correspond precisely to lunar and solar events. Moray, an area of terraced natural depressions, was probably designed to use sun and shade as part of an agricultural laboratory. The Inca went to great effort to redirect the Río Urubamba into a stone channel—to maximize farming land, but also probably to reflect the shape of the Milky Way. The great care the Inca took in aligning buildings with the sun, moon, and stars reflects their vision of the Sacred Valley as a sacred, celestial landscape.

PLANNING YOUR TIME

Most travelers arrive at the giddy heights of Cusco (3,400 meters) and plan their trip from there, visiting the Sacred Valley on day trips and seeing Machu Picchu in one very long day. This is the worst way of doing it. You are far better off getting out of Cusco as soon as you arrive and staying in the warmer, lower towns of the Sacred Valley. The first reason is that altitude sickness is far less of a problem below 3,000 meters. You may experience light-headedness and breathlessness, but it will be far less severe than in Cusco.

Additionally, by staying in Pisac, Urubamba, or Ollantaytambo, you are afforded far more time to see these spectacular sets of ruins. The standard one-day Sacred Valley tour from Cusco is far from ideal; this tour whisks visitors through the Pisac ruins and market, lunch in Urubamba, and an afternoon visit to the Ollantaytambo ruins, which are very busy by lunchtime and heaving by midafternoon. By staying overnight in town, we were at Ollantaytambo ruins at 8am and were the first tourists there.

Furthermore, visiting the Sacred Valley first is infinitely preferable to seeing it after Machu Picchu, as any ruins seem modest in comparison to the region's main attraction. It's far better to build upwards in scale, seeing Pisac, Moray, and Ollantaytambo before Machu Picchu. Finish up in Cusco, which will keep you busy for several days when you are acclimatized and ready to tackle this fascinating city. The best plan is to start your Peru trip with 2-3 days in the Sacred Valley and then take a train from Ollantaytambo to Machu Picchu. Return can be from Machu Picchu directly to Cusco, or you can go back to Ollantaytambo and take a *taxi colectivo*.

Pisac and Vicinity

Pisac is an attractive Andean town with a pleasant center and the most important Inca ruins in the Sacred Valley besides Ollantaytambo. A bigger draw for tourists used to be the Pisac market, but its popularity has waned, not least because similar wares can be found all over the Sacred Valley. Some day tours now bypass the market altogether. The town still swells with day-trippers on Sunday, Tuesday, and Thursday mornings but is very quiet later in the day. Aside from the market, there is little to see in Pisac itself, but it is a very agreeable town in which to spend a few hours.

The Inca fortress above town contains a rare combination of residential, military, and religious construction that sheds light on the daily life of the Inca. In the high plains beyond the fortress, there are remote villages that can be reached only on foot. Several hotels lead trips into the surrounding countryside to visit these Quechuan villages, spectacular mountain lakes, and the remote ruins of Cuyo Chico and Cuyo Grande.

SIGHTS
Pisac Market

Pisac used to be one of the biggest *artesanía* markets in South America, but it is quieter than it used to be. The market begins every day at 9am when the first tour buses arrive from Cusco and winds down around 5pm

Pisac

To ✚ PISAC RUINS

ATM
ULRIKE'S CAFÉ
BLUE LLAMA CAFÉ
HORNO COLONIAL
ATM
PISAQ INN/
CUCHARA DE PALO
TINKUY/AYSANA
ORGANICS
MARISCAL
Plaza
Consti-
tución
● HOSPEDAJE
SAMANA WASI
CAFÉ MULLU
● HOSTAL KINSA
CCOCHA
CASTILLA
AREQUIPA
BOLOGNESI
GRAU

To Urubamba,
Chinchero, and
Huchuy Cusco
←

BUSES TO CUSCO/
URUBAMABA

RESTAURANT
VALLE SAGRADO
TAXI STAND
AMAZONAS
MUSEO ★

Río

To Paz y Luz, Hotel
Royal Inka III, and
✚ PISAC RUINS

Urubamba

To Cusco
0   50 yds
0   50 m

© AVALON TRAVEL

when the last tourists leave. The town's main square is filled with stalls selling the full range of Peruvian *artesanía:* carved gourds *(mates burilados),* ceramics, felt hats, alpaca sweaters and mittens, musical instruments, paintings, antiques, a huge variety of trinkets, and, most of all, weavings and jewelry. Even if you are not buying, the café balconies overlooking the market offer superb people-watching as hundreds of camera-toting tourists haggle with Quechuan-speaking merchants. Quality tends to be in the low to middle range—the good stuff is found in the homes of the *artesanos* themselves or in upscale city galleries—but, after a bit of bargaining, prices can be very reasonable, especially if buying in quantity.

More interesting is the authentic Sunday market, when campesinos from surrounding villages set up a barter market, or *mercado de treque,* which is an ancient Peruvian custom and an interesting example of the informal economies upon which highlanders depend. Quechuan-speaking people sit behind piles of vegetables in one corner of the square. They sell these products to buy essentials (salt, sugar, kerosene, matches, and medicines) but also trade to acquire other foods, such as oranges from the Quillabamba Valley. It exists side by side with the Pisac market but ends by 3pm so that villagers can walk home before dark. Also on Sunday only, Masses in Quechua are held at 6am and 11am in **San Pedro Apóstol de Pisac,** the colonial church on the main square that was rebuilt after the 1950 earthquake. The church has Inca foundations and an interesting collection of colonial paintings.

TOP EXPERIENCE

★ Pisac Ruins

Pisac is one of the valley's few great Inca ruins that features all types of architecture—agricultural, hydraulic, military, residential, and religious. Little is known for certain about Pisac's precise function, and there is no mention of it in Spanish chronicles, perhaps because it was never used by the Inca in their battles against the invaders. However, it probably began as a military garrison to guard against incursion from the Anti people, who occupied the easternmost corner of the empire known as **Antisuyo** (present-day Paucartambo and the Manu jungle). Inca emperor Pachacútec probably built Pisac's imperial architecture and may have used it as a royal residence, while the temples indicate that Pisac also had religious status.

the Inca fortress above Pisac

There are two main entrances to the ruins, where you need to present or purchase the *boleto turístico*. If taking the steep walk from town, you arrive at the terraces at **Andenes Acchapata** and can climb up toward the Intihuatana, the ceremonial center, and the agricultural and urban zones. However, most people take a taxi to enter the ruins from the parking area next to the main entrance at **Qantus Raccay,** one of three residential areas in Pisac. It is composed of rough stone buildings, walls with niches, and small squares. These were probably military garrisons and, in the style of a medieval castle, shelter for villagers in times of war. From here you can appreciate some of the best views of the terraces of Pisac—there are 500 in total. Corn was grown on the lower terraces, potatoes in the middle, and quinoa grain on the high terraces. To the right, embedded in the hillside, is a huge Inca cemetery with some 3,500 tombs, although the mummies are long gone.

An Inca trail traverses the hillside, arrives at a small pass, then heads up and over a rocky summit to the sun temple. At the pass, four purification baths flow with water brought down from a lake at 4,500 meters. On the other side of the pass to the left, a 10-minute detour around the corner reveals Inca buttresses, which were once spanned by a hanging bridge made of plant fibers.

The main path crosses through a military wall with a perfect trapezoidal door, known as the **Door of the Serpent.** Above is the second residential area, **Hanam P'isaq** (upper Pisac). The path now climbs up steep staircases and niches carved out of the rock itself, alongside a cliff and through the **Q'alla Q'asa** (Split Rock) tunnel. Faced with a vertical rock face, Inca engineers decided to enlarge a rock fissure and bore through the entire cliff—how they did this, with no iron or steel implements, remains a mystery.

The best view of the **Intihuatana,** which means "sun calendar" in Quechua, is from above. Like the sun temple at Machu Picchu, the Intihuatana is an oval building of perfect masonry encasing a votive rock. The pillar atop the rock was used to track the sun's movements, and, fascinatingly, the sun rises precisely above one peak to the east on June 21 and another on December 21. The walls of five other temples surround the temple, including one that was probably devoted to the moon. To the right is a series of restored baths that flow into an underground canal. In front of the Intihuatana is a sacred *chacana* (Inca cross).

Off the easier trail back to the main entrance of the ruins is **P'isaqa,** the third and finest residential area, with its own ritual bath. These were probably homes for the elite, as opposed to the military garrisons closer to the pass. Most people head back at this point to the main entrance, though there are two trails from here that make a pleasant two-hour walk back to Pisac. One descends directly to the Río Quitamayo, with spectacular views, while the other drops through the lookout towers of Coriwayrachina and an area of steep terracing. Both trails merge on the other side of the river for the final descent into town.

There are several ways to see the Pisac ruins (7am-3pm, admission only with *boleto turístico*), but the most popular is to take a US$8 taxi up the eight-kilometer highway to the main entrance. Allow 1.5 to 2 hours to see the ruins and another 2 hours to walk downhill all the way to town (or take a taxi back for a further US$8).

Museo Comunitario de Pisac

In 2009, **Museo Comunitario de Pisac** (Amazonas and Federico Zamalloa, 8am-5pm Sun.-Fri., free) opened southeast of Pisac's center with an exhibition of traditional textiles and a small collection of ceramics from the Pisac ruins. The highlight is the exhibition of Inca mummies.

ENTERTAINMENT AND EVENTS

There are no discos in Pisac, but the cafés around the square serve beer and cocktails.

Pisac's big festival is **Fiesta de la Virgen del Carmen,** which begins on July 15 and

Natural High: Coca Tea

The coca plant's bad reputation is rather unfair. Although its most lucrative use involves refining its alkaloids into cocaine, the most natural use of the leaves is as a refreshing and useful drink.

Mate de coca is a very popular tea in the Andes, renowned for its medicinal properties and ability to combat altitude sickness. The tea itself can be made with teabags, but it's better with fresh leaves. It looks and tastes a little like Japanese green tea but sweeter. Amusingly, just like decaffeinated coffee, de-cocainized tea does exist, although it's hard to find. Coca tea containing alkaloids remains illegal in the United States, so you are inviting trouble if you attempt to take any back with you.

Although coca tea's effectiveness in combating altitude sickness has not been scientifically proven, the stimulant seems to help oxygenate the blood and ease discomfort. The average cup contains approximately 4 milligrams of alkaloids, so it is mildly stimulating. As a guide, a line of cocaine contains 20 milligrams, so five cups of coca tea could conceivably get you a little high.

runs for five days. The first day includes a horse-riding contest followed by a series of religious processions and dances.

SHOPPING

Apart from the Pisac market, there are crafts shops open all week long (10am-9pm daily) on all the main streets leading from the square, especially **Mariscal Castilla, San Francisco,** and **Bolognesi.** Contemporary art is sold in the first floor of the **Café Art Gallery Mullu** (Plaza de Armas 352, tel. 084/20-3073, www.mullu.pe).

Aysana Organics (Av. Pardo, cell tel. 984-081-970, 10am-4pm daily) is a good place to pick up healthy products. Everything from soap to chocolate, dried fruit, and coca toffee is available.

FOOD
Peruvian

The best place for trout in Pisac is **Restaurant Valle Sagrado** (Amazonas 116, tel. 084/43-6915, 8am-8pm daily, US$4-6). During lunch, this place is packed with locals who come not only for the trout but for chicken, soups, sandwiches, and lamb ribs.

The gourmet option in town is **Cuchara de Palo** (Plaza de Armas, tel. 084/20-3062, www.pisacinn.com, 7:30am-8:30pm daily, US$5-15), inside Pisac Inn. The atmosphere

(bright green walls and tree-trunk tables) and the food are all natural. Vegetarians should try the *quinoa chaufa* (fried quinoa), and meat eaters should go for *lomo saltado.*

Cafés, Bakeries, and Ice Cream

★ **Ulrike's Café** (Manuel Prado, tel. 084/20-3195, 7am-9pm daily, US$5) offers a lunch menu (US$8), vegetarian options, and pizza. Ulrike Simic, the German owner of this playful establishment, makes a delectable array of cheesecakes, including chocolate chip, coffee, and lemon. The colorful walls and laid-back atmosphere make this the perfect respite on busy market days.

★ **Café Art Gallery Mullu** (Plaza de Armas 352, tel. 084/20-3073, 9am-8pm daily, US$5) has the most diverse menu in town. Billed as an Asian fusion restaurant, it has an interesting collection of contemporary art on the first floor and a café with nice market views on the second. The menu blends Peruvian, Asian, and international dishes, including Thai curry, *tahine* lamb stew, and Kashmiri ravioli.

Blue Llama Café (Plaza de Armas, tel. 084/20-3135, 7am-8pm daily, US$5) offers good food and service. Great coffee, brownies, and pancakes go down well early in the day, and soups and mains such as teriyaki chicken, pot roast, and trout are good for dinner. It's a comfy place to hang out with a book or friends.

Tinkuy Café (Pardo, no phone, breakfast, lunch and dinner daily) is another fun place in Pisac, where owners Alfredo and Nancy offer a good range of juices, coffee, and vegetarian food. They have a daily set menu for US$5. Alfredo speaks English and can help with tours of the area.

Markets

The best supermarket is **Sofis Market** (Bolognesi s/n, tel. 084/20-3017, 6:30am-10pm daily).

ACCOMMODATIONS
US$10-25

The best budget option is **Hostel Kinsa Ccocha** (Arequipa 307, tel. 084/20-3101, US$15 s, US$20 with private bathroom), a block from the Plaza de Armas, which has several plain, clean rooms with shared or private bath. Ask for a newer room; they have higher ceilings.

Hospedaje Samana Wasi (Plaza de Armas 509, tel. 084/20-3133, US$15 s, US$20 d with private bathroom) offers small rooms overlooking the plaza with shared or private bathrooms, and a restaurant with a great value three-course set menu for just US$5 (7am-9pm daily).

US$25-50

Pisac Inn (Plaza de Armas, tel. 084/20-3062, www.pisacinn.com, US$45 s, US$55-65 d with breakfast) is owned by Roman Vizcarra and Fielding Wood-Vizcarra, a Peruvian-American couple who founded the hotel in 1993. The adobe building, covered in bright murals, includes the highly regarded Cuchara de Palo restaurant, whose balconies overlook the market square. Additional perks include a US$35 Cusco airport pickup, laundry, and a constant supply of water from the hotel's own well. Roman speaks English, Spanish, Quechua, Italian, and German and leads tours throughout the area that combine culture with spirituality (www.peruculturaljourneys.com).

New Yorker Diane Dunn's pride and joy, ★ **Paz y Luz** (off the road to the ruins 2 km outside of town, cell tel. 984-216-293, www.pazyluzperu.com, US$45 s, US$65 d with breakfast, cash in *soles* and Mastercard only on arrival, Visa in advance) is a collection of

The hotel and healing center Paz y Luz has a stunning location on the outskirts of Pisac.

earth-colored lodges on the edge of the Río Urubamba outside Pisac. Paz y Luz (peace and light) has become a center for spirituality in the Sacred Valley, and its focal point is the healing center, the inspiration for Diane's book *Cusco: Gateway to Inner Wisdom*. Diane is a kindhearted host, and the location is spectacular, with wonderful views of the mountains and Pisac ruins. The 24 rooms are located in three buildings, all comfortable and tastefully decorated, with new bathrooms. A central area has a woodstove, dining table, and polished wood staircase. The growing complex includes a restaurant, conference room, meditation room, massage, and rooms for long-term residents. Two-bedroom bungalows with their own living room, fireplace, kitchen, and bathroom are under construction at the back. Prices for long-term guests and descriptions of spiritual workshops and tailor-made tours are on the website.

US$50-100

On the outskirts of town, **Hotel Royal Inka III Pisac** (on road to the ruins 1 km outside of town, tel. 084/20-3064, www.royalinkahotel.pe, US$58 s, US$80 d) is located in a converted hacienda with a mid-19th-century chapel, but most of the rooms are in a cold and charmless modern addition. It offers an Olympic-size pool (available to nonguests), a private whirlpool tub, sauna, tennis court, horses, bikes, a game room, restaurant, bar, videos, and a spa. Without a discount, this hotel can seem overpriced, especially when compared to cheaper and more charming options nearby.

Also outside town is **Melissa Wasi** (on road to the ruins 1 km outside of town, tel. 084/79-7589 or 998-676-860, www.melissawasi.com, US$95 d, bungalow US$130), a charming hotel with eight double rooms and three separate bungalows built into the hillside. Owners Joyce and Chito have created a beautiful house with colorful gardens. Bungalows sleep up to four people, and all have WiFi and a complete kitchen.

INFORMATION AND SERVICES

Advice on Pisac and surrounding excursions is available from Tinkuy Café, Ulrike's Café, Paz y Luz, or Pisac Inn.

There is a clinic and pharmacy above the plaza near the public parking area. Other pharmacies are on Bolognesi and are generally open 8am-9pm daily, with a midday closure for lunch.

There is a **Global Net ATM** on the corner of the main square up from Blue Llama Café and a money changer on the square near the church.

A **mailbox** is on the main square inside Restaurant Samana Wasi, which also sells stamps. There are **phone booths** at Sofis Market on Bolognesi and near the municipality on the main square. **Internet** is available at several sites around the Plaza de Armas. Hours are usually 9am-10pm daily.

GETTING THERE AND AROUND

Buses for Pisac leave Cusco from Avenida Pachacútec, southwest of the center toward the bus terminal, every 20 minutes and charge US$1 for the one-hour journey. For a 45-minute ride, hire a taxi in Cusco's Plaza de Armas for US$25 or prebook with a Pisac hotel for US$30. Taxis are also available at the airport but are more expensive. Buses drop passengers off at the bridge on the main highway, from which it is a three-block walk uphill to the market and main square. Return buses to Cusco leave from the same spot every 15 minutes up until 7pm. Buses heading in the opposite direction also stop here on the way to Yucay and then Urubamba (US$0.50, 30-40 minutes). Once in Pisac, taxis can be taken eight kilometers to the main Pisac ruins entrance (US$8). *Mototaxis* offer short trips around town for US$1.

SIDE TRIPS
Huchuy Cusco

After Ollantaytambo and Pisac, Huchuy Cusco is the next most important Inca ruin in the Sacred Valley, but is not included on any day-trip itineraries and remains comparatively difficult to reach. This site features a two-story *kallanka,* or Inca hall, that is nearly 40 meters long and topped off by a well-preserved third story of adobe—it is easy to imagine this adobe painted, as were the buildings in Cusco, and topped off with a pyramid of thick thatch. There are also terraces, a square, an Inca gate, and many other ruined buildings within a few hundred meters of the hall. The whole site commands a small plateau, 800 meters above the Sacred Valley, with spectacular views.

This was probably the royal estate once known as Caquia Jaquijahuana, where, according to myth, Inca Viracocha hid when the Chancas threatened to invade Cusco in 1438. One of his sons, who later renamed himself Pachacútec ("shaker of the earth"), rose up and defeated the Chancas, thus beginning the meteoric rise of the Inca. After the conquest, the Spaniards found a mummy at this site—said to be that of Viracocha.

Reaching Huchuy Cusco is not easy. The shortest way to get there is a three-hour, uphill hike from Lamay, a village between Pisac and Urubamba. The entrance to the footbridge that crosses the Río Urubamba is marked with a large blue sign erected by the Instituto Nacional de Cultura.

Another recommended option is to approach Huchuy Cusco from the opposite direction in a two-day hike across the high plains from Cusco. The trip starts at Sacsayhuamán in Cusco and follows the original Inca Trail to Calca, heading past finely wrought canals, villages, and several 4,000-meter passes. The total trip is 27 kilometers, including the final descent to Lamay, where you can catch a bus back to Cusco via Pisac. For either route, bring plenty of water and food as there is little along the way.

Chinchero

Chinchero is a small Andean village that is about to go through major changes. The town lies along the shortest driving route between Cusco and the Sacred Valley. Chinchero is perched on the high plains at 3,800 meters above sea level and has great views over the snowcapped Urubamba range. It is nearly 400 meters above Cusco, so visitors should be aware of potential altitude sickness. Chinchero is now included on several day-trip itineraries, including the Moray and Salineras tour and some Sacred Valley tours, chiefly for demonstrations of traditional weaving techniques.

a demonstration of traditional weaving techniques in Chinchero

While some tourists stop by Chinchero today, almost all of them will in the future in order to visit Cusco and Machu Picchu. That is because the village has been chosen as the site for a new, and controversial, international airport that will replace the current airport in the city of Cusco. The airport isn't expected to be operational until 2020, but construction of the multimillion dollar project is already altering the quiet village.

Past Chinchero's less-than-appealing street front is the main square, where a handicrafts market is held on Tuesday, Thursday, and Sunday. Talented weavers in Chinchero exhibit their wares at this market, which is smaller and less touristy than Pisac's. The highlight of the square is an Inca wall with huge niches, which probably formed part of an Inca palace. Above the square is a 17th-century adobe church that was built on Inca foundations and has deteriorated floral designs painted on its interior. It is open for visitors on market days only.

On market days, you can also catch a weaving demonstration at one of the local workshops (these demonstrations are usually included on day tours). Starting as young as age 5, girls learn to wash wool; a couple of years later they are spinning the wool into thread, and finally by 12 or 15, they are weaving actual pieces. To understand the complexity and incredible skill that goes into creating these pieces, stop by **Exposición de Artesanías Mink'a Chinchero** (Albergue 22, tel. 084/30-6035, minka@hotmail.com, hours vary).

If you're looking for a more active day, and you can leave Chinchero by noon, there is a four-hour hike that drops along an old Inca trail into this valley and ends at Huayllabamba, where *combis* pass in the late afternoon for Urubamba or Pisac. From the church, a wide trail leads up the opposite side of the valley and then gradually descends into the Sacred Valley. Once you arrive at the Río Urubamba, the Sacred Valley's main river, head right (downstream) toward the bridge at Huayllabamba.

Accommodations in Chinchero are very basic, and the town's high altitude and bone-chilling nights make the Sacred Valley—almost 1,000 meters lower—a much better option. In Cusco, *colectivos* for Chinchero can be taken from the first block of Grau near the bridge (US$0.75, 45 minutes).

YUCAY

This quiet town, a few kilometers east of Urubamba, is centered on a large, grassy plaza where soccer games are played in the shade of two massive pisonay trees reputed to be 450 years old. On the far end of the square, near the highway, lies the adobe palace of Sayri Túpac, who settled here after emerging from Vilcabamba in 1558. Various colonial homes, now hotels, front the square along with the restored colonial church of Santiago Apóstol. Other than that, there is little to do in the town itself, but it makes a quieter alternative accommodation base to Urubamba. There are few services outside the hotels clustered around the square.

Food

A renowned restaurant in the Sacred Valley is ★ **Huayoccari Hacienda Restaurant** (km 64 Pisac-Ollantaytambo highway, call for directions beforehand, tel. 084/22-6241, reservas@huayoccari.com, US$45 pp). This elegant gourmet retreat, two kilometers up a dirt road near Yucay, is a converted country manor perched high on a ridge overlooking the Sacred Valley. Past a rustic courtyard, the restaurant's walls are lined with colonial paintings, altars, and ceramics collected by José Ignacio Lambarri, whose family has owned the land and nearby hacienda for more than three centuries. The garden terraces offer walks past roses and fuchsias to Inca terraces and fertile farmland.

The cuisine is completely organic, based on the hacienda's original recipes. Lunch begins with *sara lagua*, a cream soup made of local white corn, fresh cheese, and the herb *huacatay*. Main courses include steamed river trout with a sauce of herbs and fresh capers, or chicken rolled with fresh cheese and country bacon and covered with *sauco*-berry sauce. The desserts are made of delectable fruits found only in Peru: cheesecake with *aguaymanto* marmalade, *chirimoya* meringue, or a *sachatomate* compote. Though off the beaten path, Huayoccari is well worth the trek for the food, the country setting, and the private collection of art. There are only a handful of tables, so make reservations well in advance. Huayoccari is between Pisac and Urubamba and can be reached via taxi from either town.

A more conventional option, but with a diverse menu and good-value buffet lunch, is **Allpa Manka** (St. Martin 300, tel. 084/20-1258, 11am-3:30pm and 6pm-9:30pm daily, US$12-15).

Accommodations

Sonesta Posadas del Inca (Plaza Manco II, Yucay 123, tel. 084/20-1107, www.sonesta. com, US$100-180 s, US$100-190 d, prices depend on season, breakfast included) has rooms spread out among plazas and gardens, courtyard fountains, a miniature crafts market, and a chapel. The hotel is built around the charming 16th-century Santa Catalina de Sena monastery, where 21 rooms are located. The colonial-style building next door has another 40 rooms with high ceilings, cable TV, and bathrooms with tubs. Amenities include a restaurant, jewelry shop, ATM, and spa. Even if you don't stay here, stop in and see the interesting museum, which has a range of ceramics, *quipus,* and weavings from most of Peru's cultures, from the Chavín to the Inca.

The well-decorated **La Casona de Yucay** (Plaza Manco II 104, tel. 084/20-1116, www. hcy.pe, US$85 s, US$105 d with breakfast) is a colonial hacienda that has been converted into a hotel with an elegant sitting room, large guest rooms, and great views.

Getting There and Around

From Cusco, buses leave for Yucay from the first block of Grau. Frequent buses pass Yucay's main square going one direction to Pisac (30 minutes) or to Urubamba (10 minutes) in the other.

Urubamba and Vicinity

Urubamba (2,863 meters) lies in the center of the Sacred Valley. It's busier and less appealing than Ollantaytambo, 20 minutes down the valley, and Pisac, 40 minutes back up the valley. Urubamba also has too much traffic, and there is a dearth of good accommodations and restaurants for budget travelers. However, the town has a growing range of high-end accommodations, including some of the best hotels in the Sacred Valley. The masses of tourists traveling through the Sacred Valley tend to stop just for lunch at the many buffet restaurants on the edge of town, but Urubamba does have a pleasant square, colonial cathedral, busy local market, and a few bars that get going on weekends.

The surroundings of Urubamba are far more spectacular than the town itself: The snow-covered Cordillera Urubamba rises over a patchwork of russet and chocolate-brown fields. In the middle is **Maras,** a dense cluster of red tile roofs, along with two startling visual anomalies. **Moray** is a set of huge natural depressions in the earth that were elaborately terraced by the Inca. **Salineras** is a blinding-white salt mine that sprawls across the mountain slope. These three attractions are combined on a half-day trip from Cusco but can easily be explored on bicycle, horseback, or foot independently, with Urubamba as a base.

ENTERTAINMENT AND EVENTS

The best way to begin an evening is with a drink at **Red Valentina** (Grau and Palacios,

Urubamba

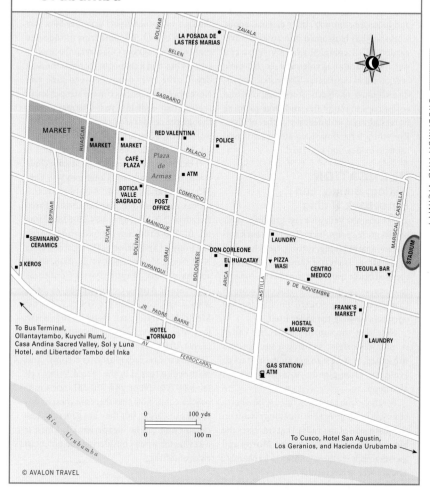

LA POSADA DE
LAS TRES MARIAS
BOLIVAR
ZAVALA
BELEN
SAGRARIO
MARKET
HUASCAR
MARKET
MARKET
RED VALENTINA
POLICE
PALACIO
CAFÉ
PLAZA
Plaza
de
Armas
■ ATM
BOTICA
VALLE
SAGRADO
POST
OFFICE
COMERCIO
ESPINAR
SUCRE
MAINIQUE
BOLIVAR
GRAU
SEMINARIO
CERAMICS
LAUNDRY
MARISCAL
CASTILLA
STADIUM
3 KEROS
YUPANQUI
BOLOGNESI
DON CORLEONE
EL HUACATAY
ARICA
PIZZA
WASI
CENTRO
MEDICO
TEQUILA BAR
CASTILLA
9 DE NOVIEMBRE
JR PADRE
BARRE
HOSTAL
MAURU'S
FRANK'S
MARKET
To Bus Terminal,
Ollantaytambo, Kuychi Rumi,
Casa Andina Sacred Valley, Sol y Luna
Hotel, and Libertador Tambo del Inka
HOTEL
TORNADO
AV
FERROCARRIL
LAUNDRY
GAS STATION/
ATM
0   100 yds
0   100 m
To Cusco, Hotel San Agustin,
Los Geranios, and Hacienda Urubamba

© AVALON TRAVEL

cell tel. 956-395-942, noon-2am Wed.-Sat.), just up from the main plaza. Around midnight, options include several places along Mariscal Castilla east of the center. The most popular is **Tequila Bar** (third block of Mariscal Castilla, tel. 084/80-1646, tequila-club@hotmail.com, 10pm-6am Fri.-Sat.).

Urubamba erupts in bullfights, dancing, and partying during the Pentecostal celebration of **Señor Torrechayoc** in late May or early June and then once again for **Urubamba Day** on November 9. An even better party, however, is Huayllabamba's **Virgen de la Natividad,** held September 7-10.

SHOPPING

When in Urubamba, do not miss the art of **Seminario Ceramics** (Barriózabal 405, tel. 084/20-1002, www.ceramicaseminario.com, 8am-7pm daily). With Pablo Seminario focusing on form and Marilú Behar on color, this husband-and-wife team began to crank out ceramics from a small home in Urubamba in 1979. Thanks to international recognition and lucrative contracts, their original adobe workshop has blossomed into an expansive, garden-filled complex where visitors can watch an educational video and see the whole ceramics-making process. The workshop produces a range of objects, from compotes and coffee cups to sculptures and large painting frames adorned with delicate touches of silver. Everything is handmade, painted with natural mineral oxides, and kiln fired.

RECREATION
Hiking, Biking, and Horseback Riding

The Urubamba Valley is a fast-growing center of adventure sports, including horseback riding, mountain biking, rafting, trekking, and paragliding. There are some highly recommended bridle trails that can also be done on foot or mountain bike. Several operators in Cusco offer daily organized tours, as do a few operators based in the valley itself.

Note that the sun in the Sacred Valley is intensely bright, so bring a sun hat and sunscreen. It is best to get an early start to avoid the often-cloudy (sometimes rainy) afternoons.

For those who can take a full day on a horse or on a bike, there is a breathtaking circuit on the south side of the valley that traverses the high plains around **Maras** and **Moray** and then descends via the salt mines to Urubamba. The scenery is spectacular.

Wayra (part of the Sol y Luna Hotel outside Urubamba, tel. 084/20-1620, www.wayrasacredvalley.com) rents mountain bikes and has the best selection of *paso* horses in the valley. Day tours cost from US$105 per person. Another good option for *paso* horses is **Perol Chico** (Carretera Urubamba-Ollantaytambo, tel. 950-314-065, www.perolchico.com). These elegant animals are best for the Maras-Moray-Salinas loop or a flat loop around the valley.

Rafting

All of the Cusco rafting agencies descend the Río Urubamba, which is at its wildest during the high-water months of December-May. Day trips run US$40-55. Some trips include one night of camping near Ollantaytambo, mountain biking, and a chance to see ruins the next day. As the river drops between June and November, the agencies run the steeper, lower section that ends just past Ollantaytambo, though the rapids rarely exceed Class III. The water itself, unfortunately, is somewhat polluted, with plastic festooning the banks.

The best rafting agencies in Cusco include **Amazonas Explorer** (Collasuyo 910, Urb. Miravalle, Cusco, tel. 084/25-2846, www.amazonas-explorer.com), **ExplorAndes** (Paseo Zarzuela Q-2, Cusco tel. 084/23-8380, Lima tel. 01/200-6100, www.explorandes.com), **Apumayo Expediciones** (Jr. Ricardo Palma N-11, Santa Monica, tel. 084/24-6018, www.apumayo.com), **Mayuc** (Portal Confituras 211, Plaza de Armas, Cusco, tel. 084/24-2824, www.mayuc.com), **Loreto Tours** (Calle del Medio 111, Cusco, tel. 084/22-8264, www.loretotours.com), **Terra Explorer Peru** (Santa Ursula D-4, Huanchac, tel. 084/23-7352, www.terraexplorerperu.com), and **Munaycha** (based in the Sacred Valley, cell tel. 984-770-108 or 984-770-381, www.munaycha.com). Note that there are cheaper operators in Cusco, but they are generally less reliable and can be inexperienced, which is a key factor when considering the potential risks of rafting.

Climbing

A new adventure in the Sacred Valley is the **Via Ferrata** (tel. 084/793-019 or 951/373-240, www.naturavive.com, US$65 pp), a system of ropes and pulleys that allows you to climb a 300-meter cliff and then rappel, or descend, about 100 meters. The whole experience lasts 3-5 hours and can be done even by small children. Reservations must be made in advance.

Peru's Battle with the Bottle

Every time travelers buy a plastic water bottle, they are contributing to a solid-waste problem that is reaching epic proportions not only in Cusco but all over Peru. The best way to understand the problem is to raft along Cusco's Río Urubamba, where tree roots are blanketed in thick gobs of plastic bags and beaches are completely covered with plastic bottles.

What resources Peru's municipal governments have are used to fight poverty, not improve the environment. Aside from an admirable local project in Ollantaytambo, there is little organized plastic recycling program in Peru. Nearly 200 million plastic bottles are produced every month in Peru alone, and a good chunk of these are consumed by tourists—who need a few liters of purified water for each day in Peru.

A boycott campaign has been initiated by longtime Ollantaytambo resident Joaquín Randall, who manages his family's El Albergue hotel in the town.

Here's how travelers can do their part to resolve Peru's plastic addiction:

· Carry a reusable hard plastic or other water bottle and fill it with treated or boiled water.

· Buy sodas and water in refillable glass bottles.

· Demand that your hotel provide water tanks (bidones) or at the very least boiled water for refilling bottles.

· Reuse plastic bags over and over and do not accept new ones.

· Spread the word.

Paragliding

The best place to get paragliding lessons in the Cusco area is **Wayra** (part of the Sol y Luna Hotel outside Urubamba, tel. 084/20-1620, www.wayrasacredvalley.com), where owners Marie-Hélène Miribel and Franz Schilter offer instruction. They are the only internationally certified instructors in Cusco. They charge US$150 for a tandem one-hour flight, taking off from a nearby mountain and landing in the valley itself.

FOOD

The Sacred Valley day tours use Urubamba as a lunch spot, so there are a half-dozen restaurants that offer good lunch buffets. These include **Alhambra** (km 74 Urubamba-Ollantaytambo Hwy., tel. 084/20-1200, noon-3:30pm and 7pm-close daily, US$12-14) and **Killa Wasi** (tel. 084/20-1620, www.hotelsolyluna.com, noon-7pm Tues., Thurs., and Sun., US$30), the restaurant connected to Sol y Luna Hotel, three kilometers from Urubamba's main plaza on the road toward Ollantaytambo and Machu Picchu.

For pizza try **Don Corleone** (Mainique and Urubamba, tel. 084/63-3783, lunch and dinner daily, US$7-14) or the most popular pizzeria in town, **Pizza Wasi** (Av. Castilla, tel. 084/43-4751, lunch and dinner daily, mains US$8-12). Pizza Wasi also does decent Peruvian meat, chicken, and fish dishes. **Café Plaza** (Plaza de Armas/Bolivar, tel. 084/20-1118, breakfast, lunch, and dinner daily, mains US$7-11) is a decent option on the main square with a range of breakfasts ($4-7) and interesting mains, including chicken in mango and beef in gorgonzola. Service is a little slack, though.

★ **3 Keros** (Sr. de Torrechayoc, tel. 084/20-1701, noon-3:45pm and 6:30pm-9:30pm Wed.-Mon., US$14-16) is renowned as one of the best restaurants in Urubamba. Ricardo, the owner of this laid-back restaurant, dishes up *cuy* specials, steak, lamb, trout, and chicken, all cooked to perfection in delicious sauces. Try the lamb in wild berries.

...ef Pio Vasquez, with the help of his ...an wife, Iris, has created an elegant res-...t and garden. Have your passion fruit ...ur on the patio of **El Huacatay** (Arica 620, tel. 084/20-1790, www.elhuacatay.com, 1pm-9pm Mon.-Sat., US$12-16) before moving into the intimate dining room for a main course based on local produce—from arugula to fresh trout. Dessert is Pio's passion, so leave room for the chocolate mousse.

ACCOMMODATIONS

Finding accommodation in Urubamba is difficult for those on a tight budget. There are very few cheap places, and be sure to avoid the *hospedajes* in the center, as these are seedy motels for local lovers. However, if you have the resources, several of the best top-range hotels in the Sacred Valley are here.

US$10-25

One of the few decent budget options is **Hostal Mauru's – Tambo del Sol** (Convención 113, tel. 084/20-1352, www.hoteltambodelsol.com, US$20 s, US$28 d), which has pleasant rooms with private bath and cable TV.

US$25-50

A midrange hotel on the main highway south of the center is **Hotel Tornado** (Av. Cabo Conchatupa and Boliva, tel. 084/20-1120, www.hoteltornadoperu.com, US$50 s, US$70 d, including breakfast). Several double rooms have a Jacuzzi ($95).

US$100-150

The **Hotel San Agustín Monasterio de la Recoleta** (Recoleta s/n, tel. 084/20-1666, www.hotelessanagustin.com.pe, US$130 s, US$154 d) occupies a stunning 16th-century Franciscan monastery. There is a modern addition with a few spectacular rooms upstairs, outfitted with exposed beams, stone showers, and sun windows; the rest of the modern rooms are nondescript. Rooms in the old section are surrounded by a stone courtyard and are superior to the blander modern rooms.

Over US$150

Kuychi Rumi Lodging (km 74.5 Urubamba-Ollantaytambo Hwy., tel. 084/20-1169, www.urubamba.com, US$120 s, US$140 d, with breakfast) offers six fully equipped houses that each have two bedrooms, a sitting room, and a kitchenette. Tastefully designed and decorated, the houses are meant for longer stays, but even if you only have a night, they are worth it for the privacy and comfort. The grounds are filled with hummingbirds.

Sol y Luna Hotel (tel. 084/60-8930, www.hotelsolyluna.com, US$350 s/d to US$660 for a deluxe suite, with breakfast), three kilometers from Urubamba's main plaza on the road toward Ollantaytambo and Machu Picchu, was opened in 2000 by Marie-Hélène Miribel and Franz Schilter. This French-Swiss couple has carefully designed every last detail of their 43 bungalows, including terra-cotta tiles, exposed beams, marble bathrooms, and king-size beds. The deluxe bungalows include a hot tub on the patio. The poolside buffet is excellent, using local produce from the valley. Groups are often treated to *pachamanca* cooking with *marinera* dance demonstrations. The hotel has extensive gardens, a pool, a gym, and a spa with whirlpool tub and massage. There are 20 Peruvian horses *(caballos de paso)* lodged in stables in the back and available for half- and full-day rides. The hotel also rents mountain bikes, coordinates cultural trips to a local school and orphanage, and offers paragliding outings with the owners, Cusco's only internationally certified instructors. Through an associated nonprofit organization, the hotel has also created a local school.

In the Sacred Valley, the **Willka Tika** (Paradero Rumichaka, 2 kilometers north of Urubamba, tel. 707/202-5340, www.willka-tika.com) is a luxury retreat that offers ceremonial activities. It has seven relaxing gardens with winding paths, a yoga studio and meditation cottages.

The best upscale hotel in the Urubamba area is the ★ **Libertador Tambo del Inka** (Av. Ferrocarril, tel. 084/58-1777, www.lux-urycollection.com/tambodelinka, US$275 s/d), designed by Bernard Fort and set on the banks of the Urubamba. It is the only hotel in Peru with a Leadership in Energy and Environmental Design (LEED) certificate, and therefore one of the most environmentally friendly hotels in the country. The elegant lobby, with 12-meter ceilings, mixes international standards with Peruvian decor. The 128 rooms and suites all have a balcony or terrace, WiFi, cable TV, and iPod docks. The buffet breakfast is a veritable feast, and a highlight is the 1,800-square-meter spa, gym, and sauna. Cool off with a dip in the pool and Jacuzzi, which command great views of the river. At night, visit the Bar Kiri, with its striking backlit onyx wall. The hotel can organize kayaking and cycling excursions.

A new option in the area is Inkaterra's **Hacienda Urubamba** (Pie del cerro Huayllawasy, Lima tel. 01/610-0400, www. inkaterra.com, US$462 s/d, US$935 suite), which offers rooms with fireplaces and sweeping views of the green countryside. The hotel opened in 2015 with 12 luxury rooms and added 24 stand-alone casitas in 2016. The hotel offers excursions for everyone from birders to guests interested in medicinal plants and *chicha de jora,* the ancient Andean beer.

Outside Urubamba

In Yanahuara, just 15 minutes outside of Urubamba on the road to Ollantaytambo, the hotel chain **Casa Andina** has constructed one of its **Private Collection** hotels (5th Paradero, cell tel. 984-765-501, www.casa-andina.com, US$116 s/d with breakfast). The result is a labyrinth of glassed lobbies, gardens, a spa center, and a planetarium. You might just have to spend two nights to take advantage of it all. It's also very child-friendly, with a small playground, llamas, and lots of open space.

In Huayllabamba, the **Aranwa** chain of hotels has a 100-bedroom, 15-suite complex (Vía Urubamba-Huayllabamba, tel. 01/434-6199, www.aranwahotels.com, US$240 s/d) that includes one of the largest spas in the Sacred Valley as well as a business center,

three restaurants, a sushi bar, and even a cinema. The newer buildings are built around a historic hacienda.

Rio Sagrado (km 75.8 Cusco-Urubamba Hwy., tel. 084/20-1631, www.riosagrado.com, US$325 s/d) is part of the Belmond line of hotels (formerly Orient-Express) and is located on the outskirts of Urubamba. It has a mixture of high-quality rooms, suites, and two-story bungalows, plus a spa.

INFORMATION AND SERVICES

There's a **police station** on Palacio (s/n, tel. 084/20-1012). The **town clinic** is on 9 de Noviembre (s/n, tel. 084/20-1032, lab open 8am-1pm). There are now tourist clinics in Urubamba, including **SOS Urgent Medical** (Mariscal Castilla, tel. 084/20-5059), which is a modern facility that works with different insurance companies. There are pharmacies all over town, but a good option is **Botica Valle Sagrado** (Bolivar 469, tel. 084/20-1830, 8am-10pm daily).

On the highway in front of Urubamba, there is a **Banco de Crédito** ATM, and in the Pesca gas station there is a **Global Net** ATM.

The **post office** is on the main square, along with several pay phones. There are several **Internet** locales, which are generally open 9am-10pm daily.

Do your laundry at **Clean Wash Laundry** (Mariscal Castilla 100, 8am-7pm Mon.-Sat.).

Volunteering

ProPeru (Apartado 70, tel. 084/20-1562, www.proworldsc.org) is a highly recommended organization arranging homestays for college students (and older folks, too) in Urubamba, Cusco, and other areas of Peru. Students take classes in art, history, anthropology, and Spanish, and work on service projects that range from reforestation to setting up a women's shelter. ProPeru receives very good reviews from its students and is one of the better foreign study programs in Peru. Other volunteer organizations in Urubamba include **Niños del Sol** (formerly Casa de los Milagros) (www.ninosdelsol.org), which works with children with disabilities.

GETTING THERE AND AROUND

From Cusco, *combis* for Urubamba leave from the first block of Grau near the bridge (US$2, 1 hour). Buses take longer and cost a little less. *Combis* drop passengers at Urubamba's bus station on the main drag, where frequent transport continues for the 20-minute ride to Ollantaytambo ($1.50) or up to Pisac (40 minutes, US$2). Taxis can be hired, costing less than US$10 for Ollantaytambo and US$20 for Pisac. To see Maras, Moray, and Salineras, a taxi costs about US$30 for a four-hour tour.

Mototaxis are ubiquitous in Urubamba and cost US$1-1.50 for getting around town.

★ MORAY AND SALINERAS

The high plains above Urubamba contain two very different attractions that are usually combined on a day trip.

First stop is **Maras,** a dusty town with a few colonial churches and *chicherías,* shops selling beer made from fermented corn. About seven kilometers farther, or a half hour along a good dirt road, lie the **four** **natural depressions of Moray** (7:30am-5:15pm daily, US$4 or included in *boleto turístico*). These sinkholes, 150 meters deep, were caused by rain eroding the calcium-rich soil. More than 20 terraces descending into concentric circles were used by the Inca to create microclimates for growing different vegetables. Gradations of sun, shade, and elevation among the terraces create dramatic differences in temperature. Irrigation canals and the discovery of different seeds on the terraces are additional clues that Moray was once a gigantic agricultural laboratory. It was here, perhaps, that the Inca learned to grow corn and potatoes in a variety of elevations, fueling the expansion of the empire. The irrigation is so good that it never floods, even in torrential storms.

On the nearby hills that lead down to the Urubamba Valley is a very different attraction, **Salineras,** unique in the Sacred Valley. Here the Inca once again transformed nature: A spring of warm, salty water was diverted into thousands of pools, where sunlight evaporates the water and leaves a thin crust of salt. The **salt mines** (entrance US$3, not included in *boleto turístico*) continue to be worked by a collective of 260 salt miners from the nearby villages of Maras and Pichinjoto. (You may see

the spellbinding salt mines at Salineras

this salt marketed overseas as "Peruvian pink salt.") Today there are 5,740 pools, or *pocitos,* each of which yields 150 kilograms of unrefined salt per month. There is a dazzling and oft-photographed contrast between the barren hillsides and the snow-white salt pools, which visitors can explore along narrow, crunchy paths. The water that flows through these mines is 60 percent salt, twice the salinity of the ocean.

Getting There and Around

To reach Moray, take a Cusco-Urubamba bus and get off at the Maras turnoff (say *"ramal a Maras, por favor"*). *Colectivos* wait here and charge US$10-12 for a half-day tour of Maras, Moray, and Salinas. A recommended company is **Empresa Transporte Moray.** To get from Moray to Salineras, car-bound travelers must return to Maras and then proceed another five kilometers downhill to the salt mines. Another option is to get a ride to Maras (four kilometers) and then walk the remaining seven kilometers to Moray (two hours, mostly uphill) through a patchwork of fields. From Moray, it is a two-hour walk—ask for directions along the way—to the salt mines. A steep but beautiful path continues for another kilometer or two from Salinas to the Urubamba Valley, ending five kilometers down from Urubamba and at the doorstep of the recommended **Tunupa Restaurant** (km 77 Pisac-Ollantaytambo Hwy., cell tel. 984-630-520, lunch daily, $15-20). This whole circuit makes for an excellent full-day tour on horse or bike, or do it yourself by electing to be dropped off at Salineras and taking the scenic, one-hour walk back to Urubamba.

Maras, Moray, Salineras, and Chinchero are combined on a half-day tour ($12) bookable with agencies in Cusco as well as with some operators in Urubamba.

Ollantaytambo and Vicinity

Ollantaytambo (2,792 meters) is the last town in the Sacred Valley before the Río Urubamba plunges through steep gorges toward Machu Picchu. It is such a shame that so many tourists rush through here on a day trip or, worse still, don't even stop on the way to Machu Picchu. More fool them, because Ollantaytambo is the best-preserved Inca village in Peru, with narrow alleys, small street canals that supply water, and trapezoidal doorways. The Inca temple and fortress above town is second in beauty only to Machu Picchu and deserves to be explored at length. In the terraced fields above town, men still use foot plows, or *chaquitacllas,* to till fields and plant potatoes. The town is overlooked by snowcapped Verónica mountain and surrounded on all sides by Inca ruins, highways, and terraces. It is well worth lingering here for a day or two.

However, Ollantaytambo also epitomizes the uneasy relationship between tradition and progress. While the town's Inca heritage stands out proudly, there are far too many pizzerias, and the streets shake under the weight of huge trucks bound for the Camisea gas pipeline in the jungle around Quillabamba. But some recent changes have been positive: After a concerted campaign, the mountain of plastic bottles and trash that filled the river around town has been reduced, if not eliminated, by a new recycling program, and the town still retains its strong sense of community. Archaeologists and philanthropists further help to preserve and strengthen the town's unique heritage.

HISTORY

Ollantaytambo (population 3,000) was occupied long before the Inca by the Quillques, who built some of the rougher buildings at Pumamarca and on the ridge near the Ollantaytambo temple itself. After Inca emperor Pachacútec conquered this area around 1440, construction began on a ceremonial

Ollantaytambo

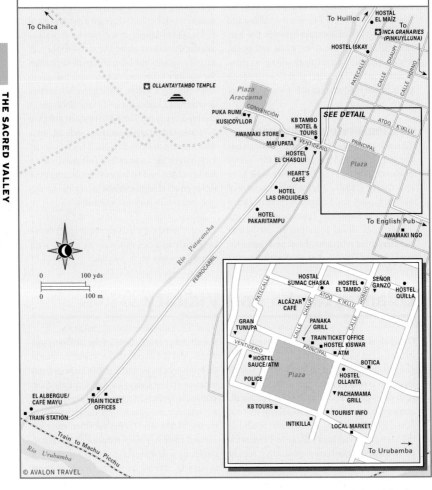

© AVALON TRAVEL

center and royal estate that housed an estimated 1,000 workers year-round. Even though it was never completed, the result is the most impressive Inca ruins in Peru after Machu Picchu.

Ollantaytambo is most famous for a 1537 battle that was the final time that the Inca defeated a Spanish army—and nearly massacred it altogether. The battle happened during the 1536-1537 Inca rebellion, when Manco Inca was forced to withdraw his troops to

Ollantaytambo after being defeated by the Spanish at Sacsayhuamán. Hernando Pizarro arrived at Ollantaytambo one morning at dawn, his brothers Juan and Francisco and his cousin Pedro among the force's 70 cavalrymen and 30 foot soldiers. But Manco Inca's men were waiting on the terraces of the sun temple, which had been hastily converted into a fort. Pedro Pizarro wrote afterward, "We found it so well fortified that it was a thing of horror."

From high on the upper terraces, Manco

The Brilliance of Inca Stone

The Inca's building work is their greatest legacy and the biggest draw for millions of tourists who flock to Peru to gaze upon these astounding architectural achievements. The central theme of Inca construction is **homage to nature. Cusco** was designed in the shape of a puma with **Sacsayhuamán** as the head, the city as the body, and the **Coricancha sun temple** as the tail. Many Inca temples, including at **Machu Picchu, Ollantaytambo,** and **Pisac,** were designed specifically to catch the light of the sun on winter or summer solstice, dates that still pull in thousands of tourists to witness the spectacle every year.

On a practical level, the Inca built on **higher ground,** mindful of the destructive power of landslides, in direct contrast to modern civilizations that continue to inadvisably live at the bottom of the valley. Size mattered for the Inca, and they used huge blocks of stone rather than the small bricks common in Europe. The best examples of this are the eight-meter blocks at **Sacsayhuamán.** The human effort involved in transporting these blocks, probably using log sleds and levers, was immense, but the result was impeccable.

The biggest stones in Sacsayhuamán are eight meters high.

Just as important, the Inca used **inclines** to increase stability. Walls were slightly inclined, with corners rounded, and the trapezoidal shape for doors and windows—wider at the bottom and narrower at the top—added crucial stability.

Most famously, the Inca did not use mortar but **cut stones precisely** to fit together. Mortar erodes in time and causes walls to become unstable, while Inca walls made of stones fitted so closely together were far sturdier. One of the most famous examples of Inca craftsmanship is the **12-sided stone** in the alleyway Hatun Rumiyoc in Cusco.

Last but not least were the **Inca roads,** many of which still exist in their original form, such as the **Inca Trail,** or have become the basis for parts of the Panamerican Highway. Overcoming the inhospitable mountain terrain, the Inca found a way to carve trails and steps as well as build bridges using natural fibers.

It wasn't just the Inca's buildings that were brilliant, but also their **agricultural terracing.** This efficient use of land increased the available space for food production and created microclimates at different altitudes for various crops—corn on lower terraces, potatoes in the middle, and quinoa higher up. The best examples of terracing are at **Moray, Ollantaytambo,** and **Pisac.** Many modern engineers in North America have since copied Inca agricultural methods.

The final proof of the superiority of Inca construction is best demonstrated by its survival in a volatile geological zone. In the 1950 earthquake, while much of the colonial architecture of Cusco collapsed, the Inca walls remained unscathed, and the foundations of the sun temple Coricancha were once again revealed to the world. Pachacútec, the Inca's greatest builder (the name means "shaker of the earth"), would have surely smiled with satisfaction.

Inca commanded his troops from horseback—co-opting the symbol of Spanish strength—as jungle archers shot volleys of arrows and Inca soldiers fired off slingshots and rolled boulders. Sensing defeat, the Spaniards retreated, but Manco Inca pulled a final surprise. In a brilliant move, he diverted the Río Urubamba through previously prepared channels and flooded the plains below Ollantaytambo, causing the Spaniards' horses to get bogged down in the mud as they beat a hasty retreat. The Spanish were pursued by thousands of Inca soldiers all the way to Cusco, where Pizarro then waited for Diego de Almagro to return from his Chile campaign with reinforcements. Manco Inca, meanwhile, recognized the growing strength of the Spaniards and withdrew to Vilcabamba.

After Manco's departure, the whole valley became an *encomienda* for Hernando Pizarro, who pursued Manco deep into Vilcabamba and raided his camp in 1539. Manco narrowly escaped, but his wife and sister, Cura Ocllo, was captured and brought to Ollantaytambo. After Manco refused to surrender, Francisco Pizarro had Cura Ocllo stripped, whipped, and killed with arrows. To make sure Manco got the message, they floated her body down the Río Urubamba toward Vilcabamba, where Manco's troops found her.

About two-thirds of the inhabitants of the Sacred Valley died of diseases brought by the Spanish over the next century. The descendants of the survivors were put to work in haciendas that sprung up in the valley, often the result of Spaniards marrying Inca elite. A road down the Urubamba Valley to Quillabamba was constructed in 1895. It was this road that Hiram Bingham took to "discover" Machu Picchu in 1911. In the 1920s, the road was converted into the rail line that now carries travelers to Machu Picchu.

Today Ollantaytambo is a busy tourist town but still preserves its unique Inca heritage. It is probably the most attractive of all Sacred Valley towns and makes a popular base to get the early morning train to Machu Picchu.

SIGHTS
City Tour

Ask your bus driver to let you off one kilometer before Ollantaytambo at the original Inca Trail, which follows the hillside on the right (north) side of town. To the left is the plain that Manco Inca flooded in the 1537 battle against the Spanish. The path leads up to the town's restored terraces and through a massive Inca gate, through which a water channel still runs. The path then joins with the road past the Wall of 100 Niches, whose inward slant indicates this was the inside—not the outside—of a roadside building (or maybe the road went through the building).

Once in the main plaza, head a half block north to the original Inca town, named **Qozqo Ayllu,** which is laid out in the form of a trapezoid and bisected by narrow, irrigated alleys. Oversized trapezoidal doorways open in the courtyards of homes, or *kanchas,* occupied continuously since Pachacútec's time.

TOP EXPERIENCE

★ Ollantaytambo Temple

The main attractions of Ollantaytambo are the ruins towering above town. The temple was still under construction when the Spaniards arrived—and was later converted into a fortress by Manco Inca.

From a distance, the most impressive part of the ruins is the agricultural terracing. Two hundred steps lead up these terraces to a double-jamb gateway and the **Temple of Ten Niches,** a long wall with odd protuberances. Some say these bumps draw heat away from the slabs, preventing them from expanding. Others say they somehow served in the transport of the blocks. Or perhaps the Inca valued them as we do today, for the graceful shadows they cast across the stone.

Above is the unfinished **Temple of the Sun,** considered one of the masterpieces of Inca stonework. Six giant monoliths of pink rhyolite are perfectly slotted together with thin slices of stone and oriented to glow with the rising sun. Traces of the *chacana* symbols and pumas that once decorated the walls can still be seen. What is unusual about the wall is the long straight lines—and the molten bronze that was poured in the T-joints to hold the wall together. These features indicate the wall was probably the handiwork of Lake Titicaca's Colla people, who were brought to work here by Pachacútec as part of the forced labor system known as *mitimayo.*

According to J. P. Protzen, the wall was probably intended to be one side of a great platform, which seems likely with the unfinished blocks, rough walls, and plaza nearby. It is impressive enough now, but one cannot help but wonder what it would have become had the Inca been allowed to finish their work. It is not entirely clear why the construction stopped—perhaps it was Pachacútec's death, a rebellion of the Colla people, the smallpox epidemic of 1527, or (most likely) the arrival of the Spaniards.

To the left of the plaza, the **Cachicata quarry** appears high on the hillside. The Inca dragged boulders weighing up to 52 tons down the mountain, across the Río Urubamba and the valley floor, and then up a steep ramp. The human effort involved in doing this boggles the mind. On the ridge above the temple are rougher buildings and the **Incahuatana,** the hitching place of the Inca, where prisoners may have been lashed into the human-sized portals. There are also the ruins of a control zone above the temple, the highest point used as a lookout to the *colcas* (storehouses) where food was kept. Walk down the terraces of **Andenes Manyaraki** to the base of the ruins. Here you'll find the **Baños de la Ñusta** (Princess Baths) and the **Water Temple;** there are a half-dozen fountains adorned with *chacana* symbols. Some of the fountains are engineered in such a way as to cause a whirlpool that allows sediment to drop before the water continues over a delicately shaped spout. From here you can walk along to the right beside a stream to a small ceremonial site, **Incamisana.** Opposite the ruins, on the steep flanks of Pinculluna, the sacred hill that rises above town, are the ruins of several granaries, which glow in the afternoon sun.

ENTERTAINMENT AND EVENTS

Bars and clubs change often in Ollantaytambo. The town has a small but lively nightlife scene on weekends, due mainly to a community of expats who live in town year-round. **Señor Ganso** (Horno Calle, 1.5 blocks from the square, 9am-11pm daily) has a great second-floor lounge.

During the **Fiesta de Reyes** (Celebration of the Kings) on January 6, a revered image of Jesus is brought down to Ollantaytambo from Marcacocha, a town high up in the Patacancha Valley. The event includes a solemn procession around Ollantaytambo's main square, which involves even more images of baby Jesus.

the unfinished Temple of the Sun

On January 6, over 200 Wallta dancers come down from the hills of Mount Pinkuylluna. These Quechua-speaking peoples, dressed in the traditional red outfits, dance and lead processions until the following day.

During the eight-day **Carnaval** season in late January and early February, the upper Patacancha Valley explodes into a series of traditions: cow branding, offerings to mountain *apus* by local priests, *wallata* (the dance of the condor), and ritual battles between towns that are now fought with mature fruit instead of rocks.

The town's most important celebration is the **Señor de Choquequilca**, which happens during Pentecost at the end of May or early June. The festival dates back to the miraculous appearance of a wooden cross near the town's Inca bridge. A chapel dedicated to El Señor de Choquequilca was completed in the main square in 1995.

SHOPPING

To find authentic, all-natural weavings and handicrafts, head to **Awamaki** (Calle Convención s/n, across from the temple, tel. 084/43-6744, www.awamaki.org). All proceeds go to the people of the communities with which Awamaki works.

RECREATION

Several agencies operate trips, including horseback riding, rafting, and biking excursions, in this area. Prices range US$50-100 for day tours. Recommended operators include **KB Tambo Tours** (Ventiderio s/n, tel. 084/20-4091, KBperu@hotmail.com, www.kbperu.com), run by a longtime resident originally from the United States; **Sota Adventures** (Procuradores 351, Office 120, cell tel. 984-455-841, www.sotaadventure.com), operated by two local brothers; and **KB Tours Travel** (Plaza de Armas s/n, tel. 084/23-3896, info@kbtourstravel.com). NGO **Awamaki** (Calle Convención s/n, across from the temple, tel. 084/43-6744, www.

awamaki.org) also organizes excursions to the communities outside Ollantaytambo.

Hikes

Ollantaytambo is a great base for a number of excellent hikes, treks, and community visits in the area. A detailed map of a dozen local hikes is available from the NGO **Awamaki** (Calle Convención s/n, across from the temple, tel. 084/43-6744, www.awamaki.org). Summaries of these hikes, taken from the Awamaki guide with permission, are listed here. Before setting out on these hikes, check with Awamaki for updated directions.

★ INCA GRANARIES (PINKUYLLUNA)

This moderate, 1.5-hour hike explores the Inca ruins that can be seen from town on the hillside opposite the Ollantaytambo fortress. The larger buildings were used for agricultural storehouses called *colcas*. Along with the multiple Inca sites, this steep hike offers great elevated views of Ollantaytambo and the fortress.

To reach the trailhead from the plaza, take Calle Principal toward Cusco. Take your first left after leaving the plaza completely on Calle Lares. After a few blocks, you will see a stone staircase on your right with a sign for Pinkuylluna. The stone staircase continues up the mountain for 10 to 15 minutes before the trail forks. The trail to the right (with the wooden handrail) will lead you around the corner to the first Inca ruins.

After exploring these, the best option is to descend back down to the fork in the trail and take the trail uphill in the other direction. The trail passes another Inca site and arrives at the large four-tiered storehouse in about 20-30 minutes. From here you can continue up the trail to the four towers that mark the crown of the head of the Tunupa, the god of abundance. If you continue up the mountain from here the views improve but the trail becomes unclear.

PUMAMARCA

The round-trip hike to the ruins of Pumamarca takes about 4-6 hours from Ollantaytambo on a moderate, steadily climbing trail. The ruins of Pumamarca sit on a hillside overlooking the convergence of the Río Patacancha and the Yuracmayo (White River). The well-preserved site was thought to be a checkpoint to control access to Ollantaytambo.

To reach Pumamarca, follow Patacalle out of town. Shortly after the first bridge, a large path leaves the main road to the right and follows the river. Follow this path for about 15 minutes until it rejoins the main road at the small town of Munaypata. Just up the road you will see an electrical pole on the left labeled 2224 and a path leading behind the adjacent house. Follow this path uphill for 15 more minutes to a blue archaeological marker for the Media Luna terraces in front of you. At this point, follow the switchback up the hill to your right (and not the path in front of you toward the terraces). The trail continues to climb steeply but soon becomes more gradual.

After another hour or so of hiking, the trail comes to a clearing with small waterfalls and the beginning of ancient aqueducts. The trail follows an aqueduct, and in 20-30 minutes the ruins of Pumamarca become apparent on the hillside in front of you. The trail becomes less clear at this point, but you can take multiple routes through the terraced fields up to the ruins (the main entrance is on the right side of the complex). At times there is someone working at the ruins who can provide information, but if not there is currently no entrance fee or hours when the ruins are closed. After exploring the ruins, return to Ollantaytambo by the same path or descend the hillside to the town of Pallata and take the road down from there.

INCA QUARRIES (CANTERAS) AND INTI PUNKU (SUN GATE)

This round-trip walk, which takes 4-6 hours to the quarries and a few more to reach the Sun Gate, begins at the Inca bridge near Ollantaytambo and along the banks of the Río Urubamba. It follows a fairly well-preserved Inca trail to Cachicata, the stone quarry 700-900 meters above the valley floor that is visible from the Ollantaytambo sun temple. It was here that the great stone blocks were slid down the hillside and hauled across the river to Ollantaytambo. There are three separate stone quarries, within half a kilometer of one another, littered with massive chiseled blocks and small *chullpas*, or burial towers. The western and highest quarry contains mysterious needle-shaped blocks that are up to seven meters long.

From Cachicata, it is possible to see that the terraces below the Ollantaytambo ruins form a pyramid shape, with one 750-meter-long wall aligning with the rays of the winter solstice. New Age theorists Fernando and Edgar Elorieta believe this is the original Pakaritampu, where the four Inca brothers emerged to found Cusco. A few hours' walk above the Cachicata is a perfect Inca gate that frames a view of Salcantay. On the trail approaching the quarries, numerous *piedras cansadas* (tired stones) that never made it to their final destination can be observed. The trail climbs high on the hillside, offering great views of Ollantaytambo and the surrounding peaks. Be prepared; the majority of the hike is fully exposed to the sun, and the only available water is near the beginning of the hike.

Begin the hike by taking a right after the Inca bridge. After about 15-20 minutes take a left at the fork up the hill (a boulder at the fork is labeled "Canteras"). Continue to stay left, following the main path when other trails diverge. In about 20-30 minutes you reach agricultural terraces and stone building foundations. Follow the trail straight past the foundations, not the smaller trail uphill. You arrive at the **first quarry** 1.5-2 hours after starting. Look for small stone buildings built on top of large boulders beneath you. Just after passing through the quarry, look for a smaller path to the left leading uphill from the large trail. If you choose to filter water, a small switchback to the left immediately after this turn will lead to the last water source.

Follow switchbacks up the hillside past the first quarry for one hour. As the grassy trail starts to level out, watch for a rounded stone resembling a primitive wheel off the trail to your left. As the trail plateaus you will see a **much larger quarry** to your left and several small fields. These flat fields are a great place to camp if you plan to spend the night. A large boulder in the middle of the quarry has "Instituto Nacional de Cultura" painted in white. Before and to the left of this boulder, a path made of smaller stones leads up though the quarry. Exploring this path, you can find a burial site with skeletons under a large boulder, along with many quarried stones that never made it to Ollantaytambo.

Looking farther ahead on the same trail, you can see **Inti Punku,** or the **Sun Gate,** on the ridge ahead. To continue to Inti Punku, pass the large boulder with "I.N.C." painted on it and head toward the largest boulder you see. Find the trail on the left side of the boulder and follow it uphill, crossing a scree field. After 30-45 minutes the trail comes to a grass field with Inca ruins (another good campsite). The trail continues just beyond and uphill from these. The trail forks once at a small ravine about 10 minutes from the Sun Gate; take a right through the ravine. About 30-45 minutes from the ruins you reach Inti Punku. From Inti Punku, return along same path to the **last quarry** (about 1 hour).

The return route from the *canteras* (quarries) should take 1.5-2 hours. Follow the trail down switchbacks to the first quarry. Take a left just past the first quarry on a small path and circle back under the quarry. From here you see two houses with metal roofs on the left hillside. Continue to descend along this ridge toward the houses and the trail improves. From the houses, continue along the trail downhill into the valley. The trail improves and continues downhill through more houses and finally to a bridge. Cross the bridge and follow the railroad tracks on your right. Turn left at a set of stone stairs reached after 10-15 minutes of walking on the tracks, and follow the path back to town.

FOOD

Ollantaytambo has an increasingly varied range of restaurants. You're never more than a few yards from a wood-fired pizza. One of the better places in town for pizza is **Intikilla** (Plaza de Armas, tel. 084/79-6062, 9am-10pm daily, US$6-12). It also does a range of meat, fish, and chicken, including trout ceviche and stroganoff. Elsewhere on the square, **Pachamama Grill** (Convención s/n, tel. 084/20-4168, 11:30am-10pm daily, US$7-10) has trout, pizza, and *lomo saltado*. The set menu for US$10 is good value. **Panaka Grill Restaurant** (Plaza de Armas s/n, 7am-10pm daily, US$11-16) is an upscale option with fine dining upstairs. They have a good-value set menu for US$14, while à la carte specialties include a range of steaks and pasta dishes.

Kusicoyllor Café-Bar (Calle Convención across from the temple, tel. 084/43-6725, 8am-10pm daily, US$5-8), located directly in front of the ruins, serves traditional dishes such as alpaca steak, as well as croissants, pancakes, espresso, and homemade ice cream. Just in front of the ruins, a favorite in town is **Puka Rumi** (Calle Convención near the entrance to the ruins, tel. 084/20-4091, 7:30am-8:30pm daily, US$6-12). The Chilean owner has brought over the traditions from his home country and is well known for his excellent *lomo saltado*. The menu is extremely varied and has options for all budgets. For dessert, try the brownies. Note that service is slow, but the food is worth the wait.

For the best meal in town, head down to the train station to the restaurant ★ **El Albergue** (Ferrocarril s/n, tel. 084/20-4077, www.elalbergue.com, 5am-9:30pm daily, US$10-20). Using organic vegetables, the menu is inventive and has great vegetarian options. Try the alpaca with *huacatay* mash or the lamb tenderloin with chimichurri and quinoa risotto. Pasta lovers can order a plate of homemade fettuccini with their favorite sauce. Reservations are recommended. The best coffee in Ollantaytambo is also found at the El Albergue's **Café Mayu** (Ferrocarril s/n, tel. 084/20-4014, 4:30am-9pm daily, US$5-15).

★ **Heart's Café** (Plaza de Armas s/n, tel. 084/43-6726, 7am-10pm daily, US$5-18) was founded by retired Brit Sonia Newhouse, an inspirational lady who has established her own charity. This place serves home-cooked meals using organic ingredients and specializes in vegetarian fare. It has everything from soups and salads to main dishes and even afternoon tea with scones. The sandwiches are particularly imaginative. Try the veggie sausage and blue cheese or hummus and chutney. Profits go to Sonia's NGO, Living Heart (www.livingheartperu.org).

Markets

The best minimarket for snacks or a picnic is **Inka Misana** on the Plaza de Armas. But head to the local market for fresh fruit and produce.

ACCOMMODATIONS
Under US$10

Unlike Urubamba, Ollantaytambo has some good budget options for backpackers. **Hostal El Tambo** (Calle Horno, 1.5 blocks from the plaza, tel. 084/77-3262, US$9 pp, www.hostaleltambo.com) is cheap and adequate. The baths are shared and have hot water. According to the owner, Hiram Bingham stayed at this hostel back in 1911. In the old Inca town, **Hostal Sumac Chaska** (Calle del Medio s/n, tel. 084/43-6739, US$8 dorm, US$20 d) has several clean rooms with wooden floors arranged around a tiny courtyard. The terrace on the top of the building has good views of the Inca granaries.

US$10-50

The best value hostel on the main square is probably **Hostal Kiswar** (Plaza de Armas, tel. 084/436-706, www.hostalkiswarperu.com, US$28 pp). It has comfortable rooms upstairs and a good café below with soups and snacks.

An excellent budget option is ★ **Hostal El Chasqui** (Av. Estación del Tren, cell tel. 984-995-031, US$20 pp). Rooms with private baths and WiFi are great value for the price. There is

a popular restaurant downstairs with a range of national and international food ($4-12).

One of the best midrange options is **Hostal Iskay** (Patacalle s/n, tel. 084/20-4004, www.hostaliskay.com, US$34 s, US$43 d with continental breakfast), a small, homely hostel with a beautiful garden and an astounding view of the ruins. The friendly Spanish owners are longtime residents of Ollantaytambo. The rooms are clean and simple, and the common living/dining area has sofas, television, books, and board games, along with real Inca walls and an open kitchen.

Another comfortable option is **KB Tambo** (Ventiderio s/n, tel. 084/20-4091, www.kbperu.com, US$28 s, US$35 d), which has cozy, unpretentious modern rooms with private bathrooms from singles and doubles to family suites. It has a pleasant garden and a rooftop with excellent views of the ruins, plus a Jacuzzi, full bar, and pizza oven.

US$50-100

Ollantaytambo's most charming and best-known hotel is ★ **El Albergue** (Ferrocarril s/n, tel. 084/20-4014, www.elalbergue.com, US$70-80 s/d with breakfast). The lodge was opened by Wendy Weeks, a painter from Seattle, who arrived here in 1976 after an overland journey with her husband, writer Robert Randall. After her husband's death in 1990, Wendy stayed to raise her two sons here—Joaquín, who now runs the lodge, and Ishmael, who is an internationally recognized sculptor. Wendy Weeks is a well-respected member of the community and a passionate spokeswoman for its preservation.

To reach El Albergue, head to the train station, through the gate, and down the tracks in the direction of an arrow and large sign for El Albergue painted on a wall. Or if you are arriving by train, simply disembark, and you'll be there. Compared to the mayhem of the station, El Albergue is a tranquil retreat. Blue-and-yellow tanagers flit among datura flowers and a huge Canary Island palm that was planted in the 1920s. The 16 rooms are spacious, with whitewashed walls, wood tables, and beds. The newest have floor heating and bathtubs. Decorations include local weavings and Wendy's paintings. The balconies are ideal for reading and taking in the breathtaking views of Mount Verónica. There is a wood-fired sauna for relaxing, and the hotel has its own organic farm out back, from which it sources most of the vegetables for the excellent restaurant. Pachamanca farm lunches are also available for groups. Book ahead because it fills up fast.

Hostal Sauce (Ventiderio s/n, tel. 084/20-4044, www.hostalsauce.com.pe, US$100 s, US$110 d with breakfast) is a serene, upscale establishment with eight sun-filled rooms overlooking the Ollantaytambo ruins. The restaurant, serving salads, meats, and pastas, has a cozy sitting area with a fireplace and couches. This hotel is deservedly very popular, so book in advance, particularly in high season.

INFORMATION AND SERVICES

There is a **municipal tourist office** (tel. 084/204030, 8am-5pm Mon.-Fri., 7am-4pm Sat.-Sun.) on the plaza.

KB Tambo (tel. 084/20-4091, www.kb-peru.com) and the NGO **Awamaki** (Calle Convención s/n, across from the temple, www.awamaki.org) also have good information. Also visit the website www.ollantaytambo.org.

The **police** and the **Botica Drugstore** (tel. 084/20-4015, 8am-9pm daily), which has public phones, are both located on the main square. For medical needs, **Centro de Salud** (Ferrocarril s/n, tel. 084/20-4090) is open 24 hours. **Banco de Crédito** has an **ATM** in Hotel Sauce, and there is another ATM on the Plaza de Armas.

Volunteer Opportunities and NGOs

There are several NGOs in Ollantaytambo worth contacting if you're looking for volunteer and homestay opportunities. Based in Ollantaytambo, **Awamaki** (Calle Convención s/n, across from the temple, www.awamaki.org), founded by American Kennedy Leavens, is a Peruvian NGO partnered with a U.S. NGO of the same name that administers a weaving project with Quechua women and promotes health, education, and sustainable tourism. They have been instrumental in helping weavers in Patacancha and other communities restore their ancient weaving techniques and find sustainable ways to market their products. Awamaki can arrange all kinds of volunteer experiences, Spanish-language programs, homestays, excursions to the communities outside of Ollantaytambo, and classes in ceramics, basket weaving, and cooking. A highly recommended experience is Awamaki's weaving class in Patacancha.

Another NGO is **Living Heart** (www.livingheartperu.org), founded by Sonia Newhouse, who owns **Heart's Cafe** on the Plaza de Armas. Living Heart aims to improve the quality of life for disadvantaged Andean children and has volunteering opportunities.

GETTING THERE AND AROUND

To get to Ollantaytambo from Cusco by bus, take the bus from the first block of Grau near the bridge (US$1.50, 90 minutes) to Urubamba and then hop another *combi* for the 20-minute, US$1 ride to Ollantaytambo. However, the most convenient option to get to Ollantaytambo from Cusco is to take a car or *colectivo* from the Paradero Pavitos (US$3.50, 90 minutes) to Ollantaytambo.

The station where you catch the train from Ollantaytambo to Aguas Calientes is a 10- or 15-minute walk down from the main square along the Río Patacancha. There are *mototaxis* if you are weary. From Ollantaytambo, various trains leave for Machu Picchu with **PeruRail** (www.perurail.com), which has the most departures, as well as **Inca Rail** (www.inkarail.com) and **Machu Picchu Train** (www.machupicchutrain.com). Prices start at US$75 per person one-way. For up-to-date prices and times, see the websites.

Note that new regulations mean that only one small piece of hand luggage weighing up to 5 kilograms is allowed on the trains. You are advised to leave the rest of your luggage at your hotel in Ollantaytambo or Cusco, or you must send it ahead on a freight train, which is inconvenient.

Reaching Cusco from Ollantaytambo is easy. *Combis* leave Ollantaytambo's main square for Urubamba, where another *combi* can be taken to Cusco. Direct buses for Cusco (US$1.75, 80 minutes) leave from Ollantaytambo when the evening trains arrive. However, the most convenient option is taking a car or *colectivo* from the train station or the main plaza ($3.50-5), but you need to wait for them to fill up (which they invariably do as soon as the train arrives).

PATACANCHA

Patacancha is a traditional Quechua community about an hour's drive above Ollantaytambo on a dirt road. People in Patacancha live much as they have for centuries, weaving, farming, and raising animals.

While in Patacancha please be aware that tourism can be harmful. Be sensitive and discreet in taking photos, avoid gaping into people's doorways, and avoid visiting the school, as this is very disruptive to classes. Be aware that you will probably be flocked by women trying to sell you things, much of it junk purchased in Cusco. Look for the naturally dyed, hand-woven textiles for which the community is known.

Patacancha is difficult to visit independently, as very little Spanish is spoken and there is no daily public transportation. *Combis* leave the plaza of Ollantaytambo Wednesday and Friday very early in the morning (around 6am). Or, just head up Patacalle. It's a four- to five-hour walk to the community, and most drivers, if you see any, are willing to pick you up for a few *soles*.

For a deeper understanding of life in Patacancha, the Ollantaytambo-based NGO **Awamaki** (Calle Convención s/n, across from the temple, www.awamaki.org) offers alternative community visits. The half-day tour, in English, includes transport, a visit to the Awamaki cooperative's weaving center, a demonstration of the weaving process, and the opportunity to buy top-quality, authentic weavings directly from the women. The tour also includes a visit to a Quechua house with permission, a respectful environment for photo-taking, and nutritious snacks and a small tip for the women who participate. All proceeds benefit the project. Cost is US$15-30 per person depending on group size. Awamaki can also arrange weaving lessons and home stays in Patacancha.

Machu Picchu

Many photographers claim that it is impossible to take a bad photo of Machu Picchu, but even the best camera cannot capture the magnificent panorama that fuses man-made and natural beauty at the lost city of the Inca.

Machu Picchu has to be seen to be believed, and despite the enormous flow of tourist traffic through here daily, it retains an awe-inspiring grandeur. Even if no Inca city had been built here, the horn-shaped, forested peak of Huayna Picchu swirling in the mist at dawn or gleaming in the sun at midday, along with the dramatic 300-meter drops from cloud forest to the Río Urubamba, would be breathtaking enough. Add the genius of Inca architecture, built in perfect harmony with earth and skies, and it's no surprise that Machu Picchu is among the New Seven Wonders of the World.

There is not a stone out of place at Machu Picchu. Terraces, gardens, temples, staircases, and aqueducts all have purpose and grace. Shapes mimic the silhouettes of surrounding mountains. Windows and instruments track the sun during the June and December solstices. At sunrise, rows of ruins are illuminated one by one as the sun creeps over the mountain peaks. The sun, moon, water, and earth were revered by the Inca, and they drive the city's layout.

A visit to Machu Picchu is many visitors' main motivation for coming to Peru. The place has a vibrant, spiritual feel and is probably the world's best example of architecture integrating with the landscape. It is in some respects the Inca's lesson to the Western world, teaching us how to build our world around nature, not against it. Today, some 60 percent of the site is original, while the rest has been restored or rebuilt.

Frustratingly though, many visitors get shortchanged on a visit to Machu Picchu. The worst way to do it is to get up before dawn in Cusco, take a bus and train to the site, arrive midmorning (when the site is already very busy), and then return to Cusco by midnight. Why, if you have traveled thousands of miles to see one of the world's great wonders, should you rush through it in one long, grueling day? It is far better

Previous: Aguas Calientes; a view of Machu Picchu. **Above:** Temple of the Sun.

Look for ★ to find recommended
sights, activities, dining, and lodging.

Highlights

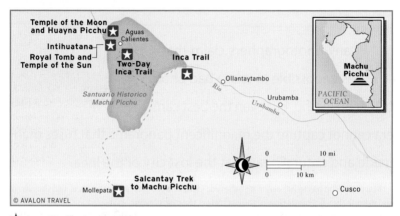

★ **Inca Trail:** This sacred path is part trek, part religious pilgrimage. Winding down from the windswept mountains to lush cloud forest, it passes 30 ruins along the way, notably Wiñay Wayna (page 115).

★ **Two-Day Inca Trail:** A great option for those short on time, or not wanting to camp, this two-day hike includes some spectacular ruins and the glorious entry to Machu Picchu via the Sun Gate (page 119).

★ **Salcantay Trek to Machu Picchu:** This five-day option offers stunning views of snow-covered mountains for hard-core trekkers wanting to get a taste of the high Andes (page 119).

★ **Royal Tomb and Temple of the Sun:** This semicircular temple aligns perfectly with the movement of the sun and sits on top of a cave, which may have once contained the mummy of Inca Pachacútec, the Inca's most revered ruler (page 123).

★ **Intihuatana:** Experts continue to debate the function of this carved stone. There are theories that it's a sundial, sacrificial altar, or a temple to the surrounding mountain gods. Whatever its purpose, it is profoundly beautiful and spiritual (page 125).

★ **Temple of the Moon and Huayna Picchu:** Towering above Machu Picchu is Huayna Picchu, a sacred summit reached via a two-hour hike up stairs, switchbacks, and, finally, a ladder. Partway up is a separate path to the enigmatic Temple of the Moon, sculpted with curving stone walls (page 127).

to hike the Inca Trail or stay overnight in Ollantaytambo or Aguas Calientes, get to Machu Picchu early, and linger longer, staying nearby in the evening.

HISTORY

Adding to the wonder of Machu Picchu is the mystery surrounding it. Nobody knows what the city was originally called or its precise purpose. In fact, the name *Machu Picchu*, which translates as "old peak" in Quechua, does not even refer to the city but the large mountain that overlooks it. The ruins were known to locals for generations, but they were never recorded by the Spanish, who probably did not venture this far into the cloud forest, and they had long been abandoned to be covered for centuries by dense foliage. All this changed forever when a certain young Yale archaeologist, Hiram Bingham, was brought to the site in 1911. Bingham cleared the site, recognized its importance, and announced Machu Picchu to the world.

Bingham, a 36-year-old adventurer who ended up being both a U.S. senator and the inspiration for the character Indiana Jones, came to Peru to find Vilcabamba, the legendary lost city of the Inca. This was the jungle enclave, well described by Spanish soldiers, to which Manco Inca and his followers retreated following their unsuccessful rebellion against the Spanish in 1537. Bingham began his search walking down the newly built road along the Río Urubamba (now the train line) and asking locals if they knew of any ruins along the way.

It was in this way that local resident Melchor Arteaga led Bingham to the vine-covered site, which Bingham would return to in 1912 and 1915 to excavate. He was convinced, to the end of his life, that Machu Picchu was the "lost city of the Inca." But historians are now certain he was incorrect. A wealth of supporting evidence indicates the real Vilcabamba was farther into the jungle at Espíritu Pampa, which Bingham also visited but dismissed at the time as too insignificant.

Bingham discovered more than 180 human skeletons in cemeteries around Machu Picchu, and an inexperienced scientist on his team incorrectly concluded that 80 of them belonged to women. The finding prompted the idea of Machu Picchu as a giant *acllahuasi*, or house for the Inca's chosen "virgins of the sun." Subsequent research on the skeletons proved that there were men, women, and children, with women being the majority.

The latest theory about Machu Picchu's original use, which is gaining widespread acceptance, is that it was a winter retreat built by Inca Pachacútec in the mid-15th century (around 1440). Scholars had long believed this, but concrete proof came in the form of a 16th-century suit filed by the descendants of Pachacútec, which University of California anthropologist Dr. John Rowe found while searching through archives in Cusco. Pachacútec was without doubt the greatest of Inca constructors, so it seems likely that this city was his work.

Machu Picchu's status as a sacred site is due to the quantities of *huacas* (shrines), and while Machu Picchu certainly had a religious sector, and probably an *acllahuasi* too, its primary purpose was likely to indulge the pleasures of the Inca and his family. Pachacútec could come here to escape the chill rains of Cusco, enjoy the jungle fruits of nearby Quillabamba, and hunt in the surrounding jungle.

It is not known if Pachacútec's successors ever used Machu Picchu, but many of them were likely too busy fighting wars to have time for a winter retreat. As the city had no military significance, the Spanish never discovered it and Machu Picchu remained untouched for centuries after the Inca's final defeat.

PLANNING YOUR TIME

According to an agreement reached by the Instituto Nacional de Cultura (INC) and UNESCO, only 2,500 people are allowed to visit Machu Picchu a day. The centenary celebrations of Bingham's discovery of the city saw 2011 visitor numbers top one million.

MACHU PICCHU

Even with restrictions, that's a heck of a lot of people tramping through a relatively small site. In order for you to get the most out of your visit to Machu Picchu, here are a few tips:

- Avoid the busiest months of June-September. The "shoulder" months of April-May and September-October are usually sunny as well.
- Avoid the Peruvian holidays, July 28-August 10. The days around Cusco's Inti Raymi festival, June 24, are also busy.
- Skip solstice days (June 21 and December 21), when the ruins are full by 6am.
- Visit on a Sunday. Although Sundays are discounted for locals, Sundays tend to draw large crowds at the Pisac and Chinchero markets, thereby pulling travelers away from Machu Picchu.
- Hike one of the Inca trails. This will give you a greater sense of anticipation, and the final arrival at Machu Picchu will be more spectacular.
- If you're not hiking a trail, at least stay the night at Aguas Calientes or Ollantaytambo and take the earliest train in the morning in order to beat the train crowds, which arrive at the ruins around 10am and start departing around 2pm. Either arrive early in the morning or linger in the late afternoon. When Machu Picchu is most crowded, you can hike to Huayna Picchu, the Temple of the Moon, the Inca bridge, or the Sun Gate. Consider staying the night nearby after your visit to avoid a long trip back to Cusco.

Machu Picchu admission is expensive by Peruvian standards and only lasts one day. Foreigners pay US$40, and nationals and students under age 26 with an ISIC card pay US$20. Including the climb up Huayna Picchu costs an extra US$10 and should be reserved at least 10 days in advance. Note that there are **no ticket sales on-site** and tickets must be bought in advance in *soles* at the **INC** office in Cusco (Av. el Sol) or in Aguas Calientes at

Centro Cultura Machu Picchu (Pachacútec s/n, tel. 084/21-1196). A passport is essential to complete the transaction, so don't leave your passport in Cusco! Tickets can also be bought online at www.machupicchu.gob.pe. The ruins are open 6am-5:30pm daily.

Shuttle

Buses to Machu Picchu leave every 5-15 minutes from just below Aguas Caliente's second bridge. **Consettur Machupicchu** (Infancia 433 – Wancha, tel. 084/22-2125, www.consettur.com) sells the tickets, US$12 one-way and US$24 round-trip, with the first bus leaving at 5:30am and the last at 5:30pm. If you want to catch the first bus up to Machu Picchu, which is a good idea, arrive at least 45 minutes early because morning lines form. The bus takes about a half hour to wind its way up the switchbacks to the ruins. It is also possible to follow the footpath to the ruins, which cuts the switchbacks. This arduous, all-uphill hike in the moist cloud forest takes about 90 minutes.

Facilities

Outside the gate of the ruins, there are bathrooms and **El Mirador Snack Bar** (US$4), which sells bottled water, sandwiches, and hamburgers that you can take away or eat at picnic tables. Note that there are no bathrooms inside the ruins (so go before you enter), although you are allowed to exit and enter as many times as you want on the same day. The gourmet **Restaurante Bufe Tinkuy** (tel. 084/21-1038, 11am-3:30pm daily, US$35) serves a huge buffet lunch open to the public that is worth the price if you have a good appetite and want to spoil yourself. There is also a separate dining room with an à la carte menu (US$40-50) serving international and Peruvian food. If you plan on eating at Machu Picchu, bring ample cash with you as prices are high. However, it is better to bring snacks and plenty of water, as it can be a long day out, and you save money by buying these in Aguas Calientes. Note: There are no ATMs at Machu Picchu, so bring cash!

Guides and Tours

During the day there are always guides, of varying quality, waiting at the entrance. A typical price is US$40 for small groups. Always check that they are registered guides with photo ID. Another option is the **Belmond Sanctuary Lodge** (tel. 084/21-1038, www.belmond.com/es/sanctuary-lodge-machu-picchu), where expensive, top-notch guides can be hired.

Trekking to Machu Picchu

TOP EXPERIENCE

★ INCA TRAIL

Though at times crowded, the hike to Machu Picchu is an unforgettable experience—both a backpacking trip and a religious pilgrimage. There are lots of ways to do it, with or without a pack on your back. All hikers on the actual Inca Trail must go with an agency to ensure everyone's safety and keep trash off the trail. The Inca Trail is part of the Santuario Histórico de Machu Picchu (Machu Picchu Historical Sanctuary), administered by the Instituto Nacional de Cultura (National Institute of Culture). There is a wide range in price and quality among Inca Trail agencies, and reservations should be made at least six months in advance.

The two- or even one-day option begins at kilometer 104 of the railroad line and includes a steep hike to reach the final stretch of the Inca Trail, including the ruins at Wiñay Wayna. Some agencies continue the same day to Machu Picchu and stay overnight in Aguas Calientes, while others camp near Wiñay Wayna to enter Machu Picchu the following morning.

The full four-day trip passes more than 30 Inca sites along the way and includes the most spectacular scenery, but it is arduous at times—day two especially—if you aren't a seasoned trekker. For a lighter experience, the two-day Inca Trail is also very good.

Trekking Agencies

Peruvian Andean Treks, ExplorAndes, and Tambo Tours are the longest-established trekking companies in Cusco; they pioneered the

Inca Trail

Trekking to Machu Picchu

TEMPLE OF THE MOON
AND HUAYNA PICCHU

MACHU PICCHU

ROYAL TOMB AND
TEMPLE OF THE SUN

Aguas
Calientes

PHUYUPATAMARKA

WIÑAY WAYNA

INTIHUATANA

SAYACMARCA

TWO-DAY
INCA TRAIL

RUNKURAKAY

CHACHABAMBA

Nevado
Salcantay

Machu   Historico

Santuario   Picchu   Machu

Inca   Trail

WAYLLABAMBA

Salcantay

Trail

SALCANTAY TREK
TO MACHU PICCHU

PATALLACTA

0
0
2 km
2 mi

INCA TRAIL

Rio   Urubamba

Nevado
Veronica

To Urubamba
and Cusco

Ollantaytambo

INCA TRAIL ELEVATION PROFILE

MACHU PICCHU

INTI
PUNKU

PHUYUPATAMARKA

WIÑAY WAYNA

INTIPATA

CONCHAMARCA

SAYACMARCA

RUNKURAKAY

PATALLACTA

Rio   Urubamba

4500m
4000m
3500m
3000m

Ollantaytambo

© AVALON TRAVEL

contemporary trekking culture. They are recommended, not only for their unsurpassed experience and professionalism, but also because they consistently recycle their trash, pack out all human waste, treat water carefully, and pay porters fair wages.

Among the more than 150 licensed agencies operating in Cusco, the standards of service and social and environmental responsibilities vary greatly. It is up to the client to be discerning and to research thoroughly before booking. All agencies listed here are recommended.

Peruvian Andean Treks (Pardo 705, tel. 084/22-5701, U.S. tel. 617/924-1974, www.andeantreks.com) is a long-standing company operating throughout South America.

ExplorAndes (Paseo Zarzuela Q-2 Huancaro, tel. 084/23-8380, www.explorandes.com) is Peru's most established adventure sports agency. It offers the traditional Inca Trail hike, as well as variations that combine it with treks above the Sacred Valley or around Nevado Salcantay and Nevado Ausangate. ExplorAndes was voted Peru's best overall tour operator by the Ministry of Tourism in 2005.

Tambo Tours (Casilla 912, tel. 084/23-7718, www.tambotours.com) is owned by Andreas Holland and has been operating for over 30 years. It offers diverse treks and tours with tailor-made itineraries (six people minimum) that accommodate group specifications and a wide range of special interests. The staff are very knowledgeable, and since its foundation Tambo Tours has had a profound commitment to helping local communities.

Andina Travel (Santa Catalina 219, tel. 084/25-1892, www.andinatravel.com) offers frequent departures for the Inca Trail as well as interesting sociocultural projects.

Auqui Mountain Spirit (José Gabriel 307, Urb. Magisterial, tel. 084/26-1517 or 084/25-1278, www.auqui.com.pe), run by Roger Valencia, has been operating for over 20 years. This high-end agency has a very experienced team and specializes in customized trips, especially for corporate clients.

Aventours (Saphi 456, tel. 084/22-4050, www.aventours.com) was founded by Ricky Schiller, who has been involved in the tourism industry for over 30 years. The expert staff provides excellent service.

Enigma (Fortunato L. Herrera 214, Urb. Magisterio 1a etapa, tel. 084/22-2155, www.enigmaperu.com) is one of the newer agencies. It offers Inca Trail treks combined with visits to Nevado Salcantay, Vilcabamba, and the ruins of Choquequirao. The company's treks include gourmet cooks.

Inca Explorers (Calle Peru W - 18 Urb. Ttio, tel. 084/24-1070, www.incaexplorers.com) has a range of longer trips to Vilcabamba, Choquequirao, and the Cordillera Vilcanota.

Perú Sur Nativa (Magisterio 2da etapa K-7-302, tel. 084/22-4156, www.perusurnativa.com) is owned by longtime Cusco adventurer Raúl Montes and has a wide range of trips.

Peru Treks & Adventure (Av. Pardo 540, tel. 084/222-722, www.perutreks.com) is also responsible for the very informative website Andean Travel Web (www.andeantravelweb.com).

Q'ente (Choquechaca 229, tel. 084/22-2535, www.qente.com) has been running since 1995 and provides good service and trained staff.

Quechuas Expeditions (San Juan de Dios 295, tel. 084/22-3548, www.quechuasexpeditions.com) is one of the most highly recommended trekking agencies in Cusco. It has a vast range of Andean treks.

United Mice (Av. Pachacútec 424 A-5, tel. 084/22-1139, www.unitedmice.com) is probably the most recommended backpacker's choice. It also offers a seven-day Salcantay trek, among others.

Xtreme Tourbulencia (Plateros 364, tel. 084/222-405, U.S. tel. 702/560-7220, www.xtremetourbulencia.com) receives good reviews and offers a range of treks and tours throughout Peru.

Four-Day Inca Trail

DAY 1

This trip traditionally begins with an early-morning three-hour bus ride to **Piscacucho,** which is at kilometer 82 of the train line at 2,700 meters (some agencies use the train instead, which drops backpackers a bit farther down at kilometer 84). The trail begins in a subtropical ecosystem, with lots of agave plants and Spanish moss hanging from the trees. Many of the cacti along the trail have a parasite that turns crimson when you crush it in your fingers, a trick local woman use for lipstick. The first ruins you pass are **Patallacta,** meaning "city above terraces" in Quechua; this middle-class residential complex was used as a staging ground for Machu Picchu. There is a modest 12 kilometers of hiking this first day, making it a relatively easy day, with an elevation gain of 500 meters to **Wayllabamba,** where most groups camp the first night with stunning views of the Huayluro Valley.

DAY 2

The 12 kilometers covered on this day are much more strenuous, because you climb 1,200 meters in elevation, including two mountain passes back to back. On the first pass, at 4,200 meters, you will pass by the ruins of **Runkurakay,** a round food storehouse strategically located at a lookout point. This site has an incredible view over a valley and nearby waterfall. The second pass, at 3,950 meters, is named Dead Woman's Pass after a mummy discovered there. In the late afternoon you will see the ruins of **Sayaqmarka** (3,625 meters), where there are good views of the Vilcabamba range. Sayaqmarka was probably used as a *tambo,* or resting spot, for priests and others journeying to Machu Picchu. The complex is divided into a rough lower section and a more elaborate upper area that was probably used for ceremonial purposes. Most trekkers camp this second night at **Pacaymayo,** with views of snow-covered peaks, including Humantay (5,850 meters) and Salcantay (6,271 meters), the highest peak in the area.

DAY 3

After a very tough second day, this is a relatively easy day with plenty of time for meandering and lots of memorable sights. You enter the cloud forest, full of orchids, ferns, and bromeliads, to reach the ruins of **Phuyupatamarka,** a ceremonial site from where you get a first glimpse of the back of Machu Picchu, marked with a flag. Look out for hummingbirds, finches, parrots, and the crimson Andean cock of the rock. Most groups rest at a halfway lookout point that is often shrouded by clouds. From here, it is a two-hour hike straight down, dropping 1,000 meters to the third campsite at 2,650 meters, where there are hot showers, cold beers, and a restaurant. There is usually plenty of time in the afternoon to see the ruins of **Wiñay Wayna,** a spectacular ceremonial and agricultural site that is about a 10-minute walk away. These are easily the most spectacular ruins on the Inca Trail. This complex is divided into two sectors, with religious temples at the top and rustic dwellings below. The hillside is carved into spectacular terraces, and the Río Urubamba flows far below.

DAY 4

Most groups rise very early in the morning in an attempt to reach the sanctuary before sunrise, and it can feel like walking in a herd of cattle. The walk is flat at the start and then inclines steeply up to **Inti Punku** (the Sun Gate), from where you will be rewarded with a 180-degree view of **Machu Picchu.** If you're lucky, you'll witness the unforgettable sight of the sun rising at Machu Picchu, although all too often the stubborn mist can leave you frustrated. Your guide will take you through the ruins, leaving you time to wander on your own and to climb **Huayna Picchu** or **Cerro Machu Picchu** if you still have the energy after a four-day trek.

★ Two-Day Inca Trail

This two-day trip consists of one day of trekking and one day of visiting Machu Picchu. It is a fairly easy hike, and for those who like to avoid camping, there's the advantage of staying in a hotel.

DAY 1

A short train ride from Ollantaytambo brings you to kilometer 104 (altitude 2,100 meters) of the train tracks. Your trek begins across the river at the ruins of **Chachabamba,** where visits to the complex are offered by most trekking agencies. From here, an eight-kilometer ascent through orchids, waterfalls, and hummingbirds in the cloud forest brings you to the impressive site of **Wiñay Wayna.** In Quechua this means "forever young," and it is home to the beautiful bright purple Wiñay Wayna orchids. Most people stop here for lunch before continuing along the Inca trail to **Inti Punku** (the Sun Gate), after which trekkers arrive at **Machu Picchu** itself. Due to changes in regulations, everyone who does the short Inca Trail now hops on a bus and stays in a hotel in **Aguas Calientes.**

DAY 2

Return early by bus for a full day to see **Machu Picchu** and its surroundings.

★ SALCANTAY TREK TO MACHU PICCHU

This five-day trek, which includes one day in Machu Picchu, is one of the latest alternatives in the area and is becoming increasingly popular. As there are no restrictions, unlike on the Inca Trail, you can do this trek on your own or with a guide or agency. If you don't like camping, there are now high-quality lodges along the route operated by **Mountain Lodges of Peru** (Av. El Sol 948, Centro Commercial Cusco Sol Plaza, tel. 084/262-640, www.mountainlodgesofperu.com).

Day 1

Leaving Cusco, take the road heading toward Lima to the town of Limatambo and the site of **Tarawasi,** named after the berry *tara,* which grows in the area. Continue on to **Soraypampa** (3,869 meters), which is above the nearby herding village of Mollepata. At Soraypampa there is a campsite and a lodge operated by Mountain Lodges Peru. This

a hut on the Salcantay trail

company offers luxury high-altitude trekking, with four lodges located along the Salcantay route. Their lodges are all designed with elements of environmental sustainability in mind. With heating, hot showers, incredibly comfortable beds, and Jacuzzis, this is a great option for trekkers who either do not want to camp or don't want to carry the gear on the way to Machu Picchu.

In Soraypampa, you have wonderful views of both **Salcantay** (6,264 meters) and **Humantay** (5,917 meters) mountains. If you are staying in the lodge, you can hike to the beautiful multicolored lake at the foot of Humantay glacier as an acclimatization tour. Some trekkers prefer to push on past Soraypampa to a campsite at **Soyroccocha** (4,206 meters). The campsite is at a very high altitude, so come acclimatized and bring plenty of warm clothing.

Day 2

This is the day of the **high pass** (4,300 meters) and possible sightings of the intriguing Andean chinchilla, a furry rodent that resembles a baby rabbit. Switchbacks take you up to the pass to spectacular snowy views of the mountain. From here, it is a steep 3.5-hour downhill walk through both barren high plains and cloud forest to the campsite of **Colpapampa** (2,682 meters).

Day 3

Colpapampa to **La Playa** is a breathtaking trek. You are now well into the cloud forest. This agricultural area is awash with coffee, avocados, citrus fruits, and wild strawberries. This day is the easiest, as it is only a slight descent to La Playa (2,042 meters).

Day 4

Today you get to **Aguas Calientes.** Follow an old trail for about two hours to the pass (2,743 meters) and down to the Inca town of **Llaqtapata.** Here there is a small archaeological site and a spectacular view of Machu Picchu. After Llaqtapata, the trail is hard, steep, downhill, and very slippery in the rainy

season. The elevation decreases 914 meters over the three-hour hike to the train station at the hydroelectric plant. From here, to get to Aguas Calientes most people take the 4:30pm train (US$8); however, some people choose to walk along the train track, which takes approximately three hours and covers eight kilometers. Most tours offer a night in a hotel in Aguas Calientes before going to Machu Picchu the next day.

Day 5

Early in the morning, you take the short bus trip from Aguas Calientes up to **Machu Picchu** to spend the day.

INCA JUNGLE TRAIL

The latest route to Machu Picchu is locally known as the Inca Jungle Trail. This is a four-day trip that includes biking, hiking, and trains. The advantage of this route is the comparatively lower altitude. It is a completely different experience, with the emphasis on cloud forest scenery, plus a welcome dip in thermal baths. Unlike on the other trails, archaeology is scarcely visible before arriving at Machu Picchu.

Day 1

After 10 years, a decent road to Quillabamba has finally been constructed. A bus ride of about three hours passes Urubamba and Ollantaytambo to the new road, which leads to the **Abra Málaga** (4,300 meters), a high pass into the jungle. Most tours bike 80 kilometers down this road to the town of Santa María, which is a vertical drop of 3,000 meters. Be very careful since this road is very busy with speeding minibuses and trucks.

Day 2

This day is a six- to seven-hour trek through cloud forest. An old Inca trail has been discovered here and is currently being restored. The walk itself takes you through coffee plantations, coca fields, and fruit farms. This walk is a hiker's favorite because it leads directly to the **Cocalmayo hot springs** in Santa Teresa.

Floods in January 2010 washed the baths out completely; they have since been restored, although they are more modest now.

After a morning of trekking, you will finally arrive at the hydroelectric plant, where a train takes you to **Aguas Calientes.**

Day 3
This is another day of trekking; the geography is very similar to that of the previous day.

Day 4
Early in the morning, you head by bus to **Machu Picchu** to do the normal day tour.

Ruins Tour

CARETAKER'S HUT
(LOS CUARTELES)
From the ticket booth, the path enters the south side of Machu Picchu through the Guards' Quarters, which are two-story storehouses orientated to the June solstice. There are many different ways to continue through the ruins from here—some tours begin with the agricultural area, but it's preferable to begin with the Caretaker's Hut, which commands the best views of the entire site.

The zigzag path is usually marked with white arrows on the left just after walking through the ticket area and before arriving at the Guards' Quarters. The 10-minute hike switchbacks up alongside the terraces and arrives at a lookout. This hut is one of the highest points in Machu Picchu, which allowed a caretaker to see a large stretch of the Río Urubamba in addition to the main entrance from the Inti Punku (Sun Gate). The Caretaker's House is built in the *wayrana* style, whereby one of the four walls is left completely open to promote ventilation. It opens up to the **Terrace of the Ceremonial Rock.** The significance of the rock itself is unknown. Nowadays, the terrace acts as the most popular spot to take panoramic photos of the city.

From here, it is easy to understand Machu Picchu's basic layout: A large grassy square divides the city in three areas. To the left are the **Royal and Sacred Areas,** which probably reserved for the Inca emperor and his court. To the right is the **Secular Area,** where the workers lived, and below the lookout itself is the **Agricultural Area.** Running

near the lookout area is the main Inca Trail, which comes all the way from Cusco. Looking left, you can see the trail coming down the terraced hillsides from the **Inti Punku,** or Sun Gate, the ceremonial entrance to Machu Picchu. On the other side of the Inca Trail are smaller paths that lead uphill to the Caretaker's Hut and another that leads across the terraces to the **Inca drawbridge.**

FUNERARY ROCK
(ROCA FUNERARIA)
A carved slab is situated on the left-hand side of the Caretaker's Hut. It is a large, white, granite altar with carvings of three steps and a large, flat bed on top. There is also a ring pointing in the direction of the solstice; its significance remains unknown. The Funerary Rock is surrounded by many other foreign rocks, such as limestone, which is found in Sacsayhuamán and other quarries far from Machu Picchu. These rocks are believed to have been left over from Inca offerings. Above the rock is a small, four-sided building whose function also remains unknown.

AGRICULTURAL AREA
(SECTOR AGRICOLA TERRAZAS)
Beneath the lookout and above the Guards' Quarters are more than 100 agricultural terraces that face the sun year-round and were used to grow multiple crops. These terraces used fertile dark earth brought from the valley below; the earth's porous quality drains waters efficiently, so despite the region's wet climate, Machu Picchu's terraces were not prone

Machu Picchu

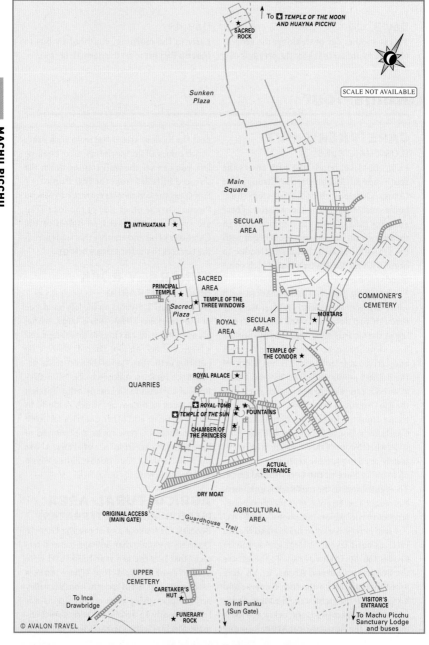

SACRED ROCK

To ✪ *TEMPLE OF THE MOON AND HUAYNA PICCHU*

SCALE NOT AVAILABLE

Sunken Plaza

Main Square

SECULAR AREA

✪ *INTIHUATANA* ★

SACRED AREA

PRINCIPAL TEMPLE ★

★ TEMPLE OF THE THREE WINDOWS

Sacred Plaza

COMMONER'S CEMETERY

MORTARS ★

ROYAL AREA

SECULAR AREA

TEMPLE OF THE CONDOR ★

QUARRIES

ROYAL PALACE ★

✪ ROYAL TOMB ★
✪ TEMPLE OF THE SUN ★ FOUNTAINS
★
CHAMBER OF THE PRINCESS

ACTUAL ENTRANCE

DRY MOAT

AGRICULTURAL AREA

ORIGINAL ACCESS (MAIN GATE)

Guardhouse Trail

UPPER CEMETERY

CARETAKER'S HUT ★

To Inca Drawbridge

FUNERARY ROCK ★

To Inti Punku (Sun Gate)

VISITOR'S ENTRANCE

↓ To Machu Picchu Sanctuary Lodge and buses

© AVALON TRAVEL

to flooding. In 2002, Cusqueñan archaeologist Elva Torres took samples from different terraces to determine what crops the Inca cultivated in Machu Picchu. The results showed that they cultivated pumpkins, squash, tomatoes, peppers, and other indigenous tubers, such as *yacon*, which is used to treat diabetes.

MAIN GATE
(LA PUERTA PRINCIPAL)

Continuing from the Caretaker's Hut, follow the Inca Trail downhill to the Main Gate to Machu Picchu. A gigantic entrance door with locks on its inner part was used to close Machu Picchu. This is where the Inca rulers would have entered the city with great pomp. Looking through, there is a great photograph opportunity of Huayna Picchu framed by the gate. Passing through, continue on for about 40 meters, where, to your right, you will find a building with many doors on the first floor. The ground floor of this building was probably used as a meeting area, while the second floor was a storage room where produce was dried by ventilation. Below these storehouses, there are more than 15 constructions on different levels that were used as housing. Going back up to the main trail, continue three minutes until you arrive at an open area with numerous rocks. This area is the quarry of Machu Picchu.

QUARRIES
(LAS CANTERAS)

The main quarry of Machu Picchu lies on the hillside just past the Main Gate. However, there are two more quarries beside the **Sacred Rock** and another below the **Secular Area.**

There are some houses in the Main Gate quarry, and they probably belonged to the workers. One noteworthy highlight of the quarry is the **Serpent Rock;** if you look closely you will see it is etched with snake designs.

Returning to the main path, walk down the main stairway of the citadel, which has 16 different fountains that are all interconnected. The first fountain is on the right-hand side

before arriving at the rest hut. From this first fountain, walk downhill, following the water into the **Royal Tomb** and **Temple of the Sun,** the most sacred of Machu Picchu's religious areas.

FOUNTAINS
(LOS FUENTES)

There are two different theories behind the fountains. Some say they were used to supply drinking water to the people of Machu Picchu, and others say that they were ritual baths.

The fountains have two very distinct styles. The first three fountains are constructed in fine stone, and the rest are built in a more rustic style using stone and mortar. Walk down 10 steps, where you will see a small entrance to the right that will take you to the impressive natural cave that the Inca fashioned into the Royal Tomb.

★ ROYAL TOMB AND TEMPLE OF THE SUN
(LA TUMBA REAL Y EL TEMPLO DEL SOL)

Here you will find a beautiful chamber where the mummy of Inca Pachacútec may have been stored, although no remains were ever found. The stonework and overall design of the building make it one of the Inca's most famed and elaborate constructions. The rocks are elegantly fitted into the contours of the natural cave, a perfect example of the Inca using carved stone to enhance the beauty of natural stone. The tomb contains three long niches and one smaller one, which has its own altar. At the entrance of the cave, there is bedrock with three long steps believed to have been used to give offerings to the dead. Inside the tomb is a chalk grid, which has been drawn by the government to determine any seismic movement in Machu Picchu.

Straight ahead is a wooden stairway next to an Inca stairway; both lead to the Temple of the Sun. *Please note:* It is forbidden to use the Inca stairway.

The Temple of the Sun, also called El Torreón (The Tower) in Spanish, is above the

Royal Tomb and is unmistakable thanks to its perfect circular walls, which lean inwards for stability and recall the Coricancha in Cusco. The temple has two windows. One faces the sunrise at Inti Punku (the Sun Gate) on the December solstice, and the other is oriented to the June solstice. These windows created rays of light inside the temple during these sacred days. Therefore, the temple is considered a solar observatory.

The temple was excavated to strengthen the walls. During this process, three niches were discovered, of which the middle niche has the distinctive double jamb. The authorities have covered this new discovery with glass. On the left side of the temple is a small, two-story building that is believed to have been the house of either a princess or a high priest. Near the sun temple is an exquisite fountain that unifies the sacred elements of Inca cosmology (sun, rocks, water, and wind).

Royal Tomb

ROYAL PALACE
(PALACIO REAL)

The buildings on the other side of the main staircase are known as the Royal Palace, because it is here that Inca Pachacútec and his family must have lived while visiting Machu Picchu. There are a few beautiful trapezoidal doorways and perfect Inca stonework, both telltale signs of royal architecture. Follow the doorways and staircases to a large stone patio.

On the right-hand side of the patio there is a large, fine door that is presumed to be the entrance to the Inca's bedroom. There are a few other rooms, including a bathroom with its own drainage system and a cooking area.

Climb to the top of the main staircase and turn right before the quarry. Continue about 60 meters to the botanical garden, where you may see various species of native flora. There are orchids, passion fruit trees, and a coca plant.

Beyond the garden to the left is the Sacred Plaza, containing both the Temple of the Three Windows and the Principal Temple.

SACRED PLAZA
(PLAZA SAGRADA)

This square has major buildings on three sides, making it one of the more important ceremonial areas of Machu Picchu. As you enter the plaza, the main attraction is the temple on the right, known as the Temple of the Three Windows.

Temple of the Three Windows
(EL TEMPLO DE LAS
TRES VENTANAS)

On the northern side of the plaza, this temple overlooks the main square of Machu Picchu and is built of gigantic stones like the structures in Sacsayhuamán. The three giant trapezoidal windows were perfectly fitted, and there are two additional windows, which were later filled to make niches. Although the exact purpose of this building is unknown, ritual ceramics such as *keros* (drinking cups) were found in the foundations in the 1980s. The view through the windows is impressive, taking in an expanse across the Main Plaza to the eastern urban sector.

The construction here was never completed. We know this because a marker that indicates where a rock should have been chiseled is still visible on the northwestern wall. To the west of the Sacred Plaza is a circular wall similar to Cusco's Coricancha (sun temple).

Principal Temple
(TEMPLO PRINCIPAL)

This building is on the western side of the Sacred Plaza and is composed of enormous horizontal stones hewn from bedrock. The temple faces Cerro Machu Picchu and has an enormous altar on the back wall. Some scholars believe that this temple was dedicated to Pachamama (mother earth). Above the altar are very high niches where ceremonial items were placed. The wall is collapsing on the right side; damage sustained to the stonework is due to insufficient foundations (an uncommon problem at Machu Picchu, where an estimated 80 percent of all stonework is underground and used to shore up the buildings on extremely steep and uneven ground).

The House of the Priest

On the eastern side of the plaza, directly opposite the Principal Temple, is a rustic house. It is believed to have been the house of the priest.

The Sacristy

Leaving the Sacred Plaza, going west behind the Principal Temple, you will come to a small construction on the right-hand side known as the Sacristy.

The Sacristy is the only room within the city that has the Inca imperial style but that is not a temple or a palace. If you look carefully, you may notice the anti-seismic construction using bedrock, keystones, and the famous 32-sided stone. Also note the unfinished polishing on the rocks.

Leaving the Sacristy, go to your right and climb up the impressive stairway to the top. On your right-hand side, there is a rock that represents the mountains of Putucusi and Yanantin. Continue upwards to the home of the Intihuatana.

★ INTIHUATANA

To the west of the Principal Temple, climb the staircase of the Intihuatana pyramid to the highest point in the urban area. The

Intihuatana

centerpiece is the fascinating four-sided sculpture, probably considered the most sacred in Machu Picchu. It was named by Hiram Bingham—the Quechua name translates as "place to which the sun was tied." Scholars dispute the function of this stone and have largely dismissed the view that it was used as a sundial. More plausible theories include a solar observatory, sacrificial altar, or a temple aligned with the surrounding mountains and their resident *apus* (gods). There is no obvious logical explanation for its careful but bizarre shape, although if you stand facing Huayna Picchu, the stone's form could be a replication of the mountain's. Whatever its use or meaning, the Intihuatana is a deeply spiritual work of art, and perhaps the world's first abstract sculpture.

In front of the Intihuatana there is a stone on the ground that looks like an arrow and points directly south, similar to a stone found on Huayna Picchu. This observatory is surrounded by two three-walled constructions, one of which is completely intact. Follow the white arrows down the stairs to the bottom. Turn right and cross the plaza. To the north, two more *wayrana* buildings surround the Sacred Rock.

SACRED ROCK
(LA ROCA SAGRADA)

The form of the Sacred Rock, which is 25 feet long and flanked by sacred *wayrana* buildings, is identical to the form of the mountain Yanantin in the background. Before this rock was protected a few years ago, hundreds of Machu Picchu visitors every day would spread their arms across it to feel its energy. Behind the Sacred Rock to the left is the entrance to Huayna Picchu and the Temple of the Moon, and to the right is a short trail that heads back in the direction of the Guards' Quarters (the entrance to Machu Picchu). This trail leads past a quarry with the **Main Plaza** on the right and **Secular Area** on the left. The grass lawns of the Main Plaza are no longer accessible to visitors, but if you keep walking in the direction of the Guards' Quarters,

you will have a great view of the **Artisans' Wall,** which runs along the perimeter of the Secular Area. It is one of the finest walls in the whole site.

SECULAR AREA
(SECTOR URBANO)

The Secular Area is where hundreds of workers and servants for Machu Picchu lived and worked. Many visitors miss out this area and walk straight down the stairs parallel to the outside wall. If you decide to explore, the area is divided between *kanchas* (living compounds) for the *ayllus* (clans), or Inca elite. The design is broken up and chaotic, and it's difficult to follow a set route through the area. Think of this area as the bustling, populated part of the citadel where most people lived and worked. If you lose track of the directions, head to the general areas indicated by the map.

After the narrow entrance, there is a large open area with two enormous buildings that probably functioned as *kallancas* (great halls). These buildings were used by workers for celebrations and doubled as large rain shelters.

Returning to the trail and heading in the direction of the Guards' Quarters, continue until you find a series of two-story *colcas* or storehouses. Continue along this trail for about 50 meters until you reach a corner. Head left on the steps and then head right, again in the direction of the Guards' Quarters. Continue ahead for about 60 meters until you reach an area known as the Mortars.

MORTARS
(LOS MORTEROS)

In the open space to the east, there is a large *wayrana*. Mortars that are sculpted in a circular shape with a concave base are found in the ground. While Bingham thought they were grinders, the modern-day hypothesis is that they were filled with water and used as earthquake detectors. Another theory is that they were mirrors to view constellations.

This area is also the *acllahuasi*, the "house of the chosen ones." If you explore the area, you will see that it has a large, secure doorway. Exiting the principal door, head left to the corner and go down the stairs, where you will see a tomb, known as **Intimachay** or Cave of the Sun. This was an important burial site in the citadel, and it contains a window that aligns perfectly with the first sunlight of the December solstice. Next to Intimachay is a large cave that contains a well-carved altar where many remains were found.

Back up the stairs and to your left is a large rock that has a slide on it. On top you will find an altar. From here, go down the stairs to the left, following the arrows to the Temple of the Condor.

TEMPLE OF THE CONDOR
(TEMPLO DEL CONDOR)

At the entrance, there is an open area with a sculpted rock on the ground known as the head of the condor, a bird still revered by Andean people. Directly behind are the wings of this impressive Andean bird, which in real life has a wingspan of over eight feet. Below the wings is a cave with stairs and niches on the wall believed to have been a tomb. In 1975, this cave was excavated by Alfredo Valencia, who found the bones of both llamas and guinea pigs. Experts believe the flat rock outside was used as a sacrificial table.

Above the condor, three very unusual niches have two holes on either side. While Hiram Bingham thought this was the prison, it is now believed to have been a place to worship mummies.

To the left of the condor, there is a large two-story building. To enter the building, you must climb down the stairs, where you will find another tomb inside the house. Under the stairs, there are small holes in the base of the wall that were used to farm *cuy* or guinea pigs, a method still used in communities throughout the Andes.

If you return to the Temple of the Condor and go to the far left, there is another cave. Go inside to find yet another tomb. To exit this chamber, duck under the small door, turn left, and then go directly to the right, where there is another secular area that offers a fabulous view of the Agricultural Area and the Temple of the Sun. Climb the stairs in the direction of the Temple of the Sun, but before arriving, turn left and follow the arrows to exit back to the Guards' Quarters, from where you started your walk.

Hikes at Machu Picchu

★ TEMPLE OF THE MOON AND HUAYNA PICCHU
(EL TEMPLO DE LA LUNA Y HUAYNA PICCHU)

The hike from the Machu Picchu ruins to the summit of Huayna Picchu (elevation 2,740 meters, or 290 meters above Machu Picchu) is approximately 1.9 kilometers round-trip. It takes over an hour to get up and just under to come down again. It is not a difficult hike, but if the sun is baking down by late morning, it can be a little tough, especially if you have been trekking for several days. It starts at the Sacred Rock and passes through a gate that is open 7am-1pm. However, most people arrive before 10am with a prebooked ticket (you can pay extra for your Machu Picchu entrance ticket to include Huayna Picchu). Only 400 adults a day are allowed to do this climb (children are not allowed), 200 at 7am and 200 at 10am. If you haven't got a ticket, head there at 10am to see if there are any spaces left, but be aware that it is often completely booked, even outside high season. It makes sense to climb Huayna Picchu in the morning and then see the ruins in the afternoon to avoid missing this hike.

While it is steep, the path is in good shape, although the last 20 meters include a steep rock slab that must be climbed with a ladder and a rope. Take extra care in the rainy season. The Inca built retaining terraces, buildings, tunnels, staircases, and a shrine on the top of the mountain. Human remains were also found in caves. The splendor of Huayna Picchu is the breathtaking view of the entire complex, which spreads out before the summit like a map.

Farther down on the slopes of Huayna Picchu is the Temple of the Moon, a construction almost as impressive as the Temple of the Sun but with an entirely different mood. The easiest way to visit the Temple of the Moon is to retrace your steps down from Huayna Picchu and take the marked trail turnoff halfway down, which leads directly to the site. Visiting the Temple of the Moon adds about 1-2 hours onto the Huayna Picchu hike. If you visit both Huayna Picchu and the Temple of the Moon, expect to spend 3-4 hours, so take plenty of water and food.

The Temple of the Moon is a medium-sized natural cave where rocks have been fitted perfectly in flowing, gentle shapes. Instead of the tower and bright sunlight of the Temple of the Sun, everything here is recessed and dark with sinuous lines. The Temple of the Moon itself is a wall of doors and windows sculpted perfectly into the space created by a giant overhanging rock. A bit below there is a doorway that leads to other structures, including a lower cave that is near where the trail from Huayna Picchu descends.

INTI PUNKU
(SUN GATE)

For a less strenuous hike, head to the Caretaker's Hut and hike up the Inca Trail, which arcs across the mountain slope to a high pass. It is about a one-hour walk to this pass, where there is a stone construction known as the Sun Gate or Inti Punku (2,720 meters). From here you can appreciate a spectacular view of the ruins from high above. This view is the first glimpse of Machu Picchu for hikers on the classic Inca Trail. If you have enough energy you can hike a little of the Inca Trail

backwards, but be aware that the checkpoint officially closes at 3pm. After visiting Inti Punku, go back down the same trail to the Caretaker's Hut.

CERRO MACHU PICCHU

Cerro Machu Picchu (3,051 meters) is the mountain above Machu Picchu in the direction of Inti Punku. This moderate three-hour hike is a good alternative to climbing Huayna Picchu, with the added bonus that you can say you've climbed the real Machu Picchu. Unknown to many visitors, this hill actually gave the city its name (Old Peak). The hike is a good way to escape the crowds, and there's a great view at the top. To get there take the Inca Trail out of the Machu Picchu ruins past the Caretaker's Hut and toward Inti Punku. About 150 meters past the Caretaker's Hut, head right up a set of stairs with a sign that says "To Machu Picchu Mountain." Follow the trail for one hour through a habitat of exotic birds, orchids, lichen, moss, and trees, until arriving at the bottom of a set of Inca stairs. From here, it is a steep, 45-minute uphill walk. This is an excellent acclimatization hike for anyone preparing for a post-Machu Picchu trek. Hiram Bingham's expedition revealed skeletons at the base of Cerro Machu Picchu. This area is therefore called **Upper Cemetery.**

INCA DRAWBRIDGE

A shorter and gentler hike than Inti Punku or Cerro Machu Picchu is along the path branching off to the right as you climb up to the Caretaker's Hut from the ruins. After you sign in at a checkpoint, the path heads into the forest before arriving at a path with sheer cliff walls. At one point, it even passes over a man-made ledge, like that found on the upper route at the Pisac ruins. The trail ends near a gap at the stone ledge, where the Inca evidently placed a drawbridge or a series of logs that could be withdrawn if necessary. It's not possible to cross the gap, and the sheer drops down to the valley far below remind you to take care on the trail. Retrace your steps back to the Caretaker's Hut.

Getting There and Around

There are various ways to reach **Aguas Calientes,** the town at the base of Machu Picchu. You can take the Inca Trail or the Salcantay route, ride the train from Ollantaytambo (90 minutes) or from near Cusco (2.5 hours), take the Inca Jungle Trail, or take the bus through Santa Teresa. In Aguas Calientes, there are frequent bus shuttles to Machu Picchu, though some choose the two-hour forest hike that cuts across the road's switchbacks. Once inside Machu Picchu, the only way to get around is by foot.

TRAIN

The breakup of the longtime PeruRail monopoly has so far failed to bring down prices, and there is no escaping that the train is expensive by backpacker standards. Expect to pay US$75 one-way (US$120 round-trip). Before booking train service to Machu Picchu or asking your hotel to book trains for you, check the websites of the companies.

Inca Rail (Portal de Panes St. 105, Plaza de Armas, Cusco, tel. 084/58-1860) has two trains that offer a number of daily departures from Ollantaytambo to Machu Picchu. The **Machu Picchu Train** leaves Ollantaytambo daily at 7:20am, arriving in Aguas Calientes 90 minutes later. It leaves for Ollantaytambo on the return trip at 4:12pm. Prices vary according to time but are approximately US$75 one-way.

The second train, **Inca Train,** offers three daily departures from Ollantaytambo at 6:40am, 11:15am, and 4:36pm, as well as three daily departures from Aguas Calientes at 8:30am, 2:30pm, and 7pm. The trains have an executive class (US$50 one-way) and a first class (US$75 one-way).

The traditional option is **PeruRail** (Av. Pachacútec, Cusco, tel. 084/58-1414, www. perurail.com), which offers train service from Ollantaytambo, Pachar (about an hour and a half from Cusco), and Poroy (near Cusco) to Aguas Calientes. The price varies depending on the station and train; the company offers the **Expedition** (US$140-240 round-trip, US$70 one-way), the **Vistadome** (US$160-260 round-trip, US$90 one-way), and the luxury **Hiram Bingham service** (US$588 round-trip, US$334 one-way). The Expedition train is nearly as comfortable as the Vistadome, with large, soft seats and plenty of legroom. Food for sale includes sandwiches (US$4) and candy bars (US$2). The perks of the Vistadome include large viewing windows in the ceilings, shows put on by train attendants (including fashion walks to promote alpaca clothing), luxurious seats, lights snacks and beverages, and live Andean music.

The Hiram Bingham service is in a whole different league. A full brunch is served on the ride from Poroy (15 minutes outside Cusco) to Machu Picchu, where guests are treated to a deluxe ruins tour and a full tea at the Sanctuary Lodge. On the ride home, predinner pisco sours are served in the elegant dark-wood bar, accompanied by a live band and dancing. A gourmet four-course dinner follows at your private table, accompanied by a selection of wines. Afterwards, there is live music and dancing for those with energy. Hands down, this is the most luxurious train service in Latin America. If it feels like the Orient Express, that's because it is—PeruRail has been operated by Orient-Express Ltd. since the late 1990s.

All trains depart from Ollantaytambo or Pachar except the Hiram Bingham service. The Hiram Bingham luxury train avoids the famous (or infamous) switchbacks out of Cusco by leaving from the Poroy station, which is a 15-minute drive from Cusco. Its bus departs Cusco at 8:10am. The train leaves Poroy at 9:40am and arrives in Aguas Calientes at 12:30pm. On the return, the train departs Aguas Calientes at 5:50pm and gets to Poroy at 8:50pm. The bus returns to Cusco at 10pm.

Sinking Like Stone: The Weight of Tourism

The phenomenal beauty of Machu Picchu attracted over a million tourists in 2011, a huge increase on the previous year, and that number had increased to nearly 1.2 million in 2014. More than 3,000 tourists per day trample the grounds of the ancient Inca city, well above the limit that Peru agreed to with UNESCO. Such popularity comes at a price. Because Machu Picchu is built on a man-made mound of earth, the ground is comparatively soft and the site is actually sinking, albeit very slowly. Some of the Inca stonework already shows signs of damage, and there is evidence of soil erosion and damage to surrounding vegetation.

After pressure from UNESCO, the Peruvian government introduced the first restrictions on the Inca Trail in 2001, limiting numbers to 500 people per day, including guides and porters. At Machu Picchu, luxury helicopter rides have been banned and total visitor numbers limited to 2,500 per day. But this is still a huge number of people, and such is the value of Machu Picchu to the local economy that it seems unlikely there will be further restrictions.

In fact, the government is now looking to implement strict new measures to visit Machu Picchu that would allow for a significant increase in tourists. In 2015, Peruvian media reported the findings of a government-commissioned study that said Machu Picchu could withstand 5,940 daily visitors if managed correctly. That would be a whopping 2.2 million visitors a year.

How are they going to do it? In 2015, the government approved a US$40 million master plan for Machu Picchu that would overhaul the management of the complex and the tourist experience. The plan envisions changing the entry point to Machu Picchu and adding new routes to and around the citadel, as well as building a help center and adding toilets within the ruins.

For tourists, the biggest change would be once they are inside the complex. The plan calls for creating three marked paths, and time limits at each part of Machu Picchu to keep the flow moving. It is unclear when this could happen, but what is certain is that the old days of moving freely within Machu Picchu are likely numbered as the longstanding tension between profiteering and preservation continues.

The Cusco-Machu Picchu train crosses high, desolate plains before descending to meet the Urubamba Valley. Once past Ollantaytambo, the rail enters a gorge that grows narrower and deeper as it continues its descent. Look for occasional glimpses of snow-covered Verónica (5,750 meters) to the right. At kilometer 88 there is a modern bridge built on Inca foundations. As the vegetation and the air grow thicker, the train descends into what the Peruvians call the *ceja de selva* (eyebrow of the jungle), and the Río Urubamba starts crashing over house-sized boulders. The train continues until reaching Aguas Calientes.

BUS JOURNEY FROM SANTA TERESA

The elaborate bus ride to Machu Picchu via Santa Teresa is hardly worth it unless you are really counting your pennies. From the Terminal de Santiago in Cusco, take a bus to Santa María (six hours, US$3). From Santa María, it is a two-hour bus ride to Santa Teresa. From there, shared taxis called *colectivos* will take you across the river to Oroya, where you can take a 5:30pm train to Aguas Calientes (US$8), or where you can walk three hours to the town. No matter what, if you choose this route, you will need to spend the night in Aguas Calientes, which may put another dent in your pocket.

Aguas Calientes

Ever since a landslide destroyed the railway past Machu Picchu to Quillabamba, Aguas Calientes is literally the end of the line for the Cusco-Machu Picchu train. While the Sacred Valley towns of Pisac and Ollantaytambo boast a vibrant Inca heritage, the town that is the gateway to Machu Picchu is unashamedly modern. There is nothing authentically indigenous about Aguas Calientes; it is a pure tourist town that has sprung up to accommodate the hordes of tourists—over one million per year at the last count—who flock to Machu Picchu.

That said, Aguas Calientes is not a disagreeable place. Its isolation and complete lack of cars make it relaxing to wander around, and there is an ever-increasing range of hotels and restaurants for all budgets. At 2,000 meters, it's also considerably lower and warmer than the Sacred Valley and Cusco. Few people stay here for longer than one night before or after a day at Machu Picchu, which is infinitely preferable to rushing to Machu Picchu on a day trip. But factor in the hair-raising climb up Putukusi, the Mandor waterfalls, and the thermal baths that give the town its name (Hot Waters), and you could do worse than stay here for two nights.

SIGHTS

The town spreads uphill from the tracks alongside the Río Aguas Calientes past a square and up the main drag of Pachacútec, which is lined with hotels and restaurants. On the other side of the river, the Orquídeas neighborhood is quieter, with a few new hotels, and is also home to the new stadium.

At the top of Pachacútec are the town's **thermal baths** (US$4 with towels, 5am-8pm daily). The six baths are cleanest in the morning and are usually quite grimy by evening. A dirt trail leads uphill for several hours to a string of remote but attractive waterfalls.

Follow the road toward Machu Picchu, and just before the uphill zigzag road to the ruins is **Museo del Sitio Machu Picchu** (highway to Machu Picchu at Puente Ruinas, 9am-4:30pm daily, US$8). The English-Spanish signs in this small, modern museum lead you geographically, culturally, and historically through Machu Picchu. Dioramas explain a typical Incan day in Machu Picchu, and enlarged photos explain the site's investigation. There is also an attached orchid garden, which contains some 300 species.

ENTERTAINMENT AND EVENTS

The disco **Wasicha** (Lloquey Upanqui, 6pm-late) is one of the few spots for dancing. **Big Brother** (6pm-midnight) at the top of Pachacútec has a pool table and is a good place for a drink. Most people, however, simply hang out in the town's many restaurants that stay open until midnight.

SHOPPING

Most Machu Picchu travelers pass through the Aguas Calientes **market,** which lies between the train station and the town itself. The market has touristy knickknacks for sale, as well as some good jewelry and textiles, but better quality can be found in the Sacred Valley and in Cusco.

RECREATION
Putukusi

This forested rock dome 400 meters above Aguas Calientes is a superb but spine-chilling half-day hike that offers great views of Machu Picchu and a chance to see many different cloud forest birds. However, you must negotiate 200 meters (600 feet) of wooden ladders nailed to the near-vertical cliff face. The trailhead is signed and is 150 meters past the control point on the railroad tracks. The walk is approximately three hours, allowing you to arrive in leisure and get a very different

To Museo del sitio Machu Picchu,
Belmond Sanctuary
Lodge, and Machu Picchu

RUPIWASI/
TREE HOUSE

THE TREE HOUSE

MACHUPICCHU HOSTAL

EL TOLDO
PACHAMAMA
APU INKA
SPA

HOSTAL LOS
CAMINANTES

HUANACAURE

TOURIST
INFORMATION

IPERU/
IMPERIO DE LOS INCA

COLLASUYO
CONSTISUYO

GRINGO BILL'S

Plaza
Principal

TOTO'S HOUSE

ATM

CENTRO
MEDICO

FORTALEZA

ANTISUYO

PERU RAIL
OFFICE

CENTRO CULTURA
MACHU PICCHU

WASICHA

INDIO FELIZ

Río Urubamba

SINCHI ROCA

PUEBLO
VIEJO

LLOQUEY UPANQUI

INKATERRA
EL MAPI

PIZZERIA
INKA WASI

MAYTA CAPAC

PIZZERIA
KEROS

AV. CAPACYUPANQUI

PACHACUTEQ

IMPERIO DE LOS INCA

Río
Alcamayo

To Sacred Valley
and Cusco

TRAIN
STATION

Artesian
Market

Río Aguas Calientes

INCA ROCA

YAHUAR HUACA

EL KINTU
INN

INTI
WIRACOCHA

CHEZ
MAGGY

Hospedaje
Inti Wasi

HOSTAL
QUILLA

LA CABANA

HOSTAL
PIRWA

INCA YUPANQUI

BIG BROTHER

EL PUEBLO
MARKET

CANDELA'S

HOSPEDAJE
Q'ENTE

PACHAMAMA INN

MACHU PICCHU
PUEBLO HOTEL

KANTU
INN

YAHUAR HUACA

Soccer
Field

LAS ORQUIDEAS

HOSPEDAJE
INTI WASI

WIRACOCHA

© AVALON TRAVEL

0   50 yds
0   50 m

photo of Machu Picchu. Note that this hike is dangerous after heavy rains, so always check locally with the tourist office for the latest conditions.

Cataratas de Mandor

Another option for out-of-town recreation is the Mandor waterfalls. About a one-hour walk (five kilometers) along the railway track in the direction of the hydroelectric plant brings you to a small house where you pay the entrance fee ($3.50). From here, it is a 45-minute hike through a banana plantation and jungle that starts from kilometer 115 off the tracks. Make sure to take the trail on the right-hand side.

FOOD

Along the railroad tracks and up on the main street, Pachacútec, Aguas Calientes is packed with restaurants. Most have a range of Peruvian meat, chicken, and fish specialties as well as the standard pizza, pasta, steaks, and other international fare. There are so many options that it seems that you are spoiled for choice. However, be advised that hygiene in Aguas Calientes is hit-and-miss, so take care where you eat. For your Machu Picchu tour, various hotels and restaurants prepare box lunches, including Gringo Bill's, Rupa Wasi, La Cabaña, and Inkaterra Machu Picchu Pueblo Hotel.

International

For something different, try ★ **The Tree House** (Huanacaure 180, in the Rupa Wasi hotel, tel. 084/21-1101, 5:30am-3pm and 7pm-11pm daily, mains US$20-25). The ecologically minded restaurant brings a fine selection of wines and pisco to accompany its high-quality food. Try the delicious trout coated in quinoa, Thai chicken, Asian soup, or sushi. They can also provide a very good box lunch for visits to Machu Picchu.

The French-Peruvian-owned ★ **Indio Feliz** (Lloque Yupanqui 103, tel. 084/21-1090, www.indiofeliz.com, 10am-6pm Mon.-Fri., US$12) is easily the best restaurant in town, combining the best of Peruvian and French

food, but served in American-sized portions. The two-story restaurant has a peaceful, homely feel, with tables in a sunny upstairs dining room. The three-course set menu is outstanding value for US$22 and includes a wide selection. Start with French onion soup and follow with salmon, trout, or chicken breast cooked in a wide range of sauces—lemon, garlic, mango, ginger, pineapple, pisco, or rum. The apple and orange pies with custard are delicious desserts. If you get a chance, talk to the French owner, Patrick, a very entertaining, friendly man who is passionate about his restaurant.

Pueblo Viejo (Pachacútec s/n, tel. 084/21-1193, 10am-11pm daily, US$5-10) is at the bottom of the restaurant row and has a cozy atmosphere with live music and a fireplace. There is a huge range of food here, from vegetarian and pizza to grilled meats. There are affordable lunchtime menus as well. Also check out **Toto's House** (tel. 084/22-4179, www.grupointi.com, 9am-11pm daily, US$18-25), a more upscale restaurant on the tracks specializing in grilled meat. It offers a US$20 lunch buffet along with river views.

Pachamama (Av. Imperio de los Incas 145, tel. 084/21-1141, 9am-9pm daily, US$8-10) has been part of Aguas Calientes for many years. It offers ceviche, deep-fried trout, and good desserts, and is a great place for groups. And yet another restaurant on the tracks, **El Kintu** (Av. Pachacútec 150, tel. 084/21-1336, 8am-10pm daily, US$7-10) is an interesting establishment with an Inca decor, open kitchen, and barbecue. It has a very relaxed atmosphere and a wide-ranging menu—trout, quinoa soup, lasagna, fajitas. There's also a small hostel attached to the restaurant. Across the tracks is **Fortaleza** (Av. Pachacútec, tel. 084/21-1119, US$14-17), a popular place for food or just an alfresco drink. Specialties include trout ceviche and *ají de gallina* (chicken in spicy sauce).

Pizza

Restaurant-Pizzeria Inka Wasi (Imperio de los Inkas 123, tel. 084/21-3322, www.

The Camisea Gas Field

Up until the discovery of the Camisea Gas Field, few outsiders had ever entered the lower Urubamba basin, a vast swath of rainforest downriver from Machu Picchu. A treacherous river gorge deterred boat traffic, and the sheer flanks of the **Cordillera Vilcabamba** hindered would-be colonists.

Thanks to its geographic isolation, the lower Urubamba has evolved over millions of years into one of the world's top 25 megadiversity hot spots, according to Conservation International. Biologists continue to discover an unprecedented variety of endemic plant and animal species in the area.

This swath of mountains and jungles is also home to several thousand seminomadic indigenous people. Some of these groups fled to these remote headwaters a century ago to escape the disease and slavery of the rubber boom. Their way of life was supposedly protected in the 1970s when the Peruvian government declared the area a cultural reserve for the Yine, Nahua, and Kirineri peoples.

The area has come under pressure ever since engineers discovered an estimated 11 trillion cubic feet of gas under the jungle floor, now known as the Camisea Gas Field. After more than two decades of negotiations, the Peruvian government signed an agreement to develop Camisea in early 2000. The lower Urubamba hasn't been the same since.

Dynamite explosions replace the murmur of rivers and shrieking of parrots, as engineers map the contours of the vast gas deposit along a checkerboard of paths spaced a mere 300 yards apart. Chainsaws and bulldozers clear forest to make way for unloading zones, a processing plant, and drilling platforms, several of which are inside the cultural reserve. Helicopters routinely buzz the canopy. A 25-meter-wide corridor of cleared land reaches over the Cordillera Vilcabamba and down into the jungle below.

The lead Camisea players are Texas-based **Hunt Oil** and the Argentine companies **PlusPetrol** and **Grupo Techint,** which led the US$1.6 billion effort to drill the gas and then ship it to the coast via two separate pipelines. Hunt built a US$2.1 billion liquefied natural gas plant on the coast south of Lima. Another Texas company, the KBR division of **Halliburton,** runs a Camisea gas plant next to **Paracas,** Peru's most important marine reserve. Conservationists

---

inkawasirestaurant.com, 9am-10pm Mon.-Sat., 1pm-10pm Sun., US$15) offers a US$13 buffet but also serves trout, chicken brochettes, ceviche, pastas, pizzas, and their specialty dish—guinea pig. Along Pachacútec, other recommended places include **Pizzeria Keros** (Pachacútec 116, tel. 084/21-1374, 9am-11pm daily), which also serves Peruvian dishes like guinea pig and grilled alpaca, and **Chez Maggy** (Pachacútec 156, tel. 084/21-1006, 11am-4pm and 6pm-11pm daily, US$10). Along with its sister restaurants throughout the country, Chez Maggy has an established reputation for great pastas and wood-fired pizzas.

Markets and Shops

The biggest minimarket is **El Pueblo,** next to the main market. With juices, yogurts, fresh bread, deli meats, and cheeses, it's a good place to put together a picnic.

ACCOMMODATIONS

Lodging in Aguas Calientes is expensive. The town lacks good-value budget accommodations, and those at the higher end are overpriced. However, it's possible to find some good deals. Note that the train is loud, so staying right next to the tracks is not appealing.

The biggest cluster of budget places is in the Orquideas neighborhood, across from the Río Aguas Calientes, but still choice is limited. Aguas Calientes itself is more expensive, offering plenty of midrange options, while the most upscale hotels are slightly outside of town. The Inkaterra Machu Picchu

opposed the project on the grounds that a single tanker spill could wipe out Paracas's already endangered marine life. The project went ahead regardless and began operation in 2004.

During the early stages of the project, U.S. media coverage focused on the behind-the-scenes lobbying, from both the Bush administration and the Inter-American Development Bank (IDB), which helped make the project happen. For some environmentalists, the real story, however, is the destruction in the lower Urubamba. They fear the same pattern of destruction that destroyed parts of the Amazon in the 20th century.

The pipeline was built with aging pipework, and since December 2004, there have been at least five ruptures of the Camisea pipeline, which sent thousands of barrels of gas into the pristine Urubamba River and polluted local water supplies. Unchecked erosion from the pipeline has also muddied water supplies and decimated fish, a main food source. A Peruvian government report estimated that 17 indigenous people have died of diseases brought to the area by oil workers. The government has promised to build fish farms to replace the extinct river fish, but these promises have yet to be fulfilled.

The Peruvian government has defended the Camisea project for producing valuable foreign revenue and helping Lima make its transition to cleaner-burning fuels. The government has received billions of dollars in royalties from Camisea, while the cheap gas has helped fuel Peru's economic growth during the past decade, allowing millions of people to escape poverty.

At the same time, not all environmentalists are opposed. Some conservationists have pointed to Camisea as a model for hydrocarbon development in fragile ecosystems through its "offshore-inland" method, which means no roads. Instead, transportation is done by helicopter to minimize environmental damage.

The oil companies, meanwhile, have promised to minimize impact by using lateral drilling technology and oil platforms normally used for deep-sea drilling. And the IDB has also monitored the environmental impacts of Camisea as part of the bank's latest US$800 million loan.

However, Peru's politicians have focused far more on the availability of gas for local people than on environmental issues. In April 2012, President Humala announced a deal to guarantee that supplies from the largest block of the gas field would be used for domestic purposes.

Pueblo Hotel is upstream from town, and the Machu Picchu Sanctuary Lodge is next to the ruins themselves.

US$10-25

Hospedaje Inti Wasi (Los Artesanos 102, tel. 084/21-1036, www.intiwasispiritualcenter.com, US$25 pp) is a step up from some of the bare-bones options in town due to the natural surroundings. To get there, walk from the train station up the right side of the Río Aguas Calientes until it dead-ends at a point a few hundred meters below the hot baths. The main sitting area is a plant-filled courtyard. The bunk rooms are small and sparse, with foam beds, and have a tendency to heat up in the sun. Bathrooms are clean and have electric showerheads. Down by the train tracks, on the other side of town, is **Hostal Los Caminantes** (Imperio de los Incas 140, tel. 084/21-2007, US$20 pp). This old wooden building has been receiving backpackers for decades and has friendly management. The older rooms with shared bath are a little tired, while newer rooms with private baths are good value.

Hostal Pirwa (Tupac Yupanqui s/n, tel. 084/244-315, www.pirwahostelscusco.com, dorms US$13 pp, private rooms US$35 d) is part of the Pirwa chain of hostels found throughout Peru.

Off the road to Machu Picchu, just before Puente Ruinas, there is a **municipal campground** (US$10 pp). Some Inca Trail tours choose to camp here as part of the package. If you opt to camp, make sure you have plenty of bug repellent; the campground is right next to the river.

US$25-50

Hostal Quilla (Aymuraypa Tikan 109, tel. 084/21-1096, hostalquilla1@hotmail.com, US$30 s, US$45 d including breakfast) has rooms with tile floors and colorful bedspreads, and service is friendly.

Machupicchu Hostal (Imperio de los Inca 313, tel. 084/21-1034, www.hostalmachupicchu.com, US$50 s, US$65 d with breakfast) has rooms arranged around a plant-filled courtyard overlooking the river. There is a sitting area with a great river view, while the rooms themselves are plain, clean, and comfortable.

US$50-100

One of the best midrange hotels in town is ★ **Wiracocha Inn** (Calle Wiracocha 206, tel. 084/21-1088, www.wiracochainn.com, US$80 s or d), which has 25 rooms, many overlooking the river. With feather pillows, Wi-Fi, cable TV on plasma screens, walls adorned with paintings, and a decent buffet breakfast, it's a very good choice.

Next door to Machupicchu Hostal is its sister property, **Presidente Hostal** (Imperio de los Inca 135, tel. 084/21-1212, www.hostal-presidente.com, US$90 s, US$110 d), a similar production with carpeted, bigger rooms with earth-colored walls—ask for one that overlooks the river.

The clean and modern **Pachamama Inn** (Las Orquideas Chaskatika s/n, tel. 084/21-1141, hostalpachamamainn@hotmail.com, US$80 s, US$100 d, plus US$20 for a Jacuzzi in your room) has 24-hour hot water, a money exchange, tourist information, and a restaurant. Strangely, all rooms are equipped with mirrors on the bathroom ceiling.

Even though the gringo owner is long gone, the charming ★ **Gringo Bill's** (signed well off one corner of the main square, tel. 084/21-1046, www.gringobills.com, US$98-190 d with breakfast) continues to be one of the best hotels in the center of town. It is also one of the oldest hotels in Aguas Calientes, with large rooms, balconies, a roof terrace, and great views over the town and surrounding hills. The newer suites on the top floors are the best.

US$100-150

Rupa Wasi (Huanacaure 180, tel. 084/21-1101, www.rupawasi.net, US$110 s/d, suites US$190) has great views of town, a stringent ecological policy, and nice though overpriced rooms. However, the attached restaurant, The Tree House, is one of the best in town.

La Cabaña (Pachacútec 805, tel. 084/21-1048, www.lacabanamachupicchu.com, US$140 s/d with breakfast) is a friendly place at the top of the main street. Rooms have tile floors, textured walls, and wood ceilings. The owners, Beto and Marta, take an eco-friendly approach. Additional services include guides for walks, security boxes, laundry, and a DVD player. They also offer better rates in the restaurant for guests of the hotel.

Over US$150

A formerly state-owned hotel has been taken over by the Inkaterra Group to create **El Mapi** (Pachacútec 109, tel. 084/21-1011, www.inkaterra.com, US$220 s/d with breakfast buffet). This hotel is by far the most modern looking of the Inkaterra Group, with a beautiful bar, restaurant, and wooden fencing along the windows. To get there from the main square take the main road, Pachacútec; the hotel is on the right-hand side.

★ **Inkaterra Machu Picchu Pueblo Hotel** (railroad km 110, tel. 084/21-1132, www.inkaterra.com, US$433 s, US$547 d) is one of Peru's best hotels. It has a tranquil, natural setting in the cloud forest teeming with birdlife, and it contains top-notch facilities. Stone paths wind through the forest past fountains and pools and up to secluded bungalows with colonial-style furniture, spacious bathrooms, outdoor hot tubs, and couches on your own private patio. The hotel has an eco-friendly philosophy that includes building all of its furniture on-site; it has received the Sustainable Travel award from *National Geographic Traveler*.

This is also the only Machu Picchu hotel that gives visitors a taste of the jungle. The biologist guides lead early-morning bird-watching walks and nature walks that include the biggest orchid collection in Peru (372 species), a butterfly house, and a miniature tea plantation. The hotel has reintroduced the *Oso anteojos* (Andean spectacled bear) to the area; three bears now live in the grounds of the hotel, and you can also take a tour to visit them. Facilities include an excellent restaurant and bar, as well as a spa, sauna, springwater swimming pool, and hot tub.

The latest five-star hotel in Machu Picchu, which took two years to build, is **Sumaq** (Av. Hermanos Ayar s/n, tel. 084/21-1059, www. sumaqhotelperu.com, US$480 s, US$600 d). The hotel has spacious rooms, each with its own range of amenities, beautiful king-size beds, and bathtubs. The hotel offers cooking classes, bird-watching tours, and access to a spa equipped with a sauna, massage service, and Jacuzzi. Dinner is also included.

If you have deep pockets and want to stay within a stone's throw of the lost Inca city, check out the **Belmond Sanctuary Lodge** (next to the entrance to the ruins, tel. 084/21-1038, www.belmond.com, US$1,025 s/d with full board). The lodge is owned by Belmond (formerly Orient-Express Hotels), which also operates Cusco's finest hotel, Hotel Monasterio. Belmond is not allowed to make any additions to the building, so it remains a small, modest hotel on the outside with an elegant interior. The 31 rooms have been outfitted with antiques, king-size beds, and cable TV, and the slightly more expensive rooms have views over the ruins. One advantage of staying here is a night excursion to the ruins, hosted by a local shaman, which is difficult to do from Aguas Calientes. There are two restaurants, one serving gourmet à la carte items (US$40-50) and the other offering an extraordinary buffet. The hotel also offers trekking, river rafting, and mountain-biking trips; walking paths behind the hotel lead through an orchid garden. In high season, this hotel is booked solid, so make reservations at least three months in advance.

INFORMATION AND SERVICES

There is a helpful **Iperú** office (Pachacútec s/n, tel. 084/21-1104), which hands out free maps (just up the main street from the square). If you haven't bought your Machu Picchu entrance ticket, you can do it at **Centro Cultura Machu Picchu** (Pachacútec s/n, tel. 084/21-1196, US$37). Tickets *must* be purchased before heading to the ruins. They can also be bought online in advance at www.machupic-chu.gob.pe.

Where the tracks cross the Río Aguas Calientes is an **EsSalud** clinic (tel. 084/21-1037) with emergency 24-hour service, and on the other side is the **Ministerio de Salud clinic. Señor de Huanca drugstore** (8am-10pm daily) is on the tracks across from the Hostal Presidente. If they don't have what you need, the **Pharmacy Popular** (Puputi s/n, tel. 084/22-8787, 8am-10pm daily) is just off the plaza.

Banco de Crédito has an **ATM** on Imperio de los Incas near Toto's House.

The **post office** (10am-2pm and 4pm-8pm Mon.-Sat.) is on the Plaza de Armas.

There are **Internet** places around the main square.

Laundry Angela (Pachacútec 150, tel. 084/21-2205, US$2/kg) washes clothes the same day.

GETTING THERE AND AROUND

The only way to reach Aguas Calientes is by trekking or taking the train from Ollantaytambo. There are few vehicles and taxis in Aguas Calientes; the place is small enough that most visitors walk everywhere.

Cusco

Cusco more than lives up to its Inca name, which translates as "navel of the world." No visit to Peru is complete without a stay in this fascinating city.

This ancient capital of the Inca culture remains the center of backpacker trails. Whichever direction you arrive from—Bolivia and Lake Titicaca to the south, Lima to the west, or the jungle to the east—all roads lead to Cusco.

Cusco stands today as one of the most beautifully schizophrenic cities in the world—a devoutly Catholic community that is extremely proud of its Inca heritage. Hispanic and Inca architecture and traditions live side by side in an alluring cultural mix. While Cusco is filled with well-preserved architecture, one can only wonder at what it must have looked like in 1533 when Spanish conquistadores arrived. As Francisco Pizarro marched wide-eyed through the Inca empire, Cusco became the holy grail of his conquest. Two scouts sent ahead told him the city was as elegant as a European city and literally covered in gold. Before the scouts left Cusco, they used crowbars to pry 700 plates of gold off the walls of Coricancha, the sun temple.

During four centuries of domination, the Spanish tried their best to subjugate the Inca legacy, but even they could not deny the brilliance of Inca construction, leaving the perfect stonework to serve as foundations for churches and to line Cusco's cobblestone alleys. In a way, it was poetic justice that when the great earthquake shook the city in 1950, the Inca structures stood firm, including the foundations of Coricancha, while more than a third of the colonial buildings were destroyed, including many Spanish churches.

Cusco is seen as the gateway to exploring Machu Picchu and the Sacred Valley, and there are more hotels, restaurants, and tour operators in the city than anywhere else in the region. However, Cusco's altitude at 3,400 meters (11,150 feet) is a major obstacle to overcome. At the airport, vendors even sell oxygen canisters and masks, and *soroche* (altitude sickness) is not to be taken lightly—it can range from a headache and lethargy to dizziness and disorientation. The last thing most travelers want to do when they finally make a Mecca-style entrance to Cusco is to leave, but

Previous: courtyard and tower of the Santo Domingo church; women in traditional dresses dancing in a festival near the Plaza de Armas. **Above:** statue of Pachacútec in the Plaza de Armas.

Look for ★ to find recommended
sights, activities, dining, and lodging.

Highlights

★ **Catedral de Cusco:** Cusco's baroque cathedral, built atop a former Inca palace, dominates the town's Plaza de Armas and is filled with paintings from the Cusco School, elegant carved choir stalls, and a gold altar (page 146).

★ **San Blas:** This charming neighborhood is quieter and quainter than the city center. Escape the urban bustle in its narrow cobblestone streets, lined with stunning colonial architecture (page 148).

★ **Coricancha and Santo Domingo:** Nowhere is the uneasy fusion of Inca and Spanish architecture more evident than at Coricancha. The foundations of the Inca sun temple, once covered with thick plates of solid gold, are topped by a Dominican church (page 150).

★ **Sacsayhuamán:** This stone fortress of huge zigzag walls, carved from stone blocks weighing hundreds of tons, was the scene of the Inca's last stand in Cusco (page 153).

★ **Centro de Textiles Tradicionales del Cusco:** This pioneering center not only sells Cusco's finest textiles but also supports local weavers, helping them recover their ancient techniques in the process (page 157).

that's exactly what you should do, unless you have arrived from a high-altitude destination such as La Paz, Puno, or possibly Arequipa. Instead of suffering for a couple of days, head to the Sacred Valley and Machu Picchu first, and return to Cusco after getting accustomed to the altitude.

The heart of Cusco is its **Plaza de Armas,** which stands out for its huge 16th-century cathedral. Beyond the Plaza de Armas, and opposite the cathedral, are two charming squares, **Plaza Regocijo** and **Plaza San Francisco.** Farther along in this direction lies the market of San Pedro. To the side of the cathedral, a narrow pedestrian street named **Procuradores** is nicknamed Gringo Alley. Behind the cathedral, steep alleys lead up to the bohemian neighborhood of **San Blas.**

Cusco's people are very welcoming, but bear in mind that the hassle level in the center is quite high. It's not for nothing that a local Irish bar sells T-shirts with the simple words "No gracias" on the front. This is exactly what you should say, firmly if necessary, if you aren't buying. Understand, though, that vendors are just trying to make a living, and don't let them get in the way of enjoying the many delights of this elegant Andean city.

HISTORY

As with most empires, the foundation of the Inca empire is shrouded in myth, and there is a tendency to romanticize what was a brutal period in history. The story of its beginning famously tells that around AD 1100, Manco Cápac and Mama Oclla, children of the sun and the moon, arose from the waters of Lake Titicaca and searched the land for a place to found their kingdom. The first place that Manco Cápac was able to plunge his golden staff into the ground was this fertile valley, and the newly founded city was christened Q'osqo, or "navel of the world."

The seeds of truth in this legend are that the **Tiwanaku** people (AD 200-1000), from the south shores of Lake Titicaca, were the first advanced culture to reach the Cusco area. Around AD 700 an even more potent culture,

the **Huari** (AD 700-1100) from Ayacucho, spread here and built aqueducts, the large city of Pikillacta, and probably the first water temple at Pisac. The Inca, sandwiched between these two advanced cultures, rose out of the vacuum created when both collapsed. The Inca combined the Tiwanaku stonework and farming techniques with the Huari highway system; the result was the greatest empire South America had ever seen.

Because the Inca had no written language, little is known about Inca history, though it is believed Manco Cápac existed and was indeed the first Inca. There were probably 13 Inca emperors, but the first of great significance was **Inca Yupanqui,** the ninth Inca leader and one of the younger sons of **Inca Viracocha.** Around 1440, the Chancas, the tribe that toppled the Huari, had amassed a large army that was poised to overrun Cusco. Inca Viracocha fled, probably to his estate at Huchuy Cusco in the Sacred Valley, but Inca Yupanqui stayed on to defend Cusco. Of the ensuing battle, mestizo chronicler Inca Garcilaso de la Vega reports that even the stones of Cusco rose up and became soldiers. Against overwhelming odds, Inca Yupanqui and a team of seasoned generals beat back the Chancas.

After the battle, Inca Yupanqui changed his name to **Pachacútec** ("shaker of the earth" in Quechua), took over Cusco from his disgraced father, and launched the Inca's unprecedented period of expansion. Pachacútec created a vision of the Inca people as a people of power, ruled over by a class of elites. He used a carrot-and-stick strategy, learned from the Huari, of conquering territories peacefully by bearing down on them with overwhelmingly large armies but offering the rich benefits of being integrated into a well-functioning web of commerce in return for loyalty. Well-behaved tribes were rewarded and resistance crushed with devastating force. Pachacútec also pioneered the *mita* system, whereby troublesome tribes were exiled to far-flung parts of the empire.

Pachacútec was an even greater builder

Cusco

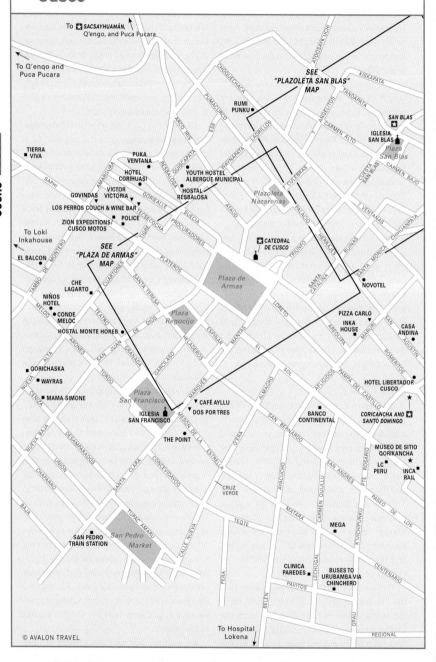

© AVALON TRAVEL

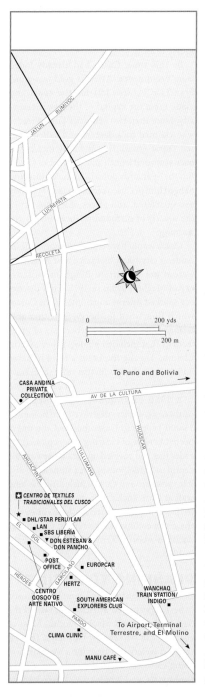

than he was a soldier. He fashioned the city of Cusco into the shape of a puma, a sacred animal admired for its grace and strength, with Sacsayhuamán as the head, the city as the body, and the Coricancha sun temple as the tail. He built a huge central plaza, which included both today's Plaza de Armas and the Plaza Regocijo, and also somehow devised a way to move the giant stones to begin construction of Sacsayhuamán. He is credited with building nearly all of the other major Inca monuments in the area, including Pisac, Ollantaytambo, and probably even Machu Picchu. Pachacútec's armies conquered the entire area between Cusco and Lake Titicaca and also spread north through the central highlands. He died in about 1472 and remains perhaps the most respected figure in Inca history. A statue of him was unveiled, despite objections from the government in Lima, in the center of Cusco's Plaza de Armas.

Pachacútec's son, **Túpac Yupanqui,** was less of a builder and even more of a warrior. He spent most of his life away from Cusco in long, brutal campaigns in northern Peru against the stubborn Chachapoyans. He dominated the entire coastline, including the Chimú empire based at Chan Chan, and pushed all the way to Quito, in present-day Ecuador.

His son, **Huayna Cápac,** the last Inca to rule over a unified empire, seemed to be ruling over a territory that had extended itself almost to the breaking point. Nevertheless, he continued the campaign in the north, fathering a son named **Atahualpa** in Quito, and pushed the Inca empire to its last limits, up against what is now the Ecuador-Colombia border.

Huayna Cápac's death in 1525 was the turning point. The empire had grown rapidly in less than a century from the Cusco area to cover most of modern-day Peru, Ecuador, Bolivia, and parts of northern Chile and Argentina—but it then began to tear itself apart. The strong-willed Atahualpa challenged his half-brother **Huáscar,** the legitimate heir in Cusco, and a disastrous civil war broke out, killing thousands of Inca and badly damaging the empire's infrastructure.

In the end, Atahualpa was victorious. He might even have been able to unify the empire again if it were not for the fact that **Francisco Pizarro** and a small Spanish army had begun their march across Peru. Pizarro and his men took Atahualpa hostage in November 1532 as he was making his way slowly south and held him until an entire room was filled with gold, much of which was taken from Cusco and carried by llama trains to Cajamarca. Then the Spaniards murdered Atahualpa anyway and continued their march to Cusco.

To maintain stability, Pizarro needed to find a new Inca ruler, and he befriended **Manco Inca,** another son of Huayna Cápac in Cusco, who was grateful to Pizarro for having routed Atahualpa's army of Quito-based Inca. Under the guise of liberators and with Manco Inca's blessing, Pizarro and his men entered Cusco and took full and peaceful possession of the city in November 1533.

It didn't take long, however, for Manco Inca to grow resentful. The Spaniards had sacked Cusco for all of its gold and silver in the first month, picking clean the gold-filled sun temple and even the sacred Inca mummies. They melted everything into bars for shipping to Spain, lived in the palaces of the former Inca emperors, and forced Inca nobles to hand over their wives.

Manco Inca escaped from Cusco and by May 1536 had amassed an army estimated at 100,000-200,000 soldiers, who used slingshots to throw red-hot coals onto Cusco's thatched roofs, burning their beloved city to the ground. Trapped, the Spaniards made a last-ditch effort against the Inca, who had occupied the fortress of Sacsayhuamán. During a battle that raged for more than a week, the Spaniards prevailed against overwhelming odds, causing Manco Inca to retreat to Ollantaytambo, where he won the last important victory for his people before retreating to the jungle enclave of Vilcabamba. The Inca resisted for more than three decades until their last leader, Inca **Túpac Amaru,** was captured in the Amazon and executed in Cusco's main square in 1573.

By this time, Cusco had already faded from prominence. After its gold was gone, Francisco Pizarro left for the coast and made Lima the capital of the new viceroyalty. More than two centuries later, a leader who claimed Inca descent and called himself Túpac Amaru II would rally Inca fervor once again and launch another siege of Cusco. But the Spaniards quickly captured him and hanged him in Cusco's main square. His body was quartered, and pieces of it were left in the squares of surrounding Inca villages as a warning.

Cusco would have ended up another quiet Andean city like Cajamarca and Ayacucho were it not for Hiram Bingham's discovery of Machu Picchu in 1911. That discovery sparked international interest in Cusco, which flourished in the 1920s with a glittering café society and a generation of intellectuals that included photographer Martín Chambi. During the 1920s a train line was built past Machu Picchu that still carries travelers today.

A **1950 earthquake,** the most severe in three centuries, destroyed the homes of 35,000 people in Cusco but had the unexpected benefit of clearing away colonial facades that had covered up Inca stonework for centuries. Much of the Inca stonework visible today around Cusco, including the long wall at Coricancha, was discovered thanks to the earthquake. Based on these ruins, and the city's colonial architecture, Cusco was declared a **UNESCO World Heritage Site** in 1983.

PLANNING YOUR TIME

Because of its altitude and complexity, Cusco is best experienced after having visited the Sacred Valley and Machu Picchu. Most of the city can be seen in two days, though many travelers stay here for a week or two, using Cusco as a base for trekking, adventure sports, and jungle trips. Cusco's *boleto*

The Right Attitude Toward Altitude

The last thing you want when arriving in Cusco, the cradle of Inca civilization and archaeological capital of the Americas, is to feel lousy, but if you're arriving from sea level or an altitude lower than 2,000 meters, that is exactly what can happen. The percentage of oxygen in the air remains roughly the same until about 2,400 meters, but at heights above that, oxygen levels decrease and fail to sustain the body's normal function.

Cusco sits at nearly 3,400 meters, and the altitude will hit you within hours of arriving. The most common symptoms are headache, nausea, dizziness, fatigue, insomnia, and loss of appetite. It can be dangerous, though, so you need to be prepared and take care of yourself, otherwise the first few days of your Peruvian adventure could be ruined. Here are some tips:

- **Leave Cusco as soon as you arrive.** Go to the Sacred Valley, where most towns are below 3,000 meters, and return to Cusco after a few days.

- **Take it easy.** Your body is starved of oxygen, so don't put it under further strain. All those hikes and adventure sports can wait a few days.

- **Drink lots of water.** Altitude sickness is usually accompanied by dehydration. Water oxygenates the blood.

- **Drink coca tea.** The locals swear by it and they should know.

- **Eat light food and plenty of carbohydrates.** Heavy foods, especially meat, make you more lethargic, while carbs give you more energy.

- **Avoid alcohol and smoking.**

- **Pack the medication acetazolamide** (Diamox) to alleviate symptoms. Take the first pill on the plane. Aspirin is a milder alternative.

CUSCO

turístico gets you into many of the major sites in and around Cusco and the Sacred Valley for US$45.

Most city attractions are clustered close to the Plaza de Armas and nearby squares Plaza Regocijo and Plaza San Francisco. There are plenty of tourist services along Avenida del Sol, which heads down toward the bus terminal and airport. For a quieter experience, head uphill on the narrow cobbled streets to San Blas, a neighborhood blissfully removed from the noise and traffic of the center. Even though cars still try to squeeze along San Blas's narrow streets, it's comparatively quiet in this area. Getting around town on your own two feet is easy enough for the majority of the city sights, but outlying sights such as Sacsayhuamán and other ruins outside the city require a taxi, bus, or guided tour, though hiking back downhill into Cusco is an enjoyable way to return.

The most popular time to visit Cusco is during the driest and sunniest season May-August, and the best weather is in June and July. Avoid the last week in July when Peru's hotels are often booked solid for Peru's Fiestas Patrias celebration around July 28. An increasing number of visitors are enjoying the solitude of Cusco during the rainy season November-March, but it can get very wet, particularly at lower-altitude sights such as Machu Picchu, and the Inca Trail closes completely during February. The "shoulder months" of April, May, September, and October are in between the dry and rainy seasons. You'll find generally good weather during these months and few crowds.

Cusco is not a particularly dangerous city, but you should still keep your wits about you. Be careful in the area around San Pedro market and, in particular, around the bus terminal. Avoid wandering into any of the poor neighborhoods on the hills. Assaults have occasionally been reported in San Blas at night, so avoid walking alone in deserted side streets. Taxi hijackings, where taxi drivers kidnap and rob their unsuspecting clients, also happen from time to time in Cusco. Never take an unmarked cab; it's preferable to ask your hotel or restaurant to call a taxi rather than hailing one on the street.

Sights

PLAZA DE ARMAS

Cusco's Plaza de Armas is the heart of the city in terms of both architecture and tourism. It is framed by elegant colonial stone arcades and dominated by not one but two stunning churches, the Catedral de Cusco and the Jesuit Iglesia de la Compañia. A statue of Pachacútec has been unveiled in the center, gesturing in the direction of the old Inca fortress Sacsayhuamán. The central government has requested its removal because it was added without permission. The square is a lively place—there are plenty of locals sitting together, attending church and regular religious and patriotic celebrations. Note that the level of vendors in the plaza is high—everything from paintings and ornaments to tours and massages. Politely decline if you're not interested.

★ Catedral de Cusco

Cusco's baroque **cathedral** (Plaza de Armas, 10am-6pm daily, US$8.50 or *boleto religioso*) sits between the more recent **Iglesia de Jesús María** (1733) on its right and, on its left, **Iglesia del Triunfo** (1539), the first Christian church in Cusco. El Triunfo was built to celebrate the victory over Manco Inca. The cathedral was built on top of Inca Viracocha's palace using blocks of red granite taken from Sacsayhuamán and took more than a century to construct, from 1560 onwards. At least four earthquakes from 1650 to 1986, along with damp and neglect, had taken a serious toll on the building. Fortunately, Cusco's archbishop organized a complete renovation 1997-2002, which removed much of the grime that had covered chapels and paintings over

time. For the first time in a century, it is possible to make out the unique **Cusco School** paintings, including unique works such as Christ eating a guinea pig at the Last Supper and the Virgin Mary wearing a mountain-shaped skirt, thus identifying her with the Inca Pachamama (mother earth). There is also an interesting painting, reported to be the oldest in Cusco, showing the city during the 1650 earthquake; the townspeople are praying in the Plaza de Armas with a crucifix named El Señor de Los Temblores (Lord of Earthquakes). Locals still parade this crucifix every year on Holy Monday. The church also contains considerable gold and silver, a 17th-century carved pulpit, choir stalls, and an original gold-covered Renaissance altar. In the bell tower is the huge **María Angola bell,** one of the largest bells in the world, over two meters high, made with 27 kilograms of gold and reportedly audible from a distance of 30 kilometers. If you don't want to pay the entrance fee for a full tour, you may be able to sneak in discreetly to see the cathedral's interior during morning Mass if you are Catholic, but put the camera away.

Iglesia de la Compañía

Around the corner from the cathedral is the 17th-century **Iglesia de la Compañía** (9am-11:30am and 1pm-5:30pm daily, US$3.50 or *boleto religioso*), which was built on top of the palace of Inca Huayna Cápac. This church was built by the Jesuits, who were expelled from Latin America in 1767, but not before they built a series of churches in Peru's principal cities as well as in Ecuador's capital, Quito. This graceful, ornate facade has a spectacular

Plaza de Armas

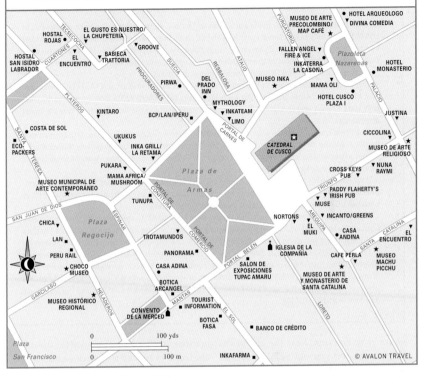

baroque altar, although the interior is considerably darker than that of the cathedral. Near the main door is a 17th-century painting depicting the wedding of Inca princess Beatriz Clara Coya to Spanish *captín* Martín García de Loyola, grandnephew of San Ignacio de Loyola.

NORTHEAST OF THE PLAZA DE ARMAS
Museo Inka

Head up the alley to the left of the cathedral to reach **Museo Inka** (corner of Ataúd and Túcuman, tel. 084/23-7380, www.museoinka. unsaac.edu.pe, 8am-7pm Mon.-Fri., 9am-4pm Sat., US$4). This ornate colonial home contains an interesting collection of Inca objects, including jewelry, ceramics, textiles, mummies, and a variety of metal and gold artifacts. It also has the world's largest collection of *qeros,* wooden cups the Inca used for drinking.

Museo de Arte Precolombino (MAP)

Farther up the alley to the left of the cathedral, on the Plaza de las Nazarenas, is the impressive **Museo de Arte Precolombino** (MAP, Plaza de las Nazarenas 231, tel. 084/23-3210, www.map.museolarco.org, 9am-10pm daily, US$8, US$4 students). The Museum of Pre-Columbian Art contains an array of ceramics, painting, jewelry, and objects made of silver and gold. The museum has an elegant layout designed by Fernando de Szyszlo, one of Peru's most respected contemporary painters, and in the courtyard is a glass box containing the MAP Café, one of Cusco's best

Cuso's Tourist Ticket

Cusco's *boleto turístico* covers admission to 16 sites. At first glance, it seems overpriced at US$40 (US$20 for students under age 26 with ISIC card), but when you consider the total number of sites, it is worth it. More importantly, rules have changed, and individual entrance fees are no longer possible at most of the included sites, so you cannot get into must-see ruins such as Sacsayhuamán, Pisac, and Ollantaytambo without this ticket.

The ticket can be bought at the entrances to most major sites or at COSITUC (Av. El Sol 103, #102, www.cosituc.gob.pe, 8am-6pm Mon.-Sun. tel. 084/22-7037). Unfortunately, the pass only lasts 10 days and this is strictly enforced. If you are doing the Inca Trail first, buy the ticket afterwards.

The ticket covers these 16 sites: Museo Municipal de Arte Contemporáneo, Museo Histórico Regional, Museo de Arte Popular, Museo de Sitio Qorikancha, Centro Qosqo de Arte Nativo, Monumento a Pachacútec, Sacsayhuamán, Q'enqo, Puca Pucara, Tambomachay, Pisac, Ollantaytambo, Moray, Chinchero, Tipon, Pikillacta.

If you don't plan on visiting both Cusco and the Sacred Valley, consider purchasing a lower-priced **circuit ticket** (US$27). There are three circuits to choose from: the Sacred Valley (over two days), Cusco Inca sites, and Cusco museums (one day only).

Notable sites that are, rather frustratingly, **not included** in the ticket are the unmissable Coricancha temple (US$3.50) and the interesting Museo de Arte y Monasterio de Santa Catalina (US$2.50), but if you go to both you only pay US$5. The Catedral de Cusco (US$8.50), Iglesia de la Compañía (US$3.50), Iglesia San Blas (US$6), and the Museo de Arte Religioso (US$6) are not covered either, but if you plan to go to all four you can buy the *boleto religioso* at the entrance of any of these sites for US$15 (US$6 for students under age 26 with ISIC card). Other interesting sites not included are the Iglesia de la Merced (US$2.50), Museo Inka (US$4), and the Museo de Arte Precolombino (US$8).

gourmet restaurants. Near the end of the plaza is the 400-year-old **Seminario San Antonio Abad,** which has been converted into the Hotel Monasterio, Cusco's first five-star hotel. Even if you are not a guest, you can sneak a peek at the courtyard and the 17th-century **Iglesia San Antonio Abad.**

Museo de Arte Religioso

Just one block downhill from MAP along Palacio, the Museum of Religious Art, also known as the **Palacio Arzobispal** (Archbishop's Palace, Palacio and Hatun Rumiyoc, 8am-6pm daily, US$6 or *boleto religioso*) resides in a colonial building built by the Marquis of Buenavista and later occupied by Cusco's archbishop. Its handsome salons showcase religious paintings from the 17th and 18th centuries. Walk up the alleyway Hatun Rumiyoc toward San Blas and you will see that the entire museum is built upon a foundation of Inca stones that fit perfectly into one another. Near the end of the street is the famous **12-sided stone,** whose sides conform perfectly to the neighboring stones. If you can't locate it, street vendors will be happy to point it out and take your photograph for a small tip.

★ San Blas

Walk away from the Plaza de Armas up along Hatun Rumiyoc to reach Cuesta San Blas, which leads to Cusco's San Blas neighborhood. The square, known as **Plazoleta San Blas,** is home to several artisan families who have been operating here for decades. San Blas is a great neighborhood to find accommodations and restaurants, or just to wander around the steep cobblestone alleys and take in the excellent views over Cusco.

Iglesia San Blas (Plazoleta San Blas, 8am-6pm daily, US$6 or *boleto religioso*) is a small, whitewashed adobe church built in 1563. One

Plazoleta San Blas

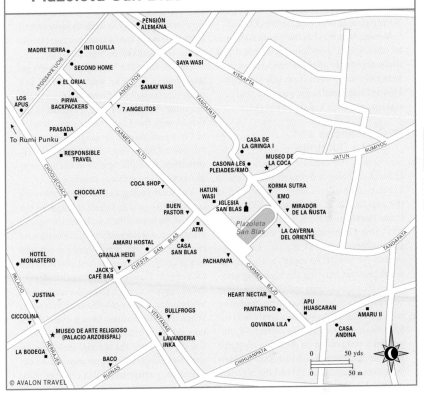

of the New World's most famous works of art is found here, a carved pulpit made from the trunk of a single tree. There is also a gold-covered baroque altar.

Another interesting place to visit is **Museo de la Coca** (Palacio 122, tel. 084/50-1020, www.museodelacoca.com, 9am-7pm daily, US$3.50, free Sun.). This interesting exhibition demonstrates the history of the coca leaf from its ancient use through to the modern production of refined cocaine. Highlights include ceramics of ancient tribesmen chewing coca leaves and an exhibition on celebrities who have fallen victim to the perils of addiction. It also has a boutique filled with a large selection of coca products—from wine and tea to candy.

EAST OF THE PLAZA DE ARMAS
Museo de Arte y Monasterio de Santa Catalina

From the Plaza de Armas, head down Arequipa to the **Santa Catalina Convent and Art Museum** (Arequipa, 8:30am-5:30pm Mon.-Sat., 2pm-5pm Sun., US$3 or US$6 with entry to Coricancha), built on top of the enclosure where the chosen virgins of the Inca lived, known as the *acllahuasi*, or "house of the chosen ones." In a strange historical twist, the Spaniards converted the building into a convent, where 30 nuns remain cloistered to this day. Holy women have thus lived in this building for at least five centuries. The museum has a good collection of

Cusco School paintings and an impressive Renaissance altar. A highlight is a trunk, used by Catholic missionaries, that contains miniature figurines depicting the life of Christ.

Museo Machu Picchu (Santa Catalina, tel. 084/25-5535, 9am-5pm daily, US$8, US$4 student) proudly displays hundreds of artifacts returned to Peru from Yale University. They include metallurgy, ceramics, and several Inca skeletons and deformed skulls.

★ Coricancha and Santo Domingo

Nowhere is the delicate cultural and architectural balance between the Inca and Spanish colonial eras more evident than at the sun temple of **Coricancha** (Plazoleta Santo Domingo, 8:30am-5:30pm Mon.-Sat., US$3.50 or US$6 with entry to Museo de Arte y Monasterio de Santa Catalina). As you approach the temple, its most striking aspect is the contrast between the brooding gray-brown Inca foundations and the lighter, beige colonial walls of **Santo Domingo,** topped by an elegant dome. The building symbolizes the Spanish subjugation of Inca culture—a convent built bang on top of the Inca's most important Cusco temple. This was the greatest prize in the Spaniards' 1533 sacking of Cusco,

and for centuries, most of Coricancha's walls were hidden beneath a convent. But the superiority of Inca architecture could not be hidden forever, and in 1950 an earthquake caused large sections of the convent to crumble, exposing Inca walls of the highest quality.

For the Inca, the building, which translates from Quechua as "gold enclosure," had many functions. It was foremost a place where offerings were burned to give thanks to the sun, though there were also rooms devoted to the moon, stars, lightning, thunder, and rainbows. Like so much Inca ceremonial architecture, the building also served as a solar observatory and mummy storehouse.

The south-facing walls of the temple were covered with gold to reflect the light of the sun and illuminate the temple. Inside was the **Punchaco,** a solid-gold disk inlaid with precious stones, which represented the sun and was probably the most sacred object in the Inca empire. Pizarro's scouts had already produced approximately a ton and a half of gold by stripping the inner walls of Coricancha. When the main Spanish force gained Cusco, they gathered hundreds of gold sculptures and objects from the temple, including an altar big enough to hold two men and an extraordinary artificial garden made of gold,

the Inca sun temple of Coricancha and the colonial church and convent of Santo Domingo

Colonial Painting: The Cusco School

The religious paintings that cover the walls of Peru's colonial churches are more than decoration. For centuries after the conquest, painting was the Catholic church's main tool for converting Peru's native peoples, who for the most part did not read or speak Spanish. The church's religious campaign produced thousands of now-priceless works and renowned schools of painting in Cusco and Quito, in present-day Ecuador.

Shortly after the conquest, the different orders of the Catholic church began importing paintings into Lima from well-known painters of the ongoing European Renaissance. The museum at Iglesia de San Francisco in Lima contains works by European painters who influenced the American schools of painting, collectively known as the Spanish American baroque. These 16th-century European masters included the Spanish painters Francisco de Zurbarán and Bartolomé Esteban Murillo and Flemish master Peter Paul Rubens.

By 1580, demand for European paintings had so outstripped supply that European painters began arriving to Lima in search of lucrative commissions. One of these was Italian Jesuit **Bernardo Bitti** (1548-1610), who was a disciple of Caravaggio and the brightly colored, emotional works of the Italian baroque. He was probably the single most influential European painter to work in Peru, and his paintings can be seen at Iglesia de la Merced in Cusco, Iglesia de la Compañía in Arequipa, and Lima's Museo San Francisco. With the guidance of Bitti and other European masters, the church orders set up convent studios around Peru where indigenous and mestizo artisans cranked out a staggering quantity of paintings in serial fashion—one painter would specialize in clothing, another in landscape, and still another in face and hands.

Right from the start, the workshops in Cusco began developing a unique style that blended the European baroque with images from Peru, including local trees, plants, animals, and foods. Cusco's cathedral, for instance, contains a painting that shows the Last Supper served with roasted guinea pig and *chicha,* the local corn beer. In another painting nearby, there is a pregnant Virgin Mary with the lustrous, smooth hair of Andean women. Often the dress of the Virgin Mary has a triangular shape, which art scholars believe is a transformation of the ancient Andean practice of worshipping *apus,* or sacred mountains.

The painters of the Cusco School also used a lot of gold to highlight their paintings and create a richly decorated surface. Most paintings pictured the Virgin Mary, scenes from the life of a saint, or panoramas of devils and angels. A unique invention of Cusco's painters was the archangels, flying through the air wearing ornate Spanish clothing and armed with muskets. Far from the tranquil realism of the Flemish baroque, these paintings portrayed a dazzling otherworld, filled with powerful spiritual beings, which were meant to awe, stun, and frighten indigenous viewers into accepting Catholicism. The most famous painters of the Cusco School were Diego Quispe Tito, Juan Espinosa de los Monteros, and Antonio Sinchi Roca, though it is difficult to decipher who did what because paintings were rarely signed.

In Quito, new-world painters embarked on a different course. The founder of the Quito School was **Father Bedón,** who studied with Bitti in Lima but quickly dropped the Italian mannerist style upon returning to Quito. Instead he ushered in a type of religious painting that combined the gold decorations of the Cusco School with the colder colors and shadowy depths favored by Peter Paul Rubens and other Flemish painters. The cathedrals in northern Peru, including Cajamarca and Trujillo, often feature paintings from both schools side by side.

including cornstalks with silver stems and ears of gold. It must have been a wonder to behold, but we will never know, because tragically, everything was melted down within a month—except for the Punchaco, which disappeared from the temple. Its whereabouts are unknown to this day. The Dominicans took over Coricancha and dismantled most of it, using the polished ashlar to build their church and convent of Santa Domingo on top of the sun temple's walls.

It requires considerable imagination today

to picture how the Inca's most important temple must have once looked. The eight-sided sacrificial font, stripped of the 55 kilograms of gold that once covered it, stands in the middle of the Coricancha's main square. The rooms that surround it may once have been covered with silver and dedicated to the moon, stars, and thunder. The wall running along the temple's eastern side is 60 meters long and 5 meters high, and each block is perfectly interlocked with its neighbor. But the highlight is the curved retaining wall beneath the facade of the church, which has not budged an inch in all of Cusco's earthquakes.

Many tourists see Coricancha as part of the Cusco city tour, but this is far from ideal because you get rushed through in the early afternoon when all the day tours converge at once between 2pm and 3pm. Even on a day tour, you have to pay separately for Coricancha, so it's preferable to visit independently in the morning when it is quieter.

Museo de Sitio Qorikancha

Reached through an underground entrance across the garden from the Coricancha is the modest **Museo de Sitio Qorikancha** (Av. El Sol, 9am-6pm Mon.-Sat., 8am-1pm Sun., entry with *boleto turístico*), which exhibits a few artifacts from the excavation of Coricancha, a model of the sun temple, and blueprints of its floor plans. Of particular interest are the mummies in fetal positions and deformed skulls. There are no guides available here, and explanations are in Spanish only.

On your way back to the Plaza de Armas, walk down the narrow alley of **Loreto.** To your right are the Inca walls of the *acllahuasi,* now the Santa Catalina convent. To the left are the walls of the palace of Huayna Cápac, now the Iglesia de la Compañía.

SOUTHWEST OF THE PLAZA DE ARMAS

From the Plaza de Armas, walk up Mantas one block to the **Iglesia de la Merced** (tel. 084/23-1821, 8am-12:30pm and 2pm-5:30pm Mon.-Sat., US$2.50), which was completely rebuilt following the 1650 earthquake. Inside the church lie two conquistadores, a father and a son who were executed by the Spanish shortly after the conquest. Diego de Almagro the Elder was hanged after he rebelled against Francisco Pizarro's authority, and his son, Diego de Almagro the Younger, was executed four years later for murdering Francisco Pizarro in revenge. Hanging on the walls nearby the tombs are paintings by the 16th-century master Bernardo Bitti. The church's elegant cloisters contain a small museum, which showcases a magnificent monstrance made of gold, silver, and precious stones.

From the Iglesia de la Merced, head down Heladeros to the **Plaza Regocijo,** where there are three museums. **Museo Histórico Regional** (Heladeros, tel. 084/22-5211, 8am-5pm Tues.-Sun., entry with *boleto turístico* only) was once the home of one of colonial Peru's most famous and eloquent writers, mestizo Inca Garcilaso de la Vega, the first Peruvian to publish a book in Spain. The museum charts the history of his life and work and also provides a fine survey of Peru's pre-Inca cultures, starting with preceramic arrowheads and continuing with artifacts from the Chavín, Moche, Chimú, Chancay, and Inca cultures. The holdings include a Nasca mummy and, on the second floor, colonial furniture and paintings from the Cusco School.

A museum that will give a different taste of Peruvian history is the **ChocoMuseo** (Calle Garcilaso 210, tel. 084/24-4765, 10:30am-6:30pm daily, free). Here you can learn about the history of the cocoa bean, from its medicinal Mayan origins to current mass production. Interestingly, 40 percent of the world's organic chocolate comes from Peru. There are classes on how to make chocolate (two hours, US$25) and a well-stocked shop to satisfy the appetite.

Across the Plaza Regocijo in the municipality is the **Museo Municipal de Arte Contemporáneo** (Plaza Regocijo, 9am-6pm Mon.-Sat., entry with *boleto turístico*), which contains a less-than-impressive exhibition of contemporary art of varying quality.

From Plaza Regocijo, walk down Garcilaso to **Iglesia San Francisco** (8am-noon and 3pm-5pm daily), a convent and church that stands above the plaza of the same name. This church, with three naves and in the shape of a Latin cross, was built in 1572 and is one of the few churches in Cusco to survive the 1650 earthquake. As a result, its convent is one of the few remaining examples of the ornate 16th-century plateresque style, complemented here by *azulejo* tiles imported from Seville.

OUTSIDE CUSCO

There are four highly recommended Inca ruins outside of Cusco, which most Cusco agencies offer as part of a rushed half-day tour that also takes in Coricancha ($6-8, not including entrance to Coricancha). These ruins accept only the *boleto turístico* for admission and are open 7am-6pm daily.

All the ruins lie close to the road that runs between Cusco and Pisac. An enjoyable way to see them is to take a Pisac bus or taxi to the farthest ruins, Tambomachay, and walk the eight kilometers back to Cusco, visiting all the ruins along the way (this walk can be shortened considerably by starting at Q'enqo and Sacsayhuamán, which are only one kilometer apart). Robberies are occasionally reported in this area, so it is better to walk in a group of two or more during the early part of the day.

★ Sacsayhuamán

Looming over the city to the north are the most impressive ruins in the Cusco area: **Sacsayhuamán** (7am-6pm daily), a hilltop fortress with three ramparts of zigzag walls that run for nearly 300 meters on the complex's north side. The Quechua name means "satisfied falcon," although most guides can't resist drawing attention to its similarity in sound to "sexy woman." Most striking about the site are the enormous stones—the largest are nearly 8.5 meters high, weighing 361 tons, placed at the apex of the walls to strengthen them. Every Inca citizen had to spend a few months of the year on public works, and the Inca used this tremendous reserve of labor to move the stones, using log sleds and levers. But even engineers have a hard time understanding how the Inca fitted these huge stones so perfectly together.

Only the largest stones of Sacsayhuamán remain. Up until the 1930s, builders arrived

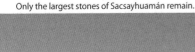
Only the largest stones of Sacsayhuamán remain.

at Sacsayhuamán to cart away the precut stone of this apparently limitless quarry, so it is difficult to appreciate how impregnable Sacsayhuamán must have been. Three towers once crowned the top of Sacsayhuamán, and the foundations of two of them are visible. During Manco Inca's great rebellion in 1536, the Spaniards managed to establish a base on the opposing hill and spent two days charging across the plain on horseback and attempting to scale the defensive walls. On the first day, one of the stones fired by the Inca slingshots struck Juan Pizarro, Francisco's younger brother, who died that night. On the evening of the second day, the Spaniards launched a surprise attack with ladders and successfully forced the Inca into the three stone towers. As the Spaniards massacred the estimated 1,500 soldiers trapped inside, many Inca preferred to leap to their deaths from the high tower. The next morning, condors feasted on the dead bodies, and this grisly image is emblazoned on Cusco's coat-of-arms. Manco Inca himself escaped to Ollantaytambo, where he later recorded a famous victory over the Spanish before retreating into the jungle. However, as far as Cusco was concerned, the battle at Sacsayhuamán was the Inca's last stand at the former seat of their power; it was a crushing defeat in the supposedly impregnable fortress.

These days the flat fields outside of Sacsayhuamán, where the Inti Raymi culminates each June, make for a peaceful stroll. In the mornings, Cusco residents come here to jog or do yoga on the grassy lawn, which is considerably larger than a soccer field. A huge trapezoidal door leads up a walkway to the top of the ruins, which commands marvelous views over Cusco. Because many tourists come here in the evening, guards are posted to put visitors at ease as dusk falls. If you have time, visit the top of Rodadero hill, where the Spaniards based themselves during their assault on Sacsayhuamán (guides will point it out). There is a rock outcrop on top, beautifully carved with sacred steps.

Sacsayhuamán is a steep, two-kilometer walk from Cusco or a 10-minute taxi ride (US$3). Taxis wait in the parking lot for the return trip to Cusco.

Q'enqo

One kilometer past Sacsayhuamán is the shrine of **Q'enqo** (7am-6pm daily), which means "zigzag" in Quechua. It is a large limestone outcrop carved with enigmatic steps leading nowhere, a sacred motif that is found on nearly every *huaca*, the sacred stone revered by the Inca. On the top of the rock are faint carvings of a puma and a condor. Carved into the rock are perfect zigzag channels, which probably flowed with *chicha* or llama blood during ceremonial rituals, much like the Sayhuite Stone between Cusco and Abancay. Below the rock are caves carved with niches where mummies of lesser nobility may once have been kept. Nearby is an amphitheater with niches framing an upright stone, which was probably defaced long ago by Spanish extirpators of idolatry. Q'enqo is about four kilometers northeast of Cusco.

Puka Pukara

The least significant of the ruins outside Cusco, **Puka Pukara** (7am-6pm daily), meaning "red fort" in Quechua, was probably not a fort at all but rather a storage facility or an Inca *tambo*, or lodge. Perhaps when the Inca emperor came to visit the baths of Tambomachay, his court waited here. There are several chambers below and a platform on top with excellent views. The distance between Puka Pukara and Q'enqo is six kilometers along the road.

Tambomachay

Known as the Inca's Bath, **Tambomachay** (7am-6pm daily) lies about 300 meters off the Pisac road and is the farthest of the Inca ruins on the outskirts of Cusco, although it is well marked with a sign. It is a well-preserved example of the sacred water fountains found at nearly every important Inca temple, including

Pisac, Ollantaytambo, and Machu Picchu. The Inca took a natural spring and painstakingly channeled the water through three waterfalls, which continue to work perfectly today. There is a fine Inca wall above with ceremonial niches. The Inca worshipped water as a vital life element, and this site no doubt formed part of a water cult. From here you can see Puka Pukara, which is on the other side of the road.

Entertainment and Events

FOLKLORIC MUSIC AND DANCE

The **Centro Qosqo de Arte Nativo** (El Sol 604, tel. 084/22-7901, included in *boleto turístico* or US$8 separately), founded in 1924, has a highly recommended music and dance show 6pm-8pm on most evenings. It was founded in 1924 as the first organized music and dance center in Cusco. In addition to the offerings here, most of the Peruvian restaurants in the Plaza de Armas have live Andean music during dinner.

BARS, PUBS, AND LIVE MUSIC

Cusco's steady stream of backpackers and robust student population means it has a lively nightlife scene, although it's far more low-key than Lima. During the week, most tourists frequent one of the many pleasant bars on or near Plaza de Armas. Many of them have draft beers, including Old Speckled Hen and Abbot Ale for a taste of home. Many restaurants have live Andean music, and the venues listed here get busy later in the evening.

At present the best expat pub, hands down, has to be **Paddy Flaherty's Irish Pub** (Triunfo 124, tel. 084/24-7719, 11am-2am daily), which claims to be the highest-elevation 100 percent Irish-owned pub in the world. Draft beer and canned Guinness, as well as Irish and British pub food such as shepherd's pie and stuffed potato skins, go down well. There's the obligatory happy hour 7pm-8pm, and it's a good place to meet other travelers over a drink. The T-shirts emblazoned with "No gracias" are popular for fending off street vendors.

There are a few other decent pubs close to Paddy's, notably American-owned **Nortons** (Santa Catalina Angosta 116, 7am-2am daily), with an impressive selection of imported beers, a classic English breakfast, darts, and, best of all, balconies overlooking the plaza.

The English **Cross Keys Pub** (Triunfo 350, 2nd Fl., tel. 084/22-9227, 10am-2am daily), owned by Barry Walker, British owner of Manu Expeditions, is good for a quiet drink, but it has seen better days and is waning in popularity. However, the dartboards, typical pub fare, and English beer on tap mean it remains an authentic pub experience.

Up Procuradores (Gringo Alley), there are a few bars in the quiet cobbled street of Tecsecocha. One of these is **Los Perros Couch & Wine Bar** (Tecsecocha 436, tel. 084/24-1447, 11am-midnight daily, US$5). The relaxed atmosphere and comfy couches make an inviting backdrop for a glass of red.

Plenty of places offer live music, and a popular spot is **Ukukus** (Plateros 316, tel. 084/25-4911, www.ukukusbar.com, 8pm-late daily, sometimes a small cover on weekends), a live music venue and bar that has been a classic of Cusco's nightlife scene since it opened in 1993. Shows range from Afro-Peruvian to rock, with affordable drinks. **The Muse** (Triunfo, 084/242-031, www.themusecusco.com, 8am-late Wed.-Sat.) is a lounge bar with eclectic decor, couches, a varied menu in the restaurant, and regular live music.

In San Blas, a local expat favorite and a good live music spot that has been around for years is **7 Angelitos** (Siete Angelitos 638, tel. 084/23-6373, 3pm-late daily). There are two-for-one happy hours (7:30pm-9:30pm and

11pm-11:30pm); the mojitos are excellent and there are regular live bands.

Another popular spot is **Frogs** (Warankallki 185, tel. 084/22-1762, 3pm-late daily), a large, gay-friendly bar with stone walls and colorful beanbags. It has good cocktails, a pool table, foosball, movies during the day, and regular live music.

Above the Plazoleta San Blas, **KMO** (Tandapata 100, tel. 084/23-6009, 3pm-2am daily) is small but a good spot for live music.

DISCOTHEQUES

For most travelers in Cusco, the altitude and long days of sightseeing and trekking mean that there is little energy left after a few drinks at the pub. However, there are many places to dance until dawn on weekends. The Cusco nightclub scene is constantly changing; clubs open and close monthly, and the popular places change regularly. The local government has been threatening to move discos out of the historic center due to noise levels, but amid substantial opposition, it is unclear if this will happen. A good local website to check out for nightlife is www.keytocusco.com.

One of the most frequented dance spots and therefore extremely crowded is **Inkateam** (Portal de Carnes 298, 9pm-5am daily). Tourists and locals dance to the blasting sounds of techno, reggae, and electro. Happy hour is 9pm-midnight, and there are free salsa classes every night 9pm-11pm. It's officially for over-23-year-olds only. Next door, **Mythology** (Portal de Carnes 298, 9pm-5am daily) has a similar offering but is not quite as busy.

Mama África (Portal de Panes 109, 3rd Fl., 9pm-6am daily) has been around since the mid-1990s but is constantly moving and has at various times been the place to go. It still fills up, and every Wednesday at 2am they have electronic sessions. Upstairs, **Mushroom** (6:30pm-late daily) is a very popular bar with locals, has happy hour until 11pm, and offers a pool table and a wide selection of music.

FESTIVALS

Celebrated continuously since the devastating quake of 1650, Cusco's procession of the **Señor de los Temblores** (Lord of the Earthquakes) traditionally begins at Cusco's cathedral on the Monday before Easter.

One of Peru's most enigmatic festivals is **Qoyllur Ritt'i,** which takes place in May or June before Corpus Christi on the slopes of the Nevado Ausangate at 4,800 meters. During the three-day festival, elaborately costumed men climb in the middle of the night to hew huge blocks of ice, which they carry on their backs down the mountain at dawn. Thousands of campesinos from neighboring communities come to this spot to bring ice down from the mountain or participate in the colorful masked dances. This festival, Christian only on the surface, grew out of the Andean tradition of worshipping mountains, or *apus,* to ensure rains and good harvests. The pilgrims trek toward the mountain from the town of Tinki, which is several hours away from Cusco on the rough road to Puerto Maldonado. If you are in Cusco during this time, you can find agencies along Plateros in Cusco that sell transport-and-camping packages.

During Cusco's **Corpus Christi,** which usually happens in early June, elaborate processions fill the streets of Cusco as all the bells in the city ring. Each procession carries a different saint, which is treated as if it were a living person, in the same way the Inca paraded their ancestors' mummies around these same streets five centuries ago.

A country festival that is straightforward for travelers to attend is the June 15-17 festival of the **Virgen del Carmen** in Paucartambo, a pleasant colonial town that is a four-hour bus ride from Cusco on the way to the Manu. The festival includes an extraordinary range of dances and costumes. Many Cusco agencies offer inexpensive lodge-and-transport packages to the festival, which include a dawn trip to Tres Cruces, a fabulous place to watch the sun rise over the Amazon basin.

Cusco's biggest festival is **Inti Raymi,** the Inca celebration of the June 21 winter solstice. Because Peru is in the Southern Hemisphere, some chroniclers, including Garcilaso de la Vega, have claimed that it is akin to the Incan New Year. The festival is celebrated throughout the Peruvian and Ecuadorian Andes, and lasts 10 days on either side of the solstice. It was banned by the Spaniards in 1535, but in 1944, a group of Cusco intellectuals re-created the sacred ceremony by studying chronicles and historical documents. Each year, hundreds dress up as Inca priests, nobles, and chosen women, and one man, chosen by audition, gets to be Inca Pachacútec. The main day, June 24, begins at 10am at the Coricancha (the sun temple) and ends around 2pm at Sacsayhuamán, where thousands of tourists sit on the fort's walls for a good view as a man dressed as Pachacútec speaks with a sun god through a microphone. It is a highly staged, touristy production, completely unlike the more down-to-earth countryside festivals.

Fiestas Patrias, the national Peruvian holiday at the end of July, is one of Peru's most important holidays. The festival honors Peru's independence on July 28 and Peru's armed forces on July 29. A large number of Peruvians travel in the week that falls around these dates, and it is usually the busiest week of the year in Cusco. Hotels, transport, and other services are often booked during this time.

Santuranticuy, on December 24, is one of the largest arts-and-crafts fairs in Peru. Nativity figures, miniature altars, and ceramics are laid out on stalls in the Plaza de Armas by hundreds of artists.

Shopping

Crafts shops are wall-to-wall along Triunfo, which leads from the Plaza de Armas and becomes Rumiyoc and Cuesta San Blas before reaching Plazoleta San Blas, the center of Cusco's bohemian/art district. Several families who have been producing crafts for decades have their workshops here and can often be seen at work.

CERAMICS AND WEAVINGS

The family workshop **Artesanía Mendívil** (Plazoleta San Blas 634, 9am-6pm Mon.-Sat.) is known worldwide for its religious sculptures made of plaster cloth, rice paste, and wood. The figures have long, mannerist necks. Hilario Mendívil began working as a craftsman at the age of 10 in 1939; though he has passed away, his sons continue the tradition.

World-acclaimed ceramicist Pablo Seminario, whose studio is in Urubamba, has a showroom on the Plaza de Armas.

A great association run by the altruistic Franco Negri is **Casa Ecológica** (Portal de Carnes 236, interior 2, cell tel. 984-117-962, www.casaecologicacusco.com, 9am-9:30pm daily), which was created to promote sustainable development in rural communities. The shop sells traditional handicrafts produced with natural fibers, as well as organic cosmetics and food products.

For mainstream touristy products, there are crafts markets in Cusco where bargaining is standard procedure. **Salón de Exposiciones Tupac Amaru** is right on the Plaza de Armas next to Iglesia de la Compañía (10:30am-1pm and 3:30pm-9pm Mon.-Sat., 4pm-9pm Sun.). A 10-minute walk down Avenida El Sol takes you past many more markets, but the biggest is **Centro Artesanal Cusco** (El Sol and Tullumayo, 8am-10pm daily).

★ Centro de Textiles Tradicionales del Cusco

The highest-quality textiles for sale in all of Cusco are at the **Centro de Textiles Tradicionales del Cusco** (Av. El Sol 603, tel. 084/22-8117, www.textilescusco.org,

7:30am-8:30pm Mon.-Sat., 8:30am-8:30pm Sun.). Nilda Callañaupa, a weaver and scholar from Chinchero, set up the center with the admirable goal of recovering ancient technologies, showcasing high-quality weavings, and sending revenue straight back to the remote, neglected villages that produce them. Local weavers give daily demonstrations, and there are displays that explain all the plants, minerals, and berries used for natural dyes. The textiles here are far better than those found elsewhere in Cusco and only slightly more expensive.

ALPACA PRODUCTS, CLOTHING, AND JEWELRY

For the finest alpaca clothing, head to **Kuna,** which has shops all over Cusco. The most central is on the Plaza de Armas (Portal de Panes 127, tel. 084/24-3191, www.kuna.com. pe, 9am-10pm daily). Another reliable option is **Sol Alpaca** (Plazoleta Nazarenas 167, tel. 084/23-2687, www.solalpaca.com, 9am-9pm Mon.-Sat.).

Werner & Ana (Plaza San Francisco 295-A, tel. 084/23-1076, 9:30am-9pm Mon.-Sat.) is a clothing boutique with styles in alpaca and other fine materials.

Hilo (Carmen Alto 260, tel. 084/25-4536, 10am-1pm and 2pm-6pm Mon.-Sat.) is a funky little shop with original clothes handmade by self-taught Irish designer Eibhlin Cassidy. Browse through her unique collection of dresses, blouses, and belts while sipping on a cup of tea.

There are exclusive jewelry shops all around the Plaza de Armas and up Cuesta San Blas; they mostly sell works of silver. The most well-known and ubiquitous is **Ilaria** (Portal Carrizos 258, tel. 084/24-6253, www.ilariainternational.com, 8am-9:45pm daily).

CONTEMPORARY ART AND HANDICRAFTS

Contemporary art can be found in several shops along Triunfo, between the Plaza de Armas and San Blas. **Primitiva** (Hatun Rumiyoc 495, tel. 084/26-0152, www.coscio.com, 10am-9pm Mon.-Sat.) features the art of Argentine painter Federico Coscio, who captures the landscapes and people around Cusco.

If you are looking for something a little different, **Indigo** (Plazoleta de Limacpampa chico 473 www.galeriaindigo.com.pe, 9am-10pm daily) has modern housewares and

traditional weaving

handicrafts inspired by traditional Andean designs.

BOOKSTORES

SBS Bookshop (Av. El Sol 864, tel. 084/24-8106, www.sbs.com.pe, 9am-8:30pm Mon.-Fri., 9:30am-1:30pm and 4pm-8pm Sat.) is Peru's foremost importer of English-language books and has a good collection at its small Cusco shop.

With choices in English, French, German, Portuguese, Spanish, and Quechua, you'd be hard pressed not to find a book at **CBC La Familia** (Tullumayo 465, tel. 084/23-4073, 10am-2pm and 4pm-8pm Mon.-Sat.). Genres include novels, cookbooks, art, and even photography.

The largest book exchange in Cusco can be found at **Libreria Puro Peru** (Heladeros 167, tel. 084/22-1753, librarypuroperu@hotmail.com, 9am-10pm daily).

MUSIC STORES

Director Kike Pinto has collected more than 400 instruments for the **Taki Andean Music Museum (Museo Taki Musica Andina)** (Pumakurku 519, tel. 084/226-897, www.institutotaki.blogspot.com, pinto.kike@gmail.com, 10am-8pm Mon.-Sat.), some of which are for sale, along with CDs, books, and music lessons.

OUTDOOR AND TRAVEL GEAR

The best shops for getting high-end outdoor apparel and equipment, although expensive, are **Tatoo** (Triunfo 346, tel. 084/22-4797, 10am-9pm Mon.-Sat., 2pm-9pm Sun.), **Cordillera** (Garcilaso 210, shop 102, tel. 084/24-4133, 9am-9:30pm daily), and **The North Face** (Portal Comercio 195, Plaza de Armas, tel. 084/22-7789, 9am-9pm Mon.-Fri., 9:30am-9pm Sat., 10am-9pm Sun.).

CUSCO
RECREATION

Recreation

Along with Huaraz in the Cordillera Blanca, Cusco is Peru's main adventure travel center. The variety of intriguing options and high-quality agencies are heaven for adrenaline-seekers. Options include rafting down rapids, climbing Andean peaks, biking, horseback riding, paragliding, and trekking in the nearby Amazon jungle.

Among the more than 150 licensed agencies operating in Cusco, the standard of service and handling of social and environmental responsibilities vary greatly. It is up to the client to be discerning and to research thoroughly before booking. The agencies listed here are all recommended.

For your safety, and for the environment, choose your agency carefully. If you choose to raft a serious river, like the Class IV Río Apurímac, go with accredited agencies, and before you depart check the equipment. An average of two tourists a year die on the Apurímac alone, and though not even the

best agency can take away all the risk, a new raft, full safety equipment, and, most importantly, an experienced guide will make a big difference.

Fly-by-night agencies, with which Cusco is crawling, offer incredibly cheap prices but usually at the expense of your comfort and safety—and at the expense of the environment. This is especially true on the Inca Trail, where trash and human waste is becoming a serious problem. These low-budget agencies do not tend to follow the principles of sustainable adventure travel, nor do they treat their staff fairly. The porters and cooks are not paid enough, they are not provided with acceptable standards of food and camp accommodation, and they do not receive proper training. Most agencies' websites claim to practice responsible tourism, but these claims are probably unfounded if their prices are bargain-basement.

Dozens of these agencies are closed down each year once the rangers in the Machu

Picchu sanctuary catch on. However, the same agency can open again under a new name, which often mimics the high-quality leaders in the field. The excellent Trek Peru, for instance, is often confused with Peru Trek, Peruvian Trek, Trekking Peru, etc. The courts are so backlogged with copyright cases that rarely do agencies defend their name. So the confusion lingers. Travelers who spend a bit more money to go with reputable agencies are helping to raise the bar of quality for all of Cusco's agencies.

Most of the agencies offer a variety of activities, but they are organized here according to their main focus.

TREKKING

The Inca Trail is by far the most popular trekking route in the Cusco area because of its spectacular route of ruins and varied ecosystems, but there are other excellent treks worth considering. Though they do not have the Inca Trail's variety of ruins or the unbeatable culmination at Machu Picchu, they are less crowded and plunge into remote areas of Andean villages, tumbling jungle, and out-of-the-way archaeological sites. While all hikers on the Inca Trail must go with a licensed agency, the other routes described here can be done independently by those with enough Spanish to ask directions, although most travelers tend to go with an agency. The best time to trek in the Cusco area is during the dry winter months April-November; the most crowded months on the Inca Trail are June-August.

Make sure your agency is one of those licensed by INRENA, the government conservation agency. A list of approved agencies can be obtained through **Iperú** (www.peru.info). Before scheduling your trip, ask your chosen agency pertinent questions: What is included in the price (e.g., train fares and entry fees), what type of tents and general equipment do they provide, what is the maximum number of trekkers in a group? Also very important is to confirm that your operator is bringing a bathroom tent. The most reputable and

responsible agencies do not use the public bathrooms but instead carry PETT toilets, which use organic compounds to break down human waste so that it can be packed out of the trail and disposed of properly. Groups are accompanied by porters, and there is a legal limit of 20 kilograms (44 pounds) for group gear and 5 kilograms (11 pounds) for personal gear, per porter, which is checked at the beginning of the trail.

Nevado Salcantay, at 6,271 meters, is the sacred mountain that towers above the Inca Trail and eventually drops to Machu Picchu itself. Many agencies offer a four- to five-day trek starting from Mollepata, a town 3.5 hours from Cusco in the Limatambo Valley. If you are trekking on your own it can be reached by any bus heading from Cusco to Abancay. In Mollepata, you can hire mules and local guides. The route traverses part of the Cordillera Vilcabamba, including spectacular views of several snow-covered peaks. It crests the 4,700-meter Salcantayccasa Pass before descending between the stunning glaciers of Humantay and Salcantay. The trek then goes through the lovely Huyracmachaypampa and down through forested slopes to the hot springs at Colpapampa. From here the trail follows the Santa Teresa River to the humid lowlands with the option to trek a little farther to the Inca ruins of Patallacta. From here you descend to the hydroelectric station at Intihuatana to board a train for the short journey to Machu Picchu. The alternative is to walk 2-3 hours along the train track to Aguas Calientes.

Choquequirao is a huge Inca complex perched on a ridge in the Vilcabamba area that includes many fine Inca walls and double-recessed doorways. It was probably built as a winter palace by Inca Túpac Yupanqui, in the same way that his father, Pachacútec, probably built Machu Picchu. It was discovered by Hiram Bingham in 1911, though it was lost again until the 1980s when a series of explorers trudged through this rugged territory to find this and other ruins in the area. The Peruvian government (INC), backed by

UNESCO, launched a campaign to restore the ruins, and much of the work has been completed to a very high standard. It is worth spending a full day exploring this site as it has some unique features, such as the wonderful stylized white stone llamas.

The most common approach is from Cachora, where guides and mules can be rented, reached by taking a bus to Abancay and getting off at a road past the Sayhuite Stone. The first day is spent hiking down to the Río Apurímac, and the second continues straight up the other side, a long six-hour slog uphill onto the cloud forest ridge. Some agencies offer a combined 10-day trek that leads from Choquequirao all the way to Machu Picchu. Another option is to reach Choquequirao from Huancacalle, near the Inca ruins of Vitcos, a spectacular eight-day traverse of the Cordillera Vilcabamba.

There are various trekking routes through the **Cordillera Vilcanota,** the range to the east of Cusco that is dominated by the sacred **Nevado Ausangate** (6,384 meters). Trekking guides say that this is one of the more untouched and spectacular areas of Peru.

The classic route is a seven-day loop around the peak of Ausangate, which begins at the town of Tinqui in the high puna grasslands and crosses four passes between 4,300 and 5,500 meters. The views include the fluted faces and rolling glaciers of all the mountains of the range, including Colquecruz and Jampa, and the route passes through remote hamlets of llama herders and weavers. This area is famous for its **Qoyllur Ritt'i** movable festival in May or June, when thousands of campesinos converge on the slopes of Ausangate.

The truly adventurous and fit may want to try reaching **Espíritu Pampa,** the actual "Lost City of the Inca" that served as the base for the Inca's 35-year rebellion against the Spanish. Gene Savoy's discovery of the ruins in 1964 made world news, and several subsequent expeditions have tried, in vain, to keep the jungle from growing over the immense site.

The trip starts from the village of Huancacalle, which can be reached by taking a truck or bus from Cusco over the Abra Málaga to Quillabamba and hopping off at the Huancacalle turnoff. The Cobos family, which has guided all the Vilcabamba explorers since Gene Savoy, operates a small hostel in Huancacalle and rents mules for US$7 a day. From Huancacalle, a path leads to the Inca ruler's original exile at Vitcos, where Manco Inca was murdered by the Spanish, and the exquisite sacred rock of Chuquipalta (the subject, among others, of Hugh Thomson's book *White Rock*). The path heads to **New Vilcabamba,** a colonial-era mining town, and then ascends a 3,800-meter pass before plunging into the jungle below. The path includes sections of fine Inca staircases along a steep and tortuous valley to the ruins, which are in mosquito-ridden rainforest at 1,000 meters. Instead of walking back all the way to Huancacalle, it is possible to walk for a day or two alongside the river on good paths until you reach the town of Kiteni on the Río Urubamba. From here, a bus goes back to Quillabamba. This trip takes 7-10 days.

Trekking Agencies

Peruvian Andean Treks, ExplorAndes, and Tambo Tours are the longest-established trekking companies in Cusco; they pioneered the contemporary trekking culture. They are recommended, not only for their unsurpassed experience and professionalism, but also because they consistently recycle their trash, pack out all human waste, treat water carefully, and pay porters fair wages. Over the last three decades, these operators have developed ties with a number of Quechua communities in the Cusco area, where they are embarking on a new brand of participatory cultural activities, such as harvesting potatoes, building adobe homes, and even herding llamas.

Trekking prices vary greatly based on the season, the number of people in the group, the length of the trek, the trek itself, and other factors. Because of licensing requirements, the four-night Machu Picchu trek now costs US$1,500, though most agencies charge US$500-650 for group bookings. The shorter two-day Inca Trail is around US$250-300 for group bookings. The alternative five-day Salcantay trek to Machu Picchu is in the US$300-850 range, though most operators offer group Salcantay treks for around US$500. Other treks in the Cusco area, such as in the Lares Valley, generally run about US$100 per day. Be careful to ask your agency whether the price includes all entry fees (an important consideration for Salcantay in particular).

Peruvian Andean Treks (Pardo 705, tel. 084/22-5701, U.S. tel. 617/924-1974, www.andeantreks.com) is owned by American and longtime Cusco resident Tom Hendrickson. It operates on the Inca Trail and runs treks through jungle areas and the Lares Valley in the Cordillera. It is also the best option for climbing expeditions in the snow-covered peaks around Cusco.

ExplorAndes (Paseo Zarzuela Q-2 Huancaro, tel. 084/23-8380, www.explorandes.com) is Peru's most established adventure sports agency. It offers the traditional Inca Trail hike, as well as variations that combine it with treks above the Sacred Valley or around Nevado Salcantay and Nevado Ausangate. Kayaking on Lake Titicaca, rafting down the Tambopata or Apurímac, and llama-supported treks around the Cordillera Blanca and Huayhuash near Huaraz are also offered. It also operates special-interest tours around Peru, focusing on orchids, potatoes and maize, camelids, ceramics, cacti, textiles, and coca and other medicinal plants.

Tambo Tours (Casilla 912, tel. 084/23-7718, www.tambotours.com) is owned by Andreas Holland and has been operating for over 30 years. It offers diverse treks and tours with tailor-made itineraries (six people minimum), which accommodate group specifications and a wide range of special interests. The staff are very knowledgeable, and since its foundation Tambo Tours has had a profound commitment to helping local communities. Most importantly, however, the welfare of all their staff has always been a priority, as has working in an ecologically sustainable and responsible manner. Tambo Tours' sister company, Tambo Film (www.tambofilm.com), specializes in outfitting film and television productions throughout Peru.

Andina Travel (Santa Catalina 219, tel. 084/25-1892, www.andinatravel.com) offers frequent departures for the Inca Trail and interesting sociocultural projects.

Auqui Mountain Spirit (José Gabriel 307, Urb. Magisterial, tel. 084/26-1517 or 084/25-1278, www.auqui.com.pe), run by Roger Valencia, has been operating since 1992. This high-end agency has a very experienced team and specializes in customized trips, especially for corporate clients.

Aventours (Saphi 456, tel. 084/22-4050, www.aventours.com) was founded by Ricky Schiller, who has been involved in the tourism industry for over 30 years. The expert staff provides excellent service.

Enigma (Fortunato L. Herrera 214, Urb. Magisterio 1a etapa, tel. 084/22-2155, www.enigmaperu.com) employs gourmet cooks. It offers Inca Trail treks combined with visits to Nevado Salcantay, Vilcabamba, and the ruins of Choquequirao. Alternative adventures include horseback riding, ayahuasca therapy, and bird-watching.

Inca Explorers (Calle Peru W - 18 Urb. Ttio, tel. 084/24-1070, www.incaexplorers.com) has a range of longer trips to Vilcabamba, Choquequirao, and the Cordillera Vilcanota, as well as participative tourism such as weaving, farming, and traditional healing.

Perú Sur Nativa (Magisterio 2da etapa K-7-302, tel. 084/22-4156, www.perusurnativa.com) is owned by longtime Cusco adventurer extraordinaire Raúl Montes. Montes has a real eye for adventure and an unflappable sense of humor (we confirmed this after spending two weeks with him on a balsa raft in the Manu jungle eating only green bananas and red-bellied piraña!). Perú Sur Nativa also runs trips in other

Río Urubamba offers great white-water rafting.

United Mice (Av. Pachacútec 424, tel. 084/22-1139, www.unitedmice.com) is a recommended backpacker's choice. It also offers a seven-day Salcantay trek.

Xtreme Tourbulencia (Plateros 364, tel. 084/22-2405, U.S. tel. 702/560-7220, www.x-tremetourbulencia.com) receives good reviews and offers a range of treks and tours throughout Peru.

RAFTING AND KAYAKING

There are many excellent rafting and kayaking options around Cusco. The easiest, and most common, are day trips along the Class III rapids of the **Río Urubamba** in the Sacred Valley (US$50-70). They often include one night of camping near Ollantaytambo, mountain biking, and a chance to see ruins the next day. December-May, when the river is swollen, agencies tend to raft the upper section above Pisac. When the water drops after June, they run the section of the river lower down between Ollantaytambo and Chilca. Farther downstream, the water rushes onward to Machu Picchu in great cataracts of unnavigable Class VI water.

Another day option is the easier stretch of the **Río Apurímac** below the Cusco-Abancay highway, a gentle stretch that passes the foundations of an Inca hanging bridge made famous by Thornton Wilder in his classic *The Bridge of San Luis Rey*. The Apurímac here is generally sunny and subtropical, so bring sunscreen, a hat, mosquito repellent, and swimwear, because a quick dip in local hot springs is often included.

A popular three-day rafting trip is on the upper Apurímac (US$400-650), which can only be run between June and October. The Apurímac plunges through a steep and wild gorge and an endless series of Class III-V rapids. Agencies that operate this section of the river usually also offer trips on Río Cotahuasi (US$1,950 approximately), a similar though more exacting canyon near Arequipa that takes 10 days to navigate in a full-scale, supported expedition.

parts of South America as well as nearby Choquequirao, Carabaya, and Vilcabamba, and to the Manu rainforest.

Peru Treks & Adventure (Av. Pardo 540, tel. 084/22-2722, www.perutreks.com) is also responsible for the very informative website Andean Travel Web (www.andeantravelweb.com).

Q'ente (Choquechaca 229, tel. 084/22-2535, www.qente.com) has been running since 1995 and provides good service and trained staff.

Quechuas Expeditions (San Juan de Dios 295, tel. 084/22-3548, www.quechuasexpeditions.com) is one of the most highly recommended trekking agencies in Cusco, with a vast range of Andean treks as well as jungle tours.

Trek Peru (Republica de Chile B-15, tel. 084/26-1501 or 800/566-1305, www.trekperu.com) has been leading high-quality tours since the mid-1990s. It offers a wide range of Inca Trail options, as well as treks to Lares, Salcantay, and Ausangate. Treks start at $460.

The most spectacular rafting expedition is the **Río Tambopata** (US$1,500-2,500), which is a great way to combine a mountain rafting adventure with world-class Amazon biodiversity. This 10- to 12-day trip begins in cloud forest north of Lake Titicaca with a few days of Class III-V rapids and ends floating on torpid jungle waters through the pristine Parque Nacional Bahuajua Sonene. Participants usually stay at the Tambopata Research Center, a rustic lodge operated by Rainforest Expeditions that is minutes from the world's largest macaw clay lick. Floating silently through this untouched rainforest provides a good opportunity to spot a jaguar or tapir and a huge range of birds and more common animals, such as capybara, turtles, and giant otters. The trip includes a flight back to Cusco from the jungle city of Puerto Maldonado.

If you want to go kayaking instead of rafting, agencies will often loan you a kayak on the easier rivers such as the Urubamba and lower Apurímac.

Rafting and Kayaking Agencies

Like trekking prices, rafting rates vary greatly based on the season, the number of people in the group, the difficulty of the rapids, and the section of the river. Prices for a daylong rafting trip on the Urubamba River are typically US$35-100 per person per day, including lunch. For the four-day Río Apurímac trip, which includes Class III-IV rapids, prices are typically US$300-1,100. Most operators, however, charge US$500-600.

One of the most professional rafting companies in Peru is **Amazonas Explorer** (Collasuyo 910, Urb. Miravalle, tel. 084/25-2846, www.amazonas-explorer.com). It runs a variety of innovative trips in Peru, Chile, and Bolivia, including canoeing, mountain biking, trekking, and rafting. One of the best trips is a 16-day expedition that begins with sightseeing in Cusco and Lake Titicaca and ends in rafting down the Río Tambopata

and two nights at the Tambopata Research Center.

ExplorAndes (Paseo Zarzuela Q-2 Huancaro, tel. 084/23-8380, www.explorandes.com) also offers high-end rafting trips.

The following are less expensive but also experienced agencies. They are recommended for easier trips.

Apumayo Expediciones (Jr. Ricardo Palma N-5, Santa Monica, tel. 084/24-6018, www.apumayo.com) is run by Pepe López, a kayaker with a lot of experience on Peru's rivers. He built an adventure center on the banks of the Río Urubamba, downstream of Ollantaytambo. The center, which shares profits with the nearby community of Cachiccata, offers hikes and mountain biking for the rafters who arrive here after descending the Río Urubamba. Apumayo runs trips down the Apurímac, Tambopata, and Cotahuasi and offers reforestation cultural treks and the classic Inca Trail.

Loreto Tours (Calle del Medio 111, Cusco, tel. 084/22-8264, www.loretotours.com) provides varied rafting itineraries and good-quality equipment.

Mayuc (Portal Confituras 211, Plaza de Armas, tel. 084/24-2824, www.mayuc.com) is one of the pioneering rafting companies and operates an excellent day trip on Río Urubamba. It also does rafting trips on the Apurímac and in Tambopata.

Terra Explorer Peru (Santa Ursula D-4, Huanchac, tel. 084/23-7352, www.terraexplorerperu.com) is owned by Piero, the youngest of the Vellutino brothers, all dedicated and well-known adventure sportsmen and white-water rafters. Terra Explorer offers all kinds of rafting trips, including Cotahuasi and Tambopata, mountain treks, and mountain biking. **Munaycha** (based in the Sacred Valley, cell tel. 984-770-381, www.munaycha.com) belongs to Duilio, the oldest Vellutino brother, and also offers rafting on Peru's best-known rivers as well as sea kayaking trips off the coast of Arequipa and on Lake Huyñaymarca, a rarely visited part of the Titicaca.

MOUNTAIN CLIMBING

Cusco is surrounded by majestic snow-covered peaks that offer outstanding mountaineering possibilities, though none should be tried by people without mountaineering experience—even with a good guide. Unlike many of the mountains in the Cordillera Blanca, these Andean routes are steep, icy, and complicated. Avalanches are common, especially on Salcantay. Several international climbing agencies operate in Peru.

Mountain Climbing Agencies

Licensed mountain guides in Peru, working on an independent basis, will charge US$100-150 per day. An agency that arranges a technical climb will generally charge twice or three times that rate on a daily basis. For climbing in Cusco, it's a good idea to inquire with agencies in Huaraz, Peru's climbing headquarters. Huaraz agencies are often able to lead climbing trips all over the country.

The best local mountaineering agency is **Peruvian Andean Treks** (Pardo 705, tel. 084/22-5701, www.andeantreks.com), owned by climber Tom Hendrickson.

The best way to contact internationally certified guides is through **Camp Expedition** (Triunfo 392, office 202, tel. 084/43-9859), which leads rappelling, climbing, and canyoneering adventures in the Cusco area.

BIKING

Nearly all of the rafting and kayaking agencies do bike tours and rent bikes. A highly recommended company is **Loreto Tours** (Calle del Medio 111, Cusco, tel. 084/22-8264, www.loretotours.com, US$100 per day for guided tours). Peru's best-known mountain biker, **Omar Zarzar Casis** (omarzarzar@aventurarse.com), has written a book describing routes in Cusco and across the country. He is a good English-speaking contact for those planning a major ride in the area. **Gravity Assisted Mountain Biking** (Santa Catalina Ancha 398, tel. 084/22-8032, www.gravityperu.com, US$100 per day for guided tours) has great equipment and experienced guides for adventure mountain biking tours.

Many of the Manu tour operators give clients the option to bike partway down the magnificent dirt-road descent from Acanaju Pass, at 3,800 meters, into the jungle. This route, which also passes through Pisac and Paucartambo, provides a stunning glimpse of more than a dozen ecosystems.

Many agencies also offer mountain biking in the Sacred Valley, especially on the Chinchero plateau around Moray and Maras, with a final descent past the salt mines (Salineras) to Urubamba. The Abra Málaga (4,300 meters), which lies along the highway between Ollantaytambo and Quillabamba, is another of Peru's spectacular mountain-to-jungle descents. This trip is now part of a bus/biking/walking alternative to the Inca Trail, called the Inca Jungle Trail, which takes you past the pristine Colcamayo hot springs in Santa Teresa, from where you can either walk or catch the train to Machu Picchu.

BIRD-WATCHING

The Cusco area has one of the world's highest areas of bird biodiversity, particularly where the high Andes meet the Amazon rainforest. Particularly rich environments are the Abra Málaga (4,300 meters) area, en route to Quillabamba, and the Acanaju Pass (3,800 meters), en route to Parque Nacional Manu. Barry Walker, owner of Manu Expeditions and author of *A Field Guide to the Birds of Machu Picchu, Peru,* leads excellent birding. Barry can be reached through **Manu Expeditions** (Pardo 895, tel. 084/22-6671, birding@manuexpeditions.com, www.birdinginperu.com, US$250 per day for guided tours with more than six people).

The high-quality **InkaNatura** (Ricardo Palma J1, Urb. Santa Monica, tel. 084/25-5255, www.inkanatura.com, US$275 per day for guided tours with more than six people) and **Gran Peru** (www.granperu.com.pe, US$175 per day for guided tours with more than six people) also run birding trips throughout the country. Leo Oblitas is an excellent birding guide and works for some of the leading bird-watching agencies.

HORSEBACK RIDING

Adventure Specialists (U.S. tel. 719/783-2076, www.adventurespecialists.org, prices vary, call ahead) leads highly recommended, custom horse-packing trips all over Peru and especially in the Cusco area. Founder and co-owner Gary Ziegler is a true adventurer, archaeologist, and noted Inca expert.

Manu Expeditions (Los Geranios 2-G Urbanizacion Mariscal Gamarra 1ro etapa, tel. 084/22-5990, www.manuexpeditions. com, prices vary, call ahead) offers a range of horse-riding expeditions that explore areas of the Vilcabamba and Choquequirao (17 days), as well as Machu Picchu and the surrounding cloud forest (15 days). Another of its itineraries is from the Andes to the Amazon (14 days). One- and two-day rides around Cusco are also offered.

The best options for riding Peruvian *paso* horses are **Wayra** (part of the Sol y Luna Hotel outside Urubamba, tel. 084/20-1620, www.wayrasacredvalley.com, US$210 per day) and **Perol Chico** (Carretera Urubamba-Ollantaytambo, cell tel. 950-314-065, www. perolchico.com, prices vary, call ahead).

EXTREME SPORTS

A wacky adventure opportunity is **Action Valley** (Santa Teresa 352, tel. 084/24-0835, www.actionvalley.com, US$75 bungee jump, US$22 paintball). This park, 11 kilometers from Cusco on the road to Chinchero, has a 107-meter bungee drop, a catapult that throws people 120 meters into the air with 3.2 G's of force, a 36-meter climbing pole, a 124-meter rappel wall, and a 10-meter climbing wall.

There are some beautiful paragliding spots in the Cusco area. **Leo Paragliding School** (UV Santiago 302-2B, tel. 084/23-9476, www. flyingexpedition-org, US$75 pp) offers tandem flights as well as paragliding training courses. Another recommendable option for

tandem paragliding flights over the Sacred Valley is **Viento Sur,** run by the European owners of Sol y Luna Hotel in Urubamba (tel. 084/20-1620, www.hotelsolyluna.com, US$195 pp).

Via Ferrata (tel. 084/79-3019, www. naturavive.com, US$55 pp, family rates available) is a 300-meter rock face located in Pacha between Urubamba and Ollantaytambo. It is equipped with wire cables and footholds to allow people with no previous experience to enjoy the adrenaline rush of rock with all the necessary safety equipment.

ESOTERIC EXPERIENCES

Cusco is a center for a range of spiritual and esoteric activities, though the main operators seem to change constantly. Tourists are shown traditional practices by native healers with **Back2Nature** (Alto Los Incas Calle Arequipa J-3, tel. 084/24-4454, back2nature. com.pe, prices vary, call ahead), owned by Norwegian Irene Kingswick and Peruvian Dennis Alejo.

Leslie Myburgh at **Another Planet** (Triunfo 120, tel. 084/24-1168, www.anotherplanetperu.net, prices vary, call ahead) and Diane Dunn at **Paz y Luz** (cell tel. 984-216-293, www.pazluzperu.com, prices vary, call ahead) in Pisac are other good contacts for ayahuasca and San Pedro ceremonies. In the Sacred Valley, the **Willka Tika** (Paradero Rumichaka, 2 kilometers north of Urubamba, tel. 707/202-5340, www.willkatika.com) is a luxury retreat that offers ceremonial activities. It has seven relaxing gardens with winding paths, a yoga studio, and meditation cottages.

MASSAGES AND SPAS

Plaza de Armas and the streets close by are filled with so-called massage therapists. Quality is variable, and most are unqualified, but for US$8 per hour, you can't really complain. For a higher level of service, try Olga Huaman and her team at **Yin Yang** (El Sol 106, Galerias La Merced, Office 302, 3rd Fl., tel. 084/25-8201, cell tel. 984-765-390, yinyang_masajes@hotmail.com, 9am-10pm daily), who give very professional massages as well as reiki; they offer room service or sessions at their premises. **Angel Hands** (Heladeros 157, tel. 084/22-5159, 6am-10pm) offers similar services. The **Siluet Sauna and Spa** (Quera 253, Interior 4, tel. 084/23-1504, 10am-10pm daily) offers massages along with a whirlpool tub and hot and dry saunas.

If you really want to treat yourself to a day of luxurious pampering, try **Samana Spa** (Tecsecocha 536, tel. 084/23-3721, cell tel. 984-389-332, www.samana-spa.com), located in a nicely renovated colonial house. They offer professional massages, steam and dry saunas, Jacuzzis in the lovely stone patio, and all sorts of beauty treatments, including facials and manicures. In addition to the providers listed here, most top-class hotels in Cusco offer massage services.

The leading chiropractor in Cusco is Canadian expat Howard Levine at **Heart Nectar** (Carmen Bajo 184-F, San Blas, cell tel. 984-791-288, heartnectarperu@hotmail.com). He offers consultations and treatment for US$40, and offers a range of natural therapies, including crystal healing and energy work. Massages are also available for US$25-30, and Howard leads shamanic workshops using ayahuasca and San Pedro cactus.

SIGHTSEEING TOURS

There is fierce competition, along with frequent price wars, between Cusco's agencies for general sightseeing tours. Most of the agencies are clustered around the Plaza de Armas and offer competitive prices. There are also luxury tours.

The most popular tours include the full-day tour of the Sacred Valley (US$14), which includes Pisac, lunch in Urubamba, Ollantaytambo, and sometimes Chinchero as well, but this is a very rushed way to see the valley. A half-day tour is also offered to Maras, Moray, and Salineras (US$12, US$4 entrance to Salineras not included). The half-day city tour (US$8) takes in the ruins outside Cusco, including Sacsayhuamán, Q'enqo,

Puca Pucara, and Tambomachay as well as Coricancha in Cusco itself ($3.50 entrance not included in tour). For all of these tours you will need the *boleto turístico* to gain entry to various ruins that do not offer separate entrance fees. Another half-day tour explores the ruins heading toward Puno, including the magnificent church in Andahuaylillas, along with Pikillacta and Tipón. Or take the full-day bus tour taking in the ruins along the way and finish in Puno.

Several agencies in Cusco cater to groups and also reserve tickets and provide tours for independent travelers. The highly recommended **Fertur** (Simon Bolivar F23, tel. 084/22-1304, www.fertur-travel.com) has friendly, knowledgeable staff that offers private day tours, with a long list of additional cultural and adventure options.

Condor Travel (Saphy 848, tel. 084/24-8181, www.condortravel.com, US$35 daylong group tour) is one of the most established and professional operators of traditional tourism. **Orellana Tours** (Garcilaso 206, tel. 084/22-1544, www.orellanatour.com, US$20 daylong group tour) is an inexpensive agency with a good reputation. **Milla Turismo** (Urb lucrepata E-16, tel. 084/23-1710, www.milla-turismo.com, US$32 daylong group tour) is well established and very professional.

JUNGLE TRIPS

Many people who visit Cusco do not realize how close they are to the Amazon jungle. There are two options within easy reach. The most popular is a trip via Puerto Maldonado to **Tambopata Reserve.** This can be reached by a half-hour plane ride or a whole day on the bus now that the highway has improved markedly. A few hours more in a boat take you to a jungle lodge with outstanding opportunities to see birds, mammals, and insects. Recommended lodges include **Explorer's Inn** (Circunvalación Mz: L, Lote 1 – Terminal Terrestre 2nd Fl., Office 111, Puerto Maldonado, tel. 082/57-3029, www.explorersinn.com) and **Libertador Tambopata Eco Lodge** (Nueva Baja 432, Cusco, tel.

084/24-5695, www.tambopatalodge.com), both of which have offices in Cusco.

A longer trip to **Parque Nacional Manu** offers a chance to see a greater variety of animals, especially predators such as the black caiman as well as parrots drinking at clay licks. However, beware of Cusco operators selling Manu packages for around US$300, because these short tours only go to the edge of the park, even though they claim it's still a Manu tour. To go deep inside and get the best experience, you need at least five to seven days. Recommended Cusco-based agencies include **Manu Nature Tours** (Pardo 1046, Cusco, tel. 084/25-2721, www.manuperu. com), **Manu Expeditions** (Los Geranios 2-G Urbanización Mariscal Gamarra 1ro Etapa Cusco, tel. 084/22-5990, www.man-uexpeditions.com), **Pantiacolla Tours** (Garcilaso 265, interior, 2nd Fl., Office 12, Cusco, tel. 084/23-8323, www.pantiacolla. com), and **Caiman Tours** (Garcilaso 210, Office 207, Cusco, tel. 084/25-4041, www. manucaiman.com).

Food

CENTRAL CUSCO
Peruvian
On the ground floor of Portal de Panes is the hugely popular ★ **Inka Grill** (Portal de Panes 115, tel. 084/26-2992, www.inkagrill-cusco.com, 11am-11pm daily, US$10-16), the first restaurant to bring Novoandino cuisine to Cusco and one of passionate restaurateur Rafael Casabonne's six restaurants (www.cus-corestaurants.com). Try the trout *tiradito* to start, followed by chicken Milanese with gnocchi. Alpaca medallions and roasted guinea pig are for the more adventurous. There is regular live Andean music.

Pucara (Plateros 309, tel. 084/22-2027, lunch and dinner daily, US$8-12) has a decent lunch menu for US$6 and offers local dishes such as *chicharron* (fried pork) and *seco de pollo* (chicken stew). **Café Restaurant Victor Victoria** (Tecsecocha 474, tel. 084/25-2854, 7:30am-10pm daily) has a reasonable lunch menu for US$5. The food is homey and there is an ample salad bar.

A recommended, unpretentious restaurant that serves fantastic Peruvian food is **Trujillo** (Tullumayo 543, tel. 084/23-3465, 9am-8pm Mon.-Sat. and 9am-5pm Sun., US$10-15). The menu is vast and servings are generous. It is particularly famous for its *ají de gallina* and the meat of the *asado a la olla*.

Nuna Raymi is another good place to eat local specialties (Triunfo 356, tel. 084/22-4644, www.nunaraymicusco.com, 9am-10:30pm daily, delivery 11am-10:30pm, US$10-15), including *ají de gallina, lomo saltado,* and trout in a variety of delicious sauces. Set menu is US$6.

For Andean music accompanying dinner, head to **Tunupa** (Plaza de Armas, tel. 084/25-2936, noon-10:30pm daily, US$15-20), right on the plaza. It specializes in fish and seafood. Try the candied trout. Prices are a little steep, but it has a great atmosphere.

Peruvian Fusion and Fine Dining
Fallen Angel Fire & Ice (Plazoleta Nazarenas 221, tel. 084/25-8184, www.fallenangelin-cusco.com, 11am-11pm daily, US$15-20) is a fascinating artistic creation. Decor includes glass-covered bathtub fish tanks instead of tables and a feast of artwork on the walls in a rotating exhibition. The atmosphere is set by techno music and multicolored daiquiris. The steaks are the specialty of the creative dinner menu.

At ★ **MAP Café** (Plaza Nazarenas 231, tel. 084/24-2476, www.cuscorestaurants. com, 11am-10pm daily, US$20-30), one of Cusco's best gourmet restaurants, dinner guests sit in a perfectly proportioned glass box in the stone courtyard of the Museo de

Arte Precolombino. The food is a gourmet interpretation of traditional Andean cuisine. The glazed and deep-fried *cuy* legs on a *choclo* foam with *tarwi* salad is a tasty and less confrontational way to try guinea pig. A favorite dish on the menu is *capchi de setas,* a mouthwatering creamy mushroom, potato, and broad bean casserole topped with a buttery pastry. Other specialties include the *tiradito* of sea bass in chili and *tumbo* sauce, and the roast lamb and quinoa cannelloni with truffles. The desserts are some of the most creative and delectable in Cusco. The specialty is hot truffle balls with *aguaymanto* and pisco, served with vanilla ice cream and a surprise shot.

Cicciolina (Triunfo 393, 2nd Fl., tel. 084/23-9510, www.cicciolinacuzco.com, 8am-11am, noon-3pm, and 6pm-10pm daily, US$15-20) is one of the most happening restaurants in town, popular with tourists and locals alike. A casual lunch here might be a sandwich, salad, and smoothie or their daily set menu. For dinner, try the cracked black pepper tagliatelle, grilled scallops in an Asian sauce, barbecued trout in coconut milk, or beetroot ravioli, accompanied by a glass of wine. For dessert try the strawberries and port. If you leave satisfied, come back the following morning for breakfast and delicious croissants at the Cicciolina bakery. They also provide a picnic catering service.

For an evening meal with an entertaining and operatic twist, **Divina Comedia** (Pumacurco 408, tel. 084/43-7640, www.restaurantcusco.com, 11:30am-3pm and 6:30pm-11pm Wed.-Mon., US$12-16) is a lot of fun. The Divine Comedy theme, medieval-influenced decor, and waiters dressed in period clothing are a fitting backdrop to the talented opera singers who entertain you while you dine. The menu ranges from tapas and ceviche to pasta and steak.

For an all-around great dining experience, easily the best fusion restaurant in Cusco is ★ **Limo** (Portal de Carnes 236, 2nd Fl., tel. 084/24-0668, www.cuscorestaurants.com, 11am-3pm and 6pm-midnight daily,

US$15-18). Rafael Casabonne's latest project is a tastefully decorated restaurant with a great view over the Plaza de Armas. The service is excellent, but most importantly the food is superb. Start the evening with a plate of exquisite sushi rolls. The *tiraditos* and ceviches, especially the *ceviche oriental,* are delicious. As a main, try the crab meat and breaded shrimp bathed in *leche de tigre* or the trout in passion fruit-infused white wine. For dessert, you can't go wrong with the *lasaña de suspiro* (wonton filled with fruit and strawberry coulis).

Peru's most famous chef and the man responsible for introducing the country's cuisine to the world is Gaston Acurio. His best-known, world-class restaurants are in Lima, but in Cusco he also has the recommended **Chicha** (Plaza Regocijo 261, 2nd Fl., tel. 084/24-0520, noon-10:30pm daily, US$15). The menu here is as diverse as Peru's geography, offering local favorites and international dishes with a twist. Try the alpaca tartare, pachamanca (meat dish), and rocoto relleno (stuffed peppers) for a flavor of Cusco. For international dishes, there is duck pizza, lamb ravioli and a loin rump with carmelized onions in red wine sauce.

International

An excellent Italian restaurant with a varied fusion menu is ★ **Incanto** (Santa Catalina Angosta 135, tel. 084/25-4753, www.cuscorestaurants.com, 11:30am-11pm daily, US$11-17). The minimalist decor shows off the original Inca walls, and the food is delicious. Choose from inventive Peruvian-Italian dishes, such as smoked trout fettuccine, ravioli *de ají de gallina,* and vegetable cannelloni. The *lúcuma* bar crunch is a delicious dessert. Above Incanto and belonging to the same owner is ★ **Greens** (Santa Catalina Angosta 135, 2nd Fl., tel. 084/24-3379, www.cuscorestaurants.com, 11am-11pm daily, US$13), the best organic restaurant in town. All dishes are a minimum of 90 percent organic. Choose from a wide variety of fresh vegetable and fruit juices from produce taken from the restaurant's own organic gardens in the Sacred Valley. The trout is delicious, and you should round off your meal with a dish invented by the chef: mango ravioli.

Peruvian cuisine is full of sushi-influenced dishes, but for real Japanese-style sushi, head to ★ **Kintaro** (334 Plateros, tel. 084/26-0638, www.cuscokintaro.com, noon-3pm, 6pm-10pm Mon.-Sat., US$6-15). The US$6 lunch menu is an excellent value, or try the range of rolls. Tea, extra bowls of rice, and Wi-Fi are all free.

Pizza

Pizza Carlo (Maruri 381, tel. 084/24-7777, noon-3pm and 5pm-11pm Mon.-Sat., 5:30pm-11pm Sun., US$10) has traditional Italian wood-fired pizzas with thin, smoky crusts. Those meat lovers who like a bit of spice should try the Diablo.

Babieca Trattoría (Tecsecocha 418-A, tel. 084/50-6940, 11am-midnight, US$12) has excellent dough, gourmet toppings such as alpaca and trout, and a gigantic pizza called the Kilometriza for US$20.

Vegetarian

Although most restaurants in Cusco have vegetarian options, there are few places dedicated exclusively to vegetarian cuisine. A popular option is **Govinda** (Saphy 584, tel. 084/79-0687, 8am-10pm daily, US$3-5), a few blocks up from the Plaza de Armas. This small Indian-inspired restaurant has flavorful dishes, including curry, paella, pasta, and wonton with tofu. The US$4 lunch menu is a very good value.

A worthwhile and economical option is **El Encuentro** (Santa Catalina Ancha 384, tel. 084/24-7977, 9am-3pm and 6pm-9pm Mon.-Sat., US$3-6). It has a salad bar, soups, sandwiches, falafel, and pasta.

Cafés, Bakeries, and Ice Cream

For a light lunch on Plaza de las Nazarenas, head to **Mama Oli** (Plaza Nazarenas 199, no phone, 9am-8pm Mon.-Fri. and 9am-5pm Sat.-Sun., US$4). This Peruvian-French-owned café has great juices, fresh soups, quiches, and desserts.

The classic Cusqueño **Café Ayllu** (Almagro 133, tel. 084/25-5078, 6:30am-10:30pm Mon.-Sat., 6:30am-1:30pm Sun., US$4) opened in the 1970s, and its glass cases still display pastries made from the age-old recipes. Be sure to try the *ponche de leche,* a pisco-and-milk cocktail, or a sliced roast suckling pig sandwich. **Dos Por Tres** (Marquez 271, tel. 084/23-2661, 9am-9pm daily, US$2.50) is another Cusco classic and artist hangout, good for drinks, cakes, and ice cream. The coffee, usually made by the owner, is cheap and delicious.

Directly across from the post office, **Don Esteban & Don Pancho** (Av. El Sol 765-A, tel. 084/25-2526, 8am-10pm Mon.-Sat., 8am-7pm Sun., US$5) has a varied menu of sandwiches, empanadas, desserts, and bread made on the premises.

Dolce Vita (Santa Catalina Ancha 366, tel. 084/63-9334, 10am-9pm daily, US$3) is the best place for homemade ice cream. Your only trouble will be deciding on a flavor: *chicha,* pisco sour, *lúcuma,* and coca are just a few of the exotic creations. It also has a new store at Maruri 276.

A good place for coffee, cakes, pancakes, and empanadas is the ideally located **Café Perla** (Plazoleta Santa Catalina 215, no phone, 7am-11pm daily, US$3-8). Peruvian main courses are available too.

SAN BLAS
Peruvian

Pacha Papa (Plazoleta San Blas 120, tel. 084/24-1318, www.cuscorestaurants.com, 9am-10pm daily, US$7-12) occupies a sunny courtyard across the street from the Iglesia San Blas. It's a good place for breakfast, with everything from Peruvian specialties (such as tamales, *chicharron,* and beef stew) to French toast and granola. For dinner, specialties range from oven-baked trout to a whole roasted *cuy.* Note that service can be slow.

International

If you are after Indian food, British-run **Korma Sutra** (Tandapata 909, tel. 084/23-3023, 6pm-10pm Mon.-Sat., US$8-12) is a good option. The curries are a little overpriced but very tasty, especially the onion *bhaji* and the *tikka masala*.

The German-owned **Granja Heidi** (Cuesta San Blas 525, tel. 084/23-8383, 8:30am-9:30pm Mon.-Sat., US$6-10) has farm-fresh produce, including delicious natural yogurt, homemade granola, and a light and tasty midday lunch menu. Prices are a little steep.

Australian Tammy Gordon's **Baco Wine Bar and Restaurant** (Ruinas 465, tel. 084/24-2808, bacorestaurante@yahoo.com, 3:30pm-10:30pm Mon.-Sat., US$10-15) has a relaxing atmosphere. There are thin-crust pizzas topped with such options as duck prosciutto and mushrooms or blue cheese, marinated figs, and basil. The organic salads and grilled meats are also delicious accompanied by a great wine from an extensive list.

A very cozy and affordable pizzeria in San Blas is **Justina's** (Palacio 100, interior, tel. 084/25-5475, 5pm-11pm daily, US$9-13). Or go to the extremely popular **La Bodega 138** (Herrajes 138, tel. 084/26-0272, noon-10:30pm daily, US$8-14), which has a great atmosphere and is renowned as the best pizzeria in town.

Cafés, Bakeries, and Ice Cream

The most popular café in Cusco is Irish/Australian-owned ★ **Jack's Café Bar** (Choquechaca 509/Cuesta San Blas, tel. 084/25-4606, www.jackscafecusco.com, 7:30am-11:30pm daily, US$6-10), and with good reason. It is famous for big breakfasts, such as El Gordo: a huge pile of eggs, homemade baked beans, fried potatoes, bacon, and sausages. For lunch there are great soups, salads, and sandwiches made with homemade bread. Don't miss the Tuscan veggie soup.

There is a fully stocked bar, as well as milk shakes, fruit juices, and coffees. At peak periods, you have to wait to be seated, an indication of how good this place is.

Along Cuesta San Blas, you'll eventually walk into the warm baking aromas of **Buen Pastor** (Cuesta San Blas 575, tel. 084/24-0586, 7am-8pm Mon.-Sat., US$2-4). This bakery run by nuns has warm empanadas and sweet pastries at very affordable prices.

To satisfy a chocolate craving, stop in the tiny ★ **Chocolate** (Choquechaca 162, tel. 084/25-8073, 7am-11pm daily), a shop serving steaming mugs of hot chocolate and chocolates by the piece. If you fancy sampling some creative coca-flavored chocolate and baked goods, head to the **Coca Shop** (Carmen Alto 115, 9am-8pm Mon.-Fri.).

If you are after a hefty sandwich, try **Juanito's** (7 Angelitos 638, tel. 084/25-5343, 11am-10pm Mon.-Sat., US$5). There is a selection of 30 fillings both meaty and vegetarian, including alpaca and *lechón.*

Markets

The **Mercado San Pedro** (Túpac Amaru, 6am-7pm), near the San Pedro train station, has a wide selection of fruit and vegetables. Come here to try the unique and delicious *granadilla* and *chirimoya* and cheap juices, but keep your eyes out for pickpockets and those who silently slice backpacks with razors to steal the goodies within.

Several blocks past Mercado San Pedro toward Avenida Ejercito is the black market **El Baratillo,** which on Saturday morning is full of the most fascinating secondhand wares. If you have time to browse properly you can find some real treasures, but be careful with your valuables.

The largest supermarket is **Mega** (Plaza Túpac Amaru and Matara); **Market** (Portal Mantas 120) is on the Plaza de Armas. They're small and pricey but stock some hard-to-find imported products.

Accommodations

Cusco is awash in tourist accommodations, and there is huge variation, from bare-bones dorms to some of the best hotels in Peru. There is a sufficient range of hotels and hostels in the tourist center, so there is no need to stay outside this zone. Your biggest decision is between staying close to Plaza de Armas, which is busy and noisier, or heading up the hills north, south, or west of the main plazas to seek out quieter lodgings, many of which have great views. The most pleasant of these outlying areas is the bohemian neighborhood of San Blas, which has a relaxing, artsy vibe. Its narrow streets keep out the traffic and smog of central Cusco.

Traffic has made parts of Cusco unpleasant. These areas include the extension of Plateros and Avenida El Sol, where even the back rooms of hotels hum with the noise of taxis and amplified advertisements. Outside of San Blas, Cusco's nicest lodging is along out-of-the-way streets like Suecia, Choquechaca, or Siete Cuartones/Nueva Alta, where classy bed-and-breakfasts line charming cobblestone streets. Try to make a reservation ahead of time in Cusco, and ask for the kind of room you want (e.g., with a view or with a double bed). Quality is variable, so try to check the room before paying. Despite a steady increase in the number of Cusco hotels, the best ones are increasingly booked solid May-November. If you arrive and don't like your room, you can usually wriggle out of your reservation after your first night and head elsewhere—there are lots of good options, especially among the newer, lesser-known hostels.

CENTRAL CUSCO
Under US$10

For budget accommodations, backpacker hostels are a good option, and there are now quite a few in Cusco. Bear in mind that these places tend to be noisier with regular parties, which may or may not suit you. The most popular are **The Point** (Meson de la Estrella 172, tel. 084/25-2266, www.thepointhostels.com, US$8-13 dorms) and **LOKI Inkahouse** (Cuesta Santa Ana 601, tel. 084/24-3705, www.lokihostel.com, US$9-13 dorm, US$33 d private bath). Both have locations in Lima and Máncora and include dorm rooms (and a few private rooms) that open onto TV rooms, Internet stations, shared kitchens, and bars. They have a reputation for their parties, and you are bound to meet other travelers.

Youth Hostal Albergue Municipal (Quiscapata 240, San Cristóbal, tel. 084/25-2506, albergue@municusco.gob.pe, US$6 dorm, US$8 d), part of Hostelling International, has great views from the balcony, clean bunk rooms, and a shared kitchen. A discount is given to Hostelling International members.

US$10-25

The name of ★ **Hostal Resbalosa** (Resbalosa 494, tel. 084/22-4839, www.hostalresbalosa.com, US$20 s shared bath, US$30 d private bath) translates as "slippery hostel," which might not seem immediately inviting. But it is appropriate for the steep walk up here. The hostel itself is one of the best budget options in town. Service is friendly, and rooms are well-equipped with orthopedic mattresses, hot water, and cable TV—but the highlight is the sweeping view over Cusco from the terrace. The rooms at the top are better.

Pirwa Backpackers (Portal de Panes 151, tel. 084/24-4315, www.pirwahostelscusco.com, US$12 dorm, US$35 d) has four central locations: the Plaza de Armas, Suecia, San Blas, and San Francisco. They all have a variety of dorms and private rooms, most with shared kitchen, common rooms, and a travel desk.

A great backpacker option is ★ **Ecopackers** (Santa Teresa 375, tel. 084/23-1800, www.ecopackersperu.com,

US$12-15 dorms, US$40-55 d), set in a beautiful colonial home. It offers a courtyard with games, a travel agency, Wi-Fi, and a decent, well-priced restaurant. Dorms and showers are well equipped. The private rooms are overpriced, but for backpacker groups, the dorms are a very good deal.

Mama Simona (Ceniza 364, tel. 084/26-0408, www.mamasimona.com, US$10-15 pp) has a selection of dorms and private rooms, plus a colorful sitting room. **Che Lagarto** (Siete Cuartones 284, tel. 084/23-3251, US$12 dorms, US$45 d) is another hostel. The dorms are a good value but private rooms are overpriced.

The charming **Sihuar** (Tandapata 351, tel. 084/22-7435, www.sihuar.galeon.com, US$25 d) is a two-level building that looks out over a patio and garden. The good-value rooms are pleasant and tastefully decorated, with wooden floors, woven rugs, and hot water.

US$25-50

A very good value hotel is **Conde Meloc** (Meloq 420, tel. 084/22-1117, www.hostalcondemeloc.com, US$26 s, US$39 d), which has elegant rooms and a cozy atmosphere.

Niños Hotel (Meloq 442, tel. 084/23-1424, www.ninoshotel.com, US$50 s or d) is a remarkable place with a cause: Its Dutch owner uses hotel revenue to feed, clothe, and provide medical assistance to street children. Just four blocks from the Plaza de Armas, this restored colonial home is a very attractive setting. With large, stylish rooms, hardwood floors, and a pleasant courtyard for taking breakfast, it's easy to make yourself at home. There is a second location at Fierro 476 (tel. 084/25-4611) and a Niños Hotel Hacienda in Huasao.

US$50-100

A lovely place in Tandapata is **Casona les Pleiades** (Tandapata 116, tel. 084/50-6430, www.casona-pleiades.com, US$77 s/d). Whether it be Melanie or Philip who opens the door for you, the welcome is bound to be warm and friendly. This young French couple has made their seven-room home into a guesthouse, and their aim is to make you feel right at home. There are down comforters on the beds and eggs made to order for breakfast.

The good-value European/Peruvian hotel **Madre Tierra** (Atocsaycuchi 647-A, tel. 084/24-8452, www.hostalmadretierra.com, US$49 s, US$58 d) has seven comfortable carpeted rooms. Cozy and inviting communal areas have white sofas, exposed beams, and open fireplaces.

★ **Hostal El Balcon** (Tambo de Montero 222, tel. 084/23-6738, www.balconcusco.com, US$60 s, US$75-125 d) is a restored colonial house with rustic charm and a pretty, flower-filled garden. This 16-room hostel is quaint and homely, and rooms are decorated simply with weavings on the beds.

The unpretentious **Hostal Corihuasi** (Suecia 561, tel. 084/23-2233, www.corihuasi.com, US$45 s, US$55 d) is a quick, steep walk up from the Plaza de Armas and has an old-world charm that beats Cusco. The rooms of this rambling, eclectic colonial house are connected by verandas and walkways. Some of the rooms are nicer with views over the city; others are dark, with porthole windows, so make sure you check your room before paying.

MamaSara Hotel (Saphy 875, tel. 084/24-5409, www.mamasarahotel.com.pe, US$90 s, US$110 d), a short walk from the plaza up Saphy, is very pleasant and comfortable. The rooms are heated and spacious, and they come with flat-screen TVs, good showers, and oxygen on request. Another good option right off the plaza is **Del Prado Inn** (Suecia 310, 084/224-442, www.delpradoinn.com, US$65 s, US$95 d), with stylish, warm rooms and an ideal location.

For a location one block from the Plaza de Armas, look no further than **Hostal Rojas** (Tigre 129, tel. 084/22-8184, www.hotelrojascusco.com, US$60 s, US$85 d with private bath), with clean, carpeted rooms around a sunny courtyard inhabited by an entertaining parrot.

An impressive original Inca doorway, once the entrance to a sacred place, is now the way into the hotel **Rumi Punku** (Choquechaca

339, tel. 084/22-1102, www.rumipunku.com, US$80 s, US$100 d). Light-filled terraces, a garden with an original Inca wall, and a gym and spa make this a pleasant place to stay.

Another midrange hotel with an excellent location is **Cusco Plaza** (Plazoleta Nazarenas 181, tel. 084/24-6161, www.cuscoplazahotels. com, US$55 s, US$65 d). The rooms are relatively simple, but the views are great and it's perfect to be on the quiet square.

US$100-150

The well-known national hotel chain ★ **Casa Andina** (www.casa-andina.com) has four of its Classic Collection hotels at ideal locations in the center of Cusco. Two are within one block of the Plaza de Armas (Santa Catalina Angosta 149, tel. 084/23-3661, and Portal Espinar 142, tel. 084/23-1733), one is near Coricancha (San Agustín 371, tel. 084/25-2633), and the fourth in San Blas (Chihuampata 278, tel. 084/26-3694). These well-designed, comfortable hotels provide excellent service, and all have the same prices (US$140 s/d). The aim of the hotels is to reflect the local character of a place and give a genuine experience using local ideology and local products where possible, without sacrificing comfort and convenience. All rooms have down comforters, heating, and cable TV, and a generous breakfast buffet is included. Prices may be cheaper booking online.

A good option in this range is **Tierra Viva** (Saphi 766, tel. 084/24-1414, and Suecia 345, tel. 084/24-5848, www.tierravivahoteles.com, US$129 s, US$141 d), which has two hotels near the center with impeccable rooms and a buffet breakfast.

The **Hotel Arqueologo** (Pumacurco 408, tel. 084/23-2569, www.hotelarqueologo.com, US$120 d standard, US$140 d superior) occupies an old colonial building. Rooms with high ceilings wrap around a rustic stone courtyard or overlook a grassy garden. The hotel tries to maintain an eco-friendly philosophy by having its own bio-veggie garden, recycling rubbish, providing a fountain with drinking water to refill bottles, and only providing TVs

in rooms upon request. The first-floor café, **Song Thé,** has comfortable sofas, a fireplace, and French pastries.

US$150-250

The **Novotel** (San Agustín 239, tel. 084/58-1030, www.novotel.com, US$240 d modern room, US$320 d colonial room) is in a restored colonial manor that has a patio lined with stone arches and decorated with lamps and wicker furniture in which guests can enjoy evening drinks. Undoubtedly the best rooms are those on the second floor around the stone courtyard, with wood floors, high ceilings, king-size beds, sitting areas, and all creature comforts (security box, minibar, cable TV, heating). The other 82 rooms are comfortable but bland, small, and sterile, housed in an unfortunate five-story modern addition.

Equal in elegance and similar in layout, but cheaper and better value is **Costa del Sol Ramada** (Santa Teresa 344, tel. 084/25-2330, www.costadelsolperu.com, US$140 d modern room, US$159 d colonial), which has an ideal location one block from Plaza Regocijo and a two-minute walk from the Plaza de Armas. This 17th-century colonial mansion, which once belonged to the Spanish noble Marquis de Picoaga, has been well restored with stone archways and columns wrapping around a classic colonial patio. Costa del Sol, the Peruvian hotel chain, recently acquired it.

Over US$250

The five-star ★ **Hotel Libertador Palacio del Inka** (Plazoleta Santo Domingo 259, tel. 084/23-1961, www.libertador.com.pe, US$305 d) has a great location next to Coricancha, the Inca sun temple. It occupies the Casa de los Cuatro Bustos, Francisco Pizarro's last home. It is built on the foundation of the *acllahuasi*, "the house of the chosen ones," where virgins picked by the Inca lived in seclusion from society. The entrance to the Hotel Libertador is spectacular. A stone portal leads into a glass-roofed lobby, lined on one side by Spanish stone arches and on the other by exposed portions of stone Inca walls. There is an excellent buffet breakfast served alongside another large square, ringed with two stories of stone arcades. Throughout the hotel are examples of original colonial furniture, artifacts, and paintings. Ask for rooms in the colonial section, with views of the sun temple. The suites are larger and have sitting areas and marble bathrooms, and are probably worth paying extra for.

The new exclusive hotel in town is none other than the **Hilton Garden Inn** (Santa Ana, Avenida Apurimac 207, tel. 084/ 58-0130, call for rates), located on a hill overlooking Cusco and about a kilometer from the main plaza. The rooms have all of the comforts of Hiltons around the globe: 47-inch TVs, comfy beds with crisp sheets. There is excellent Wi-Fi and a good restaurant.

★ **Casa Andina Private Collection** (Plazoleta Limacpampa Chico 473, www.casa-andina.com, tel. 084/23-2610, US$320 s/d) is the best of Casa Andina's hotels in town. This beautifully renovated 18th-century manor house is just three blocks from Cusco's Plaza de Armas, and it offers the intimacy of a boutique hotel but the comforts and services of a much larger property. The hotel has three interior patios with wooden balconies and a stone fountain. In the hotel's cozy lounge

and reading room is a massive stone fireplace that's always crackling, while the gourmet restaurant offers candlelit dinners in one of four connected salons richly decorated with 18th-century Cusco School paintings. Several rooms in the original structure of the hotel feature surviving colonial frescoes unearthed during renovation.

One of the more memorable places to stay in Cusco is ★ **Hotel Monasterio** (Palacio 136, Plazoleta Nazarenas, tel. 084/60-4000, www.belmond.com, US$634 basic d or US$806-2,232 suites), a 415-year-old monastery that has been converted into an elegant five-star hotel. The stone lobby leads to a dramatic stone courtyard, graced with an ancient cedar tree and lined with two stories of stone archways. Colonial paintings line long hallways, which wrap around two other stone patios. The rooms are decked out in old-world Spanish decor, including carved wooden headboards and colonial paintings, and include all the plush five-star comforts. They can even be pumped with oxygen, simulating an altitude 900 meters lower and allowing guests to sleep more soundly.

The hotel occupies the former Seminario San Antonio Abad, which was built in 1595 on top of the Inca Amaru Qhala Palace but

Hotel Libertador Palacio del Inka occupies the former home of Francisco Pizarro.

was badly damaged in the 1650 earthquake. During the restoration, a colonial baroque chapel was added, which remains open to guests and has one of the most ornate altars in Cusco. After yet another damaging earthquake in 1950, the building was condemned and auctioned by the Peruvian government in 1995. It eventually landed in the hands of Orient-Express Hotels, which carefully restored the stonework, planted fabulous gardens, and converted the former cells into 126 plush rooms. These days, guests take lunch in the main square, which is shaded by a giant cedar, scented by a rose garden, and filled with the gurgling of a 17th-century stone fountain. The hotel hosts one of Cusco's three gourmet restaurants, and also includes a small massage room. It's a few minutes' walk from the Plaza de Armas.

Diagonally opposite the Monasterio on Plaza de las Nazarenas is **Inkaterra La Casona** (Plaza de las Nazarenas 113, tel. 084/23-4010, www.inkaterra.com, US$720 patio suite, US$924 balcony suite, US$1,128 plaza suite). Literally named "the big house," it offers a homely but luxurious atmosphere. This beautiful colonial mansion was built in 1585. Following the Spanish conquest it was possessed by Francisco Barrientos, lieutenant to Diego de Almagro. It has now been officially named a historic monument by the Instituto Nacional de Cultura, and has been exquisitely restored into 11 luxurious suites with original caoba doors. The doors to La Casona are closed to the outside world, ensuring the utmost privacy. The philosophy of the hotel is to provide a personalized service; you'll struggle to find the front door, and there is no reception, just a butler and concierge who prioritize individuals' needs. Rooms are decorated with faded frescoes, colonial tapestries, Persian rugs, and antiques, ensuring the original feel of the home without sacrificing modern comfort and luxury. Every suite has thermostat-controlled heated floors, a flat-screen TV with DVD player, iPod speakers, Wi-Fi, and a minibar. There is also a private spa and

massage room. La Casona also prides itself on being one of Peru's first carbon-neutral hotels.

SAN BLAS
US$10-25

Samay Wasi (Atocsaycuhi 416, tel. 084/25-3108, www.samaywasiperu.com, US$10-11 dorm, US$26-34 d) is about a 10-minute walk from Cusco's Plaza de Armas in San Blas. It offers shared and double rooms and has nice gardens.

Mirador de la Ñusta (Plazoleta San Blas, tel. 084/24-8039, US$15 pp) is a budget hotel on the main plaza of San Blas. It's very basic, and hot water is available only in the mornings, but it's a great price for the location.

US$25-50

Probably the best value for money is **Inti Quilla** (Atocsaycuhi 281, tel. 084/25-2659, www.intiquilla.8m.com, US$14-20 s, US$25-30 d). This very basic but clean hostel has two triple rooms and five double rooms arranged around a colorful lounge area. Some rooms have private bathrooms, and there is 24-hour hot water.

In the center of San Blas is **Casa de la Gringa** (Tandapata 148, tel. 084/24-1168, www.casadelagringa.com, US$24-30 s, US$30-40 d), owned by Lesley Myburgh. It is recommended for its colorful rooms, friendly staff, and small gardens. There is a New Age, spiritual air about the place.

A very popular hotel right on the square is **Hatun Wasi** (Plazoleta San Blas, tel. 084/25-3585, www.hotelhatunwasi.com, US$50 s, US$76 d), with comfortable rooms and an ideal location.

In lower San Blas, one of the nicer hotels in Cusco is ★ **Amaru Hostal** (Cuesta San Blas 541, tel. 084/22-5933, www.amaruhostal.com, US$50 s, US$60 d with private bath). The 27 rooms, with balconies, are spread around two sun-filled patios overflowing with geraniums and roses. The rooms have comfy beds and wood floors, and are small but generally pleasant. However, note that rooms vary widely—ask for the corner rooms with sun porches, wicker furniture, and vistas on both sides. For those on a budget there are cheaper rooms with shared bathrooms. The hostel has two more locations in San Blas: **Amaru Hostal Colonial** (Chihuampata 642, tel. 084/22-3521) and the private **Hostería de Anita** (Alavado 525, tel. 084/22-5499).

US$50-100

Charming, German-owned **Pensión Alemana Bed and Breakfast** (Tandapata 260, tel. 084/22-6861, www.cuzco-stay.de, US$63-68 s, US$70-75 d with breakfast) is the closest thing to a European pensione in Cusco. There are 12 light and airy rooms (many with incredible views over the city) with comfortable beds and hot showers. A pleasant garden looks out over the red-tiled roofs of the city, and a nightly fire crackles in the dining room.

Apu Huascaran (Carmen Bajo, tel. 084/23-5825, www.apuhuascaranperu.com, US$65 s, US$75 d) is a midrange hotel in San Blas with decent rooms with cable TV and private baths, a small courtyard, and a rooftop terrace with great views.

Encantada (Tandapata 354, tel. 084/24-2206, www.encantadaperu.com, US$90 s, US$115 d) is a pleasant hotel in a modern building with great views and minimalist decor. The hotel also doubles as a massage and spa center.

US$100-150

As the name suggests, **Second Home Cusco** (Atocsaycuchi 616, tel. 084/23-5873, www.secondhomecusco.com, US$110 s, 120 d) in San Blas really is a home away from home. This highly recommended bed-and-breakfast, owned by artist Carlos Delfin, son of the famous sculptor Victor Delfin, has three very simple but nicely decorated, light-filled junior suites: the skylight suite, the patio suite, and the balcony suite. Each has its own special charm. There is another Second Home located in Lima.

At the Swiss-managed **Los Apus** (Atocsaycuchi 515, tel. 084/26-4243, www.losapushotel.com, US$100 s, US$120 d), the rooms have wood floors, heating, comfortable beds, and cable TV. Breakfast is served in a glass-roofed courtyard.

The attractive boutique hotel **Casa San Blas** (Tocuyeros 566, tel. 084/23-7900, www.casasanblas.com, US$136 d, US$198 suite) prides itself on providing personalized service. The hotel is ideally located, set back off the Cuesta San Blas, and has great views of the city from its sunny roof terrace. Its eighteen rooms are comfortable, have all the necessary amenities, and are decorated simply with traditional weavings on the walls. There are also self-catering suite apartments with kitchenettes. Sustainability issues are addressed by giving guests the option to reuse bedding and towels and refill water bottles. Light bulbs are energy-saving, and there are double curtains to reduce the need for heating.

The finest of the Casa Andina Classic Collection hotels is the ★ **Casa Andina San Blas** (Chihuampata 278, tel. 084/26-3694, www.casa-andina.com, US$140 s/d), built around a colonial stone courtyard with great views of Cusco. The cozy sitting areas with wood-burning fires, a rustic bar, and a terrace make this a great place to relax.

Information and Services

TOURIST INFORMATION

The **South American Explorers Club (SAE)** (Pardo 847, tel. 084/24-5484, www. saexplorers.org, 9:30am-5pm Mon.-Fri., 9:30am-1pm Sat.) is a gold mine of information. It costs US$60 to join as an individual for a year, US$90 for a couple, though nonmembers are allowed to look around as well. This is definitely worth the cost if you will be in Peru for any length of time, and is a recommended first stop in Cusco. No matter how much research you have done, you will always learn something here and, at the very least, meet some interesting people. Club members can peruse trip reports for all over the Cusco area, use the well-stocked library, make free calls to the United States and Canada, and receive discounts at a wide range of restaurants, language schools, hotels, and agencies. It is also the only place in Cusco that sells topographical maps ($25). There are trekking sheets available (members US$2, nonmembers US$4), and the clubhouse can advise you on the best local tour operators. The club hosts weekly events, and there is a new volunteer room that helps travelers become involved in children's, women's, and environmental projects.

If all you need is some basic tourist information and a map, services are free at the friendly **Iperú** (Portal Harinas 177, Plaza de Armas, tel. 084/25-2974, www.peru.travel/iperu.aspxwww.promperu.gob.pe, 9am-6:50pm Mon.-Fri., 9am-12:50pm Sat.-Sun. or at the airport (tel. 084/237-364, 6am-5pm daily). You can also try the city tourist office, **Dircetur** (Plaza Tupac Amaru Mz. Lote 2, Wanchaq, tel. 084/22-3701, www.dirceturcusco.gob.pe, 8am-8pm Mon.-Sat., 8am-2pm Sun.).

POLICE

Travelers can contact the tourist police through the Iperú office, but a larger,

24-hour tourist police office is at Saphi 510 (tel. 084/24-9659), where officers speak some English.

IMMIGRATION

Tourist visa inquiries can be made at the **Oficina de Migración (Immigration Office)** (Av. El Sol 612, tel. 084/22-2741, 8am-4:15pm Mon.-Fri., 8am-noon Sat.).

HEALTH CARE

One of the major hospitals of Cusco is **Hospital Lorena** (Plazoleta Belén 1358, in the Santiago neighborhood, tel. 084/22-1581 or 084/22-6511, www.hospitalantoniolorena.com). Another is the **Regional Hospital** (Av. de la Cultura, tel. 084/22-3691).

One recommended clinic is **Cima Clinic** (Pardo 978, tel. 084/25-5550 or cell tel. 984-651-085, www.cima-clinic.com), which specializes in altitude problems.

The best pharmacies are **InkaFarma** (Av. El Sol 210, tel. 084/24-2631, www.inka-farma.com.pe, 24 hours), **Boticas Arcangel** (Mantas 132, tel. 084/22-1421, 7am-11pm daily), and **Boticas Fasa** (Av. El Sol 130, tel. 084/24-4528, www.boticasfasa.com.pe, 7am-11pm Mon.-Sat., 8am-9pm Sun.).

A recommended dental clinic is **Vivadent Clínica Odontológica** (El Sol 627-B, 2nd Fl., tel. 084/23-1558 or cell tel. 984-746-581, www.vivadentcusco.com). Dr. Virginia Valcarcel Velarde is expensive but very professional and experienced.

BANKS AND MONEY EXCHANGE

Getting money out of an ATM usually means a stroll down the first few blocks of Avenida El Sol, where **Banco de Crédito** is on the first block and **Banco Continental** and **Interbank** are on the third. The Banco de Crédito and Interbank are open all day 9am-6:30pm (the others usually close 1pm-3pm),

City Safety

It is a common misconception that traveling through Peru's remote countryside is risky while spending time in a tourist town like Cusco is safe. In fact, the exact opposite is true. Taxi assaults, where cab drivers rob their passengers, are on the rise in Cusco. Most of these are simple robberies, though some have involved violence. Here are some tips for staying out of trouble:

· Take only authorized taxis; these can be easily recognized by a hexagonal yellow sticker on the windshield. Even better, go with a radio taxi company—these have advertising and phone numbers on their roofs.

· Look at the taxi driver and decide whether you feel comfortable. If you feel nervous, wave the taxi on and choose another.

· Always take a taxi late at night, especially after drinking. Night taxis anywhere in town cost about US$2.

· Walk in a group at night. Women should never walk alone.

· Carry your wallet in your front pocket and keep your backpack in front of you in a market or other crowded area. In markets, it is often better to leave most of your money and your passport at home.

· Walk with purpose and confidence.

· Stay in the main tourist areas. Avoid lesser-known suburbs and take care in the areas around San Pedro market and the bus terminal.

· When riding on a bus, store your luggage below or keep it on your lap. Do not put it on the racks above you where others can reach it as you sleep.

· Be wary of new friends at bars and on the street—many scams involve misplaced trust or the lure of drugs and sex and are hatched over the space of hours. Think twice before you go somewhere out of the way with someone you just met.

with Saturday hours 9am-1pm. All the banks are closed on Sunday. For wire transfers, there is a **Western Union** (Av. El Sol 627-A, tel. 084/24-4167, 8:30am-7:30pm Mon.-Fri., 8:30am-1:30pm Sat.).

There is an overwhelming number of money exchange places, especially along the Avenida El Sol, and they are all much the same. A reliable option is **Panorama** (Portal de Comercio 149, 9am-10pm daily). The rate is always fair, and the bills are brand new because they come directly from the bank.

COMMUNICATIONS

Cusco's main **post office** is the Serpost (Av. El Sol 800, tel. 084/22-5232, www.serpost. com.pe, 7:30am-8pm Mon.-Sat. and 9am-2pm Sun).

The city has plenty of Internet places, all of which have cable connections and are generally good, although the availability of Wi-Fi in hotels and hostels makes them less and less important. Most are open 9am-9pm daily. Long-distance and international calls can be made at many Internet places, which are all similar in price.

LANGUAGE SCHOOLS

Cusco has more Spanish schools than any other city in Peru, though it is hard to be truly immersed in Spanish unless you can somehow isolate yourself from English speakers. Considering what they include, the school packages are inexpensive: prearranged hostel accommodations or homestay with local family, breakfast, airline reservations, volunteer work options, city tours, dance and cooking classes, lectures, and movies. An intensive group class with all these perks runs around US$200-300 per week with 20 hours of classes, while a private package is around US$300-400 for the same schedule. A private teacher, without lodging or food, is US$10-13 per hour.

Academia Latinoamericana de Español (Plaza Limacpampa Grande 565, tel. 084/24-3364, www.latinoschools. com, US$300 private classes, US$185 group classes) is a professional, family-run business with schools in Peru, Ecuador, and Bolivia. They have great host families in Cusco and offer volunteer programs as well as university credits through New Mexico State University. **Amigos Spanish School** (Zaguan del Cielo B-23, tel. 084/24-2292, www.spanishcusco. com, US$150 group) gives half of its income to children with disabilities and has highly recommended teachers.

Centro Tinku (Nueva Baja 560, tel. 084/24-9737, www.centrotinku.com, US$165 group) is a cultural institution that offers standard and custom-made Spanish and Quechua classes. All the teachers are fully certified. Off the Plazoleta San Blas is the affordable and quaint yet professional **Mundo Antiguo Spanish School** (Tandapata 649, tel. 084/22-5974, www.learnspanishinperu. net, US$70-120 group, US$90-175 private), run by a friendly Peruvian-Dutch couple; the school keeps its programs intimate, personal,

and welcoming. **Maximo Nivel** (El Sol 612, tel. 084/25-7200, www.maximonivel.com) has schools all over North and South America.

LAUNDRY

Most Cusco hostels offer laundry service for the going rate of US$2 per kilogram. Otherwise the best place for washing clothes (although a little more expensive) and especially for dry cleaning is **Lavandería Inka** (Ruinas 493, tel. 084/22-3421, 8am-1pm and 3pm-8pm Mon.-Sat.). For just regular washing, **Lavandería Louis** (Choquechaca 264-A, tel. 084/24-3485, 8am-8pm Mon.-Sat.) is a reliable and cheaper option.

PHOTOGRAPHY

It's a good idea to download your photos, particularly after visiting Machu Picchu, just to be safe. Digital photographers can download their full media cards to a CD in 20 minutes at many camera shops in Cusco. Sometimes you need the USB cord that works with your camera. An exception is **Foto Panorama** (Portal Comercio 149, in front of the cathedral, tel. 084/23-9800, 8:30am-10pm), which accepts most different media cards. Another highly recommended place for developing or digital services and products is **Foto Nishiyama** (Triunfo 346, tel. 084/24-2922). It has other locations around town, including on Avenida El Sol.

Getting There and Around

AIR

Cusco's airport, **Aeropuerto Internacional Alejandro Velasco Astete** (tel. 084/22-2611), is 10 minutes south of town, and the taxi ride costs about US$4.50.

All Cusco-bound travelers must first arrive in Lima and then board another plane in Cusco, for which there are currently three main operators. To approach Cusco's airport, planes must fly at considerable altitude and down a narrow valley, passing ice-covered

Nevado Salcantay en route. Because of the tricky approach and winds, afternoon flights are frequently canceled. If possible, fly in and out of Cusco in the morning.

LAN (Av. El Sol 627-B, tel. 084/25-5552, Lima tel. 01/21-38200, www.lan.com) is the most reliable airline but also the most expensive, and has more than 10 Cusco-bound flights a day. Published fares are as high as US$400 return, but it often has special offers if you book ahead of time, plus it works out cheaper to book the international flight and internal flight to Cusco together. **Star Perú** (Av. El Sol 627, tel. 084/25-3791 or 084/23-4060, www.starperu.com) and **Avianca** (Av. El Sol 602-B, tel. 084/24-9921 or 084/24-9922, Lima tel. 01/21-37000, www.taca.com) are also reliable and usually have cheaper flights, starting from US$200 return. **LCPeru** (Av. El Sol 520, tel. 084/23-5584, www.lcperu.pe) is a small Peruvian airline, but a reliable and economical option. It offers round-trip flights between Lima and Cusco starting at about US$130.

In addition, LAN has daily flights from Cusco to Puerto Maldonado and Arequipa, as well as various other destinations around Peru from Lima. Star Perú and Taca also fly from Lima or Cusco to Puerto Maldonado and from Lima to other Peruvian destinations.

BUS
Long-Distance Buses

The long-distance bus terminal, the **Terminal Terrestre**, is on the way to the airport (Vía de Evitamiento 429, tel. 084/22-4471). This huge building is busy, safe, and crammed with all of the long-distance bus companies, along with bathrooms and a few stores selling snacks. Companies generally are open 6am-9pm and accept reservations over the phone, with payment on the day of departure (you have to speak Spanish, though). Note that the area around the bus terminal is not particularly safe, so take a taxi directly to and from the terminal. When you have the option, traveling in the highlands is best done during the day.

A recommended way to get to **Puno** is with one of the tourist buses that visit the ruins on the way. These buses include a buffet lunch and an English-speaking guide, and they stop at most of the major ruins along the route. **Inka Express** (Platteros 320, tel. 084/24-7887, www.inkaexpress.com, US$50) makes stops at the exquisite colonial church of Andahuaylillas and the Inca ruins of Raqchi, and includes a buffet lunch stop in Sicuani. In the afternoon the bus stops at La Raya pass and the ruins of Pukará before arriving

in Puno. The buses generally leave Cusco at 8am and arrive at 5pm in Puno, including hotel pickup and drop-off. There is usually a 10 percent discount for groups of more than four people.

For direct services to Puno, **Ormeño** (tel. 084/22-7501) has a daily bus leaving at 9am, which arrives in Juliaca at 1:30pm and Puno at 2pm (US$14 for Royal Class, which has onboard food service and plusher seats than even the Imperial buses). **Turismo Puma** offers a similar service. **Imexso** (tel. 084/22-9126, imexso@terra.com.pe), for the most part, has good service and new buses, with English-language videos.

Many of these companies offer transfer buses leaving for **Bolivia,** though some go through Desaguadero and others through Copacabana (launching point for Isla del Sol). **Ormeño** (tel. 084/22-7501) has a direct business-class bus (no meals) through Desaguadero to La Paz, leaving daily at 9pm. To head through Copacabana, try **Tour Peru,** which leaves at 10pm daily (US$28). Another recommended company for getting to Bolivia is **Litoral,** though there are many more options in Puno's excellent Terminal Terrestre. The border crossing, which is open between 8am and 3pm, is quick and easy: Passengers need only get off the bus for a few minutes on each side of the border to have their passports stamped. Remember to ask for the maximum number of days (usually 90).

Buses for the 20-hour haul to **Lima** now head to Abancay before crossing the mountains to the coast at Nasca and then heading north for Lima. Ormeño offers the extra-plush Royal Class service, which leaves at 10am and arrives in Lima the following day at 6am for US$50. There are also plain, one-story buses with a stop in Abancay. Another recommended company is **Expreso Wari** (tel. 084/24-7217), which has buses with seats that recline into beds. Trips including meals leave at 12:30pm and 8pm for US$52. They also have a less luxurious service leaving at 2pm and 4pm for US$28. **Cruz del Sur** (tel. 084/24-8255) has a good Imperial service leaving at 3:30pm and 6:30pm. **Tepsa** (tel. 084/22-4534, www.tepsa.com.pe) is also a reliable option for Lima. The only company with transfer service through Abancay on to **Ayacucho** is **Expreso Los Chankas** (tel. 084/24-2249).

The journey between Cusco and Nasca takes 13 hours along some pretty dicey roads. It costs US$35 during the day and a little more at night. Turismo Internacional and all companies listed above for Lima go to Nasca.

The journey to **Arequipa** via Juliaca takes 9.5 hours ($12). **Cruz del Sur** (tel. 084/24-8255) has Imperial buses that include dinner leaving at 2pm for US$34, and Ormeño offers a similar-quality service. **Enlaces** (tel. 084/25-5333) and **Cial** (tel. 804/22-1201) also have Imperial buses leaving daily.

The only direct option for Tacna, the border town for Chile, is **Cruz del Sur** (tel. 084/24-8255), which leaves at 4:30pm and arrives at 8:30am the following day.

The trip to **Puerto Maldonado** used to take two days, but with the construction of the Lima-to-São Paulo highway, known as the Inter-Oceanic Highway, it now only takes 10 hours ($25-30). **Transzela** (Terminal Terrestre, 084/238-223, www.transzela.com.pe) is a good company in the terminal. Atalaya, the gateway to the Parque Nacional Manu, is hard to reach, but the journey can generally be made in a long day. Travelers must first head to Paucartambo. For Quillabamba, **Ampay** (tel. 084/24-9977) has buses leaving for the 8.5-hour journey for US$7 from the Terminal Terrestre.

Regional Buses

For destinations in the Cusco region, find the informal *terminales,* where buses, *combis,* and *colectivos* leave when full. These are often located in places that are unsafe at night or early in the morning. They generally operate from 5am until as late as 7pm Most taxi drivers know where these *terminales* are.

For **Quillabamba,** there is a roadside pickup spot, called a *terminal de paso,* at the last block of Avenida Antoñia Lorena, the principal exit road for the route that goes through the Sacred Valley before heading over Abra Málaga into the jungle (7 hours, US$6).

For **Urubamba,** there are two options. Buses for the shorter, 1.5-hour route, through Chinchero, leave from the first block of Grau near the bridge (45 minutes, US$1 for Chinchero; 1.25 hours, US$2 for Urubamba). Collective taxis at Pavitos do the same route but go all the way to **Ollantaytambo** (1.5 hours, US$3.50 pp).

Collective taxis and buses for **Pisac** and **Calca** via Urubamba leave from Avenida Pachacútec on the way to the airport (one hour, US$1.50 for Pisac; 1.5 hours, US$2 for Urubamba).

For **Andahuaylillas** and **Urcos,** on the way to Puno, buses leave from Avenida de la Cultura in front of the regional hospital (1.5 hours, US$1).

Note that pickup points for some of these services change, and there are new collectives offered regularly, so it's always a good idea to ask in your hotel for the latest recommendations.

TRAINS

The train service between Cusco and Machu Picchu, while overpriced, is a spectacular route. The **PeruRail** monopoly has been consigned to the past with the emergence of a new train company: **Inca Rail.** However, prices remain high—US$75 one-way, US$120 return. Trains back from Aguas Calientes can be a little cheaper ($50) due to the volume of travelers returning from the Inca Trail.

If you're not hiking the Inca Trail, then the train is the only way to get to Machu Picchu, although most people don't take it all the way from Cusco. A major problem with trains from Cusco, especially during high season, is availability. The easiest way to get tickets is through a hotel or a travel agent. Otherwise visitors should make reservations online. The third, and least desirable option, is to head down to the Cusco train station, a process that, especially during high season, can take an hour or two.

PeruRail still operates trains from Cusco, but most Machu Picchu travelers now depart farther down the line at Ollantaytambo in the Sacred Valley. From Ollantaytambo the train enters the narrow Urubamba gorge, which offers spectacular views of snowcapped Verónica peak (5,710 meters or 18,865 feet) on the right (eastern) side of the train as the landscape transforms into the lush and humid *ceja de selva,* or "eyebrow of the jungle." By the time the train reaches Aguas Calientes, the town closest to Machu Picchu, the scenery has changed remarkably from high Andean plains to verdant cloud forest.

The other major train service is the Cusco-to-Puno service. It is a spectacular route up through the high plains of southern Peru above 4,000 meters. However, prices are very steep—$150-220 one-way. Compare this with only US$50 for the bus and it's obvious why most backpackers now take that option instead.

PeruRail

PeruRail (www.perurail.com), a division of Belmond, offers many train services to Machu Picchu: the **Expedition** (US$70 one-way, leaves Ollantaytambo six times daily, first at 5:05 am, leaves Aguas Calientes six times daily, first at 5:35 am), the **Vistadome** (US$85 one-way, leaves Ollantaytambo six times daily, first at 7:05am, leaves Aguas Calientes six times daily, first at 10:55am), and the luxury **Hiram Bingham service** (US$380 one-way, leaves Poroy 9:40am, leaves Aguas Calientes 8:50pm). The Expedition and Vistadome can also be caught from Pichar

For trains to Puno, the PeruRail deluxe **Andean Explorer** (US$306 one-way) departs on Monday, Wednesday, and Saturday (and Friday April-October) from Wanchaq Station (Av. El Sol s/n, tel. 084/23-3592) at 8am and arrives at 6:30pm in Puno. This spectacular 10-hour trip winds through the vast altiplano past snowcapped mountains.

Inca Rail

Inca Rail (Portal de Panes St. 105, Plaza de Armas, tel. 084/23-3030, Lima tel. 01/61-35288, www.incarail.com) offers three daily departures from Ollantaytambo (6:40am, 11:15am, and 4:36pm) and three daily departures from Aguas Calientes (8:30am, 2:30pm, and 7pm) on its Inca Train. The trains have an Executive Class (US$75 one-way) and a First Class (US$135 one-way). Inca Rail has ticket offices in Ollantaytambo and Aguas Calientes next to the train line.

Inca Rail's Machu Picchu Train leaves daily from Ollantaytambo for Aguas Calientes at 7:20am, and from Aguas Calientes for Ollantaytambo at 4:12pm. Prices are also about US$75 one-way.

CAR AND MOTORCYCLE RENTAL

Through its Cusco operator, at **Hertz** (Av. El Sol 808, tel. 084/24-8800, www.inkasrac.com) you can rent a Toyota, be it a Corolla or a Land Cruiser. Rental rates include insurance, taxes, and 250 free kilometers per day. **Europcar** (Saphy 639, tel. 084/26-2655, www.europcarperu.com) also operates in Cusco. Motorcycles can be rented at **Cusco Moto** (Saphi 592, tel. 084/22-7025, www.cuscomototourperu.com). The rental includes helmet, gloves, goggles, jacket, and medical and legal insurance. It also offers tours of the Sacred Valley, Maras and Moray, and even Colca Canyon.

LOCAL TRANSPORTATION

A taxi anywhere in Cusco's center costs US$2-3 at night. Always be careful with taxis, especially at night. Never take unmarked cabs, and be sure to check the taxi's credentials. It's preferable to ask your hotel or restaurant to call a taxi from a reputable company. The extra dollar is worth it for guaranteed security. Because Cusco's center is so compact (and congested), few travelers find the need to take buses or *combis*—though the ones that head down Avenida El Sol toward the Terminal Terrestre and airport are useful.

Vicinity of Cusco

There are very interesting ruins along the road that heads south from Cusco to Lake Titicaca. These cultural sites, from pre-Inca, Inca, and colonial times, form an interesting day tour from Cusco that an increasing number of agencies are offering. These landmarks can also be visited on the highly recommended special tourist buses between Cusco and Puno, which hit all the sights described, head over La Raya Pass, and then keep going to Puno and Lake Titicaca.

Tourist bus services that travel the route and visit the sites for about US$60 one-way include **Inka Express Bus** (tel. 084/43-1398 or 084/23-3498, www.inkaexpressbus.com, Mon.-Sat. 9am-1pm and 3pm-6pm) and **Peru Bus Tickets** (Triunfo 392, Office 212, Cusco, cell tel. 974-334-261, www.cuscopunobus. com, Mon.-Sat. 9am-8pm).

Or, ask any number of travel agencies in Cusco, including **Inkas Destination** (Urb. Zaguan del Cielo F-13, Cusco, tel. 084/50-5819, www.inkasdestination.com, US$20 day tour) and **Machu Picchu Travel** (Tomasa Tito C. Av. 1430, B-601, tel. 084/26-4242, www.machupicchuviajes.com, US$32 day tour).

Alternatively, you can also rent a car and visit the sites on your own. Major rental companies include **Hertz** (tel. 084/24-8800, www. inkasrac.com), **Avis** (tel. 01/207-6000, www. avisperu.com), and **Budget** (tel. 01/444-4546, www.budgetperu.com).

Tipón

One of the most elaborate and well-preserved examples of Inca agricultural terracing is **Tipón** (7am-5pm, US$4 or included in *boleto turístico*), which lies 22 kilometers south of Cusco and then another 4 kilometers up a valley via a switchbacking gravel road. The terraces, finely fitted and incredibly tall, run in straight lines to the head of a narrow valley. They are irrigated by an elaborate aqueduct that still runs from Pachatusan, the sacred mountain that looms over the site, whose name in Quechua means "cross beam of the universe." There are remains of a two-story house on the site and other ruins, possibly a fort, near the top of the aqueduct.

Rumicolca and Pikillacta

Though the Inca refused to admit it, much of their highway network and organizational know-how was based on the **Huari empire,** which spread across Peru AD 500-1000. An example of Huari engineering is **Rumicolca,** a huge aqueduct that sits on a valley pass on the side of the highway about 32 kilometers from Cusco. The Inca altered the construction, added a few stones, and converted it into a giant gateway to Cusco, though the remains of the old water channels can still be seen.

Nearby is **Pikillacta** (6am-6pm, US$4 or included in *boleto turístico*), the largest provincial outpost ever built by the Ayacucho-based Huari. This curious walled compound, with nearly 47 hectares (116 acres) of repetitive two-story square buildings, sprawls across the rolling grasslands with little regard to topography. The floors and walls, which are made of mud and stacked stone, were plastered with white gypsum and must have gleamed in the sun. But the Inca so thoroughly erased evidence of the Huari that little about their empire is known today. For many years Pikillacta was thought to be a huge granary, like the Inca site of Raqchi. But excavations have revealed evidence of a large population that left behind refuse layers as deep as three meters. Part of the city caught fire between AD 850 and 900, and the Huari withdrew from the city around the same time, bricking up the doors as they went. Whether they abandoned the city because of the fire or burned it as they left is unclear. Some historical information is available at the museum at the entrance. In the valley below is Lago Sucre and, even farther on, Lago Huacarpay. On the far shores of this lake are the ruins of **Inca Huáscar's summer palace,** much of which continues to be enjoyed today by locals as the Centro Recreacional Urpicanca, the local country club. From the shoulder of the highway, it is possible to see ceremonial staircases the Inca built into the landscape above the lake.

Andahuaylillas

The colonial village of Andahuaylillas, 37 kilometers south of Cusco, has a charming plaza shaded with red-flowered pisonay trees and an adobe church, **San Pedro** (8:30am-noon and 2pm-5pm Mon.-Sat., 8am-10am and 3pm-5pm Sun., free), which is built on the foundations from the early Inca empire. Though it's unremarkable on the outside, the doors open to a dazzling painted ceiling, frescoes, and wall-to-wall colonial paintings. This is the most finely decorated church in all of Cusco, probably in all of Peru, though its nickname, "Sistine Chapel of the Americas," is going a bit far. One highlight is a mural by Luis de Riaño depicting the road to heaven and the road to hell, with a full-blown display of all the respective rewards and punishments.

There is a well-known natural healing center just off the square, **Centro de Medicina Integral** (Garcilaso 514, tel. 084/25-1999, 9am-7pm daily, medintegral@hotmail.com), with a charming stone courtyard with gardens and plain rooms for US$8 per person. The center attracts a considerable number of overseas visitors for massage, meditation, harmonizing energy therapy, and other treatments.

Urcos

Driving through the main square of this small village, 47 kilometers south of Cusco, it is hard not to notice Urcos's tidy colonial church with a public balcony on the second floor and stone steps in front. On the outskirts of town, there is the beautifully decorated chapel at Huaro, which is on a hilltop overlooking a small lake. According to legend, Inca Huáscar threw a huge gold necklace into these waters to protect the treasure from the Spaniards. The story seemed probable enough that *National Geographic* funded an exploration of the lake's bottom by scuba divers—though thick mud prevented them from finding anything.

Raqchi

Raqchi (119 kilometers south of Cusco, 8am-6pm, US$3) is a ceremonial center built by Inca Pachacútec that offers a fascinating glimpse into the ambition and organizational skills of his budding empire. Rising above the humble village of Raqchi, a wall of adobe nearly 15 meters high and 90 meters long sits on a carved Inca wall. This was once the center of a huge hall, the roof of which was supported by adobe columns—one of which has been restored—on either side. On the side are six identical squares, each with six stone buildings, which probably served as a soldiers' barracks. But the most impressive part of Raqchi is line after line of round stone houses—200 in all—that once were filled with a gargantuan amount of quinoa, freeze-dried potatoes, and corn.

Sicuani

There are several nice lunch spots in Sicuani, 138 kilometers south of Cusco. At the **Casa Hacienda Las Tunas** (J. C. Tello 100, tel. 084/35-2480, US$4), there is a huge, scrumptious buffet of Peruvian food from 11:30am onward, when the Inka Express bus pulls in. There are good trout and meat dishes at the **Cebichería Acuarios** (Garcilazo de la Vega 141, 2nd Fl., tel. 084/80-9531, US$3) on the plaza.

Lake Titicaca and Canyon Country

S outhern Peru is the country's second travel destination after Cusco
and Machu Picchu. Breathtaking land-
scapes and geography, elegant and exquisite architecture, colorful people, and centuries-old traditions are all present in this

vast region where the Colca Canyon, the deepest on the planet, and Lake Titicaca, the highest navigable lake in the world, attract thousands of nature lovers and adventure seekers every year.

Arequipa is Peru's most elegant city and seems at times more like southern Spain than South America. It's a wonderful place to come to enjoy the extraordinary cuisine, stroll the elegant streets, and soak in the romance of this city. Laid-back and sunny, Arequipa is known as the "white city," as it is constructed entirely of white volcanic stone. Colonial churches and *casonas* line the street leading to the elegant Plaza de Armas, where a stately cathedral is flanked by palm trees and framed by three volcanoes: Chachani, Pichu Pichu, and Misti. The city's architectural highlight is the Monasterio de Santa Catalina, a maze of churches, plazas, and homes where cloistered nuns have lived since 1579.

Arequipa is surrounded by some of the country's most bizarre and remote landscapes: snowcapped volcanoes, lava fields, high-altitude deserts, and two of the deepest canyons on the planet. Stone villages, graced with co-lonial churches and elaborately carved altars, dot the rim of the Colca Canyon. The Río Colca leads into Colca Canyon, which is twice as deep as Arizona's Grand Canyon. Andean condors, the world's largest flying bird, can be watched soaring just meters away from those assembled at La Cruz del Cóndor, a morning lookout point on Colca Canyon.

In the southeast region of the country, Lake Titicaca, a massive expanse of water, sprawls across the middle of a Peruvian high plateau known as Meseta del Collao. While boating across the lake's sapphire waters, it is easy to understand why the Inca consid-ered this their sacred, foundational land-scape. Lake Titicaca is one of Peru's cradles of civilization, and staying with families—who speak either Quechua or Aymara—on

Previous: Islas Uros; woman weaving in Arequipa. **Above:** pack horses on a trek into the Colca Canyon.

Look for ★ to find recommended sights, activities, dining, and lodging.

Highlights

★ **Plaza de Armas:** Any tour of Arequipa should begin in Peru's most elegant urban square, with its neoclassical cathedral, arcades, palm trees, flowers, and fountains (page 191).

★ **Monasterio de Santa Catalina:** Since the 16th century, nuns have lived cloistered amid the timeless archways and chapels of this miniature city, built entirely of white volcanic stone (page 194).

★ **Monasterio de las Carmelitas Descalzas de Santa Teresa de Arequipa:** This 300-year-old Carmelite monastery, recently opened to the world, offers a rare collection of colonial art (page 195).

★ **La Cruz del Cóndor:** Nowhere can the Andean condor, the world's largest flying bird, be seen so reliably as from this spot perched on the rim of the Colca Canyon (page 219).

★ **Folklore Festivals:** Lake Titicaca is Peru's Folklore Capital, so don't miss a chance to take in one of the local festivals, such as Puno's Fiesta de Virgen de la Candelaria, when devils and angels dance in the streets (page 223).

★ **Kayaking Lake Titicaca:** The only way to see the emerald waters and snow-covered mountains of the world's highest navigable lake is by boat. Kayaking gives you the view from the water's edge (page 225).

★ **Islas Amantaní and Taquile:** Stay with a family on one of Lake Titicaca's islands to

immerse yourself in the lake's natural beauty and ancient lifestyle (page 235).

★ **Isla Suasi:** Lake Titicaca's only privately owned island boasts awesome views of Bolivia's Cordillera Real, a eucalyptus steam sauna, lakeside cottages, and gourmet cuisine (page 237).

Lake Titicaca and Canyon Country

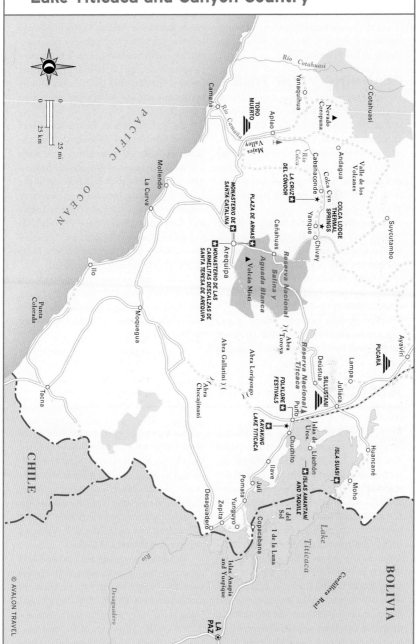

© AVALON TRAVEL

the lake's islands or peninsulas is a good way to experience ways of life that extend back thousands of years. It is also the best way to see the lake's bucolic scenery of winding country lanes, transparent waters, and Mediterranean-like sunlight.

PLANNING YOUR TIME

Many travelers take the bus from Lima to Arequipa and stop along the coast at Paracas, Ica, or Nasca before heading up to Lake Titicaca and Cusco. Bus companies in Peru offer extremely comfortable double-decker buses with nonstop itineraries and VIP service including 180-degree reclining seats, food, and Wi-Fi. Traveling by bus on these routes is completely safe.

Because of the dramatic changes in altitude between Peru's coast and highlands, staying at least two days in Arequipa before continuing to Puno or Cusco is a must. At an elevation of 2,300 meters, Arequipa is a good place to acclimatize before heading to Lake Titicaca (3,800 meters) or Cusco (3,300 meters).

Travel options between Arequipa and Puno—a five-hour drive—include a wide variety of good buses too, with comfy seats on a very good highway with breathtaking views of the Reserva Nacional Salinas y Aguada Blanca. The travel options between Puno and Cusco include the Andean Explorer, a deluxe train service with excellent views, or a high-quality tourist bus that has the advantage of stopping at a string of interesting ruins along the way. Travelers with less time can also fly between Arequipa, Juliaca (an hour from Puno), and Cusco.

Lake Titicaca has an increasingly large share of tourist traps these days. Puno, the gateway city, though quite grimy, is the starting point for most of the off-the-beaten-path adventures, such as kayaking in the lake and arranging homestays on Taquile or Amantaní islands, the lesser-known Anapia and Yuspique islands, or the Península de Capachica. Traveling by bus on either shore of Lake Titicaca and stopping in towns along the way is another interesting option.

The best time to visit is between March and November, the sunny winter months. Bring lots of warm clothing for the freezing nights and a wide-brimmed hat and sunscreen for the intense sun.

Arequipa

Arequipa has a long tradition of producing Peru's presidents, laureate writers, poets, and artists. Like other great coastal cities such as Trujillo and Lima, Arequipa was founded shortly after the Spanish conquest and has a wealth of convents, churches, colonial homes, and fine art. But Arequipa is the most subdued and relaxed of Peru's coastal cities. Constructed entirely of white *sillar* stone, the city gleams in the sun and is home of the most stunning Plaza de Armas in Peru. Some blocks behind the main square, light shifts delicately across the arches, streets, and homes inside the 400-year-old **Monasterio de Santa Catalina,** a citadel that could have been lifted right out of southern Spain.

Arequipa is for adventurers. One of the three volcanoes that tower above the city, **Chachani,** is the most attainable 6,000-meter mountain in Peru. A bit farther away lie some of the country's most extraordinary landscapes, including high-altitude deserts, a magical place called the **Valley of the Volcanoes,** and two of the world's deepest canyons: **Cotahuasi** and **Colca.**

The better known and more accessible of these two, the Colca Canyon, is five hours away. The canyon was only connected to the modern world in the late 1970s, and villagers living in the valley adhere to their centuries-old ways of life. This is one of the most spectacular and safe places in Peru for trekking and mountain biking. Rafting is also possible in the canyon and lower down on the Río Majes.

Arequipa is also for foodies, and Arequipeños are extremely proud of their culinary tradition. Products such as *cuy* (guinea pig), *rocoto* (a bell pepper-shaped chili), and *camarones* (freshwater prawns) are the foundation of a richly made, exquisite gastronomy, with recipes and cooking techniques traced back to pre-Hispanic times.

The Collagua people occupied the Arequipa area for millennia, as evidenced by the extensive terracing in the Colca valley, which was improved by the Inca. But the name for Arequipa apparently comes from Inca Mayta Cápac, who reportedly arrived at present-day Arequipa with his army and uttered the Quechua phrase *"ari, que pay"* meaning "yes, stay here." After conquering the area in the 15th century, the Inca began the practice of sacrificing children atop the area's highest volcanoes. **Juanita,** the mummy of a 13-year-old girl, captured worldwide attention in 1995 when she was discovered atop Volcán Ampato at 6,380 meters. Her mummy can now be seen in Arequipa's **Museo Santuarios Andinos** of the Santa María Catholic University.

The city of Arequipa was founded on August 15, 1540, by Captain Garcí Manuel de Carbajal after disease forced the Spaniards from an earlier settlement near Camaná, near the coast. Arequipa blossomed as a trade hub between Lima and southern Peru, including Cusco, Puno, and the rich silver mines in Potosí, in modern-day Bolivia.

Arequipa has a long history of earthquakes. More than 300 buildings collapsed after a major earthquake in 1588, which prompted King Charles V to issue a royal order limiting building height. The city was covered with ash by erupting Huaynaputina a few decades later and leveled by earthquakes roughly once per century—in 1687, 1788, 1869, 1958, and 1960. The latest earthquake, in 2001, measured 7.5 on the Richter scale and knocked down one of the towers of the cathedral, which has since been repaired.

SIGHTS
★ Plaza de Armas
The horizontal white facade of the neoclassical cathedral is nearly as long as a football field and features pointed bell towers, ornate square windows, and huge columns. *Portales* or arches take up the other three sides of the square, which overflows with palm trees, flowers, and a fountain in the middle topped

Plaza de Armas in Arequipa

Arequipa

Río Chili

LORETO

PUENTE SAN MARTIN

LA PLAZUELA

LIMA

SAN MARTÍN

LUNA PIZARRO

ANDRÉS MARTÍNEZ

QUEEN'S VILLA

CASAGRANDE

SALAVERRY

CASA DE AVILA

PARRA

LIMA

CRUZ VERDE

SUCRE

PUENTE

LA MERCED

CASA GOYENCHE

CONSUELO

FORY FAY

CASONA TERRACE HOTEL

PALACIO VIEJO

TACNA Y ARICA

MUSEO DE ARTE CONTEMPORANEO

To Terminal
Terrestre and
Terrapuerto

28 DE JULIO

ALVAREZ THOMAS

LA MERCED

TRISTAN

CASONA SOLAR HOTEL

QUINOZ

ANGAMOS

BONIFAZ

MALECON

SAN JUAN DE DIOS

TAMBO VIEJO

PIEROLA

ALTO DE LUNA

SAN CAMILO

VALDIVIA

SAN CAMILO MARKET

PERU

2 DE MAYO

To Puno

To Tradición Arequipeña

PIZARRO

CALLE NUEVA

JORGE CHAVEZ

SAN FRANCISCO

UGARTE

MORAL

BOLIVAR

PSJE. CATEDRAL

ZARATE EXPEDITIONS

COLONIAL TOURS

EL CAMINANTE

MONO BLANCO

SANTA CATALINA

CASONA DE SANTA CATALINA/IPERU/CHICHA

EL TURKO/COLIBRI/PALADAR1900

MONASTERIO DE SANTA CATALINA

LA CAFE ART

HATUNPA

LOS BALCONES DE MORAL Y SANTA CATALINA

CREPISIMO

POSADA DE SANCHO

CHACHAO

ZARATE ADVENTURES

MONTREAL

ISTANBUL

LIBRERIA EL LECTOR

HOSTAL LE FOYER

HOSTAL REGIS

MILLMA'S BABY ALPACA

GOVINDA

MIXTOS/FARREN'S

CASA TRISTÁN DEL POZO

LA CATEDRAL

PLAZA DE ARMAS

CASA ANDINA SELECT

IBERIC

© AVALON TRAVEL

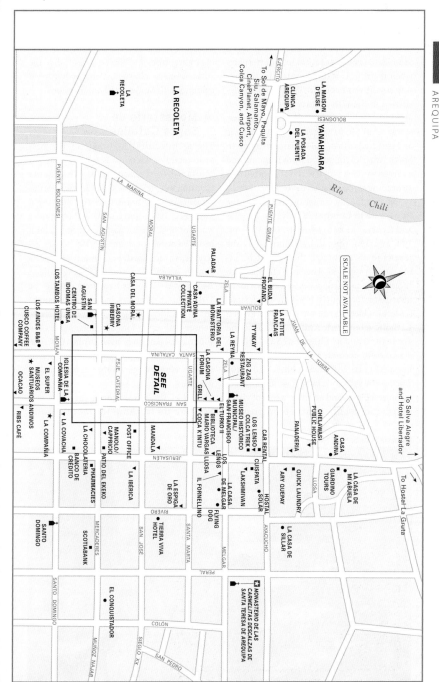

SCALE NOT AVAILABLE

LAKE TITICACA AND CANYON COUNTRY

Río Chili

To Sol de Mayo, Paquita Siu, Salamanto, CinePlanet, Colca Canyon, Airport, and Cusco

LA RECOLETA

YANAHUARA

LA RECOLETA

CLINICA AREQUIPA
LA MAISON D'ELISE
LA POSADA DEL PUENTE

BOLOGNESI

PUENTE BOLOGNESI
PUENTE GRAU
PUENTE BOLOGNESI

LA MARINA
SAN AGUSTIN
MORAL
UGARTE
VILLALBA
ZELA
BOLIVAR
JUAN DE LA TORRE

PALADAR

CASA DEL MORAL
SAN AGUSTIN
CENTRO DE IDIOMAS UNSA
CASONA IRIBERRY
LA TRATTORIA DEL MONASTERIO
CASA ADINA PRIVATE COLLECTION
EL BUDA PROFANO
LA PETITE FRANCAIS

LOS TAMBOS HOTEL
LOS ANDES B&B
CUSCO COFFEE COMPANY
OCACAO
MUSEOS SANTUARIOS ANDINOS
LA COMPAÑIA
RIBS CAFÉ

MORAN
PSJE. CATEDRAL
SANTA CATALINA
UGARTE
SAN FRANCISCO

SEE DETAIL

IGLESIA DE LA COMPAÑIA
LA COVACHA
LA CHOCOLATERIA
MANDALA
POST OFFICE
MANOLO/CAPRICIO
PATIO DEL EKEKO
PHARMACIES
BANCO DE CREDITO
EL SUPER

TY'NKAY
LA REYNA
LA CASONA FORUM
GRILL
ZIG ZAG RESTAURANT
ZELA

MUSEO HISTORICO MUNICIPAL/
SAN FRANCISCO
EL TURKO II
BIBLIOTECA MARIO VARGAS LLOSA
COCA K'INTU
LOS LEÑOS
LOS LENSO
COLCA TREK
LA CASA DE MELGAR

CAR RENTAL
CHELAWASI PUBLIC HOUSE
PANADERIA
CASA ANDINA

CUISPATA
LAKSHMIVAN
FLYING DOG
IL FORNELLINO

HOSTAL SOLAR

QUICK LAUNDRY
ARY QUEPAY
GIARDINO TOURS
LA CASA DE MI ABUELA
LA CASA DE SILLAR

LA IBERICA
LA ESPIGA DE ORO
TIERRA VIVA HOTEL
SCOTIABANK
SANTO DOMINGO
EL CONQUISTADOR

SAN JOSE
RIVERO
JERUSALEN
MERCADERES
SANTO DOMINGO
COLON
SAN PEDRO
MUÑOZ NAJAR
PERAL
SANTA MARTA
MELGAR
AYACUCHO
LLOSA

To Selva Alegre and Hotel Libertador

To Hostal La Gruta

MONASTERIO DE LAS CARMELITAS DESCALZAS DE SANTA TERESA DE AREQUIPA

with an usual character—some say it is a soldier, others an angel—known as *el tuturutu*.

La Catedral (tel. 054/21-3149, 10am-5pm Mon.-Sat.) is most beautiful in the afternoon when its front is stained orange by the setting sun. It was begun in 1544, partially destroyed in the 17th century by earthquakes, and then completely burned in an 1844 fire. It was rebuilt in its present neoclassical style and outfitted with one of the largest organs in South America, imported from Belgium, and a carved wooden pulpit that is supported by a swimming serpent-tailed devil.

On an opposite corner of the plaza is the **Iglesia de la Compañía** (Álvarez Thomas and General Morán, tel. 054/21-2141, 9am-1pm and 3pm-6pm daily), founded by the Jesuits in 1573, though the present building dates from 1650. The large church, with threes naves and a cupola, is best known for its mestizo facade (church fronts in which stone sculptures blend traditional Jesuit or Roman Catholic icons with Andean imagery and symbolism) and its **Chapel of San Ignacio de Loyola,** decorated with works from the mannerist master Bernardo Bitti (1550-1610). The nearby sacristy contains vivid murals of rainforest plants and animals, a sort of visual introduction for missionaries being prepared

for the Amazon. The Jesuits' minor cloisters—now a crafts market—lie a few doors down General Morán. There are gargoyles depicting figures from pre-Inca cultures and, in the adjacent major cloisters, elaborately carved columns with Mudejar (Islamic) designs.

★ Monasterio de Santa Catalina

The architectural highlight of the historic center of Arequipa is the 425-year-old **Monasterio de Santa Catalina** (Santa Catalina 301, tel. 054/22-1213, www.santa-catalina.org.pe, 10am-1pm and 3pm-6pm Mon.-Fri., 10am-1pm Sat., US\$12.50, guides work for tips). The monastery is a citadel built in 1579 entirely of *sillar* with 100 houses, 60 streets, three cloisters, a main square, a church, a cemetery, and a painting gallery. As many as 175 nuns lived here during the 17th and 18th centuries, including the daughters of wealthy families, who lived in private houses with up to four servants. More than 400 colonial paintings, mostly from the Cusco School, hang in a gallery that was once a shelter for widows, single mothers, and homeless women.

One of the most prominent nuns was **Sor Ana de los Ángeles Monteagudo**

Monasterio de Santa Catalina

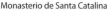

The Ice Maiden of Ampato

Juanita was only 12 when she walked up a staircase onto the snowy summit of Ampato (6,380 meters), accompanied by Inca priests intent on making a sacrifice to the mountain god. She wore a feathered headdress and an elaborate shawl and skirt, decorated with gold. An Inca priest gave her a narcotic potion, which probably put her to sleep after days of fasting—and then killed her with a precise blow to her head. Juanita was wrapped and surrounded by objects needed for the afterlife: pots of food, gold and wood figurines, textiles. The tomb was sealed by rocks and time.

After being frozen in ice for five centuries, Juanita's concealment ended when neighboring Volcán Sabancaya showered ash onto Ampato's summit, gradually melting snow to uncover a trail of curious objects that would lead archaeologists to the tomb. In 1989, climber Miguel Zárate discovered a stone ceremonial square on a ridge at 5,000 meters. On a subsequent trip, he found ceramics and bones at 5,800 meters, along with the remains of stairs. Miguel's father, Carlos Zárate Sandoval, found similar evidence before discovering a tomb atop Volcán Picchu in 1964. Joined by archaeologist Johan Reinhard, of Chicago's Field Museum of Natural History, Zárate returned in 1995 to retrace the path up Ampato. Near the summit, Miguel spotted a fan made of red feathers poking out of the snow. Juanita's stone tomb had melted out of the snow and slid downhill toward the crater, scattering the fan, gold plates, and three figurines. But the mummy was nowhere to be seen.

To locate Juanita, the climbers wrapped rocks in yellow plastic and rolled them downhill. Near where the rocks came to rest, they found Juanita, who was still wrapped in her Inca shawl. Miguel and Johan carried the 36-kilogram mummy to the base of Ampato and then on to the village of Cabanaconde, the city of Arequipa, and eventually Johns Hopkins University in Baltimore. The fact that the Inca climbed to 6,380 meters, sacrificed children in the snow, and then buried them in elaborate tombs made news around the world.

Archaeologists believe the Inca sacrificed children as part of *capac-cocha*, a ceremony to appease the gods, often in response to earthquakes, volcanic eruptions, droughts, or floods. Each child was carefully chosen (on the basis of beauty, innocence, and intelligence), taken to Cusco for a ritual, and then paraded through towns on the way to the mountain. Participation in *capac-cocha* was an honor because the child, after death, became a spiritual go-between for the people and their gods.

(1620-1686), who was elected Mother Prioress of the monastery. A series of miracles was attributed to this nun, even after her death, which made the nuns of the monastery write a petition to the Vatican to try to make her saint; the process continues.

Today, there are a few nuns living in modern quarters in the convent; they subsist on the visitor entry fees. The nuns were shut off from the rest of the city until 1985, when they became half-cloistered, meaning they can now leave and shop for food or visit relatives (up until that year, they spoke with their families only through screened windows). Photographers should visit late in the afternoon, when the light falls across the buildings at interesting angles.

★ Monasterio de las Carmelitas Descalzas de Santa Teresa de Arequipa

The **Monasterio de las Carmelitas Descalzas de Santa Teresa de Arequipa** (Melgar 303, tel. 054/28-1188, 9am-5pm Tues.-Sun., US$3.50, guides work for tips), founded in 1673, is not as ostentatious as Santa Catalina but is definitely fascinating. The monastery suffered considerable damage in the earthquake of 2001. This is when, after 295 years of total seclusion, and after restoring the religious site, the Carmelite nuns decided to open part of the convent to the world as a museum. The nuns still keep partially cloistered.

More than 300 works of art are exhibited in the long *sillar*-built hallways with decoratively painted walls. Carmelite nuns still meander during certain hours of the day, and thus visitors can hear them crossing galleries behind closed doors. If you happen to be there around noon, you will hear, but never see, 21 cloistered nuns and five novices singing the *Angelus* in Latin. A gallery exhibits techniques and materials used to make effigies, paintings, sculptures, murals, and metalwork during the 17th and 18th centuries.

Student tour guides, who deserve to be nicely tipped, are available and are fluent in English, French, German, and Portuguese. A nice shop in the front patio sells delicious pastries and empanadas baked by the nuns, books about the monastery, and rose-scented soap also made by the Carmelites.

Other Churches

Iglesia de San Francisco (Zela 103, tel. 054/22-3048, 9:30am-12:30pm and 3pm-6:30pm Mon.-Fri., US$1.75) is a 16th-century Franciscan church with a Latin cross shape and an unusual brick entranceway. The next-door convent, also designed in 1569 by Gaspar Báez, is worth visiting if it's open, as is the adjacent **Chapel of the Third Order,** built in 1777.

Other convents and churches worth visiting include **Santo Domingo** (Santo Domingo and Piérola, tel. 054/21-3511, 6:45am-noon and 3pm-7:45pm Mon.-Fri., 6:45am-9am and 3pm-7:45pm Sat., 6:45am-1pm Sun.), which was built around 1680 and has the oldest mestizo-style facade in the city. Another fine mestizo facade is to be found at **San Agustín** (San Agustín and Sucre, tel. 054/22-0066, 9am-1pm and 4pm-7pm Mon.-Fri., 9am-1pm Sat.), for which construction began in 1576. **La Merced** (3rd block of La Merced, tel. 054/21-3233, 7am-8am and 5pm-8pm Mon.-Sat., 6am-noon and 7pm-8pm Sun.) has fine carved wooden sculptures and a colonial library. **La Recoleta** (Recoleta 117, tel. 054/27-0966, 9am-noon and 3pm-5pm Mon.-Sat., US$1.50) is a Franciscan convent built in 1648 with beautiful cloisters, a library, and a museum of Amazonian artifacts

collected by missionaries. It is located across the Río Chili, about a 10-minute walk east from the Plaza de Armas.

Museums

One of Peru's most interesting museums, dedicated to the high-altitude archaeology pioneered by U.S. anthropologist Johan Reinhard, is the **Museo Santuarios Andinos** (La Merced 110, tel. 054/28-6613 or 054/21-5013, http://www.ucsm.edu.pe/museo-santuarios-andinos, 9am-6pm Mon.-Sat., 9am-3pm Sun., US$7, US$3.50 students). The museum contains the mummy of 13-year-old Juanita, an Inca human sacrifice victim recovered from the 6,312-meter summit of Ampato. The discovery was chosen by *Time* magazine as one of the world's 10 most important scientific discoveries of 1995.

There are also 18 other mummies discovered on volcano tops in Peru, Chile, and Argentina, along with the textiles, gold, wood carvings, and ceramics found in their tombs—a rare chance to see Inca art overlooked by both the Spaniards and modern-day grave robbers. Included in the entry fee is an obligatory, excellent one-hour tour that includes a documentary made by *National Geographic.*

Near San Francisco Church is the **Museo Histórico Municipal** (Plaza San Francisco, tel. 054/20-4801, 9am-5pm Mon.-Fri., 9am-3pm Sat., US$3.50), with a naval museum, a portrait gallery of Arequipa's elites, historical photographs of the city, and a series of caricatures and paintings by local artist Jorge Vinatea Reynoso (1900-1931).

The **Museo de Arte Contemporáneo** (Arica 201, near Arequipa, tel. 054/22-1068, 9am-2pm Mon.-Fri., US$1) is across from the old train station, housed in a 1900s mansion built for the manager of the Peruvian Corporation, the English train company that built most of Peru's rail lines from the 1870s onward. The museum has an interesting collection of 20th-century art, including photographs by the brothers Miguel and Carlos Vargas, who mentored Martín Chambi, the famed Cusco photographer. The museum showcases an interesting range of young local artists heavily influenced by the horrors of the Shining Path terrorist movement, along with a few paintings from Peru's most famous painters, such as Fernando de Szyszlo and Carlos Enrique Polanco, among others.

For fans of Peruvian author Mario Vargas Llosa, who received the Nobel Prize in literature in 2010, check out his personal library of some 45,000 of his books, donated to Arequipa, city of his birth. At the **Biblioteca Mario Vargas Llosa** (San Francisco 308, www.bibliotecaregionalmariovargasllosa.org, 8:30am-8:30pm Mon.-Sat., 9am-1pm Sun., bring your passport to be admitted), you can browse his collection.

Colonial Mansions

Arequipa, like Trujillo and Lima, has several colonial mansions, or *casonas,* worth visiting. Many of them were expropriated by President Juan Velasco in the late 1960s and have subsequently been converted into banks. The best of the houses is the **Casa del Moral** (Moral 318, tel. 054/21-0084, 9am-5pm Mon.-Sat., US$1.75, US$1.25 students), which was built around 1700 and takes its name from a graceful *moral* (mulberry tree) in a courtyard paved with *canto rodado* (river stones) and lined with beautiful ocher walls. The elaborate and dense carving over the front door includes pumas spitting out serpents, and the rooms are restored and decorated with period art and furniture.

Casona Iriberry (San Agustín, on the Plaza de Armas, tel. 054/20-4482, 10am-3pm and 4pm-8pm daily, free), has a series of graceful stone patios and spacious rooms built in 1793 and recently converted into the Centro Cultural Chávez de la Rosa. Try to read the messages carved above the doorways—one says, in old Spanish, "This house was made in the year 1743. I ask God that he who would live in it, recite an Our Father."

Casa Tristán del Pozo (San Francisco 108, tel. 054/21-5060, 9am-6pm Mon.-Fri., 9am-1pm Sat.) receives its name from General Domingo Tristán del Pozo—member of one of Arequipa's most prominent and powerful families—who commissioned it in 1738. The house has been converted into a cultural center and offices for the BBVA Banco Continental and includes a stately portico, entryway, and double patios.

Over the door of **Casa Goyeneche** (La Merced 201, tel. 054/21-1101, ext. 223, 9:15am-1:30pm and 2:30pm-4pm Mon.-Fri.) is an ecclesiastical coat of arms of Arequipa's bishop José Sebastián Goyeneche (1784-1872). This home, with a large and graceful patio, is occupied by the Banco Central de Reserva del Perú and contains a good collection of paintings from the Cusco School.

Yanahuara

A jaunt across the Río Chili for lunch at La Nueva Palomino restaurant can easily be combined with a digestive stroll, a few blocks north, to the charming square of the Yanahuara neighborhood. It is graced with stone archways, views of Misti, and the 18th-century **Iglesia San Juan Bautista** (7am-6pm Mon.-Fri., 7am-5:30pm Sat., 6am-11am and 6:30pm-7:30pm Sun.). The church's walls are nearly two meters thick, and the roof's arch was built with a flat shape to accommodate the relative weakness of *sillar* (this shape was found to be stronger than the perfect arch). The elaborately carved facade is considered one of Peru's masterpieces of religious art. Look closely to find a cherub with feathered crowns, which is a pre-Hispanic symbol of power outlawed in Peru during colonial times.

About five minutes away by taxi (US$1.50) is the **Mirador de Carmen Alto,** a lookout point that offers views of all the volcanoes, the city of Arequipa, and a *sillar* quarry used by the Spaniards. There are Collagua terraces nearby, a few resident alpacas and llamas, and a small snack bar.

La Mansión del Fundador

A restored church and home, **La Mansión del Fundador** (Huasacache, 6.5 kilometers

The Republic of Arequipa

Arequipeños stick out in Peru, much in the same way that it is hard to miss a Texan in the United States. Arequipeños seem more Spanish, more confident, and have a fierce regional pride that manifests itself in passports for the "Republic of Arequipa." No one jokes, however, about the several revolutions that have been plotted here over the last two centuries. Nor about the fact that the mayor of Arequipa, as recently as 2001, publicly discussed secession and that two of Peru's most controversial recent historical figures—Shining Path head Abimael Guzmán and Fujimori henchman Vladimiro Montesinos—both hail from here.

One theory behind Arequipeñismo—as the local braggadocio is called—is population-based. There have always been more Spaniards in Arequipa. In the mid-18th century, for instance, there were 22,000 Spaniards out of a total population of 37,000 (Lima, at the same time, had only 18,000 Spaniards out of a total population of 62,000). Arequipa received even more European immigrants after independence, when numerous English families settled in Arequipa and set up trading houses for the area's alpaca wool.

Probably the main reason for Arequipa's distinct feel is its geographic and economic isolation from the rest of the country. It is closer to Bolivia and Chile than to Lima, for instance, and Arequipeños have long complained that they are neglected by the centralized powers that be in Lima. The huge haciendas that dominated other parts of Peru have always been balanced by small landowners and merchants who have depended on an internal southern economy among Tacna, Moguegua, Mollendo, and Puno—not to mention La Paz, Bolivia, and Arica, Chile.

from Arequipa, tel. 054/44-2460, www.lamansiondelfundador.com, 9am-5pm daily, US$5), 20 minutes outside town, was first owned by Garcí Manuel de Carbajal, who founded Arequipa in 1540. The house later became a Jesuit retreat before being bought and restored by the city's illustrious Archbishop José Sebastián de Goyeneche in the early 1800s. The church is plain, with an arching stone ceiling, and the home has a large patio flanked with rooms filled with original paintings and furniture. A taxi from Arequipa costs around US$4 one-way.

Sabandía

This pleasant country town has a 17th-century flour mill, **El Molino de Sabandía** (8 kilometers southeast of Arequipa, cell tel. 959-839-545, www.elmolinodesabandia.com, 9am-6pm daily, US$3.50), which still turns under the power of water. A bit farther down the road, the hamlet of **Paucarpata,** surrounded by Collagua terracing, is a favorite weekend lunch spot with locals. *Combis* head frequently to Sabandía from Independencia and Paucarpata or Jorge Chávez and Víctor

Lira (US$1) in Arequipa, or a taxi charges around US$5 for the 15-minute trip.

ENTERTAINMENT AND EVENTS
Nightlife

Arequipa has great nightlife, with ground zero on the streets San Francisco, Zela near Plaza San Francisco, and Santa Catalina. Walk down these streets to survey the options, as bars start up and shut down constantly and vary depending on the night of the week. **Déjà Vu** (San Francisco 319-B, tel. 054/22-1904, www.dejavuaqp.com, 9am-close Mon.-Sat., 6pm-close Sun.) is popular with young tourists and Arequipeños lured by its second floor terrace with comfy seating and good views, as well as its crowded dance floor.

A better option is next door at the **La Casona Forum** (San Francisco 317, tel. 054/20-4294, www.casonaforum.com), which is home to a variety of bars and discotheques, including **Zero Pub & Pool** (cell tel. 959-174-964, www.zeropub-pool. com, 6:30pm-1am Mon.-Sat.), on the second floor, which is a glitzy rock-and-roll pub with pool tables and live music. **Forum** (tel. 054/20-4294, 10pm-2am Mon.-Sat.), on the first floor, is Arequipa's best discotheque for salsa and other Latin rhythms; it gets going after 11:30pm, offering different levels and even a waterfall. Another option for salsa, or bachata, is **Latino Salsa Club** (cell tel. 987-332-110, 10pm-close Fri.-Sat.), which is more intimate than Forum. **Club 80s** (cell tel. 958-012-123, 6pm-1am Mon.-Sat.), for drinks and chatting, and retro music, of course. **Terrase** (from 6:30pm Mon.-Sat.), a karaoke bar, and **Chill Out** (from 7pm Mon.-Sat.), a bar with sofas, round out the mix.

Nearby are several other bars, including **Istanbul** (San Francisco 231A, tel. 054/21-4622, 6pm-4am daily), with charming sofas on the first floor and a nook upstairs, the perfect place for an early-evening drink. Locals hang out at **Ad Libitum** (San Francisco 233, tel. 054/28-5814, 6pm-4am daily), a dimly lit, laid-back place with a wide range of affordable cocktails.

An excellent place for craft beer and huge burgers that can compete with anything back home is **Chelawasi Public House** (102 Campo Redondo, tel. 054/23-2778, 4pm-10:30pm Tues.-Thurs., 4pm-11pm Fri., noon-11pm Sat., noon-7pm Sun.). For a beer, try the Coca Golden or the Dark Jesus.

A great live music and drinks place is **La Café Art Montréal** (Ugarte 210, tel. 054/20-6652, 4pm-late daily). This swanky colonial space, built of *sillar* in the 19th century and divided up into rooms with vaulted ceilings, swings with Cuban protest, Latin rock, and other live music Wednesday to Saturday. There is a light menu including burritos, guacamole, pizza, pastas, and crepes.

If you want to see a movie on a big screen, go to the eight-theater **CinePlanet** (Ejército 1009, Real Plaza, tel. 054/60-3480, www.cineplanet.com.pe, US$5). Movie times and options can be found in *El Pueblo*, the local newspaper, or on the theater's website.

Arequipa has a lean but worthwhile cultural calendar that is promoted in the newspaper *El Pueblo* and in *El Búho* (www.elbuho.

pe), an extremely smart weekly publication that is a good source of information as well. **Teatro Municipal** (Mercaderes 239, tel. 054/21-3298, 7pm daily, free) has weekly concert listings at the door, with live string orchestras, big bands, guitar ensembles, and other Latin groups. Other exhibits and performances are held at **Instituto Cultural Peruano Alemán** (Ugarte 207, tel. 054/21-8567, www.icpa.org.pe), **Centro Cultural Peruano Norteamericano** (Melgar 109, tel. 054/39-1020, www.cultural.edu.pe), and **Alianza Francesa** (Santa Catalina 208, tel. 054/21-5579, www.afarequipa.org.pe).

Festivals

Arequipa's main festival is **Founders Day** (Aug. 15), which includes a week of fireworks, parades, dancing, and bullfights. One of Peru's more famous pilgrimages is the **Virgen de Chapi** (May 1). Pilgrims trek 45 kilometers, about 15 hours, from Arequipa to the small town of Chapi, which is blanketed with flowers by day and lit by fireworks at night. Other local festivals include **Virgen de la Candelaria** in Cayma (Feb. 2), the **bullfighting festival** in Characato (June 24), and the **Virgen del Rosario** in Yanahuara (Oct. 8).

SHOPPING

Arequipa continues to thrive, as it has for centuries, as the center of Peru's wool industry. Wools and fine clothing shops are all over town, and for the real aficionados, the main wool producers can arrange visits to factories and highland ranches with alpacas and vicuñas. Apart from wool products, the city produces high-quality jewelry and chocolates.

Shopping Centers

Across the street from the Monasterio de Santa Catalina is the **Casona Santa Catalina** (Santa Catalina 210, tel. 054/28-1334, www.santacatalina-sa.com.pe, 9am-9pm daily). Once a colonial house, this building now houses a variety of upscale shops, including

Don't Look a Camelid in the Mouth

The most honored gift, and most common form of tribute, among the Inca was not gold but finely woven garments of alpaca or, even better, vicuña wool. A relative of the camel, the llama was also the Inca's only beast of burden and their primary source of meat. These high-altitude camelids made the Inca empire possible.

Arequipa, surrounded by high-altitude grasslands, has been the center of Peru's lucrative wool industry since colonial times and even before. Now that alpaca ranches are spreading across the United States like wildfire, some of Arequipa's main wool exporters—such as Grupo Inca and Michell—occasionally lead tours up to highland alpaca ranches. Participants help round up and shear wild vicuñas and learn how to spin wool and loom-weave.

The finest fiber of any wool-producing animal comes from the **vicuña**, which was brought back from the verge of extinction in the 1960s. Each of these camelids is sheared every three or four years and only yields a mere 250 grams of wool. Shearing vicuñas was only made legal again in 1995, and the wool remains highly regulated. Clothing made from their wool, considered the world's most luxurious animal fiber, can cost several thousand dollars. The Inca would have been pleased—they only let nobles wear vicuña clothing.

The vicuña herds typically consist of one male who walks in front of a harem of up to six females, though it is not uncommon to see mixed herds of up to 50 vicuñas. A good place to see them in herds is Pampa Cañahuas, en route to Colca Canyon from Arequipa.

The largest camelid, with fiber nearly as fine as the vicuña's (around 16 microns), is the **guanaco.** Like the vicuña, it is difficult to domesticate and has a thin orange-brown wool of incredible fineness. There are only 500,000 guanacos, mostly in the highlands of Chile and Argentina, and their wool is highly regulated on the international market.

The **alpaca** is a whole other animal. For starters, there are more than 10 million alpacas in the world—more than three-quarters of them in Peru. Their wool has a delightful range of browns, blacks, whites, and grays. The wool fiber also has a dramatic range of fineness, which is carefully measured by merchants in determining the value of the wool.

All over Peru's highlands, women can be seen weaving in fields as they tend a flock of grazing alpacas, which have a sheep-like abundance of wool that fluffs up even around their eyes. The *suris* (long-haired alpacas) can produce over three kilograms of wool every two years. On the other hand, grilled alpaca meat has been popping up in restaurants around Peru, overtaking llama as the meat of choice.

Because **llamas** have much coarser wool than alpacas, they are used for their meat and as pack animals. Llamas and alpacas can intermingle—the result is called a *huarizo*—and can be difficult to tell apart. But llamas are larger, have much less hair, and have a small tail that sticks out in the back. Dried llama meat, a traditional Andean food, is called *charqui*—perhaps the only Quechua word to have made its way into the English lexicon (as beef "jerky").

A final word of caution: Llamas and alpacas, even the ones with pink tassels tied on their ears, are not always friendly creatures. They have a well-deserved reputation for spitting grass loogies at anyone who comes too close. If the cheeks puff out and the ears flatten, back off.

Gastón Acurio's Chicharestaurant. If you are looking to buy alpaca products, jewelry, or art, this could be your one-stop shopping.

Patio de Ekeko (Mercaderes 141, tel. 054/21-5861, www.elekeko.pe, 10am-9pm Mon.-Sat., 11am-8pm Sun.) is a touristy complex near the square. Its multiple floors are filled with classy crafts, alpaca shops, a high-end jewelry store, an Internet café, a restaurant, and even a big-screen cinema showing documentaries on Arequipa.

Alpaca Wool

Michell & Cia (www.michell.com.pe) is the world's leading producer and exporter of alpaca fiber. The company started in 1931 and now has a top-end outlet chain named **Sol Alpaca** (Santa Catalina 120B, tel.

054/20-2525, www.solalpaca.com, 8am-1pm and 1:45pm-4:30pm Mon.-Fri.), with stores in Cusco, Lima, Santiago de Chile, and Bogotá. In Arequipa, it has other locations, including **Mundo Alpaca** (Alameda San Lázaro 101, tel. 054/20-2525). Sweaters, scarves, coats, and even carpets are sold, with people on hand to demonstrate the hand sorting of alpaca fiber and loom weaving. At the shop, ask about a tour of the factory, located in Parque Industrial.

Grupo Inca (www.grupoinca.com) is a series of companies that also produce and export alpaca fiber. **Inca Tops** (Francisco la Rosa 120, Parque Industrial, tel. 054/60-2500, www.incatops.com, 8am-12:30pm and 2:30pm-5:30pm Mon.-Fri., 9am-noon Sat.) sells world-class tops and yarns of alpaca wool and cotton. **Incalpaca TPX** (Juan Bustamante s/n, Tahuaycani neighborhood, tel. 054/60-3000, www.incalpaca.com, 9:30am-7pm Mon.-Fri., 10:30am-3:30pm Sat.), on the other hand, produces the finest cloth, outerwear, knitwear, and home items. It is the only company in Peru licensed to sell vicuña wool. A vicuña scarf can cost US$1,250, while a coat will run over US$7,000. That is still a lot less than buying vicuña abroad, where a men's sports coat can cost US$21,000. It has shops named **Kuna** (Patio del Ekeko; Casona Santa Catalina; Libertador Hotel; Arequipa Airport; www.kuna.com.pe), and you can visit the factory (Condor 100, Tahuaycani), but you need to set it up a week or so in advance.

Jewelry and Antiques

For jewelry, **Ilaria** (Mercaderes 139-141, Patio del Ekeko, tel. 054/28-7749, tel., 9:45am-9pm daily) has high-end jewelry and wood sculptures decorated with silver. **L. Paulet** (workshop Urb. La Marina D-25, Cayma district, tel. 027/22-5098, www.lpaulet.com, 9am-1pm or 4pm-6pm Mon.-Fri.) specializes in gold and silver handmade jewelry as well as hand-knit and handwoven baby alpaca textiles. It is best to call ahead as visiting hours may change.

There are several antiques shops clustered on Santa Catalina. **Alvaro Antiq**

(Santa Catalina 204, tel. 054/22-9103, 9am-8pm daily), **El Anticuario** (Ugarte 213, tel. 054/23-4474, 9am-7pm Mon.-Sat.), and **Arte Colonial** (Santa Catalina 312, tel. 054/21-4887, 10am-8pm Mon.-Fri., 10am-5pm Sun.) all sell everything from small crafts to antique furniture. A wide range of inexpensive crafts can be found at or around the **Fundo de Fierro** handicraft market, on the corner of the Plaza San Francisco.

Chocolate

La Ibérica (Jerusalén 136, tel. 054/21-5670, www.laiberica.com.pe), Arequipa's century-old chocolate company, produces the best bitter chocolate in the country. It has shops on Mercaderes, at the Saga Falabella Mall, and at the airport. The dark fondant bars are irresistible, and the small chewable toffees come in five flavors. A newer favorite is **Chaqchao Organic Chocolates** (Santa Catalina 204, tel. 054/23-4572, www.chaqchao.wordpress.com, 11am-9pm Tues.-Sat.), which has a nice second-floor café and several different chocolate workshops (from US$15 pp).

Bookstores

Along with Lima, Arequipa has the largest concentration of bookstores in Peru, the best of which is **Librería el Lector** (San Francisco 213, tel. 054/28-8677, www.libreriaellector.com, 9am-8pm Mon.-Sat.), with European charm. Owner Fernando Rosas has a great collection of books on Peruvian culture—including many in English—and on archaeology, politics, cooking, music, flowers, photography, and travel. The shop also has an English-language fiction section and a book exchange. There are several other bookshops along San Francisco near the plaza. **Crisol** (Ejercito 1009, Cayma, tel. 054/27-5653, www.crisol.com.pe, 10am-10pm daily), one of Peru's chain bookstores, also has a location at the Real Plaza mall.

RECREATION

Colca Canyon and other stunning areas near Arequipa, like the Majes Valley, are one big adventure playground. There is a huge range of options, including Class III-V rafting, mountain biking, trekking, climbing, and good agencies to make it happen. Before you go, remember the altitude: Acclimatize in Arequipa.

Climbing

The closest volcano to Arequipa, **Misti** (5,830 meters) can be climbed in two days, one night. There are a few routes, but the easiest begins from a road that reaches 3,400 meters. From here, climbers ascend six or seven hours to make base camp around 4,700 meters before climbing at dawn up Misti's snowy south side. It is possible to be back in Arequipa by the afternoon.

The easiest 6,000-meter peak—perhaps in all of Latin America, maybe in the world— is **Chachani** (6,095 meters). Three hours of driving from Arequipa brings climbers to 5,100 meters, from which they ascend two more hours to base camp. The summit is another five or six hours farther the following morning. Although it's possible to climb Chachani in a single day from Arequipa, it seems safer (and more enjoyable) to plan on at least two.

Another popular mountain that can be combined with a trekking circuit through Colca Canyon is **Ampato** (6,312 meters). A car can be driven to 4,900 meters, from where climbers ascend for two hours to base camp at 5,200 meters. The summit is then another six hours. Another route from Cabanaconde, in the Colca Canyon, begins at an Inca ceremonial center at 5,000 meters elevation near the northeast side of the volcano. The summit is about seven hours from here, and the neighboring volcanoes of **Sabancaya** (5,995 meters) and **Hualca Hualca** (6,095 meters) can also be climbed from this camp. Colca is also the launching point for **Mismi** (5,597 meters), the source of the Amazon.

Coropuna (6,425 meters), Peru's second-highest peak, is rarely climbed because it is 10 hours from Arequipa. But its slopes are gentler than those of many of the other volcanoes, and it is on the way to, and sandwiched by, Cotahuasi and Valley of the Volcanoes.

Most of Arequipa's volcanoes are gentle and relatively free of ice, so few climbers rope up, though crampons might be required for the summit push. Although not as technical as the mountains around Huaraz, any mountain near 6,000 meters elevation demands caution and experience. Only go without a guide if you have climbing

climbing the Misti volcano that overlooks Arequipa

experience and have done your homework ahead of time.

There are several adventure agencies in downtown Arequipa. **Zárate Adventures** (Jerusalén 505-A, tel. 054/20-2461, www. zarateadventures.com), founded by legendary mountain climber Carlos Zárate, offers guided expeditions to all the local volcanoes, along with a range of treks, and its services include food and transportation. The agency offers trips to Misti, Chachani, and Colca-Ampato. There is an interesting antiques shop in the courtyard where the agency is located. **Colca Trek** (Jerusalén 401-B, tel. 054/20-6217, www.colcatrek.com.pe) can arrange customized treks to Colca as well as part-biking, part-trekking expeditions or a biking countryside tour. The shop has the best range of camping gear for sale and rent in the area, and it also rents bikes and usually has white gas. Both **Land Adventures** (La Peña A-20, Sachaca, tel. 054/66-5548, www.landadventures.net) and **Carlitos Tours** (Urb. Nuevo Peru M-15, Paucarpata, tel. 054/33-8255, www.carlitostours.com), led by experienced guide and chef Arturo Carlos Muñoa, get good reviews for guided treks in the Colca.

Trekking

The areas around Arequipa, such as Colca Canyon, offer fabulous trekking for those who like views of canyons and volcanoes and a hot, sunny climate. Unlike in the more popular Cordillera Blanca, trekkers have no problem getting off the beaten path and need not worry much about robbery or other safety issues. The views range from immense canyon rims to wide valleys studded with volcanoes. The villages, isolated for centuries, are friendly and unforgettable.

Zárate Adventures (Jerusalén 505-A, tel. 054/20-2461, www.zarateadventures.com), **Carlitos Tours** (Urb. Nuevo Peru M-15, Paucarpata, tel. 054/33-8255, www.carlitostours.com), and **Colca Trek** (Jerusalén 401-B, tel. 054/20-6217, www.colcatrek.com.pe) offer the best organized treks and are glad to answer questions for those going on their own. Topographical maps can be bought at the South American Explorers clubhouses in Cusco and Lima, or the Instituto Geográfico Militar in Lima (or, in a pinch, copied in Arequipa). Ask for detailed information—especially concerning the availability of water—at each village you pass. Apart from running out of water, the main things to watch for are sunburn and getting cold at night. Bring a wide-brimmed hat, sunscreen for the day, a warm sleeping bag, and a jacket.

Rafting and Kayaking

Expert boaters rank **Cotahuasi Canyon** up with Cusco's Río Apurímac, another extraordinarily beautiful wilderness river with a steady series of Class IV rapids. Colca, on the other hand, is a steeper and more closed canyon with unavoidable Class V rapids. Rafting guides prefer Cotahuasi over Colca because there are portages around all the Class V rapids, the hillsides offer more ruins and terracing, and the river is doable even for first-time rafters. That doesn't mean, however, that it's not hard.

The best rafting operator in Arequipa is **Cusipata** (Jerusalén 402A, tel. 054/20-3966, www.cusipata.com), run by Gian Marco Vellutino. From April to December, Cusipata has daily three-hour trips (US$35 pp) down the Río Chili, which tumbles through Arequipa and includes one Class IV chute. Ask if the agency is offering trips down other rivers.

Cycling

The standard Colca mountain-bike route begins at Patapampa, at 4,950 meters elevation, and drops into the Colca Valley at Chivay at 3,650 meters. Cyclists follow dirt roads along the north side of the river and cross the bridge to Yanque. The third day includes the Cruz del Cóndor and Maca, and ends in Cabanaconde. **Cusipata** (Jerusalén 402A, tel. 054/20-3966, www.cusipata.com) can also design extraordinary routes in Cotahuasi and the Valley of the Volcanoes. Cusipata also rents bikes. **Land Adventures** (La Peña A-20, Sachaca, tel. 054/66-5548, www.landadventures.net) offers a technically demanding ride (US$85 pp, minimum 2 people) 2,500 vertical meters down from a station at Chachani (4,800 meters) to Arequipa.

Tour Guides and Agencies

The standard Arequipa tours are the city tour and the countryside tour, both about three hours. The city tour includes Yanahuara church and lookout, the Compañía church, and the Santa Catalina Monastery—ask for your guide to visit colonial homes as well. The country tour includes the mill at Sabandía and the Mansión de Fundador. The most reputable agency is **Giardino Tours** (Jerusalén 604-A, tel. 054/20-0100, www.giardinotours.com), run by the same owners as La Casa de mi Abuela in Arequipa and La Casa de Mama Yacchi in Colca Canyon. Another agency with a good reputation is **Colonial Tours** (Santa Catalina 115-B, tel. 054/28-6868, www.colonialtours-peru.com). Another option is **Ricketts Turismo** (Moral 229, tel. 054/22-2208, www.rickettsturismo.com).

FOOD

Arequipeños are proud of their cuisine, and rightly so, but besides traditional food, there are innovative chefs whipping up Turkish, French, Japanese, Thai, Moroccan, and Italian food in the city. Additionally, Arequipa has a hidden culinary gem: *picanterías,* holes-in-the-wall, which range from very modest to fancier and are where the real Arequipeño cuisine is made and can be enjoyed. While in town, don't miss the *chupe de camarones* (prawn chowder) and *rocoto relleno* (baked stuffed chilies).

Picanterías

The name refers to a place where spicy food is sold (*picante* means spicy), even if all meals are not necessarily hot. The origin of these eateries can be traced back to at least 19th-century Arequipa, where artists, bohemians, and foodies would gather for a bite during the day or Sunday lunch. *Picanterías* still hold

a food vendor in the Yanahuara neighborhood

much of Arequipa's culinary essence. They only open for lunch.

Sabor Caymeño (Plaza de Armas de Cayma 112, tel., 6am-4pm Mon.-Fri., 3am-4pm Sat., 3am-6pm Sun., US$3-8) is probably one of the last genuine *picanterías* in the city, located in the upper district of Cayma. The unusual opening hours are because the featured dish is *adobo*—macerated pieces of pork in corn beer, served in a soupy sauce in which you dip crusty bread—a typical meal eaten after a night of partying, and this is one of the best places to try it. But this eatery, owned by friendly María Meza, who is still in charge of the cooking, also has *caldo* (meat broth), *costillares* (fried ribs with potatoes), and smaller appetizers. As in other *picanterías,* the place is open as long as there is food.

La Lucila (Grau 147, Sachaca, tel. 054/20-5348, www.picanterialalucila.com, 11am-close daily, US$3-6), on the outskirts of Arequipa in Sachaca, is the most celebrated of all *picanterías,* due to its former owner, the late Lucila Salas Valencia (1917-2012), a legend of Arequipa's culinary heritage. Doña Lucila cooked on a woodstove in an old artisan-made kitchen where you could see guinea pigs running between your legs. While some things have changed, the kitchen is still essentially the same. Lucila's five children, who now manage the place, are trying to preserve tradition in the food-making, but some complain about a drop in quality and slow service. Specialties include *rocoto relleno*, duck, *camarones, cuy chactado* (fried guinea pig), and a soup du jour. Wash it down with a *chicha*.

La Nueva Palomino (Pasaje Leoncio Prado 122, Yanahuara, tel. 054/25-2393, noon-5pm Wed.-Mon., US$6-10) has been in business for three generations. The Palomino family, made up of savvy cooks, has opened other restaurants with similar names; for example, La Palomino, on the corner of Leoncio Prado and Misti, is much more traditional and owned by a cousin. The menu includes boiled lima beans with mint and *chupe de camarones* (prawn chowder). Portions are huge, so order a few dishes and share.

Tradición Arequipeña (Dolores 111, tel. 054/42-6467, www.tradicionarequipena.pe, noon-4pm daily, US$5-10) is less traditional but still well reputed for its food. The menu includes *adobo,* 11 versions of *camarones,* and a range of *chupes* (soups). Food is served either indoors under bamboo ceilings or in a cactus-lined garden.

Over 100 years old, **Sol de Mayo** (Jerusalén 207, Yanahuara, tel. 054/25-4148, 11am-6pm daily, US$7-10) is the result of a long road of transformation from hole-in-the-wall to sophisticated restaurant. Still a *picantería* at heart, this eatery is probably the most popular with visitors. Try the *ocopa con queso frito, rocoto relleno,* and *camarones.* The service is excellent.

Peruvian

Peru is home to potatoes, with some 4,000 different varieties that fed the Inca empire before nourishing people around the globe. In Arequipa, **Hatunpa** (Ugarte 208, tel. 054/21-2918, 12:30pm-9:30pm Mon.-Sat., US$5-8)

is passionate about potatoes, paying homage to the humble spud with delicious results. Its dishes include some of Peru's lesser-known native varieties, like the purple-colored Leona potato, with a range of toppings such as *lomo saltado, aji de gallina,* and stroganoff.

Ary Quepay (Jerusalén 502, cell tel. 959-672-922, www.aryquepay.com, 12:30pm-10pm daily, US$8-13) is a good traditional Peruvian restaurant in the historic center, despite being very touristy. The varied menu features Arequipeño cuisine as well as dishes from other regions in Peru. Live folkloric music starts at 6:30pm daily.

Peruvian Fusion and Fine Dining

With a menu initially designed by Peru's iconic chef Gastón Acurio and a location in the Monasterio de Santa Catalina, **La Trattoria del Monasterio** (Santa Catalina 309, tel. 054/20-4062, www.latrattoriadelmonasterio.com, noon-3pm and 7pm-11pm Mon.-Sat., noon-3pm Sun., US$10-15) was bound for success. But the clean white tablecloths, attentive service, and precise dishes have closed the deal. Specialties include *tagliolini* with lamb *ragù,* prawn risotto with artichokes, and the extraordinary *rocoto relleno de camarones* with *pastel de papas* (baked potato cake). Owner Verónica Luque also runs a café inside the Santa Catalina Monastery and owns Cappricio.

For a romantic evening, head to **Salamanto** (León XIII, H-11 Cayma, tel. 054/34-0607, www.salamanto.com, 4pm-midnight Mon.-Sat., US$10-14), a new option launched by local chef Paúl Perea, who studied in cooking in Lima and wines in Buenos Aires. Perea's philosophy aims for modern cuisine with a creative twist inspired by local ingredients and traditional recipes. Options include seven-course menu (US$35) that starts off with ceviche, followed by colorful dishes featuring everything from stuffed peppers and prawns to guinea pig and alpaca.

Zíngaro Restaurant (San Francisco 309, tel. 054/21-7662, www.zingaro-restaurante.

com, 11:30am-11pm Mon.-Sat., noon-10pm Sun. US$8-12) is a highly acclaimed restaurant, based in a colonial house, that serves an interesting fusion of Peruvian and Mediterranean gastronomy. Order anything from Novoandino selections or a *chupe de camarones*. Don't miss the delicious coca or *rocoto* sours.

Zig Zag (Zela 210, tel. 054/20-6020, www.zigzagrestaurant.com, noon-11pm daily, US$5-12) is a cozy place right across from Plaza San Francisco, with house specialties such as stone-cooked alpaca, ostrich, and lamb, served carpaccio-style or sizzling on a stone slab. Its claim to fame is an iron spiral staircase supposedly built by famed French architect Gustave Eiffel.

Chicha por Gastón Acurio (Santa Catalina 210, Int. 105, tel. 054/28-7360, www.chicha.com.pe, noon-11pm Mon.-Sat., noon-8pm Sun., US$6-15) is a popular restaurant in town with a very chic atmosphere and impeccable service. The food can be an explosion of flavors for the uninitiated in world cuisine, but the result of a fusion between Arequipeño, Mediterranean, and Asian flavors can be a blast. Cocktails are superb and desserts even better.

Paladar 1900 (San Francisco 227, tel. 054/22-6295, www.paladar1900.com.pe, noon-midnight daily, US$10-18) is a beautiful restaurant that gives you the option of eating inside under arched ceilings or outside in a courtyard decorated with flowers. The menu is fusion, and options include everything from sushi to an alpaca steak with quinoa risotto.

International

Middle Eastern food is not easy to find in Peru, but in Arequipa it exists due to a century-old tradition of immigrants; all the restaurants are clustered around the street San Francisco. **El Turko** (San Francisco 223, tel. 054/25-0055, www.elturko.com.pe, 7:30am-midnight Sun.-Wed., 7:30am-3am Thurs., 7:30am-5am Fri., US$3-5) is the best place to go for a quick delicious bite. Try the *dönner* kebab or *cacik* salad, made with cucumber, yogurt, and garlic.

The best place for sushi is **El Buda Profano** (Bolívar 425, cell tel. 977-228-590, www.elbudaprofano.com, noon-3:30pm and 6pm-9pm daily, US$5-10), which specializes in a vegan sushi menu created by chef Jimbo Echevarria. Another excellent option for Japanese-Peruvian fusion is **Ty'nkay** (Puente Grau 304 A, tel. 054/31-3835, noon-10pm daily, US$3-5). In addition to sushi, it has delicious ceviche, hearty soups, make-your-own salads, and vegetarian options. A Maracuya sour is a good cocktail to accompany your meal.

For some American comfort food, stop by **Chelawasi Public House** (102 Campo Redondo, tel. 054/23-2778, 4pm-10:30pm Tues.-Thurs., 4pm-11pm Fri., noon-11pm Sat., noon-7pm Sun., US$5-8) for a juicy hamburger, wings, and even chili. The burgers are the best in Arequipa, and probably southern Peru. It also has a good selection of craft beer.

Crepisimo (Santa Catalina 208, tel. 054/20-6620, www.crepisimo.com, 8am-midnight daily, US$3-5) is inside the colonial house of the Alliance Française. In this tiny café, with a definite French atmosphere, you can watch as your savory or sweet crepes are made.

There are several restaurants with rooftop and sidewalk seating on Pasaje La Catedral, the charming pedestrian alley behind the cathedral. The best views are at **Mixto's** (Pasaje La Catedral 115, tel. 054/20-5343, 9am-9:30pm daily, US$5-8). The menu offers everything from ceviche to pastas and pizzas. Live folkloric music is featured from 7pm Monday-Saturday. There is also an Irish pub, **Farren's** (tel. 054/23-8465, 10am-midnight Mon.-Sat.), on the *pasaje,* serving Guinness.

Pizza

For pizza, a local favorite is **Marengo** (Santa Catalina 221, tel. 054/28-4883, 1pm-11pm daily, US$5-10) which also has locations in Cusco and Cajamarca. The most laid-back of the pizzerias is the cave-like **Los Leños**

(Jerusalén 407, tel. 054/45-9049, 4pm-11pm daily, US$4-6), serving great wood-fired pizzas. The dim lighting and graffiti on the *sillar* walls give it a pub atmosphere. **Il Fornellino** (Melgar 108, cell tel. 975-666-669, 4:30pm-10pm daily, US$3-7) is a tiny restaurant with some of the best pizza and pasta in town.

Vegetarian

Mandala (Jerusalén 207, tel. 054/28-7086, 11am-6pm daily) is a cozy and centrally located vegetarian option. Mandala has been around for several years and is a great option for the price; a lunch *menú* here costs about US$3. **El Buda Profano** (Bolívar 425, cell tel. 977-228-590, www.elbudaprofano.com, US$5-10) has a vegan sushi menu.

Cafés, Bakeries, and Ice Cream

Arequipeños take their desserts very seriously, as is evident by the colorful window displays along the first block of Mercaderes or on Portal de Flores on the Plaza de Armas. The lineup on this street starts with **Manolo** (Mercaderes 107, tel. 054/21-9009, 7am-1am daily, US$6-10), a relaxed diner where locals come to indulge in inexpensive Peruvian meals and decadent desserts. **Cappricio** (Mercaderes 121, tel. 054/27-2387, www.cappriccioperu.com, 9am-midnight Tues.-Sun., US$5) serves espresso, Italian food, and great pastries and desserts in a diner-like atmosphere.

But the best café in the city is beautiful **La Petite Francaise** (Santa Catalina 413, cell tel. 952-167-232, 7am-9pm Mon.-Fri., 8am-9pm Sat.-Sun., US$5-10). Relax with a book under its arched ceiling while enjoying a delicious crepe and coffee. In the mood for chocolate with your coffee? Head to the second-floor terrace of the **Chaqchao Organic Chocolates** (Santa Catalina 204, tel. 054/23-4572, www.chaqchao.wordpress.com, 11am-9pm Tues.-Sat.). It also has a great selection of craft beer. Another chocolate-inspired café, **OCacao** (Palacio Viejo 205A, tel.

054/22-0774, www.o-cacao.com, 9am-9:30pm Mon.-Fri., 10am-9:30pm Sat.) has waffles, muffins, and hot chocolate. Try the Bonbon Pisco Sour. For great empanadas, head to **Ribs Cafe** (Álvarez Thomas 107, tel. 054/28-8188, 8am-10pm Mon.-Sat., 9am-3pm Sun.). As the name implies, it also serves good ribs.

Markets

Over 130 years old, the **Mercado San Camilo** (San Camilo between Nicolás de Piérola and Perú, 7am-7pm Mon.-Sat., 7am-5pm Sun.) is the main market in the city, where you can find meat, vegetables, fruits, good cheese, and anything you can think of. There are also *juguerías,* or juice stands, where you can drink any kind of mix for US$1.50. On the Plaza de Armas, **El Super** (Portal de la Municipalidad 130, tel. 054/28-6616, 9:15am-9:15pm Mon.-Sat., 9:15am-1:30pm Sun.) can fill in with dry goods, yogurt, tuna, beer, and wine.

ACCOMMODATIONS

As one of Peru's top business centers, Arequipa has dozens of hotels, including many charming options under US$50 for a double as well as more upscale options, including the beautiful *casona* of Casa Andina Private Collection Arequipa and the outstanding five-star Hotel Libertador.

Under US$10

A good backpacker option in Arequipa is the **Flying Dog** (Melgar 116, tel. 054/23-1163, www.flyingdogperu.com, US$8 dorm, US$25 s with private bath). The hostel is located in a colonial house with a nice courtyard that has a fountain in the middle. It's four blocks from the Plaza de Armas and offers buffet breakfast, very hot water, and a game room with cable TV, a DVD player, and a pool table. Two blocks from Arequipa's Plaza de Armas is **Wild Rover** (Ugarte 111, tel. 054/21-2830, US$7-11 dorm, US$25 private room), which has a reputation as a fun, loud party hostel with friendly staff. It has Wi-Fi, a TV room, a free pool table, same-day laundry service, and an on-site bar with inexpensive drinks. Both places are great options to meet other backpackers.

US$10-25

El Caminante Class (Santa Catalina 207-A, 2nd Fl., tel. 054/20-3444, www.elcaminante-class.com, US$20 s, US$25 d) is a very good deal, conveniently located in an old 18th-century house between Plaza de Armas and Santa Catalina Monastery. Rooms are comfy and have private baths. Amenities include a laundry and a book swap. There are also cheaper rooms with shared baths.

Los Andes Bed & Breakfast (La Merced 123, tel. 054/33-0015, www.losandesarequipa. com, US$17 s, US$25 d, with breakfast) is an excellent option, with comfy, very clean single, double, or larger rooms for groups, with and without private baths. Features include an open kitchen where you can cook meals, safes, luggage storage, laundry service, an impressive library and reading lounge, a book exchange, cable TV, and Wi-Fi.

La Casa de Sillar (Rivero 504, tel. 054/28-4249, www.lacasadesillar.com, US$25 s or d, with breakfast) has nine rooms, some with private baths, in a colonial house opening onto a sunny patio. Four rooms have traditional *sillar* arches and construction. The rooms are simple, and the breakfast is more than ample: yogurt, fruit, and hash browns. There is Wi-Fi, along with a TV room and laundry service.

US$25-50

The great deal in Arequipa is found at the beautiful **Casona Solar Hotel** (Consuelo 116, tel. 054/22-8991, www.casonasolar. com, US$50 s, US$80 d). The walls in this restored 18th-century colonial house, located only blocks from the central plaza, are made of large *sillar* stones, while the rooms have arched ceilings. There is a pleasant courtyard for Arequipa's sunny days, and a fireplace for its chilly nights.

Nearby is the **Casona Terrace Hotel** (Álvarez Thomas 211, tel. 054/21-2318, www. hotelcasonaterrace.com, US$43 s, US$52

d), also housed in a former colonial home. Rooms here have a more modern feel. There is a nice terrace, buffet breakfast, cable TV, and Internet access.

La Casa de Melgar (Melgar 108, tel. 054/22-2459, www.lacasademelgar.com, US$45 s, US$65 d with breakfast), is worth it for a fascinating glimpse into 18th-century Arequipa. The house has 1.5-meter-thick *sillar* walls, vaulted ceilings, wood floors and shutters, and six interior patios. Each room is unique, with antique rocking chairs and armoires, vaulted stone showers, rotary phones, and funky stained-glass skylights. Room 104 is huge and has a fireplace. An added bonus to staying here is the on-site Italian restaurant Il Fornellino, with some of the best pizzas in Arequipa.

For those who prefer to be out of the city center, **Vallecito** is a quiet, relaxed neighborhood with homes built in the early 20th century, about a five-minute taxi ride south of town. **La Plazuela** (Plaza Juan Manuel Polar 105, Vallecito, tel. 054/22-2624, www.hostal-laplazuela.com, US$35 s, US$50 d, with breakfast) is a large home from the early 1900s that has been converted into a bed-and-breakfast with a nice lawn, a sitting area, and a dining area. The rooms are all painted in light pastel colors and have individually controlled heating, a minibar, and cable TV; La Plazuela also has Wi-Fi and currency exchange.

Hostal Solar (Ayacucho 108, tel. 054/24-1793, www.hostalsolar.com, US$38 s, US$45 d, with breakfast and airport transfer) is a charming hostel some blocks away from the center of town, with a small library, a sitting room, and rooftop terraces. The 15 rooms have wood or carpeted floors, *sillar* walls, high ceilings, Wi-Fi, and TVs. The kitchen is available for guest use, and there is a 24-hour doctor on call.

The entry to the **El Conquistador** (Mercaderes 409, tel. 054/21-2916, www. hostalelconquistador.com, US$45 s, US$60 d, with breakfast) is quite stunning, crossing an elegant colonial patio and entering into the reception and dining area with vaulted *sillar* construction built in the 1770s. The owners recently renovated the baths and carpeted the rooms. Prices online are higher than listed above, but if you call they should give you a lower rate. Even if you don't plan to stay the night, the original building is worth a visit.

Los Balcones de Moral y Santa Catalina (Moral 217, tel. 054/20-1291, www. losbalconeshotel.com, US$38 s, US$49 d, with breakfast) is an excellent choice, located in a beautiful and well-preserved colonial house on a corner. It has a quiet reception room, a simple breakfast area, and a row of huge, comfortable rooms overlooking the cathedral bell towers as well as Volcán Chachani. Apart from being large, the 17 rooms have gorgeous wood floors, nice beds and furniture, Wi-Fi, cable TV, and phones.

US$50-100

Six blocks from the Plaza de Armas, **La Casa de mi Abuela** (Jerusalén 606, tel. 054/24-1206, www.lacasademiabuela.com, US$59 s or d, with breakfast) has a delightful oasis of gardens and lawns. Rooms, which wind around the gardens, are of varying quality and age. The newer rooms are bigger and modern. Older rooms are darker but more homey. The hotel offers every conceivable service for travelers: excellent beds, cable TV, phones, laundry, massages, a library, a game room, Internet, a pool, and one of the best tour agencies in Arequipa—Giardino Tours. Because of all the activities, this is an especially good place for families.

In the Vallecito neighborhood is **Queen's Villa** (Luna Pizarro 512, Vallecito, tel. 054/28-3060, www.queensvillahotel.com, US$53 s, US$60 d, with breakfast), with rooms and a handful of bungalows surrounded by pleasant gardens, sitting tables, palm trees, and a nice pool. The rooms vary in quality and have parquet, tile, or carpeted floors. The tranquil setting and amenities, such as inexpensive laundry, cable TV, Wi-Fi, and kitchenettes in some bungalows, make the place worth the money.

A charming option in the upscale neighborhood of Selva Alegre, just north of the city center, is **La Gruta Hotel** (La Gruta 304, tel. 054/28-9899, www.lagrutahotel.com, US$55 s, US$75 d, with breakfast). This cozy hostel offers 16 rooms in a discreet 1970s house. Each room is different; one has an interior garden, another has a fireplace. All have carpet, fridges, and cable TV and open up to a small garden. It doesn't really feel like a hotel; it's more like staying in a guest room. Also in Selva Alegre, **Villa Elisa** (Manuel Ugarteche 401, tel. 054/22-1891, www.villaelisahb.com, US$58 s, US$88 d, with breakfast) is a restored villa with a relaxing garden and helpful staff.

Casa Andina Classic-Arequipa Jerusalén (Jerusalén 603, tel. 054/20-2070, www.casa-andina.com, US$80 s or d, with buffet breakfast) is a modern hotel that stands out for the bright red-and-orange blocks designing its facade. Its comfortable 94 rooms have safes, cable TV, Wi-Fi, and comfy beds, and many have tubs.

A solid mid-range option near the Plaza de Armas is the **Tierra Viva Arequipa Plaza** (Jerusalén 202, tel. 054/23-4161, www.tierravivahoteles.com, US$65 s, US$75 d). The recently renovated rooms come with flat-screen TVs, desks, and simple but nice baths. The hotel has Wi-Fi and laundry service as well as currency exchange and medical assistance if needed. Half a block from the main plaza is the popular **Los Tambos** (Bolognesi 129, tel. 054/60-0900, www.lostambos.com.pe, US$85 s or d). The hotel has standard amenities that include flat-screen TVs and Wi-Fi. It also has two terraces and a comfortable lobby with a chimney, and the rooms have large windows that allow in natural light. On the other side of Río Chili is **Hotel La Maison D'Elise** (Bolognesi 104, tel. 054/25-6185, www.hotelmaisondelise.com, US$95 s, US$120 d, including breakfast). The modern, blocky exterior contrasts with the architecture of the rooms, which attempts to imitate the local colonial construction. All 48 rooms have cable TV, phones, Wi-Fi, large baths, and easy access to a grassy lawn with a small pool and good views of Misti. Amenities include 24-hour free medical service, laundry, and a parking lot.

US$100-150

Casa Andina Select (Portal de Flores 116, tel. 054/41-2930, www.casa-andina.com, US$140 s or d, with breakfast) has a privileged location right on the Plaza de Armas. Recently acquired by Casa Andina, the hotel's 58 rooms have been remodeled. There is still a rooftop terrace with a small pool where you can be served lunch overlooking the square. A handful of rooms have private terraces over the square; the remaining rooms look into a modern interior courtyard. Amenities include air-conditioning, mini fridges, cable TV, Wi-Fi, and safes. Depending on the time of year, you can find nonrefundable rates below US$100 s or d.

West of town is the charming **La Posada del Puente** (Esquina Puente Grau, Av. Bolognesi 101, tel. 054/25-3132, www.posadadelpuente.com, US$130 s, US$140 d, with breakfast), across the Puente Grau. The landscaping is well done, and the modern rooms with vaulted ceilings overlook Volcán Misti and Río Chili. All have cable TV and Wi-Fi. The elegant dining room has a view of the river as well. **Casa de Avila** (San Martin 116, Vallecito, tel. 054/21-3177, www.casadevila.com, US$135 s, US$180 triple) gets good reviews for its family-like atmosphere and relaxing garden.

Over US$150

Three blocks from the Plaza de Armas, **Casa Andina Private Collection Arequipa** (Ugarte 403, tel. 054/22-6907, www.casa-andina.com, US$159 s or d, US$269 senior suite, buffet breakfast and airport transfer included) is the finest hotel in Arequipa's historic center and one of the best in the city. Declared a historic monument, this colonial mansion was Arequipa's Casa de Moneda, the old Mint House, built in 1794. Restored and remodeled in 2008, the hotel features two ample colonial courtyards, original frescoes, and an exquisite chapel long hidden from

view. The hotel boasts five spectacular large suites, a skylight shielding the main courtyard from Arequipa's intense sun, and 40 spacious rooms, all with Wi-Fi, flat-screen TVs, and bathtubs. Amenities include an Internet center, an ATM, a fourth-floor terrace, a handicraft and gift shop, a colonial-style bar, and an excellent gourmet restaurant called Alma, with superb regional food.

The grand **Hotel Libertador** (Plaza Bolívar s/n, Selva Alegre, tel. 054/21-5110, www.libertador.com.pe, US$160 s or d, US$200 duplex suite, with buffet breakfast) is the only five-star hotel in Arequipa. It sits next to one of the city's largest and prettiest parks yet is only a 15-minute walk to the Plaza de Armas. The rose-colored republican-style building, built in the 1940s, has a grand lobby with elegant details carried throughout. The rooms and suites are decorated soberly with dark wood furniture, deep red carpets, and huge baths with tubs, among the many amenities of this kind of hotel. The big outdoor pool is surrounded by gardens and a playground. There is a Sunday buffet at the restaurant.

INFORMATION AND SERVICES

Visitor Information and Police

Thorough up-to-date information is available at **Iperú** (Portal de la Municipalidad 110, tel. 054/22-3265, www.turismoperu.info, 9am-6pm Mon.-Sat., 9am-1pm Sun.). There is a second **Iperú** (tel. 054/44-4564) at the airport. The **tourist police** (tel. 054/20-1258) are at Jerusalén 315.

Immigration Office

Tourist visas can be extended at the **Migraciones** (J. L. Bustamante and Rivero, Urb. Quinta Tristán, tel. 054/42-1759, 8am-4:15pm Mon.-Fri., 9am-noon Sat.).

Health Care

For health care, **Clínica Arequipa** (Puente Grau and Bolognesi, tel. 054/59-9000, www.clinicarequipa.com.pe, 24 hours daily) is a fully equipped hospital and pharmacy with some of the better doctors in town. **PAZ-Holandesa** (Urb. Villa Continetal, Calle 4, N. 101 Paucarpata, tel. 054/43-2281, www.pazholandesa.com, 24 hours daily) is another well-equipped medical practice founded by a Dutch neurosurgeon from Rotterdam. It began as a children's hospital but is now seeing travelers and providing dental care as well.

At the corner of Jerusalén and Mercaderes are two reliable pharmacies: **Boticas Fasa** (Mercaderes 145, tel. 054/20-5061, www.boticasfasa.com.pe, 7am-midnight Mon.-Sat., 9am-11pm Sun.) and **Boticas BTL** (Mercaderes 200, tel. 054/20-2024, 24 hours daily).

Banks and Money Exchange

There are many money exchange offices around the first block of San Francisco, and most of the banks with ATMs are near the Plaza de Armas, including Interbank (Mercaderes 217), **Scotiabank** (Mercaderes 410), **Banco de Crédito** (San Juan de Dios 123), and **BBVA Banco Continental** (San Francisco 108). Money wires can be received at **Western Union** (Santa Catalina 115, 8:30am-7:30pm Mon.-Sat., 9am-1pm Sun.).

Communications

Mail can be sent at the post office, **Serpost** (Moral 118, tel. 054/21-5427, www.serpost.com.pe, 8am-8pm Mon.-Sat., 8am-1pm Sun.). International Internet calls can be made at **Catedral Internet** (Pasaje La Catedral 101, tel. 054/22-0622, 8am-11pm daily). In Vallecito, Internet is available at San Martín 222. Shipping services are available at **DHL** (Santa Catalina 115, tel. 054/23-4288).

Language Schools

There are many language schools in Arequipa. Some offer group lessons and other individual classes. If you are interested in a homestay, ask the school if it arranges them; many do. The **Centro de Intercambio Cultural** (Los Arces 257-A, Cayma, tel. 054/25-0722, www.ceica-peru.com) offers one-on-one or group lessons and can organize family homestays

and volunteering. Besides Spanish, **Centro de Idiomas UNSA** (San Agustín 106, tel. 054/24-7524) offers English, French, Portuguese, and Chinese classes. **Rocio Language Classes** (Ayacucho 208, Of. 22, tel. 054/22-4568, www.spanish-peru.com) is a more affordable option, and classes cater to students' flexibility. The best is **Centro Cultural Peruano Norteamericano** (Melgar 109, tel. 054/39-1020, www.cultural.edu.pe), which offers Spanish and English courses.

Laundry

A good laundry is **Quick Laundry** (Jerusalén 520, tel., 7am-8pm daily, US$1.50 per kilogram), which has same-day service. **Magic Laundry** (Jerusalén 404) is another good option.

Car Rental

You don't need a 4WD vehicle for the beautiful drive to Colca Canyon, but it is recommended. Companies include **Genesis Rent A Car** (Puente Grau 100, Cercado, tel. 054/20-2033, www.genesisrentacar.com) and **Hertz** (www.hertz.com, 7am-8pm Mon.-Fri.) is at the airport.

GETTING THERE AND AROUND
Air

The **Alfredo Rodríguez Ballón International Airport** (AQP, Aviación s/n) is seven kilometers northwest of the city, about a US$3 cab ride. **LATAM** (Lima tel. 01/213-8200, www.latam.com) has six or eight daily flights between Arequipa and Lima, and several others to Cusco via Juliaca. StarPerú doesn't fly to Arequipa, but **Avianca** (www.avianca.com), **Peruvian Airlines** (www.peruvianairlines.pe), and **LCPeru** (www.lcperu.pe) have daily flights to and from Arequipa.

Bus

There are daily departures to Lima, Tacna, Cusco, and Puno from the two bus terminals in Arequipa—the **Terrapuerto** and **Terminal Terrestre**—right next to each other on Jacinto Ibañez, a five-minute taxi ride (US$3) outside town. Most companies have offices in the Terminal Terrestre that are open 7am-9pm daily.

Most bus companies make the 15-hour direct trip to Lima overnight, with different services, including buses stopping along the way in Nasca and Ica. The best option is **Cruz del Sur** (Terrapuerto, tel. 054/72-0444, www.cruzdelsur.com.pe), with seven daily departures to Lima, which has nearly full beds on the first floor for US$54 and reclining seats on the second floor for US$40.

Oltursa (Terminal Terrestre, tel. 054/42-6566, www.oltursa.pe) is also a good option, with seven daily departures. Prices range US$30-50, depending on the floor. Other Lima options include **Ormeño** (Terrapuerto, tel. 054/42-7788, www.grupo-ormeno.com.pe), **Tepsa** (Terrapuerto, tel. 054/42-4135, www.tepsa.com.pe) and **Civa** (Terrapuerto or Terminal Terrestre, tel. 054/42-6563, www.civa.com.pe).

Direct buses also leave Arequipa for the five-hour journey to Tacna, a border town that has a duty-free port but has little of interest to visitors besides the heaps of imported, almost-new Toyota station wagons. From Tacna, a 30-minute taxi ride (US$5) can take you across the border to Arica, Chile, where most travelers continue south in Chile by bus or by domestic flight. Ormeño has direct buses to Tacna every day, as well as one that has a stopover in Moquegua (3.5 hours).

For the Colca Canyon, **Turismo Milagros** (Terminal Terrestre, tel. 054/42-3260) has buses leaving at 3:30am and 2pm daily for the three-hour journey to Chivay. The buses wait there 30 minutes and then continue two hours on to Cabanaconde. Return buses leave Cabanaconde at 11am and 10pm daily, and from Chivay at 1:30am and 2:30pm daily.

Local Transportation

Arequipa is a safe city, by Peruvian standards, so you can either call a taxi or flag one down on the street. Just be sure to get an official taxi, which has a sign on the top of the car. Consider **Taxi Remisse 21** (tel. 054/21-2121).

Colca Valley and Canyon

Road engineers could hardly believe their eyes when they visited the Colca Valley in the late 1970s to build the area's first road. Condors cruised in the brilliant blue skies. A river lay hundreds of meters below at the bottom of an impenetrable canyon. Potatoes and corn overflowed from thousands of stone terraces. Stone-and-adobe villages, each with a small but elegant colonial church, were strung like pearls along the valley rim. Women herded alpacas while dressed in fantastically embroidered skirts and hats with ribbons and sequins.

Even with a spate of new roads and tourist hotels, Colca Valley and Colca Canyon are still an odd combination of historical time warp and geological anomaly. The Collagua and Cabana peoples who lived here for at least 2,000 years, from 800 BC onward, built an ingenious terracing system on the valley walls that collects snowmelt from nearby volcanoes. Inca Mayta Cápac arrived here with his army in the 15th century and, according to Spanish chronicler Francisco Jerónimo de Oré, sealed the conquest by marrying Mama Tancaray Yacchi, daughter of a local Collagua chief. The Inca built for her a house of copper that, according to legend, was melted to make the gigantic bells that still hang in Coporaque's towers.

The Spaniards, a century after the Inca, were less kind: They herded villagers into *reducciones* (new settlements) and put them to work in plantations or the nearby Caylloma silver mine. All the while, the Collaguas absorbed Roman Catholic imagery into their

Colca Valley and Canyon

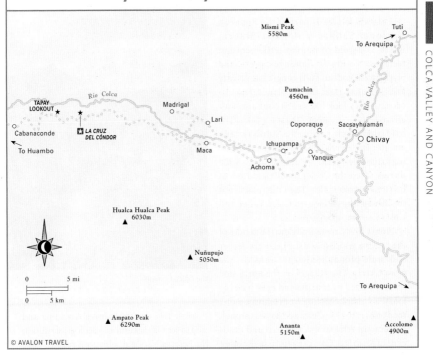

© AVALON TRAVEL

festivals. The women copied the petticoats of the Spanish women, adding their natural indigos and bright blues and their fine paisley-like embroidery. And then Colca, with neither roads nor communications, was forgotten.

In 1979, shortly after the road was built for the Condorama Dam, a motley crew of six Polish adventurers, led by Piotr Chmielinski and Andrzej Pietowski, with Peruvian Antonio Vellutino (the owner of recreational outfitter Cusipata), discovered another side of Colca: adventure. They made the first river descent of the Colca Canyon. In a grueling five-week journey, they navigated the Class V waters of the canyon and confirmed that the Colca Canyon was at least 3,400 meters deep—more than twice the depth of Arizona's Grand Canyon. Since that expedition, Colca Canyon has become, along with Cusco and Huaraz, a center for adventure sports. From Cabanaconde, near the end of the canyon road, climbers begin to climb Ampato, the 6,300-meter volcano where the Juanita mummy was discovered. Numerous other hikes and mountain-bike routes lead throughout the canyon and its spectacular villages.

PLANNING YOUR TRIP

The shortest way into Colca is a three-hour journey (but longer with stops) on a newly paved road from Arequipa to the town of Chivay. The lunar landscape along the route is decorated only with rocks, *ichu* grass, and the blob-like *yareta* plant. The fluorescent green *yareta* appears to be a moss-covered boulder but is actually a plant that lives for centuries but only grows to about one meter in size. It requires a very specific climate: the dry, desolate tundra over 4,200 meters elevation. The plant survives because of its hundreds of tightly bunched waxy leaves, which trap moisture inside and allow the plant to withstand temperatures down to -50°C.

This whole area is part of the **Reserva Nacional Salinas y Aguada Blanca,** which is devoid of human settlement but teems with animals: flamingos, geese, and black-faced Andean gulls congregate at salty lakes, vicuñas graze the grasslands, and viscachas—they look like rabbits but are actually rodents—dart among the stony fields. The road climbs high, passing the **Sumbay cave** and its petroglyphs at 4,000 meters, then rising to the lonely plain of **Patapampa** at 4,900 meters, where the Collagua built hundreds of mysterious stone piles. Then the road drops to **Chivay,** the gateway to Colca Valley and Colca Canyon, at 3,650 meters.

From Chivay, roads lead down both sides of the canyon, which gradually becomes deeper and more pronounced as it works its way from Chivay. The villages on the north side are less visited by tourists and have nice colonial churches. Starting from Chivay, a dirt road crosses the Río Colca and passes through Coporaque, Ichupampa, and Lari and dead-ends in Madrigal. Cars can return to the other side of the canyon via bridges near Ichupampa and Lari. The more often visited side of the canyon is the south side, leading to **Cruz del Cóndor,** where a 60-kilometer dirt road leads from Chivay to Yanque, Achoma, Maca, Pinchollo, and Cabanaconde.

Colca is spread out, and churches keep odd hours, so it's best to rent a car (US$100 per day) to explore the valley and canyon at your own pace. A second option is a two-day agency tour, which is usually cheaper. The standard two-day tour, offered by many agencies in Arequipa, ranges US$25-60, depending on the hotel and what is included. Apart from lodging, the price usually includes transportation, a guide, and breakfast. Ask if it includes the tourist ticket (US$25) and access to the hot springs (US$5). The better agencies, such as Giardino and Colonial Tours, have new buses and better-informed guides. Groups are often just a few people.

the Colca Canyon

Most two-day tours leave Arequipa and stop to see vicuñas and archaeological ruins in the Reserva Nacional Salinas y Aguada Blanca before exploring the Inca ruins and churches around Chivay. But the highlight is a starlit evening soak in thermal hot springs, either near Chivay or, better yet, at the Colca Lodge near Coporaque. Groups rise early the next morning to drive an hour or two down the canyon to the Cruz del Cóndor. Afterward, groups visit the churches in Yanque, Maca, or Pinchollo and then head back to Arequipa. Because of road conditions, few agencies take the longer **Pulpera** return route, which takes adds another day but passes through the interesting villages of Callali, Sibayo, and Tuti and tours the petroglyphs at Mollepunko Cave.

If you are traveling on your own, it is easy to take a bus to Chivay or Cabanaconde and travel around on foot or by *colectivo*. **AUTOCOLCA** (www.colcaperu.gob.pe), the Colca Canyon managing authority, requires visitors to buy a US$25 tourist ticket to access Cruz del Cóndor as well as the area's churches.

Mismi: The Source of the Amazon?

The Río Colca, like Cusco's Urubamba, has different names on each of its sections. Up high it's the Colca, then the Majes, and finally the Camaná, but it all flows into the Pacific Ocean. On its way to the ocean, the Colca slices past several volcanoes, including Ampato (6,380 meters) and Mismi (5,597 meters). But not all of the rain and snow that falls on Mismi ends up in the Colca. Some of it collects in two lakes on the north side, which are often frozen and shrouded in fog. After months of studying aerial photographs and making precise measures, a National Geographic Society expedition tromped up to these lonely lakes in 1975 and declared them the official source of the Amazon. Incredibly, water from these lakes drains into a small stream that eventually, after hundreds of kilometers, ends up in Cusco's Río Apurímac. So, depending on its position, a snowflake that falls on Mismi's summit can either have a brief but bumpy 75-kilometer trip to the Pacific Ocean, or it can have a meandering journey of more than 7,000 kilometers, passing first through endless stretches of high-altitude desert, then down the Sacred Valley and past Machu Picchu and into brown rivers that lazily wind their way to Brazil.

Proceeds supposedly maintain the valley and canyon's historical sights.

Colca's skies are sunny and deep blue April to October, making a wide-brimmed hat and sunscreen essential. Make sure to bring plenty of warm clothing, as temperatures can drop below freezing at night. If you are not coming from Cusco, stay in Arequipa for a few days to avoid *soroche*, or altitude sickness. Chivay is at 3,652 meters elevation.

ENTERTAINMENT AND EVENTS
Festivals

The Colca Valley has a well-deserved reputation for beautiful festivals. **La Virgen de Candelaria** is celebrated in Chivay, Acoma, and Maca on February 2-3. Both **Carnaval,** in late February, and **Semana Santa,** the week before Easter, usually in April, are lively in Colca. **La Fiesta de San Juan** is celebrated in Yanque and several other Colca towns on June 13.

The celebration of the **Virgen del Carmen** (around July 16) is a huge event in Cabanaconde and Chivay, along with that of **Santiago Apóstol** (July 25) in Coporaque and Madrigal. An interesting eight-day festival takes place in Chivay, starting on August 15, in honor of the town's patron saint, **La Virgen de la Asunción,** with simultaneous celebrations taking place in Coporaque, Maca, and Yanque.

Yanque's **Spring Festival** happens September 23. **La Fiesta de la Virgen del Rosario** (Oct. 7) takes place in Chivay, Achoma, Ichupampa, Maca, and Yanque. **Todos Santos** (All Saints' Day) and **Los Fieles Difuntos** (All Souls' Day) can be enjoyed throughout Colca Valley on November 1-2. The final big event is a celebration for **La Virgen Inmaculada** in Chivay and Yanque, during which time the five-day Wititi dance is performed. The Wititi is also performed in Yanque from December 25 onward. **PromPeru** (www.peru.info), the government promotion agency, maintains an updated list of festivals.

RECREATION
Trekking

Those who enjoyed hiking in Arizona's Grand Canyon will love Colca Canyon, which has the added beauty of volcanoes and untouched villages.

A popular short trek drops 1,200 vertical meters down into Colca Canyon from the village of Cabanaconde to **Sangalle,** a riverside oasis where three campgrounds with pools have sprung up since 2000. Their names—Paradise, Oasis, and Edén—play off the same theme and are easy to confuse.

Sangalle, which feels subtropical even when Chivay is chilly, is a great place to lounge by the pool and read books, but don't expect any cross-cultural encounters. You can camp for a few dollars or rent cane huts with rickety beds, and the campgrounds also sell beer and food. As they are close to one another, check out each campsite before you choose. You will need to pack out all solid waste, including organic waste, cans, glass, and plastic—a look at the riverbanks will demonstrate the area's trash management problems. Hiking down takes two or three hours, but returning to Cabanaconde, which most people do the second day, can take twice as long.

A longer, more interesting option is to cross a footbridge at Sangalle and hike up the other side of the Colca Canyon to the charming village of Tapay. Another path leads from Tapay back to a good camping spot farther upstream on the Río Colca. From here the path winds uphill, approximately 1,200 vertical meters, to the Cruz del Cóndor. This trip could be done in two or three days, though getting to the Cruz del Cóndor by 8am means breaking camp by 4am.

Other interesting treks involve hiking along the canyon rim between various towns. Despite what your maps say, there are ancient Collagua paths connecting most villages together. Because most visitors travel along the Cruz del Cóndor side, the best trekking is on the north side of the canyon—though it is easy to cross back and forth at the bridges near Maca and Yanque.

A truly adventurous four- or five-day route leads from Cabanaconde to the Valley of the Volcanoes and retraces the steps of Robert Shippee and George Johnson, who flew over and mapped the area in 1929. They were so intrigued by the Valley of the Volcanoes that they forged out from Cabanaconde to find it. Their route drops west (downstream) into the Colca Canyon and then back up the other side to the village of Choco, at 2,473 meters elevation. After camping here, hike up and over a 4,500-meter pass and then on to the village of Chacas, at 3,100 meters. A road with sparse traffic leads from here to Andagua, at the head of the Valley of the Volcanoes, one day's hike away.

CHIVAY

The village of Chivay, at 3,652 meters elevation, lies where the main road to Arequipa meets the Colca Valley. It is the traditional base for exploring either the valley or the canyon, and it has become a bit touristy in recent years. Many backpackers are now heading to Cabanaconde, closer to the Cruz del Cóndor, or to excellent new lodges near Coporaque or Yanque. Chivay has the best-equipped health clinic (with a laboratory), and it's the headquarters for the police and mountain rescue.

Sights

Chivay has an interesting 18th-century church, **Nuestra Señora de la Asunción,** and a bridge with Inca foundations right outside town that once supported a hanging bridge made of plant fibers. Immediately on the other side of the bridge is the Inca road to Cusco, marked by a path leading up to stone grain stores. On the hillside above are several round Inca storehouses.

Chivay's main draw, however, is **La Calera thermal baths** (5am-7pm daily, US$5), two kilometers outside town. There are five hot pools, including a couple designed for travelers. The first is an outdoor pool at the river's edge, and the second is round and enclosed with a domed ceiling. Both are clean and kept at 40°C, though they can become quite packed with travelers in the evening. Other hot baths in the area are the riverside tubs at **Colca Lodge** (tel. 054/28-2177, www.colca-lodge.com, US$12), which are 30 minutes' drive away. It's a good idea to call ahead, as use of the hot springs by nonguests depends on space. If there is space, the entry fee includes lunch at the lodge.

After stargazing from the hot springs, why not head to **Casa Andina's Planetarium** (Huayna Cápac s/n, tel. 054/53-1020, www.casa-andina.com, showings 7pm daily in Spanish and 8:30pm daily in English, US$7) and learn what you were looking at? Nightly shows explain the ancient Andean culture's understanding of the star-filled Colca sky. The presentation involves both an indoor and an outdoor viewing through a telescope.

For the more adventurous, the newest activity in the Colca Canyon is zip-lining over the Rio Colca. This takes place near the La Calera thermal baths and is run by **Colca Zip-Lining** (cell tel. 958-989-931, www.colcaziplining.com).

Food

Many restaurants in Chivay have lunch buffets. One spot that has been around for a while is **El Balcón de Don Zacarias** (22 de Agosto 102, tel. 054/53-1008, www.balconcolca.com, 7:30am-9pm daily). The restaurant is frequented by travelers for its US$11 lunch buffet. Another place is **Los Portales** (Arequipa 603, tel. 054/53-1101, 11am-3pm and 7pm-9pm daily, US$9), located in a hotel by the same name, which serves a lunch buffet of *comida típica*. There is also **Yavarí** (Plaza de Armas 604, tel. 054/48-9109, 7am-10pm daily, US$4), the locals' favorite lunch spot that serves spit-roasted chicken or a delicious daily *menú* (US$4) with lots of options. You can normally find a decent cup of coffee on the Plaza de Armas. One option on the plaza is **Innkas** (8am-11pm daily).

Accommodations

The best choice in town for those on a budget is the friendly **La Casa de Lucila** (Grau 131, tel. 054/28-4211, www.casadelucila.com, US$55 d, with breakfast). The comfortable homelike hotel is very clean and has carpeted rooms. The **Colca Inn** (Salaverry 307, tel. 054/53-1111, www.hotelcolcainn.com, US$38 s, US$48 d, with breakfast) is a reliable mid-range choice with large rooms and good beds. The baths and carpet are in need of an update, but the downstairs bar has a pool table. **Casa Andina** (Huayna Cápac s/n, tel. 054/53-1020, www.casa-andina.com, US$81 s or d, with breakfast), part of a well-run national chain, is a charming complex of rooms

and 30-odd bungalows connected by stone-lined walkways. The rooms are tastefully decorated, with modern baths, beds with down comforters, and heaters. A peaceful option is **Pozo del Cielo** (tel. 054/53-1041, www.pozodelcielo.com.pe, US$88 s, US$135 d, with breakfast). The hotel is right across the Inca bridge from Chivay, perched up on a bluff that is an easy walk to the nearby Inca ruins. The lodge is laid out like a small stone-and-adobe village, with rooms of whitewashed walls, exposed beams, and excellent canyon views. The cozy dining room serves typical Andean food.

Information and Services

The office of Colca's main **tourist police** (24 hours daily) and mountain rescue are on the main plaza. Beside the municipality on the Plaza de Armas is the office of **AUTOCOLCA** (tel. 054/53-1143), which sells the mandatory US$25 Colca tourist ticket. For health issues, there is a **health center** (Puente Inca s/n, tel. 054/53-1074), and a good pharmacy is **Botica Rivera** (Salaverry 123, 9am-10pm daily). There is a **Banco de la Nación** on the plaza with an ATM.

Getting There and Around

Chivay's bus station, with good restrooms and snack shops, is a five-minute walk on the outskirts of town. **Empresa de Transportes Reyna** (tel. 054/53-1014, www.reyna.com.pe) has three daily buses leaving for Arequipa (US$5). Another option is **Transportes Andalucia** (tel. 054/53-1106), whose buses leave for Arequipa twice daily.

Once in Chivay, there are travel agencies on the main square that can provide transportation to the Cruz del Cóndor lookout point.

YANQUE

Yanque, 10 kilometers west of Chivay, is a simple town with dirt streets and a baroque church, **Inmaculada Concepción** (Plaza de Armas), which was rebuilt in 1702 and has a mestizo facade carved with various saints, including Santa Rosa de Lima. The main in-town attraction is the **Museo de Yanque** (Plaza de Armas, 9am-6:30pm daily, US$2), which illustrates the area's history through displays and videos. From the east side of the Plaza de Armas, a one-kilometer path leads to an ancient stone bridge over the Río Colca. From the bridge, the adobe walls of Inca hanging tombs are perched on the cliff face. Those with energy and two free hours can cross the Río Colca and climb up to the ruins at **Uyu Uyu,** where the Collagua lived before the Spanish forced them to settle in present-day Coporaque. Return by walking over the car bridge just downstream of Yanque, where there are public **hot springs** (4am-7pm daily, US$3).

Food and Accommodations

The best backpacker hostel is the simple and clean **El Tambo** (San Antonio 602, tel. 054/78-6887 or 959/68-8125, www.tambohostelcolcaperu.com, US$5 s, US$10 d), whose rooms face a grassy garden. Though a bit isolated on the road at the outskirts of town, **Tradición Colca** (Colca 119, tel. 054/42-4926, US$30 s, US$40 d, with breakfast) has a charming feel, with comfortable rooms with large beds. The central stone building has a thatched roof, a fireplace, and a nice sitting area with games. **Eco Inn** (Lima 513, tel. 051/36-5525, US$95 s or d, with breakfast) is four blocks from Yanque's square and has views over the canyon.

Las Casitas del Colca (Fundo la Curiña s/n, cell tel. 996-998-355, www.lascasitasdelcolca.com, US$450 superior bungalow) is Colca's most elegant lodge. The hotel, which was recently acquired by Colombia's **GHL Hoteles** from the Orient-Express, includes a series of luxurious bungalows perched on a secluded bench above the Río Colca. Push open the door to your bungalow and you'll find a comfortable sofa across from a fireplace. At night, watch the stars from the whirlpool on your private terrace. The Samay Spa offers a range of massages, including an hour-long treatment with warm river stones. You could easily spend a few days here, walking through the gardens and admiring the Peruvian *paso* horses in the hotel's stable.

COPORAQUE

Across the river from Chivay and about eight kilometers west is the tiny village of Coporaque. There are not many services here. Coporaque's church, **Santiago Apóstol,** was built in 1569 and is the oldest in the valley. Its false balconies seem almost medieval, and the towers contain bells said to be melted from the copper palace of a Collagua princess, Mama Yacchi. Inside there is a fascinating and primitive altar and a variety of 16th-century images. Around the corner is the facade of **La Capilla de San Sebastián.**

Food and Accommodations

Some of the best food in Colca Canyon is cooked at **La Casa de Mama Yacchi** (8 kilometers from Chivay, on right side of Colca river, Arequipa tel. 054/24-1206, www.lacasademamayacchi.com, US$70 s or d, with breakfast). This hotel is within walking distance of Coporaque's main square and is a great base for day hikes through the Colca Valley. The whitewashed rooms are comfortable and clean and have great valley views. The kitchen churns out a variety of fresh salads, perfectly cooked meat dishes, and homemade sauces. An unlikely staff member is Manchita, the pet llama who greets guests at the front door.

Colca Lodge (Mariscal Benavides 201, Arequipa tel. 054/20-2587, www.colca-lodge.com, US$82 s, US$92 d, with breakfast) has the distinct advantage of being the only place in Colca to have world-class thermal baths. The hotel, owned by Grupo Inca, has a fabulous riverside location and hands out fishing poles and floatable duckies for guests who want to play. The rooms have wood floors, lofts, and excellent river views. There are also suites with fireplaces and family cottages. The restaurant's buffet breakfast is sensational. Upstairs, the lounge, with a fireplace and a cozy bar, has a nightly informational slide show. The hotel can arrange horseback rides and mountain biking, as well as walking tours to the ruins of Uyu Uyu, the Inca bridge, and Yanque. But its best feature is down a stone trail near the river, where boiling hot springs

The village's charming church, **Santa Ana,** is damaged but still standing. The facade is decorated with miniature false pillars, carved flowers, and a curious balcony that was used by missionaries to preach and present images to the natives. On the way out of town, the **Choquetico Stone** is a carved Collagua model of nearly 10,000 hectares of terracing in the Colca Canyon. This rock was perhaps used for prophetic or rainmaking rituals, perhaps in conjunction with *chicha* or llama blood. On the surrounding hills are ancient *colcas,* adobe-and-stone granaries for which the canyon is named.

The 17th-century **San Sebastián** church in **Pinchollo,** 27 kilometers west of Chivay, is another church worth visiting, with a baroque altar and a baptistery with an elaborately painted entrance.

Geyser

This nameless geyser lies up an incredibly bumpy road, which turns off the main road before reaching La Cruz del Cóndor. Pushing up the road is certainly worth it; just make sure you have a guide.

On stepping out of the car, the walk to the geyser is about one hour. The skinny dirt trail winds through green and yellow brush, arriving first at small bubbling pools and finally at the geyser. However, the telltale steam gives away the site of the gushing water long before your arrival. This is an excellent place to spot condors.

★ La Cruz del Cóndor

Colca's main draw, the condor lookout, has become touristy beyond belief and, most mornings, teems with vendors and tour buses. Still, this spot, perched 360 meters above the Colca Canyon and about 60 kilometers (1.5 hours) from Chivay, commands a spectacular view over the canyon and is one of the best spots to see the Andean condor. Enormous vultures with a silver collar and a wingspan of nearly 3.3 meters, the condors zoom past the lookout nearly every morning—usually around 8am, again at 10am, and sometimes

La Cruz del Cóndor

bubble into stone pools and steam into the cool river air. Nonguests can use the baths for about US$12, which includes lunch. The hotel also has a new Alpaca Ranch, with several grazing camelids on-site and an exhibit on the different types of alpaca fiber.

MACA TO CABANACONDE

While there is no place to stay in Maca or anywhere along the road until Cabanaconde, this stretch of the canyon is the area that draws the most attention from visitors. The dramatic views, the Cruz del Cóndor viewpoint, and an impressive hike up to a steaming geyser are worth the haul from wherever happens to be your base point.

Maca and Pinchollo

Maca, 23 kilometers west of Chivay, was nearly destroyed by repeated eruptions of nearby Volcán Sabancaya in the late 1980s. Because it sits on a geological fault line, it is continually disturbed by earthquakes.

in the late afternoon. The birds sleep on the canyon walls at night and, after the sun heats the air, ride thermals up into the sky until they are nearly out of sight. At least a pair, but sometimes as many as a dozen, show up in the morning during the nonrainy months between April and December. Fewer show up during the September-October mating season. Farther up the road is the less mobbed Tapay lookout, where condors also fly, but less frequently. Any bus headed to Cabanaconde will let travelers out at either of these spots.

Getting There and Around

If you do not come with an organized tour, your option for seeing this section of the canyon is a Chivay- or Cabanaconde-based bus company. There are two that run regularly: **Empresa de Transportes Reyna** (Chivay tel. 054/53-1014) and **Transportes Andalucia** (Chivay tel. 054/53-1106). Catch an early morning bus from one of the base towns and ask to be let off at La Cruz del Cóndor. For the return, stand by the side of the road and flag down one of the same companies, whose buses make a return trip in the late morning.

CABANACONDE

Cabanaconde, at 3,287 meters elevation and 65 kilometers west of Chivay, is the last of the five villages strung out along the southern edge of the Colca Canyon. The road doesn't end here, but it does become rougher and heads away from the canyon, which becomes much deeper and more serpentine. Buses do travel the 12 hours to Arequipa along this road, however. Cabanaconde is a great place to stay because it is quiet, has a few inexpensive hostels, and is only 15 minutes from La Cruz del Cóndor and adventure activities. The town's church, **San Pedro Alcántara,** was rebuilt after a 1784 earthquake and has the sun, moon, and stars carved onto its imposing front.

Food and Accommodations

The best food in Cabanaconde is in hotel restaurants, even at the budget level.

One of the town's better known accommodations is **Valle del Fuego** (Grau and Bolívar, 1 block from the plaza, cell tel. 958-962-369, Arequipa tel. 054/20-3737, www.valledelfuego.com, US$25 s, US$32 d), which is basic and clean. The owner, Pablo Junco, is a great source of information, and he also operates the Pablo Tours agency. Another place is **La Posada del Conde** (San Pedro and Bolognesi, tel. 054/63-1749, Arequipa tel. 054/40-0408, www.posadadelconde.com, US$25 s, US$30 d), with private baths. The nicest and most upscale place to stay is **Kuntur Wassi** (Cruz Blanca s/n, tel. 054/69-6665, www.arequipacolca.com, US$8 dorm, US$50 s, US$61 d). This friendly, well-run hotel is one block uphill from the plaza and has adobe-and-stone rooms. The nice bathtubs feel great after a long walk out of the canyon.

Getting There and Around

For the six-hour journey from Arequipa, options include **Empresa de Transportes Reyna** (Chivay tel. 054/53-1014) and **Transportes Andalucia** (Chivay tel. 054/53-1106). These companies have at least a couple of buses daily. For the return trip, contact the same agencies, all of which have offices in the Arequipa bus stations and on Cabanaconde's main plaza.

COTAHUASI CANYON AND VICINITY

Cotahuasi Canyon, the deepest in the world at 3,354 meters, is more rugged than Colca. Since it was overlooked by the Spanish, there are few churches here. The Inca, however, built a highway along much of the canyon for transporting dried fish from Puerto Inca on the coast all the way to Cusco. Today, the ruins of these roads connect several villages that grow citrus fruits on 1,000-year-old terraces.

The main town is Cotahuasi, at 2,680 meters elevation, which is a 12-hour bus ride from Arequipa. There are a few simple places to eat, sleep, and buy groceries here. The best is **Hotel Vallehermoso** (1st block of Tacna, tel. 054/58-1057, www.hotelvallehermoso.com, US$25 s, US$45 d, with breakfast).

The road continues up the canyon to the villages of Tomepampa, Lucha, and Alca. One good **trek** heads down the canyon from Cotahuasi along a path that crosses the river several times and leads, after a few hours, to the village of **Sipia**. Nearby is the thunderous 60-meter-high **Cataratas de Sipia**. Trekkers can continue downstream to more isolated villages and ruins—and, with enough time, all the way to the Pacific, as the Inca did. Agencies in Arequipa, including Cusipata, offer treks to these areas.

Buses for Cotahuasi leave in the evening from Arequipa's bus terminal (12 hours) and arrive at dawn. Return buses to Arequipa leave Cotahuasi daily. If you can, travel this route during the day. The spectacular road passes over a 4,650-meter pass between Coropuna (6,425 meters) and Solimana (6,093 meters) before dropping into Cotahuasi.

VALLEY OF THE VOLCANOES

Partway along the Arequipa-Cotahuasi Canyon route, the road branches off for **Andagua,** a small village at the head of the Valley of the Volcanoes. The small valley, sandwiched between Colca and Cotahuasi and only 65 kilometers long, is a seemingly endless lava field, lorded over by the snow-capped Coropuna and Escribano and punctuated by more than 80 perfect volcanic cones. In the middle of it all is a lake and the gentle Río Andagua, which runs underground through much of the valley. Few people travel here, and those who **trek** along this valley need to carry a tremendous amount of water. Near the village of Ayo, a few days' trek from Andagua, the valley leads to Lago Mamacocha. There is also an adventurous five-day route that retraces the 1929 route of Shippee and Johnson and passes through Chacas to Cabanaconde in Colca Canyon. Andagua-bound buses leave several times a week from Arequipa's bus station.

For those with a 4WD vehicle, a fascinating circuit connects Cotahuasi and Andagua and then heads to the Colca Canyon via Cailloma. Except in Chivay, there is probably no gasoline along this route, and not even the best maps are completely accurate, but the scenery is legendary.

Puno

The first impression you get when you arrive in this city is of a sprawling, somewhat unappealing city surrounded by an extraordinary landscape. It has a few colonial churches and an incredible number of religious festivals. Because it is Peru's only major city on the shores of Lake Titicaca, most travelers pass through here en route to more interesting destinations. As a result, there is a good range of hotels, restaurants, and agencies.

Great efforts have been made to improve Puno's attractiveness. The wooden lake boats, powered by converted car engines from the 1950s, are safer now that they are equipped with life jackets, fire extinguishers, and cell phones. They also float higher out of the water with an enforced limit on passengers. The terminal on the edge of town brings all of the major bus companies together and is just a few minutes' walk from the port, where boats leave for Amantaní and Taquile islands.

During the early days of the Peruvian viceroyalty, Puno was a stopover for those traveling between Arequipa and the Potosí mine, in present-day Bolivia. In 1688 a silver deposit was discovered at nearby Laicota, and the town was renamed San Carlos de Puno. During this time, important churches were built in Puno and around the shores of Lake Titicaca, with mestizo facades similar to those in Arequipa.

Puno

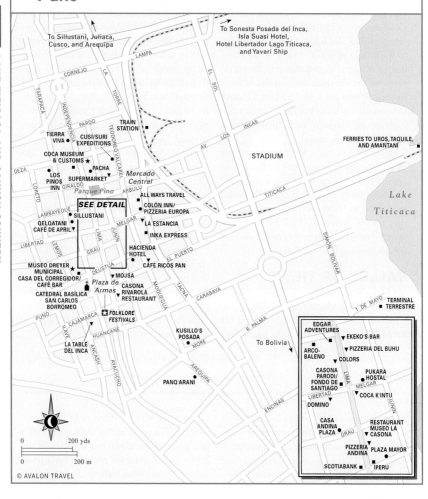

To Sillustani, Juliaca,
Cusco, and Arequipa

To Sonesta Posada del Inca,
Isla Suasi Hotel,
Hotel Libertador Lago Titicaca,
and Yavari Ship

FERRIES TO UROS, TAQUILE,
AND AMANTANÍ

STADIUM

TRAIN
STATION

TIERRA
VIVA
CUSI/SURI
EXPEDITIONS
COCA MUSEUM
& CUSTOMS ★
PACHA
LOS
PINOS
INN
SUPERMARKET
GIRALDO
Mercado
Central
Parque Pino
ALL WAYS TRAVEL
SEE DETAIL
SILLUSTANI
COLÓN INN/
PIZZERIA EUROPA
QELQATANI
CAFÉ DE APRIL
LA ESTANCIA
INKA EXPRESS
HACIENDA
HOTEL
MUSEO DREYER
MUNICIPAL
CAFÉ RICOS PAN
CASA DEL CORREGIDOR/
CAFÉ BAR
MOJSA
Plaza de
Armas
CASONA
RIVAROLA
RESTAURANT
CATEDRAL BASÍLICA
SAN CARLOS
BORROMEO
FOLKLORE
FESTIVALS
KUSILLO'S
POSADA
To Bolivia
LA TABLE
DEL INCA
PANQ'ARANI

Lake
Titicaca

TERMINAL
TERRESTRE

0   200 yds
0   200 m
© AVALON TRAVEL

EDGAR
ADVENTURES
EKEKO'S BAR
ARCO-
BALENO
PIZZERIA DEL BUHU
COLORS
CASONA
PARODI/
FONDO DE
SANTIAGO
PUKARA
HOSTAL
COCA K'INTU
DOMINO
CASA
ANDINA
PLAZA
RESTAURANT
MUSEO LA
CASONA
PIZZERIA
ANDINA
PLAZA MAYOR
SCOTIABANK
IPERU

SIGHTS
City Tour

One of Puno's most interesting sights, just outside town, is the *Yavarí* (behind Sonesta Posada Hotel, cell tel. 994-622-511 or 989-289-524, www.yavari.org, 9am-5pm daily, free), one of the world's great antique ships. Sent in pieces from England in 1862, the *Yavarí* took six years to arrive at its destination. First, it was sent around Cape Horn, then carried by porters and mules over the Andes, and finally assembled on Lake Titicaca. For a unique experience, there is the option of spending the night on the *Yavarí* in one of its four cabins, which can each host up to seven people.

If you have the time and the energy, start your tour three blocks from the Plaza de Armas at **Parque Huajsapata,** the mirador overlooking Puno with a huge sculpture of Manco Cápac, the first Inca. Take extra precaution here and ask about safety before visiting, as there have been assaults on tourists.

In the Plaza de Armas is the city's **Catedral Basílica San Carlos Borromeo** (7:30am-noon and 3pm-6pm Sun.-Fri., 7:30am-noon and 3pm-7pm Sat.), which was built in the 17th century by Peruvian master stonemason Simón de Asto. The interior is rather Spartan in contrast to the carved facade but contains an interesting silver-plated altar. Next to the cathedral is the 17th-century **Casa del Corregidor,** built by Father Silvestre de Valdés, who was in charge of the cathedral construction. It has a pleasant courtyard, now occupied by Puno's most charming café.

At the corner of Conde de Lemos and Deústua is the **Casa Conde de Lemos** (8:30am-12:30pm and 1:30pm-5:30pm Mon.-Fri.), which is part of a building where Peru's viceroy lived when he first stopped in the city. It is now the headquarters of Puno's Regional Culture Office and includes the **Francisco Montoya Riquelme art gallery.** Across the street from the balcony is the **Museo Dreyer Municipal** (Conde de Lemos 289, next to Plaza de Armas, 9am-7pm Mon.-Sat., US$5), which has a collection of pre-Inca and Inca ceramics, gold, weavings, and stone sculptures, as well as stamps and documents on the history of the Spanish foundation of Puno.

Puno's **pedestrian street,** Lima, connects the Plaza de Armas to **Parque Pino** and has the city's best restaurants and cafés. The 18th-century church gracing Parque Pino is dedicated to San Juan Bautista and contains the Virgen de Candelaria, Puno's patroness and center of its most important festival. Past Parque Pino is the **Coca Museum & Customs** (Deza 301, no phone, www.museodelacoca.com, 9am-8pm Mon.-Sat., US$1.75). This excellent family-run museum has two parts: Half the exhibits explain the history of the coca plant, and the other half, accompanied by a movie, displays the foloric costumes used in traditional dances. Silva, the museum coordinator and director, speaks English and reads coca

leaves. The street, which switches names to Independencia, leads to Arco Deústua, a huge stone arch dedicated to those killed in the battles for independence in Junín and Ayacucho. Another option from Parque Pino is to head a few blocks downhill, toward the lake, to Puno's huge **central market,** which is especially busy in the mornings. Puno visitors may also want to take half a day and see the ruins of Sillustani.

ENTERTAINMENT AND EVENTS
Nightlife

The second-floor lounge of **Colors Restaurant Lounge** (Lima 342, tel. 051/36-9254, 9am-10pm daily) is the best place for evening drinks and appetizers. The black sofas are showcased against white walls, the cocktails are varied, and some evenings there's a DJ. The best pub in Puno is **Kamizaraky** (Grau 148, cell tel. 950-077-173, 5pm-midnight Tues.-Sun.). For dancing, there's **Ekeko's Pub** (Lima 365, tel. 051/36-5986, 5pm-close daily), which ladles out free drinks 7:30pm-9:30pm daily. The best and one of the only discos in Puno is the salsa-influenced **Domino** (Libertad 443, 7pm-3am Tues.-Sun.).

TOP EXPERIENCE

★ Folklore Festivals

A highlight of any visit to Lake Titicaca is seeing one of 300 traditional festivals that happen in this area each year. **PromPeru** (www.peru.info), the government promotion agency, keeps an updated list of festivals. Lake Titicaca has the richest and most vibrant dances and celebrations in all of Peru, and it is worth timing your trip to see one. With precision and endurance, entire towns participate in the orchestras, musical groups, and elaborately costumed dances. Though performed on Roman Catholic holidays, most of the dances in Puno are rooted in pre-Columbian rituals of harvest, planting, herding, and magic.

The most famous dance is **La Diablada** (Feb. 2), performed yearly during Puno's

Iron Boats Up and Over the Andes

Peru is filled with stories about large iron boats lugged to improbable places. In 1890, rubber baron Carlos Fermín Fitzcarrald and an army of 1,000 indigenous Piro people lugged a steamship up and over a ridge, nearly 10 kilometers, to connect two river basins. This harebrained scheme became the subject of *Fitzcarraldo*, the 1982 movie directed by Werner Herzog.

An even crazier but less well-known scheme was concocted by the Peruvian navy in 1861, when it ordered not one but two huge iron gunboats—the *Yavarí* and the *Yapura*—for patrolling the waters of Lake Titicaca. Within two years, the Thames Iron Works and Ship Building Company in London had the gunboats shipped, in crates, around Cape Horn to Arica, the Peruvian port that would later be snatched by Chile in the War of the Pacific.

This is where the story becomes surreal. From the desert coast, with the Andes looming before them, porters hefted the crankshafts to their shoulders, while mules stood, knees quivering, under the weight of hull sections and crates containing more than 2,766 ship parts. The 466-kilometer journey, up and over the Andes, wound up steep and treacherous trails and included a final 4,700-meter pass. Not surprisingly, getting everything to the shores of Lake Titicaca took more than six years. With much fanfare, the *Yavarí* was launched on Christmas Day 1870 and the *Yapura* three years later.

Because of a lack of coal, the navy began shoveling a more abundant local fuel source into the ship's boilers: dried llama dung. But more space was needed to accommodate the manure piles. The *Yavarí* was cut in half in order to add 12 meters to her hold, bringing her to a total length of 50 meters. Finally, in 1914, her steam engine was replaced by a Swedish-made Bolinder, a four-cylinder diesel. Half a century later, the boats were decommissioned. The *Yapura* was sold for scrap metal, and the *Yavarí* was abandoned on the lake's shores, its instruments carted off to Arequipa's municipal museum.

The sight of the forgotten ship, whose hull had rusted little in the lake's fresh waters, moved Englishwoman Meriel Larken to action in the early 1980s. She launched the Yavarí Association to save the old ship and attracted the financial support of Britain's Prince Philip, who had visited Lake Titicaca in 1962. In 1999, more than 40 years after her last voyage, the *Yavarí* once again slipped her moors and began plying the waters of Lake Titicaca.

The *Yavarí* is, without a doubt, the most interesting thing to see in Puno, and it's a one-of-a-kind in the whole world. The bunk, engine, and map rooms have been meticulously restored, and the bridge has all the ship's original navigation equipment, including an old-fashioned sextant and compass. The Bolinder engine, lovingly restored by Volvo engineers, is considered the oldest working ship engine in the world.

Fiesta de la Virgen de la Candelaria. The dance is essentially a struggle between dozens of elaborately costumed angels and bug-eyed horned devils, along with an ever-growing cast of new characters: the Widow, the Skeleton, the Old Man, the Mexican, the Redskin, Batman, and so on. Other dances include **Choq'elas,** which is performed before the roundup of the vicuñas, and **Q'ajelo,** which ends when the gun-toting shepherds steal the dancing maidens before them and carry them off over their shoulders.

The musical instruments used are a good example of the intermingling of Spanish with Inca and Aymara. The trumpets, tubas, saxophones, and stringed instruments are recent European contributions, but the flutes, panpipes, and drums have evolved over thousands of years. The flutes range from the tiny *quena*, which looks like a pennywhistle, to the huge *pincullo*, made out of a chunk of algaroba wood. The panpipes range from the handheld *zampoñas* or *antaras* to the *sicus*, which are almost as tall as their players. There is also a huge range of drums, rattles, and bells.

SHOPPING

Puno has two old buildings that have been renovated into small shopping centers with cafés. **Casa del Corregidor** (Deústua 576, www.casadelcorregidor.pe, 10am-9pm Mon.-Fri., 10am-8pm Sat.-Sun.) is near the plaza, and **Casona Parodi** (Lima 394, no phone, 9am-10pm daily) is on the main drag. In addition to a restaurant, the Casona Parodi houses artisans shops that sell alpaca products and silver jewelry.

Puno is a good place to buy alpaca wool clothing and weavings. The highest quality is found at the expensive **Kuna** (tel. 051/36-8422, www.kuna.com.pe, 7am-10am and 5pm-10pm daily), which sells nice sweaters, scarves, and shawls from the Hotel Libertador on the Esteves Island. A place with a social cause is the **Casa de la Mujer Artesana** (Puno 645, tel. 051/36-4196, 11am-9pm Mon.-Fri., 4pm-9pm Sat.)

RECREATION

The turquoise waters of Lake Titicaca are Puno's main draw, and there are two ways to get out on them: the traditional large motorized boats or a kayak. The kayak route is strongly encouraged. There are also opportunities for horseback riding, cycling, and even bird-watching.

TOP EXPERIENCE

★ Kayaking Lake Titicaca

There is no better way to see the beauty of Lake Titicaca than by sea kayak. You can start your kayaking trip far from the hustle and bustle of Puno at **Llachón,** a Quechua village on the lake's shore. At dawn, with Bolivia's snow-covered mountains aglow, instead of chugging across the lake on a diesel-powered boat, glide on the glassy waters past boulders covered with bright-green algae, breathe in the musty air, and watch waves fold onto the white-sand beaches. We would have sworn we were on an ocean were it not for the impossibly thin air—and the fact that our guide kept drinking the crystal-clear lake water from his cupped hands. You can leave the shoreline and begin to paddle across the lake, as deep as 275 meters in some places, toward the rising hulk of **Isla Amantaní.** By evening, the lake is glassy calm and stained red by the setting sun.

ExplorAndes (Bolognesi 334, Lima tel. 01/200-6100) offers a variety of safe and organized kayak trips leaving from Llachón. A half-day trip tours the shores of the peninsula, a full-day trip goes back and forth to Taquile or Amantaní, and a three-day trip explores the islands in detail. Longer 10-day trips to out-of-the-way places can be arranged. The company has excellent equipment and provides everything needed. **Valentín Quispe** (cell tel. 951-821-392, llachon@yahoo.com) in Llachón is the kayak caretaker, and trips can also be arranged directly through him.

Motorboat Tours

An early morning start to the day will find you, and 10 to 20 others, at the Puno port boarding a double-deck motorboat and throwing on a life jacket. On the typical tour, in an hour you'll be at the **Islas Uros.** From there, it is another two or three hours on to **Islas Amantaní and Taquile.** The motorboat's enclosed first floor is often the DVD room, where educational films about the lake and its cultures are shown. The second floor is an open-air deck for sightseeing. Tours can be arranged as day trips or overnights. Some travel agencies have high-speed boats, which greatly reduce travel times.

Horseback Riding

Enjoy horseback riding at **Fundo Chincheros** (Puno-Juliaca Hwy., 9 kilometers north of Puno, tel. 051/35-1921, www.fundo.casadelcorregidor.pe, US$25 pp half-day tour), a country hacienda in the valley just north of Puno operated by the owners of the café Bar in La Casa del Corregidor. Apart from trail rides, the day is spent hiking through cactus forest, seeing vicuñas, and having a garden picnic next to a rare 17th-century *capilla abierta,* or open chapel.

Lake Titicaca: Folklore Capital of Peru

The festivals and celebrations at Lake Titicaca are some of the most vibrant and spirited in Peru. It's worth timing your visit to the region to coincide with one of the 300 annual festivities. **PromPeru** (www.peru.info), the government promotion agency, maintains an updated list of festivals.

- January, 3rd Thursday: **Pacha Mama ceremony** on Isla Amantaní

- February 2-19: **Virgen de Candelaria** in Puno

- February, 2nd Thursday: *Ispalla* **dance** to Pachamama at hilltop pre-Inca temple in Llachón

- All February: **Carnaval** in Puno and surrounding areas

- May 2-3: **Alasitas,** a festival featuring good luck charms to be hung on the Aymara Ekeko doll in Puno

- May 3-8: **Fiesta de la Cruz y de San Martín de Porras** in Ilave

- May, 1st week: **Fiesta de San Bartolomé** in Chucuito

- May 5-17: **Pentecostal celebration of San Isidro Labrador** on Isla Taquile

- May, 4th week: **Roundup *(chacu)* of vicuña** on Isla Umayo, near Sillustani; visitors are invited to join

- June 10-14: **Founders Day** celebration in Llachón with dances and bullfights

- June 23-25: **Festival de San Juan** in Puno

- July 2: **Founders Day** celebration in Capachica, en route to Llachón

The controversial constructions, which were banned after 1680, allowed Spanish priests to baptize indigenous people without having to let them in the church.

Tour Guides and Agencies

All Ways Travel (Deustua 576, 2nd Fl., tel. 051/35-3979, www.titicacaperu.com) can also arrange kayak trips, but its specialty is socially conscientious tourism. Managed by Víctor Pauca and his entrepreneurial daughter Eliana, a graduate of the International Development Policy School at Duke University, the agency offers slightly more expensive trips that are worth it for their quality and community benefits. A two-day trip to Uros, Amantani, and Taquile, with an overnight on Amantani, costs US$35 pp plus US$17 to be paid to the Amantaní host family.

Run by a Peruvian husband-wife team, **Edgar Adventures** (Lima 328, tel. 051/35-3444, www.edgaradventures.com) focuses on activity. If you want to visit Lake Titicaca, Edgar will take you to the noncommercialized island of Ticonata, where you will spend the afternoon farming with locals. Or you can do a one-day trip that combines a visit to the Urumayo Island, where you can see vicuñas, and then check out Sillustani, a pre-Inca burial ground. Apart from these and other specialty trips, the agency also offers conventional tours.

Dozens of agencies offer the traditional day or overnight trips to the lake's islands and the surrounding sites of Sillustani and Chucuito. Be sure to use a recommended guide, and remember; you get what you pay for. One reliable agency is **Inca Lake**

- July 25 onward: **Fiesta de Santiago Apóstol** on Isla Taquile, in Chucuito, and in Lampa
- August 1-3: **Fiesta de la Octava de Santiago,** on Isla Taquile
- August 6: **Fiesta Niño de Praga** in Capachica, en route to Llachón
- August 10-17: **Fiesta de San Simón** on Isla Amantaní
- August 15: **Festividad de la Virgen de Cancharani** in Puno
- August 15-18: **Festividad de la Virgen de Asunción** in Chucuito
- September 15: **Fiesta de la Virgen de la Natividad** in Acora
- September 24: **Festividad de Nuestra Señora de las Mercedes** in Juliaca
- September 29: **Fiesta de San Miguel Arcángel** in Ilave
- October 2: **Fiesta de Nuestra Señora del Rosario** in Acora
- October 12-19: **Fiesta de Nuestra Señora del Rosario** in Chucuito
- October, 3rd week: **National road rally** around Lake Titicaca, with dances in Puno
- November 1-7: **Puno Week,** including the arrival by raft of the legendary founders of the Inca empire, Mamo Ocllo and Manco Cápac, on November 5
- November 1-2: **Fiesta de Todos los Santos** throughout the area
- December 5: **Fiesta de Santa Bárbara** in Chucuito, Ilave, and Puno
- December 6-8: **Fiesta de la Inmaculada Concepción** in Puno, Lampa, and other villages

(Cajamarca 619, cell tel. 956-060-988, www.incalake.com, 9am-1pm, 3pm-7pm Mon.-Sat.). It offers trips to Uros; Uros and Taquile; Uros, Amantaní, and Taquile; and to Sillustani. It can also do private tours. **Suri Explorer** (Teodoro Valcárcel 158, tel. 051/36-8188, www.suriexplorer.com) offers similar trips at comparable prices.

FOOD

Most of Puno's best restaurants are along Lima, the upscale pedestrian street off the Plaza de Armas. A good local dish to try is *chairo,* a soup of beef or lamb, potatoes, beans, squash, cabbage, *chuño* (dried potato), wheat, and *chalona* (dried mutton). *Trucha* (trout), *pejerrey,* and *ishpi* are excellent local fish, and *sajta de pollo* is a chicken stew mixed with potatoes and peanuts.

Peruvian

Famous for its antique iron collection, which hangs on the walls of its new location, **Restaurant Museo La Casona** (Lima 423, 2nd Fl., tel. 051/35-1108, www.lacasona-restaurant.com, noon-9:45pm daily, US$5-7) is an institution in Puno. This is your chance to try guinea pig, garlic alpaca meat, and *anticuchos.* Off Lima, **La Estancia** (Libertad 137, tel. 051/36-5469, 11am-10pm daily, US$6-8) serves excellent *parrillas* (grilled meats) and trout, and has an unlimited salad bar. Friendly ★ **Mojsa** (Lima 635, 2nd Fl., tel. 051/36-3182, www.mojsarestaurant.com, noon-9:30pm daily, US$3-7) makes a good afternoon coffee stop, with a view over the Plaza de Armas and the Cathedral. **La Table del Inca** (Ancash 239, cell tel. 994-659-357, 6pm-10pm Mon.-Sat., US$20) is a bit pricy, with classic options like *lomo saltado*, but it also has quinoa risotto and stuffed guinea pig.

International

Flip open the artsy black-and-white menu of **Colors Restaurant Lounge** (Lima 342, tel. 051/36-9254, 9am-10pm daily, US$8-10) and you'll quickly realize that the same artistic sensibilities have reached the food. A *lomo saltado* is whipped into a sandwich, and trout and beef are sliced thin into carpaccio. The most popular dish is the Andean cheese fondue, but the menu also offers Greek- and Thai-inspired dishes. A few doors down, and by the same owners, is **IncaBar** (Lima 348, tel. 051/36-8031, 7am-10pm daily, US$6), which has really good food: Greek salads and *pomodoro* pasta with plum tomatoes, basil, and garlic are just a few of the tempting dishes. Unfortunately, time has begun to wear on the restaurant and it is not as popular as it once was.

Pizza

Locals say the cozy **Machu Pizza** (Arequipa 409, cell tel. 951-390-652, www.tumachu-pizza.com, 4:30pm-11pm daily, US$5) holds the honor for best pizza; it also delivers. **Pizzeria Andina** (Lima 525, cell tel. 951-515-844, US$5) has good wood-fired pizza and other pastas.

Cafés, Bakeries, and Ice Cream

The most charming place to hang out is **Café Bar** (Deústua 576, tel. 051/35-1921, www.cafebar.casadelcorregidor.pe, 9am-9pm Mon.-Sat., US$1), in the 17th-century Casa del Corregidor. The café is an NGO whose 5,000 members work in the Puno coffee industry. All eight types of coffee are local and delicious. The menu also offers Greek salads, gourmet appetizers, and a range of teas. There is no place better to enjoy a snack than on the café's sun-filled patio. **Café Ricos Pan** (Arequipa 332; Moquegua 326, tel. 051/35-4179, www.ricospan.com.pe, 6am-10pm Mon.-Sat., 3pm-9pm Sun., US$2) serves good

milk shakes, quiche, and espresso drinks at incredibly cheap prices. Standouts include the gooseberry cheesecake and pisco sours (US$1.50).

Markets

Near the **Mercado Central** (Tacna and Arbulu, 7am-6pm daily), where you can buy produce, cheeses, and meats, there is a **Supermarket** (Oquendo 226, 8am-10pm daily) that sells yogurts, cold cuts, and dry goods.

ACCOMMODATIONS
US$10-25

Kusillo's Posada (Federico More 162, tel. 051/36-4579, www.kusillosposada.com, US$20s, US$30 d, with breakfast), a backpacker's hostel, has a very homey feeling. The first-floor living room, dining room, and kitchen are open for guest use, and the upstairs bedrooms are bright and clean with telephones and Wi-Fi. This is a good place for a long-term stay. **Pacha Hostel** (Lima 106, tel. 051/35-1087, www.pachahostel.com, US$10 dorm, US$15 s) is centrally located and gets good reviews for its clean rooms and helpful staff.

US$25-50

Casa Panq'arani (Arequipa 1086, tel. 051/36-4892, www.casapanqarani.com, US$30 s, US$50 d, with breakfast) "is not a restaurant, neither a hotel," the owners claim. "It is grandma's house for you to stay in." Nothing could be truer. Consuelo Giraldo and her family live in this beautiful dreamlike house, which has some extra rooms with private baths and a terrace, giving you the feeling that you are not staying at a bed-and-breakfast. You can order meals cooked by Doña Consuelo, including local traditional food or other dishes. This is one of the best places to stay in Puno.

★ **Posada Don Giorgio** (Tarapacá 238, tel. 051/36-3648, www.posadadongiorgio.com.pe, US$33 s, US$42 d, with breakfast) is another cozy option some blocks from downtown, with great service in a very relaxed and quiet atmosphere. Rooms are quite simple but with comfortable beds and very clean baths. There is Wi-Fi, a small business center, a good restaurant, and rent-a-car service.

For a more traditional hotel, the quiet **Sillustani** (Tarapacá 305, tel. 051/35-1881, www.sillustani.com, US$35 s, US$46 d, with breakfast) has comfortable carpeted rooms with bathtubs and cable TV. A buffet breakfast is served in a formal dining room.

The bed and breakfast at the **Yavarí** (behind Sonesta Posada Hotel, cell tel. 994-622-511 or 989-289-524, www.yavari.org, US$40 pp, with breakfast) is the most unique place to stay in Puno. The 19th-century antique ship, which was hauled up the Andes, includes bunks in four cozy cabins, with a capacity for seven guests. Staying here is an unforgettable night, with great sunsets.

US$50-100

The most elegantly old-fashioned place in town is the Belgian-owned **Colón Inn** (Tacna 290, tel. 051/35-7090, www.coloninn.com, US$45 s, US$55 d, with breakfast). This hotel's large rooms are arranged around a marble-floored lobby, sun-filled sitting rooms, and atrium. Rooms have cable TV and writing desks.

Plaza Mayor Hotel (Deústua 342, tel. 051/36-6089, www.plazamayorhotel.com, US$60 s, US$80 d, with breakfast) has king beds, feather pillows, bathtubs, and cable TV. Breakfasts are served in a window-lined dining room. The hotel has all major amenities, including Wi-Fi and heaters in the rooms.

Casona Plaza Hotel (Puno 280, cell tel. 951-751-818, www.casonaplazahotel.com, US$90 s, US$100 d, with buffet breakfast) has 64 comfy and spacious rooms with very nice baths, blow-dryers, room heating, cable TV, Wi-Fi, and 24-hour room service. The hotel has a restaurant-bar, laundry service, Internet access included in the rates, a private garage, and medical assistance. It is conveniently located one block from Puno's Plaza de Armas.

Sol Plaza Puno (Puno 307, tel. 051/35-2658, www.solplazahotel.com, US$65 s, US$80 d, with buffet breakfast), half a block

from the Plaza de Armas, is another option in town, with nice comfortable beds in the rooms, despite the decor, which is quite cheesy. Services in this three-star hotel include baths with showers and bathtubs, room heating, Wi-Fi, cable TV, oxygen on request, a bar, a restaurant, and massage services on request.

On a cold evening, the fireplace at the **Casa Andina Classic-Puno Tikarani** (Independencia 143, tel. 051/36-7803, www.casa-andina.com, US$61 s or d, with buffet breakfast) will come in handy. The 50 rooms at this hotel, which has a nicely decorated courtyard, are spacious, quiet, and comfortable. Its amenities include an Internet center, Wi-Fi, an ATM, and laundry service.

The new **Tierra Viva Puno Plaza Hotel** (Grau 270, tel. 051/36-8005, www.tierraviva-hoteles.com, US$60 s or d, with buffet breakfast) is a block from the Plaza de Armas, with 30 brightly lit and carpeted rooms that have baby alpaca blankets, heaters, and flat-screen TVs with cable. The hotel has Wi-Fi and an elevator (very useful if you've just arrived in Puno).

US$100-150

An affordable luxury option, on the lake near Hotel Libertador Lago Titicaca, is **Sonesta Posada del Inca** (Sesqui Centenario 610, tel. 051/36-4111, www.sonesta.com, US$105 s or d). The carpeted rooms are comfortable, with a small desk, a flat-screen TV, heaters, and many other amenities. An exquisite breakfast buffet is served on a lakeside dining room or outdoors on an open porch. The hotel also has oxygen and Internet access (US$4 per hour). The *Yavarí*, Puno's most interesting attraction, is docked a few meters away.

Over US$150

If it is a chilly day on the lake, you can slip down to the lobby of **Casa Andina Private Collection** (Sesqui Centenario 1970, tel. 051/36-3992, www.casa-andina.com, US$155 s or d) for a hot cup of tea. But if it is bright and sunny, throw open your windows and step out onto your lakeside balcony. Half the rooms face the lake, and all have down comforters, cable TV, telephones, and writing tables. The bar serves an excellent *muña* sour, the local take on pisco sour, and the lakeside restaurant serves a flavorful Novoandino menu. There is also a business center with fast Internet, a jewelry shop, and a small gift store.

Of all the former state-owned hotels, the five-star **Hotel Libertador Lago Titicaca** (Isla Esteves s/n, tel. 051/36-7780, www.libertador.com.pe, US$160 s or d, US$200 suite, with breakfast) is one of the more stunning. It is like a huge alabaster cruise ship, perched on its own island jutting into Lake Titicaca. From the marble lobby, the rooms rise on both sides over a huge glass-enclosed courtyard and an expansive, elegant area with a bar and couches. Lying in the king beds surrounded by five-star amenities with the sun rising over Lake Titicaca is truly deluxe—especially when you consider the spa and whirlpool tub awaiting you. The hotel even has its own dock, where tours leave for the islands.

INFORMATION AND SERVICES

Free visitor information and maps are available at **Iperú** (Deústua and Lima, tel. 051/36-5088, www.peru.info, 9am-6pm Mon.-Sat., 9am-1pm Sun.). A concise and interesting pamphlet that explains life on the islands and shore is Juan Palao Berastain's "Titikaka Lake: Children of the Sacred Lake," available in bookstores and tour agencies.

Both the **national police** (Sol 450, tel. 051/35-3988) and the **tourist police** (Deústua 558, tel. 051/35-2303) are available 24 hours daily. **Peruvian Immigration** (Ayacucho 270, tel. 051/35-7103) can extend tourist visas, but expect a wait. Americans, Canadians, Britons, New Zealanders, and Australians do not need visas to enter Bolivia but can ask for information at the **Bolivian Consulate** (Arequipa 136, 2nd Fl., tel. 051/35-1251, 8am-4pm Mon.-Fri.).

For health care, there is the 24-hour **Medicentro** (Moquegua 191, tel. 051/36-5909) tourist clinic, where English is spoken. Other options include **Hospital Manuel Nuñez Butrón** (El Sol 1022, tel. 051/36-7128, emergency tel. 051/36-8682), **Hospital Regional Essalud** (Parque Industrial Salcedo s/n, tel. 051/35-2661), and **Clínica Los Pinos** (Los Alamos B-2, tel. 051/35-1071). For pharmacy needs, **Inkafarma** (Lima 364, 10am-10pm daily) is a good option located a block from the Plaza de Armas.

For money matters, head to Lima, the pedestrian street, for **Interbank** (Lima 444) and **Banco Continental** (Lima 400), as well as **Scotiabank** on the Plaza de Armas; all have ATMs. The post office is **Serpost** (Moquegua 269, tel. 051/35-1141, 8am-7:45pm Mon.-Fri., 9am-noon Sat.).

There is fast **Internet** access at several cafés along Lima. At many cafés you can also make international calls. Laundry can be done at **Don Marcelo** (Ayacucho 651, 10am-6pm Mon.-Sat.) and **Lavandería América** (Moquegua 175, 10am-5:30pm daily).

GETTING THERE AND AROUND

Air

Unfortunately, Puno does not have an airport. The closest is **Aeropuerto Manco Cápac** (JUL, tel. 051/32-8226) in Juliaca, about 45 minutes north of Puno. **LATAM** (Tacna 299, Lima tel. 01/213-8200, www.latam.com) flies the routes Lima-Juliaca and Juliaca-Arequipa several times a day. LATAM also has a Cusco-Juliaca flight. **Avianca** (www.avianca.com) also has daily Lima-Juliaca flights.

Bus

Puno's **Terminal Terrestre** (1 de Mayo 703, at Bolívar, tel. 051/36-4733 for schedules) opened in 2001 and has greatly improved the pleasure of busing into Puno. It is safe, with restaurants, snack bars, and even a clean, though noisy, hostel. From here buses arrive from and depart for Juliaca, Arequipa, Tacna, Cusco, and Lima, as well as La Paz, Bolivia, through both Desaguadero and Copacabana.

The travel times given here are accurate; if a bus company promises you a dramatically shorter ride, do not believe it. Traveling at night is also not recommended.

If you're going to spend a day riding to Cusco, why not make a trip of it? There are two tourist buses that include a huge buffet lunch, an English-speaking guide, and stops at most of the major ruins on the way. **Inka Express** (Tacna 346, tel. 051/36-5654, www.inkaexpress.com, US$60) makes stops in Pukará and La Raya before a buffet lunch in Sicuani. The bus then continues to see the extraordinary Inca ruins at Raqchi and the exquisite colonial church at Andahuaylillas. Buses generally leave Puno at 7am and arrive at 5pm, and include hotel pickup and drop-off. Some buses even have onboard oxygen tanks for passengers with altitude sickness.

Ormeño (tel. 051/36-8176, www.grupoormeno.com.pe) has a direct seven-hour bus to Cusco. It is the best bus option. There are many options for the five-hour trip to Arequipa. **Cruz del Sur** (tel. 051/35-3542, www.cruzdelsur.com.pe) has buses that leave at 3pm (US$20-25) for Arequipa. If you are continuing on to Lima, you can catch Cruz del Sur's night bus (US$39-54) that leaves Arequipa at 10pm daily. **Ormeño** has a bus that leaves from Puno at 6:30am daily for Lima (US$43), with a brief stopover in Arequipa.

Train

One of the highest passenger trains in the world, the *Andean Explorer* runs between Cusco and Puno. The views along this route are fantastic, although the train rolls right by a series of interesting ruins. It does stop briefly, however, at the high pass of La Raya (4,314 meters), where a colonial chapel stands alone in the middle of the high plateau. Trains depart on both the Puno-to-Cusco route and the Cusco-to-Puno route on Monday, Wednesday, Friday, and Saturday. From Cusco, the train leaves at 8am, stops in La Raya at 12:15pm, and arrives in Puno

at 6pm. Another train leaves from Puno at 8am, stops in La Raya at 12:45pm, and arrives in Cusco at 6pm. This deluxe train costs US$256 one-way, including lunch. This first-class service has elegant dining cars, an open-air bar car, and luxurious coaches designed by James Parks and Associates, the same company that designed the first-class cabins for Singapore Airlines. Tickets can be bought at the **Puno train station** (La Torre 224, 7am-noon and 3pm-6pm Mon.-Fri., 7am-3pm Sat.) or reserved online or by phone through **PeruRail** (tel. 084/58-1414, www.perurail.com).

Boat

Two luxury boat companies offer interesting, though expensive, options for traveling between Puno and La Paz, Bolivia, in a single day. The trips include a bus to **Copacabana**, boat rides and tours of **Islas del Sol y de la Luna,** and a final bus journey to **La Paz** (about 13 hours). It can also be done in the opposite direction if you want to, for example, fly into La Paz and out of Cusco.

Crillon Tours (Tarapacá 391, tel. 051/35-1052, www.crillontours.com), takes passengers from Puno to Copacabana by bus, from Copacabana to Isla del Sol to Huatajata, Bolivia, by high-speed hydrofoil, and then on to La Paz (US$189). The total journey is about 13 hours. At Huatajata, Crillon also operates the five-star Inca Utama Hotel & Spa and La Posada del Inca, a restored colonial hacienda on Isla del Sol. Crillon has offices in La Paz (Camacho 1223, tel. 591-2/233-7533, titicaca@entelnet.bo).

Transturin (www.transturin.com) has buses and slightly slower mini cruise ships, or catamarans, working the same basic route, although they dock at Chúa, Bolivia. This can either be a day tour or include a night aboard a catamaran docked at Isla del Sol. Transturin has an office in Puno through **Leon Tours** (Libertad 176, tel. 051/35-2771, www.peru-titicaca.com). Transturin also offers day trips from Puno to La Paz that visit

Isla del Sol (US$264 pp), and a variety of all-inclusive package tours.

Local Transportation

Rent a taxi for about US$7 per hour. Try **Taxi Tours** (tel. 051/36-7000) or **Aguila Taxi** (tel. 051/36-9000).

Inexpensive, safe boats leave from Puno's public dock, at the end of Avenida Titicaca, for most of the surrounding islands. The dock facilities include police, a health clinic, restrooms, and stalls that sell food, sweaters, hats, and more. Boats leave for a 2.5-hour tour of Uros (US$5) between 8am and 4pm daily. There are *colectivo* boats that leave for the 3.5-hour trip to Taquile (US$8), including a stop at Uros, at 7am daily. Those who want to overnight on Amantaní can take a boat (US$11) at 8am daily that visits Uros en route to Amantaní. To travel from Amantaní on to Taquile the next day, you need to arrange transportation with a travel agency. A private boat for a one-day trip to Taquile and back costs around US$100.

Lake Titicaca

TOP EXPERIENCE

Lake Titicaca seems more like an ocean than a lake. Bright-green algae blankets beach boulders and fills the air with a musty seaside smell. Waves lap sandy beaches. The intense blue waters, as deep as 270 meters, stretch endlessly in all directions. The only reminders that Lake Titicaca is a lake are the impossibly thin air and a backdrop of snow-covered mountains—and the sight of islanders drinking the lake's clear waters out of their cupped hands.

The best way to experience Lake Titicaca is to leave behind the bustle of Puno and escape to the lake's placid shores and islands. Here you will find paths bordered by stone walls, a crystal-clear sky, and sweeping views of arid sunbaked terraces. The land, shaded in places by groves of eucalyptus, plunges into waters below. On sunny days, the air is perfectly still and the sky blends with the water to form a single expanse of blue. The mood changes quickly, however, when squalls swoop in from the high plateaus, plunging temperatures and whipping the lake into a froth of gray waters. By evening, when the lake is calm again, the sunset appears as a line of fire around a half moon, the curvature of the earth plainly visible.

It is no coincidence that the Inca decided first to conquer this lake, nor that they formed a creation myth around it. The Inca contend that the sun sent his son, Manco Cápac, and the moon sent her daughter, Mamo Ocllo, to emerge from the waters of Lake Titicaca and found the Inca empire. It is also no coincidence that the Spaniards decided to bequeath this lake and its people directly to the king and not to a conquistador, as was usually the case; despite its altitude and barren appearance, Lake Titicaca has traditionally been a cradle of civilization and a center of wealth. The dense populations of Quechua- and Aymara-speaking indigenous people around this lake have a unique place in Peruvian culture because their ways of life go back at least 3,000 years.

By 600 BC, the Chiripa and Pukara populations were already building temples around the lake, which offered a perfect combination of grasslands for llamas and alpacas, an ample supply of fish, and good growing conditions for potatoes and quinoa. By AD 200 the gold-covered carved stone blocks were being raised on the shores of Lake Titicaca to build Tiwanaku, a city in present-day Bolivia that lasted 1,000 years. The Tiwanaku empire, along with the Ayacucho-based Huari, would later spread its deities and urban ways of life across Peru, laying the foundation for the Inca empire. The Tiwanaku empire collapsed around AD 1000, perhaps because of a

Lake Titicaca

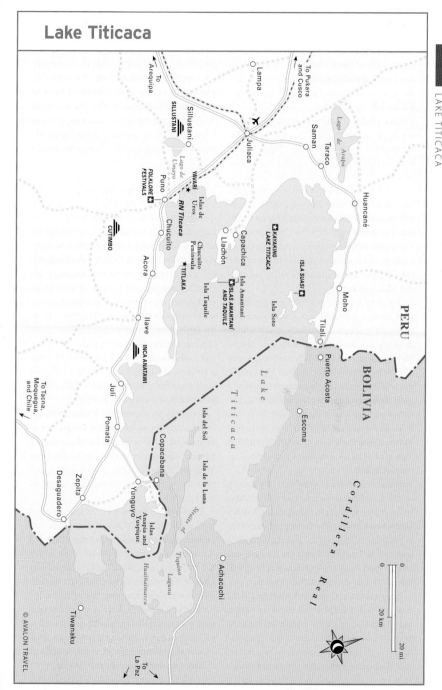

To Arequipa

Lampa

To Pukara and Cusco

Lago de Arapa

Saman

Taraco

Juliaca

Huancané

SILLUSTANI
Sillustani

Lago de Umayo

YAVARI
FOLKLORE FESTIVALS
Puno

RN Titicaca

Islas de Uros

Capachica

KAYAKING LAKE TITICACA

ISLA SUAS

CUTIMBO

Chucuito

Llachón

Chucuito Peninsula

Isla Amantani

ISLAS AMANTANI AND TAQUILE

Isla Soto

Moho

Acora

TITILAKA

Isla Taquile

Tilali

Puerto Acosta

Ilave

INCA ANATAWI

PERU

BOLIVIA

Escoma

Juli

Lake Titicaca

Pomata

Copacabana

Isla del Sol

Isla de la Luna

Cordillera Real

To Tacna, Moquegua, and Chile

Zepita

Desaguadero

Yunguyo

Islas Anapia and Yuspique

Straits of Tiquina

Huiñaimarca

Achacachi

© AVALON TRAVEL

Tiwanaku

Tiquina Laguna

To La Paz

0   20 km
0   20 mi

drought, and the Lupaca and Colla emerged to build the tombs at Sillustani and other monuments. These proud people would become famous for their bloody rebellions against both the Inca and the Spanish.

ISLAS UROS

Visitors tend to find the bizarre sight of floating Islas Uros (Uros Islands), about a 20-minute boat ride from Puno, either depressing or very interesting. The Uros, an ancient lake people who were harassed by the Spanish to near extinction, probably fled to these islands to escape forced labor in Spanish silver mines, although they may have come here earlier to isolate themselves from the Collas or Inca. Their way of life revolves around the *tótora*, or reed, which they cut and pile to form giant floating islands that are anchored to the shallow lake bottom.

The true Uros people, whom legends say were protected from cold by their thick black blood, have long since intermingled with the Aymara, whose language they now speak. Nevertheless, the islanders preserve a way of life that is probably based on Uros traditions. They live in family units governed by a grandfather, and they prearrange marriages—sometimes right after the births of the future bride and groom. They fish, hunt birds, and move around the lake in huge *tótora* rafts that look almost like Viking ships with their huge dragon heads.

Many visitors find it disconcerting to walk on the springy, waterlogged reeds, which have to be continually replenished as the bottom layers rot, creating the fermented odor that is peculiar to the islands. But the scenery is spectacular and the islands are unique—the largest even has a health clinic, a school, and a Seventh-Day Adventist church on it.

Tourism to the islands, which began in the late 1960s, has helped pull the Uros people out of grinding poverty and maintain their population of several hundred. But it has also brought problems. Thousands of tourists arrive each year with camcorders, creating a generation of begging children and adults who aggressively push miniature reed boats and other trinkets. Do not give money to begging children—give them fruit or school supplies, or buy something from them instead. The islanders also offer US$2 boat rides in their reed boats to neighboring islands. Most Puno agencies offer guided tours for the Uros Islands, and cheap public boats to the islands leave frequently from the Puno public pier.

LLACHÓN

Villagers in Llachón, a charming village on a peninsula near Puno and Juliaca, may not wear traditional clothing anymore, but staying with families is every bit as interesting, and less touristy, than visiting Islas Amantaní and Taquile. Valentín Quispe, who lives outside town near a cemetery, runs a rustic lodge (US$22 pp room and board) with fabulous views over the lake. The little cabins, with whitewashed walls and thatched roofs, are at the top of a hill and seem like stone huts in the sky. Nearby, an adobe arch supports nothing and leads nowhere—but it beautifully frames a piece of the lake itself. At night a billion stars come out, including the Southern Cross, pointing the way to Isla Amantaní.

Valentín also arranges homestays with other Llachón families, and his lodge serves as the point of departure for kayak trips to the islands. The kayaks can also be rented from Valentín for the day for a reasonable price, and the ruins of a pre-Inca temple are at the top of a nearby hill.

Llachón can be reached by taking a bus in Puno from the corner of Costanera and Lampa. Buses leave here for the village of Capachica (1.5 hours, US$1.50), from which the half-hour taxi ride to Llachón should cost US$7-8. There is a nice beach at Llachón with free camping and a French-owned campground at one end that can rent tents or provide meals. Anglers are glad to take travelers to nearby Islas Taquile and Amantaní, only 11 kilometers away from Llachón, by sailboat (US$6) or private motorboat (US$36).

★ ISLAS AMANTANÍ AND TAQUILE

Staying for a night or two with a family on Isla Taquile, about 35 kilometers from Puno, or the slightly farther Isla Amantaní, has become a classic Lake Titicaca experience that some travelers may consider excessively touristy nowadays. On these islands, visitors are picked up at the dock by a family member and led home to clean but rustic accommodations: a simple adobe room next to the family house, a lumpy mattress, and an outhouse without running water. With luck, visitors are invited to help herd the sheep, work in the terraced fields of potatoes and quinoa, or learn how to weave with back-strap looms. Evenings are spent watching the sunset, and usually there is music and dancing, arranged for the visitors, in the town square at night.

Taquile is closer to Puno and has been receiving increasing numbers of overnight visitors for nearly three decades. Because Taquile is just six kilometers long and one kilometer wide, it is possible to walk around the island in two hours on walled paths carved into the hillside that bob up and down along its contours. There are a few beaches, which can be nice on sunny days and conducive to a plunge in the lake's icy waters. There are pre-Inca ruins, though not very elaborate, on the tops of the hills, and an elegant stone arch at the high pass separating the two sides of the island. Everyone speaks Quechua, some speak Spanish, and almost no one speaks English. Taquile can receive as many as 500 overnighters during the high season (June-Aug.), so during high season it can be hard to have a secluded experience. Restaurants have sprung up in recent years, locals pose for photos, and people hawk handicrafts in the village and along popular walks.

The slightly larger Isla Amantaní, about 40 kilometers from Puno, rarely hosted foreigners for overnight visits, but since 2000, travelers have begun to stay the night here, and homestays have become an important means of making a living on the island. The quality of each homestay experience often depends largely on the family you are offered when you arrive. Your host family might teach you how to weave blankets and farm potatoes at high altitude. Or you might join them for family meals, with guinea pig as the main course.

As tourism has become an increasingly important source of income for the islands, the local elders, or *varayocs,* have struggled to find a system to spread the new wealth evenly among all families or, as they say, ensure that

gate on Isla Taquile

"todos comemos el mismo pan" ("all of us eat the same bread"). Their solution, based on the communal *ayllu* system, is run by the *varayocs,* who meet boats at the docks and rotate visitors to nearly 100 families. This equitable system has faltered somewhat in recent years because travel agencies are allowed to do direct deals with certain families, which end up getting a disproportionate share of guests. These family homes can have as many as four guest homes, which seems to water down the homestay experience.

Taquile has a true guest lodge, **Taquile Sumaq Wasi** (Sector Chuñopampa, cell tel. 996-662-956), with an on-site restaurant with homemade dishes, comfortable rooms with simple designs, a small garden and great views. On Amantaní, **Kantuta Lodge** (tel. 051/63-0238, www.kantutalodge.com) has a similarly elaborate setup. Though comfortable, these kinds of lodges represent a critical challenge to islands' communal way of life.

If you go on a prepaid tour to one of the islands, go with a socially responsible agency and ask a few questions beforehand. Ensure, for instance, that the agency pays the islanders the going rate—US$6 pp per night for lodging, US$3 for breakfasts, and US$4 for lunches and dinners. Ensure also that no more than two people will stay with each family and preferably away from the touristy area. Otherwise, arrange your own homestay by hopping aboard the boat (US$6) that leaves from Puno's public pier every morning between 7:30am and 8am—you will be assigned a family on arrival and will need to pay an arrival fee.

Whether you stay with a family or eat at one of Taquile's restaurants, you are likely to be served the same delicious and wholesome food: quinoa soup, steamed or fried *pejerrey* (the local fish), an omelet, or tortilla mixed with potatoes and vegetables. The main handicrafts are elaborately woven hats (*chullos*) and cloth belts, both of which play an important role in island culture. Travelers are advised to bring their own snacks and beverages— even a small bottle of beer can cost US$2 on Amantaní. Beds are likely to have a woolen blanket or two, but it is a good idea to bring a sleeping bag to stay warm, as well as a water bottle, soap, and toilet paper.

PENÍNSULA DE CAPACHICA

Six indigenous communities situated on the **Península de Capachica** (http://turismocapachica.wordpress.com), northeast of Puno, have organized themselves in tourism associations to offer the real thing: a genuine homestay experience with no intervention of travel agencies, as it used to be decades ago on Taquile and Amantaní. Each community offers different tours and services, totally independent of one another, some of them quite isolated without phone or Internet access, but truly well organized and ready to host travelers in comfortable lodgings with homemade meals and an extremely hospitable and friendly crowd of villagers that will surely make this an amazing and revealing experience. The six communities are Paramis, Chifrón, Escallani, Ccotos, Isla Tikonata, and Ccollpa.

Paramis (cell tel. 950-949-705, contact: Balbino Quispe), 67 kilometers from Puno, offers meals (US$3-4 each) and lodging (US$8 s, US$12 d) as well as a series of activities (US$1-4 each) that include the P'utin-Canjarno trek, artisanal fishing, adobe brick-making, farming, and bonfires.

Chifrón offers three different experiences: **Flor de Lago** and **Casa Rural Inti Wasi** (cell tel. 950-936-611, contact: Walther Pancca Páucar, titikakaintiwasi@hotmail.com), and **Playa Chifró.** They all offer meals (US$3-4 each) and lodging (US$5-13 s, US$11-22 d) and similar activities (US$5-8) such as walking the Centilinayok circuit and its spectacular views of the lake, boat rides around Isañata island, storytelling of local myths and legends, and a ceremony to Pachamama, among other things.

Escallani is the northernmost and remote community, grouped in **Munay Suyo** (contact: Rufino Paucar Pacompia), without phone or Internet access. This is probably the most interesting village; you could go and try your luck just dropping by and staying for a night or two. Ask for the **Asociación Turística Munay Suyo** when you arrive at Escallani. You can join families to sail in the lake in traditional boats through the *tótora* wetlands, where a wide variety of birds can be observed. Circuits to Apu Wiracochani or Kawayojapina cost US$4-7; meals are US$3-5 and lodging US$7 pp.

On the eastern side of the peninsula, **Ccotos** also has two groups: **Inca Samana** (cell tel. 951-856-462, contact: Alfonso Quispe Acuña) and **Posada Ccotos** (cell tel. 951-620-826, contact: Santos Ramos). This community offers activities (US$4) such as walks, fishing and sailing in the lake, and the experience of milking cows or farming. Typical foods (US$3-5 per meal) are served, and lodgings (US$5 s, US$9 d) are quite comfortable.

Isla Tikonata (cell tel. 951-664-881, contact: Marino Humpiri Charca) is an island off the coast of Ccotos and northwest of Amantaní. You can participate in activities (US$2-4) such as sailing around the island, fishing, and even shearing sheep or helping building a house. Food is about US$4 per meal and lodgings US$5 pp. Transportation from the peninsula to the island costs US$5.

Ccollpa is down south of the peninsula and has two groups hosting travelers: **San Pedro Ccollpa** (cell tel. 951-637-382, contact: Richard Cahui Flores, ccollpallachon@hotmail.com) and **Pacha Ccollpa** (cell tel. 951-311-622, contact: Dorca Cahui Padillo). Both offer food (US$2.50-5 per meal) and lodgings (US$6.50 s, US$13 d) along with activities (US$3-5) such as artisanal fishing, learning to dye wool, and sailing in the lake.

★ ISLA SUASI

If you are looking for an upscale Titicaca island experience, step onto the Isla Suasi, and all the stresses of the real world will disappear.

Suasi is the lake's only privately owned island, and the location of the exclusive **Hotel Isla Suasi** (tel. 051/35-1102, www.islasuasi.pe,

US$200 for 2 people). The lodge has a gourmet restaurant and 23 rooms, including a two-room lakeside cottage. Enjoy a massage, relax in a hammock in the gardens, or take a kayak out onto the lake. Despite all the development, the island trails, Andean cultural center, and gardens remain the same.

A walk or kayak trip around Suasi affords incredible views of distant blue mountains, islands in Bolivia, and orange-tinged sunsets. The dry air and the rustic smell of grasses remind you that, while you are in the lap of luxury, you are in the middle of nature.

The trip may be a splurge, but it's completely worth it. The lake's natural beauty is never as perceptible as it is here on the island. You'll return to the mainland with a spirit as clean as the Suasi air.

ISLAS ANAPIA AND YUSPIQUE

The trip to Anapia and Yuspique islands, in southern Lake Titicaca, begins with a two-hour drive along the Lake Titicaca's south shores, visiting the towns of Juli and Pomata, before passing through Yunguyo to the port of Punta Hermosa. Visitors then hop aboard a sailboat for a two-hour ride to Anapia's beach, where the father of each family leads each visitor to their new home. That afternoon, families and guests go hiking on nearby Isla Yuspique, which has a large herd of vicuñas, and have a beach picnic to try *huatia*, potatoes cooked in a natural oven with pieces of hot soil.

The trips are not staged or overly planned, which seems like a good thing, so the activities vary: There is usually an evening meeting of neighbors, with conversation and music, or a chance to herd animals, fish, or help build a house. Depending on the time of the year, visitors also help plant or harvest crops.

All Ways Travel (Deustua 576, 2nd Fl., Puno, tel. 051/35-3979, www.titicacaperu.com), managed by a father-and-daughter team in Puno, runs a socially responsible homestay program on Islas Anapia and Yuspique. As a mark of its success, the company has won an award from the Ford Foundation for the Best Community-Based Project in Peru. Since the project began in 1997, All Ways participants have helped to build a library and a puppet theater and to paint the local school. This trip also works well for travelers either coming from or continuing on to Bolivia and can be combined with a visit to Tiwanaku or the Islas del Sol y de la Luna. **Edgar Adventures** (Lima 328, Puno, tel. 051/35-3444, www.edgaradventures.com) also leads trips to the islands.

PUNO TO BOLIVIA

Travelers make a mistake when they breeze between Puno and the Bolivian border without stopping. The road passes through a string of quaint towns, with interesting colonial churches and a seemingly continuous schedule of festivities.

The south shores of Lake Titicaca are the center of Peru's Aymara people, who have a distinct language and culture. They have a historical reputation for repelling domination, be it the Inca 500 years ago or the Shining Path in the 1980s and 1990s. In 2004 several towns in this area rose in protests against allegedly corrupt leaders. In the worst instance, the mayor of the town of Ilave was dragged from a house and lynched by a mob of Aymara people. In 2011, large protests erupted against a Canadian-owned silver mining project, resulting in several deaths and damage to property. Before visiting these towns, inquire in Puno beforehand about the present situation.

Chucuito

Located 18 kilometers south of Puno, Chucuito is one of the oldest towns in the area and is surrounded by farming fields that slope gently down to Lake Titicaca. The town was once the capital of the whole province and has colonial churches on its two main squares. **Nuestra Señora de la Asunción** has a Renaissance facade from 1601 and sits near the upper Plaza de Armas. The second church, **Santo Domingo,** is L-shaped with

beautifully painted stone arches, a wooden altar carved in *pan de oro,* and a single ancient stone tower.

Chucuito's lead attraction, however, is **Inca Uyo** (7am-sunset daily, free), a walled enclosure next to Santo Domingo that looks, at first glance, like a garden of giant mushrooms. On closer inspection, the mushrooms are carved stone penises, some pointing up at the sky (presumably toward Inti, the Inca sun god), and others are rammed into the ground (toward Pachamama, mother earth goddess). At the center of this obvious fertility temple is the largest phallus of all, placed atop a platform carved with the outlines of a human figure. Village children, who work as the temple's very charming and dead-serious guides, claim that women still sneak into the temple at night, with coca leaves and *chicha,* to perform a ceremony designed to help them get pregnant. The essence of the ceremony, they contend, is that the women sit atop the head of the giant phallus for several hours. The origin of this temple is hotly debated; some say it was built by the Aymaras or the Inca. Others contend that cannot be possible, because the priests, who built the church next door, had a fondness for destroying idols that surely would have included phallus-shaped rocks. Whatever you believe, the site is still interesting.

FOOD AND ACCOMMODATIONS

There are two great lodging options near Chucuito. The best place to stay in town is ★ **Las Cabañas** (Tarapacá 538, near Plaza de Armas, or Bolognesi 334 in Puno, tel. 051/36-8494, www.chucuito.com, US$25 s, US$37 d, with breakfast). Inside high adobe walls is a charming garden of yellow *retama* and *queñua* flowers surrounding bungalows with wood floors, hearths, exposed beams, and new baths. The owner, Juan Palao Berastain, has authored the highly informative pamphlet about the area, "Titikaka Lake: Children of the Sacred Lake," on sale at the hotel. Members of Hostelling International receive a discount.

★ **Titilaka** (Lima tel. 01/700-5100, www. titilaka.com, US$301 s or US$530 d, including all meals), which is part of the exclusive Relais & Châteaux group, is a one-of-a-kind lodging situated on the shore of Lake Titicaca on the Chucuito Peninsula. The hotel offers 18 lake-view suites with heated floors and oversize tubs. The hotel also offers a series of half-day and full-day excursions to surrounding villages. The best restaurant in town is at Titilaka.

Crossing into Bolivia

From Puno, there are a few ways to make the border crossing to Bolivia. The most popular is to go from Puno to Yunguyo to Copacabana to La Paz, Bolivia, a route that leads through a series of interesting villages on the lake's south shore before a scenic ferry ride across the **Straits of Tiquina.** From Copacabana, it is easy to visit the **Isla del Sol** (Island of the Sun), a 20-kilometer boat ride from Copacabana. This island, covered in Inca ruins and graced by a sacred stone, was revered by the Inca as the place from where Manco Cápac emerged to found the Inca empire. Nearby is the smaller but interesting **Isla de la Luna** (Island of the Moon), birthplace of Mama Ocllo.

Panamericano (Tacna 245, tel. 051/35-4001, www.tourpanamericano.s5.com) buses leave Puno for this seven-hour trip at 7am and 7:30am daily. Or explore the towns along the way by hopping on and off a local bus from Puno to Yunguyo (2.5 hours, US$4). These *colectivo* buses leave from the local bus station, two blocks from the main Terminal Terrestre (1 de Mayo 703, at Bolívar). From Yunguyo, take a *colectivo* from the border to Copacabana (30 minutes, US$1). There are several buses daily from Copacabana to La Paz (5 hours).

A more direct, but less scenic, five-hour route to La Paz goes through **Desaguadero,** an ugly duckling of a town that straddles the border. Buses along this route pass **Tiwanaku,** the capital city of an empire whose deities and monumental architecture spread throughout Peru nearly a millennium before the Inca. Though ravaged by grave robbers and modern-day reconstructions, the ruins here were once so impressive that even the Inca thought them constructed by giants. What stands out today is the **Kalasasaya temple,** a rectangular temple surrounded by pillars, monolithic figures, and the renowned Gateway of the Sun, chipped from a single piece of andesite and adorned with a carved deity. *Combis* run from Puno to Desaguadero (2.5 hours, US$4) frequently, leaving from the terminal zonal station, located a few blocks from Terminal Terrestre on Simón Bolívar. After crossing the border, you can catch another *combi* to La Paz.

Crossing is usually a 20-minute, hassle-free process at either place—as long as you have your passport and a valid tourist visa and the border is open (protests in Peru and Bolivia are common, meaning that main roads can be blocked and even borders can be temporarily shut down). Because travel requirements can change quickly, it is best to check with the consulate for updated travel requirements before you go. You can also consult the website for the Bolivian embassy in Peru (http://boliviaenperu.com), which has listings of the visa requirements in Spanish.

The Amazon

Nearly 60 percent of Peru is rainforest, whether it is the montane cloud forest or the deep lowland rainforest known simply as *selva*. Peru's Amazon basin is quite accessible and is one of the most biodiverse spots on earth, with an ample variety of excellent lodges and activities.

In as little as three hours after landing in Iquitos or Puerto Maldonado, travelers can be boating down a winding chocolate-brown river with the endless rainforest rising on both sides. Animals that you are most likely to see on any trip are monkeys, capybaras, turtles, caimans, *pirañas,* gray and pink river dolphins, hundreds of bird species, and many insects. Large mammals like anteaters, ocelots, and tapirs can be spotted at least a day's travel away into more remote areas. The jaguar, king of the Amazon, is stealthy and rarely seen. Seeing these animals through all the greenness of the rainforest is a serious challenge, but being on a river or lake with good binoculars and an experienced guide greatly increases the odds.

First-time rainforest visitors are usually concerned about suffocating heat, malaria, mosquitoes, yellow fever, bugs, and other discomforts. But Peru's Amazon is mostly malaria-free—at least the places travelers tend to roam. The mosquito issue can be minimized by wearing light-colored long clothing and a head net during outdoor walks in the evenings, and a yellow fever vaccination is strongly suggested before visiting the rainforest; check with the Centers for Disease Control and Prevention (www.cdc.gov) for full recommendations. Other than that, the new generation of superb eco-lodges and deluxe river cruises offer the experience of visiting Peru's Amazon in quite comfortable conditions.

There are dozens of well-run lodges, ranging from stylish top-end bungalows with electricity, air-conditioning, hot water, and tile floors to simple, more adventuresome wood cabins with cold water (which actually isn't that cold), hammocks, kerosene lamps, and a

Previous: small village on the shore of the Manu River; hammocks on a ship traveling between Yurimaguas and Iquitos. **Above:** macaw.

Look for ★ to find recommended
sights, activities, dining, and lodging.

Highlights

★ **Wildlife:** The Amazon's wildlife will amaze you, whether you observe a giant otter, a pink river dolphin, a *taricaya* turtle, or the giant capybara rodent (page 249).

★ **Rainforest Eco-Lodges:** Spend a few days learning at one of the myriad eco-lodges deep inside the Amazon rainforest (page 253).

★ **Canopy Walks:** Climb up into the rainforest canopy, whether by ladder or ropes, to have a closer look at the amazing biodiversity 35 meters off the ground (page 254).

★ **Manu Expeditions:** Spend a two-week birding trip observing Manu's speckled and cinnamon teal or the red-backed hawk, among hundreds of other species (page 269).

★ **Aqua Expeditions:** Become a privileged observer of the Amazon rainforest through an unforgettable journey on a top-end river cruise, available in three-, four-, and seven-night travel packages (page 296).

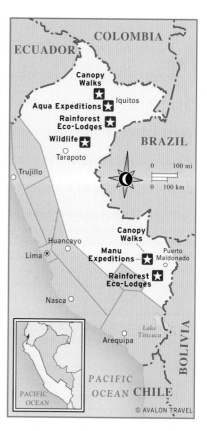

mosquito net over the bed. River cruises, on the other hand, are a comfortable and luxurious way to see the Amazon rainforest, with all imaginable amenities on board, including gourmet cuisine and savvy bilingual guides.

Peru's Amazon, though under siege from oil and gas drilling as well as illegal logging and gold mining, continues to host the planet's most concentrated levels of biodiversity. Humans have been part of this web of life for thousands of years, and 56 indigenous nations—of which the largest are the Asháninka, Aguaruna, and Shipibo-Conibo—still populate a considerable area of the rainforest. Small pockets of indigenous people in isolation, such as the Isconahua, Kugakapori, and Mashco-Piro, roam as nomads in remote areas north of the Reserva de Biósfera del Manu (Manu Biosphere Reserve), the lower Urubamba basin, or the higher Ucayali basin, close to the border with Brazil.

Responsible and sustainable tourism is a much better option for the Amazon than the traditional industries of informal gold mining, illegal hardwood logging, and drug trafficking. But the integration of Amazonian indigenous communities into Peru's economy has been a longtime struggle due to the immense—and, in some instances, deserved—distrust they have of the Peruvian government.

In June 2009, Peru's congress revoked two legislative decrees that sparked a violent indigenous uprising. In the melee, 23 police officers, 5 nonindigenous civilians, and 5 indigenous people were killed, and 200 people were injured. The revoked decrees, which were later reinstated by Peru's congress, were a bungled attempt to open vast tracts of the Amazon rainforest to oil and gas developers as part of the free trade agreement with the United States. The problem resulted when legislative action was taken without consulting the indigenous nations in the area. In mid-2016, indigenous communities in northern Peru blocked rivers during weeks-long protests over spills from an oil pipeline.

Unlike the oil and gas industry, ecotourism has expanded in the Peruvian Amazon with little conflict. Some lodges share profits or have as an aim to transfer ownership to the community after a certain number of years. Others work to provide local employment and fund local schools and health clinics.

It is important to cross-check the credentials of the lodge or tour operator you choose. Choose a lodge that is respectful of the environment and works with local communities. By supporting sustainable lodges, you will be helping preserve the Amazon as well.

PLANNING YOUR TIME

Your visit to Peru's Amazon largely depends on the money you want to spend, the time you have, and what season you are traveling. If you only have three to five days and a few hundred dollars, look into lodges around Puerto Maldonado or Iquitos. If you have a week or more and a bigger budget, go to the Reserva de Biósfera del Manu (Manu Biosphere Reserve) or indulge yourself with a river cruise on the Amazon. There are exceptions to this rule, however. High concentrations of wildlife can also be found in the Reserva Nacional Pacaya Samiria, southwest of Iquitos, or the Reserva Nacional Tambopata, farther south of Puerto Maldonado. Either way, the best time to visit Peru's rainforest is during the dry months, May to October, though Iquitos can be visited year-round.

Where to Go

To figure out where to go, it helps to understand Peru's different rainforest zones. Prevailing winds in South America move west, not east as in North America. Amazon humidity cools and condenses as it is forced over the eastern slopes of the Andes. This gives rise to the damp and chilly **montane cloud forests** perched between 700 and 2,900 meters elevation. This is the habitat of the cock of the rock, a crimson chicken-shaped bird; the Andean bear, the only surviving bear species of South America; and a huge range of colorful orchids, bromeliads, and hummingbirds. Peru's most accessible montane cloud forests are around Tarapoto,

The Amazon

PACIFIC OCEAN

LIMA

San Vicente de Cañete

Pisco

Chincha

Cordillera Yauyos

Huancavelica

Abra Apacheta

Chincheros

Andahuaylas

Abancay

Ayacucho

Pampas

Huancayo

La Oroya

Junín

Jauja

Tarma

San Ramón

La Merced

Satipo

Huánuco Viejo

Cerro de Pasco

Zona Reservada Pampa Hermosa

Oxapampa

Pozuzo

Huánuco

Tingo María

La Unión

Chiquián

Cordillera Huayhuash

Cordillera Raura

Cordillera Blanca

P.N. Huascarán

P.N. Tingo María

Aucayacu

Progreso

Tocache

Cordillera Azul

P.N. Yanachaga Chemillén

Res. Comunal Yanesha

Puerto Ocopa

Reserva Comunal Ashaninka

Reserva Comunal Machiguenga

P.N. Otisi

Río Tambo

Río Urubamba

Atalaya

Shapahua

San Luis

Puerto Inca

Iparia

Puerto Bermúdez

Masisea

Pucallpa

Ucayali

Cordillera Vilcabamba

Quillabamba

Aguas Calientes

MACHU PICCHU

ESPIRITU PAMPA

Ollantaytambo

Urubamba

CUSCO

Urcos

Paucartambo

Ocongate

Cordillera Vilcanota

Nevada de Ausangate

Quincemil

Atalaya

Tres Cruces

Boca Manu

Santuario Nacional Megantoni

Parque Nacional Manu

Manu Multiple Use Zone

Reserva Comunal Amarakaeri

Río Azul

Río Colorado

Río Alto Madre de Dios

MANU EXPEDITIONS

RAINFOREST EXPEDITIONS

THE TAMBOPATA RESEARCH CENTER

RAINFOREST ECO-LODGES

Río Tambopata

RESERVA AMAZONICA

La Torre

Parque Nacional Bahuaja Sonene

Río Heath

Río Las Piedras

Puerto Maldonado

CANOPY WALKS

Puerto Heath

Reserva Nacional Tambopata

Iberia

Guayos

Madidi

BOLIVIA

Parque Nacional Alto Purús

Alerta

Reserva Comunal Purús

Taumaturgo

Puerto Portillo

San Gregorio

San Vicente

Río Tambo

© AVALON TRAVEL

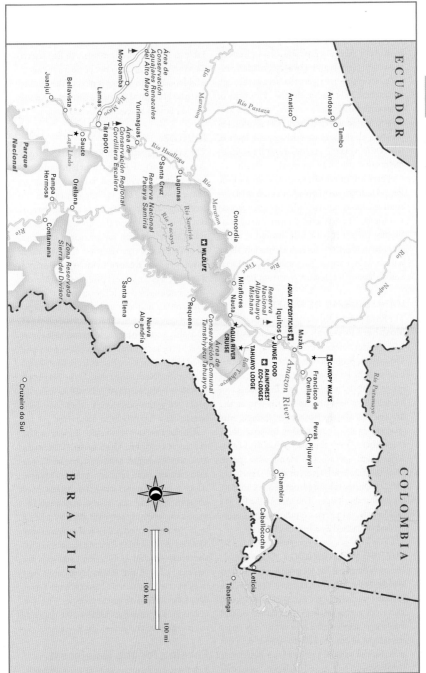

Tingo María, Machu Picchu, and the drive into the Reserva de Biósfera del Manu.

Lower down in the rainforest, clear mountain streams cascade through steep mountain forests, giving way to broader, progressively muddier rivers that weave through the increasingly flat landscape. This type of **lowland rainforest** occurs in Manu and Puerto Maldonado but reaches its greatest expression all the way downriver near Iquitos, where the Amazon reaches around two kilometers in width and the forest is perfectly flat.

There are interesting access points to the Peruvian **high rainforest** or *selva alta,* including Chanchamayo Valley in Peru's central rainforest; Tingo María, a former drug trafficking zone that is rapidly becoming a safe and low-budget rainforest destination along with nearby Parque Nacional Tingo María; and Tarapoto, located upriver from Iquitos.

MANU BIOSPHERE RESERVE

The **Reserva de Biósfera del Manu (Manu Biosphere Reserve),** which stretches from 4,000 meters elevation all the way down to 150 meters, protects one of the most pristine swaths of the Peruvian Amazon, where a wide range of birds, primates, and mammals can be seen. The best time to visit is during the dry season, May to November, though only sporadic rains occur starting in November-December. There are only a handful of licensed tour operators in Manu, who charge US$800-2,250 for five- to nine-day tours with amenities ranging from beach camping to comfortable lodges. The Manu, like Puerto Maldonado, is in Peru's southeastern rainforest and is reached by a full-day bus ride.

PUERTO MALDONADO

The advantages of the lodges around **Puerto Maldonado,** downriver from the Reserva de Biósfera del Manu, are cost and access: Travelers arrive within 30 minutes of flying from Cusco, and a two-night stay costs anywhere from US$80 to US$450. This area, on the edge of the **Reserva Nacional Tambopata,** has a good variety of monkeys, birds, caimans, and small mammals. As at Manu, the best time to visit here is May to November. There are levels of wildlife comparable to Manu at the **Tambopata Research Center,** a 7- to 10-hour boat ride from Puerto Maldonado. This center is next to the remote **Parque Nacional Bahuaja Sonene** and the world's largest macaw clay lick, or *collpa.*

IQUITOS

The city of **Iquitos,** in Peru's northeastern Amazon, forged Peru's tourism industry back in the late 1960s but has grown so large that visitors have to go a long way to find interesting rainforest. There is a wide variety of cost and quality in this area. If you don't mind traveling a bit longer, some of Peru's best lodges are upstream on the Marañón River, near the **Reserva Nacional Pacaya Samiria,** Peru's largest protected rainforest area. Endangered wildlife such as the rare Amazonian manatee or sea cow can be observed here. Close to the **Reserva Comunal Tamshiyacu Tahuayo,** a reserve self-managed by the local communities, there are some good lodges. An hour by car from Iquitos, on the Iquitos-Nauta highway, is the **Reserva Nacional Allpahuayo Mishana,** the only protected white-sand forest, where new bird species have recently been discovered.

Unlike Puerto Maldonado, Iquitos can be visited year-round. The Puerto Maldonado area, which is higher rainforest, has an intense rainy season from January to April. Iquitos, which is much farther downstream, has more constant weather year-round. Although the weather is relatively constant, the river rises 7 to 15 meters during the November-May rainy months in the Andes. During these months, the forests around Iquitos flood and soils are replenished with silt. Animals can most easily be spotted on the mud banks after the river drops, between June and September. The cost of Iquitos lodges ranges US$60-200, depending on the distance from Iquitos.

Packing for the Rainforest

Yes, there are biting insects in the rainforest,

so bring plenty of repellent (20 percent DEET is what the Centers for Disease Control and Prevention recommends). The best defense, however, is to cover your body with light-colored long clothing and, in the evenings, cover up with a mosquito head net. Apart from two or three pairs of long pants and shirts, other items include T-shirts, lots of socks, a swimsuit, one pair of shorts, a sweater or fleece for chilly evenings, hiking or tennis shoes (rubber boots are normally supplied by the lodge or river cruise you choose), a rain suit or poncho, toiletries, sunglasses, sunscreen, binoculars, a headlamp, a water bottle, a photocopy of your passport, a camera, and one or two memory cards. Most agencies require that you keep your luggage to a minimum because of tight space on the planes and boats. You can usually store your extra luggage at the agency's main office. Better, though, is to pack lightly.

HISTORY

There are 56 indigenous nations living in the Peruvian Amazon basin, most of which have been here for thousands of years. Still, it is largely a mystery as to when and exactly how human civilization fanned out through the waterways of the rainforest. The **Inca** were aware of the geographic challenges and the skilled archers that were hidden in the **Antisuyo**—"land of the east," as they named the Amazon in Quechua. Inca Garcilaso de la Vega, a mestizo chronicler of the 16th century, reports that Inca Túpac Yupanqui crushed an insurrection of the Manu people and ordered the construction of two fortresses that have yet to be discovered. From Pisac, an Inca road led to Paucartambo and on to coca plantations maintained in the high rainforest at Pilcopata. This is still the main route to reach the Reserva de Biósfera del Manu.

Apart from Pilcopata, the Inca conquered, in some of the most bloodiest campaigns they waged, other rainforest fringe areas, including **Moyobamba** and the montane cloud forests where the **Chachapoya** flourished. As a result, the Inca had rainforest archers in their army, as the Spanish learned

the hard way at the battles of Sacsayhuamán and Ollantaytambo. But even before the Inca, trade routes were established from the rainforest to the coast to export exotic woods and animals, cacao, natural dyes, and medicinal plants, among other products.

The Spanish conquistadors explored the rainforest recklessly and paid a heavy cost in their feverish search for fabled gold cities such as **Paititi** and **El Dorado.** One of these adventurous deeds was conducted by **Francisco de Orellana.** If Vicente Yáñez Pinzón was the first European to see the Amazon River in 1500, Orellana was immortalized as the first European to navigate the whole length of the "sea river" 41 years later.

A cousin of Francisco Pizarro, according to some historians, Orellana accepted in 1541 to head an expedition in search of El Dorado. With a party of only 49 men and under constant threat from the Omagua indigenous people, Orellana sailed down the Río Napo until he finally reached the confluence with the Amazon in 1542, not far away from present-day Iquitos.

According to the Spanish friar Gaspar de Carvajal, who traveled with Orellana's men, they were attacked by "women warriors." The Spanish Jesuit Cristóbal de Acuña wrote that the area close to the Amazon River, rich in gold, was dominated by Yacamiaba people, whose name in their language meant "women without husbands." The fierce Yacamiaba women that battled Orellana's expedition inspired the explorer to baptize the river as **Río de las Amazonas,** after the Greek myths of the mighty Amazons. Orellana never found any golden city, but managed to sail the complete length of the Amazon to the Atlantic, one of the great epic journeys of human history.

Orellana's report of vast uncivilized territory triggered what is perhaps the largest missionary effort ever. Jesuit and Franciscan missionaries hacked their way down into nearly all of the Amazon's important tributaries from Peruvian cities such as Cajamarca, Chachapoyas, Moyobamba, and Huancayo, which became important bases for these evangelical missions.

The suppression and expulsion of the **Jesuits** from Latin America in 1767 left not only an intellectual abyss but also large tracts of the Amazon nearly abandoned. At one point, much of what is now the Peruvian Amazon was attached to the Viceroyalty of Santa Fe (present-day Argentina). But because access to the Amazon was easier from Peru, a royal dictate of 1802 transferred much of the Amazon basin to the Viceroyalty of Peru.

In 1839, U.S. citizen **Charles Goodyear** vulcanized rubber by heating natural rubber and sulfur to create an elastic, durable substance that could be fused into objects for real use. Suddenly *caucho,* as the gooey white latex from the rubber tree was known, became a valuable commodity. First Brazil and later Peru became the center of the **rubber boom** (1879-1912), which caused Iquitos to explode in size and fortunes overnight. Within a decade, Iquitos became the second-richest city in Latin America after Manaus, Brazil, another rubber boomtown.

During the rubber boom, Iquitos's wealthiest families built elaborate mansions decorated with tiles imported from Seville and Portugal, and large public buildings were commissioned, such as Gustav Eiffel's **Casa de Fierro,** or Iron House. Rubber barons, such as **Julio César Arana del Águila** and **Carlos Fermín Fitzcarrald,** headed a class of "new rich" that accumulated big fortunes founded on slavery and extremely cruel treatment of indigenous populations. Extravagant stories from this time abound, such as families who sent their laundry each week to Paris, or the rubber baron who ordered a crate of expensive beaver-skin hats from Europe and tossed all but the perfect-fitting hat into the river.

During the rubber boom, millions of indigenous people were coerced to collect *caucho* in the forest. These people became some of the most abused, wretched workers in Peru's history, and their sufferings have not been sufficiently researched and studied. Enslaved by debt, malnourished, and diseased, the workers often faced the choice of perishing or attempting an often fatal escape through the rainforest.

The rubber boom collapsed in 1912 as rapidly as it had begun. The Dutch and English smuggled *caucho* plants out of Peru and Brazil and successfully cultivated them in Malaysia. Thanks to a railroad network and orderly rows of trees, collecting latex became far easier in Southeast Asia than among the wild vegetation of the Amazon forest.

A decade after the rubber collapse in the 1920s, oil was discovered in the Amazon. Engineers from international petroleum companies, along with Mormon missionaries, were among the first outsiders to explore many remote headwaters of the Amazon. Since then, huge pipeline projects such as the **North Peruvian Oil Pipeline,** completed in 1996, and the **Camisea Pipeline,** operational since 2004, have brought foreign revenue to Peru but have also affected huge areas of virgin Amazon lands. Whenever a large pipe has to be filled with fossil fuel, a network of roads, platforms, testing paths, helicopter pads, and pumping stations springs up in front of it.

A major threat to the Peruvian Amazon today is illegal **gold mining.** The activity took off during the past decades as metal prices soared to new highs, luring thousands of workers to the Amazon in a modern-day gold rush. Some economists estimate that illegal gold miners reap billions of dollars in profits ever year. With no environmental oversight, the miners have turned lush, green rainforest into barren landscape in their pursuit of the precious metal. Mercury used to extract gold has created alarming rates of pollution in some of the region's waterways and a toxic mix for the health of indigenous communities that rely on fish for their diet. Government efforts to crack down on the activity, which has fueled human trafficking, forced labor, prostitution, and corruption, have been met with violent protests.

The future of Peru's Amazon is quite uncertain, trapped between an unstoppable exploitation of resources—a result of the country's modernization and need for foreign currency—and the urgent need to protect the most biodiverse rainforest on the planet.

Exploring the Rainforest

TOP EXPERIENCE

★ WILDLIFE

The Amazon rainforest, blanketed in a brilliant uniform shade of green, depends on its inhabitants to give it color and noise. Strange, noisy, and even stinky, Amazon wildlife is often colorful—and loud. Birds squawk, beetles wiggle across the ground, and monkeys howl at sunrise. The wildlife is the energy of the rainforest.

Although the rainforest is home to thousands of creatures, the ones discussed here are especially noteworthy. We recommend exploring the rainforest with a guide. His or her trained eye is likely to see twice as much as what your beginner vision will spot.

Hoatzin

Known locally as *shansho,* few birds are more common and bizarre in the rainforest than the hoatzin, a chicken-like bird with a spiky crest that can often be seen flapping noisily around bushes at water's edge. They make odd grunting noises and eat only leaves, which are digested by a system of three stomachs, or "crops." The leaves ferment inside their crops, thus giving these birds a bad odor. The hoatzin doesn't mind being smelly because its scent is its main protection from predators.

Hoatzin chicks are born with claws on their wings like the flying pterodactyl. When an anaconda or other predator comes to the nest to eat the chicks, they dive into the water. When the danger is past, they use their claws to climb back into their nest. Scientists once thought the hoatzin was a descendant of the prehistoric bird, but recent DNA analysis indicates the hoatzin is a strange member of the cuckoo family. Its claws are probably a relatively recent adaptation.

Macaws, Parrots, and Parakeets

There are few natural sights more remarkable than a *collpa,* or a macaw clay lick, covered very early in the morning with dozens of brightly colored macaws, parrots, and parakeets jostling with each other for access to the mineral-rich clay mud they eat. The

hoatzin

world's largest *collpa* is near the Tambopata Research Center, on the Río Tambopata, about a seven-hour boat ride upstream from Puerto Maldonado. At dawn, as many as 600 birds perch on surrounding trees before they cautiously descend to the riverbank. By 7am the show is over. There are similar but smaller *collpas* spread throughout the Parque Nacional Manu and the Reserva Nacional Tambopata.

Why do these birds eat the clay? The current theory is that the birds are attracted to the clay licks for sodium, which is deficient in the eastern Amazon region.

The most common macaws found in the Peruvian Amazon are the **red-bellied macaw,** which is mostly green with a dullish yellow color on the underside of its wings and tail, and the **blue-and-yellow macaw,** which is bright blue on top and yellow underneath. Less common are the **chestnut-fronted macaw,** which is mostly green but with a reddish color on the underside of its wings and tail; the **scarlet macaw,** with yellow median upper wing coverts; and the **red-and-green macaw,** which is deep scarlet with green median upper wing coverts.

Piraña

There are 20 species of *piraña* in a rainbow of colors, though the most common in Peru is the **red-belly *piraña,*** which is crimson on the bottom and silvery-green on the sides. This *piraña* hunts in schools and eats whatever it can: mollusks, crustaceans, insects, birds, lizards, amphibians, rodents, baby caimans, and other *pirañas.* During the Amazon's high-water months, they also eat submerged fruit.

Contrary to the pop culture image of *pirañas* devouring people in a bloody maul of frothy water, these fanged creatures rarely bother humans, as proved by troops of Amazon children that play each day in the river. Nobody remembers a human being killed by a *piraña,* although plenty have been viciously nipped. If you swim in a rainforest river, avoid the warm, still waters favored by these fish. *Pirañas,* like sharks, are attracted

piraña

by blood and splashing in the water. They can become especially aggressive when food is scarce, such as when trapped in a drying lake. They are most active at dawn and dusk and sleep at night.

A must-do activity at most rainforest lodges in the Peruvian Amazon is *piraña* **fishing.** You will be provided with a string, a hook, and a chunk of red meat. Just plunk the baited hook into the still waters of nearly any Amazon backwater and presto! Once you feel the aggressive tug of these palm-size fish, the fun has just begun. Before you grab hold of your catch, ask your guide to do so instead. With a bulldog face, powerful lower jaw, and a set of razor-sharp teeth, these little creatures will nip at anything in reach and cause a nasty bite. Leave the fish handling to the guide.

Giant Otter

Once found throughout thousands of kilometers of Amazon waters, the populations of river otters have been reduced to only two species, found mainly in remote headwaters

taricaya turtles

1940s and 1970s, otter populations have plummeted, and they have been declared an endangered species. Even though it is illegal to hunt otters and sell their pelts, river otter populations continue to decline in some areas. Because they are at the top of the food chain, many biologists consider their decline to be a worrisome sign of watershed contamination from the mercury used in gold mining.

Taricaya Turtle

Fossils indicate that earth's first turtles could not withdraw their heads into their shells. Instead they tucked their heads to one side, as the *taricaya* turtle still does. These creatures eat meat but also chomp on fruits and seeds, which they can reach during the high waters of rainy season. They are solitary nesters and lay approximately 30 to 50 eggs, which have been an important source of protein for Peru's indigenous Amazon peoples. Thanks to programs in Reserva Nacional Pacaya Samiria, they have been brought back from the edge of extinction in some parts of Peru, though they remain common along the Madre de Dios and Manu Rivers. Look for groups of this aquatic turtle, stacked on top of each other like fallen dominos, on logs jutting from the water. They sun themselves in order to increase body temperature and probably also to eliminate the buildup of algae on their carapaces.

Caiman

This reptile is a crocodilian that can reach an astonishing six meters in length. Caimans live in the still waters of oxbow lakes and rivers and are very good swimmers, with long slender bodies and powerful tails that propel them through the water. They crush their prey with their powerful jaws and, along with their staple diet of fish, will eat anything they can get their jaws on, including capybaras, juvenile otters, birds, insects, and mollusks. Caimans may be such fierce predators because they have such a hard time growing up. The eggs are eaten by snakes, fish, and hawks. After hatching, baby caimans hide in the water grass, coming out only at night to avoid being

and oxbow lakes. The larger species, the giant otter, is most commonly seen in lakes in Parque Nacional Manu, Reserva Nacional Tambopata, and in remotes areas of the Reserva Nacional Pacaya Samiria.

A family generally consists of a pair of adults plus a few juveniles. Their home is a mud cave in a lake bank marked by trampled vegetation and carefully placed boundaries of feces and urine. The giant otter has stubby feet, which makes it an awkward land traveler, but a powerful flat tail, which makes it an impressively fast and acrobatic swimmer. With luck, otters can be seen and heard chomping on their fish catch from their log perches or even taking sunbaths. Otters hunt baby caimans, snakes, and young turtles. Though extremely inquisitive animals, they steer clear of predators such as adult black caimans and anacondas. If attacked, however, a group of otters can use their powerful jaws and swimming abilities to prevail over these much larger predators.

Because of intense hunting between the

eaten by a turtle, otter, or wading bird. A very small percent of caimans survive the ordeal.

Caimans can easily be spotted by the red reflection of their eyes in a flashlight beam, a common night activity at many lodges. With a fast hand jab into the water, most Amazon guides are capable of pulling a juvenile caiman up to a half meter out of the water for inspection.

There are four species of caiman in Peru: the dwarf (1-5 meters), the smooth-fronted (2 meters), the spectacled (5 meters), and the black (up to 6 meters). This last, rarest of all, has black marks, a spiky tail, and a short snout. After being hunted relentlessly for their skins in the first half of the 20th century, the Amazon's caiman population is a fraction of what it was in 1900.

Capybara

The cuddly shape and peaceful demeanor of the capybara seems out of sync with the brutal anaconda-eat-jaguar world of the Amazon. Troops of capybaras can be seen munching on the lush grasses and aquatic vegetation at the banks of most rivers. At the first whiff of danger, these timid animals scurry into the muddy water and sink like submarines out of sight. Though they are mammals, they can hold their breath underwater and even sleep underwater, their snouts barely protruding above the surface.

The capybara, which in Guaraní means "master of grasses," is the largest rodent in the world. It grows to about the size of a large pig and is covered with a thin layer of reddish brown hair. It has a small nose and ears, and eyes that are perched at the top of its barrel-shaped snout for swimming. Though clumsy on land, capybaras are agile swimmers thanks to their webbed toes.

Capybaras are prized bush meat among the Amazon's indigenous people and a food source for anacondas, big cats, harpy eagles, and caimans. Despite all the hunting, the capybara remains common thanks to its rapid reproduction. Females begin mating in the water a year after they are born and have

capybara

two to eight offspring at a time. Capybaras can live up to 10 years.

Pink River Dolphin

One of the Amazon's most flabbergasting sights is the pink river dolphin rising above the waters of lakes or rivers. Unlike their ocean-going relatives, these dolphins have a strange dorsal hump that gives them an S-shape and a huge set of flippers. Their elastic vertebrae allows them to contort their pinkish bodies nearly in half in search of crustaceans and fish in the grassy waters and flooded forests of the Amazon. Their pink color comes mainly from capillaries near the surface of the skin.

Pink river dolphins occupy a special place in Amazon mythology. Some indigenous cultures consider it a sacred animal, while others regard them as an evil spirit that seduces young women. Regardless of its exact reputation, the pink river dolphin has never been hunted by the Amazon's indigenous people. As a result, it was extremely common in the lower waterways of the Amazon up until

jaguar

about 30 years ago. The biggest enemies of the dolphin these days are deforestation, which has damaged its aquatic home, and gill nets, which ensnare and drown dolphins.

Jaguar

Known as *otorongo* in Peru, derived from the Quechua word *uturunku*, the jaguar is the biggest spotted cat in the Americas and probably the hardest animal to spot in the rainforest. They are solitary and keen hunters, feeding chiefly on capybaras, deer, and tapirs—their favorite—but also fish, caimans, and smaller mammals.

Jaguars are mostly spotted at night. But during the months of May and June, 30 percent of Manu visitors report seeing these felines stretching out on a river log under the morning sun. Most jaguars will flee quickly from human presence once spotted.

Considered a deity in pre-Hispanic cultures such as Chavín or Cupisnique, the jaguar has been overhunted for centuries for its fur and is listed as endangered.

★ RAINFOREST ECO-LODGES

Most of the lodges in the northern rainforest are clustered in the area around **Iquitos.** In the southern patch of the rainforest, east of Cusco, lodges are located in the **Reserva de Biósfera del Manu (Manu Biosphere Reserve)** or farther south in the **Puerto Maldonado** area. Lodges arrange transportation such as motorboats with canopy shades, 4WD trucks (in Manu), and small canoes. Food is included in the package and normally is a nutritious combination of veggies, beans, rice, fish, chicken, and local foods such as *yuca frita* (manioc root fries), palm heart salad, and *cecina* (tender smoked pork meat).

Most lodge programs include early-morning bird-watching, a visit to an oxbow lake or a macaw clay lick, day hikes through the forest, *piraña* fishing, and evening boat rides to spot caiman and other night creatures. Some lodges also have canopy walks, zip lines, or observation towers. A visit to a shaman for a talk about medicinal plants or a visit to a local farm or village crafts market is also common. A key component of any rainforest experience is a knowledgeable English-speaking guide, whose job is to spot wildlife and introduce the extraordinary web of connections among plants, trees, animals, and insects.

The lodges in this guide all have a strong environmental commitment, a sustainable approach and design, and have forged strong and supportive relationships with surrounding communities. Recommendations also consider the amount of wildlife and primary forest that can be seen nearby, along with the quality of food and lodging. Finally, the recommendations consider whether lodges work with fully licensed and professional guides, who are essential for spotting wildlife and understanding how the rainforest works. A good guide should give the local, English, and scientific name for all birds, talk about a wide range of trees and medicinal plants, and boil down the complexity of symbiotic relationships and rainforest ecology.

Avoid private guides who promise trips down remote rivers for an unbelievably low price. There have been numerous reports of clients robbed at gunpoint and left stranded on a riverbank. More common experiences include mediocre food, faulty equipment, and unfulfilled promises. Use only private guides recommended by a trusted source. The agencies in this book are professional, safe, and worth the money.

★ CANOPY WALKS

Visitors to the Amazon are often surprised by how dark, gloomy, and colorless the rainforest ground can be. The situation is completely different 30 meters or more up in the air, where a dazzling array of orchids, bromeliads, and mosses hang out on the treetops and soak in the scorching sunlight. The fragrant scents of these epiphytes and the succulent fruit of the ubiquitous *matapalo* or strangler fig lure monkeys and a huge range of pollinators, including birds, bats, and insects.

Most of the Amazon's biodiversity is in the canopy, which U.S. biologist Bruce Rinker describes as a "leafy aerial continent, elevated on stilts, called the treetops." Biologists have come up with ingenious ways to explore this airy world with a combination of suspended cable walkways, tree house-like platforms, and rope-climbing techniques adapted from rock climbing.

In the early 1990s the nonprofit ACER organization funded the Amazon's longest canopy walkway, which was built 80 kilometers northeast of Iquitos at the **Explorama Lodge.** It is a cable bridge, suspended among a series of giant rainforest trees, that runs for nearly 500 meters and reaches 35 meters above the ground. Visitors hang out for hours on the walkway, peering down the sides of trees to the rainforest floor below or scanning over the treetops for hundreds of different birds.

The bridge is completely safe, even for children. There are safety cables at shoulder height to grab onto, a wooden floor, and thick mesh stretched between. The whole thing is like a giant channel of mesh out of which it would be hard to climb, much less fall. Visitors climb up a wooden tower with a wide staircase to access the bridge, and no harnesses or other safety precautions are necessary. Guides usually let visitors wander wherever they want on the bridge.

Reserva Amazónica east of the Puerto Maldonado area has built a similar canopy walkway. A dozen other lodges in Peru's rainforest offer observation platforms. These platforms, such as the one at the **Manu Wildlife Center,** are up to 35 meters off the ground and are usually reached via a circular staircase that is made of steel and held upright via steel cables. Again, no safety harnesses are required, and as long as you are not terrified of heights, getting to the platform is easy.

There are plenty of other adventurous canopy options in Peru's rainforest, including the wooden platforms at **Cocha Salvador** in the Parque Nacional Manu. To reach these airy tree houses, you must don a rock-climbing harness and climb the rope via a set of Jumars, ascending devices used most commonly in rock climbing. It is a completely safe, though strenuous, experience that allows you to appreciate how high 35 meters off the ground really is. For those uncomfortable with climbing the rope, another option is to be pulled up into the tree house by a geared contraption that is cranked by the guide.

The **Tahuayo Lodge,** 145 kilometers upstream of Iquitos, has a zip line, which is essentially a harness that slides along a set of steel cables about 30 meters above the ground. From a wooden platform, visitors launch into space and can either zing through the canopy or stop and hang quietly in order to observe wildlife. Obviously, this is for those extremely comfortable with heights.

Southern Amazon Basin

For the quality of the lodging and the amount of wildlife that visitors see, the rainforest lodges around the Southern Amazon basin represent an excellent value. This is one of the most biologically diverse areas in the world. And with the Interoceanic Highway, it is increasingly close to Cusco and other tourism hotspots.

PUERTO MALDONADO AND VICINITY

Just a half-hour plane ride or a 10-hour drive from Cusco, Puerto Maldonado is the place for people with limited time but who are keen to take in an amazing variety of flora and fauna. In an action-packed stay of two or three nights, visitors are likely to see a few types of monkeys (there are seven species in the area), capybaras and other rainforest rodents, a wide variety of water and forest birds, caimans, and turtles. Large mammals such as tapirs and jaguars are seldom seen, though chances become better farther into the rainforest at the Tambopata Research Center, which is inside the **Parque Nacional Bahuaja Sonene.**

Although there are fewer species here than in Manu, getting to Puerto Maldonado's rainforest is a heck of a lot easier. Visitors arrive at the airport, where they are picked up by their lodge and taken up a river in a motorboat. In as little as three hours after leaving Cusco, visitors can be in a comfortable rainforest lodge surrounded by miles of Amazon rainforest. Standard features of most trips include early-morning bird-watching followed by a nature walk, *piraña* fishing, and a visit to a local community or medicinal plant talk by a local shaman. If guests have energy, guides lead night rainforest walks or boat rides to spot baby caimans, a close relative of the alligator, along the river bank. Prices include airport transfers, boat transportation, lodging, and food.

There are two main protected areas near Puerto Maldonado. The 275,000-hectare

Reserva Nacional Tambopata stretches east from Puerto Maldonado all the way to the Río Heath on the Bolivian border. It serves as a buffer zone around the 1.1-million-hectare **Parque Nacional Bahuaja Sonene.** The whole area of 1.4 million hectares is across the Río Heath from the **Parque Nacional Maididi** in Bolivia, forming the largest patch of protected rainforest in South America.

The rainforest lodges are clustered in two areas on the edge of the Reserva Nacional Tambopata. The first group is an hour's boat ride down the Río Madre de Dios. The lodges here include some of the most comfortable in the Amazon, including Reserva Amazónica and Sandoval Lake Lodge.

The other main group is three or four hours up the Río Tambopata, on the way to the Parque Nacional Bahuaja Sonene. In general, wildlife-spotting opportunities are about equal between these two groups of lodges—all of them are near the reserve's buffer zone and are mostly surrounded by secondary forest.

An exception is **Explorer's Inn,** built in 1976, which is the only lodge inside the Reserva Nacional Tambopata and seems to have more bird and animal species than the other lodges—including frequent sightings of the giant otter and world-record levels of birds and butterflies. The reserve also includes areas of virgin forest, unlike the other lodges, whose large mahogany and cedar trees were cut down years ago.

The world's largest macaw clay lick, which attracts nearly all the area's species of macaws, parrots, and parakeets, is seven hours up the Río Tambopata near the **Tambopata Research Center.** Most Puerto Maldonado lodges offer two-day trips to the lick, which include a night of camping on a sandy beach, a guided hike through the forest, meals, and a morning visit to the lick.

A relatively new option for those who want to be closer to the city and who have a smaller

Puerto Maldonado and Vicinity

© AVALON TRAVEL

Map information courtesy of
InkaNatura Travel

budget is the **Tambopata Ecotourism Corridor.** Only 15 minutes up the Río Tambopata from Puerto Maldonado, 17 local families have created interesting homestay programs with an environmental cause.

History

Puerto Maldonado began as a rubber boom-town in 1902 after a mule road was built from the coast to the headwaters of the Río Tambopata. After the rubber craze ended, gold mining and logging took its place and continue today, though fortunately tourism and Brazil nuts are increasingly important. The wide avenues of Puerto, as locals call the city, quickly peter out into mud lanes and ramshackle rows of wooden buildings. Instead of cars, mostly scooters and three-wheeled *mototaxis* buzz the streets. Puerto Maldonado is smaller and infinitely more relaxed than the Amazon megalopolis of Iquitos, however the city and its services have been expanding with the recent completion of the Interoceanic Highway. Most travelers still fly into Puerto

Maldonado and transfer immediately to one of two dozen lodges in the area, but it is now possible to travel comfortably from Cusco to Puerto Maldonado on the new highway. Avoid staying the night in Puerto, as the rainforest is more interesting.

There were two explorers with the surname Maldonado who explored the Madre de Dios. The first, Spaniard Juan Álvarez Maldonado, came in 1567 in search of gold. He was the first to make it all the way to the Río Heath, the present-day Bolivian border, but in the process he lost 250 Spaniards to disease and conflicts with indigenous people. He returned to Cusco months later, half-crazed and in rags, and claimed to have found a sophisticated wealthy rainforest city known as Paititi.

Though the legend of Paititi grew, the memory of Maldonado's hardships prevented the Spaniards from returning to the area for nearly three centuries. In the mid-19th century, Colonel Faustino Maldonado returned to make the first map of the area. But he perished, along with his valuable journals, in a rapids on the Río Madre de Dios. He carved his name on a tree trunk where the Río Tambopata meets the Madre de Dios, where the town named in his honor is located today.

Entertainment and Events

By far the best way to spend a night in Puerto Maldonado is to find a quiet spot and relax under the starry sky and take in the sounds of the rainforest. But if you really want to go out, there are a few pubs and discotheques on the boulevard next to the main plaza. For dancing, options include the **Witite Bar** (cell tel. 987-405-521, 9:30pm-close Fri.-Sat.), which fills up during weekend evenings with locals and visitors. Another spot across the boulevard from Witite is the more relaxed **Vikingo** (noon-11pm Mon.-Fri., noon-close Sat.).

Food

Locals and visitors all flock to **Los Gustitos** (Loreto block 2, Plaza de Armas, 11am-10pm daily), which has the best rainforest fruit-flavored ice cream and juices in the city. Grab a seat in its airy courtyard and try a scoop of *cupuazú* ice cream and a glass of *aguajina* juice; they are fantastic. A good place for breakfast, hamburgers, or a light lunch is **La Casa Nostra** (León Velarde 515, tel. 082/57-3833, 7am-1pm and 5pm-11pm Mon.-Sat., US$4), a small café with good service and good coffee.

The best food in town is at **Burgos's Restaurant** (León Velarde 127, tel. 082/57-3653, www.burgosrestaurant.com.pe, 7am-10pm daily, US$4), which offers large portions of local cuisine made in its open kitchen. It also has a location at Avenida 26 de Diciembre 195. The wide-ranging menu includes local dishes like *patarashka de pollo,* and the chicken brochettes with Brazil nut sauce are scrumptious. Other hotels such as Wasaí, Don Carlos, and Cabaña Quinta also have good restaurants.

Another good option, and a local favorite, is **El Califa** (Piura 266, tel. 082/57-1119, noon-midnight daily, US$6-10), which serves local rainforest cuisine and good Peruvian menus. The best bet for pizza is **Hornito** (Daniel Carrión 271, Plaza de Armas, tel. 082/57-2082, 6pm-midnight daily, US$6-8), with good music and a cozy pub-like interior. The best spit-roasted chicken is at **La Estrella** (León Velarde 474, tel. 082/57-3107, 5pm-10pm daily, US$3 for half a chicken and fries). For delicious hamburgers, marinated steaks, and yummy chicken wings there is **La Vaka Loca** (1st block of Loreto, cell tel. 993-560-109, noon-10pm Mon.-Sat., US$5-7).

Accommodations
US$10-25
The best of the budget options is **Royal Inn** (Dos de Mayo 333, tel. 082/57-3464, www.royalinnpuerto.com, US$15 s, US$20 d), with shared baths and cold water. It can get noisy, so ask for a room away from the street and the central courtyard. A good new budget option is the **Tambopata Hostel** (26 de Diciembre 234, tel. 082/57-4201, www.tambopatahostel.com, US$10 dorm, US$15 s, US$25 d), with clean rooms and hammocks in a pleasant courtyard.

Choosing an Eco-Lodge

There are dozens of eco-lodges in the Peruvian Amazon, many of them excellent choices. That can make deciding on where to stay difficult. Here is a list of just a few to help get you started in picking a place based on your needs.

BEST FOR WILDLIFE-VIEWING

- **Tambopata Research Center** (page 262) is near the world's largest clay lick, offering some of the best viewing anywhere of macaws, parrots, and other species.

- The **Manu Lodge,** owned by **Manu Nature Tours** (page 268), is the only lodge inside the Manu Nature Reserve, a hotspot for wildlife.

BEST FOR FAMILIES

- **Refugio Amazonas** (page 261) is a comfortable environment with plenty of educational activities and fun experiences for children. Identify new species with the resident researcher, walk on a no-adults-allowed trail, go mountain biking, climb the canopy, and get a temporary tattoo from a rainforest fruit.

- **Reserva Amazónica** (page 263) has 15 activities, including *piraña* fishing, canopy walks, and a treasure hunt for children.

MOST REMOTE

- Perhaps not the most remote, but at **Amazon Villa** (page 261) you'll be secluded with a private bungalow in the rainforest with your own guide.

US$25-50

Cabaña Quinta (Cusco 535 or Moquegua 422, tel. 082/57-1045, www.hotelcabana-quinta.com, US$32 s, US$54 d, with breakfast) has smallish tile-floored rooms and nice gardens. Rooms have hot water, cable TV, and optional air-conditioning for US$15-20 more. The setting is quiet, and the hotel restaurant is one of the better ones in town.

The best mid-range option in town is the **Perú Amazónico** (Ica 269, tel. 082/57-1799, www.peruamazonico.com, US$35 s, US$42 d, with breakfast), whose tiled-floored rooms are clean and comfortable. Rooms have air-conditioning, hot water, satellite TV, and a mini fridge. The hotel can pick you up at the airport.

US$50-100

Don Carlos Hotel (León Velarde 1271, tel. 082/57-1029, www.hotelesdoncarlos.com, US$50 s, US$60 d, with breakfast) is a pleasant hotel perched on a hilltop on the edge of town. There is a nice wood porch for having a drink, and a decent restaurant. The rooms have wood floors, nice beds, optional air-conditioning, and clean baths with a limited hot water supply. Rates include airport transfer.

The most charming and expensive place in town is **Wasaí Maldonado Lodge** (Guillermo Billinghurst, tel. 01/436-8792, www.wasai.com, US$60 s, US$70 d, with breakfast), a mini rainforest lodge overlooking the Río Madre de Dios. Stilts and wooden ramps support and connect 16 wooden bungalows and rooms, which include minibars,

BEST LODGES ON A BUDGET

- **Refugio Kerenda Homet** (page 263) offers excellent rates and the opportunity to learn about the Amazon's challenges from conservationist Victor Zambrano.

- Only 45 minutes by boat from Iquitos, the **Ceiba Tops Lodge** (page 299) offers a good inexpensive taste of the rainforest.

- The **Cumaceba Lodge** (page 300) is a quick trip from Iquitos that offers a chance to see dolphins, caimans, and several bird species.

MOST LUXURIOUS LODGES

- The private bungalows at **Reserva Amazónica** (page 263) have ceiling fans and hot showers, which guests take before sitting down for an elegant dinner with candles and butler service after a day of activities. There are also cooking classes.

- A river cruise rather than a lodge, the *Aria Amazon,* operated by **Aqua Expeditions** (page 296), offers one of the most exclusive experiences in the Amazon, with onboard whirlpool tubs and meals inspired by one of Lima's top chefs.

CULTURAL EXPERIENCES

- Owned by the indigenous Ese-Eja community, visitors to **Posada Amazonas** (page 261) learn about medicinal plants from a shaman and see a rainforest farm to learn about local agricultural practices.

- The **Casa Machiguenga** (page 270), in the Manu biosphere, is operated by the Machiguenga indigenous people, offering activities to learn about their life in the Amazon.

cable TV, hot water, and a choice of air-conditioning or fan. Features include a tiny pool with a waterfall, Puerto's fanciest restaurant, and a gazebo bar with great views.

Information and Services

The **Tourism Ministry** (San Martín s/n, tel. 082/57-1164, 7am-3:30pm Mon.-Fri.) has an office in Puerto Maldonado and a small booth at the airport, but visitors should do their research before arriving in Puerto Maldonado. The national park service, **SERNANP** (8th block of San Martín), has an office in Puerto Maldonado that can provide information on national reserves.

The **police** (tel. 082/57-1022) are at Carrión 410 and can be called by dialing 105. You'll find an office of **Peruvian immigration** (Av. 28 de Julio 467, tel. 082/57-1069, 8am-4:15pm Mon.-Fri., 9am-noon Sat.). The **Bolivian consulate** is on the main square on Loreto.

Puerto's best medical care is at **Hospital Santa Rosa** (Cajamarca 171, at Velarde, tel. 082/57-1046, www.hospitalsantarosa.gob.pe, 24 hours daily). For medical emergencies, dial 117. **Clínica Madre de Dios** (28 de Julio 702, tel. 082/57-1440) is a private clinic.

The **Banco de la Nación** (Carrión 233), **Banco de Crédito** (Carrión 201), and **Interbank** (León Velarde and Carrión) are located on the Plaza de Armas and have ATMs. **Banco Continental** also has an ATM on the main plaza. There are several currency exchange houses on Puno. Few places in Puerto Maldonado accept credit cards, so bring cash.

The **post office** is at León Velarde 675 (tel. 082/57-1088, 8am-8pm Mon.-Sat.), and there are pay phones on the main square. **Internet** access is available at businesses around the plaza and on León Velarde. Laundry is available at **Lavandería Silán** (León Velarde 930, Mon.-Sat.) and several other places down the street.

Getting There and Around

As it is a short flight, most travelers arrive via plane to **Puerto Maldonado's airport** (PEM, tel. 082/57-1531 or 082/50-2029), which is eight kilometers from town, about US$3 by taxi. Airline routes are Lima-Cusco-Puerto. **LATAM** (Lima tel. 01/213-8200, www.latam. com) has regular flights and a local office (León Velarde 503, 8:30am-1pm and 4pm-7:30pm Mon.-Fri., 8:30am-1pm Sat.). The cheaper option is **StarPerú** (Lima tel. 01/705-9000, www.starperu.com), with flights from Lima and Cusco.

The road between Cusco and Puerto Maldonado is part of the **Interoceanic Highway,** a massive project that has connected Peru's Pacific coast to Brazil. The road, which cost some US$3 billion to complete, was inaugurated in 2011 and promises to transform Peru's southern Amazon, for both good and bad. From Cusco, the bus journey to Puerto Maldonado is now far easier: instead of a 20-hour trip on a rough bumpy road, it only takes 10 hours on a paved highway. A few interesting spots have popped up along the route. One of these is the **Mirador Cuyuni** (www.miradorcuyuni.com), located an hour outside Cusco. It offers nice views of the snow-covered Ausangate peak. The Mirador is owned by the nearby Cuyuni indigenous community, which sells crafts at the lookout point.

If traveling by bus, the best option is **Móvil Tours** (Av. Tambopata 428, www.moviltours.com.pe), with night and day buses (US$18-25 one-way). From Puerto Maldonado, the road continues to Peru's border town of Iñapari and into Brazil, where it connects with Rio Branco.

the Interoceanic Highway in Puerto Maldonado

The Bolivian border is six hours downstream from Puerto Maldonado, and boats sporadically leave from Puerto's port of Capitanía. Before you leave, however, you must get your passport stamped with an exit stamp at Peruvian immigration.

Mototaxis are everywhere and cost US$0.75 for a jaunt across town. *Colectivo* boats ferry passengers across the Tambopata and Río Madre de Dios and can be hired at the Capitanía port for local tours (US$20-25 per day). There are a few places in town to rent **scooters** (US$3 per hour), including the intersection of Gonzáles Prada and Puno.

RÍO TAMBOPATA LODGES

There are lodges on two rivers around Puerto Maldonado: the Río Tambopata and the Río Madre de Dios. On both rivers you will find a variety of accommodations, but for the most part, the rainforest activities remain the same.

Rainforest Expeditions

★ **Rainforest Expeditions** (Lima tel. 01/719-6422, www.perunature.com) is a top-notch outfit that operates three excellent well-managed lodges on the Río Tambopata as well as a private bungalow, providing biologist guides, excellent boats, and reliable service. In addition to its classic tours, Rainforest now offers soft adventure trips that involve kayaking, canopy climbing, and drifting down the Río Tambopata on a stand-up paddleboard. Programs include active and educational tours aimed at families, and wildlife photography trips with professional photographer Jeff Cremer. A five-day, four-night photography tour includes visits to the three lodges, professional tips on taking nature shots, and the use of professional cameras and super telephoto lenses, including a Canon 600 mm.

The four lodges are listed below in order of distance from Puerto Maldonado. There are several packages offered at the lodges, with prices starting at about US$220 per person per night.

POSADA AMAZONAS

Posada Amazonas is a groundbreaking experiment in cooperation with the community of Infierno, two hours upstream from Puerto Maldonado. The people of Infierno, mestizo descendants of Ese Eja indigenous people, receive training, jobs, and a share of the profits, while the lodge gets use of the land. Posada Amazonas is owned by the community and managed in partnership with Rainforest Expeditions, with the goal being to integrate the community into ecotourism and the overall preservation of rainforest.

The elegant lodge, located 45 minutes by boat from Puerto Maldonado, has 30 thatched rooms, with the outside wall completely open to keep guests in contact with nature. They have private baths with hot water and beds with mosquito canopies. Some rooms are lit by candlelight while others have electricity. There is a hammock lounge, a library, an open-air dining room, and a permanent snack and hot drink table. Tours include visits to an oxbow lake to see otters, an ethnobotanical center at Infierno, a canopy tower 35 meters off the ground, and walks in the effervescent rainforest. A parrot clay lick is a 15-minute walk from the lodge.

For families with teens, Posada has a five-day, four-night option that offers kayaking on the river, canoeing on an oxbow lake, and climbing a 30-meter Brazil nut tree.

REFUGIO AMAZONAS

Rainforest Expeditions' **Refugio Amazonas** is located four hours from Puerto Maldonado in a 200-hectare private reserve next to the Reserva Nacional Tambopata. The 32-room lodge has hot water, electricity, and Internet access in the common area. Each room comes with a private bath. There is an open dining room and a loft on top of the building providing a view of the surrounding rainforest. After a day of activities in the rainforest, the lodge offers massages at its wellness center. There is also a four-person private villa in the middle of the rainforest for those who want a little more privacy.

Refugio is a great option for parents that want to provide their children with an active and highly educational vacation in the rainforest. One day on the four-day, five-night family program includes a visit to the 25-meter canopy tower (walking up the tower in a spiral staircase is perfectly safe), where you can see toucans and macaws. Later there is a children's game to identify seeds and understand their use in the rainforest. After lunch, children will learn how people live in the Amazon during a guided walk on Refugio's rainforest trail, specially made for kids. After dinner there is the option of a night walk. Other activities include paddling on an oxbow lake, visits to a parrot clay lick, and searching for caimans at night. Children can also visit a nearby farm and make tattoos from rainforest fruits.

AMAZON VILLA

The newest offering from Rainforest Expeditions is the **Amazon Villa,** about 3.5

hours from Puerto Maldonado. Stay at the private bungalow nestled into the rainforest, with tropical hardwood floors, a king bed, and hammocks for relaxing. It offers a lot of the same activities as the other lodges: visit a macaw clay lick, climb up a canopy tower, river kayaking, a sunset cruise, and a rainforest night walk. The difference is you'll have a private guide, without larger groups.

TAMBOPATA RESEARCH CENTER

Also operated by Rainforest Expeditions, the **Tambopata Research Center** offers three-to seven-day packages where guests will experience a huge range of biodiversity that is comparable to the Parque Nacional Manu or Reserva Nacional Pacaya Samiria. Compared to those areas, the seven-hour journey up the Río Tambopata is a relatively short trip there and back, with a one-night stop in Refugio Amazonas. It is the only lodge near the Parque Nacional Bahuaja Sonene, a rainforest wilderness the size of Connecticut. The lodge is also 500 meters from the world's largest clay lick, where dozens of species of macaws, parrots, and parakeets come to get their sodium. The clay lick is amazing and well worth the long trip by river.

The lodge has 18 double bedrooms with shared baths (no hot water). The rooms have one wall completely open to the forest. The lodge also has a wellness center and offers sunset cruises. Photography trips are also offered, where almost all guests spot the white-lipped peccary and a quarter of the visitors will get a glimpse of the elusive jaguar. The center hosts the Tambopata Macaw Project, a research project established in 1989 that studies and promotes the conservation of macaws and parrots. The project is led Donald Brightsmith, a professor at Texas A&M University who did his PhD research at Manu.

Tambopata Eco Lodge

With more than 20 years' experience, **Tambopata Eco Lodge** (Nueva Baja 432, Cusco, tel. 084/24-5695, www.tambopata-lodge.com, 3 days, 2 nights US$437 pp), three

hours upstream from Puerto Maldonado, is a well-established rainforest option on the Río Tambopata. The older wooden bungalows are charming, with porches, hammocks, and thatched roofs. At night, the lodge is lit by flame lanterns and candles, and some buildings have solar energy. The hotel has plans to install solar panels to supply energy to all the rooms. The bungalows are spread out in a rainforest clearing, with the cozy bar and dining room a short walk away along a wooden ramp.

The lodge is surrounded by 100 hectares of secondary forest in which a few old trees remain. Highlights of a visit are bird-watching at Lago Condenado, swimming in the nearby Gallucunca stream, a bird-watching platform that is 24 meters high, and heading out on a night excursion on the Río Tambopata to spot caimans. An excursion to the macaw clay lick, several hours farther upstream, costs US$400-500 pp extra.

Explorer's Inn

Built in 1975, **Explorer's Inn** (Alcanfores 459, Miraflores, Lima, Lima tel. 01/447-8888, www.explorersinn.com, 3 days, 2 nights US$300 pp s) is the oldest, most experienced eco-lodge in Puerto Maldonado and has a comfortable worn-in feel. The palm-thatched wood-rich bungalows have foam mattresses, palm-wood walls, en suite baths (but no hot water), and are romantically lit by candles at night. They are comfortable but not luxurious. The central dining room is made entirely of wood and has an upstairs library with a number of natural history exhibits left behind by biologists and other researchers who have worked here over the decades.

Compared to other Amazon lodges, Explorer's Inn has the best combination of convenience, rates, and biodiverse rainforest. It is one of few located within Reserva Nacional Tambopata, and it carefully manages 5,500 hectares of pristine rainforest that began as a private reserve and has since been incorporated into the new Reserva Nacional Tambopata (the private property of the lodge is 105 hectares). The owner, Max Gunther, speaks flawless English as well as German and has been a leading figure in Peruvian ecotourism and conservation for three decades.

Biologists have proclaimed the 5,500 hectares surrounding the lodge to be "the most biodiverse place on the planet" because of a number of Guinness World Records that have been set here for animal species, including 600 bird species and more than 1,235 types of butterfly. The lodge also runs a volunteer resident naturalist program designed to appeal to graduates of the environmental sciences eager to gain experience in the Amazon rainforest.

There are 37 kilometers of well-marked trails that lead to huge tracts of virgin forest, a small macaw clay lick, and two lakes where giant otters live. During the walks, you can see several bird species, including macaws and toucans, as well as howler monkeys and otters. The guides are extremely knowledgeable. The lodge also arranges other trips, including a mystic adventure with an ayahuasca session, a trip to the macaw clay lick on the Río Tambopata, a six-night bird-watchers program, and a variety of camping trips with the chance of observing tapirs at a salt lick at night. The lodge is 1.5 hours upstream from the indigenous community of Infierno.

Inotawa

About 15 minutes before Explorer's Inn, **Inotawa** (tel. 082/57-2511, www.inotawaexpeditions.com, 3 days, 2 nights US$340 pp), which is 3.5 hours upstream from Puerto Maldonado, has a main thatched building with open-air rooms and single beds with mosquito-net covering. Baths are shared, with flush toilets but no hot water. There is a small bar, a restaurant with vegetarian food, and an option to visit the clay lick near the Tambopata Research Center. Inotawa offers two- to five-night lodge-based and expedition trips.

Tambopata Ecotourism Corridor

Only 15 minutes from Puerto Maldonado's main plaza are a number of budget homestay options along the banks of the Tambopata River. Families here have created small rustic lodges aiming to push back against encroaching urbanization. These are great options if you don't have the budget or time for the traditional lodges. Take note, however, that these are more rustic options than the traditional lodges and that there is less wildlife due to its location near the city. If you decide to stay on the corridor, one option is to rent a taxi and check out a few places before you pick your spot. For more information on the homestays, visit the **Tambopata Ecotourism Corridor**'s website (www.tambopataecotours.com). Puerto Maldonado travel agency **Mundea Tours & Travel** (Dos de Mayo 282, tel. 082/63-7112) can help book a homestay and organize transportation.

One of the first families to settle in the area was the Balarezo Yabar's. When you walk into **El Parayso** (about US$45 pp), or paradise, you really feel like you're entering the family home. Percy, a highly professional and knowledgeable guide, takes care of guests, who stay in one of two small but comfortable cabins (no electricity) overlooking the Tambopata river. A typical day could involve a trip up the river in Percy's canoe, and a night walk on a three-kilometer trail where we spotted noisy night monkeys, an armadillo, and a wax-tailed plant-hopper.

Another option is Víctor Zambrano's **Refugio Kerenda Homet** (www.refugiokerenda.com, from US$50 pp). Over several years Víctor planted some 19,000 trees, turning the area damaged by cattle ranching back into forest. Today, he's a well-known conservationist at the forefront of efforts to stem the expansion of illegal gold mining, a major source of environmental destruction in this part of the Amazon. In 2016, he was awarded the Buffett Award from National Geographic Society for his work.

RÍO MADRE DE DIOS LODGES
Reserva Amazónica

The fabulous ★ **Reserva Amazónica** (Lima tel. 01/610-0400, U.S. tel. 800/442-5042, www.

The Ecological Toll of Amazon Gold

The endless carpet of green Amazon rainforest, seen from above, is violently interrupted by the view of thousands of hectares of denuded brownish-black sand and earth, with lifeless pools of water contaminated with mercury. Tens of thousands of people involved in illegal gold mining in the last decade have destroyed at least 150,000 hectares in the Madre de Dios region, where 40,000 kilograms of mercury is dumped into the environment annually. Peruvian authorities have lost control over large areas of land and the activities that take place, driven by the high price of gold.

For every gram of gold extracted, up to three times more mercury is needed. The toxic metal is used to bind with the gold particles, forming an amalgam that makes them easier to extract. The process is cheap and efficient. But the leftovers are thrown into rivers and lagoons, poisoning flora and fauna and in turn passing into the food chain. The impact of mercury poisoning on the local population was documented in a 2013 study by Luis Fernandez, a research associate at Stanford University. Using hair samples, Fernandez found that over three-quarters of adults in Puerto Maldonado, the capital of Madre de Dios, had mercury concentrations higher than the international reference limit due to their consumption of contaminated fish. Perhaps unsurprisingly, the study found that indigenous communities are among the most vulnerable. Mercury contamination in indigenous communities was five times the maximum limit, compared to 2.3 times among nonindigenous people.

Despite the negative impacts, government efforts to stop the mining have so far been unsuccessful. Efforts to bring the activity under control have come face to face with violent protests from the estimated 30,000 informal miners. Meanwhile, the massive profits from the activity have corrupted local officials. While it's difficult to determine the size of any illicit activity, economists estimate that illegal gold mining accounts for 10 to 15 percent of Peru's total gold production, bringing in annual profits of US$1.8 billion, which would be more than Peru's cocaine trade.

These miners are often armed and go about their work without any restrictions, much as in the U.S. Wild West of the mid-19th century. Anyone who comes in their way is a target. Victor Zambrano, a local conservationist, told the BBC in 2016 after receiving an award from the National Geographic Society that he has faced several death threats. The Peruvian government recognizes the problems but does not have the power or staff to stop the thousands of miners operating illegally. Antonio Brack Egg, a late Peruvian conservationist and Peru's first Minister of the Environment, warned of grave repercussions for Madre de Dios, which is one of the most biologically diverse spots on earth. "Within 20 years Madre de Dios will be an ecological disaster like mankind has never seen before," Egg warned.

inkaterra.com, 3 days, 2 nights US$541-879 pp d, US$674-1,147 pp s) lodge is the most luxurious, and most romantic, in the Peruvian Amazon. It was founded in 1975 and is the oldest in the area. The hotel was the brainchild of José and Denise Koechlin, Peruvian eco-pioneers, who also own the elegant Inkaterra Machu Picchu Pueblo Hotel.

Near the riverbank, a sophisticated round dining building sets the tone for this lodge. This is not the kind of place where guests sit around in mud-spattered rubber boots; after long walks or boat rides, guests take hot showers, get cleaned up, and take cocktails in the dining loft with hip lounge music. The elegant dinner buffet, served downstairs, features organic salads and gourmet rainforest entrées like *paca,* which is *doncella* fish, tomatoes, and onions cooked inside a bamboo tube over an open fire. There are 35 private wooden bungalows with wood porches and hammocks, beds with mosquito netting, hot showers, ceiling fans, kerosene lamps, and interesting touches like wooden sinks and the hotel's own line of organic shampoo and conditioner.

The lodge has several unique attractions. First, it is surrounded by 200 hectares of private land plus a 10,000-hectare reserve.

Second, it is the only lodge with a hanging canopy walk: 344 meters of swinging bridges that, at 30 meters off the ground, connect six treetop platforms and two towers and truly allow for a bird's-eye view. If you want to spend the night in the canopy, there is the option of sleeping in the tree house. Guests have the options of some 15 different activities while staying at the lodge, including several that are good for families with children. You can trek seven kilometers through the rainforest, learn about the flora and fauna, go *piraña* fishing on Lake Sandoval, and take part in a nighttime caiman-spotting cruise.

Just downstream from the lodge, InkaTerra maintains the **Hacienda Concepción** (US$429 pp s, US$720 d), a former cacao and rubber plantation. The lodge has an environmental research and education center run jointly with the U.S.-based ACER. The main building is the restored home of Arturo Gonzáles del Rio, a beloved local doctor who bought a steamship from the Bolivian navy in the 1930s and used it as an ambulance for local indigenous people. The rusty girders and boilers of the boat can be seen during the walk into the center, which also has the area's largest garden of medicinal plants.

Sandoval Lake Lodge

The comfortable **Sandoval Lake Lodge** has a privileged location on Lago Sandoval, a crystal-clear lake fringed with *muriti* palms and teeming with aquatic birds. The lodge's operator, InkaNatura, often combines a trip to this lodge with a sister operation near the Bolivian border, the Heath River Wildlife Center. A two-night program (US$288 pp) can be booked through **InkaNatura Travel** (Lima tel. 01/440-2022, U.S. tel. 888/870-7378, www.inkanatura.com).

The lodge has clean rooms made of recycled cedar, with electricity and hot water. The lake itself is an enchanting place, especially when waters turn pink and orange with the sun's rising and setting, forming a perfect mirror for the elongated palms at the water's edge. About 30 bird species, mostly aquatic,

can be seen on a typical boat ride, including several species of kingfisher as well as herons and egrets. There are giant otters on the lake, but they are hard to see. Trails from the hotel's backyard lead into the Reserva Nacional Tambopata, which backs up against the property.

Reaching the lodge is the best part. Boats drop guests off at a dock, from where they walk three kilometers through a rainforest lane flitting with butterflies. Then guests board a canoe, which is paddled across the lake to the lodge. Each leg of the journey—motorboat, walking, and canoe—takes about 45 minutes.

The lodge is the result of a deal struck in 1996 with the Mejía family, who homesteaded around the lake in the 1950s and now operate their own lodging nearby.

Heath River Wildlife Center

Off the beaten path and in a seldom-visited part of the Amazon, the **Heath River Wildlife Center** is run by a local community of Ese Eja indigenous people. This community works closely with InkaNatura Travel, which guides the lodge's management. The lodge is a 4.5-hour boat journey from Puerto Maldonado and is sandwiched between Bolivia and Peru and in the middle of South America's largest patch of protected rainforest. The lodge has six bungalows with hot showers and a rustic communal space. The basic program is three nights, and longer programs often include the associated Lake Sandoval Lodge. Trips can be booked through **InkaNatura Travel** (Lima tel. 01/440-2022, U.S. tel. 888/870-7378, www.inkanatura.com).

MANU BIOSPHERE RESERVE

Sprawling across the eastern slope of the Andes, the **Reserva de Biósfera del Manu (Manu Biosphere Reserve)** is one of the most biodiverse corners of the planet. Roughly the size of New Hampshire, the park begins at high-altitude grasslands at 4,100 meters elevation, drops through cloud forest and mountainous rainforest, and then fans across a huge swath of rainforest at around 350 meters. There are 13 species of primates (more than anywhere else in the country), 15,000 plant species, 1,300 butterfly species, and more than one million insect species that are not even close to being documented. In May and June, the beginning of the dry and colder season, the odds increase of seeing jaguars, which come out to sun themselves on river logs. From July to November, near the end of the dry season, macaws, parrots, and parakeets are especially abundant around the riverside clay licks. Other frequently seen megafauna include giant otters, black caimans, lowland tapirs, armadillos, anteaters, sloths, wild pigs, and the endangered harpy eagle. As if that were not enough, Manu is one of world's top birding spots, with more than 1,022 confirmed species—almost 15 percent of the world's total.

The **Parque Nacional Manu** was created in 1973, but the area was deemed so biodiverse that UNESCO incorporated the whole surrounding area into a biosphere in 1977. Then Manu won the ultimate accolade when the International Union for the Conservation of Nature declared it a **World Heritage Site,** one of only 200 in the world.

These days the biosphere is classified into several areas. The section along the Río Alto Madre de Dios is the **Multiple Use Zone,** commonly referred to as the **Cultural Zone** or **Buffer Zone,** where there are a few villages and a variety of eco-lodges. The more pristine section up the Río Manu is the Parque Nacional Manu, to which access is strictly controlled. To enter the area, travelers must be with one of Manu's licensed operators, who have built comfortable safari camps and a few lodges alongside oxbow lakes. The lower part of the Río Manu, formerly known as the Reserved Zone, is used for sustainable eco-tourism and research.

The vast majority of the 1.5-million-hectare Parque Nacional Manu is closed except to licensed biologists and anthropologists. This chunk of rainforest shelters at least two ethnic groups who have had almost no contact with Western civilization, the Kogapacori people and the Mashco Piro people. Other groups have only limited contact with the modern world.

Only a handful of companies are allowed to operate in Parque Nacional Manu. They offer trips from 5 to 10 days that range from US$600 for camping to US$2,250 for more comfortable, high-end tours that include

Manu Biosphere Reserve

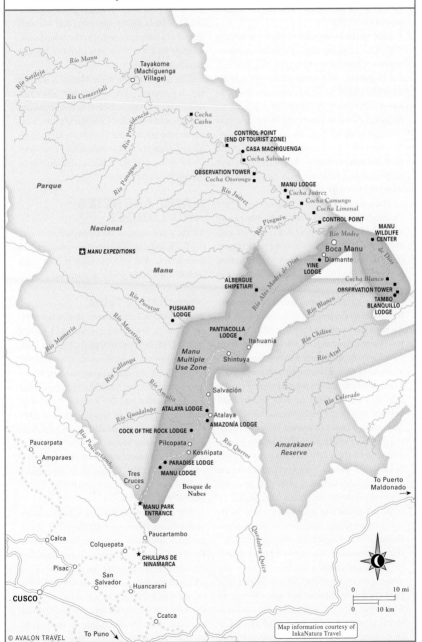

Manu Biosphere Reserve

Río Manu
Río Sotileja
Río Comeerjali

Tayakome
(Machiguenga
Village)

Río Providencia

Cocha
Cashu

**CONTROL POINT
(END OF TOURIST ZONE)**

CASA MACHIGUENGA

Cocha Salvador

OBSERVATION TOWER
Cocha Otorongo

Río Juárez

MANU LODGE
Cocha Juárez
Cocha Camungo
Cocha Limonal

CONTROL POINT

**MANU
WILDLIFE
CENTER**

Río Madre

Boca Manu
de Dios

Diamante

**YINE
LODGE**

Cocha Blanco

OBSERVATION TOWER

**TAMBO
BLANQUILLO
LODGE**

**ALBERGUE
SHIPETIARI**

Río Alto Madre de Dios

Río Blanco

Río Chilive

Río Azul

Río Colorado

**PUSHARO
LODGE**

**PANTIACOLLA
LODGE**
Itahuania

**Manu
Multiple
Use Zone**

Shintuya

Salvación

ATALAYA LODGE
Atalaya

AMAZONÍA LODGE

COCK OF THE ROCK LODGE

Pilcopata

Kosñipata

PARADISE LODGE

MANU LODGE

Tres
Cruces

Bosque de
Nubes

**Amarakaeri
Reserve**

To Puerto
Maldonado

**MANU PARK
ENTRANCE**

Paucarpata

Amparaes

Río Mameria

Río Maestrón

Río Callanga

Río Amalia

Río Guadalupe

Río Paucartambo

Río Queros

Quebrada Quico

Paucartambo

Calca

Colquepata

**CHULLPAS DE
NINAMARCA**

Pisac

San
Salvador
Huancarani

CUSCO

Ccatca

To Puno

Parque

Nacional

Río Panagua

Río Porotoa

Manu

★ **MANU EXPEDITIONS**

Río Pinguén

0   10 mi

0   10 km

© AVALON TRAVEL

Map information courtesy of
InkaNatura Travel

lodges with cotton sheets, electricity, and hot water. Some of the agencies offer adventure options, from rafting and trekking to extreme mountain biking.

One of the best parts of Manu is getting there and dropping through the dizzying sequence of ecosystems along the way. The first day is spent driving seven hours through the altiplano near Cusco and down into the rainforest. This takes you to one of a handful of lodges perched in the cloud forest and surrounded with orchids, hummingbirds, butterflies, and the crimson Andean cock of the rock. From here, visitors descend to the lower rainforest and take a several-hour boat ride down the Río Alto Madre de Dios.

There used to be the option of flying into the small town of Boca Manu, which has a tiny airport. While the airport is still operational, there haven't been any commercial flights over the last few years. The only other option for flying is to charter a plane, which is very expensive.

In the national park, guests commonly stay in safari camps, but on trips to both the national park and the Cultural Zone, participants spend their days exploring oxbow lakes with floating platforms and spotting scopes.

Because of the lack of air service to Boca Manu, companies are now wrapping up the tour by traveling both by boat and by road vehicle to Puerto Maldonado, which can take several hours (duration varies depending on where you leave from). Once in Puerto Maldonado, there is the option to fly to Lima or Cusco, or you can take a private bus on the paved highway to Cusco. Ask your operator about the route for returning from Manu.

Apart from the operators listed here, many other Cusco agencies sell Manu trips. Some of these agencies simply "endorse" their clients over to a licensed Manu operator at an additional cost. Others only take passengers through the Cultural Zone of the park, which is cheaper because there is no US$60 park fee and less gas is used. You will have better guides, see more wildlife, and be more comfortable if you stick with one of the operators listed here, who also offer budget options. It is not recommended to visit Manu on your own or with a private guide. Boat traffic is highly sporadic, and without one of the licensed agencies, the rangers absolutely will not allow you into the Parque Nacional Manu.

The best time to visit Manu is during the dry season, May to October, although rains only become unbearably heavy during January and February. Considering how hard Manu is to reach, it does not make sense to go for less than six days—except for those who fly in and out of Boca Manu and choose to bypass the cloud forest.

MANU AGENCIES AND LODGES

All the prices quoted are all-inclusive, covering food, lodging, and transportation to and from Manu. Ask your operator if their rates include the US$60 park entrance fee.

Manu Nature Tours

Manu Nature Tours (Pardo 1046, Cusco, tel. 084/25-2721, www.manuperu.com, 5 days, 4 nights US$1,678 pp, not including the park fee) has the most comfortable trips and the only lodge inside the Parque Nacional Manu (except for the rustic Casa Machiguenga at the Cocha Salvador and the Romero Rainforest Lodge). The company was launched in 1985 by Boris Gomez with funding from American biologist Charlie Munn, who has been a key force behind preservation of the Manu and other rainforests. It has been repeatedly named the best Manu operator by Peru's Ministry of Tourism.

The company was the first to build a lodge in the cloud forest, and all the other Manu agencies followed suit. **The Manu Cloud Forest Lodge** is a magnificent thatched structure with a glass atrium and view over a white-water creek. Guests can try a half-day or one-day **rafting trip** down two rivers in the area, the Kosñipata and the Tono, which are Class III or IV depending on the season. In 1987 Manu Nature Tours also built the first lodge inside the Parque Nacional Manu. **Manu Lodge** is built of salvaged mahogany next to a lake where guests can see black caimans, brown capuchins, and giant otters.

In addition, Manu Nature Tours offers **trekking** and **mountain biking trips** from the grasslands into the Manu, a brain-spinning descent of hundreds of vertical meters through the cloud forest.

★ Manu Expeditions

Manu Expeditions (Los Geranios 2-G, Urb. Mariscal Gamarra Primero Etapa, Cusco, tel. 084/22-4135, www.manuexpeditions.com, 7 days, 6 nights US$2,485 pp) is run by English ornithologist Barry Walker and has a solid reputation for high-quality tours and world-class bird guides. On their way to Manu, guests first stay at the **Cock of the Rock Lodge,** a wood building in the cloud forest with cozy, simple rooms lit by candles and kerosene lamps. Once in the rainforest, guests typically stay nights at the Romero Rainforest Lodge and the company's own safari camp near Cocha Salvador in the Parque Nacional Manu. Manu Expeditions is the owner of the new Romero Rainforest Lodge, which is about a 45-minute boat ride from Boca Manu at the old park station of Romero.

Manu Expeditions also sends guests to the **Manu Wildlife Center,** which it owns along with Peru Verde (www.peruverde.org), a nonprofit Peruvian conservation group. The 44-bed wooden lodge is 90 minutes downriver from Boca Manu in a section of rainforest adjacent to the Manu Biosphere Reserve. There are 35 kilometers of trails through mature forest, two 35-meter-tall canopy platforms, and oxbow lakes with giant otters and floating observation platforms. A natural clay lick near the lodge offers the best chances in Manu for seeing the tapir, a 250-kilogram cousin of the hippopotamus. Because tapirs mainly forage at night, guests camp out in a comfortable nearby blind, which is outfitted with mosquito netting, snacks, and mattresses. The lodge is also 20 minutes from Manu's largest macaw lick.

Barry personally leads private birding tours to Manu and all over Peru and Bolivia, which are described on the website www.birding-in-peru.com. An 18-day odyssey through the central Peruvian highlands and cloud forest costs US$5,795.

InkaNatura

The other high-end Manu operator is **InkaNatura Travel** (Lima tel. 01/440-2022, www.inkanatura.com, 5 days, 4 nights US$1,475 pp), which is one of Peru's leading ecotourism operators, with programs in Chachapoyas, Puerto Maldonado, and the rainforest around Quillabamba as well.

InkaNatura is the profit-making arm of the Peru Verde conservation organization that owns Manu Wildlife Center. It offers a four-day trip to a tented camp at Cocha Salvador with a round-trip flight between Cusco and Boca Manu and an optional two-day extension to the Manu Wildlife Center.

Early mornings are spent in boats, birdwatching; afternoons are filled with rainforest walks, where, with binoculars in hand, you are likely to see a variety of monkeys, butterflies, and even more birds; and evenings are spent looking for tapirs or other nocturnally active animals. With such full days, it is a good thing that InkaNatura provides for all your other needs: refreshing snacks, filling meals, comfortable bedding, and excellent guides.

Pantiacolla Tours

Pantiacolla Tours (Garcilaso 265, 2nd Fl., Cusco, tel. 084/23-8323, www.pantiacolla.com, call for tour prices) was started in 1991 by conservationist Gustavo Moscoso, who was born in Boca Manu, and his Dutch wife, biologist Marianne van Vlaardingen. The company funds conservation in Manu and is currently involved in a legal case to prevent gas drilling in the Amarakaeri communal reserve, located east of Manu.

Pantiacolla offers a series of excellent trips that range from three to nine days and include stays at its rustic lodges. The three-day trip involves spending two nights at its Posada San Pedro lodge in Manu's cloud forest, while a five-day trip adds a stay at its Pantiacolla lodge in Manu's Cultural Zone. Its seven-day journey into Manu adds two nights in Manu's Reserved Zone, with a stay at its rustic tented camp near Cocha Salvador and a visit to the Blanquillo macaw clay lick.

Crees

Crees (Urb. Mariscal Garmarra B-5, Zone 1, Cusco, tel. 084/26-2433, www.crees-manu. org, 8 days, 7 nights US$2,630 pp) is a non-profit organization created in 2002 that does environmental research and community projects in Manu to promote conservation and sustainable development. Its tours to Manu help to fund its research. Participants in the tours stay at the organization's Manu Learning Center, an eco-lodge that houses the research facilities. It is also a bird-watcher's paradise. Crees claims that almost 130 bird species can be spotted just from lounging in the hammocks in its gardens, while more than 360 species have been recorded in the area over the last three years. The lodge has received a verification mark from the Rainforest Alliance. Longer trips also include a stay at the comfortable Romero Rainforest Lodge, which it manages with Manu Expeditions. In addition to its six-day tour, it also offers a four-day and a nine-day package. Ask about its volunteer programs for longer stays.

SAS Travel

SAS Travel (Garcilaso 270, Cusco, tel. 084/24-9194, www.sastravelperu.com, 6 days, 5 nights US$1,400 pp) has tours led by naturalist rainforest guides that range from three-day tours of the Manu cloud forest to an eight-day trip that includes a visit to the Blanquillo macaw clay lick and stops at oxbow lakes to see giant otters and black caimans. SAS also offers tours in Cusco and to Machu Picchu.

Expediciones Vilca

Another Manu operator is **Expediciones Vilca** (Plateros 361, Cusco, tel. 084/25-3773, www.peruvilca.com, manuvilca@terra.com. pe, 5 days, 4 nights US$1,000), which offers Manu trips at the Casa Machiguenga and Tambo Blanquillo Lodge. It also offers Inca Trail and other adventure trips.

Independent Lodges

There are a few independent lodges that the licensed Manu operators often use in their packages.

CASA MACHIGUENGA

Casa Machiguenga is a lodge built and operated by the Machiguenga people in the communities near Yombebato and Tayakome, with financial assistance from a German nonprofit organization. Various agencies use the facilities they have on offer. The wooden lodge, with adequate baths, is more rustic than other Manu lodges but offers a good chance to glimpse the lifestyles of Manu's true local people. Book through an agency such as **Manu Expeditions** (www.manuexpeditions.com).

TAMBO BLANQUILLO LODGE

Tambo Blanquillo Lodge (www.tambob-lanquillo.com) has an observation tower and is a 10-minute boat ride from the largest of Manu's macaw clay licks.

ALBERGUE PANKOTSI LODGE

The Shipetiari community's **Albergue Pankotsi Lodge** (www.alberguepankotsi. com) is located on the edge of Manu but provides good opportunities for spotting wildlife and is a good way to learn about community life.

Selva Alta

One of the most breathtaking areas of Peru is on the Eastern side of the Andes, where the cold mountain air suddenly gives way to the lush vegetation of the warm rainforest. Peru's high rainforest, or *selva alta,* typically extends from about 600 meters elevation to around 2,500 meters, running the length of Peru from North to South. Here, you'll find beautiful waterfalls, orchids, and dancing butterflies. It is also fertile terrain for coca leaves, creating a few remote valleys that are rife with drug trafficking and best avoided.

The places included here, however, are completely safe and are some of Peru's best off-the-beaten path rainforest destinations. Unlike the Amazon basin, the *selva alta* doesn't have as broad a choice for eco-lodges. But there are several towns worth exploring, including the coffee-growing region of Chanchamayo, and Tarapoto, which is easily accessible by plane from Lima.

CHANCHAMAYO AND VICINITY

From Lima, the closest shot of rainforest warmth is Chanchamayo, an area that includes the towns of **San Ramón** and **La Merced** on the Río Chanchamayo. The paved highway has shortened the drive from Lima to eight hours.

There are lots of interesting things to see and do around Chanchamayo, including 100-meter waterfalls in the nearby **Perené Valley,** virgin forest with colossal cedars in the **Zona Reservada Pampa Hermosa,** and visitor-friendly Asháninka villages. There are Class III-IV rafting rivers, great mountain biking, and a bizarre Austrian-German colony from the mid-19th century, where villagers still speak German and hold on to their Tyrolean customs. Via a network of roads and rivers, truly wild rainforest on the Río Tambo can be reached in a day or two. The best time to visit is during the dry months, April to October.

The **Franciscans** who came here in 1635 had to leave after Spaniards entered the area looking for gold and were slaughtered by local indigenous people. By 1750 a few plantations in the valley were growing sugarcane, cocoa, coffee, and coca leaves. But the settlers were massacred during the indigenous rebellion led by **Juan Santos Atahualpa,** a local and legendary indigenous hero, raised by the Jesuits, who claimed kinship with Inca Atahualpa. Colonists entered the area permanently after 1850 when a rough road from Tarma down into the valley was constructed. The area today is famous for its tropical fruits, avocados, *rocoto,* and high-octane coffee.

Sights
PERENE VALLEY

Several agencies have put together one-day tours into the valley below Chanchamayo that pack an extraordinary number of activities into one day. These include crossing a river on a wire trolley, sunbathing on a sandy beach, traveling by boat from the river port of Pichanaki to an Asháninka community, and swimming or even rappelling off a set of extraordinary 120-meter-high waterfalls known as Bayoz and Velo de la Novia (Bride's Veil). The closest waterfall is Cascada El Tirol, just outside San Ramón.

SAN MIGUEL

This interesting Asháninka village in the Perene Valley has a lodge recommended by Norwegian anthropologist Ole Steinert as an excellent way to understand the daily life of this indigenous group. **Ñapirori Lodge,** which means "strong man" in the Asháninka language, consists of three houses built in indigenous style, each with a double bed and a balcony out front. Around the lodges are mango trees, coffee plants, tropical flowers, and spectacular views of the Perene Valley. The 40 families that live in San Miguel are very friendly and proud of their uncommercialized settlement. Men still hunt with bows and arrows and, during communal meetings, show up in traditional dress. This is a great place to stay for some days and be enriched by the Asháninka way of life.

Colectivos leave frequently from La Merced to Santa Ana, also called Villa Perené, and then from Santa Ana to San Miguel throughout the afternoon. The dirt road to San Miguel is about five or six kilometers up in the hills. From here it is a 500-meter walk farther to the village, where guests should ask for the lodge owners.

POZUZO-OXAPAMPA

In 1857, after a formal invitation from the Peruvian government, a group of German and Austrian immigrants from Prussia and Tyrol hacked their way into a remote rainforest enclave northeast of the Chanchamayo Valley. They survived despite the odds, were largely forgotten, and over time developed a charming and somewhat bizarre Bavarian village in the Amazon that they christened **Pozuzo.**

Where else in the Amazon can you find three-story Tyrolean homes with carved wooden rafters, blond damsels who speak German, and huge wheels of cheese? The blue-eyed villagers have built comfortable Alpine guesthouses that charge as little as US$10 pp, including breakfast. There are also caves, ox-driven sugarcane mills known as *trapiches,* waterfalls, and German dancing contests during holidays.

Oxapampa, founded by Pozuzo settlers in 1891, is a two-hour, 80-kilometer journey from Chanchamayo on a paved road. Pozuzo is another four hours (80 kilometers) farther on spectacular bumpy roads that cross several streams. The best lodging in Oxapampa is **Albergue Turístico Böttger** (Mariscal Castilla, block 6, tel. 063/46-2377, www.oxapampaonline.com/bottger, US$35 s, US$50 d, with breakfast), with six beautiful wooden-made rooms, hot water, laundry service, a small TV lounge, and a big backyard. The owner, Doris Böttger, is a very warm host and

extremely resourceful, with information about what to see and what to do around the area.

Since 2010, quiet Oxapampa gets a big wake-up every June with a music festival called **Selvamonos** (www.selvamonos. org), which includes everything from rock to electronic and reggae. Check www.oxapampaonline.com, in Spanish, which has good information about Oxapampa and Pozuzo, including other lodgings, restaurants, and places to visit.

ZONA RESERVADA PAMPA HERMOSA

A two-hour drive, about 24 kilometers, along a rough road from San Ramón's Victoria Bridge, followed by a steep two-hour walk, leads to a stunning patch of high cloud forest known as Pampa Hermosa. This reserved zone, with almost 10,000 hectares, protected since 2005 by the Peruvian government, contains primeval cedar, walnut, and strangler fig trees. It is oddly flat, like an island of rainforest perched 1,600 meters in the air. Steep access has kept loggers away. Nearby communities are now protecting this last patch of virgin primary forest, which is filled with the noises of monkeys and the musky odor of the white-collared peccary.

Recreation

Undisturbed rainforest areas can be found within the **Parque Nacional Yanachaga Chemillén,** three to four hours from Chanchamayo. More remote rainforest is a day's journey from Chanchamayo. A seven-hour *combi* ride leads to Puerto Bermúdez, a lazy settlement on the Río Pachitea. Both the river and the dirt road (not passable in rainy season, Nov.-Mar.) lead all the way to Pucallpa, an adventurous journey that runs through the town of Puerto Inca. Another option is to head to **Satipo,** two hours along paved road from Chanchamayo, and then to travel farther by *combi* to the riverside town of Puerto Ocopa. From here, boats can be hired to descend the Río Tambo, a remote corner of Peru's Amazon.

If you are driving, or not shy about hitch-hiking, there is a spectacular dirt road to Huancayo from Satipo, which leads up and over a 4,320-meter pass, **Abra Tortuga,** in the Huaytapallana range. No regular transportation follows this route, a 10-hour journey between Satipo and Huancayo.

TOUR AGENCIES AND GUIDES

Agencies tend to come and go in Chanchamayo, but the friendly Rodolfo May, owner of **Hostal Golden Gate** (just west of Herrería Bridge, outside La Merced, tel. 064/53-1483), can give excellent information about activities in the area and, with advance notice, can arrange trips.

Lucho Hurtado, the owner of **Incas del Peru** (Av. Giráldez 675, tel. 064/22-3303, www.incasdelperu.org) in Huancayo, takes groups into the Chanchamayo area for a five-day action-packed stay at his father's farm near Pozuzo.

San Ramón and La Merced

The launching points into the Chanchamayo rainforest are the nearby towns of San Ramón and La Merced. Although there are only 11 kilometers between both towns, they are drastically different. San Ramón is a sleepy town with a good restaurant and hostel. The bigger and much more hectic La Merced has more restaurants and agencies, along with a collection of drab hostels. The best accommodations are the nice hotels on the road between the towns.

FOOD

La Merced has three safe and well-known restaurants, all lined up near the main square and specializing in rainforest cooking, including ceviche made from *doncella* fish as well as deer and wild pig dishes. The first, **Los Koquis** (Tarma 376 interior, tel. 064/53-1536, 7am-10pm Mon.-Sat., 7am-6pm Sun., US$3-6), has excellent *comida criolla*. The second, **Shambari-Campa** (Tarma 389, tel. 064/53-1425, 7am-midnight daily, US$3-6), has an even more extensive menu and an interesting

series of old historical photos on the wall. The third, **El Sabroson** (no phone, 10am-10pm daily, US$5-8), is next door with a similar menu but a cleaner, less cluttered interior.

The quieter San Ramón also has two excellent options. If you are leery of the sketchy sanitary habits of most *chifas,* you can dive in head first at **Felipe Siu** (Progreso 440, tel. 064/33-1078, 11:30am-3pm and 6:30pm-11pm daily, US$3-5). This charming, decades-old establishment is known for *pollo chijau kay* (fried chicken with ginger sauce) and *limón kay* (strips of chicken in lemon sauce). You would call it a hole-in-the-wall. It now also has a spot in La Merced (Junín 121).

ACCOMMODATIONS

La Merced is a pleasant town but its lodging options are lackluster. San Ramón is quieter and cleaner but has few services. If at all possible, spring for the charming hotels and bungalows between the towns.

In La Merced, the new **Heliconia Hotel** (Junín 922, Parque Integración, tel. 064/53-1394, www.heliconiahotel.com, US$35 s, US$50 d, with breakfast) is a good option. The tiled rooms have comfortable beds, private baths with hot water, air-conditioning, and views over a park. **Hotel El Rey** (Junín 103, tel. 064/53-1185, www.hotelrey.net, US$21 s, US$29 d) has been in business 30 years and has excellent service. It has retiled all of its rooms, which have private baths, hot water, and Wi-Fi. On the outskirts of La Merced is the ★ **Hotel Presidente** (tel. 064/53-1686, www.hotelpresidente.com.pe, US$80 s, US$90 d, with breakfast buffet). While it is more expensive than other options, the tiled rooms are very comfortable with large beds, air-conditioning, cable TV, and baths with a tub. It has a small pool and a comfortable area for reading in the evening.

In San Ramón, you'll find peaceful, quiet, and friendly ★ **Hospedaje El Parral** (Uriarte 355, tel. 064/33-1128, www.elparralhotelyparrilladas.com, US$20 s, US$33 d). A good bungalow option about one kilometer outside San Ramón is the **Rio Grande**

Lodge (Carretera Central, Km 97, tel. 064/33-2193, www.riogrande-bungalow.com, US$45 s, US$53 d). There are stone paths to the wood-paneled bungalows, which surround a nice pool and are close to the Río Chanchamayo. In San Ramón, **El Refugio** (El Ejército 460, tel. 064/33-1082, www.lodgeelrefugiochanchamayo.com.pe, US$22 s, US$36 d) is a very good choice, with 21 bungalows, gardens, swimming pool, Wi-Fi, and a good restaurant.

GETTING THERE AND AROUND
La Merced's main bus station is on the eastern end of town, at the triangular intersection of Fitzgerald and Carmen. From here *combis* can be taken nearly anywhere: to Satipo (2 hours, departures throughout the day, US$4), Oxapampa (3 hours, departures 4am-6am, US$5), Puerto Bermúdez (7 hours, departures 4am-5am, US$8), or Huancayo (3 hours, US$5).

Double-decker buses from **Empresa de Transportes Junín** also leave from La Merced to Lima (US$10), an eight-hour trip. **Transportes Chanchamayo** (www.transporteschanchamayo.com) also travels the Lima to La Merced route.

Mototaxis are everywhere in La Merced but are not really needed unless you want to take the US$1 ride to the hilltop cross, a fabulous lookout over the Chanchamayo Valley that is not safe at night. *Combis* are also frequent between La Merced and San Ramón and leave when full from the corner of Junín and Arica in La Merced, about every 15 minutes.

FROM LIMA TO PUCALLPA
Built on the shores of the Río Ucayali, Pucallpa is the east-central gateway to the Amazon rainforest and the launching point for a four-day cargo boat journey down the Río Ucayali to Iquitos.

Pucallpa can be reached from Lima by daily flights or by bus. The area has become safer for travelers, and the overland journey from Lima to Pucallpa is interesting. A good way to break up the journey is to stay in Huánuco, with its ideal climate, or Tingo María, which is surrounded by gorgeous natural settings. Both towns are in the Huallaga Valley and were off the tourist circuit until the end of the 1990s because of intense drug trafficking and terrorist violence. Since then the situation has changed slowly but dramatically for the better. Huánuco and Tingo María are becoming off-the-beaten-path destinations for bird-watchers, nature lovers, and adventure seekers.

Huánuco
The 410 kilometers—about 10 hours on a bus—between coastal Lima, up the **Carretera Central,** and all the way to Huánuco is a magnificent day trip and crosses at least five different geographic regions. After passing Chosica and San Mateo, among other smaller towns, the highway makes a winding ascent on its way to Ticlio and the Anticona Pass, at 4,820 meters. At the mining center of La Oroya (3,700 meters), the highway detours north to Huánuco. It crosses the high-elevation puna at 4,000 meters and runs next to the **Reserva Nacional Junín,** which protects wetlands and the highly endangered Junín grebe in Lake Junín. The Carretera Central passes by the detour road to Cerro de Pasco before descending the Río Huallaga, which eventually broadens into a fertile valley where Huánuco is located.

Situated at 1,894 meters elevation, the inhabitants of this small city on the Upper Río Huallaga Valley boast that they have the best climate in Peru due to its warm weather all year round. Founded in 1541, the town itself has some churches and old historic buildings, but its major interesting sites are located in the surrounding area.

SIGHTS
The **Temple of Kotosh,** known in Spanish as **Templo de las Manos Cruzadas** (8:30am-5pm daily, US$1 pp), is five kilometers west of the city and is one of Peru's oldest

the Temple of Kotosh, one of Peru's oldest archaeological sites

archaeological sites. It was intensely studied by Japanese archaeologists, led by Seichi Izumi, in the 1950s and 1960s. It can be easily visited hiring a taxi (US$8 round-trip, including a 30-minute wait).

South of the city lies a long and wide stretch of the fertile Upper Huallaga Valley, where the **Cachigaga Hacienda** is located and which can be reached by taxi (US$5 one-way). It is well reputed for its *aguardiente* (distilled sugarcane alcohol) and rum, which are sold here. The owner, **Honorato López** (cell tel. 962-947-140), is a friendly man who doesn't speak English, but he will gladly tour you around his small hacienda, showing you the process to make his spirituous drinks, if he is around and you know some Spanish.

About 20 kilometers up from **Cachigaga** are the **Lagunas de Pichgacocha,** a beautiful set of five waterfalls and lagoons, that you can reach by trekking from Conchamarca (5-6 hours) or by hired taxi (US$30 round-trip). It is possible to camp, explore, and trek around the lagoons.

FOOD

El Bambú (Av. Universitaria, Km 2.2, tel. 062/51-6097, 9am-7pm daily, US$3-8), a bit outside the city, is an excellent place to try regional food such as fried or stewed *cuy* (guinea pig). If you prefer pizzas or pasta, **Pizzería Don Sancho** (General Prado 645, tel. 062/51-6906, US$3-6), just across Hotel Trapiche Suites, is your place.

ACCOMMODATIONS

Huánuco has a couple of mid-range hotels, such as the central **Grand Hotel Huánuco** (Dámaso Beraún 775, tel. 062/51-4222, www. grandhotelhuanuco.com, US$60 s, US$75 d). The best is **Hotel Trapiche Suites** (General Prado 636, tel. 062/51-7091, US$45 s, US$55 d), with extremely comfy beds (with lots of pillows) in cozy rooms, impeccable private baths, cable TV, Wi-Fi, and mini fridges.

INFORMATION AND SERVICES

Huánuco does not have an Iperú office, but **Dircetur** (Bolívar 381, tel. 062/51-2980) can offer some guidance about tourism destinations and services. The **police station** (tel. 062/51-3480) is at Constitución 621. **Scotiabank** (28 de Julio 1016-1018), **Banco de Crédito** (Dos de Mayo 1005), and **BBVA Banco Continental** (Dos de Mayo 1137) have 24-hour ATMs.

Tingo María

The 135-kilometer drive between Huánuco and Tingo María takes about two hours and ascends the **Cordillera Carpish** before plunging into the cloud forest. Tingo María is gradually shaking off its unfortunate reputation as one of Peru's biggest drug-trafficking hubs. Tourism started to pick up in the late 1990s due to this town's extraordinary natural surroundings, including waterfalls, an amazing population of birds, and the Parque Nacional Tingo María, which was established in 1965 and is Peru's second-oldest park. The whole Huallaga region still has its share of coca plantations, but tourism is growing quickly.

SIGHTS

The main attraction, without doubt, is **Parque Nacional Tingo María**, 12 kilometers southeast of the city, with almost 4,800 hectares of protected montane cloud forest that lies around the mouth of the **Río Monzón**, a tributary of the Huallaga. The park has lots of caves, and the most popular to visit is the **Cueva de las Lechuzas** (Owl Cave, park fee US$2), which is inhabited by oilbirds instead. The best time to visit the cave is early in the morning or in the afternoon; taxis or *mototaxis* (US$3-5) will take you. Additionally, Tingo María has at least a dozen waterfalls that can be visited and accessed by *mototaxis,* including **Cueva de las Pavas** (8 kilometers south), **Santa Carmen** (30 meters high, 13 kilometers south), and **Velo de las Ninfas** (15 kilometers south). About 20 kilometers north of Tingo María, on the newly paved Carretera Marginal heading to Tocache, is **Laguna El Milagro,** a lagoon in the middle of a beautiful high rainforest setting where you can either take a canoe ride or a paddle boat (US$1.50 for 30 minutes).

The **Market** (between Alameda Perú and Tito Jaime Fernández) in downtown Tingo María is an interesting place to observe and buy rainforest products such as fruit, river fish, bush meat, and other exotic products.

FOOD

If Tingo María is the first rainforest town you go to, be ready for the explosion of fruits and fish you have as eating options. Explore your senses. **D'Tinto & Madero** (Alameda Perú 391, 2nd Fl., tel. 062/56-3012, US$3-10) has *picuro a la parrilla,* which is grilled *picuro* (also named *majás*), a medium-size rodent, and grilled deer as well as beef, lamb, chicken, and pork.

ACCOMMODATIONS

Tingo María's downtown has a variety of low-budget hostels, most of them clean, with private baths and fans. **Eco Albergue Villa Jennifer** (Km 3.4, Sector Monterrico, Castillo Grande, tel. 062/79-4714, www.villajennifer.com, US$55 s or d, with breakfast) is undoubtedly the best option on the outskirts. Owned by a friendly Peruvian-Danish couple, Graciela and Erlan Ohlsen, this place has a swimming pool, delicious food (try the banana lasagna), and hectares of green to stroll and relax.

INFORMATION AND SERVICES

The Municipalidad de Tingo María has a **Tourism Office** (Alameda Perú 525, tel. 062/56-7589) that can provide information and some brochures. **Banco de Crédito** (Raimondi 249) and **BBVA Banco Continental** (Raimondi 555) both have ATMs. The **public hospital** (tel. 062/56-2018) is at Ucayali 144. Branches of the pharmacy chains **Inkafarma** and **BTL** are both on Raimondi. There are **Internet cafés** all over the town, with decent speed, charging US$0.60 per hour.

PUCALLPA AND VICINITY

From Tingo María to Pucallpa is a 282-kilometer, five-hour drive. The highway, also known as **Carretera Federico Basadre,** is paved but with some sections that are constantly being repaired. Once you pass by **Boquerón del Padre Abad,** a river gorge that cuts through the southern tip of the **Cordillera Azul,** the rainforest opens into a flat plain of endless vegetation, passing through the town of Aguaytía before reaching Pucallpa.

Sights

Pucallpa, which means "red dirt" in Quechua, became a city in 1883, during the rubber boom. Today, it is still underdeveloped despite being the Ucayali region's capital city. Tourist attractions are limited to **Yarinacocha,** an oxbow lake 10 kilometers northeast of the city, with boat rides available to go fishing or visit nearby Shipibo communities. Pucallpa is the last town where you can get provisions and money before embarking in a cargo boat to do a river cruise on the Río Ucayali and the

Amazon River toward Iquitos. If you decide to stay for a day or two, there are comfortable lodgings and good restaurants.

Food

On the Puerto Callao lakeside village in Yarinacocha are some inexpensive restaurants. The better ones are Anaconda (no phone) and Puerto Rico (no phone) on the waterfront. In Pucallpa, Parrilladas Orlando (Aguaytía y 28 de Julio, tel. 061/59-6577, US$3-8) has superb grilled meats, including *majás*. Chez Maggy (Inmaculada 643, tel. 061/57-4958, 5pm-midnight daily, US$3-6) is a good option for pizzas and pasta. Restaurante Golf (Huáscar 545, tel. 061/57-4632, 10am-5pm Tues.-Sun., US$3-7) has delicious river fish dishes, including *doncella* and *paiche*. For breakfast, including really good coffee, there is C'est Si Bon (Independencia 560, tel. 061/57-4049, 8am-midnight, US$3-5). It also has good selection of ice cream.

Accommodations

The city has a wide range of hotels for all budgets. Hotel Los Gavilanes (Ipuatía 370, Yarinacocha, tel. 061/59-6741, www.losgavilaneshotel.com, US$36 s, US$40 d, breakfast and airport transfer included) has rooms with fans and air-conditioning, cable TV, and mini fridges, along with a swimming pool, a bar, and a restaurant in a relaxed atmosphere. Antonio's Hotel (Progreso 545, tel. 061/57-3721, www.antonioshotel.com.pe, US$35 s, US$44 d, with breakfast) has big rooms with Wi-Fi and cable TV and a nice swimming pool. Another good option is Manish Hotel Ecológico (Av. Centenario, Km 4800, tel. 061/57-7167, www.manishhotel.com.pe, US$65 s, US$83 d), which has comfortable rooms with air-conditioning, cable TV, flat-screen TVs, Wi-Fi, and ample gardens. Bungalows with double rooms are available. One of the bungalows has been turned into a small workout room.

Information and Services

Banks with ATMs in Pucallpa are Scotiabank (Raimondi 466-468), Interbank (Independencia 560), and BBVA Banco Continental (Ucayali con Raimondi 699). Clínica Monte Horeb (Inmaculada 529, tel. 061/57-1689, 24 hours daily) is a good health clinic for emergencies. The police station is on Independencia (block 3, tel. 061/59-1433).

Getting There and Around

Pucallpa has daily flights from Lima, but the trip can also be done by bus. It takes around 17 hours from desert coast to rainforest. Transmar (Raymondi 793-795, tel. 061/57-9778, www.transmar.com.pe) has nonstop buses between Lima and Pucallpa (US$45).

Boats from Pucallpa to Iquitos leave from the wharf. Consider *Gilmer I, IV,* and *V,* owned by Transportes Eduardo, and the *Baylón I* and *II.* There is no office or phone available to book a ticket; you need to approach the decks and talk to the captain or the second in command. Both companies sell tickets offering closed decks to hang your hammock on (US$35 pp); there are also cabins with a bunk bed, TV, and private bath in the *Baylón* boats (US$64 pp) and better cabins on the *Gilmer* boats (US$145 pp).

MOYOBAMBA AND VICINITY

The less-visited area of northeastern Peru is a good stopover for travelers en route from the coast to Chachapoyas or vice versa. The Moyobamba cloud forest, along with Tarapoto, is Peru's best off-the-beaten-path rainforest. While the cities themselves are only a mild draw, the surrounding areas are rich in activities and natural beauty.

For travelers coming over the Andes from Peru's northern coast or Chachapoyas, Moyobamba is the first city with an unmistakable rainforest feel. The air is warm and humid, cooled by rains that fall heaviest between January and March. Travelers also encounter exotic new fruits and an explosion of animals and plants. In the cloud forest surrounding Moyobamba are more than 2,500 recorded types of orchids. The long riverboats common to the lower Amazon also navigate the lazy meanderings of the **Río Mayo,** fringed by alternating patches of fields and high rainforest.

Moyobamba was one of the few rainforest areas occupied by the Inca. Túpac Yupanqui conquered the local indigenous **Motilones** and **Muyupampas** people in the mid-15th century. The city of Moyobamba was founded by Spanish captain Juan Pérez de Guevara in 1540. In Quechua, Moyobamba means "circular plain," which makes sense because the city is situated on a flat area perched above the Río Mayo. Various streets dead-end into spectacular views of the muddy, snaking river, which offers a good range of white-water rafting and kayaking. There are also thermal baths, caves, and waterfalls in the area, with relatively pristine patches of cloud forest that harbor orchids and endangered or extremely rare mammal species such as the yellow-tailed monkey.

Sights

The best of Moyobamba lies outside the city. In the town there is little to see besides the modern cathedral on the Plaza de Armas and a municipal museum (Benavides 380) with sporadic hours.

For a pleasant view of the Río Mayo, and the tiny river port of Puerto Tahuishco, head to **Punta de Tahuishco,** 20 minutes northeast of the Plaza de Armas (US$1 by *mototaxi*). The municipality has built a variety of gardens and pleasant overlooks in this neighborhood, known as Zaragoza. Nearby is **Agroriente Viveros** (Reyes Guerra 900, tel. 042/56-2539, www.orquideasamazonicas.com), a commercial greenhouse featuring a wide range of local orchids. Another place to check out more than 150 orchid species is **Waqanki** (www.waqanki.com), which has a 100-hectare property about two kilometers outside town.

Recreation

The **Gera Waterfalls,** once a tourist favorite, have been reduced to a trickle due to hydroelectric construction. But a good hike can be done all the way to the top of **Morro de Calzada,** an isolated humpbacked mountain that rises above the landscape 12 kilometers from Moyobamba. There is a pleasant two-hour walk through cloud forest to the top, past a few small waterfalls and a variety of orchids. There are caves at both the top and bottom of the hill and an incredible panoramic view from the summit. This overlook is a launching point for hang gliders and paragliding aficionados. You can also camp on the top. **Selene Tours** (25 de Mayo 254, tel. 042/56-4471, www.selenetours.com) offers tours to all the sites outside Moyobamba.

Food

La Olla de Barro (Pedro Canga and Serafín Filomeno, 8am-11pm Mon.-Sat., 8am-4pm Sun., US$3-7) serves traditional food as well as pizzas and pastas in a charming rainforest-themed atmosphere. **El Avispa Juane** (Alonso de Alvarado and 25 de Mayo, 9am-9pm daily, US$2-7) is another good option for regional food, with a set menu (US$2) and a variety of dishes, including *juanes,* of course. The restaurant at **Hotel Puerto Mirador** (Sucre s/n, tel. 042/56-2050, 6:30am-11pm daily, US$5-10), serves Peruvian dishes and international food in a peaceful setting. Juices are great, and the fish is pretty good. It has a daily lunch menu (US$9).

Accommodations

The budget hotels are all pretty standard in Moyobamba, and the best options can be found along Alonso de Alvarado.

A mid-budget option is **Río Mayo Moyobamba Hotel** (Pedro Canga 415, tel. 042/56-4193, www.hotelriomayo.com, US$30 s, US$50 d), quite a modern hotel with a swimming pool, laundry service, a garage, Internet access, and a café-restaurant.

The resort option in Moyobamba is **Hotel Puerto Mirador** (Sucre s/n, tel. 042/56-2050, www.hotelpuertomirador.com, US$47 s, US$86 d, with breakfast). In a peaceful setting on the outskirts of town, this hotel offers brick bungalows and a swimming pool overlooking the Río Mayo. Rooms are large, with cable TV and private terraces surrounded by generous amounts of green. The main lodge has access to Wi-Fi, a good restaurant, and a full bar. The hotel offers tours to various lakes, waterfalls, and thermal baths as well as boat tours on the Río Mayo.

Information and Services

The **tourist police** (tel. 042/56-2508) office is at Pedro Canga 298. For medical issues, **EsSalud** (tel. 042/56-1079) is in the first block of Grau.

Both **Banco de la Nación** (Plaza de Armas) and **Banco de Crédito** (Alonso de Alvarado 903) have ATMs. There is also a **Banco Continental** (San Martín 490-494), **Interbank** (San Martín 535-537), and **Scotiabank** (Alonso de Alvarado 866-868). The post office is **Serpost,** (Serafín Filomeno 501). For a high-speed Internet connection, go to the **Internet café** (Alvarado and Benavides, 9:30am-midnight daily, US$0.75 per hour).

La Popular Lavandería (Alvarado 874, tel. 042/56-2440) does washing (US$1.50 per kilogram). If you are in need of long pants or shirts for the rainforest, try the **street market** (25 de Mayo and Callao).

Getting There and Around

The nearest airport is at Tarapoto, 105 kilometers or 2.5 hours away by bus. All the buses between Chiclayo and Tarapoto pass through Moyobamba. **Móvil Tours** (Grau 547, tel. 042/56-3720) has the best bus service from Moyobamba to Chiclayo (US$23). **Transportes Cajamarca** (Serafín Filomeno 298, tel. 042/56-1496) has modern, reliable station wagons on their routes from Moyobamba to Tarapoto (US$7) and from Moyobamba to Nueva Cajamarca (US$2). Moyobamba is teeming with cheap *mototaxis* (US$0.75) for local trips.

Tingana

About two hours away from Moyobamba, Tingana is in the heart of an amazing patch of flooded forest and swamps abundant with *aguaje* and *renaco* palm trees. Almost 3,500 hectares of this fragile and endangered ecosystem is currently protected in the **Área de Conservación Regional Municipal Aguajales Renacales del Alto Mayo,** a long name for an area with extensive flora and fauna, including orchids, bromeliads, river otters, monkeys, snakes, and a great variety of birds, which can be observed on canoe rides along the Río Avisado.

Tingana (cell tel. 931-033-884, www.tingana.org) is run by its own nonprofit organization with the support of San Martín's regional tourism office. Tours (full-day US$54 pp, 2 days, 1 night US$90 pp), are available and include transportation from Río Huascayacu to Tingana and back, all meals, lodging in cabins with mosquito nets, a guide, and boat trips. The organization can coordinate transportation from Moyobamba to Río Huascayacu.

TARAPOTO

Tarapoto is the main gateway to the northeastern high rainforest, situated in the lower Río Mayo watershed, surrounded with pristine montane cloud forest that tumbles into the flat, steamy lowlands of the Amazon rainforest. This area, with daily flights to and from Lima, is well known for waterfalls, orchids, very good food, and unusual birds.

Tarapoto was founded in 1782 at the base of the Ríos Cumbaza and Shilcayo. It was named after the native *Taraputus* palm tree. The surrounding valley has rich agricultural lands that yield corn, bananas, manioc, cocoa, tobacco, tea, coffee, palm oil, and tropical fruits. Its role as a commercial hub between the Amazon and the northern regions of Peru was cemented by the construction of the **Carretera Marginal** (Marginal Highway) to the northern coast, known today as **Carretera Fernando Belaúnde Terry** in honor of the president who built it in the 1960s.

Coca cultivation began in the nearby upper Huallaga Valley in the 1970s, and much of the area's valuable lands were destroyed by slash-and-burn agriculture. Tarapoto became the place where the drug traffickers built their lavish homes and laundered their money in all kinds of real estate projects that dot the city. During the 1980s, Tarapoto was at the center of the territory dominated by the **Movimiento Revolucionario Túpac Amaru** (MRTA), a left-wing terrorist organization that occupied the cities and towns surrounding the city. Eventually, the MRTA developed close ties to the area's drug lords.

During the Fujimori regime, Tarapoto's prominent drug traffickers were jailed and the MRTA was completely defeated—a small remaining faction was wiped out after taking over the Japanese ambassador's residence in Lima in 1996.

Tarapoto is now a safe place to visit and an increasingly popular tourist destination, especially for those who fly in from Lima with a few days on their hands. The leader of the tourism comeback in Tarapoto is the resort **Puerto Palmeras** (Carretera Fernando Belaúnde Terry, Km 614, tel. 042/52-4100, www.puertopalmeras.com.pe), which operates several lodges in the region. Some now get mediocre reviews, however.

Sights

If you want to see the elusive cock of the rock, head out at dawn or dusk to **Aguashiyacu Waterfalls** (US$1, paid at trailhead hut), about 14 kilometers outside Tarapoto on the winding highway to Yurimaguas. If you are quiet, you have a good chance of spotting these crimson birds flying in and out of their nests on the rock wall below the waterfall. If you have a bird guide, available at Puerto Palmeras, there is also excellent bird-watching on nearby ridges.

This area, along with **Huacamaillo Waterfalls**, is part of the **Área Regional de Conservación Cordillera Escalera**, which protects big patches of cloud forests, indigenous communities, flora, and fauna. The Huacamaillo falls can be reached after a two-hour walk from the village of San Antonio de Cumbaza, 18 kilometers north of Tarapoto. This waterfall jets forth from a stunning rock gorge and is well worth the walk.

An interesting destination is **Laguna Sauce**, a two-hour trip south from Tarapoto that involves crossing the Río Huallaga by steel barge. There are several hotels and restaurants around the town of Sauce, and canoe rental is available. At the far end, accessible via narrow channel, is the more remote **Lago Lindo**, a 5,300-hectare private reserve, accessible only through Puerto Palmeras (Carretera Fernando Belaúnde Terry, Km 614, tel. 042/52-4100, www.puertopalmeras.com.pe). The beautiful bungalows, resembling an Amazon lodge, are surrounded by 15,000 mahogany trees that have been planted in an effort to reintroduce this endangered species. The place is peaceful and ideal for bird-watching. There are rafting opportunities on the nearby Río Huallaga and Río Mayo.

Tarapoto is also home to two unusual sites. The first is the village of **Lamas**, 21 kilometers north of Tarapoto, an isolated village of people known as the Lamistas, who speak a mixture of Quechua and rainforest dialects. They are grouped together in one half of the town, have their own museum, and have a sense of community and identity that never fails to impress visitors.

The second is the **Takiwasi Center** (Alerta 466, tel. 042/52-2818, www.takiwasi.com, call before visiting), a drug rehabilitation center that uses ayahuasca and other hallucinogenic rainforest medicines as a central part of its treatment. The center also caters to the growing number of travelers interested in taking ayahuasca. Because of its highly experienced staff of authentic rainforest *curanderos* (healers) and a serious philosophy that includes post-experience debriefing with a psychoanalyst, participants almost invariably have a safe, meaningful experience.

Outside Tarapoto is the nationally renowned **Orquídea Chocolate Factory** (Santa Mónica 200, tel. 042/52-6573, www.orquideaperu.com, 9am-noon and 3pm-5pm Mon.-Fri., 9am-noon Sat.). Here you can see demos and hear explanations of how cacao is processed into chocolate, melted into a bar, and eventually prepared for export. Most of the chocolates are organic.

Entertainment and Events

Stonewasi (Lamas 222, tel. 042/52-4681, 10pm-close daily) is a Tarapoto institution and a great place to grab a beer and listen to 1980s music. **Musmuki** (Arias de Morey 173, cell tel. 951-902-028, 10pm-close daily), on the other side of the Plaza de Armas, has cocktails mixed with *aguardiente* (sugarcane distilled alcohol). Drinks are good and strong. A few meters away is **Café d'Mundo** (Arias de Morey 179, tel. 042/52-4918, 6:30pm-midnight daily), probably the smartest bar in Tarapoto. You ring a button to be let in to a very relaxed setting.

Tarapoto's most festive day is its birthday, July 16, which comes in the middle of **Tourist Week.** Lama's **Fiesta de Santa Rosa** at the end of August is said to be spectacular.

Recreation

A handful of agencies in Tarapoto offer excellent, reasonably priced tours to the area, which include lunch and have a three-passenger minimum. **Puerto Palmeras** (Carretera Marginal Sur, Km 3, tel. 042/52-4100, www. puertopalmeras.com) has well-maintained Land Rovers that head to Lama, Huacamaillo, and Ahuashiyacu waterfalls as well as Lago Lindo.

Adventure options include guide César Reategui, owner of hostel and restaurant **La Patarashca** (Lamas 261, tel. 042/52-8810, www.lapatarashca.com). He is willing to go anywhere, including out-of-the-way river spots and visits to Tingana, near Moyobamba. He also leads backpacker treks to Reserva Nacional Pacaya Samiria.

The best rafting outfitter in town is **Los Chancas Expeditions** (Rioja 357, tel. 042/52-2616, www.chancas.tripod.com), which organizes day trips on the Río Mayo, which gets up to Class III during the rainy months, November to March.

Food

If you like pork and *camarones* (freshwater prawns), this is definitely your town. On Moyobamba, right on the Plaza de Armas, there are three good eating options. **Real Grill** (Moyobamba 131, tel. 042/52-2714, 8am-midnight daily 8, US$5-8) has a decent variety of food, including meats, seafood, salads, and pastas. The best option is **Doña Zully** (Moyobamba 253, tel. 042/59-0827, 8am-midnight daily, US$3-12), with large portions of delicious fish, pork, and chicken dishes, salads, soups, and great juices.

A good option for meat eaters and from the same owner of Doña Zully is **Parillas El Rincón Sureño** (Leguía 458, tel. 042/52-2785, 11am-12:30am Mon.-Sat., noon-11pm Sun., US$6-10), which serves Peruvian food and grilled meats. The best place for Italian food is **Café d'Mundo** (Arias de Morey 157, tel. 042/52-4918, 6:30pm-midnight daily, US$5-15), with a relaxed ambience, illuminated at night by candles. It has a good and varied option of starters, thin-crust pizzas, and pastas.

A good option for local dishes is **La Collpa** (Av. Circunvalación 164, 10am-11pm daily, US$6-10), strategically located over a balcony overlooking the Río Shilcayo and a patch of the Cordillera Escalera rainforest. The best dishes are meat, freshwater prawns, and fish. A new hamburger spot in Tarapoto is **Brava Grilled** (San Martín 615, cell tel. 952-273-816, 5pm-midnight daily, US$6). It also serves hot wings, quesadillas, and chicken burgers at its small locale, located about six blocks from the plaza, or by delivery.

For great ice cream and other desserts, head over to **Heladeria Sandoval** (Manuela Morey 133, cell tel. 979-776-117, 10am-11pm Mon.-Sat., 10am-10pm Sun.), located a couple of blocks from the Plaza de Armas.

Accommodations
US$10-25

La Posada Inn (San Martín 146, tel. 042/52-2234, laposada_inn@hotmail.com, US$23 s, US$27 d) is a renovated colonial house a few meters from the Plaza de Armas. Off the busy street, guests enter a hushed atmosphere of orchids, stained wood floors, and comfortable rooms with hot water, fridges, TVs, phones, Wi-Fi, and air-conditioning or fans. The landings outside the rooms are a great place to relax and chat.

US$25-50

★ **Hostal Casa de Palos** (Leoncio Prado 155, cell tel. 942-666-453, www.casadepalos. pe, US$34 s, US$50 d) is the best option for a mid-range budget lodging. Opened in 2009, this seven-room hostel has really nice and comfy beds, impeccable baths, hot water, Wi-Fi, remote-control fans, flat-screen TVs, and cable TV. It is conveniently two blocks from the Plaza de Armas.

Plaza del Bosque (Av. Circunvalación 2449, tel. 042/52-3448, www.plazabosque. com, US$33 s, US$50 d, with breakfast) is in the high part of town, five minutes from the Plaza de Armas. It has 31 brick-built bungalow rooms surrounded by dense vegetation. Amenities include cable TV, Wi-Fi, laundry, a garage, a swimming pool, and a restaurant. Rates also include free transfer to the airport.

Cordillera Escalera Lodge (Prolongación Alerta 1521, tel. 042/78-0168, www.cordilleraescalera.com, US$45 s, US$55 d, breakfast and airport transfer included) is a good option if you want to be outside the city, savoring nature, without spending loads of money in a lodge. Overlooking the Cordillera Escalera, on top of a small hill, this lodge is 15 minutes east of Tarapoto and can accommodate 14 people.

US$50-100

About 10 minutes outside the city is **DM Hoteles Tarapoto** (Pasaje las Flores 224, Banda de Shilcayo, 2 kilometers outside Tarapoto, tel. 042/52-2225, www.dmhoteles. pe, US$100 s or d, buffet breakfast and airport transfers included), with five hectares of green. Brick buildings surround a round pool with a bar, thatch-shaded tables, and well-maintained palm groves and lawns. There are

22 rooms with all modern amenities, including air-conditioning, cable TV, mini fridges, and Wi-Fi. Another option is one of the 15 more private bungalows (US$107), which sleep up to three.

US$100-150

Puerto Palmeras (Carretera Fernando Belaúnde Terry, Km 614, tel. 042/52-4100, www.puertopalmeras.com.pe, US$130 s or d, breakfast and airport transfer included) is a tasteful and relaxed resort, tucked into a river bend far from the hustle and bustle of Tarapoto. This resort is a perfect getaway for both couples in search of solitude and families looking for a range of well-organized activities. There are stone courtyards and open-air sitting areas decorated with a collection of paintings from local artists. The sprawling grounds around the resort also include playing fields, a lake with canoes, and an island population of monkeys. Check the website for programs and other travel options.

★ **PumaRinri Huallaga Lodge** (tel. 042/52-2225, www.pumarinri.com, US$100 s or d, US$120 suite, including breakfast) is 35 kilometers southeast of Tarapoto, on the road that leads to Chazuta. It is in the middle of a 62-hectare private reserve situated in the canyon stretch of the Río Huallaga. Surrounded by montane cloud forest, rivers, and streams, the lodge is very close to the **Área Regional de Conservación Cordillera Escalera** and **Parque Nacional Cordillera Azul,** both protecting unique ecosystems. PumaRinri offers three all-inclusive programs: Tarapoto Adventure, combining stays at Tucán Suites with the lodge (from 3 days, 2 nights) and Tarapoto Amazonía, exclusively at PumaRinri, with a variety of outdoor activities, including rafting on the Huallaga (from 3 days, 2 nights). There is another all-inclusive program that focuses on coffee and cacao production in Tarapoto. The program includes visits to plantations and a chocolate workshop (from 3 days, 2 nights).

Information and Services

There is no Iperú office in Tarapoto, but most mid-range hotels have general information about what to do and where to go. A good website with information on hotels, restaurants, tourism and shopping in Tarapoto (Spanish only) is www.vivetarapoto.com.

Police (tel. 042/52-4436 or 042/52-2141) are at Ramírez Hurtado 296. There is a **state hospital** (Delgado, block 3, tel. 042/52-2071), but the best option is the private **Clínica del Oriente** (Alonso de Alvarado 209, tel. 042/52-1250). On the Plaza de Armas, there are branches of pharmacy chains **Inkafarma, Boticas Arcángel,** and **MiFarma.**

The best supermarket is **La Inmaculada** (Martinez de Compagñon 126, tel. 042/52-3216). Banks with ATMs are **Banco de Crédito** (Maynas 140), **Scotiabank** (Ramírez Hurtado and Grau), and **Interbank** (Grau 119), which also has an ATM at the airport. The post office is **Serpost** (San Martín 482, tel. 042/52-2021, 8am-8pm Mon.-Sat.).

Getting There

Tarapoto is connected by air to Lima and Iquitos, and the **Tarapoto Airport** (TPP, Av. Aviación s/n, tel. 042/53-2206) is a US$3 *mototaxi* or US$6 taxi ride from town. **LATAM** (Ramírez de Hurtado 183, Lima tel. 01/213-8200, www.lan.com) has at least three daily flights to Tarapoto. **StarPerú** (Lima tel. 01/705-9000, www.starperu.com) has two daily flights. **Peruvian Airlines** (Lima tel. 01/716-6000) also has daily flights.

Buses move in and out of Tarapoto on a daily basis on a good highway. Most of the bus companies are lined up along Salaverry (blocks 6 and 7). **Móvil Tours** (Salaverry 880, tel. 042/52-9193) is the best and safest bus service to Chiclayo (12-15 hours, US$25) and Lima (US$60).

Transportes Cajamarca (Alfonso Ugarte 1438, tel. 042/52-9122) has *colectivos* that travel to Yurimaguas (US$7 pp) from Tarapoto. Vehicles leave when full. There are other companies located on Alfonso Ugarte that do the Yurimaguas route. The journey to

Yurimaguas takes two hours on an excellent paved but winding 120-kilometer highway.

YURIMAGUAS AND VICINITY

At an elevation of 180 meters, Yurimaguas is the northeastern gateway to the Amazon rainforest, accessible from Tarapoto via a two-hour drive on a serpentine 120-kilometer highway that crosses the Cordillera Escalera.

Founded by the Jesuits in 1710, Yurimaguas is a sleepy town that still contains remnants from the golden rubber boom days, on Avenida Arica. Popularly known as *la perla del Huallaga*, "the pearl of the Huallaga River," the main reason to go to Yurimaguas is to hop on a cargo ship and head toward Iquitos or the Reserva Nacional Pacaya Samiria, via Lagunas. Depending on what time you arrive from Tarapoto, you might have to sleep overnight to catch your boat.

Cargo boats from **Transportes Eduardo** (Elena Pardo 114-116, tel. 065/35-1270 or 965/63-5356) depart Yurimaguas around noon, with accommodations ranging from covered decks for slinging hammocks (US$38 pp) to cabins with huge beds and private baths (US$60 pp). The company has seven boats and different services available on each. Even if departures are confirmed, boats get delayed quite often. Be prepared to stay overnight in this town.

Food and Accommodations

There are budget restaurants around the marketplace, but **El Dorado** (Aguirre 126, Barrio La Loma, tel. 065/35-1023) is worth visiting for a superb lunch if you want to try some of the exotic Amazon delicacies. The decor is surreal, with stuffed *carachamas* (a prehistoric-looking armored catfish) hanging from the roof. Specialties include *huevos de charapa* (turtle eggs) and *guiso de majás* (a stew made out of a medium-size rodent). There is also fish, chicken, and pork for the less adventurous.

Posada Cumpanamá (Progreso 403, tel. 065/35-2957, www.posadacumpanamaperu.

com, US$30 s, US$36 d, with a/c) is a nice place, with 13 rooms and a swimming pool. Internet costs US$1.50 per hour, and breakfasts range US$3-4.50. **Puerto Pericos** (San Miguel 720, Malecón Paranapura, tel. 065/35-2009, www.puertopalmeras.com.pe, US$100 s or d) is the top-end hotel in town; you will probably stay here if you hook up with a travel program at Puerto Palmeras in Tarapoto.

Information and Services

The **Municipalidad Provincial de Alto Amazonas** (town hall, Plaza de Armas 112-114) can give visitor information during office hours. **BBVA Banco Continental** (Sargento Lores 132) and **Banco de Crédito** (Julio C. Arana 143) both have ATMs.

Getting There and Around

Transportes Gilmer (Víctor Sifuentes 580, cell tel. 942-627-415) has daily departures to Tarapoto (US$5.50) every hour 5am-6pm. The journey to Tarapoto takes two hours along a 120-kilometer paved highway.

Iquitos

Iquitos is a swanky and sassy place to go, with around half a million inhabitants and hemmed in by muddy rivers and flooded rainforest on all sides. Being the largest city in the world that cannot be reached by road, Iquitos's only bridges to the outside world are planes and boats. It is the launching pad for exploring Peru's northern Amazon.

Because of its isolation, terrorism never reached the city during the 1980s and 1990s. Perhaps as a result, Iquitos has a relaxed, laid-back vibe that seems much closer to Bangkok than, say, Cusco. The air is thick and steamy, and the noisy buzzing of the *mototaxis* invades all your senses. Life revolves around the Amazon River, a couple of kilometers wide after collecting water from all of Peru's major rivers. People are descended from a dozen different indigenous groups and waves of European and Chinese immigrants.

The weather in Iquitos, even during the October-May rainy season, is fairly predictable. The sky dawns blue most days, but by late afternoon fills with the clouds of convection storms, which release sheets of cool rain. Between mid-December and June, the Amazon rises anywhere from 7 to 15 meters, carrying silt and fallen trees brought down from the Andes. The river floods hundreds of kilometers of forest around Iquitos. Oil

supertankers and huge passenger cruisers make the 3,600-kilometer odyssey from the Atlantic.

The floods enrich the surrounding fields, which are planted with rice, peanuts, watermelons, and pumpkins as soon as the water begins to recede in July. Fish leave the oxygen-poor oxbow lakes in the low season and concentrate in the river, prompting huge harvests of corvina (bass), dorado, catfish, and *paiche* (a prehistoric-looking fish, quite tasty, and the biggest in the Amazon).

After Francisco de Orellana's epic descent down the Amazon River in 1542, the Spaniards left the area to the Jesuits, who founded a settlement here in the 1750s before being expelled from Latin America shortly thereafter. Two hundred years later, the ramshackle settlement exploded into one of Peru's richest cities thanks to the rubber boom. The flip side of the opulence was the oppression and abject poverty of the indigenous and mestizo rubber tappers, who lived in virtual enslavement and frequently died of malaria and other diseases. The floating city of **Belén,** which some call the Venice of South America but which is really a slum, is a leftover from that era.

Iquitos is the pioneer of Amazonian tourism, which began in the 1960s, and is the base for a variety of lodges, cruise ships, and

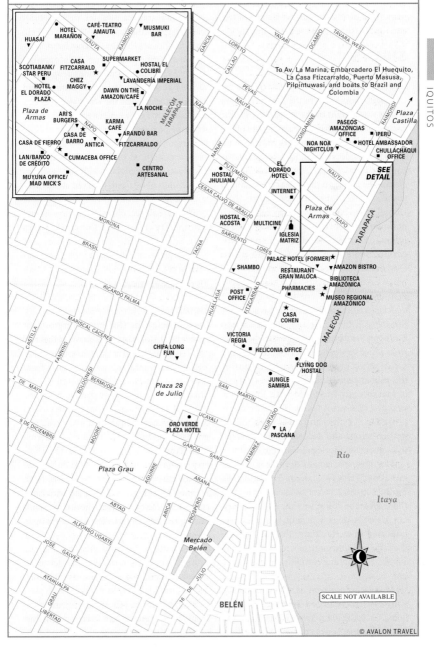

Iquitos

HUASAÍ ▼

HOTEL MARAÑON ●

CAFÉ-TEATRO AMAUTA

▼ MUSMUKI BAR

SCOTIABANK/ STAR PERU ■

CASA FITZCARRALD ★

SUPERMARKET

HOSTAL EL COLIBRÍ ●

HOTEL ● EL DORADO PLAZA

CHEZ MAGGY

LAVANDERÍA IMPERIAL ▼

DAWN ON THE AMAZON/CAFÉ ■

Plaza de Armas

ARI'S BURGERS ▼ ★

LA NOCHE ▼

KARMA CAFÉ

MALECÓN TARAPACÁ

CASA DE BARRO

ARANDÚ BAR ▼

CASA DE FIERRO ★

ANTICA FITZCARRALDO

LAN/BANCO DE CRÉDITO ■

CUMACEBA OFFICE ●

MUYUNA OFFICE/ MAD MICK'S ■

CENTRO ARTESANAL ●

To Av. La Marina, Embarcadero El Huequito, La Casa Ftizcarraldo, Puerto Masusa, Pilpintuwasi, and boats to Brazil and Colombia

Plaza Castilla

PASEOS AMAZÓNICAS OFFICE ■

IPERÚ ■

NOA NOA NIGHTCLUB ▼

● HOTEL AMBASSADOR

CHULLACHAQUI OFFICE ■

EL DORADO HOTEL ●

HOSTAL JHULIANA ●

INTERNET ■

Plaza de Armas

SEE DETAIL

TARAPACÁ

HOSTAL ACOSTA ▼

MULTICINE ■

IGLESIA MATRIZ ♦

PALACE HOTEL (FORMER) ★

SHAMBO ▼

RESTAURANT GRAN MALOCA ▼

▼ AMAZON BISTRO

BIBLIOTECA AMAZÓNICA ■

POST OFFICE ■

PHARMACIES ■

★ MUSEO REGIONAL AMAZÓNICO

CASA COHEN ★

VICTORIA REGIA ▼

CHIFA LONG FUN ▼

HELICONIA OFFICE ■

FLYING DOG HOSTAL ●

JUNGLE SAMIRIA ▼

Plaza 28 de Julio

ORO VERDE PLAZA HOTEL ●

▼ LA PASCANA

Río

Plaza Grau

Itaya

Mercado Belén

SCALE NOT AVAILABLE

BELÉN

© AVALON TRAVEL

adventure agencies. Other industries include lumber, agriculture, and the export of exotic fish and birds and *barbasco,* a poisonous plant used by indigenous people to kill fish and which is now being used as an insecticide.

SIGHTS
City Tour

In the center of the **Plaza de Armas** is the Obelisk, a monument to the Iquitos military heroes who fought in the War of the Pacific against Chile in 1879. The south side of the plaza is marked by the **Iglesia Matriz,** built in 1919. Inside are religious paintings by Américo Pinasco and César Calvo de Araujo. Across the plaza, on the corner of Putumayo and Próspero, is the **Casa de Fierro** (Iron House). It was bought by wealthy rubber businessman Anselmo del Águila and shipped in pieces to be reassembled on its current site. Around the corner is the **Casa de Barro** (Napo and Raimondi), the mud-and-wood house used as a warehouse by rubber baron Fermín Fitzcarrald.

A block from the Plaza de Armas along the **Río Itaya** is the hectic and busy pedestrian **Malecón Tarapacá,** also a prime viewpoint from which to view the river's landscape. The construction of this walkway began during the rubber boom in the late 19th century; it was recently improved with fountains, benches, and street lamps. The promenade is lined with 19th-century mansions built by rubber barons and decorated with *azulejos* (tiles imported from Spain and Portugal).

The most spectacular of these is the former **Palace Hotel** (Malecón Tarapacá 208). Built 1908-1912 in art nouveau style, this three-story building was the most luxurious in Peru's Amazon. Its iron balconies were imported from Hamburg, the marble from Carrara, and the multicolored mosaics from Seville. The building currently serves as a military base.

Along the *malecón* is the **Biblioteca Amazónica** (Malecón Tarapacá 354, tel. 065/23-1259, 8:30am-1pm and 2:30pm-5pm Mon.-Fri., but hours change), an excellent library containing a range of books, maps, old photographs, newspapers, and films.

The **Museo Regional Amazónico** (Malecón Tarapacá 386, tel. 065/23-4031, 8:30am-1pm and 2:30pm-5pm Mon.-Fri., US$1.50) houses the *Sons of Our Land,* a selection of 76 fiberglass statues out of approximately 300 statues of indigenous people from various communities in Peru, Brazil, and Venezuela, created by the eccentric Peruvian-Swedish artist Felipe Lettersten in 1987 to preserve the memory of these rapidly vanishing cultures. The historic building was built in 1863 and restored in 1996 to be converted into a museum. It contains wall panels, doors, and ceilings of intricately carved old-growth mahogany.

There are elegant old rubber barons' homes near the city center. **Casa Cohen** (Próspero 401) was built with Moroccan tiles and Parisian grates in 1905, and now houses a supermarket. Another is the neoclassic **Casa Morey** (Próspero 502).

Belén

This is a gigantic floating shantytown of homes built atop rafts of balsa wood that rise and fall with the river. It is an exotic sight, with children jumping into the water from their front porches and entire families paddling along the waterways in dugout canoes. Closer to the riverbank, other families live in thatched homes lifted above the water on rickety stilts. Because of the recent meandering of the Amazon away from Iquitos, the whole area becomes a gigantic mudflat during the dry months of July to December. Although the municipality does a good job with trash collection, there are serious health problems during the dry months because of the open sewers.

To visit the floating city, head down Próspero south from the Plaza de Armas to Belén's raucous and colorful market, which begins around García Sanz. Along with plastic kitchen items and cheap clothing imported from Brazil, vendors sell every imaginable: rainforest fruit and vegetables, dried fish, medicinal herbs, and contraband meat of *sajino* (wild pig) and *venado* (deer). The smells of garbage, mud, and all of these foods baking in the sun can become overpowering at times, so visit in the morning when the market is cleanest and most active.

Once in the market, head left toward the waterfront along 9 de Diciembre and walk out on wooden walkways toward the water. Here, people with canoes will paddle you around Belén for US$4 for a half hour. Another, easier option is to head to the *malecón* near the Plaza de Armas. From there, head toward the river by walking down some stairs. Near the bottom of the stairs are boats that can take you on a tour through Belén and back to the *malecón*. Make sure to bring sunscreen, glasses, and a hat because the sun on the river is powerful. Ask your hotel for the latest updates on security in the Belén area. Locals will insist that you should not go on your own. It is best to leave valuables and most of your money behind.

Pilpintuwasi Butterfly Farm and Animal Orphanage

The best day trip from Iquitos is **Pilpintuwasi** (tel. 065/23-2665 or cell tel. 965-932-999, www.amazonanimalorphanage.org, 9am-4pm Tues.-Sun., US$7 adults, US$3.50 students), which means "butterfly's home" in Quechua. Huge mesh tents contain numerous butterfly species fluttering above the stone paths that lead through exotic gardens. The facility was founded by an Austrian-Peruvian couple, Gudrun Sperrer and Roblar Moreno, who have designed the garden to contain all the fruits, flowers, and leaves that caterpillars and butterflies need for survival.

Apart from butterflies, the place also receives rescued wild animals, including Pedro Bello, a jaguar; Chavo, a red uakari monkey; Rosa, an anteater; and a dozen other animals that Sperrer and Moreno adopted to save from being sold or killed. Pilpintuwasi is in Padre Cocha and always welcomes volunteers who want to work in the butterfly farm or help take care of the animals.

To reach the farm, head to the port of Bella Vista-Nanay, 15 minutes out of town and accessible by *colectivos* along Próspero that read "Bella Vista-Nanay." It is about a 20-minute boat ride (US$14 return for 4-5 people) from here, passing Bora and Yagua villages along the way, although in low-water months passengers have to disembark early and walk along a path for 15 minutes.

Amazon Golf Course

Located around 30 minutes by taxi from Iquitos's downtown, the nine-hole **Amazon Golf Course** (Malecón Maldonado 185, cell tel. 965-943-267, www.amazongolfcourse. com, 6am-6pm daily, US$25 for 18 holes) is the only golf course in the Peruvian Amazon. Started in 2004 by a group of expats, it offers almost 10 hectares of flat green. There is a clubhouse, a putting green, and a driving range. Watch out for the snakes!

Other Side Trips

There are a number of places to visit outside Iquitos, though frankly the surrounding rainforest is far more interesting. About 15 minutes west of the city is the **Quistococha Tourist Center** (7am-5pm daily), which has a lake with rowboats, a fish farm, and a small zoo. Iquiteños head here and to **Lago Moronacocha,** three kilometers east of the city, on the weekends to swim, sunbathe, and water-ski. There are a few bars at Moronacocha that offer bath services for guests. **Santo Tomás** is a lakeside village 15 kilometers northeast of Iquitos known for carved root and ceramics handicrafts.

ENTERTAINMENT AND EVENTS
Nightlife

All along the first block of Malecón Tarapacá are small bars and restaurants with tables on the walkway where locals and travelers sit, enjoy a beer, and watch the people stroll by. **Arandú Bar** (Malecón Tarapacá 113, tel. 065/24-3434, 3:30pm-midnight Sun.-Thurs., 3:30pm-3am Fri.-Sat.) is a classic, decorated with kitschy rainforest-motif wall paintings by renowned artist Christian Bendayán. It has hip music, pretty good drinks, and a friendly crowd.

The Karma Café (Napo 138, tel. 065/60-0576, 12:30pm-late Tues.-Sun.) has become a popular spot day and night for travelers and local expats. There is often live music on the weekends. During the day, it is a good place to stop by for lunch, where curry is on the menu.

At **Musmuki Bar** (Raymondi 382, 6:30pm-3am daily), all cocktails are mixed with *aguardiente,* sugarcane-distilled alcohol. The drinks are good and the ambience quite hip. On Plaza Castilla, there are some small bars selling cheap beer to plenty of thirsty locals and backpackers.

For a night of dancing, **El Pardo** (Mariscal Cáceres 1046, cell tel. 965-676-867, 6pm-3am Thurs.-Sun.) is a local favorite. It is actually a huge fenced open space where local salsa and *cumbia* bands play all night. Any *mototaxi* can take you there for US$1.50. Tickets go for US$1.50-6, depending which band plays.

Iquitos also has a big-screen movie theater, **Cine Star Iquitos** (Arica 258, 2pm-10pm daily, US$3), that shows the latest Hollywood blockbusters.

The Festival of San Juan

Celebrated on June 23-25, this festivity overlaps with winds that originate in the southern Atlantic and Patagonia, sweeping northwest and across the Amazon basin with temperatures as low as 8°C. These cold spells or *friajes* can happen anytime from May to August but are most common around San Juan's birthday in late June. Don't expect to see many animals during a *friaje*—the monkeys huddle up together in balls to stay warm and the birds roost until it's all over.

The religious and meteorological coincidence has merged over the centuries into Iquitos's biggest party, celebrated these days at the Mercado Artesanal de San Juan (Av. Quiñones, Km 4.5), on the road to the airport. Dance competitions from indigenous groups and rock concerts are enjoyed while eating *juanes,* rice tamale-like bundles of chicken, tomato, and onion wrapped in a *bijao* palm leaf, which imparts a delicious flavor to the concoction. A sweater or a windbreaker is quite handy, because *los vientos de San Juan,* "the San Juan winds," make the place feel more like Seattle or London than Iquitos.

Iquitos also has a Founders Day celebration on January 5 and a Carnaval in late February or early March. Santo Tomás has a handicraft fair on August 21 and a festival in honor of its patron saint September 23-25.

SHOPPING

Market stalls on stilts hovering above the Amazon make up the **Centro Artesanal Anaconda** (Malecón Tarapacá, 8am-10pm daily). Vendors sell jewelry, sandals, paintings, beaded curtains, shoulder bags, and other souvenirs. There is also a line of crafts stores along Próspero south of the Plaza de Armas, though Iquitos's largest handicraft market is the **Mercado Artesanal de San Juan** (Av. Quiñones, Km 4.5, 7am-8pm daily), on the road to the airport. The colorful native rainforest seeds sold by the kilogram are a notable find here. These can be used to make your own jewelry or for other artistic endeavors.

For books and drawing and writing materials, go to **Librería Tamara** (Próspero 268, tel. 065/24-2999, 8am-1pm and 3:30pm-9pm daily). Rubber boots, binoculars, and other rainforest equipment can be purchased with a buyback guarantee at **Mad Mick's Trading Post** (Putumayo 163, 2nd Fl., cell tel. 965-754-976, 8am-8pm daily), near the Iron House. Locals do their food shopping at the colorful **Belén Market,** which is liveliest in the mornings. Much of Iquitos slows down, or shuts down, in this area during the afternoon, 1pm-4pm. There is a cluster of **handicraft stores** (generally 8am-9pm daily) on the sixth block of Arica.

FOOD

Iquitos's most famous dish is the *juane,* and restaurants serve a variety of exotic rainforest juices made from the *cocona* and *camu camu* fruits. Main plates include *paiche con chonta* (fish with palm-heart salad) and *tacacho con cecina* (fried banana mixed with smoked pork meat). *Inchicapi de gallina* is chicken soup with peanuts, cilantro, and manioc root; it is quite good, as is *picuro* or *majás* rodent stew, which actually tastes more like pork.

Apart from these typical foods, many restaurants offer bush meat, including alligator, deer, turtle stew, and even grilled monkey. Eating these dishes only encourages illegal hunting. There is a ban on fishing or serving *paiche* during its reproductive season, October to February. If you order it during this time, ensure that it comes from one of the fish farms and not from the river.

Peruvian

A block off the Plaza de Armas is **Huasaí** (Fitzcarrald 131, tel. 065/24-2222, 7am-4:30pm daily, US$5), a bustling family-owned restaurant whose tables fill up very quickly at the lunch hour. Most people come for the US$3 lunch menu, with fish, chicken, beef, and vegetarian options. It also serves tamales, ceviche, sandwiches, and juices.

On the *malecón,* there are a couple of good restaurants with outdoor seating. **La Noche** (Malecón Maldonado 177, tel. 065/22-2373, 7am-1am daily, US$5-7) opens early for breakfast, serves refreshing fruit drinks throughout the day, and draws its biggest crowd in the evening.

Peruvian Fusion and Fine Dining

Fitzcarraldo (Napo 100, on the *malecón,* tel. 065/22-6536, 8am-11:30pm daily, US$5-7) has become a classic, with a stylish decor from the rubber boom days. The restored colonial house has a pleasant open-air atmosphere, and there are also tables outside on the *malecón.* The menu includes brochettes of meat, fish, chicken, and *pescado en salsa de maracuya,* an Amazonian fish with passion-fruit sauce.

Located in a grand tile-covered 19th-century house, **Restaurant Gran Maloca** (Lores

178, tel. 065/23-3126, 9am-11pm Mon.-Sat., noon-7:30pm Sun., US$6-10) serves a wide variety of rainforest dishes. If bush meat does not appeal to you, there are also pastas, fish, and meat. The formal dining room is air-conditioned. The restaurant offers an affordable three-course lunch menu.

For a true night on the Amazon, take a boat out to the extravagant floating restaurant-bar **Al Frío y al Fuego** (Embarcadero el Huequito, tel. 065/26-2713 or 965/60-7474, www.alfrioyalfuego.com, noon-4pm and 7pm-11pm Tues.-Sat., noon-5pm Sun., US$7-15). Built in 2006, the place also has a floating swimming pool. The specialties are regional fish, meat, and exotic drinks from the rainforest. It's a good treat.

Chifa

The best place for Peruvian-Chinese food is **Chifa Long Fung** (San Martín 454, in front of Plaza 28 de Julio, tel. 065/23-3649, 11:45am-2:30pm and 6:45pm-midnight daily, US$4-6), claimed to be one of the best in the Amazon.

International

Despite all the restaurant options in Iquitos, you only really need **Dawn on the Amazon Café** (Malecón Maldonado 185, tel. 065/23-4921 or 065/60-0056, www.dawnontheamazoncafe.com, 7:30am-10pm Mon.-Sat., US$8-12). For breakfast, there is everything from granola with fruit and yogurt to pancakes and bacon and eggs. You can wash it down with one of the 16 fruit-flavored smoothies. For lunch, there is a wide selection of soups, salads, and sandwiches. And for dinner, options include *cecina* with sweet potatoes and passion fruit sauce, a tenderloin steak, beef fajitas, or vegetable stir-fry with a pisco sauce. There is a good vegetarian selection, and diet options for those who plan to do ayahuasca.

Another top restaurant is ★ **Amazon Bistro** (Malecón Tarapaca 268, tel. 065/60-0785, amazon.bistro@gmail.com, 6am-midnight daily, US$8-11), which has a good selection of international dishes and French-inspired ambiance.

Pizza

Good wood-fired pizzas, lasagna, and ravioli are served in a cozy atmosphere at **Chez Maggy Pizzeria** (Raimondi 177, tel. 065/24-1816, 6pm-1am daily, US$4). Colorful art and a full bar make this a great place to have a leisurely dinner. ★ **Antica Pizzeria** (Napo 159, tel. 065/25-8659, www.anticapizzeria.com.pe, 7am-midnight daily, US$5-14) is the more hip pizza choice. They have delicious thin-crust pizza, great salads, fresh pasta, and more.

Cafés, Bakeries, and Ice Cream

A main Iquitos hangout for both locals and gringos is **Ari's Burgers** (Próspero 127, tel. 065/23-1470, 7am-1am daily, US$1-7). This open-air establishment resembles a rainforest version of a greasy spoon. It is strategically located on the Plaza de Armas with its fluorescent lights. The huge menu includes burgers and fries, milk shakes, vegetarian dishes, and a huge range of desserts.

Ice cream in Iquitos is ubiquitous. The hot, humid climate invites pushcart ice cream vendors, a number of gelato shops on the Plaza de Armas, and lots of popsicle stations. The best of these is **Shambo** (Morona 396, 9am-11pm daily, US$0.30), which sells only natural fruit-juice popsicles. Your flavor choices range from grape and strawberry to *aguaje* and beer.

Markets

The largest supermarket is **Supermercado Portales** (Próspero 401, tel. 065/23-1552, 7am-11pm daily), located in the Casa Cohen. If you are looking for imported favorites, you might likely find them in **Inversiones Saby** (Raimondi 195, tel. 065/23-1823, 6am-midnight daily).

ACCOMMODATIONS

Most hotels in Iquitos will pick you up at the airport and save you the hassle of dealing with taxi drivers. In general the area north of the Plaza de Armas is safer and more attractive. There are dozens of hostels clustered around the Belén Market, south of the Plaza de Armas, but they are mostly grimy and filled with the drone of passing *mototaxis*.

Under US$10

The popular Peruvian hostel chain **Flying Dog** (Malecón Tarapacá 592, tel. 065/22-3755, www.flyingdogperu.com, US$9 dorm, US$27 s, with breakfast) has a location in Iquitos. Just a few blocks from the Plaza de Armas, the hostel has a riverfront view. Guests enjoy all the amenities that are offered at its other hostels: clean and safe rooms, free Wi-Fi, hot water, and a shared kitchen. It also has a shuttle that can pick you up at the airport.

US$10-25

Hostal El Colibrí (Raimondi 200, a new entrance but in same location, tel. 065/24-1737, hostalelcolibri@hotmail.com, US$18-25 s, US$23-31 d) is a longtime favorite. It has a homey feeling not found in many other Iquitos hotels. Rooms are small but have big windows and fans, and there are also nice rooms with air-conditioning (US$20 s, US$27 d) and writing desks. The hostel is small but clean and with friendly staff. There are only a few rooms with hot water, but all rooms have private baths and cable TV.

Hostal Baltazar (La Condamine 265, tel. 065/23-2240, hostalbaltazar@hotmail.com, US$18 s, US$25 d) has clean rooms, cable TV, private baths with hot water, and rooms with fans or air-conditioning.

US$25-50

Hotel Marañón (Nauta 285, tel. 065/24-2673, www.hotelmaranon.com, US$40 s, US$58 d with breakfast) is quite central and a bit of an oasis in this hot, sticky town. Large rooms with clean white walls are kept cool with tile floors and air-conditioning. Amenities include fridges, comfortable beds, hot water 24 hours daily, Wi-Fi, and a nice outdoor pool with an adjoining Peruvian restaurant. Rooms on the fourth floor have a view of the

Amazon. Make advance reservations, as this hotel frequently fills up.

Hostal Jhuliana (Putumayo 521, tel. 065/23-3154, US$40 s, US$47 d, with breakfast) has carpeted rooms with comfortable beds, air-conditioning, fridges, and hot water. There is a full-service restaurant and bar as well as a swimming pool. The best mid-range option is ★ **Nativa Apartments** (Nanay 144, tel. 065/60-0270, www.nativaapartments.com, US$43 s, US$50 d). This family-run place has mini-apartment suites, with kitchenettes, cable TV, hot water, laundry service, and Wi-Fi. It has a nice courtyard with plants, and staff can help you organize city and rainforest tours.

US$50-100

La Casa Fitzcarraldo (Av. La Marina 2153, Punchana, tel. 065/60-1138, www.lacasafitzcarraldo.com, US$65-90 s or d, with breakfast and airport pickup) is perhaps the most interesting hotel in Iquitos. It is owned by Walter Saxer, the former producer of Werner Herzog's most famous films, including *Fitzcarraldo*. Self-defined as a "jungle oasis" due to the intense vegetation that surrounds the house, built in the 1960s, this place hosted Mick Jagger, Klaus Kinski, and Herzog himself. The rooms are huge, with high ceilings, painted with pastel colors and decorated with indigenous arts and crafts. The amenities include a pool, satellite TV, Wi-Fi, airport transfer, and a privileged peek into photos of the film shoot, when Jagger and actor Jason Robards were in the cast. If you stay here, with a bit of luck you might bump into Saxer; he might tell you a tale or two, if he is in the right mood.

Oro Verde Plaza Hotel (Ucayali 315, tel. 065/22-1616, www.hoteloroverdesuitesiquitos.com, US$80 s, US$100 d, with breakfast) is near the Plaza 28 de Julio, a bit off the main drag; its big rooms, firm mattresses, and bright reading lamps are worth the extra walk. The hotel has some rooms that face the street, which are well lit but a bit noisier. Room rates include airport transfers.

Hotel Acosta (Huallaga 254, tel. 065/23-1761, www.terraverde.pe, US$50 s, US$78 d, with breakfast) is a modern and comfortable three-star hotel that includes air-conditioning, hot water, cable TV, phones, fridges, Internet access, laundry, and safes. The rates include airport transfer.

US$100-150

A newer option in town is **Jungle Samiria** (Ricardo Palma 159, tel. 065/22-3232, www.samiriajunglehotel.com, US$86 s, US$115 d). Rooms have hot water, cable TV, Wi-Fi, and air-conditioning. There is also a pool, a restaurant, and a bar.

Victoria Regia Hotel and Suites (Ricardo Palma 252, tel. 065/23-1983, www.victoriaregiahotel.com, US$95 s, US$115 d, with breakfast), owned by the Acostas, one of the pioneering Peruvian families in tourism in the rainforest, is an upgraded version of its sister property, Hotel Acosta. In addition to all amenities imaginable, it has a pool and comfy suites, making this place one of the best hotels in the city. The same owners manage Heliconia Lodge, 80 kilometers downriver from Iquitos.

Over US$150

The five-star hotel of Iquitos is **El Dorado Plaza Hotel and Business** (Napo 258, Plaza de Armas, tel. 065/22-2555, www.grupo-dorado.com, US$250 s or US$280 d, with breakfast). Extremely overpriced for what it is, the 65 rooms are divided between the newly remodeled, with huge windows, and the older ones, which are not as nice. The upper floors have nice views toward the Amazon River. Additional services include a gym with a sauna, a boutique, Wi-Fi, air-conditioning, a business center, a huge sun-filled atrium in the lobby, and an outdoor pool with a bar and a whirlpool. It has a sister hotel about a block away called **El Dorado Isabel** (Napo 362, tel. 065/23-2574, US$88 s, US$105 d) that is more affordable.

INFORMATION AND SERVICES

The Iperú office (Loreto 201, at Raimondi, tel. 065/23-6144, www.turismoperu.info, 9am-6pm Mon.-Sat., 9am-1pm Sun.) is located near the Plaza de Armas. There can be updated visitor information and maps at the Dircetur office (Nanay 461, tel. 065/23-4609, 7am-3pm Mon.-Fri.).

A good English-language resource is the Iquitos Times (www.iquitostimes.com), a free newspaper that provides up-to-date information; it is available at many cafés or Mad Mick's Trading Post (Putumayo 163, cell tel. 965-754-976, 8am-8pm daily). Mick himself is also an excellent source on activities around town, including his annual Longest Raft Race in the World.

In an emergency, call the tourist police of Iquitos (Lores 834, tel. 065/24-2081) or the national police (Morona 126, tel. 065/23-1123). For health care, the Hospital Regional de Iquitos (28 de Julio s/n, tel. 065/25-1882 or 065/25-2744) is open 24 hours daily. The Ana Stahl Adventist clinic (Av. La Marina 285, tel. 065/25-2535, emergency tel. 065/25-2518, www.caas-peru.org, 24 hours daily) offers the best care. There are reliable pharmacies near the corner of Morona and Próspero: Inkafarma, Boticas Arcángel, and MiFarma, open approximately 8am-midnight daily.

Scotiabank and Banco de Crédito, both located on the Plaza de Armas, have ATMs. Farther south are the BBVA Banco Continental (Lores 171) and Interbank (Próspero 336). Banks are typically open 9am-6pm Monday-Friday, with some of them closing for a couple of hours at 1pm. On Saturday, banks are open only in the morning.

Iquitos's post office is at Arica 402 (tel. 065/23-4091, 8am-7pm Mon.-Fri., 8am-4:30pm Sat.). There are plenty of fast Internet cafés around town; the local and traveler favorite is on the Plaza de Armas at the intersection of Napo and Arica. The Peruvian immigration office (Avelino Cáceres 18, tel. 065/23-5371) is where tourist visas can be extended.

For a choice of full-service or coin-operated laundry, go to Lavandería Imperial (Nauta 125, tel. 065/23-1768, 8am-7pm Mon.-Sat.).

GETTING THERE AND AROUND

Because Iquitos has no road access, nearly all visitors arrive by plane. Iquitos's airport is seven kilometers out of town, a 20-minute cab ride (US$5).

Three airlines fly to Iquitos Airport (IQT) from Lima. LATAM (Próspero 232, Lima tel. 01/213-8200, www.latam.com) has four daily flights. Peruvian Airlines (Próspero 215, Iquitos tel. 065/23-1074, www.peruvian.pe) has three daily flights. StarPerú (Napo 260, tel. 065/23-6208, Lima tel. 01/705-9000, www.starperu.com) has two daily flights. From Iquitos, StarPerú also flies to once daily to Tarapoto and once daily to Pucallpa. There are also international flights to Iquitos from Panama on Copa Airlines (www.copaair.com).

The only other way to enter or leave Iquitos is by boat. From Puerto Masusa, on the north end of Iquitos, boats leave for Pucallpa and Yurimaguas (US$35-60) and sporadically for the seven-day trip to Pantoja (US$29-37), on the border with Ecuador, up the Río Napo. Public colectivo boats head upstream to Nauta from the Puerto Bella Vista-Nanay, 15 minutes out of town and reachable by buses that run along Próspero. Boat tickets should be bought the day of departure or the day before.

Covered passenger boats also go down the Amazon from Iquitos to Pevas and the border towns of Leticia, Colombia, and Tabatinga, Brazil. Most of these companies have their offices in the third block of Raimondi. Golfinho (Raimondi 378, tel. 065/22-5118, www.transportegolfinho.com) schedules departures at 5am Wednesday, Friday, and Sunday. The boats leave from a small dock on Avenida La Marina, called Puerto Huequito, which is beside the Petroperu gas station.

Visiting Amazon Villages

If your Iquitos tour operator says the package may include a visit to a "native" community, you should know what to expect. "Native" these days means a highly staged experience, where Yagua or Bora people emerge in grass skirts, explain a few aspects of village life, do a quick song and dance, and then try to sell their handicrafts. Some foreigners feel awkward with the situation. But before misjudging or making assumptions, here's a review of the pros and cons of such experiences.

There are few remote indigenous communities left in the Amazon, and tourists, missionaries, and even anthropologists frankly should leave them alone. On the other hand, the indigenous communities that have chosen to contact the Western world are extremely glad to have the extra resources that come from tourism income. For them, it is an important means of acquiring the cash to buy city items such as sugar, salt, gasoline, and medicine, which otherwise they simply could not acquire.

The benefits of tourism for these people are even clearer with the visits to the mestizo or mixed-race towns that have sprouted up along tributaries of the Amazon. Many of them began three or four decades ago with a few thatched huts but now boast soccer fields and schools. Many are close to lodges that employ villagers or have markets that are visited by tourists. These new sources of tourism income have helped change local economies and lessen the prevalence of game hunting.

Amazon visitors should choose lodges that employ local villagers with fair wages and are actively involved in improving the quality of life for nearby villages. It is also a good idea to carry Peruvian *soles*, and not dollars, as the exchange rate between the dollar and the Peruvian *sol* can be volatile. Dollars are also hard to exchange in the Amazon, and exchange is done only at a steep discount in Iquitos and other cities.

Rather than taxis, the most common way to get around town is in one of the hundreds of noisy *mototaxis,* which provide cheap and quick transportation. A ride anywhere in the city costs US$0.50-2, depending where you go. To rent a motorcycle or a 4WD vehicle, head to **River Fox** (La Condamine 300, tel. 065/23-6469, 7am-11pm daily, US$1.50-5 per hour for a motorcycle).

PEVAS SIDE TRIP

The best place to stop for a night or two for those traveling to Brazil is Pevas, a laid-back village 145 kilometers downstream of Iquitos that was founded by missionaries in 1735. Pevas's main attraction is **La Casa del Arte,** a huge thatched structure on the banks of the Amazon that serves as the studio and home of **Francisco Grippa,** a well-known painter. Born in Tumbes in the 1940s, Grippa attended art school in Los Angeles and somehow ended up in Pevas, where he paints the extreme beauty and destruction of the Amazon on canvases he makes himself from tree bark. His work ranges from the mystical to the abstract, although his best-known works portray Amazon indigenous people, animals, or landscapes with explosions of color reminiscent of Jackson Pollock. A sampling of Grippa's work can be seen in the lobby of the El Dorado Plaza Hotel.

IQUITOS RAINFOREST

The rainforest in the northeastern Amazon can be explored in a number of ways: by visiting a rainforest lodge, cruising on a riverboat, or going on a camping trip. What you see depends in large part on how far you travel from Iquitos. The riverbanks that were mostly wilderness in the 1960s are now wall-to-wall farms and cow pastures. Most of the rainforest within 80 kilometers of Iquitos is secondary forest, but dolphins, monkeys, and birds can still be seen. The rainforest gets more interesting the farther you travel. **Reserva Nacional Pacaya Samiria** (12 hours upstream) and the

Iquitos Rainforest

Reserva Comunal Tamshiyacu Tahuayo (4-6 hours) have wildlife and pristine rainforest comparable to Parque Nacional Manu in Peru's southern Amazon.

One advantage that this rainforest region has over Peru's southern Amazon is that even during the rainy season, it typically only rains in the afternoon, so lodges can be visited year-round. It's also the only place in Peru where pink river dolphins live. There is a high-water season, however, between January and June,

when the Amazon rises 15 meters and floods much of the surrounding forest. Guides say there are more birds during these months, though mammals are easiest to see during the low-water months of July-December, when they hang out on the muddy riverbanks. The number of monkeys seems to hold steady year-round.

The land that does not become flooded is called terra firma or *restinga,* and it has different animals. Typical birds in a flooded forest include flycatchers, tanagers, wood-creepers, kingfishers, finches, woodpeckers, parrots, macaws, and all species of cotingas. Because there is more food in a nonflooded forest, there is a greater variety of mammals and reptiles and different birds, including antbirds, manakins, curassows, guans, foliage cleaners, and all species of woodcreepers and woodpeckers. To see the greatest range of wildlife and birds, choose lodges that have access to both flooded forest and terra firma.

Competition is intense among the rainforest outfits in Iquitos, and discounts are sometimes handed out to those who make their reservation in town as opposed to over the Internet. If you come into town without a reservation, use the agencies, lodges, and guides recommended in this book and, when in doubt, consult the Iperú or Dircetur offices listed.

Reserva Nacional Pacaya Samiria

One of the most pristine areas of Peru's northern Amazon is the Reserva Nacional Pacaya Samiria, an immense wedge of flooded rainforest between the Ucayali and Marañón Rivers. At just over two million hectares, it is still Peru's largest nature reserve. Its vast network of lakes, lagoons, swamps, and wetlands harbors many endangered animals, with good chances for spotting wildlife rivaling that in Parque Nacional Manu, although there are no lodges in the reserve.

Commonly seen animals in the reserve include huge Amazon manatees, tapirs, gray and pink river dolphins, black and white caimans, giant otters, at least 12 types of monkeys, the *paiche* fish, and hundreds of aquatic birds. The best times to visit the park are the low-water months of July to December, when animals can often be spotted on the riverbanks. The reserve began in the 1940s in an effort to save the endangered *paiche*. After biologists realized it has world-class biodiversity, the present reserve was officially established by the Peruvian government in 1972. More than 30,000 colonists and indigenous inhabitants live inside the reserve, including Cocama, Huitoto, Bora, and Yagua peoples.

Visitors to Pacaya Samiria require a guide, a US$33 entrance fee, and at least five days, whether you motor the 300 kilometers upriver from Iquitos (15-18 hours) or downriver from Yurimaguas (10 hours). Because there are no lodges in the reserve itself, options range from deluxe cruises to rustic camping trips. Trips usually travel up the Río Ucayali to the town of Requena and then enter the heart of the reserve through the Canal de Puinahua and the Río Pacaya. Generally speaking, this southern side of the reserve has more wildlife than the northern area along the Río Samiria.

A fast access point for the reserve is **Yurimaguas,** which lies two hours from Tarapoto. Cargo boats that leave here most afternoons chug down the northern border of the park for nearly two days. The fringes of the park, however, have been heavily impacted by colonists, and the more pristine areas can now only be reached by a two- to three-day canoe journey inside the reserve. In the middle of the first night after leaving Yurimaguas, cargo boats stop in the small village of **Lagunas.** From here it is possible to contract a local guide and a canoe for about US$30 per day, though there are no guarantees on the quality of service. A surer bet is to set up a guide and transportation in Tarapoto through either Puerto Palmeras resort (Carretera Fernando Belaúnde Terry, Km 614, tel. 042/52-4100, www.puertopalmeras.com.pe) or adventure guide César Reategui (La Patarashca hostel and restaurant, Lamas 261, Tarapoto, tel. 042/52-8810, www.lapatarashca.com). From Lagunas, a half-hour *mototaxi* ride will take you to the headwaters of the Río Samiria. From here, it is a three-day paddle to Laguna Pastococha, a huge oxbow lake teeming with wildlife. Fewer tourists enter the park via this route, so this is more of a wilderness experience. The farther you go, the more you are likely to see.

Camping and canoeing through the reserve is an amazing experience with the right equipment and a good operator. When combined with a stay at a community-based lodge, it is one of the best ways to understand the rhythms of life in a flooded forest.

Reserva Nacional Allpahuayo Mishana

Created in 2008, this national reserve encompasses 58,068 hectares of rainforest, protecting the scarce white-sand forests, exceedingly rare in Peru, and flooded forests by the Río Nanay. Allpahuayo Mishana is famous for its variety of soil types, from white quartz sands to red clays, which makes it a very biodiverse spot in the Amazon.

Located 23 kilometers south of Iquitos, beside the highway to Nauta, this protected area has surprisingly copious flora and fauna despite being surrounded by farms. At least four new species of birds have been discovered in the reserve, including the ancient antwren, Mishana tyrannulet, allpahuayo antbird, and the northern chestnut-tailed antbird. Allpahuayo Mishana also contains other protected primate species, including the collared titi monkey and equatorial saki.

River Cruise Agencies

Cruises on the Amazon are a great option for those who are lured to the romance of traveling by boat on the world's largest river and want to indulge themselves in deluxe comfort. Some boats bear an uncanny resemblance to Mississippi paddleboats without the paddle but with air-conditioning, such as the Jungle Expedition boats, while others are more sophisticated vessels with a lounge-like atmosphere and a minimalist touch. The most popular trips are upriver to the Reserva Nacional Pacaya Samiria, where passengers disembark for walks into the rainforest and village visits. The smaller boats can enter shallow rivers where more wildlife can be seen. It is hard to see much wildlife from a boat deck, apart from dolphins and birds.

★ AQUA EXPEDITIONS

For years, the ultimate luxury cruise experience in the Amazon was with **Aqua Expeditions** (Iquitos 1167, tel. 065/60-1053, www.aquaexpeditions.com). That is still the case, but in 2016, one of the company's ships, *Aqua Amazon,* sank after an explosion, tragically killing six crew members. No passengers were on board. Aqua Expeditions took the incident and a subsequent investigation seriously. Today, it is still operating its other vessel, the *Aria Amazon,* which continues to provide a top-notch experience. The *Aria*

Travel in comfort on an Amazon River cruise.

(3 nights from US$3,645 pp, 7 nights from US$8,505) measures 147 feet long and was completely refurbished in 2015. The voyages on the *Aria* depart year-round out of Iquitos, offering three-, four-, and seven-day itineraries to Reserva Nacional Pacaya Samiria. It has 16 stylishly designed suites accommodating 32 passengers. It also features an outdoor whirlpool tub, an exercise room, and a reference library. All meals on board are highlighted by fresh, delicious Peruvian fare created in partnership with Pedro Miguel Schiaffino, one of Peru's top 10 chefs. Complimentary South American wines are paired with dinner each evening.

GREENTRACKS

GreenTracks (U.S. tel. 970/884-6107, www. greentracks.com), a Colorado-based ecotourism agency, offers cruises on its luxurious and modern *Delfin I* and *Delfin II* ships. All-inclusive tours begin and end with airport transfer and include good food, cabins with private baths, excellent guides, and a full program of activities. The basic trip offered by GreenTracks includes early-morning canoe trips to see monkeys, hoatzin viewing, a visit to a local village, and, of course, some lounging on the boat deck. A four-day, five-night tour on *Delfin I* costs US$3,360 pp, and a five-day, six-night tour costs US$4,200 pp. On the *Delfin II*, a four-day, five-night tour starts at US$2,750 pp and a five-day, six-night tour costs US$3,550 pp.

DAWN ON THE AMAZON

After a career in Indiana farming, Bill Grimes left the United States for a leisurely life on the Amazon, and he arrived in style with his cruise boat company **Dawn on the Amazon** (Malecón Tarapacá 185, tel. 065/22-3730, www.dawnontheamazon.com). Unfortunately, Bill unexpectedly died in 2016. His enthusiasm for the Amazon continues to be echoed by the staff at Dawn on the Amazon. Bill built a tropical hardwood boat whose carved beams constantly catch the eye of travelers and whose elegance even

piqued the curiosity of a Peruvian reality TV show. The *Dawn I* is an open-air boat that can be contracted for day trips or adventure overnights. For the day trip (US$80 pp), chairs are set up in the boat's main hull; for the overnights, hammocks or mattresses are set out. There are also trips on the *Selva Viva*, which has private cabins. All trips, regardless of length, provide food and cover entrance fees.

INTERNATIONAL EXPEDITIONS

The 15 air-conditioned cabins on luxurious *La Estella*, by **International Expeditions** (U.S. and Canada tel. 800/234-9620, worldwide tel. 205/428-1700, www.ietravel.com), all have their own private balconies equipped with comfy chairs perfect for taking in the rainforest scenery. Rooms are equipped with handcrafted furniture, and baths are decorated with Italian tile. Another highlight includes the large observation deck, the biggest of any Amazon cruise ship, measuring over 93 square meters. Activities include predawn birding, rainforest walks, kayaking on the Amazon, and visits to indigenous communities and shamans. In the evenings, there are nature presentations and live music on board.

International Expeditions offers a 7-day package that includes three nights on the *La Estella* and a night at the Ceiba Tops Lodge (from US$3,698 pp). There is also a 10-day package with seven nights on *La Estella*.

Rainforest Lodges

Though more expensive than Peruvian hotels of the same category, rainforest lodges are an excellent deal when you consider that transportation, an English-speaking guide, food, lodging, and a full range of activities are included in the rates.

In general, you get what you pay for, and the better guides tend to work at the more expensive lodges. Because the main cost of any lodge is gasoline for the outboard motor, the lodges farther away from Iquitos become progressively more expensive but offer the chance to see a wider array of animals.

Adventurous River Travel to Iquitos

To reach Iquitos, you have two options: travel by air or travel by water; there are no highways. There are plenty of direct flights from Lima, but if you are looking for adventure, you can hop aboard a cargo boat from either **Yurimaguas** or **Pucallpa.** As you lounge in a hammock, the rainforest will pass by while the ship meanders through the muddy waters of the Marañón or Ucayali River, flowing into the Amazon under a bright blue sky. Just when the heat and humidity become unbearable, a refreshing afternoon rain might fall to reveal a spectacular clear sky dominated at night by the Southern Cross. With a little preparation, the right attitude, and some patience, a river journey through the rainforest can be a comfortable, safe, and a unique travel experience.

Yurimaguas is located in northeastern Peru, two or three days from Iquitos down the Río Marañón. This small city is reached by a two-hour drive from Tarapoto. Comfy minivans and *colectivo* station wagons offer daily trips on the 120-kilometer highway that crosses the **Cordillera Escalera,** the last mountain range with cloud forests, before descending into the Amazon basin.

Cargo boats from **Transportes Eduardo** (Yurimaguas tel. 065/35-1270 or 965/63-5356) depart Yurimaguas around noon, with accommodations ranging from covered decks for slinging hammocks (US$38 pp) to cabins with huge beds and private baths (US$60 pp). The company has seven boats (*Eduardo I, II, III*, and so on) and different services available in each. Be warned, however, that boats wait until their cargo deck is full, and confirmed departures are quite often be delayed.

The other option is Pucallpa, on the shores of the Río Ucayali, a commercial hub four to five days upstream of Iquitos. The city is unattractive but is the southern gateway to the northeastern Amazon rainforest. The wharfs are always busy loading and unloading goods—bananas, cars, passengers—to and from Iquitos and other small towns along the river.

From Lima, Pucallpa is reached by daily flights or by a gorgeous 15-hour bus journey from the desert coast to the Andes to the rainforest, reaching an elevation of almost 5,000 meters crossing Ticlio. The bus ride can be broken up in two parts with an overnight stop in Huánuco or Tingo María, which are opening up to travel after being shut down for years by drug trafficking in the area.

Gilmer I, IV, and *V,* also owned by Transportes Eduardo, and the *Baylón I* and *II* are the boats we recommend. Unlike in Yurimaguas, there is no office or phone available to book a ticket. You need to approach the decks and talk to the captain or the second in command. Both companies sell tickets offering closed decks to hang your hammock on (US$29 pp); there are also cabins with a bunk bed, TV, and private bath in the *Baylón* boats (US$64 pp) or better cabins on the *Gilmer* boats (US$145 pp).

Regardless of whether you travel from Yurimaguas or Pucallpa, the ticket includes three hot meals a day on any of these vessels, served up by the boat's cooks and announced by a bell or a hammer blow on some metal surface. Passengers must bring their own spoon, bowl, and mug (US$2-3), available from the vendors roaming on the boat before departure. The food is pretty good: mostly stews with chicken, fish, and rice. If you need a special diet, do not rely on the boat food. Buy fruit or whatever you think you might want to eat during your journey. As long as you consume bottled water, you won't get sick on board. The *Baylón II* has a small restaurant offering set-up dishes, cold beer, and other beverages.

Hammocks can be bought on board or around the wharf (US$11-21). The upper decks get less crowded than the lower ones. If you travel in a group, you might consider the security of a locked cabin and alternate beds and hammocks to sleep.

EXPLORAMA

Founded by U.S. anthropologists Peter Jenson and Marjorie Smith in 1964, **Explorama** (La Marina 340, tel. 065/25-2530 or 800/707-5275, www.explorama.com) has grown into a large, highly professional organization, with four lodges, great cooking, huge boats, and some of the Amazon's best guides. As a bonus, all of the lodges offer access to both flooded and terra firma forest. Explorama's claim to fame is one of the longest canopy walkways in the world, 500 meters of continuous hanging bridges suspended among more than a dozen giant trees. At 35 meters off the ground, the walkway is an excellent way to spot birds and see tremendous rainforest vistas.

Explorama's **Ceiba Tops Lodge** (2 days, 1 night US$390 pp) is 40 kilometers downriver from Iquitos on the north shore of the Amazon. With modern air-conditioned bungalows, Wi-Fi access, a hammock house, a swimming pool with a slide, and a huge dining room and full bar, it is the only resort along Peru's Amazon River. Activities include nature walks through the lodge's 40 hectares of old-growth forest, bird-watching, and village visits. This lodge is a good option for people who don't really want to rough it. With Explorama's fast boat, it can be reached in 45 minutes from Iquitos.

TAHUAYO LODGE

Operated by Amazonia Expeditions, ★ **Tahuayo Lodge** (10305 Riverburn Dr., Tampa, FL 33647, tel. 800/262-9669, www. perujungle.com, 8 days, 7 nights US$1,295, extra days US$100 per day) is 145 kilometers south from Iquitos on the Río Tahuayo, near the Área de Conservación Regional Comunal Tamshiyacu Tahuayo, where it has been operating since 1981, started by U.S. naturalist Paul Beaver, author of the autobiographical book *Diary of an Amazon Jungle Guide*.

Tamshiyacu Tahuayo is a communal reserve, created by the Peruvian government in 1991, to protect, among other species, the rare uakari monkey. Biologists have since recorded 500 bird species and exceptional levels of biodiversity in this area.

This lodge has 15 wooden rooms, some with private baths. Amenities include a dining room where very good food is served, a hammock hall, a small library, and a laboratory with a terrarium that contains tarantulas and other creepy crawlies. There is access to both flooded and terra firma forest in the area, and a controlled zip line that allows guests to cruise safely through the canopy at 35 meters off the ground. With a good team of experienced guides, a wide variety of activities can be done on request; they are listed on the website.

A stay in Tahuayo Lodge can also include one to three days at the **Amazon Research Center,** 45 minutes upstream of the Río Tahuayo, a stone's throw from the reserve. Here, a **trail grid** has been completed covering almost 84 kilometers over an area of 400 hectares, with at least four different rainforest ecosystems. A vast amount of fauna can be spotted exploring this trail grid, including primates, birds, and small mammals.

MUYUNA AMAZON LODGE

At 140 kilometers upriver from Iquitos on the Río Yanayacu, **Muyuna Amazon Lodge** (Putumayo 163, tel. 065/24-2858, www. muyuna.com, 3 days, 2 nights US$440 pp) lodge has developed a solid reputation for excellent guides, simple but comfortable rooms, and affordable rates. The lodge is nestled in an interesting swath of flooded forest that has several types of monkeys, a large variety of birds, caimans, sloths, pink dolphins, and a good chance of seeing a giant otter, armadillo, or porcupine. There are two- to six-bed bungalows with private baths, and food is served buffet-style. Guides are well-spoken and energetic, willing to make late-night forays into the rainforest or spend time visiting the local community of San Juan.

AMAZON YARAPA RIVER LODGE

One of the best Amazon options is the **Amazon Yarapa River Lodge** (La Marina

124, U.S. tel. 315/952-6771, www.yarapa.com, 4 days, 3 nights US$800-880 s). This lodge, around the corner from the Reserva Nacional Pacaya Samiria on the pristine Río Yarapa, is surrounded by world-class rainforest and oxbow lakes teeming with exotic birds, pink dolphins, sloths, and monkeys.

Along with Explorama, Amazon Yarapa River Lodge probably has the most experienced and eloquent guides in the Amazon, and they are absolutely relentless in their efforts to pinpoint as many species as possible. In a single morning you might see 30 bird species, including the rare Amazonian umbrella bird, which has a crest of black hair that earns it the nickname "the Elvis bird."

The lodge itself is a magnificent structure with huge bungalows with private baths and private rooms with shared baths. Solar-powered electricity heats the showers. The food is excellent, consisting of fresh fish and a large range of salads, and there are nice small details—like icy towels after each rainforest outing. The lodge has a good relationship with villages in the vicinity, and has even acquired the titles of nearby villages so that it can help villagers stop poachers and illegal hunters. There is also a green system for everything from local building materials to flush compost toilets.

There is a research station adjacent to the lodge, which was built by Cornell University and which is used today mainly by professors and graduate students from local universities. The lodge is entirely surrounded by flooded rainforest, but guests who stay a few days often make trips to remote areas of terra firma upstream.

PASEO AMAZÓNICOS

Another well-managed outfit that has been around since 1975 is **Paseos Amazónicos** (Pevas 246, tel. 065/23-1618, www.paseosamazonicos.com). It has excellent guides and two lodges, built in indigenous style and purposefully left rustic with simple rooms and kerosene lamps. The lodges are listed from most comfortable to most adventurous.

Amazonas Sinchicuy Lodge (3 days, 2 nights US$313 pp, 4 days, 3 nights US$435 pp) is located on the Río Sinchicuy, about 30 kilometers from Iquitos. It has 32 pleasant wooden rooms with mosquito screens, thatched verandas, private baths, and kerosene lamps. The lodge organizes a visit to a local shaman, who gives a talk on medicinal plants. There are also visits to Yagua villages close to the lodge. There isn't much wildlife in the area other than dolphins and birds.

Tambo Yanayacu Lodge (3 days, 2 nights US$362 pp) is on the shores of the Río Yanayacu, about 60 kilometers from Iquitos in a patch of flooded rainforest. It has 10 wooden rooms with private baths, kerosene lamps, and a simple dining room where all food is cooked over an open hearth. There are many birds here, and at night the stars are reflected in the black, still waters alongside the lodge.

CUMACEBA LODGE

A good option for a one-night stay is **Cumaceba** (Putumayo 184, tel. 065/23-2229, www.cumaceba.com, 2 days, 1 night US$208 pp), which is 35 kilometers downstream of Iquitos. The thatched lodge has nice rooms with private baths, cold water, and kerosene lamps, along with a dining area and hammock hall. The lodge's packed one-night, two-day tour includes a walk through a patch of primary rainforest, caiman and dolphin spotting, bird-watching, and a visit to a Yagua village. To make up for a general lack of wildlife, guests visit a nearby family that keeps monkeys, turtles, sloths, parrots, and a pet anaconda.

HELICONIA AMAZON RIVER LODGE

Heliconia Amazon River Lodge (Lima tel. 01/421-9595, www.amazonriverexpeditions.com, 3 days, 2 nights US$426-529 pp) is owned by the same group that operates the Acosta and Victoria Regia Hotels in Iquitos. Heliconia, 80 kilometers downriver from Iquitos, is a good mid-range resort with a comfortable lodge, rooms with private baths, and well-guided tours. Trips can be arranged and leave the same day.

Heliconia offers excellent river sportfishing programs that start from four days, three nights but can be extended as many days as you want. You are required to bring your own fishing equipment, or you can rent it. One of the most valued river fish to catch is the *tucunaré* or peacock bass, but other catches include *pacaya* (giant wolf fish), silver arowana, and pike cichlid, among others.

PACAYA SAMIRIA AMAZON LODGE

The **Pacaya Samiria Amazon Lodge** (Urb. Las Palmeras A-9, Iquitos, tel. 065/22-5769, www.pacayasamiria.com.pe, 3 days, 2 nights US$600 pp d) is 190 kilometers southwest of Iquitos—one hour upriver from Nauta on the banks of the Río Marañón—just past the village of San Isidro, on the outskirts of the Reserva Nacional Pacaya Samiria. The lodge is surrounded by high-ground secondary forest, but a good hour's walk will lead you into primary forest. Bungalows have a porch, a private bath, a shower, and hammocks, and there is electricity in the evenings. There is a small library with interesting books about birds, plants, and mammals of the rainforest. The lodge is clean and well run and offers camping trips into the reserve.

Nasca and the Desert Coast

Peru's southern desert coast is sucked dry by the frigid Humboldt Current. Rivers here often disappear into the sand before reaching the Pacific Ocean.

To solve their water problem, ancient cultures such as the Paracas, Nasca, and Chincha moved inland and built aqueducts from the mountains. The Panamericana follows the ancient inland migration, veering away from the coast toward the towns of Ica and Nasca, and in the process isolates a huge chunk of spectacular wild desert wedged against the Pacific. A handful of qualified guides with 4WD trucks are now leading travelers into this ocher lunar land. Dunes for sandboarding, star-filled nights, the spiritual stillness of the desert, and the world's greatest collection of marine fossils, including giant teeth from a gigantic extinct shark known as megalodon, all can be unveiled in the sea of sand.

On the northern edge of this desert is the Reserva Nacional de Paracas, a series of bluffs that drop to long desert beaches teeming with 200 bird species, sea lions, seals, and the endangered Humboldt penguin. Camping, hiking, or mountain biking here is an unforgettable and safe experience.

Just up the coast at El Carmen, thousands of enslaved people from Africa stumbled off boats in the 17th and 18th centuries to work in the sugarcane plantations. These days, El Carmen is a center of Afro-Peruvian dance and music. Down the road is Hacienda San José, which was restored and reopened as a beautiful hotel in early 2013 after being severely damaged during the 2007 earthquake.

The highlight of the south coast, however, is the Nasca Lines, giant enigmatic drawings of hummingbirds, whales, and mythical beings etched onto the desert floor and surrounded by a maze of lines and triangles. Although theories range from extraterrestrial landing strips to sacred water symbols, the riddle of the Nasca Lines remains unsolved. The Nasca people, who supposedly made the lines, produced some of the finest ceramics and textiles in pre-Columbian Peru, which are on display in excellent museums in Paracas, Ica, and Nasca.

Previous: Lago Huacachina; dune buggies in the Ica desert. **Above:** Peruvian pelican on the Islas Ballestas.

Highlights

★ **Reserva Nacional de Paracas:** This coastline of rugged cliffs and islands is a good place to see a wide array of birds and marine mammals and, in the process, camp or hike amid the spectacular surroundings (page 310).

★ **Islas Ballestas:** These islands in the brilliant blue waters of the Pacific are filled with marine mammals and birds—including sea lions and penguins (page 311).

★ **Pisco Bodegas:** Ica's wineries welcome visitors with tours, followed by hearty home-cooked Peruvian food, port wines, and a shot of pisco to wash it all down (page 318).

★ **Ica Desert:** This ancient ocean floor is littered with marine fossils, sculpted hills, and towering dunes. Those who venture into this remote sand-scape return dazzled by the experience (page 320).

★ **Nasca Lines:** There are certain mysteries, like huge "astronauts" and hummingbirds etched onto the desert plain, that stagger belief (page 326).

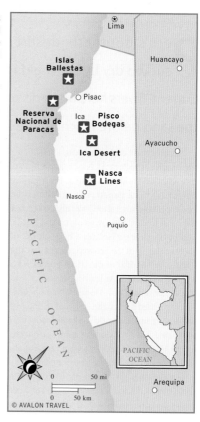

Nasca and the Desert Coast

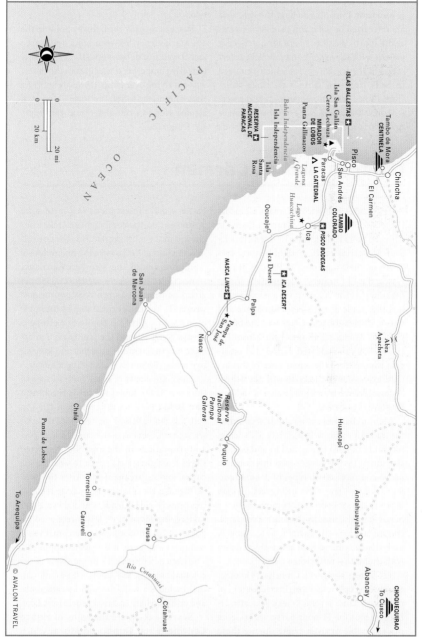

PACIFIC

OCEAN

ISLAS BALLESTAS
Isla San Gallán
Cerro Lechuza
MIRADOR DE LOBOS
Punta Gallinazos
Isla Independencia
RESERVA NACIONAL DE PARACAS
Bahía Independencia
Isla Santa Rosa

Tambo de Mora
CENTINELA
Pisco
Paracas
LA CATEDRAL
San Andrés
Laguna Grande
El Carmen
Chincha
TAMBO COLORADO
PISCO BODEGAS
Lago Huacachina
Ica
Ocucaje

Ica Desert
ICA DESERT

NASCA LINES
Palpa
Pampa de San José
Nasca

San Juan de Marcona

Huancapi

Abra Apacheta

Reserva Nacional Pampa Galeras

Chala

Puquio

Andahuaylas

Punta de Lobos

Torrecilla

Caravelí

Pausa

To Arequipa

Río Cotahuasi

Cotahuasi

Abancay

CHOQUEQUIRAO
To Cusco

© AVALON TRAVEL

0
20 km
0
20 mi

PLANNING YOUR TIME

More travelers are hopping aboard a bus for at least one leg of this entertaining journey to and from Lima. If you have the time and are interested by what you read here, points at the south coast can make for quick, easy visits—with the exception of a 4WD desert safari in the Ica desert, for which you need three to five days. Chincha is three hours from Lima, boasting good food and pisco, with new hotels. Pisco is a mid-budget place to stay in order to explore Ballestas Islands and the Reserva Nacional de Paracas. Ica's main attractions are its artisan-made pisco bodegas, which you can visit in a day or two.

Nasca is roughly the halfway point in the 20-hour journey between Lima and Cusco and is well worth the stop—there is no way to really comprehend the lines in the desert without flying over them. If you are short on time and prefer to fly, the Nasca Lines can also be seen in a one-day round-trip package from Lima.

Chincha and El Carmen

Roughly three hours from Lima is Chincha, the center of Afro-Peruvian culture. If Chincha is its center, then El Carmen is its soul. Most travelers blow right by these two towns on their way south to Paracas, Ica, or Nasca. But El Carmen, 10 kilometers off the highway past Km 202, is worth a stop, because it is the cradle of Afro-Peruvian dance and music. This laid-back village was the birthplace of Amador Ballumbrosio Mosquera (1933-2009), the talented dancer and musician who sparked the renaissance of this artistic expression in the 1970s with the help of Spanish-Peruvian rock musician, DJ, and guitarist Miki González.

Many of Ballumbrosio's children continue the tradition today with a variety of dancing, including *zapateo* (tap dancing) and percussive music that involves seven instruments: *bongo* and *tumba* (two types of drums), *quijada* (a burro's jaw with rattling teeth), *cajón* (a box that is sat upon and drummed with the hands, now also used by flamenco musicians), *cincero* (a large bell), *castañuela* (castanets), and *cabaza* (a hand-held sheet-metal drum with chains that rattle when twisted).

El Carmen, along with Chincha, 15 kilometers away, erupts into all-night celebrations of music and dance several times a year, attracting Limeños for 24-hour partying. Lodging prices double or even triple during these parties—make reservations well in advance or, as many do, dance all night and take a bus onward in the morning. Outside the festivals in Chincha and El Carmen, the Ballumbrosio family hosts music and Afro-Peruvian dance shows, called *baile de los negritos* (US$60 per group, home-cooked lunch US$9 pp), on most weekends. You can also just stop by the home of this warm, generous family. Something is always going on, and the family even offers basic lodging to music students and inquisitive souls who simply want to linger longer.

There are plenty of other things to see in the area. At the top of the list is **Hacienda San José** (Panamericana Sur, Km 203 s/n, cell tel. 940-234-957 or tel. 056/31-3332, www.casahaciendasanjose.com), one of several plantations in the area that imported slaves from Africa via Spain to work in the cotton and sugarcane fields. After the 2007 earthquake, the Cilloniz family, proprietors of this century-old hacienda, shut it down. After undergoing restoration, it was reopened for guests in 2013 under new ownership. Even if you don't stay here, it is worth stopping by. The hacienda offers a 45-minute tour of the colonial house (US$8 adults, US$4 children) that includes a walk through its catacombs and an area where enslaved people were kept.

Near the coast are the ruins of **Huaca Centinela** and **Tambo de Mora,** which

The Forgotten Chincha

During the time of the Inca conquest, the Chincha kingdom flourished on the coast, stretching from Río Cañete at least as far south as Nasca, with its ceremonial centers at Tambo de Mora and Centinela. Once painted dazzling white and covered with friezes of stylized birds, fish, and geometric designs, the deteriorated adobe mounds still offer commanding views over the ocean today.

Legends about the Inca conquest of the Chincha may have some truth. They say that the emperor's son Inca Túpac Yupanqui marched troops into the Ica Valley to take it by force. However, the young Inca was struck by the beauty of Chincha lord Aranvilca's daughter, Chumbillalla. He called off the invasion and began courting the princess. When she explained her people's lack of water for farming, the Inca ordered his 40,000 soldiers to build an aqueduct from the mountains through the desert. This aqueduct, known as the Achirina del Inca, still runs 30 kilometers through the desert, irrigating 11,000 hectares of fields.

There is well-documented evidence of the grandeur of the Chincha. In his *Crónica* of 1533, Pedro de Cieza de León comments that "as soon as the Inca had finished their conquest, they took from [the Chincha] many customs and copied their clothing and imitated them in other things." The map made by Diego Rivero of Peru in 1529, three years before the conquest, marked the location of the Chincha kingdom but made no mention of the Inca. On November 16, 1532, the date of at the fateful first meeting between the Inca and the Spaniards, two litters were carried into the square of Cajamarca. One held the emperor of the Inca and the other lord of Chincha. The two litters were so luxurious that the Spaniards became momentarily confused as to who was the real Inca. In the ensuing slaughter, the lord of Chincha was killed.

By 1550, the valley's population had plummeted five to one, according to Cieza de León. In *Conquest of the Incas*, historian John Hemming asserts that after suffering enslavement by the Spaniards, the ravages of European diseases, and profound culture shock, the Chincha simply lost the will to live. In *A Short Account of the Destruction of the Indies*, written in the 1560s, Dominican priest Bartolomé de las Casas estimated that the population in the Chincha Valley, about 40,000 when the Spanish arrived, had dropped to 1,000. Centinela and Tambo de Mora were already in ruins.

formed the capital of the Ica-Chincha culture, which was incorporated into the Inca empire in the late 14th century. The adobe ruins, once painted a dazzling white and covered with friezes of fish and birds, are badly deteriorated but offer commanding views over the Pacific Ocean on one side and Inca roads that wind up the valley on the other.

Grocio Prado, a small village just north from Chincha along the Panamericana, is a good place to see traditional basket weaving, and farther along is the long wide beach at Jahuay. Finally, there are several pisco bodegas near Chincha, including **Tabernero** (tel. 056/26-1602 www.tabernero.com), right off the highway at Chincha, and **Naldo Navarro** (tel. 056/27-1356, www.vinosnaldonavarro. com, 8am-6pm Mon.-Fri.), in Sunampe. All these places can be reached from Chincha by inexpensive taxis (US$30 for 1 day) or through tours offered by hotels in Chincha.

ENTERTAINMENT AND EVENTS

The biggest festivals in the Chincha-El Carmen area are **Verano Negro,** also known as **La Vendimia,** at the end of February and the beginning of March; the festival of **Virgen del Carmen** in the middle of July; **El Carmen's festival** (late Aug.); and an elaborate **Christmas** celebration that begins in mid-December and ends January 6. For more information, see **PeruTravels** (www. perutravels.net).

FOOD

Aside from the lunches offered by the Ballumbrosio family, there are few eating options in El Carmen. The exception is during festival times. In Chincha, **El Batán** (Panamericana Sur, Km 200, tel. 056/26-1967, 6:30am-11pm Mon.-Sat., 6:30am-6pm Sun., US$5-8) may be next to a gas station, but the food is gourmet with large portions. Try a ceviche, a *tacu tacu*, or grilled sole, and if you sit in the sunny walled-in patio, you can almost forget the highway traffic. Another great option is **Restaurant Chicharronería Lorena** (Panamericana Sur, Km 196.5, tel. 056/27-1549, 7:30am-4:30pm Tues.-Sun., US$7-10). You'd be silly not to try the house specialty—*chicharrones,* of course—but don't forget to accompany them with excellent tamales or *seco de arroz,* the local specialty.

ACCOMMODATIONS

Chincha has dozens of hotels, but none of them seem a very good value for what they offer, especially considering the noise and confusion of the city itself. Some excellent options nowadays are outside the city, at either Hacienda San José, La Estancia Sur, the Casa Andina Classic-Chincha, or the beachside Wakama Eco Playa.

US$25-50

One of the more pleasant lodging options, despite being a bit overpriced, is **Lega's Hostal** (Benavides 826, tel. 056/26-1984, www.legashostal.com, US$40 s, US$47 d, with breakfast), a miniature walled compound with modern rooms, a terrace, gardens, a cozy bar, and a small pool. The rooms are large, decorated with pastels and flowers, and include cable TV, Wi-Fi, tables, and nice baths. It is on the Panamericana Sur, next door to the Soyuz bus station and in front of the Plaza Vea grocery store. It is a five-minute walk from the center.

US$50-100

Five minutes before arriving to Chincha from Lima is **La Estancia Sur** (Panamericana Sur, Km 192.5, tel. 056/26-6148, www.laestancia-sur.com, US$40 s, US$60 d, with breakfast), a beautiful hotel with five hectares of green areas. Despite the fact that the rooms are built with brick, they have been painted white and decorated in a rustic colonial style with comfy beds and baths. Facilities include a swimming pool, a bar, an outdoor terrace, a pool, and a children's area with a trampoline, Ping-Pong tables, and a kid-size pool. They also arrange tours around Chincha.

US$100-150

For a taste of colonial Peru, stay at the ★ **Hacienda San José** (Panamericana Sur, Km 203 s/n, tel. 01/705-8563 or 056/31-3332, www.casahaciendasanjose.com, US$120 s or d, US$165 suite, with breakfast), the 17th-century sugarcane plantation where more than 100 enslaved people worked the fields. The hotel has been restored under the ownership of Spanish hotel company Hotusa, which took it over following the devastating 2007 earthquake. This is a perfect place to disconnect for a few days in a beautiful colonial estate with flower gardens, an outdoor swimming pool, and a restaurant. Its rooms are spacious and include Wi-Fi and flat-screen TVs. Guests receive a free tour of the hacienda, an eerie and grim experience taking in the slave tunnels and catacombs.

The **Casa Andina Classic-Chincha** (Panamericana Sur, Km 197.5, tel. 056/26-2451 or 01/213-9739, www.casa-andina.com, US$120 s or d, US$155 superior, with breakfast buffet), has ample gardens and a swimming pool, plus a bar, a billiards room, and a karaoke salon. There are 50 rooms, all with air-conditioning, Wi-Fi, and minibars in the superior rooms. This is, without doubt, the best hotel in the city. If you book online, you can find promotions starting at US$63.

Over US$150

If you want a place literally on the beach, **Wakama Eco Playa** (Panamericana Sur, Km 178.5, Lima cell tel. 998-386-154, www.wakamaecoplaya.com, US$380 4-person cabin, US$550 8-person cabin, higher Fri.-Sat.) is about 20 kilometers before Chincha. Once you get here, you will never want to wear shoes as you trek back and forth to your beachside hammock, as you stop by the bodega, and even as you set the table for dinner. There are 21 brilliantly colored bungalows built meters from the beach, where the floors of the sitting and dining rooms are sand, and the service is spectacular. There is a wonderfully long list of activities: horseback riding, sunset hikes, ocean-side massages, afternoon volleyball games, and evening bonfires with Afro-Peruvian music.

INFORMATION AND SERVICES

Banks in Chincha with ATMs include Scotiabank (Plaza de Armas 194), Banco de Crédito (Castilla 185-195), and Interbank (Benavides 288). The post office, Serpost, is on the Plaza de Armas, as is the police station (tel. 056/26-2458). Chincha has several fast Internet places; walk around the Plaza de Armas to find one. The hospital is south of the center on the Panamericana. Chincha has a Plaza Vea supermarket (Benavides Block 8).

GETTING THERE

Most of the major bus companies stop in Chincha en route to Ica and Nasca, though Soyuz and Ormeños have the best and most frequent service. *Combis* leave the Panamericana in Chincha frequently for the 30-minute drive to El Carmen (US$2).

The Paracas Peninsula

TOP EXPERIENCE

This sledgehammer-shaped chunk of desert coastline jutting into the Pacific Ocean is surrounded by frigid waters of the Humboldt Current, causing a rich upwelling of mineral waters. The rich waters feed phytoplankton, which in turn feed huge schools of anchovies, which in turn feed one of the world's largest collection of seabirds—about 216 resident and migratory species, including the Andean condor—two types of sea lions, and the endangered Humboldt penguin.

From 1000 BC onward, the area's rich waters also sustained the Paracas culture, which inhabited the surrounding coastline before being subsumed by the Nasca culture in AD 200. In 1925, a Peruvian archaeologist, Julio C. Tello, discovered 400 mummy bundles in an ancient cemetery on the peninsula. The bodies were preserved in the bone-dry climate and hidden by windblown sand. The most extraordinary discovery was the textiles wrapping each mummy, woven from cotton or camelid fiber and decorated with birds, fish, and other designs. They remain today the finest and most richly decorated textiles produced in pre-Columbian Peru.

The Reserva Nacional de Paracas was set up in 1975 to protect 335,000 hectares of this spectacular area from the peninsula south to Bahía de la Independencia, or Independence Bay. It is Peru's largest chunk of continuous protected coastline, and its attractions include the Museo Julio C. Tello, containing Paracas textiles, and El Candelabro, a huge hillside etching of a candelabra that has a mysterious origin.

But the reserve's main attractions are its desolation and extraordinary rugged beauty. It's like the coast of Oregon or Northern California but with no trees, no people, and 10 times the marinelife. Southwesterly ocean winds blast the Paracas coastline each afternoon and, together with the surf, have sculpted promontories with tunnels and odd shapes. Cooled by the ocean, these winds are warmed when they hit the sunbaked land and their capacity to hold water rises. This is why no rain falls on Paracas and much of the Peruvian coastline, even though fog blankets the area July-October with *garúa* because of a winter temperature inversion.

Although the late-afternoon winds can be a challenge, camping or mountain biking along

The Paracas Peninsula

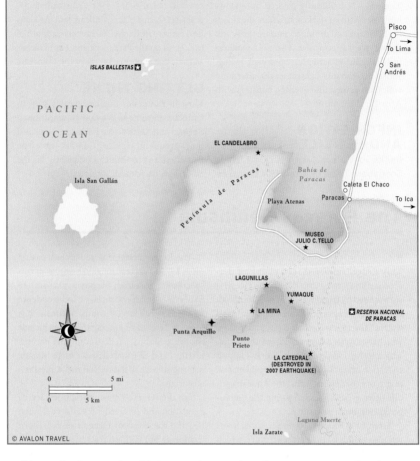

ISLAS BALLESTAS

Pisco
To Lima

San Andrés

PACIFIC

OCEAN

EL CANDELABRO

Isla San Gallán

Península de Paracas

Bahía de Paracas

Caleta El Chaco

Playa Atenas

Paracas

To Ica

MUSEO JULIO C. TELLO

LAGUNILLAS

YUMAQUE

LA MINA

RESERVA NACIONAL DE PARACAS

Punta Arquillo

Punto Prieto

LA CATEDRAL (DESTROYED IN 2007 EARTHQUAKE)

0   5 mi

0   5 km

Laguna Muerte

Isla Zarate

© AVALON TRAVEL

this coastline is a once-in-a-lifetime experience. It is not difficult at all to find a deserted beach, and the controlled access to the reserve makes this a safe place to camp overnight on a beach.

★ RESERVA NACIONAL DE PARACAS

There is a road junction right after the control booth of the **Reserva Nacional de Paracas** (8am-5pm daily, US$4). The left road leads to the remote south coast beaches, which are

anywhere from 30 minutes to three hours away on bumpy dirt roads. This road first passes a turnoff where there once used to be a rock formation known as **La Catedral** (The Cathedral), destroyed by the 2007 earthquake. The base of this million-year-old geological formation can still be seen. The road heads to Playón, the salt flats of Otuma, Mendieta, and **Bahía de la Independencia.** These are some of the more beautiful, less-visited beaches in the reserve and can be visited during a 4WD expedition through the desert to Ica.

the rugged coastline of the Reserva Nacional de Paracas

Punta Arquillo, where there is a lookout over a rocky area crowded with sea lions, especially during mating season, December to March.

Museo Julio C. Tello

The Museo Julio C. Tello (8am-5pm daily, included in park entry fee) was rebuilt after it was severely damaged in the 2007 earthquake. The museum's exhibition houses some of the finest textiles produced in pre-Columbian Peru, as well as ceramics and mummies.

The Paracas people used boards and weights to change the shape of a person's skull according to their social status. The Paracas practiced trepanation, an early form of brain surgery whereby a disk was cut from the front of the cranium. Because of scar tissue, the trepanned skulls in the museum prove that patients survived this technique, which may have been used to treat mental disorders. Nearby are Cabezas Largas and Cerro Colorado, Paracas cemeteries that were excavated by Tello and are now covered with dirt to prevent looting.

★ ISLAS BALLESTAS

Since 2010 these islands have been protected under the Reserva Nacional de las Islas, Islotes y Puntas Guaneras, a national reserve that protects all 33 islands and guano points along the Peruvian coast, including Ballestas. Sea lions can be seen from the Punta Arquillo lookout and other places around the reserve, but visitors have a good chance of seeing dozens of sea lions, seals, and even a penguin or two during a four-hour boat tour of Islas Ballestas, the islands just to the north of the peninsula.

Hundreds of thousands of birds also roost on the islands, covering them with guano, a Quechua word that has become commonly used in English. These bird droppings contain 20 times more nitrogen than cow manure, and guano is a highly coveted fertilizer that sparked Peru's 1850-1870 guano rush. Nearly 10 million tons of the stuff was dug off the Islas Ballestas, along with the Islas Chincha seven kilometers to the north, lowering the

The paved road that leads straight from the control booth heads onto the peninsula. The first stop is the museum, after a few kilometers, and farther on is Playa Atenas, a combination of rocks and sand and a favorite windsurfing spot, with its flat waters and strong afternoon winds. From Atenas a road leads to a huge etching in the hillsides called El Candelabro, on the west side of the peninsula, similar at first glance to the Nasca Lines. Because the image is of a candelabra, a rather European invention, archaeologists think pirates may have dug it into the hillside as a navigation aid. Visitors are prohibited from getting closer than 20 meters, and its huge shape, difficult to discern close up, can best be seen during a boat tour to Islas Ballestas.

At the museum, an alternative dirt road leads to Lagunillas, which has a handful of restaurants—the best of which is Tía Fela (cell tel. 956-100-915, 10am-9pm daily, US$4-6)—and two of Paracas's most beautiful (and, in the summer, crowded) beaches, El Raspón and La Mina. The road ends at

islands' height by as much as 30 meters. These days the guano is removed in a sustainable fashion by the Peruvian government.

PISCO AND PARACAS

Paracas is also the name of what used to be a small village and now is pretty much a fancy middle-class beach town. A few meters north of Paracas is the small artisanal fishing port of **El Chaco,** from where boats leave daily en route to Ballestas Islands.

Most travelers still end up staying in Pisco, a pushy little town near the highway that was almost completely destroyed during the magnitude 8.0 earthquake in 2007. Pisco's busiest evening spot is still Comercio, a pedestrian street that leads from the plaza and is lined with pizzerias and other restaurants. Pisco is 22 kilometers north from the reserve entrance.

Entertainment and Events

At Paracas, the only things happening at night are the lapping of waves and a few drinks being served at some beach restaurants. If you want something classier, simply buy alcohol from a bodega.

In Pisco, **As de Oro's** (San Martín 472, 4 blocks from the plaza, tel. 056/53-2010, www. asdeoro.com.pe) is a classic. A restaurant with a pool by day, it transforms into a discotheque on weekend nights, staying open until 6am. Catch a taxi at the door when you leave, because the surrounding neighborhood, though only four blocks from the plaza, is not safe at night.

On **June 29** fisherfolk in Pisco float the images of Saint Paul and Saint Peter into the Cove of San Andrés, as musicians perform on shore and cooks battle in a cooking contest of shellfish and fish dishes. Pisco also puts on a tourism week in September and includes **Peruvian** *paso* **horse shows, wine contests,** and an **international sandboarding contest.** The festival dates can change, so it's best to confirm with an agency.

Recreation

Camping at the Reserva Nacional de Paracas is possible and is an extraordinary experience that can be combined with a 4WD safari through the Ica deserts. Buy all your groceries ahead of time in Lima or Pisco and make sure you pack plenty of water (3-4 liters pp per day), sunscreen, clothes to protect from the wind and sun, and a camping stove—there is little driftwood on the beach. Contract with a taxi either in Pisco or the beach town of Paracas to leave you at a beach and return the next day at a prearranged time (US$15-20 one-way). The more remote beaches are on the south coast, past La Catedral, though if it is not a weekend, La Mina is a beautiful, close beach that could be empty too. Be sure to register with the reserve's visitors center.

The waters of the Paracas Bay, especially around Playa Atenas, remain flat even during stiff afternoon winds of over 30 knots. This makes for ideal **sailing** and **windsurfing** conditions. There is a good **surfing** break off San Gallán, the large island south of Islas Ballestas that can only be reached via a private boat from El Chaco fishing port.

The standard four-hour agency tour of the Reserva Nacional de Paracas includes stops at the museum, La Catedral, Lagunillas, La Mina, and the sea lion lookout at Punta Arquillo. The best way to see the reserve, however, is to contract a car with a driver. This often ends up being cheaper for a group of two or more, and allows for unscheduled stops such as lounging on the beach. For four hours, taxis from El Chaco or Paracas cost US$25-30, while drivers from Pisco can charge US$40-45. Taxis can also leave you at a beach and return for you later in the afternoon for an additional US$8.

The Islas Ballestas tours all leave from El Chaco. Before you buy your tour, inquire whether the agency has its own fast boat or you are likely to chug out of port on someone else's slow boat. Private tours are expensive and should not be done in the afternoon, when winds and seas pick up.

The Who's Who of Paracas Birds

Paracas's anchovy-rich waters attract nearly 200 bird species from around the world. Populations migrate south during El Niño years, when coastal waters warm and anchovies move offshore. Here's a who's who:

Humboldt penguins on the Islas Ballestas

- **Andean condors:** These massive vultures, with wingspans of up to 3.3 meters, descend from the high-lands and feed mainly on sea lion carcasses.

- **Boobies:** Peru has six of the world's 10 booby spe-cies, but the most common in Paracas is the Peruvian booby. These chicken-size birds have compact bodies and look like pelicans with smaller bills. These dra-matic divers eat only fish and so suffer huge declines in El Niño years.

- **Cormorants:** These long-billed divers are abun-dant in Paracas; up to four birds can nest in a single square meter. Recognizable for the sleek bodies and long necks, they dive underwater to catch anchovies and crabs.

- **Flamingos:** This wading bird, with a pink body, a long neck, and blue legs, uses its strangely bent bill to filter minute mollusks, algae, and diatoms found in brackish salt lakes. They summer in the altiplano and winter in Paracas.

- **Frigate birds:** These large birds with forked tails, hooked bills, and long V-shaped wings are aerial pirates who harass other birds until they drop their fish.

- **Humboldt penguins:** Islas Ballestas is one of the best places in the world to see this en-dangered penguin. Less than knee-high, it wobbles along on two webbed feet, but uses its wings allow it to swim at amazing speeds.

- **Inca terns:** Terns, or *zarcillos* in Spanish, are known for migrating all over the world. They look like gulls, though they have smaller bodies, pointed wings, and a pointed bill and dive after shrimps and minnows. Of the six tern species at Paracas, the Inca tern is unmistakable: red feet and bill, gray body, and white feathers that curl downward from its eyes.

- **Oystercatchers:** These birds wade around rocky coastlines, using their long red bills to open oysters and clams.

- **Peruvian pelicans:** With gray bodies, streaks of yellow on the neck, and wingspans up to 2.7 meters, these superb gliders travel up to 80 kilometers in one day, scooping fish out of the water and storing them in their large pouches.

- **Seagulls:** Paracas's most common species is the band-tailed gull, which has a black band at the end of its white tail feathers. These birds cruise the beaches for fish, though they are not above eating other birds' chicks.

- **Whimbrels:** This sandpiper scurries along the sand in search of mollusks. It has a mottled brown body, horizontal black stripes near its eyes, and blue feet. Its high-pitched scream gives it the Spanish name *zarapito trinador* (whistling sandpiper).

Most of the agencies are based in Pisco, but you can also get a tour from El Chaco. The most reputable is **Ballestas Travel** (cell tel. 998-433-385, Lima tel. 01/257-0756, www.ballestastravel.com), which has an office as you enter El Chaco. Ballestas Travel charges US$18 for a tour of the Islas Ballestas via speedboat. Another option is **Zarcillo Connections** (tel. 056/53-6636 or 998/38-1110, www.zarcilloconnections.com), which also has an office at the entrance to the Paracas beach town on the left side of the road. It offers half-day tours to Islas Ballestas (US$18) and the reserve (US$15) as well as full-day excursions to the Inca ruins at Tambo Colorado (US$25).

Paracas Explorer (tel. 056/53-1487, www.paracasexplorer.com) tours Islas Ballestas and the reserve via dune buggy. In El Chaco, the cheapest Islas Ballestas boats (US$12) leave from the town pier at 8am daily, and when there is demand, also at 10am. Tickets should be bought the day before at a green control booth near the pier. The El Chaco taxi drivers cooperative sells tickets in another booth nearby for a four-hour driving tour of the reserve (US$12).

In Pisco, all the agencies are lined up on San Francisco near the Plaza de Armas. **Paracas Overland** (San Francisco 111, tel. 056/53-3855, www.paracasoverland.com.pe) offers half-day trips to Islas Ballestas (US$20), and a full-day tour (US$25) adds a visit to the reserve. Right beside the agency is **Milsy Tours** (San Francisco 113, tel. 056/53-5204, www.milsytours.com). It has its own fleet of speedboats to tour the Islas Ballestas (US$30 pp half-day, US$40 pp full-day), including the reserve. It also offers tours of the Tambo Colorado ruins, Ica wineries and bodegas, and Nasca overflights. Ask a lot of questions beforehand: what type of airplane, where the airport is, how long the flight is, and which lines you will see.

FOOD

There are several inexpensive seafood restaurants along the waterfront in the beach town of Paracas or at El Chaco beach that have a reputation for causing traveler's diarrhea. Be cautious but not paranoid.

The best option in town is **El Chorito** (Av. Paracas s/n, Playa El Chaco, tel. 056/54-5045, 7am-9pm daily, US$4-10), one block back from the beach, which has great grilled fish and good ceviche. For a fruit smoothie and light meal, try **Fruzion** (Alan Pérez García Mz. C, Lote 8, 7am-10pm daily, US$4). It also serves pancakes, chicken wings, and hamburgers, with a vegetarian option.

If you're willing to splurge on a good meal, you might consider one of the two restaurants at Paracas Libertador hotel (Av. Paracas 173, tel. 056/58-1333): **Ballestas** (7:30am-11am, 1pm-4pm, and 7:30pm-11pm daily, US$20), with great Peruvian fish and seafood specialties and also Mediterranean cuisine, or **La Trattoria,** with good pastas and pizzas.

Worth the walk away from the center, **La Viña de Huber** (Prolongación Cerro Azul, tel. 056/53-6456, 9am-7pm daily, US$5-7) is a Pisco favorite with good prices. The lengthy menu offers plates, full enough for two, of *chicharrones,* fish, and ceviche. On the Plaza de Armas is **La Catedral** (San Juan de Dios 108, tel. 056/53-5611, 7am-11pm daily, US$8-10), with good breakfast and lunch menus and a range of chicken, beef, and seafood plates.

ACCOMMODATIONS

Most low- and mid-budget hotels are in Pisco. The upper-end hotels, mainly in Paracas, have low-season rates and also weekend packages on their websites.

US$10-25

Pisco's **Hostal San Isidro** (San Clemente 103, 5 blocks from the plaza, tel. 056/53-6471, www.sanisidrohostal.com, US$18 s, US$25 d) is a good backpacker-style place to stay. Breakfast is not included, except for free coffee in the morning, but you can get American (US$3) or continental (US$2.50) on request. There's a pool, Ping-Pong and pool tables, and a kitchen and laundry machine for the guests to use. Internet access is included, and there is a book exchange. The big rooms are nice, but because of the location, you'll want to take taxis at night.

Hostal La Casona (San Juan de Dios 252, tel. 056/53-2703, www.hostallacasona.com, US$20 s, US$25 d) is basic but has comfortable rooms with cable TV and hot water in private baths. It also offers laundry services and can help book tours.

US$25-50

In Paracas is **Hostal Los Frayles** (Paracas Mz. D5, tel. 056/54-5141, www.hostallosfrayles.com, US$28 d), which has clean rooms with great beds, private baths, hot water 24 hours, included Internet, cable TV, and several rooms with ocean views. They will pick you up from Cruz del Sur's bus stop for an additional US$3. The hotel works with Paracas Explorer to organize tours for guests.

A better option is **Hostal Residencial Santa María** (Av. Paracas s/n, Playa El Chaco, tel. 056/54-5045, www.hostalsantamariaparacas.com, US$40 s, US$47 d, with breakfast), right beside the Plaza Quiñonez. Rooms are simple but clean, with tile floors and ocean views, as well as private baths, hot water, and cable TV. Ask about the tour packages the hotel offers to the reserve and the Ballestas Islands. It also has a seafood restaurant named El Chorito.

In Pisco, **Villa Manuelita Hostal** (San Francisco 227, half block from plaza, tel. 056/53-5218, US$27 s, US$36 d) is a good option, in a century-old restored colonial house that miraculously survived the 2007 earthquake. Painted with pastel colors, this cozy hotel has large rooms with cable TV and nice baths, decorated with wooden tables and cabinets as well as fresh flowers. There are rooms with windows and skylights as well as a small patio with a fountain, elegant sitting areas, and a pizzeria.

Another option in town, a couple of blocks from the Plaza de Armas, is **Hotel Embassy Beach** (San Martín 1119, tel. 056/53-2256, www.hotelesembassypisco.com, US$50 s, US$75 d), a concrete-built, resort-like

70-room hotel with tacky decor. Rooms are enormous, with fans, mini fridges, and cable TV. There is a huge swimming pool and a restaurant with unexpectedly good seafood specialties.

Over US$150

In Paracas are three top-notch hotels. **Paracas Libertador Luxury Collection Resort** (Av. Paracas 173, tel. 056/58-1333, www.libertador.com.pe, US$225-252 d garden view, US$265-290 d ocean view, suites from US$348, with buffet breakfast) is one of the most luxurious resorts on the Peruvian coast. There are 120 rooms with great views and all amenities imaginable. The superior rooms have bamboo-covered walls. There are three kinds of suites—balcony (US$320), solarium (US$414), and plunge pool (US$470)—with highlights such as luxury baths. The hotel has two restaurants, Ballestas, with Peruvian and Mediterranean cuisine, and La Trattoria, with Italian food. Two bars and two pools offer both sides of excitement and relaxation. A travel agency, **Tikariy** (www.tikariy.com.pe), offers deluxe packages, including overflying the Nasca Lines, 4WD excursions in the desert, tours to pisco bodegas, and luxury yacht sailing. There is free kayaking for all guests and an on-site ATM. The staff is extremely friendly and helpful.

The **Doubletree Guest Suites by Hilton Paracas** (Lote 30-34, Urb. Santo Domingo, tel. 01/617-1000, http://doubletree1.hilton.com, from US$195 for garden views) is on Santo Domingo beach, in the southern section of the Paracas village. This U-shaped hotel has suites overlooking the pool and the ocean; the ocean views are more expensive. Rooms have super comfortable beds and are spacious, with a large balcony offering impressive views of the Paracas Bay or the hotel gardens. The restaurant serves a buffet and also has a menu of good but not spectacular food. Since the hotel is isolated, be prepared to have all your meals there unless you have your own transportation. Wi-Fi is available but not always reliable. There is an ATM in the hotel.

Next door to the Hilton is the **Hacienda Bahia Paracas** (Lote 25, Urb. Santo Domingo, tel. 056/58-1370, www.hoteleslahacienda.com, US$220 s or d), another luxurious option that offers comfortable rooms and excellent service. The hotel has all the amenities, like a gym and spa, a large pool, and a good restaurant overlooking the bay. There is a bar with live music and a lounge with a fireplace. If you get tired of relaxing at the pool, you can take a hotel bicycle out for a spin along the bay or do some windsurfing.

INFORMATION AND SERVICES

There is a medical post in Paracas. Internet, post office, small grocery stores, and a public phone are all within a block of the small main square. **Visitor information** is available from Pisco's municipality (tel. 056/53-2525) on the main square, although nearby agencies on San Francisco are a better bet.

Pisco's **police station** (San Francisco, tel. 056/53-2884) is on the plaza. For medical issues in Pisco, go to **Clínica San Jorge** (Juan Osores 440, tel. 056/53-6100, 8am-8pm Mon.-Sat., 8am-2pm Sun.). Reliable pharmacies are **Boticas Fasa** (Humay 521, www.boticasfasa.com, 10am-10pm daily) and **Inkafarma** (Humay 519, www.inkafarma.com.pe, 10am-10pm daily).

All the banks with ATMs are on Pisco's square, including **Banco Continental,** **Banco de Crédito, Interbank,** and **Scotiabank.** The **post office** (Callao 358, tel. 056/53-2272, 8am-6pm Mon.-Fri., 8am-4pm Sat.) is three blocks from the main square. There are private phone booths (Progreso 123A) opposite the cathedral, and **Internet** places are a half block away on Comercio.

GETTING THERE AND AROUND

To get to the Reserva Nacional de Paracas, get off the Panamericana at Km 234 and drive five kilometers to Pisco and then another three kilometers to the gate of the reserve. The town of Paracas is on the right a few kilometers before the gate.

The best bus company to go to Paracas is **Cruz del Sur** (www.cruzdelsur.com.pe), offering a stop in Paracas on their Lima-Nasca route. A cheaper option, with frequent buses to and from Lima and Pisco, is **Soyuz** (www.soyuzonline.com.pe), which has an office on the Plaza de Armas. From there, passengers are shuttled out to the highway to meet buses that are constantly rumbling north and south.

From Pisco, **taxis** charge US$5 for the 20-minute drive to Paracas. **Buses** marked "El Chaco-Paracas" leave every half hour from the market near Nicolás de Piérola and take about 30 minutes (6am-6pm daily, US$0.30). Buses return to Pisco every half hour from El Chaco's only entrance.

Ica

At 420 meters elevation, sunny Ica is an oasis of palm trees and sand dunes. The town escapes the fog, or *garúa,* that blankets Lima much of the year. To the west, the Ica desert, a moonscape of sand dunes and eroded dirt formations, stretches to the Pacific Ocean. This wilderness is known primarily to a select group of paleontologists who come to search for the fossilized bones of prehistoric sea lions and gigantic sharks. Recently the local guides of these paleontologists have begun showing travelers the paleontologists' route. On a desert safari, activities include hunting for gigantic fossilized teeth, examining the bones of marine animals scattered in the sand, and sleeping under a brilliant star-filled sky. No one who has gone on one of these trips has been disappointed—this desert, which extends from Paracas down to Nasca, is one of the wildest and most spectacular in the world.

What Ica is most known for, though, is its **vineyards,** which were planted by the Spaniards in the 16th century. Ica's 80 surrounding bodegas produce the world's best pisco, or white grape brandy, and a variety of ports and wines. There is a huge range of bodegas, from the haciendas that have been outfitted with state-of-the-art technology, such as Tacama and Ocucaje, to more rustic mom-and-pop operations where grapes are crushed underfoot and pressed with the weight of a huge *huarango* trunk. Most visitors like to see one of each.

The city of Ica changed dramatically after a wave of highland settlers came here to escape terrorism in the 1990s. The city is more crowded now, and assaults on tourists have become common. When in Ica, walk in groups, stay near the plaza at night, and avoid the whole east side of the city between the plaza and the Río Ica. The best lodging options are now outside the city, including Hotel Hacienda Ocucaje, Lago Huacachina, or the quiet Angostura neighborhood on the edge of town.

Lago Huacachina, six kilometers out of town, is a magical and incongruous sight, a lake of green waters fringed with palm trees and reed swamps and surrounded on all sides by huge sand dunes. There are excellent lodging options around the lake. During the day, the dunes are the best place in Peru to try sandboarding and dune buggy riding. For those who don't want to stay in Nasca, overflights of the nearby lines leave frequently from Ica, but the cost is slightly higher.

Ica has endured a series of natural disasters, from an earthquake that killed 500 people way back in 1664 to an El Niño flood in 1998. As a result, there are few colonial buildings or well-preserved ruins in the area, even though the valley has been home to a series of ancient cultures: the Paracas, Nasca, Huari, and Chincha. Inca Pachacútec conquered and integrated this valley into the Inca empire in the 15th century. A century later Luis Jerónimo de Cabrera founded the first city, Villa de Valverde, in 1563. The Spaniards, no doubt missing the *riojas* and *ribieros* of their homeland, planted the first South American grapes in the 1540s.

SIGHTS
City Tour

There are a few churches to see in Ica, along with two museums. The **Plaza de Armas** is lined with ancient trees and has been rebuilt with an obelisk and fountain since a 1998 flood sent a meter of water running through town. The 19th-century **cathedral** on the corner has a neoclassical facade and beautiful, though spooky, wood carvings inside. The biggest church in the city, **San Francisco,** is a block to the west of the cathedral and has a number of stained-glass windows illustrating the life of the patron saint. The most beautiful church, however, is **Señor de Luren,** which is reached by walking south on Lima for eight blocks and turning right on Cutervo. The church has a beautiful interior that holds an image that inspires a yearly October pilgrimage. There are a few colonial and republican *casonas* around town, which are not generally

Ica Wineries

open for tours but are worth viewing from the outside, including **Casa de las Cornucopias** (Dos de Mayo 158), **Casa del Valle** (San Martín 159), **Edificio del Estanco** (Lima 390), and **Casa Colonial El Portón** (Loreto 233).

The **Museo Cabrera** (Bolívar 170, on Plaza de Armas, cell tel. 999-437-702, 10am-1pm and 4pm-10pm Mon.-Sat., by appointment Sun., US$10) is an imaginative collection of thousands of stones and boulders collected by the late Javier Cabrera, a descendant of the town's founder. Carved on these stones are depictions of ancient hunts, brain surgery, and even dinosaurs. No one has been able to explain exactly who carved the nearly 11,000 stones that Cabrera claimed to have found in tombs around Ica, and archaeologists doubt their authenticity. Cabrera, who died in 2002, never revealed their exact origin. If nothing else, this idiosyncratic museum is a monument to one man's obsession.

El Museo Regional de Ica (Ayabaca, block 8, near J. J. Elias, tel. 056/23-4383, 8am-7pm Mon.-Fri., 8:30am-6:30pm Sat.-Sun., US$3) is 1.5 kilometers south of the Plaza de Armas but definitely worth the visit. It is one of Peru's best small museums and offers a fascinating glimpse into the Paracas, Nasca, Huari, Chincha, and Inca cultures. Displays include textiles, ceramics, trepanned skulls, mummies, and *quipas* (bundles of knotted strings that served as memory devices). The museum presents a good historical overview of the area, along with photos and furniture from the 19th century and a full model of the Nasca Lines. To get here, take a US$0.50 taxi or hop aboard any *combi* (US$0.15) that says "Universidad" at the cathedral in the Plaza de Armas.

★ Pisco Bodegas

Most of Ica's bodegas welcome visitors with free tours and then wine and dine them with their own wines and piscos and heaps of home-cooked food. Ica's bodegas have a charming down-home feel, and most visitors end up staying longer, and drinking more,

than they had planned. The larger wineries are the best places to understand how pisco is made, though the smaller bodegas have a more charming atmosphere for eating and tasting. Taxis from Ica are cheap and easy to hire, even for non-Spanish speakers. For the return home, if there aren't taxis lined up outside the bodega, they can be called at a moment's notice. The most interesting time to visit is during harvest, or *vendimia,* January to March. Only Tacama has English-speaking guides always on hand; the others can arrange for one with advance notice.

Just 11 kilometers northeast of Ica, **Tacama Winery** (Camino a La Tinguiña, tel. 056/58-1030, www.tacama.com, 9:30am-4:30pm Tues.-Sun., US$3) produces Peru's only dry wines and is a leading producer of pisco. There is a modern warehouse with state-of-the-art facilities, which backs up to the ocher walls of a colonial hacienda, a plaza of river stones, and a driveway lined with ancient trees. An old bell still rings every day from a tower, from which visitors can look out over 200 hectares planted with 20 different grape varieties.

The Olachea family bought the hacienda in 1898, but lost much of the original 950 hectares in the Agrarian Reform. A tour of the winery includes a visit to an old grape press made from a *huarango* tree, a 19th-century *alambique,* and a full tour of the modern warehouse. There is an interesting museum of wine technology from the past few centuries and a wine-tasting room. The blended white wines—especially the Blanco de Blancos and the lighter Gran Blanco—are very good and sold at a 50 percent off retail. Taxis cost US$6 from Ica.

Another large winery even closer to Ica is **Vista Alegre** (Camino a La Tinguiña, Km 2.5, Lima tel. 01/248-6757, www.vistaalegre.com.pe, 9am-5pm daily), only three kilometers from Ica across the Río Ica. Vista Alegre was operated by the Jesuits in the 18th century. It was then purchased by the Picasso family in 1875, which continues to operate it today. Unfortunately, the half-hour walk to

When in Peru, Drink Pisco

Peruvians are proud of pisco, a grape brandy distilled from sweet grapes cultivated in Peru's desert near Ica. When Chile tried to patent the name pisco during the 1980s, Peru protested. Experts agree that Peru makes a more delicate, aromatic pisco—the key difference is that Peru's hot climate allows it to produce sweeter grapes. Peruvian bodegas distill pisco from grape juice that has been fermented for 45 days. The Chilean grapes, in contrast, are made into wine first, distilled, and then cut with water to lower the alcohol content. The difference is noticeable. Fine Peruvian pisco, such as Biondi from Moguegua, or Castañeda or Bohorquez from Ica, has a delicate range of flavors that experienced sippers recognize immediately.

The Spaniards first planted red grapes in the Ica Valley around 1547 and began exporting wine within a decade. Someone had the idea to distill the fermented juice of the dark Quebranta grape, and pisco was born. Pisco was an immediate success, becoming an important drink in Spanish salons and even in the saloons of 1849 gold rushers in San Francisco—it was cheaper to ship pisco up the Pacific Coast than to lug whiskey across the Panama Strait from the eastern United States.

No one knows for sure how pisco got its name. The word means "bird" in Quechua, and apparently the Nasca and Paracas cultures used the word to describe the huge clay jugs they used for fermenting chicha. The Spaniards later used these same jugs for fermenting pisco.

There are five different types of pisco: Pisco puro is made from nonaromatic grapes such as mollar, quebranta, and the black grape; pisco promático is made from albilla, torontel, Italian, and moscatel grapes; pisco aromatizado gets its fruit bouquet from limes or cherries added during distillation; pisco acholado is a blend of many different grapes; and pisco mosto verde is made from partially fermented grapes.

Although fine pisco is chilled and sipped by itself, Peruvians have invented many pisco-based cocktails: They range from the algarrobina, a sweet drink prepared with the honey of the algarroba tree, to a chilcano, a simple mix of pisco and ginger ale. The favorite is the pisco sour, invented in the early 20th century in Lima's Rojo Bar at the Maury Hotel. The preparation is simple: fresh-squeezed lime juice, sugarcane syrup, egg white, and water are blended, topped with Angostura bitters, and served in a tumbler. Drink as many as possible while in Peru. The small, bitter limes essential for pisco sour—known as limón de pica—are impossible to find outside Peru.

Vista Alegre—down Grau and across the Río Ica—takes you through the unsafe side of the city. Take a taxi (US$3) instead.

One other option is the recently-opened **Hotel Viñas Queirolo** (San José de los Molinos s/n, tel. 056/25-4119, Lima tel. 01/261-3772, ext. 102, www.hotelvinasqueirolo.com). The 400-hectare winery is located about 20 minutes from the city in a beautiful valley surrounded by barren mountains, sand dunes, and bright blue sky. This is where the Intipalka wine and pisco served at Queirolo bodega in Lima are produced. The family business, which was started in 1880 by Italian immigrant Santiago Queirolo, originally had its vineyards in Lima. It moved south to Cañete in 1962 as a result of Lima's population boom. It relocated again in 2002, this time to its current location outside Ica. While tours are offered to guests of the hotel, day visitors can also take part. The tour includes a guided walk through its vineyards and wraps up with wine and pisco tasting at the hotel restaurant. The tours, which are in Spanish, start at 4:30pm and cost US$35 for nonguests.

Small Pisco Bodegas

Ica's best small bodegas are just two kilometers apart along the dirt road that leads to Tacama. The more authentic of the two is **Bodega Lazo** (Camino de Reyes s/n, tel. 056/77-1008, 9am-9pm daily). Locals come here to drink port and eat under the bougainvillea-covered bowers or inside the bodega itself, which is a charming and elegant space filled with wine barrels, presses, and other objects from the bodega's history, which began in 1809. There is a good tour here of the vines and winery, though you need to speak Spanish.

El Catador (Fundo Tres Esquinas 102, Subtanjalla, tel. 056/40-3516, www.elviejocatador.com, 10am-7pm, daily) is a more established spot on the bodega circuit, run by the Carrasco family, which has large spaces for visitors to drink and eat. But first, go on the excellent tour of the colonial wine and pisco process: The grapes are crushed underfoot and then pressed in a huge adobe platform with a 150-year-old *huarango* trunk as a weight. Then the juice is poured into clay containers, known as *botijas de barro,* which were used in this area long before the Inca. The pisco is distilled in huge brick boilers with copper basins known as *falcas.* In March, the height of the grape crushing, visitors are asked to roll up their pants and lend a foot. The food is good and reasonably priced, with entrées around US$5 and a full lunch menu for US$6.

★ Ica Desert

Ica is the best launching point for tours through the desert, which, apart from being beautiful, also happens to be one of the world's richest hunting grounds for marine fossils. You need at least three days, preferably a week, to get there and back from the truly remote wild desert, and make sure you have a hat, plenty of sunscreen, three to four liters of water per day per person, and a desert-worthy vehicle with plenty of spare tires as protection against razor-sharp volcanic rocks. The guides recommended here are intellectual but all self-taught, absolutely passionate about the desert, and safe. They make a living by guiding foreign paleontologists, and they know all the local *huaqueros* (grave robbers), who tip them off about new fossil areas.

The guide with the best transportation, and the most experience, is Roberto Penny Cabrera, alias **Desert Man** (Bolívar 178, cell tel. 956-624-868 or tel. 056/23-7373, www.icadeserttrip.com). A former prospector for mining companies, Roberto can show you detailed satellite imagery and geology maps of the whole area, and a quick glimpse of his truck is the best proof that you will not end up dying of thirst or crawling out of the desert on your hands and knees. His powerful diesel pickup has mattresses for three, a 22-gallon shower, and even an air pump for inflating his three spare tires. He speaks impeccable English and is a descendant of the

exploring the sand dunes outside Ica

The Sands of an Ancient Breeding Ground

Looking out over the endless sand dunes west of Ica, it is impossible to visualize the area as a huge ocean, with giant sharks, sea lions, penguins, dolphins, and whales. But that is what was going on here two million years ago before shifting tectonic plates heaved the ocean floor up into the hot, dry air where it is today.

After a paleontologist discovered a new dolphin species here in the 1980s, the Ica desert has produced dozens more and has become known as the best place in the world to hunt for marine fossils. There are so many, in fact, that bumpy points on the top of sand dunes are not usually rocks but rather the perfect vertebrae of some long-extinct swimming animal. Experienced guides know where the most interesting fossils are, whether it's a sea sloth (oddly similar to a rainforest sloth but with a beaver-like tail and hooked hands for excavating soil), the delicate baleen of huge plankton-eating whales, or a prehistoric pelican with a nine-meter wingspan.

Paleontologists believe that the whole area was once a shallow breeding ground for a variety of marinelife, like the bays of Mexico's Baja California. The animals died, perhaps naturally or because of storms, and sank to the bottom, where their carcasses were quickly covered with mud.

One of the more spectacular animals is the *Carcharocles megalodon,* the *Tyrannosaurus rex* of the sea. This gigantic whale-eating shark was up to 14 meters long. Like sharks today, the megalodon had more than 100 teeth, arranged in seven lines, which were constantly falling out and being replaced. These gigantic teeth, up to 20 centimeters long, are now fossils that can be picked right out of the dried mud.

Geological maps show the different formations around Ica and to which epoch they belong. The Pisco formation, a huge area of marine sediment that stretches from Arequipa to Pisco, contains mostly fossils from the Upper Miocene to the Lower Pliocene, or from about 16 million to 2 million years ago. The huge bluff closer to the coast, which forces the Río Ica south on its way to the Pacific, is the Caballo Formation. It is far older, with fossils from the Triassic (230-145 million years ago) and even the Precambrian that go back three billion years to the beginnings of life on earth. Any fossils that are found must stay in Peru; it is the law.

town's founder. He is intense, well organized, and endlessly entertaining.

Marco León Villarán (Lima tel. 01/230-8351, www.peruadventure.com) leads trips in the Ica desert and works as a professional bone hunter throughout Peru's coast. He is a genuinely nice person who leads very professional expeditions and speaks only Spanish.

ENTERTAINMENT AND EVENTS

Nightlife in Ica is a weekend affair. At Lago Huacachina, many of the bars are attached to the hostels. One option is to head to the bar at **Hostal Rocha** (Balneario Huacachina s/n, tel. 056/22-2256, 10pm-close Sat.-Sun.).

Otherwise most nightlife options are in the city of Ica itself. A locals' favorite for beers and cocktails is the dark and swanky **Pekados** (Lima 261, 9pm-close Thurs.-Sat.). The **UVK**

Multicines (Av. Ayabaca s/n, next to the INC Museum, in the San José neighborhood, tel. 056/21-7261, www.uvkmultcines.com) shows international movies.

The best Ica festival is the **International Grape Harvest Festival,** which takes place during the height of the harvest in the first half of March. There are concerts, cockfighting, and beauty pageants. The woman chosen as the queen of the festival ends up wallowing in a vat of grapes.

Ica has been a center for **Peruvian** *paso* **horses** for centuries, and the **Sol de Oro horse competition** is held here every June, though the exact date varies. Peru's **national day of pisco** is July 25, and Iqueños celebrate with raucous parties. **Our Lord of Luren** takes place the third Sunday in October and includes processions of hundreds of people and streets covered with carpets of flowers.

RECREATION
Sandboarding the Dunes

Ica is the best place in Peru to try sandboarding and dune buggy riding. There is a thrill in speeding up and down the dunes, but simply being on the dunes lets you appreciate the magnitude of the desert geography. Dune buggies are available through Mario Vera, the dune buggy pioneer of Ica, inside the **Las Dunas** (La Angostura 400, tel. 056/25-6224). Las Dunas and many of the Angostura hotels provide sandboards free of charge, though make sure they are waxed or they will not go very fast.

The best places for these sports, however, are the huge, perfect dunes around Lago Huacachina. At the green control entrance to the lake there are dune buggies for rent—the best are available through Eduardo Barco at **El Huacachinero hostel** (Perotti s/n, tel. 056/21-7435), but **Hotel El Huarango** (El Medano Y-5, tel. 056/25-6257) and **Hostería Suiza** (Balneario de Huacachina 264, tel. 056/23-8762) can also put you in touch with reliable operators. Dune buggy riding is like a roller coaster without a track, because the machines zip down 50-degree slopes at up to 80 kilometers per hour. Accidents do happen, so make sure you have seatbelts with chest harnesses and good roll bars—and don't hesitate to get out if your driver is reckless. The best times for both of these sports are early morning and late afternoon, to avoid the heat and winds that pick up around midday.

Tour Agencies and Guides

If you are short on time and don't mind spending more, Ica can also be a good base for seeing the Nasca Lines, and 35-minute overflights from here cost around US$200 pp. Because the flight is longer from Ica, pilots occasionally try to save gas by skipping some of the lines. Have the agency write down a list of lines beforehand, and pay extra if necessary to get more flight minutes. Agencies also offer US$40-50 tours to the Reserva Nacional de Paracas that include a trip to the Islas Ballestas. However, this seems like a very rushed way to see such a spectacular reserve.

Of the companies that offer these kinds of trips, the best options are **Desert Travel** (Lima 171, cell tel. 956-601-576, desert_travel@hotmail.com) and **Dolphin Travel** (Municipalidad 132, cell tel. 947-130-062 or tel. 056/21-8920, www.av-dolphintravelperu.com). The agencies offer local tours that cost US$20 and include El Museo Regional de Ica, Lago Huacachina, Cachiche (a town known for its now-disappeared tradition of witchcraft), Señor de Luren church, and a bodega or two. One option is to take this tour and then stay at the wineries and take a taxi home.

FOOD
Peruvian

First opened in 1968, **El Otro Peñoncito** (Bolívar 255, tel. 056/23-3921, noon-10pm daily, US$10) has a huge classy menu of Peruvian concoctions, including a dozen different salads, meats, pastas, fish, and vegetarian cuisine. Try *pollo a la Iqueñas*, grilled chicken with spinach covered in a pecan sauce. The Hernández family makes their own pisco, and bartender-owner Hary is one of Peru's better-known bartenders.

El Cordón y la Rosa (Los Maestros D-14, Urb. San Jose, tel. 056/21-8012, 11am-11pm Mon.-Sat., 11am-7pm Sun., US$10) is a newer popular option in Ica, with delicious servings of Peruvian dishes, specializing in fish and seafood. Accompany your dish with a *pisco sour* or *chilcano*. **Plaza 125** (Lima 125, Plaza de Armas, tel. 056/21-1816, 7am-midnight daily, US$4-7) serves salads, *adobos*, steaks, and US$2 pisco sours.

International

Restaurant Venezia (San Martín 1229, tel. 056/21-0372, 11am-3pm and 6pm-11pm Tues.-Sat., www.restaurantvenezia.com, US$6) is the best place for pizza and also serves gnocchi, homemade pasta, and ice cream. The best place for fish is **La Candela** (Túpac Amaru F-5, Urb. San José, around the corner from

Lago Huacachina: Lake of Tears

The name Huacachina is Quechua: *Wakay* means "to cry" and *china* means "young woman." According to local legend, a young woman and her lover strolled most afternoons in the countryside around Ica. But just when the couple was to be married, he dropped dead. The woman was wracked with sorrow and spent the days afterward wandering through the countryside and retracing her walks with her lover. As she walked, her tears formed a lake.

As she sat by the lake one day, an evil spirit in a man's form tried to rape her. She jumped into her lake's waters, imploring the water gods to protect her from evil spirits by covering her with a cloak of snow. Though she escaped, she drowned in the lake. Now, every full moon, she floats over Lago Huacachina, cloaked in sparkling white light. Locals say she drowns nighttime swimmers as a sacrifice to the lake gods who protect her.

Museo Regional, tel. 056/23-7853, 8:30pm-close Thurs.-Sat., US$5-8). The menu includes a range of mouthwatering ceviches, *tiraditos*, and other seafood plates. For tapas, sandwiches, and pizzas for dinner or weekend lunch, there is **Forja** (Urb. Santa Elena D-14, tel. 056/22-4303, 7pm-11:45pm Tues.-Thurs., 7pm-2am Fri., noon-4pm and 7pm-2am Sat., noon-4pm Sun., US$8). It prides itself on having the best *chilcano* in Ica.

Cafés, Bakeries, and Ice Cream

Most of the area's better restaurants are in Ica. **Anita's** (Conde de Nieva 558, tel. 056/21-8582, 10am-10:30pm daily, US$8-10) is an upscale, rather expensive café and restaurant with great service. The huge menu is good for breakfast and includes a wide range of Peruvian dishes and desserts. A local favorite for pies and empanadas is **Dulcería Pastelería Velasco** (Grau 199, tel. 056/23-2831, 9am-9pm daily), which was founded in 1936 and serves up a staggering array of local sweets. The best-known sweets maker in Ica is **Helena Chocolates & Tejas** (Nicolás de Ribera 227, Urb. Luren, tel. 056/23-3308, www.helenachocolatier.com), which offers tours of its factory, 11 blocks south of the Plaza de Armas. There is also a store (Cajamarca 139), near the plaza, which sells the local specialty *tejas*, or pecans and candied fruits—figs, lemons, grapes, oranges— filled with *manjar blanco*, a milk caramel,

and bathed in sugar. The chocolate-covered version is called *chocotejas*.

Markets

Like many midsize Peruvian cities, Ica now has a mall, **Plaza del Sol** (San Martín 727, tel. 056/23-8345, 10am-10pm daily). All the banks are here, as well as pharmacies and a grocery store. The other supermarket in town is **Plaza Vea** (Ayabaca 1180).

ACCOMMODATIONS

The best place to stay near Ica is Lago Huacachina, southwest of town and accessible by taxi (US$3). Another option is Ica's Angostura neighborhood, which is quiet and safe and only a few minutes from town.

Under US$10

For a budget hostel on Lago Huacachina, your best bet is **Desert Nights Hostel** (Malecón Principal s/n, tel. 056/22-8458, www.hihostels.com, US$10), affiliated with Hostelling International and with basic but clean dorm rooms with eight beds as well as a TV room. It is managed by an American and staff can help organize sandboarding and dune buggy trips. Because of its central location just off the lagoon, the hostel's restaurant is a popular place for breakfast, lunch, and dinner. Another option is **Hostal Rocha** (Balneario Huacachina s/n, tel. 056/22-2256, US$7 s, US$14 d), with a friendly family feel and an open-door policy for even the rowdiest backpackers. The rooms have yellow tile or polished concrete floors, and some have balconies, private baths, and hot water. Noise can be a problem due to the bar attached.

US$10-25

Located near the entrance to Huacachina is **Hotel Curasi** (Balneario de Huacachina 197, tel. 056/21-6989, www.huacachinacurasi.com, US$11 s, US$18 d). Rooms are clean and comfortable but basic, with red-tiled floors, wooden dressers, private baths, and hot water. The hotel has a pool and a small green space where you can catch some sun. It also has its own drivers for dune buggy riding and organizes sandboarding trips. **Banana's Adventure Hostel** (Balneario Huacachina s/n, tel. 056/23-7129, www.bananasadventure.com, US$20 dorm, US$45 s or d, with breakfast) has clean rooms with comfortable beds, a nice swimming pool, and an on-site café. The price may seem high, but it includes one tourist activity: a ride in a dune buggy, sandboarding, or tour of a pisco bodega.

US$25-50

In Huacachina, Eduardo Barco's **El Huacachinero** (Perotti s/n, tel. 056/21-7435, www.elhuacachinero.com, US$35 s, US$45 d) is an excellent option. Rooms are decorated with bright bed covers, the garden is full of hammocks, the pool is surrounded by lounge chairs, and the bar is never far away. Piña colada by the pool? The friendly Eduardo can arrange dune buggy rides.

In the Angostura neighborhood, **Hotel El Huarango** (El Medano Y-5, tel. 056/25-6257, www.huarango.net, US$35 s, US$60 d) offers large rooms with parquet floors, TVs, big baths, and antique furniture. Deep roof eaves make the rooms a bit dark, but it's great for sleeping. There are Internet stands and a restaurant next to the pool that serves excellent Peruvian food, and there are sandboards for surfing the dunes right next to the hotel. The owner, Antonio Carrión, can also arrange dune buggy rides (US$20 for 1.5 hours) and bodega tours (US$20 pp).

In Ica, a rather ugly modern option is **Hotel Sol de Ica** (Lima 265, tel. 056/23-2243, www.hotelsoldeica.com, US$45 s, US$57 d), a huge building a block from the Plaza de Armas that has a pool and a restaurant. The rooms are small and plain, with cable TV, clean baths, and thin stucco walls that let in the street noise.

US$50-100

Hotel Casa Sur (La Angostura 367, tel. 056/25-6106, www.casasur.pe, US$65 s, US$90 d), in Angostura, run by an Austrian-Peruvian couple, is a pleasant compound with red tile floors, large rooms with TVs, and a nice pool. Tucked in the corner of its yard is a small wooden deck with hammocks, perfect for relaxing in the shade. *Criolla* food is served for a reasonable price. This is one of the cleanest hotels in Peru, though a bit rigid in its Austrian impeccability. You will not find a speck of dust here.

On Lago Huacachina is **Hostería Suiza** (Balneario de Huacachina 264, tel. 056/23-8762, www.hosteriasuiza.com.pe, US$50-70 s or d). The Baumgartner family, which ran the Hotel Mossone in its 1940s heyday, bought this house about eight years ago and converted it into a peaceful, friendly family hotel. The 22 rooms have comfortable beds, fans, and big baths, and some have views over the lake. Though the rooms aren't particularly luxurious, the pool outside, with its beach chairs surrounded by palm trees and purple blossoming flowers, is very nice, and this place runs like a fine-tuned Swiss watch. The staff can set you up with dune buggy riding.

The Old World ambience of **Hotel Mossone** (Balneario de Huacachina s/n, tel. 056/21-3630, Lima tel. 01/614-3900, www.dm-hoteles.pe, US$100 s or d) is the pride and joy of every Iqueño and, after years of neglect, is undergoing somewhat of a Renaissance. This grand hotel was one of the country's most famous resorts from the 1920s to the 1950s, when politicians and diplomats came here to relax on the elegant colonial porch overlooking the lake and sand dunes. Present management is restoring the hotel's fabulous grounds, which include a stone patio with huge ficus and *huarango* trees, a dining room and porch overlooking the lake, and an elegant pool across the street. The colonial rooms are simple, with high ceilings, air-conditioning, TVs, fridges, and bathtubs. Guests can use bicycles and sandboards free of charge. Lower rates can be found online.

US$100-150

Just north of Ica, the luxury hotel ★ **Las Dunas** (La Angostura 400, tel. 056/25-6224, Lima tel. 01/213-5000, www.lasdunashotel. com, US$140 s or d, higher on weekends) could easily be in Marrakech, with its sparkling white buildings and looming sand dunes overhead. Rooms are shaded and cool, with red tile floors and all the comforts of a three-star hotel, including TVs, fridges, phones, and fans. Las Dunas feels at times like an American theme park, with tennis, golf, volleyball, sandboarding, horseback riding, three pools with a 37-meter waterslide and a poolside bar, a playground, bicycles, a discotheque with karaoke, a game room, and even a small golf course. As such, it's a great place for kids. An extraordinary buffet of international and regional cuisine is served on an outdoor dining terrace. Horseback riding in the desert (US$11 per hour with a guide), a sauna with a massage (US$18), and the planetarium (US$5) all cost extra. The hotel offers a variety of packages that include lodging and tours to Paracas, Tambo Colorado, Ica wineries and churches, and overflights of the Nasca Lines.

Twenty minutes outside Ica is the **Hotel Viñas Queirolo** (San José de los Molinos s/n, tel. 056/25-4119, Lima tel. 01/205-7170, ext. 209, www.hotelvinasqueirolo.com, US$140 s or d), a relaxing spot surrounded by vineyards. The owners of Lima's popular Queirolo bodega, which dates back to the late-19th century, produce their wine and pisco here. The rooms have feather comforters, flat-screen TVs, satellite TV, and Wi-Fi. Each room has its own private patio. Guests are treated to an afternoon tour of the estate, which includes pisco and wine-tasting. Sip on pisco at the poolside bar.

INFORMATION AND SERVICES

The **tourist office** (Grau 148, tel. 056/22-7287, www.dirceturica.gob.pe, 8am-2:30pm Mon.-Fri.) is helpful, and the **tourist police** (tel. 056/22-7673) office is located on the fifth block of Elias.

The best hospital is **Felix Torre Alba** (Cutervo 104, tel. 056/23-4450, 24 hours daily), and there is also a clinic in the Angostura neighborhood. There are several pharmacies on Calle Municipalidad. **Boticas Arcángel** (tel. 056/22-8700) is the only 24-hour option.

Scotiabank, Continental, and **Banco de Crédito** are all on Plaza de Armas and at the Plaza del Sol mall. Most are open 9am-6pm Monday-Friday, morning only on Saturday; travelers checks can be exchanged at the Banco de Crédito.

The **post office** (tel. 056/23-3881, 8am-7pm Mon.-Sat.) is at San Martín 521, and the best Internet places are **Internet** (Municipalidad 247, 9am-11pm daily, US$0.75 per hour), **Cabin@sClub** (Grau 175, 9am-11pm daily, US$0.50 per hour), and the quiet **Internet Callao** (Callao 128, 8am-11pm daily). The best option for international calls is **Datel** (Municipalidad 132, Plaza de Armas), which has private phone booths and crystal-clear service to the United States (US$0.15 per minute). There are private phone booths in the **Telefónica** office on Lima, in the Plaza de Armas.

There are several laundry services along San Martín, but the best is **Laundry** (Chiclayo, block 5, 8am-1pm and 4pm-8pm daily).

GETTING THERE AND AROUND

There is no main bus station in Ica, but all of the main bus companies are clustered on the east end of town, a few blocks from the Plaza de Armas near the corner of Lambayeque and

Salaverry. The best option to and from Lima is **Cruz del Sur** (Fray Ramón Rojas and Seba, tel. 056/72-0444, www.cruzdelsur.com.pe). It has several trips to Lima (about US$15) every day, and daily trips to Arequipa.

Soyuz (Matias Manzanilla 130, near Lambayeque, tel. 056/22-4138, www.soyuzonline.com.pe), has comfortable buses leaving every 15 minutes for as little as US$10, although nicer buses cost more. The four-hour trip includes stops out of Pisco (with a shuttle to the town center), Chincha, and Cañete. Another option for Arequipa and Nasca is **Flores** (Lambayeque and Salaverry 396, www.floreshnos.pe).

Ica is swimming with taxis, but for trips to the wineries or Lago Huacachina, it is best to go with a driver recommended by your hotel. Reliable **Taxi Ya** (tel. 056/23-5361) charges US$3 from central Ica to Huacachina.

Nasca

Nasca would be just another dusty highway town were it not for the enigmatic lines in the desert, which have tormented scientists ever since they were spotted by planes in the 1920s. When seen from above, the stylized forms of hummingbirds, a killer whale, a monkey, and other animals sprawl across the desert floor, surrounded by a maze of trapezoids and geometric figures and lines that recede to the horizon. The lines are so bizarre that many people, spearheaded by Danish eccentric character Erich von Däniken, believed they are landing strips for extraterrestrials. That theory has somewhat faded, along with a dozen others, but the mystery of the Nasca Lines remains.

Despite the desolate surroundings, advanced cultures have occupied the Río Nasca Valley since the Paracas culture (800-200 BC), which probably made the area's first hillside etchings around 400 BC. They also began work on Cahuachi, a huge complex of pyramids 28 kilometers northwest of Nasca. The Nasca culture (AD 100-600) continued building Cahuachi and also built an ingenious aqueduct that pipes water under the desert floor and is still used by farmers today. The Nasca are world-famous for ceramics and, along with the Paracas, weavings; excellent examples of both can be seen at the town's Museo Antonini. After the Nasca, the area fell under the successive influences of the Huari, Chincha, and Inca. A small Spanish settlement was founded here in 1591 but has been destroyed so often by earthquakes—most recently in 1942 and 1996—that no colonial architecture remains.

Nasca today is a noisy hodgepodge of concrete buildings. The best places to stay, both budget and high-end, are in the surrounding countryside. Nasca has a particularly aggressive culture of *jaladores* (salespeople) that swarm visitors when they get off the bus. The city's tourism commission has passed laws making it illegal to sell tourist services on the street, because many travelers have been ripped off, or become ticked off, by this town's informal tourism racket.

SIGHTS

TOP EXPERIENCE

★ Nasca Lines

The Spanish chronicler Pedro Cieza de León was the first European to comment on the hillside drawings that can be seen from ground level near Nasca and Paracas. Archaeologists had also studied similar hill drawings in Arequipa, Lima, Trujillo, and the mountains of Bolivia and Chile. But the profusion of lines etched onto the perfectly flat San José desert are the continent's fullest expression of this cryptic practice and were not fully appreciated until the first planes flew over the area in the 1920s. When viewed from

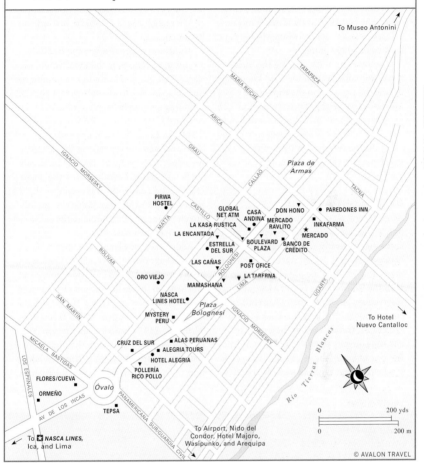

Nasca City

To Museo Antonini

Plaza de Armas

PIRWA HOSTEL

GLOBAL NET ATM
CASA ANDINA
DON HONO
PAREDONES INN

LA KASA RUSTICA
MERCADO RAVLITO
INKAFARMA

LA ENCANTADA
MERCADO

ESTRELLA DEL SUR
BOULEVARD PLAZA
BANCO DE CRÉDITO

LAS CAÑAS
POST OFICE

ORO VIEJO
LA TABERNA

MAMASHAÑA

NASCA LINES HOTEL

MYSTERY PERU
Plaza Bolognesi

CRUZ DEL SUR
ALAS PERUANAS

ALEGRIA TOURS

HOTEL ALEGRIA

POLLERÍA RICO POLLO

FLORES/CUEVA

ORMEÑO

Óvalo

TEPSA

To Hotel Nuevo Cantalloc

To ✈ NASCA LINES, Ica, and Lima

To Airport, Nido del Condor, Hotel Majoro, Wasipunko, and Arequipa

Río Tierras Blancas

0		200 yds
0		200 m

© AVALON TRAVEL

above, more than 70 giant plant and animal figures pop into view, etched impermeably onto the desert floor, along with hundreds of straight lines, trapezoids, and other figures as long as 10 kilometers. The shapes cover an astonishing 1,000 square kilometers, including a cluster of drawings farther north near Palpa.

The shapes are so visible thanks to the area's peculiar geography. A thin layer of manganese and iron oxides, called desert varnish, covers the rocky surface of the San

José desert. The Nasca people removed the dark rocks to expose the lighter-colored rocks beneath, in canals that average about 20 centimeters deep. They piled the rocks into walls about one meter high to enhance the canal's edge. The Nasca probably made the drawings in small scale and then used ropes and stakes to reproduce them larger on the desert floor.

The best way to see them is by airplane. Pilots bank sharply so that people on both sides of the plane can see the lines, and as a result, many people end up clutching barf bags.

Even those with a stomach of steel should avoid breakfast before flying and consider taking motion sickness medication beforehand. The best time to fly is in the morning before winds pick up, decreasing visibility and making the flight bumpier.

Another option for viewing the lines is a three-story observation tower 19 kilometers north of Nasca and on the way to the Casa-Museo Maria Reiche. Three small lines can be seen from here, including a set of hands, a lizard, and a tree. A few hillsides offer good views during the clearest light of the morning, especially the giant sand dune of Cerro Blanco.

OVERFLIGHT AGENCIES

After recent plane crashes over the lines, only a few companies can thoroughly guarantee flights. Nearly a dozen companies offer Nasca overflights, which start at US$80-150, depending on the time of year. Prices go up with the length of the flight. Make advance reservations June to August, when entire days can be booked by gigantic package tours. Otherwise, travelers get the best price by negotiating directly at the overflight companies. But be cautious if the price sounds too good. It is better to pay a little more with a reputable

company than to risk your safety. If you are uneasy about flying but would still like to see the lines, there is an observation tower about 20 kilometers north of Nasca, just off the Panamericana.

While every agency offers the traditional 30-minute flight over the most enigmatic Nasca Lines, it is increasingly common to find companies that offers alternative flights, including taking a helicopter rather than the standard Cessna planes. Preferential overflights, for example, last longer and see more lines, and there are flights over the Cantayoc Aqueduct or Palpa Lines. Even if you decide not to take one of these alternative flights, we recommend combining a typical overflight with a visit to the sites. This will greatly broaden your understanding of the cultures that created the lines.

Additionally, the largest agencies in Nasca have package deals that combine flights with hotel accommodations or daylong tours and lunch. Ask if the agency includes in its prices the US$10 airport tax. One of these agencies is the reputable **Alegría Tours** (Lima 166, tel. 056/52-2497, www.alegriatoursperu.com, US$100), which works with the highly professional **Alas Peruanas** airline. In addition to its standard flight over the lines, it

the Nasca Lines

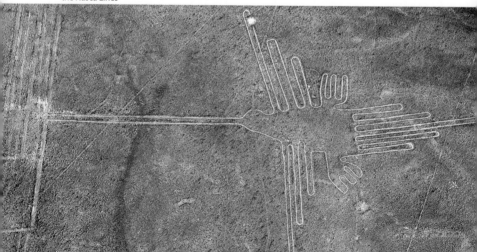

From UFO Landing Strips to Rain Ceremonies

The Nasca Lines first caught the world's attention in 1939, when American archaeologist Paul Kosok splashed their pictures across world newspapers. His translator, German mathematician Maria Reiche, was so intrigued that she moved to Nasca a year later and spent the next six decades measuring the lines under the desert sun. By the time she died in 1998, she had developed an elaborate theory to support Kosok's claim that the lines were "the biggest astronomy book in the world." She became a much-loved and venerated personality in Nasca, where her birthday remains the town's biggest celebration.

Many other researchers have come up with theories that range from clever to crackpot. In 1947 Hans Horkheimer said they were indigenous cultural symbols, while George Von Breunig likened them to a giant running track in 1980, and Henri Stirlin claimed a few years later they represented huge yarn weavings. The theory that struck the public imagination was proposed in Erich von Däniken's book and movie *Chariots of the Gods*. He claimed the pampa was a giant landing strip for extraterrestrials and that one of the drawings, which shows a snowman figure with large round eyes, was an astronaut.

Today, an emerging consensus suggests the lines are about water. Water runs from the mountains to the narrow southern valleys only during the rainy season. During a dry year, the Río Nasca may never even reach the town, much less the ocean. Because drought meant death, Nasca cosmography—as evidenced by their ceramics, textiles, and ceremonial architecture—is shaped by religious practices to ensure a steady supply of water.

The first drawings (400 BC) were spirals, a water symbol that recurs throughout South America. These later morphed into sea creatures like sharks and whales. Giuseppe Orefici, who has led excavations around Nasca since the early 1980s, says the later phase of bird images is also water-related. The hummingbirds that suck life-giving nectar from flowers are fertility symbols, he says; their wings are sacred dispensers of water. After studying lines in Chile and Bolivia, Johan Reinhard concluded all of them are part of a pan-Andean fertility tradition. This agrees with the theory of the first Nasca researcher, Peruvian Toribio Mejía Xesspe, who argued that the lines were sacred paths walked for magical ceremonies.

There are aspects of the lines that have not been fully understood, though they all seem to involve water-producing cosmic forces. Many of the lines point at sacred mountains, or *apus*, or at points on the horizon that mark important lunar or solar events. One leads to Cahuachi, the ceremonial complex of pyramids that faces the lines and is located on a sacred spot along the Río Nasca. Whatever relationship the pyramids had with the lines, archaeologists believe it too probably had to do with water.

also offers a two-day tour that adds a trip to Ica for sandboarding and a visit to the Islas Ballestas and Reserva Nacional de Paracas. **Mystery Peru** (Simón Bolívar 221, cell tel. 956-691-155, www.mysteryperu.com) offers a number of tours for a range of prices. The traditional 30-minute flight costs US$130, while an extended flight that includes Palpa runs US$250. For about double the price you can do a flyover in a helicopter. For those short on time, Mystery also offers one-day tours from Lima. **Great Nazca Tours** (Bisambra 255, tel. 056/52-3100, www.

greatnazcatours.com) can organize the classic flight over the Nasca Lines for US$100, as well as separate visits to the Cantayoc aqueducts and the Chauchilla cemetery, with mummified human remains.

Reputable airplane companies that you can contact directly for the classic half-hour or extended overflights are **Alas Peruanas** (Lima 168, tel. 056/52-2497, www.alasperuanas.com), **AeroParacas** (tel. 056/52-2688, Lima tel. 01/641-7000, www.aeroparacas.com), and **AeroDiana** (Lima tel. 01/447-6824, www.aerodiana.com.pe).

Museo Antonini

The **Museo Antonini** (Av. de la Cultura 600, tel. 056/52-3444, 9am-7pm daily, US$5) is the labor of love of Giuseppe Orefici, whose excavations at Cahuachi have been funded by the Italian government. This museum has a small but exquisite collection that sheds light on the Nasca's religious way of thinking, including a ceremonial fishing net with embroidered crimson edges and a cotton coat fringed with supernatural dolls that look like tiny cactus-like beings.

Other Nasca ceramics here portray a pantheon of seafaring creatures, pelicans, cats, birds, lizards, and snakes. These deities often have serpentine shapes emerging from their mouths, which archaeologists believe reflect the Nasca belief that blessings come from the nose and mouth. There are also elongated skulls, others with trepanation holes, and a few well-preserved mummies. Out back is a replication of a Nasca tomb, a Nasca irrigation canal, and a scale model of the Nasca Lines. Orefici has a spectacular collection of painted textiles that he hopes to put on display in the future.

Casa-Museo Maria Reiche

During much of her six decades living in Nasca, German mathematician Maria Reiche lived in a simple room in the village of Pascana, about 27 kilometers south of Nasca. When she died in 1998 at the age of 95, she was buried here, and her home was converted into the **Casa-Museo Maria Reiche** (Panamericana, Km 420, tel. 056/23-4383, 9am-6pm daily, US$2). The place now pays tribute to Reiche's life and her theories about the Nasca Lines. Another way to understand her theories is at the evening planetarium show of the Nazca Lines Hotel, but travelers complain of the high prices and lack of substance in the presentation.

Cantayoc Aqueducts and Paredones

Faced with droughts and famine, the Nasca people came up with a brilliant engineering solution around AD 300-500 to guarantee year-round water. They went to the mountains where water gurgles out of the rock and built underground aqueducts, called *puquios,* to carry this water under the desert floor. These aqueducts are an engineering marvel of pre-Columbian America and are still used today.

Some archaeologists believe the canals were originally exposed but became buried after a series of *aluviones* or muddy flash floods. The

the Cantayoc aqueducts

canals can be accessed by periodic *respidores* or spiral ramps that lead down to an exposed section of the canal. During the dry months of September to December, local farmers crawl through the tunnels between *respidores* to clean the canals, which are S-shaped to slow the flow of water during the rainy months. Today 36 of these ancient aqueducts irrigate Nasca's fields, though archaeologists believe that many others exist under the desert floor.

The aqueducts are four kilometers southwest of town near the Hotel Cantayo and reachable via taxi (US$5) or transportation that runs along the nearby Abancay highway. Guards are now charging a US$4 entrance fee, which includes two other nearby sites: the Inca ruins of Paredones, a deteriorated *tambo,* or resting place, made of adobe walls atop stone foundations; and two of the Nasca Lines, known as El Telar and Las Agujas (The Weaving and The Needles). This area is safe to walk around until the guards go home at 4:30pm.

Cahuachi

Excavations at Cahuachi, an area of low-lying hills 28 kilometers northwest of Nasca, are gradually revealing a city that, at 24 square kilometers, was even bigger than the northern Chimú city of Chan Chan. Unlike Chan Chan, however, there is no evidence of homes or food production nearby. Giuseppe Orefici, who has been excavating Cahuachi since 1985, believes the area's 40-odd pyramids were used for public ceremonies to thank the gods for water. The whole complex faces the Nasca Lines and was built on a sacred spot where the Río Nasca reemerges from under the desert floor.

Like the adobe pyramids of the Moche and Sicán in Peru's north, the Nasca pyramids are huge—the Great Pyramid is 25 meters high and 100 meters long. Orefici's team has worked to restore its elaborate north facade. These pyramids are not solid adobe, but rather a cap of adobe bricks over the existing hill. Cahuachi was built in five main phases between 400 BC and AD 400, when it was abandoned because of flooding. The site has been looted by grave robbers, but Orefici's teams have found tombs full of painted Nasca textiles. There is no public transportation to the site, though more and more agencies are including this site in their day tours. A round-trip taxi from Nasca, including the driver's waiting time, costs US$15, and the trip takes 40 minutes each way.

Cementerio de Chauchilla

Nasca agencies frequently visit this graveyard from the Chincha period (1000-1460), but more than anything it is a bleak reminder of the destructive force of grave robbers. Thousands of scraps of textiles, bones, and patches of human hair lay spread across the sands. A few of the clay tombs have been restored, and bleached skeletons, with huge dreadlocks, are on display inside. At other cemeteries, like the one near Lomas, locals have used bulldozers to unearth their ancestors, leaving skulls strewn across the sand. The cemetery is about eight kilometers off the Panamericana south of Nasca, or about 30 minutes' drive. There is no public transportation to the site, although agencies visit here frequently, and a round-trip taxi from Nasca costs US$17.

ENTERTAINMENT AND EVENTS

Discos get cranked up in Nasca only on the weekends. **Las Cañas** (Bolognesi 279, tel. 056/80-6891, 8am-8pm daily) is a restaurant that transforms into a discotheque after 9pm on weekends. If you are looking for a mellow environment, **Boulevard Plaza** (Bolognesi 388, tel. 056/52-3749, 2:30pm-1am daily, US$4-7) has a long cocktail list and a good selection of accompanying appetizers.

The biggest party in Nasca is **Fiesta Yacu Raymi,** which kicks off with Maria Reiche's birthday on May 15 and includes dances, *pachamancas,* and other celebrations. Religious holidays include the **Virgen del Carmen** on September 19 and the **Virgen de Guadalupe,** patroness of Nasca, on October 8. During the low-water months from

September to December, communities gather in the fields to clean the ancient aqueducts.

RECREATION
Trekking

Local trekking guide **Edmundo Watkin** (Wasipunko, Km 462, tel. 056/63-1183, www.waskipunko.com) has put together a range of interesting hikes, including an eight-hour jaunt from the altiplano to the summit of Cerro Blanco, one of the world's largest sand dunes, which rises 2,000 meters over the valley floor and offers good views of the Nasca Lines. He also has an interesting three-day package that includes an overflight of the Nasca Lines, a walking tour around the Cementerio de Chauchilla, and a full day of cultural tourism in a farming community near the former hacienda of the Benavides family. Although Edmundo speaks only Spanish, his brother Alan speaks English. Between the two, they can help you figure out travel plans.

Sandboarding

Alegría Tours (Lima 168, tel. 056/52-2497, www.alegriatoursperu.com) offers sandboarding on Cerro Blanco (6 hours, US$40 pp) or a four-hour cycling trip (US$20 pp) that drops 2,000 vertical meters in 45 kilometers and whizzes past Cerro Blanco.

Tour Agencies and Guides

The agencies that organize Nasca overflights, including **Alegría Tours** (Lima 168, tel. 056/52-2444, www.alegriatoursperu.com), can also arrange conventional day tours, which combine visits to the Museo Antonini, the aqueducts, and Cahuachi with a buffet lunch. **Mystery Peru** (Simón Bolívar 221, cell tel. 956-691-155, www.mysteryperu.com) is an alternate option whose tours include a bit more adventure.

FOOD
Peruvian

La Kañada (Lima 160, tel. 056/52-2457, 7am-10pm daily, US$5-6) has been operated by the

Puerto Inca

The nicest place to stop on the seven-hour drive between Nasca and Arequipa is the half-moon beach of Puerto Inca, at Km 603, 10 kilometers south of Chala. The Inca had a settlement here, where fish were caught for the Inca and carried up to Cusco along Inca roads that can still be seen receding into the mountains. Today, what's left is an area of ruins with other smaller ruins nearby—including a strange carved seat on a rocky cliff to the south. Located scandalously close to the ruins, **Hotel Puerto Inka** (Panamericana Sur, Km 610, tel. 054/69-2596 or 054/25-5732, www.puertoinka.com.pe, US$43 s, US$68 d, with breakfast) has the beach all to itself, and all rooms have ocean views. Amenities include a video library, a pool table, a discotheque with karaoke, a swimming pool, and a playground; camping with showers costs US$5 pp. The hotel rents kayaks (US$5 per hour) and Jet Skis (US$20 per hour).

Benavides family for over 40 years and serves excellent ostrich, vegetarian, and seafood dishes such as sea bass with prawns from the Río Palpa. There is live folkloric music at 8pm most nights. **La Kasa Rustica** (Bolognesi 372, tel. 056/32-4463, www.lakasarustica.com.pe, 11:30am-11pm Mon., 7am-11pm Tues.-Sun., US$7-10) has a big menu, with Peruvian classics like *causa,* ceviche, and *tacu tacu* with *lomo saltado.* It also offers lasagna and its specialty, pepper steak.

Located on a quiet street, **La Encantada** (Bolognesi 282, tel. 056/52-4216, www.hotellaencantada.com.pe, 7:30am-11pm daily, US$3-8) also serves up Peruvian fare like ceviche, *salpicón de pollo,* and *camarones.* There are also pizza and pasta dishes. Down the block, **Mamashana Restaurant** (Bolognesi 270, tel. 056/52-1286, 8am-11:30pm daily, US$5-8), gets good reviews for its fresh seafood and desserts. For *pollo a la brasa,* head over to **Polleria Rico Pollo** (Lima 190, tel. 056/52-1151, noon-1am daily,

US$4-6). It serves up juicy browned chicken with piping hot fries.

International

Looking at its graffiti-covered walls, it's easy to believe that **La Taberna** (Lima 321, tel. 056/52-3803, 11am-10pm daily, US$4-6) has been around for more than 20 years. The clean kitchen dishes up a wide-ranging menu that includes salads, pastas, and local favorites such as *lomo saltado* and *arroz con mariscos.*

Markets

The *mercado central* is between Grau and Arica. **Mercado Ravlito** (Grau 245, 8am-10pm daily) is the best-stocked grocery store.

ACCOMMODATIONS
Under US$10

A good option for a clean backpacker place is **Nasca Lodge** (El Acero Mz. B, Lote 7, tel. 056/52-4120), located three blocks from the main plaza. The white-tiled rooms have private baths, while the hostel also has Wi-Fi and a travel desk to help with tours. Get a bed (US$8) in a four-person dorm room, or a private single room (US$17). If you are arriving at night, take a taxi to the hostel. There is great camping with showers at **Wasipunko** (Panamericana Sur, Km 462, tel. 056/52-3212, www.wasipunko.com, US$5 pp).

US$10-25

The **Estrellita del Sur** (Callao 568, tel. 056/52-2764, US$15 s, US$22 d, with breakfast) is on a quiet street three blocks from the Plaza and across from the hospital. We liked this place because it was clean, fresh-smelling, and friendly, and it had big rooms with closets, cable TV, and fair baths; some rooms even have a porch.

US$25-50

The family-run **Wasipunko** (Panamericana Sur Km 462, tel. 056/63-1183, www.wasipunko.com, US$25 s, US$50 d, with breakfast), owned by Olivia Watkin, is a rustic country hostel 12 kilometers south of Nasca in a paradise of palms, acacia, and *huarango* trees that are scented by jacaranda blooms and filled with birds. The simple rooms have whitewashed adobe walls, bamboo roofs, antique furniture, clean baths, and Olivia's own watercolors of local plants. The dining room is an adobe structure with large *huarango* beams, stained glass, and a telescope for stargazing. This is a great place to hang out for a day or two, hop aboard a horse, and relax.

The charming **Oro Viejo** (Callao 483, tel. 056/52-2284, www.hoteloroviejo.net, US$40 s, US$54 d, with breakfast) is a family-run place a few blocks from the plaza but away from the noise. Rooms, arranged around a flower garden, have nice furniture, big baths, and fans. There is an outdoor bar and swimming pool. The tables in the indoor dining room are lit with candles.

The **Pirwa Hostel** (Juan Matta 611, Cusco: tel. 084/24-4315, www.pirwahostels-cusco.com, US$35 s or d, with breakfast) has 12 hotels across Peru and Bolivia, including this one in Nasca. The hotel has large rooms with private baths as well as a small garden, Wi-Fi, and a computer that guests can use. The staff is friendly and can help with travel suggestions and tours. It also has what every backpacker wants after time on the road: laundry.

US$50-100

The major agencies own hotels that are typically bundled together in the overflight packages. The best option among these agency-owned hotels is the one run by Alegría Tours, **Hotel Alegría** (Lima 166, tel. 056/52-2702, www.hotelalegria.net, US$60 s or d), in a modern building near the bus station with lots of light and a nice pool. The rooms are large and there is laundry service, a book exchange, and a cafeteria in a grassy backyard. It is centrally located, so there can be street noise.

Casa Andina (Bolognesi 367, tel. 056/52-3563, www.casa-andina.com, US$70 s or d, with breakfast when booking online), part of the national hotel chain, has an ideal location on the Bolognesi pedestrian mall. The modern rooms open onto a sunny bougainvillea-lined patio, and a small circular pool is an essential stop after a morning of sightseeing. Be sure to book online, where you can get significantly lower rates. As always, the staff is friendly and can help you plan your sightseeing.

US$100-150

Hotel Majoro (Panamericana Sur, Km 453, tel. 056/52-2490, www.hotelmajoro.com, US$100 s or d, with breakfast) is a charming country hotel whose gardens spill into pools, tennis courts, and horse corrals. The 40 comfortable, cool rooms with high ceilings have recently been remodeled. There are two nice pools, which have bougainvillea-covered rock islands shaded by fruit trees and gardens.

A good hotel in the city itself is **Nazca Lines Hotel** (Bolognesi 147, tel. 056/52-2293, www.dmhoteles.pe, US$100 s, US$110 d, with breakfast). Whitewashed arcades wrap around a luxurious patio with two pools, fountains, and tables shaded with palm trees and bougainvillea. The rooms are tastefully decorated with *sautillo* tile floors, cable TV, and baths with tubs. The restaurant (6am-10:30pm daily, US$6-9) serves excellent food in the breezy dining room.

The **Hotel Nuevo Cantalloc** (Hacienda Cantayo s/n, tel. 056/52-2264, www.hotel-nuevocantalloc.com, US$110 s, US$160 d, with breakfast) is located outside Nasca. The hotel is a good choice for a relaxing stay. From the ruins of a hacienda, the owners have saved the original archways, floor tiles, a well, and a centuries-old ficus tree. Songbirds flit around the lawn, where the huge ficus tree rises alongside two elegantly shaped pools. Other amenities include a whirlpool tub, massages (US$50 per hour),

a library, and a piano bar. The large rooms come with flat-screen TVs, mini fridges, comfortable baths with tubs, and remote-controlled air-conditioning.

INFORMATION AND SERVICES

Maps are available at the **tourist office** at Parque Bolognesi. The **police station** (Los Incas, block 1, tel. 056/52-2442) is on the highway just outside the center.

For medical issues, there is Nasca's **Hospital de Apoyo** (tel. 056/52-2010, emergency tel. 056/52-2586) on the fourth block of Callao, which is open 24 hours daily. The largest pharmacy is **Inkafarma** (Lima 596, tel. 056/52-3065, www.inkafarma.com.pe, 7:30am-11pm daily), and a smaller option is **Boticas Universitarias** (Bolognesi and Grau).

For money matters, Interbank (Bolognesi 590) and **Banco de Crédito** (Lima and Grau) both have ATMs. There is a **Global Net** ATM next to Casa Andina. Banks are generally open 9am-6pm Monday-Friday and Saturday morning.

The **post office** (Fermín del Castillo 379, tel. 056/52-2016, 9am-5pm Mon.-Fri.) is between Bolognesi and Lima. There are several Internet cafés with speedy connections; the most convenient way of finding these is by asking at your hotel which café is closest.

GETTING THERE AND AROUND

There are no flights to Nasca. All of Nasca's bus companies are congregated around the traffic circle at the end of Lima, where the Panamericana skirts around town. The bus trip between Lima and Nasca is seven to eight hours. **Ormeño** (Av. de los Incas 112, tel. 056/52-2058, www.grupo-ormeno.com.pe) has Royal Class and economy buses to Lima. **Cruz del Sur** (Lima and San Martín, tel. 056/72-0440, www.cruzdelsur.com.pe) buses to and from Lima stop in Ica, Pisco, and

Paracas. Cheaper, less direct buses are available through **Flores** (Av. los Incas 120, tel. 056/66-7202, www.floreshnos.net) or **Cueva** (Av. los Incas 108, tel. 056/52-2526), whose buses between Nasca and Ica leave approximately every 30 minutes.

Because of highway improvements, buses now travel between Lima and Cusco in 20 hours and turn toward the mountains at Nasca. In 14 hours, the highway that leads uphill from Nasca passes the Reserva Nacional Pampa, crests over the Andes at 4,400 meters elevation, and reaches Abancay before heading on to Cusco. Ormeño and Cruz del Sur travel this route. Cruz del Sur also runs Arequipa buses (9 hours).

Colectivos travel the Ica-Nasca route (US$5 pp) in two hours flat. There are unfortunately no large taxi companies in Nasca; ask your hotel to recommend a taxi.

Ayacucho and the Cordillera Blanca

This part of Peru abounds with gems, from the stunning colonial city of Ayacucho to the picture-perfect peaks of the Cordillera Blanca.

Ayacucho remains one of the least visited of Peru's Andean cities. There are 33 colonial churches in Ayacucho, a huge amount of colonial art, colorful markets, artisans' studios on every corner, and one of Latin America's most famous Semana Santa (Easter Week) celebrations.

Huancayo, farther north, is equally interesting, but for its countryside, not its city. There are a dozen or more quaint adobe villages in the surrounding Mantaro Valley where artisans make a living by carving gourds or making weavings from alpaca wool and natural dyes. There are more traditional festivals here than anywhere else in Peru, and outsiders are welcome; after such bitter years, they are overjoyed to have guests.

For outdoors enthusiasts, the Cordillera Blanca is a favorite for its jagged peaks and crystalline glaciers. The highest mountain range in the world outside the Himalayas, the Cordillera Blanca's extravagant collection of jagged pyramids, glacier domes, and knife-edge ridges runs north-south for 180 kilometers but is only 20 kilometers wide. The Cordillera Blanca contains 34 peaks over 6,000 meters, including the world-famous snow pyramids of Artesonraju, Chopicalqui, and Tocllaraju. Some of the peaks, such as Pisco and Ishinca, are accessible to first-time climbers with experienced guides, and there are even a few gentler trekker peaks, such as Urus and Maparaju. The area's most postcard-perfect peak is Alpamayo, at 5,947 meters, which lures climbers to its 70-degree face. The mountain that dominates the entire valley, however, is Huascarán. At 6,768 meters, Huascarán looms over Huaraz much like Mont Blanc towers over Chamonix, France.

To its west lies the Cordillera Negra, a humble, snowless range that reaches 5,200 meters before fading at the coast. Between the two ranges is the Río Santa Valley, also known as the Callejón de Huaylas. The highway from the coast drops into this valley near Huaraz, at the top of the valley, and leads through a string of villages before reaching the city of Caraz. At this point, the Río Santa

---

Previous: Semana Santa in Ayacucho; camping in the Cordillera Huayhuash. **Above:** *Puya raimondii*, Peru's most famous highland plant.

Look for ★ to find recommended
sights, activities, dining, and lodging.

Highlights

★ **Festival de Apóstol Santiago:** This July 25 festival features dancing and a ritualistic branding of cattle that blurs Christian and pre-Hispanic religious beliefs (page 345).

★ **Ayacucho City Tour:** The streets of this hidden jewel include Renaissance and baroque churches and the friendliest and most interesting market in Peru (page 351).

★ **Huari:** Exploring the countryside around Ayacucho leads to the ruins of Huari, the empire that made the Inca possible. Just 15 kilometers up the road, you'll find Quinua, a charming adobe village known for its red-clay ceramics (page 355).

★ **Barrio Santa Ana:** The winding streets of this charming Ayacucho neighborhood are lined with stone carvers and rug weavers and graced with Iglesia Santa Ana de los Indios, a simple baroque church with an embossed silver altar (page 359).

★ **Chavín de Huántar:** Built more than 2,000 years before the Inca, this center of the Chavín culture includes underground tunnels that lead to the Lanzón, a carved rock pillar (page 377).

★ **Cordillera Blanca:** Two days is enough time for a quick jaunt through the mountain range and its corresponding Parque Nacional Huascarán, which includes Peru's tallest peak (page 385).

★ **Cordillera Huayhuash:** Spend two weeks circumnavigating this stunning range with some of the finest mountain scenery on earth (page 388).

★ **Cordillera Negra:** This often overlooked range, just west of the Cordillera Blanca, offers challenging mountain bike routes with panoramas of glaciers and snow peaks (page 389).

Ayacucho and the Cordillera Blanca

Map labels:
Cajamarca, Celendín, Juanjuí, Bellavista, Río Huallaga, Zona Reservada Sierra del Divisor, Cruzeiro do Sul, GRAN PAJATEN, Parque Nacional Cordillera Azul, Pacasmayo, Casa Grande, Huamachuco, PN Río Abiseo, Tocache, Río Ucayali, 15 de Noviembre, Trujillo, Pucallpa, BRAZIL, Reserva Nacional de Calipuy, CORDILLERA BLANCA, PN Tingo María, Aucayacu, Chimbote, Caraz, Huaycabamba, Tingo María, Puerto Inca, PERU, Casma, Huaraz, CHAVÍN DE HUÁNTAR, Huánuco, Pozuzo, CORDILLERA NEGRA, PN Huascarán, Parque Nacional Alto Purús, CORDILLERA HUAYHUASH, Cerro de Pasco, Parque Nacional de Yanachaga, Paramonga, Barranca, Reserva Nacional de Junín, La Merced, Atalaya, Parque Nacional Otisi, Huacho, RN Lachay, Sayán, Lago de Junín, Satipo, Huaral, MARCAHUASI, Tarma, Parque Nacional Otisi, LIMA, FESTIVAL DE APÓSTOL SANTIAGO, Callao, Huancayo, PACHACAMAC, HUARI, Koshireni, AYACUCHO CITY TOUR BARRIO SANTA ANA, Santa Rosa, ESPÍRITU PAMPA, INCAWASI, Ayacucho, Quillabamba, MACHU PICCHU, Chincha, CHOQUEQUIRAO, Pisco, HUAYTARÁ, CUSCO, Abancay, TAMBO COLORADO, Ica, Reserva Nacional Paracas, Santo Tomás, Nasca, PACIFIC OCEAN

0 — 100 mi
0 — 100 km

© AVALON TRAVEL

jags toward the coast, and the road somehow follows it, through a spectacularly steep canyon known as the Cañón del Pato. Besides trekking and climbing around Huaraz, there are plenty of other adventure sports, including mountain-bike circuits and rafting down the Rio Santa.

But there's more to do. This area of Peru gave birth to one to the first advanced cultures of the Andes, the Chavín. The carved stone capital of the 9,000-year-old empire, Chavín de Huántar, can be visited from Huaraz in a day, or overnight, and is worth a look. Right outside Huaraz are also the Wari ruins of Wilcawaín.

PLANNING YOUR TIME

Reaching the central highlands can be done via plane, train, or automobile. Lima is the starting point to visit Ayacucho, south of the capital, Huancayo to the east, and Huaraz to the north.

Most travelers arrive to Ayacucho, the most interesting town in the central highlands, and in Peru's Andes, via bus from Lima, a comfortable 10-hour journey on paved roads. From here, you can continue on to Andahuaylas, and then Abancay and Cusco (10 hours) to the south. Plan on spending at least three days in Ayacucho.

Huancayo is reached by heading east from Lima for about 300 kilometers on the country's busy central highway. The Lima-Huancayo railroad, billed as the second highest in the world, is another option, but its schedule is much reduced, and the scenic trip takes almost twice as long. An increasing number of travelers are also making a direct trip overland from Ayacucho to Huancayo (8-10 hours).

Reaching Huaraz and the Cordillera Blanca, which is not easily integrated into Peru's other major travel circuits, requires departing Lima heading north. For outdoors enthusiasts, the traditional climbing and trekking season runs May to August, but the best weather and snow are in June and July. Ascents, however, can be made during the sometimes-sunny climate of September. And if you happen to hit Huaraz during low season (Sept.-Apr.), you can enjoy a series of day hikes, deep green landscapes colored by the afternoon rains, and cheaper prices.

If you are short on time or aren't keen on long bus trips, there are daily flights to Ayacucho, Huaraz, and Jauja, near Huancayo.

Lima to Tarma

If you want a crash course in Peruvian geography, take a bus up the Carretera Central, the well-paved highway that connects Lima with the interior of the country. Even on the foggiest of Lima's winter days, blue skies and sun can usually be found after less than an hour's drive inland to the towns of Chaclacayo, Chosica, and Santa Eulalia. From here the Carretera Central follows the Río Rímac through the subtropical valleys outside Lima, sheer rock canyons, desolate expanses of puna (high plains), and down into the rainforest on the other side.

This trip is not for the fainthearted: In two hours, or 126 kilometers, travelers head from sea level to the town of Ticlio and the Anticona Pass, at 4,820 meters elevation. One of Peru's greatest engineering achievements was building a railroad over this pass. When traveling this route, bring warm clothing and water, and travel quickly to avoid headaches, nausea, crabbiness, and the other effects of altitude sickness.

After passing snowcapped Nevado Anticona and Lago Huacracocha, the route drops through striking pea-green puna and a string of grimy mountain towns that end with

La Oroya, an industrial rust heap hemmed in by bare hillsides. The river that runs through it is choked with foundry runoff and crossed by a series of concrete bridges, over which miners with plastic helmets and sooty faces trudge to and from their shifts.

At La Oroya the highway branches toward two Lima weekend spots, both of which are about two hours' drive away: to the south lies the highland countryside around Huancayo; to the east lie the towns of La Merced and San Ramón, or Chanchamayo, as they are collectively known.

The Chanchamayo road winds gently to **Tarma,** a colonial city at 925 meters elevation that is famous in Peru for its Easter celebration. Past Tarma the road plunges another 2,300 meters to Chanchamayo, a fertile region for growing coffee, yuca, and bananas.

A third route to the north leads past Junín, a battlefield from Peru's war for independence, Tingo María, and the low-rainforest city of Pucallpa.

TARMA

Tarma is the first decent lodging option on the long haul between Lima and Chanchamayo, and strolling townspeople crowd the streets in the evening, a warming sight after the barren landscape of the puna above. Because of its chilly weather and elevation (925 meters), people coming from Lima occasionally feel altitude sickness here.

Tarma was founded by the Spanish soon after the conquest, though narrow streets and a handful of old homes are the only clues to its colonial pedigree. There are two churches on the main square that are worth a visit. **La Capilla del Señor de la Cárcel** (Chapel of the Lord of the Prison) was built in 1800 and remodeled in 1954 by General Manuel Odría, Tarma's most famous son and a Peruvian dictator during the 1930s. Across the Plaza de Armas is **Catedral de Santa Ana** (7am-9am and 5pm-7pm daily), also built by Odría.

What Tarma is most known for, however, is incredible festivals, starting with elaborate processions, singing contests, and water balloon-throwing during February's **Carnaval.** During Tarma's **Semana Santa,** the week before Easter, millions of flowers and seeds are carefully arranged on and around the Plaza de Armas. The resulting flower carpet—depicting everything from landscapes to religious images—sets a new world record every year, covering every inch of street in an eight-block area around the main square, an estimated 3,400 square meters. At 5am on Easter Sunday, a religious procession walks over the carpet and through a number of decorated wooden arches on its way to and from the cathedral.

Other nearby attractions include **Tarmatambo,** a collection of Inca ruins nine kilometers south of Tarma. The **Santuario del Señor de Muruhuay** is a huge white modern church with an electric bell tower, visible from the highway nine kilometers east of Tarma at **Acobamba.** This is only the latest building to cover a rock carving of Christ reputed to have miraculous properties. Tradition maintains that it was etched on a boulder by a survivor of the Junín independence battle of August 6, 1824.

There is world-class **caving** near Palcamayo, 23 kilometers north of Acobamba along a dirt road. This town is the launching point for exploring one of Latin America's largest caves, the **Gruta de Huagapo.** Cavers using scuba equipment and oxygen tanks have descended as far as 2,800 meters into the cave. Guides can be contracted locally to help descend some distance into the cave, but unguided visitors with headlamps can enter to about 300 meters.

Tarma, the city of flowers

Over the Andes by Train

One of Latin America's great engineering achievements of the 19th century was the completion of a train line across the Andes between Lima and Huancayo. The 12-hour journey begins at the desert coast around Lima and climbs through a subtropical river valley, into dozens of rock tunnels, onto the puna, and finally up and over the snow-covered cordillera. Needless to say, the 12-hour ride is a memorable experience.

The train was built between 1870 and 1908 and was the brainchild of American entrepreneur Henry Meiggs, who bragged that he could "get a train wherever a llama can walk." Polish engineer Ernest Malinowski designed most of the 61 bridges, 65 tunnels, and 21 switchbacks, built over four decades by 10,000 workers—more than half of whom were indentured workers, or coolies, from China.

The train, considered to serve the highest passenger station in the world, climbs nearly nine vertical meters per minute until reaching Ticlio at 4,758 meters. Shortly afterward it climbs to its highest point at La Galera, a tunnel through the Andes at 4,781 meters. Depending on the season, the snow line hovers a few hundred meters above.

The service was shut down in 1991 following attacks by Sendero Luminoso. It began again briefly in the late 1990s but once again fell out of service. Now the recently upgraded service is running once or twice a month. The six cars have been remodeled, and there is an onboard lookout station and bar.

If you're coming from Lima, there's really no way to acclimatize for this journey except by sipping plenty of water (or even better, *maté de coca*) and being well rested. Symptoms of altitude sickness include headaches and sometimes nausea, which usually pass once the train descends, though some passengers continue to suffer from *soroche*, or altitude sickness, even in Huancayo (3,240 meters).

Mountain guides swear the best medicine to take for altitude headaches is Excedrin. While adjusting to a higher altitude, it is always a good idea to avoid alcohol, heavy foods, and physical exertion. As the Bolivians say, *"Come poco, tome poco, y duerme solo"* ("Eat little, drink little, and sleep alone").

Food

For spit-roasted chicken, trout, meats, and meal-size soups, head to **Restaurant Senorial** (Huánuco 138, 8am-3pm and 6pm-11pm daily, US$6-10). For an option right on the Plaza de Armas, try **Chavín de Grima** (Lima 270, tel. 064/32-1341, 8am-10pm Mon.-Sat., 8am-4pm Sun., US$8), which has a good inexpensive menu for lunch. You can also try restaurants at some of the hotels, including **Hotel Los Portales** (Ramón Castilla 512, tel. 064/32-1411, 6am-11pm daily, US$10), which has two restaurants and a bar. A local favorite about 10 minutes outside Tarma, in the town of Acobamba, is **La Olla de Barro** (María Delgado De Odría 158, tel. 064/76-4071, noon-5pm daily, US$8), which serves delicious *pachamanca*, a typical Andean dish of chicken, lamb, pork and other meats slowly cooked in an open pit with potatoes, green lima beans, and other vegetables.

Accommodations

The best budget option in Tarma is **Hostal Dorado** (Huánuco 488, tel. 064/32-1914, www.hospedajeeldoradotarma.com, US$20 s, US$25 d), a colonial home with a plant-filled courtyard and wooden second-story balcony. Rooms are simple, clean, and quiet, and cheaper rooms with shared baths are available.

The luxury option in Tarma is **Hotel Los Portales** (Ramón Castilla 512, tel. 064/32-1411, www.losportaleshoteles.com.pe, US$60 s, US$90 d, with breakfast), which was built, of course, by General Odría in the 1950s on the main road just west of town.

Rooms are newly remodeled, and there is a bar with karaoke.

A German-Swiss couple are running **Hacienda La Florida** (6 kilometers north of Tarma, tel. 064/34-1041, Lima tel. 01/344-1358, www.haciendalaflorida.com, US$48 s, US$85 d, with breakfast), a colonial hacienda that once belonged to Peruvian painter José Otero. There are 12 tasteful rooms, some decorated with antiques, and courtyards and gardens for strolling.

Information and Services

There is some visitor information, as well as guides for surrounding sights, at the **information office** on the main square next to the local government building. The town's fastest Internet is at **Infomedia** (Paucartambo and Lima).

Getting There and Around

There are several transportation companies that offer daily buses between Lima and Tarma (US$11), and onward to Chanchamayo. The two best companies are **Empresa de Transportes Chanchamayo** (Callao 1002, tel. 064/32-1882, http://atchanchamayo.com) and **Empresa de Transportes Junín** (Amazonas 669, tel. 064/32-1234). The buses normally leave early in the morning or in the afternoon. There are sometimes night buses, but it's better to travel during the day. For transportation to Huancayo, **Los Canarias** (Amazonas 694, tel. 064/32-3357) has hourly buses (5am-6pm daily, US$3) leaving Tarma. A better option, but slightly more expensive, is to travel in a *colectivo,* a shared taxi, which leave from the Terminal Terrestre.

Huancayo and the Mantaro Valley

The Mantaro Valley in Peru's central highlands is one of the country's most productive agricultural areas, a giant swath of flat land famous for its potatoes, corn, barley, quinoa, artichokes, and many vegetables. The charming adobe villages of this valley are the best places in all of Peru to see a wide range of craftspeople at work and acquire the highest quality artwork at a fair price that benefits the artist, not the merchant.

Artisans here produce the ceramics, weavings, carved gourds (*mates burilados*), and silver filigree that is sold, at a considerable markup, in the crafts markets of Cusco and Lima. Many of the artisans are national champions in their disciplines and produce works of staggering beauty that are impossible to find elsewhere in the country. The artisans are glad to work and chat at the same time and gladly invite in visitors who knock on their unmarked wooden doors.

More so than residents in other more touristy areas of Peru, Mantaro Valley villagers do not behave differently in front of foreigners and go about their lives much as they have for centuries. They are proud and prosperous people. Depending on the time of the year, villagers are out in the fields planting or harvesting, threshing wheat with horses and donkeys, herding cows with colorful tassels tied to their ears, or building rammed-earth homes that are the same chocolate color as the surrounding fields. There is a festival nearly every day somewhere in the valley.

A good way to experience local culture is through one of the walking or mountain-bike routes mapped out by the energetic and affable Lucho Hurtado at **Incas del Perú** (Giráldez 675, tel. 064/22-3303, www.incasdelperu.org), the best source of information on the area. He has good contacts among local craftspeople and leads treks to the Cordillera Huaytapallana, a small but spectacular range 50 kilometers east of Huancayo that includes a number of glaciated peaks, including Mount Lasuntay (5,780 meters).

There are many local ruins from the Xauxa and later Huanca cultures, which ran a lively

Huancayo

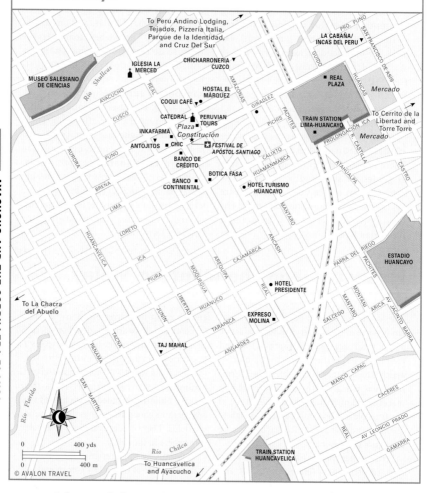

coast-rainforest trade from AD 900 until being conquered by the Inca in the 15th century. Like the Chachapoyans farther north, the Huanca resented Inca rule and sided with the Spanish, who followed the Inca roads through the Mantaro Valley en route to Cusco in 1533. The following year, Francisco Pizarro returned to the area to found Jauja, Peru's first, though short-lived, capital, and the land was divided up among the Spaniards (a source of dismay, no doubt, to Huanca elders).

During the independence struggle three centuries later, the Spanish troops based themselves in Huancayo for three years until they were defeated at nearby Junín and Ayacucho in 1824. During the War of the Pacific (1879-1883), several bloody battles were again fought in the Mantaro Valley between Chilean soldiers and the Peruvian army led by General Andrés Cáceres, who was dubbed the Wizard of the Andes for his ability to attack and quickly disappear into the mountains. During the 1980s and 1990s, Mantaro Valley villages were caught in the crossfire between the Shining Path and the Peruvian army. The area is recovering strongly, thanks in part to good farming lands, crafts production, and tourism.

The best base for touring the valley is Huancayo (3,240 meters), the regional capital that has been flirting with a more modern feel. Twenty years ago it would have been unimaginable that Huancayo would have an American-style mall, like it does now, not to mention the prospects of an urban metro train. The city's biggest attraction is the Sunday market, where fresh food is sold side by side with handicrafts. There are not many other sights, nor good lodging options, in the city itself—the best options are on the edge of town or in the nearby village of Concepción.

SIGHTS

There is not much to see in Huancayo itself. The central **Plaza de la Constitución** is nondescript, and Huancayo's churches are all modern, except **La Merced** (1st block of Real), where Peru's constitution was signed in 1839. **El Museo Salesiano de Ciencias Naturales** (Santa Rosa, El Tambo, tel. 064/24-7763, 9am-1pm and 3pm-6pm Mon.-Sat., US$3) has an amazing collection of more than 13,000 Amazon insects, rainforest birds, butterflies, fossils, and archaeological artifacts.

ENTERTAINMENT AND EVENTS
Nightlife
La Cabaña (Giráldez 652, tel. 064/22-3303, www.incasdelperu.org, 5pm-11pm daily) is an excellent drinking and dancing spot that is popular with both locals and travelers. Local bands crank out folkloric music from 9pm onward Thursday-Saturday. **Antojitos** (Puno 599, tel. 064/23-7950, 9am-4am daily), on the corner of Arequipa and Puno, serves up light food in an atmosphere of classic rock and salsa, as does **Galileo** (Paseo La Breña 378, 6pm-midnight Mon.-Sat.), which occasionally has live music.

Festivals and Events
★ FESTIVAL DE APÓSTOL SANTIAGO
Some of Peru's most interesting (and most frequent) festivals are found in the Mantaro Valley, which has more traditional festivals than there are days in the year. During the **Festival de Apóstol Santiago** on July 25, villagers throughout the Mantaro Valley brand their livestock amid much dancing and drinking of *chicha* (fermented corn beer). Although Roman Catholic on the surface, this pre-Hispanic ritual invokes the protection of Andean deities.

OTHER FESTIVALS
Other festival highlights include **Fiesta del Niño** in January, **Carnaval** in February, **Cruz del Mayo** in May, **Fiesta de San Pedro y San Pablo** on June 28-29, **La Fiesta de Santiago** on July 25, and **Todos los Santos** (All Saints' Day) on November 1. In **Jauja** there is **Jala Pato** (Pull the Duck) in late January, when horsemen compete to yank off the head of a suspended duck. The village of **Sapallanga** is known for the colorful processions of the Virgen de Cocharcas September 7-9. For a complete list of Mantaro Valley festivals, visit **Incas del Perú** (www.incasdelperu.org).

SHOPPING
Huancayo is famous for its Sunday market on Huancavelica, where fresh food is sold alongside handicrafts on three blocks from Puno to Loreto. The best time to go is around 4pm-5pm, when vendors are packing up and are eager to bargain. There are several small markets in Huancayo that sell mostly tourist items—the best place is **Casa de Artesano** (Real 495, www.casadelartesano.org) on the Plaza de la Constitución. However, you will receive better prices and have a memorable experience if you buy directly from the artists in their homes.

Villages around the Mantaro Valley have markets where crafts are sold on different days of the week, including Wednesday in **San Jerónimo de Tunán,** Saturday in **Chupaca,** and Sunday in **Concepción** and **Jauja.**

RECREATION

The peaks and valleys around Huancayo invite all sorts of excuses to escape the city. Spend the day visiting Mantaro Valley towns, learning about traditional weaving, cycling, or even exploring the neighboring rainforest.

Tour Guides and Agencies

The colorful, all-natural, traditional **weavings** from the Huancayo area draw textile experts from across the world not only to buy weavings but also to participate in hands-on classes. If you have a real curiosity in the subject, Sasha McInne's 22-day Textiles-Folk Art-Market Tour is the best option. Sasha's tours operate through her agency, **Puchka Peru Cultural Tours** (Canada tel. 250/360-1898, www.puchkaperu.com), traveling through Peru and stopping in Lima, Cusco, the Sacred Valley, and Arequipa. The energetic and knowledgeable Sasha grew up in Peru, knows the lay of the land, and exposes trip participants to a variety of weaving techniques, including knitting, braiding, embroidery, and back-strap and tapestry weaving.

For a closer-to-Huancayo weaving experience, contact **Juana Sanabria** (tel. 064/22-3956), a passionate weaver and patient teacher. She organizes in-house weaving classes, demonstrations, and tours. Contact her before your arrival so that she can gather the necessary plants and fiber to make the natural dyes, which you will in turn learn to make and mix with wools.

True adventure, however, bears the name of Lucho Hurtado. Lucho operates **Incas del Perú** (Giráldez 675, tel. 064/22-3303, www.incasdelperu.org, 9am-1pm and 4pm-7pm Mon.-Sat.), from which he rents mountain bikes and hands out free walking and biking maps to those who rent bikes or stay at his hostel, La Casa de la Abuela. The walks

include the lake-to-lake circuit near Jauja and the loop above Huancayo; ruins and hot mineral baths at Matachico, north of Jauja; and a ridge walk between the villages of Ahuac and Chupaca that passes through a line of Huanca granaries and offers views of the snow-covered Cordillera Huaytapallana and Lago Ñahuimpuquio.

FOOD

Huancayo has some excellent places for *comida típica,* all of which are a taxi ride from the center. The region's most famous dish is *papas a la huancaína,* yellow potatoes smothered with a yellow sauce made from fresh cheese, oil, ground yellow chili pepper, lemon, and egg yolk—and topped with black olives.

Peruvian

★ **Huancahuasi** (Mariscal Castilla 222, El Tambo, tel. 064/24-4826, www.huancahuasi. com, 9am-8pm daily, US$9) is a great place for Sunday lunch, with live folkloric music and steaming chunks of pork, beef, and lamb from the *pachamanca* pit, followed by *humitas.*

★ **La Tullpa** (Atahualpa 145, tel. 064/25-3649, www.latullpa.com, 11am-8pm daily, US$6) has one of the town's only chefs certified in Peruvian food. It serves the classics like *papa a la huancaína* as well as several beef and fish dishes, including trout in mushroom sauce. It also offers *cuy* (guinea pig).

Detrás de la Catedral (Ancash 335, tel. 064/21-2969, noon-11pm Mon.-Sat., noon-4pm Sun., US$6-10) is, as the name says, behind Huancayo's cathedral. It has a broad menu with homemade local dishes and international options, including hamburgers, trout, and *ají de gallina.*

Pizza

The welcoming **La Cabaña** (Giráldez 675, tel. 064/22-3303, www.incasdelperu.org, 5pm-11pm daily, US$7) is a cozy place with a fireplace, art, and great pizza. Live folk music plays from 8pm Thursday-Saturday. It also serves grilled meats, sandwiches, and pitchers of sangria.

In the San Carlos neighborhood, try **Italia** (Leandra Torres 441, at Parque Túpac Amaru, tel. 064/23-3145, 6pm-11pm daily, US$8), which delivers and has lasagna and a range of other pasta dishes. In the Plaza Real (Ferrocarril 1035) mall there is **Rustica** (tel. 064/23-4318, noon-3am daily, US$6-9), the Peruvian chain that serves a range of dishes that includes pizza, pastas, and spit-roasted chicken.

Cafés, Bakeries, and Ice Cream

The best place for a rich cappuccino, light snack, or dessert is **Coqui Café** (Puno 296, tel. 064/23-4707, www.coquicafe.com, 7am-10:30pm Mon.-Sat., 7am-12:30pm and 6pm-10pm Sun., US$4). It also makes homemade bread and sells good-for-picnics deli meats and cheeses.

Markets

The best small market is **Comercial Huaychulo** (Paseo a la Brena 174), with fruits, vegetables, deli meats, and cheeses. For a grocery store, the national chain **Plaza Vea** (8am-10pm daily) has recently opened up in the new Plaza Real mall (Ferrocarril 1035).

ACCOMMODATIONS
US$10-25

La Casa de la Abuela (Cusco 794, tel. 064/23-4383, www.incasdelperu.org, US$10 dorm, US$14 s or US$25 d, with breakfast) recently moved across town and is now about eight blocks from the Plaza de la Constitución. Staff are still helpful and friendly, and the new location is more spacious. It has a place for bonfires at night as well as for camping. Baths are shared.

US$25-50

Walking distance from the Plaza de la Constitución, **Retama Inn** (Ancash 1079, tel. 064/21-9193, retamainn73@hotmail.com, US$18 s, US$30 d, with breakfast) is centrally located. The 20 clean rooms have comfy beds, carpeting, cable TV, phones, room service, and private baths. The traditionally decorated café bar is great for evening drinks.

US$50-100

Hotel Turismo Huancayo (Ancash 729, tel. 064/23-1072, US$70 s, US$78 d) is an elegant 1930s colonial-style hotel, smack in the center of town, with good views over the Plaza Huamanmarca. The long tile hallways are a cool escape from the busy city, and rooms are genuinely comfortable: king beds, heaters, cable TV, Wi-Fi, and immaculate baths. If you want to be in the city and need some comfort, this is your place.

Located 20 minutes north of Huancayo, the **Hotel Loma Verde** (Leopoldo Peña 770, Concepción, tel. 064/58-1569, www.lomaverdeperu.com, US$60 s, US$90 d, including all meals) has plenty of country charm. The main lodge has sitting areas with fabulous views over the Mantaro Valley. Rooms are crafted from stone, plaster, and exposed beams and feature feather comforters, fireplaces, and porches with sunset views.

For those willing to forgo charm for a firm bed, plenty of hot water, and a central location, there's the modern **Hostal El Marquéz** (Puno 294, tel. 064/21-9026, www.elmarquezhuancayo.com, US$60 s, US$80 d, with breakfast). Rooms are large, carpeted, and quiet. There is cable TV and Wi-Fi.

Another three-star option in Huancayo is **Hotel Presidente** (Real 1138, tel. 064/23-1275, www.huancayo.hotelpresidente.com.pe, US$85 s or d, with breakfast). The hotel is centrally-located, only a few blocks from the train station, and its carpeted rooms have large comfortable beds. Some rooms have flat-screen TVs. There is Wi-Fi and a restaurant on the ground floor that serves Peruvian and international dishes. It has a sister hotel called **Hotel Turismo** (Ancash 729, tel. 064/23-1072, www.turistas.hotelpresidente.com.pe, US$85 s or d, with breakfast) located a few blocks away.

INFORMATION AND SERVICES

The best source of travel information in Huancayo is Lucho Hurtado at **Incas del Perú** (Giráldez 675, tel. 064/22-3303, www.

incasdelperu.org, 9am-1pm and 4pm-7pm Mon.-Sat.). The **tourist police** (tel. 064/21-9851) are at Ferrocarril 555.

For a pharmacy, **Inkafarma** (Real 537, www.inkafarma.com.pe) has several locations in the city, including one in Plaza Real. For health care, try the **Hospital de EsSalud** (Independencia 296, Tambo, tel. 064/24-8366).

Most banks are located on blocks 5 and 6 of Real, including **Banco de Crédito, Interbanc, Banco Continental,** and **Scotiabank.** In Plaza Real there is also a Western Union office. Rigged calculators are a problem in Huancayo, so change bills in a bank or at a money exchange.

The **post office** (tel. 064/23-2101, 8am-8pm Mon.-Sat.) is in the Plaza Huamanmarca, near the intersection of Real and Huamanmarca. The **Internet** places around the Plaza de la Constitución are slightly expensive, and there are several faster places along Giráldez. **Telephone cabins** at Real and Lima are open 7am-10pm daily.

Incas del Perú (Giráldez 652, tel. 064/22-3303, www.incasdelperu.org) offers a Spanish for Travelers class with courses starting every Monday. The budget course (US$110) includes three hours of daily lessons, five days' lodging at La Casa de la Abuela, and three meals a day. Additional options include homestays, weekend excursions, and field trips around town. The agency can also arrange classes in the Quechua language.

GETTING THERE AND AROUND

You have several options to get to Huancayo from Lima. **Ferrocarril Central Andino** (Jose Galvez Barrenchea 566, Lima tel. 01/226-6363, www.ferrocarrilcentral.com.pe) has one or two train services a month from March to November, stopping during the rainy season, running from Lima up into the highlands and on to Huancayo. At 12 hours, the ride is a long one, but worth it for the scenic views and a once-in-a-lifetime experience. The coaches connect to a bar and lookout deck and have tourist (US$85) and economy (US$45) seats.

There are lots of bus service options to and from Huancayo, but the best is **Cruz del Sur** (Ferrocarril 151, tel. 064/22-3367, www.cruzdelsur.com.pe), which runs half a dozen buses starting at 7:45am daily. **Oltursa** (Terminal Terrestre, Evitamiento s/n, tel. 064/60-1503) is another good choice and has three daily buses to and from Lima. By far the fastest option is by flying. **LC Perú** (Ayacucho 322, tel. 064/21-4514) does daily 45-minute flights between Lima and Huancayo. The airport is in Jauja, but the airline has shuttles to and from Huancayo.

For Tarma and the rainforest around Chanchamayo, try **Empresa Transporte San Juan** (Omaryali 159). Buses leave hourly for Tarma (5am-8pm daily, US$5), with connections to Merced (US$6) and Satipo (US$7). For Ayacucho (US$12), try **Empresa Transporte Union Molina** (Angaraes and Real). The road has been improved and the trip now takes 8-10 hours. Buses leave in the morning and evening daily.

With the Carretera Central running through Huancayo, finding transportation around the Mantaro Valley is easy. All transportation to the north (Hualhuas, San Jerónimo, Concepción, Jauja, Sicaya) passes the corner of Giráldez and Huancas. Transportation to the south passes the nearby corner of Ferrocarril and Giráldez.

TOP EXPERIENCE

THE MANTARO VALLEY

The Mantaro Valley is filled with ruins, churches, and, most important, entire villages that specialize in one type of handicraft. With an early start, it is easy to take public transportation and visit these towns on your own—many of the better artisans are now marked by yellow signs.

A spectacular way to walk between towns, and have a picnic lunch on the way, is to follow the out-of-the-way paths that have been

The Art of Natural Dyes

Weavers in Hualhuas are keeping alive a tradition of making the unmistakably vibrant natural dyes that were pioneered by pre-Inca cultures such as the Nasca and Paracas peoples. The dyes are made by grinding up roots, leaves, flowers, fruits, vegetables, minerals, and even bugs. Some of these are seasonal, so certain dyes are only available during certain times of the year. After the dye is made, hand-spun wool is soaked in the color, then fixed with minerals and hung to dry. Here are a few of the sources for the natural dyes:

- **Yellow:** crushed lichen

- **Reds and pinks:** *cochinilla* (cochineal), a parasite that lives in the prickly pear cactus

- **Green:** *chilca* plant

- **Brown:** walnuts

- **Copper:** onion

mapped out by Lucho Hurtado. If you go on your own, get recommendations ahead of time and avoid the *artesanía* stores at the entrances of the towns. The easiest way to tour workshops is with an organized tour.

Hualhuas

This **weaving** town 20 minutes north of Huancayo produces tapestries, rugs, and clothing—mostly from hand-spun wool and natural dyes. The highest quality is found at **Víctor Hugo Ingaroca Tupac Yupanqui** (Huancayo 315, Hualhuas). His weavings, based on pre-Columbian techniques used by the Nasca and Paracas cultures, are stunning. **Antonio Cáceres** (28 de Julio 888, Hualhuas) produces more affordable weavings and is an expert on the natural plants, bugs, and minerals used to make his bright natural dyes.

To reach Hualhuas, catch a *combi* (20 minutes, US$1) at the corner of Giráldez and Huancas in Huancayo.

Cochas Grande

Carved gourds (*mates burilados*) are an art form from pre-Inca times that continues to thrive in Cochas Grande and Cochas Chico, a pair of towns tucked behind the hills a half hour east of Huancayo. These gourds are carved in mind-boggling detail and usually tell a story about country life. Common stories include courtship, marriage, and childbirth; planting, harvest, and celebration; or the process of building a home. Some even include current political commentary, and gourds carved during the 1980s are rife with images of the Shining Path.

To reach Cochas, take a bus (30 minutes, US$0.50) from the corner of Giráldez and Huancas in Huancayo.

San Jerónimo de Tunán

This village, 13 kilometers north of Huancayo, is known for **silver** filigree. It is fascinating to watch **Jesús Suarez Vasquez** and his sister **Nelly Vasquez** (Arequipa 496, 3 blocks east of Plaza de Armas) make their delicate silver jewelry. A necklace that sells for US$16 in Lima can be bought here for US$6. Wednesday mornings are a good day to visit San Jerónimo, to catch the weekly market. There are many stores down the road and, on the main square, a beautiful 17th-century church with a baroque altar.

Other lesser crafts centers in the valley include **San Augustin de Cajas,** known for its wool hats; **Molinos,** near Jauja, which makes wood carvings, including masks and stools decorated with animal shapes; and **Aco,** a center of ceramics. The best time to visit Aco is during its Friday early-morning market, when ceramics wholesalers from all over the country snap up pots and other goods for cheap.

Santa Rosa de Ocopa and Ingenio Trout Farm

There is a lot to see at **Santa Rosa de Ocopa** (9am-noon and 3pm-6pm Wed.-Mon., US$1.25), a Franciscan monastery founded in 1723 that's near Concepción, about 25 kilometers northwest of Huancayo. As evangelical churches have grown, Santa Rosa has withered, and now only six monks are left. But the story behind Santa Rosa is fascinating. Franciscan missionaries embarked from here to proselytize in the Amazon rainforest, and 86 were killed in the process, according to a commemorative plaque inside.

Baroque altars adorn the chapel, and it is usually possible to descend into the catacombs. The newer convent building has a museum with stuffed rainforest animals, paintings from the Cusco school, and gruesome paintings of missionaries being tortured by indigenous Amazonians. The highlight of the convent, however, is a library that contains more than 25,000 volumes from the 15th century onward. The oldest book in the library, published in 1497, is Saint Augustine's reflections on the Bible (the convent used to have a 1454 catechism in Aymara, Quechua, and Spanish, but it was stolen in a 2002 armed robbery, along with a painting from the Flemish school). The original adobe cloisters include a stone courtyard, a metal shop, and other rooms.

The best lunch spot nearby is Ingenio, home to Peru's largest fish farms, which produce approximately 50,000 kilograms of trout per year. Most visitors tour the state-owned **Ingenio Trout Farm** (28 kilometers from Huancayo, in the Ingenio district, 8am-6pm daily, $2 pp) before sitting down to lunch at either **Ávila** or **Llao Llao,** small restaurants that serve trout heaped with local artichokes. Afterward there is a pleasant hour-long walk up a dirt road alongside the river to a set of waterfalls.

Most Huancayo agencies visit Ingenio and Santa Rosa as part of a Mantaro Valley tour, though it is easy to arrive at both places via public transportation. *Combis* for Concepción (US$0.80) leave every 30-40 minutes from Pachitea in Huancayo. In Concepción, there are nearby *colectivos* and *combis* that head to both Ingenio and Santa Rosa de Ocopa.

carved gourds, or *mates burilados*

Jauja and Laguna Paca

Peru's first capital is 45 minutes, or 40 kilometers, northwest of Huancayo on the highway from Lima. It is an alternative base for exploring the valley but has few services.

Lodging options include the excellent **Hostal Manco Cápac** (Manco Cápac 575, tel. 064/36-1620, US$15 s, US$30 d), run by Bruno Bonierbale, and **Cabezon's Hostal** (Ayacucho 1027, tel. 064/36-2206, US$5 s), with shared baths.

From Jauja there are *motocars* to Laguna Paca (US$1), the shores of which have unfortunately been marred by a line of cheap restaurants. A quick boat ride to the Isla de Amor, a tiny island in the middle of the lake, offers good views of Xauxa ruins on a nearby ridge and the mountains to the west. A good walk leads up from the lake to these and other Inca ruins in the area and passes through the villages of Acolla, Marco, and Tragadero. This is a good walk for those who want to spend the day walking through countryside and tracking down rarely visited ruins. The walk ends at a smaller, upper lake near a road where *combis* return to Jauja.

Huariwilca

Six kilometers south of Huancayo, the **Huariwilca ruins,** from the Huanca and Huari cultures, are located below the plaza of the village of Huari, which is next to Río Chancas. The ceremonial center includes a high wall, a staircase, interior passageways, and two huge *molle* trees. Huariwilca means "sacred place of the Huari," the Ayacucho-based culture that spread throughout Peru's highlands between AD 700 and 1200. The nearby **museum** (8am-1pm and 3pm-6pm Tues.-Sun., US$0.50) includes many pre-Inca artifacts found at the site, including *Spondylus* shells imported from Ecuador, ceramics, metalwork, and a female mummy, found at the site, known as **The Maiden of Huariwilca.** To get to the ruins, near the town of Huari, take a blue-and-white bus to Huari from the corner of Giráldez and Ferrocarril in Huancayo.

Ayacucho and Vicinity

It is easy to understand why Peruvians are so fond of Ayacucho. This hidden jewel of Peru's southern Andes has Renaissance and baroque churches around every corner (33 in all), its elaborate Semana Santa (Easter Week) celebration is second only to that of Seville, and one-of-a-kind Huari and Inca ruins are in the surrounding countryside. Ayacucho is colonial enough to seem like a time warp. At dawn, townsfolk stream into churches to listen to Mass. In the nearby market, campesinas in big straw hats and colorful hand-knit skirts serve up lunch: *puca picante* (a spicy red stew of chili, pork cracklings, crushed peanuts, and potatoes), sheep's head soup, and about 10 varieties of *chicha*. Quechua is spoken everywhere in the soft, swishing sounds of the local dialect.

Ayacucho is known as one of Peru's most artistic towns. Some of the country's best *huayno* singers come from here, along with world-famous harp player Florencio Coronado and the guitarist Raúl García Zárate. Nearly every man knows how to play guitar—an essential skill for evening serenades—and artisans around the city produce ceramics, weavings, miniature altars, and stone carvings in alabaster, the local stone known as *piedra de huamanga*. At 2,761 meters above sea level, the city has one of the best climates in the country—the dry landscape, scattered with cactus and agave, receives only short, if hard, storms in the rainy season, December to March. There are sunny skies and warm temperatures the rest of the year.

Ayacucho was a dangerous place to visit in the 1980s and early 1990s. The Sendero Luminoso, or Shining Path, was founded here by Abimael Guzmán, a philosophy professor from Arequipa who came to work at the local university. His movement, based on Maoist philosophy, fought an 11-year civil war that claimed the lives of 70,000 people across the country. The fighting was most intense around Ayacucho, where both guerillas and army soldiers terrorized local villages and caused widespread migration to the cities.

Ayacucho has been a safe place to visit since Guzmán's arrest in 1992 and the subsequent disintegration of the Shining Path. The U.S. Embassy has taken Ayacucho off its travel advisory. But apart from April and Semana Santa, Ayacucho still gets little attention from foreign travelers, mostly because it is isolated by rough highways and lack of an air connection to Cusco.

SIGHTS
★ Ayacucho City Tour
An Ayacucho city walking tour begins with an early-morning visit to churches—most of which open for Mass at 6:30am and close an

Ayacucho

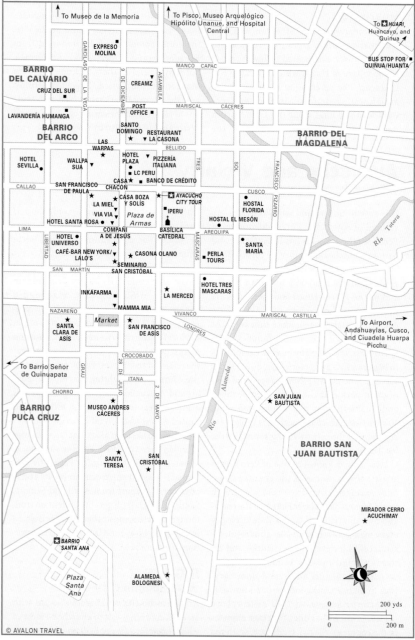

To Museo de la Memoria

To Pisco, Museo Arquelógico Hipólito Unanue, and Hospital Central

To ⊞ HUARI, Huancayo, and Quinua

BUS STOP FOR QUINUA/HUANTA

EXPRESO MOLINA

MANCO CAPAC

GARCILASO DE LA VEGA

9 DE DICIEMBRE

ASAMBLEA

CREAMZ

BARRIO DEL CALVARIO

CRUZ DEL SUR

MARISCAL CÁCERES

POST OFFICE

LAVANDERÍA HUMANGA

BARRIO DEL ARCO

SANTO DOMINGO

RESTAURANT LA CASONA

BARRIO DEL MAGDALENA

LAS WARPAS

BELLIDO

HOTEL SEVILLA

WALLPA SUA

HOTEL PLAZA

PIZZERÍA ITALIANA

TRES

SOL

FRANCISCO

CALLAO

SAN FRANCISCO DE PAULA

CASA CHACÓN

LC PERU

BANCO DE CRÉDITO

CUSCO

CASA BOZA Y SOLÍS

AYACUCHO CITY TOUR

HOSTAL FLORIDA

LA MIEL

IPERU

LIMA

VIA VIA

HOTEL SANTA ROSA

COMPAÑÍA DE JESÚS

Plaza de Armas

BASÍLICA CATEDRAL

HOSTAL EL MESÓN

AREQUIPA

LIBERTAD

HOTEL UNIVERSO

CAFÉ-BAR NEW YORK/ LALO'S

CASONA OLANO

MASCARAS

PERLA TOURS

SANTA MARÍA

SAN MARTIN

SEMINARIO SAN CRISTÓBAL

INKAFARMA

LA MERCED

HOTEL TRES MASCARAS

MAMMA MIA

NAZAREÑO

VIVANCO

MARISCAL CASTILLA

Market

SANTA CLARA DE ASÍS

SAN FRANCISCO DE ASÍS

LONDRES

To Airport, Andahuaylas, Cusco, and Ciuadela Huarpa Picchu

CROCOBADO

GRAU

28 DE JULIO

ITANA

2 DE MAYO

Alameda

Río

To Barrio Señor de Quinuapata

CHORRO

BARRIO PUCA CRUZ

MUSEO ANDRES CÁCERES

SAN JUAN BAUTISTA

BARRIO SAN JUAN BAUTISTA

SANTA TERESA

SAN CRISTÓBAL

MIRADOR CERRO ACUCHIMAY

⊞ BARRIO SANTA ANA

Plaza Santa Ana

ALAMEDA BOLOGNESI

Río Tatora

0   200 yds

0   200 m

© AVALON TRAVEL

A Troubled History... and Brighter Future

The villagers of Peru's central highlands were already hard-hit in the 1980s by bad roads, little or no phone communication, and a life that revolved around subsistence agriculture. Then came the Sendero Luminoso, the **Shining Path,** a terrorist movement based on Maoist ideals that tried to spark a nationwide revolution by destroying the state and the "old oligarchy."

During the 1980s and early 1990s, a staggering 70,000 people were killed in the crossfire between the Shining Path and the army. Sendero Luminoso began in Ayacucho and wreaked most havoc in the central highlands—more than 75 percent of those killed were Quechua-speaking villagers.

These days, terrorism has disappeared, except for a few remote rural provinces, and the highways are in better shape—thanks to the national government, which is doing everything it can to connect this forgotten part of Peru to the rest of the country. The area is safe for travel—even the conservative U.S. embassy says so. Families have moved back to their towns, and there is a sense of recovery, of wounds slowly healing.

hour or two later. Many of the churches open for an evening Mass too, so if you're not an early bird you can still get a look inside. Get up at dawn and start two blocks from the Plaza de Armas at **Santo Domingo** (Bellido and 9 de Diciembre, 6:30am-7am Mon.-Sat., 7am-8am Sun.), which has a simple Renaissance facade covered with a bizarre column-and-balcony addition. According to local legend, Spanish Inquisition judges held public trials and hung their victims from this balcony. Inside are several examples of Andean-Catholic syncretism: Profiles of Inca with headdresses abound on the altars and, on the main altar, the eagle of San Juan is replaced with a local hummingbird.

Next stop is **San Francisco de Paula** (Garcilaso de la Vega and Callao, 7am-8am and 6pm-7pm Mon.-Sat., 7am-8am, 9am-10am, and 6pm-7pm Sun.), which competes with San Blas in Cusco for Peru's finest carved pulpit. The altar is brimming with angels and is one of the few in the city that is not covered with gold plating—but the Nicaraguan cedar is just as pretty. **La Merced** (2 de Mayo and San Martín, 5:30pm-6:30pm daily) was constructed in 1542 and is the second-oldest church in town. A mark of its antiquity is its simple Renaissance facade—as opposed to the later, more effusive baroque style. It sometimes opens in the morning at around

7:30am for baptisms and other events. **Santa Clara** (Grau and Nazareño, 6:30am-7:30am Fri.-Wed., 6:30am-7:30am and 2pm-4pm Thurs.) holds the revered Jesus of Nazareth image that is the center of Ayacucho's most important procession during Semana Santa (the week before Easter). The ceiling above the altar is an intricate wood filigree of Mudejar, or Spanish-Arabic, design.

On the way to the next church, cross Grau and head into the **market,** which is clean, relaxed, and full of local foods. *Pan chapla,* a local favorite, is a round bread with a hollow center, and from August to October there is also *wawa* ("baby" in Quechua), an infant-shaped bread that is meant to be consolation for women who became pregnant during Carnaval in February and also used as a gift for godparents. There are also large rocks of mineral salt, a variety of *chichas* made from corn and grains, and huge pots of *puca picante.*

Emerge on the other side to a huge rust-colored arch next to **San Francisco de Asís** (28 de Julio and Vivanco, 7am-8am and 6pm-7pm Mon.-Sat., 7am-10am Sun.), a Renaissance church built in 1552. Next door is the related convent, open to visitors only via prior arrangement, which contains one of the country's finest collections of colonial paintings.

The final stop is the **Compañía de Jesús**

(28 de Julio, between Lima and San Martín, 6am-7:30am and 10:30am-2:30pm Mon.-Sat.), the Jesuit church built in 1605 with a facade of sculpted flowers. Next door was the Jesuit College, now the Seminario San Cristóbal, where indigenous children were taught music, Latin, painting, and wood carving until the Jesuits were kicked out of Latin America in 1767. A large international grant, interestingly, once again trained local kids to restore the building. Stop here to have breakfast at one of the cafés and shop at the stores, which are slowly paying back the costs of the restoration.

After breakfast, head down 28 de Julio to the **colonial home and museum of Andrés Cáceres** (28 de Julio 508, cell tel. 981-689-481, 9am-1pm and 3pm-5pm Mon.-Fri., 9am-1pm Sat., US$0.75), Peru's top general during the War of the Pacific, who moved troops so quickly through the mountains that he was known as the Wizard of the Andes. The home, part of which is now a museum, contains his letters, photos, travel desk, weapons, and so on, and has an excellent (and unrelated) collection of baroque paintings, alabaster stone carvings, and *petacas,* the elaborate burro satchels used by missionaries.

Go one block down from the Andrés Cáceres home to **Santa Teresa** (28 de Julio, 5:30am-6:30am Mon.-Sat., 5:30am-8am Sun., and 8am-10am Thurs.), the church and Carmelite monastery where nuns remain cloistered today. The nuns make *mazapan, turrones,* and *agua de agrás* (a *chicha* made from local flowers), sold in the convent's foyer. By knocking on the door, visitors often gain admission here during the day to see the baroque altar and a painting of the Last Supper where Jesus is seated before a roasted guinea pig. If admitted after hours, visitors should leave a small donation as a courtesy.

Farther down the street is **San Cristóbal** (1540), the city's oldest chapel, which is rarely open, and the pleasant promenade known as **Alameda Bolognesi.** From here, walk uphill on steep streets to **Barrio Santa Ana,** a neighborhood with a small-town feel, and the **Iglesia Santa Ana,** referred to commonly as the Iglesia de los Indios because of the various ethnicities the Spanish brought here in the 16th century to serve as a buffer against the attacking Inca. Working in the streets around the Plaza de Armas are some of Peru's most famous weavers, who have exhibited their work all over the world.

Ayacucho's elegant **Plaza de Armas** is bordered by the cathedral and university on one side and continuous stone arcades on the

Ayacucho's main square, the Plaza de Armas

others. The best time to visit **La Catedral,** which was completed in 1672, is in the evening, 4pm-7pm, when its huge interior is illuminated. If you try to visit during Mass in a large group taking pictures, you may be turned back. You can also visit 9am-1pm Monday-Saturday. There are two interesting examples of Andean-Spanish fusion: San Juan's eagle is replaced by a condor on top of the dome's columns, and the sacred half-moon of Andean cosmology is at the foot of the Virgin Mary.

Next to the cathedral is **La Universidad San Cristóbal de Huamanga,** which was founded in 1677 but went bankrupt and closed two centuries later during the War of the Pacific with Chile. The university was reopened in 1959.

Around 1969 the Velasco government expropriated many of the colonial mansions around the main square, forcing their families to vacate, and resold them to banks. **Casa Boza y Solís** (Portal Constitución, Plaza de Armas, 8am-1pm and 3pm-5:30pm Mon.-Fri., free) today houses government offices and stands out for its massive stone arcade and Italian tiles decorating an original stone fountain, staircase, and second floor. The Banco de Crédito occupies the **Casona del Canonigo Frías** (Plaza de Armas, 9am-6pm Mon.-Fri., 9am-1pm Sat.).

The Museo Arqueológico Hipólito Unanue (Independencia, 1 kilometer north of town, tel. 066/31-2056, 9am-1pm and 3pm-5pm Tues.-Sun., US$2) has a range of objects from the Warpa, Huari, and Chanca pre-Inca cultures: ceramics, weavings, turquoise jewelry, and seven priest monoliths carved out of volcanic stone. Plus, there is a botanical garden next door with more than 120 kinds of regional cacti.

Similarly on the outskirts of town is **El Museo de la Memoria** (Prolongación Libertad 1229, tel. 066/31-7170, 9am-6pm Mon.-Fri., US$2), which, although small and in Spanish, does a good job of showing the multisided issues of the terrorism era.

A beautiful view of Ayachucho can be had from the top of **Cerro Acuchimay,** which can be reached by taxi (US$2) and then descended via a long staircase that ends at the Plaza San Juan Bautista, near Londres. Do this walk during the day only.

★ Huari

There are three worthwhile sites north of Ayacucho that can be seen in one very full day. **Huari** (22 kilometers north of Ayacucho, 8am-6pm daily, US$2) is the sprawling capital of the onetime empire of the same name. Much of the city, which sprawled over 2,000 hectares, has been buried by drifting sands. The ruins are badly deteriorated and largely unexcavated, but what can be seen today, about 10 percent of the original city, includes huge complexes of walls up to 12 meters high.

The best place to start a visit is at the on-site museum, on the road between Ayacucho and Quinua, which contains a stone monolith, ceramics, and a few useful historical charts. A short walk away is the ceremonial center of Monqachayoc, which has an enigmatic half-moon shape. It appears to be a calendar, because it faces exactly north and contains 18 niches, which is a strange link to Mayan calendars in the Yucatán Peninsula in what is now Mexico. Holes where stone cylinders once stood were found nearby and were probably used for casting shadows onto the niches. Nearby are a few unexcavated pyramids covered with prickly pear cactus along with a huge stone table where sacrifices were probably made. Archaeologists believe the umbrella-shaped *paty* trees were used in a potion that prevented blood from coagulating during sacrifice ceremonies—a trick the Huari may have learned from the Moche in Peru's north.

A tunnel, closed to visitors, leads underground 50 meters from the ceremonial area to a labyrinth of funerary chambers that was excavated in 1997 and leads an astonishing 19 meters below ground—the hidden underground level is apparently built in the shape of a llama.

Another interesting area, called Cheqo Wasi, lies 500 meters farther up the road and

The Huari: Peru's First Empire Builders

Partly because the Inca (and the Spanish) consolidated power by erasing past history, the Huari people's role in Peruvian history has until recently been vastly underestimated. Archaeologists are still trying to explain the rise of the Huari, whose complex, polychromatic ceramics began to replace the simple two-color pots of Ayacucho's Huarpa culture around AD 500. The Huarpa were one of southern Peru's early cultures, along with the Nasca on the coast and the Tiahuanaco at Lake Titicaca. The Huari appear to have grown out of all three, combining their different technologies and religious beliefs into a more powerful system. But many of their beliefs stretch even farther back in time—Huari ceramics repeatedly portray a staff-wielding warrior deity, apparently the same one worshipped by the much earlier Chavín culture (1200-300 BC) in Peru's northern mountains.

Jokingly referred to as the Mormons of the Andes, the Huari built their empire by persistent evangelization, not by force. By AD 700 they had spread as far north as the Moche capital near present-day Trujillo, and images of the Moche decapitator god, Ai-Apaec, begin to appear on Huari ceramics. At the height of the Huari empire, around AD 900, the capital, near present-day Ayacucho, covered 300 hectares and sustained a population of anywhere from 10,000 to 70,000. The empire was connected by good roads and stretched from Arequipa in the south to Chiclayo in the north. The Huari did beautiful work in bronze, silver, lapis lazuli, and gold, made architectural models for all of their new buildings, and produced weavings with as many as 250 threads per inch.

The Huari literally paved the way for the Inca. They were the first to base their empire on large cities—and not just ceremonial centers used during festival times. Their transnational roads and advanced stone-carving techniques formed the foundation upon which the Inca empire was built. Other traditions passed on to the Inca include mummy worship and the use of *quipus*, which were bundles of brightly colored strings with elaborate knots tied in them. Ethnohistorians will probably never decipher exactly what information was catalogued by the elaborate knots and different colors of thread.

Like the Huns invading Rome, a weakening Huari state was invaded by less civilized rebel groups, probably the fierce Chancas from the Huancavelica area. Sometime between 1000 and 1200 the empire collapsed—perhaps overnight. At the capital city of Huari, some of the tunnels leading into the underground funerary chambers appear to have been hastily blocked—an effort perhaps to protect the sacred mummies. Today the city of Huari, 22 kilometers outside Ayacucho, remains largely unexcavated—most of the ruins have been literally covered by the sands of time.

includes more funerary chambers, some of which are constructed of 1.5-ton rock slabs. The joints between the rocks are perfectly smooth and rival later Inca stonework. One theory holds that the Huari used these fortified chambers to store and guard both their own mummies and those of the peoples they conquered. Like the Inca, the Huari worshipped their ancestors' mummies as a source of power and displayed them in public during sacred festivals.

Quinua

Another 15 kilometers up the road lies Quinua, a pleasant Quechua village 37 kilometers outside Ayacucho, which is known for its **iglesias de Quinua,** miniature clay churches that are placed on the roofs of homes to bring good luck. There are other hand-shaped ceramics as well, all in the region's red clay and bright mineral paint, ranging from religious images to more humorous depictions of musicians and drunken men. This remarkable town of cobblestone streets, adobe houses, and a colonial church has a few good restaurants and a few basic rooms for rent at the Hotel Qenwa. The owner is Quinua's longtime, and somewhat controversial, leader, who headed up the town's militia against the Shining Path—an 11-year battle that forced much of the town's population to flee for Ayacucho or Lima.

Pampa de Ayacucho

A short walk uphill from Quinua is the Pampa de Ayacucho, the broad plain where Spanish and patriot troops clashed on December 9, 1824, in the final battle of South America's independence. This is one of Peru's three historical sanctuaries, along with Machu Picchu and the other independence battlefield at Junín. Above the plain rises Cerro Condorcunca, where the Spanish force of 9,300 soldiers were led by Viceroy José de la Serna. On the plain below, 5,800 patriot soldiers from all over South America and Europe were led by General Antonio José de Sucre—not Simón Bolívar as is commonly believed (Bolívar was in Lima at the time). The battle began at 10am after relatives and friends on opposing sides were allowed to greet each other. After a series of tactical mistakes by the Spanish, the patriots pushed downhill and won the battle after three hours of grueling, mostly hand-to-hand fighting. By 1pm, the patriots had lost 300 men and the Spanish 1,700.

A postbattle peace treaty was signed in a room on Quinua's plaza—now glassed off for public viewing in the Casa de la Capitulación—while the wounded were being treated in the town's church. Today the battlefield is marked with a stone obelisk, 44 meters tall in recognition of the 44 years between this battle and Túpac Amaru II's indigenous rebellion against the Spanish in 1780. A two- to four-hour walk between Quinua and Huari includes good views and interesting countryside. Ask in Quinua for the start of the well-marked path.

An agency day tour to Huari and Quinua usually includes the **Pikimachay Cave,** a few kilometers past the turnoff to Quinua on the road to Huanta. Some agencies also continue on through a striking desert valley, known for its production of avocados and *lúcuma* fruit, to visit villagers and take a hike up the nearby mirador of Huatuscalla.

Buses from Ayacucho to Quinua (1.5 hours, US$3) can be taken at the Paradero Huanta (Salvador Cavero 124), next to El Niño Restaurant on the northeast edge of town. *Combis* leave when full. If you take public transportation, visit Huari on your trip out and then continue on to Quinua—*combis* passing Huari in the afternoon on their way to Ayacucho are usually full, making it hard to get home.

Vilcashuamán and Laguna Pumaqocha

After Cusco, Peru's most important Inca city is Vilcashuamán, the administrative center founded by Inca Pachacútec after the defeat of the Chanca. The present village of Vilcashuamán, site of horrific massacres during the Shining Path revolution, is built entirely on Inca ruins. There are the ruins of a fine sun temple, on top of which is the colonial church of San Juan Bautista with its carvings of serpents, monkeys, and pumas. According to the chronicler Pedro Cieza de León, this three-level sun temple was decorated inside with sheets of silver and gold, along with another, now disappeared, moon temple.

A block away is an *ushno,* a four-level Inca pyramid that can be found nowhere else in Peru and is the main reason for making the Vilcashuamán trek. A trapezoidal doorway and stairs lead to the upper platform, where the throne with two seats was probably used by the Inca administrator and his wife (*coya*). This *ushno* originally had a clear view of the temples through a single gigantic plaza and is surrounded by three sacred mountains (*apus*). Consequently, it is not surprising perhaps that President Fujimori often brought TV cameras to this place to make important announcements. The festival of the sun, or **Vilcas Raymi,** is celebrated here during the July 28 weekend, but lodging is almost nonexistent.

On the way to Vilcashuamán, it is possible to see Laguna Pumaqocha, a spectacular lake located up a side road four kilometers before the town of **Vischongo.** The detour from the main road takes about 10 minutes by car or 30 minutes walking. There are semiburied Inca

Semana Santa in Ayacucho

Peruvians regard Ayacucho's Semana Santa, the week before Easter, as Peru's most beautiful and intense religious festival. For the 10 days leading up to Easter Sunday, Ayacucho becomes a city of flower-carpeted streets, solemn processions, fireworks, and wild partying. Religious processions throughout the week depict the various passions of Christ, and there are also art shows, folk dancing, music concerts, sporting events, livestock fairs, and traditional food contests. During the festival, lodging and bus tickets triple in price and are often sold out, so book in advance. The tourist office publishes an annual brochure.

The principal events begin on the Friday before Palm Sunday, when the first religious procession starts from the Iglesia Magdalena. Palm Sunday has two important celebrations. At noon there is a huge caravan of mules and llamas carrying dried *retama* (broom) flowers and accompanied by several orchestras. After processing around the plaza twice, the *retama* is unloaded, to be burned during all-important religious ceremonies. At 4pm, Christ, on a white mule, leaves from the Carmelite monastery of Santa Teresa, along with crowds of people carrying golden palm fronds, and proceeds around the plaza to the cathedral.

The most sacred, and intense, ceremony of the week occurs on Wednesday, when the Plaza de Armas becomes a stage for the allegorical meeting of Jesus of Nazareth and the Virgin Mary. During this mystic ceremony, the images are carried on their thrones by townspeople, many in tears, watch. Because most visitors arrive the following day, there are mostly Ayacuchanos at this event.

Friday night is a candlelit procession of the deceased Jesus and the Virgin Mary, during which all the lights in the city are turned off. On Saturday morning, a bull is released every half hour from 11am onward from the Alameda Bolognesi. Surrounded by shouting kids, some of whom are injured each year, a total of six bulls run through a cordoned-off area of town. People party in the Plaza de Armas until late at night with dancing and orchestras.

At 5am on Sunday, before dawn, El Señor de la Resurrección (the resurrected Christ) is carried out of the cathedral atop a huge white pyramid adorned with 3,000 candles. As many as 250 people carry the pyramid, which goes around the plaza until 7am, amid ringing bells, fireworks, and smoke from the last bit of burning *retama*.

constructions around this sacred lake, fine walls, and a bath that features a seven-sided rock with twin water chutes.

Puya raimondii, a gigantic agave-like plant that shoots up a 15-meter flower stalk only once at the end of its life, at about age 100, can be seen on the high plains before Vilcashuamán. Titankayoq, the largest forest of these plants in the world, sprawls across 440 hectares, a two-hour uphill walk from the village of Vischongo. In August and September there is always a *Puya raimondii* in bloom—a unique and beautiful sight.

Combis to Vilcashuamán leave from the main bus station for the bumpy five-hour ride, and you can also rent a private car and driver (about US$100) in a one-day round-trip. But the best, and easiest, way is to go with an agency. This allows you to visit Lago Pumaqocha and Vilcashuamán, along with the *Puya raimondii* along the way, in a single day.

ENTERTAINMENT AND EVENTS

Bars and discotheques come and go quickly in Ayacucho, but for the moment a good option for a bar is **Magia Negra** (Independencia 65, Plaza Mayor, from 4pm Mon.-Sat.). An evening-only **pool hall** operates on the corner of Bellido and Garcilazo. A small **cinema** on the Plaza de Armas, located in the university's cultural center in the Casona Velarde Álvarez (Cusco and Asamblea), shows movies and documentaries sporadically during the week at about 6:30pm. On the weekend, traditional dances are sometimes held at the center.

Ayacucho's **Semana Santa,** the week

of weavers in their family and produce exquisite tapestries based on Huari designs. The Gallardo family makes its own natural dyes and produces only a few dozen rugs per year, which are mostly sold to galleries in Europe and the United States. Even if you are not buying (a 1.2- by 1.6-meter rug costs US$250-350 here, three times that overseas), the weaving demonstration is fascinating.

Locals also highly recommend the weavings of **Chrisantino Montes.** His production is small, and exclusively of naturally dyed pure alpaca wool. Prices are similar to those of the Gallardos. Ask around Barrio Santa Ana for directions to his workshop. **Alfonso Sulca Chávez** (Plazuela de Santa Ana 83) is another highly skilled weaver whose designs are a free interpretation of pre-Inca motifs in brilliant natural dyes. Next door is the **Huaranca family,** which focuses on animal and nature themes.

Though hard to transport, carvings in the local *piedra de huamanga* (alabaster) are made by **Julio Gálvez** (Jerusalén 12, Plazuela de Santa Ana, tel. 066/31-4278 or 966/11-1460, edgard_galvez@yahoo.es).

Other Areas

Other **crafts stores** outside the Barrio Santa Ana include **Guitarras Flores** (Miguel Grau 676, Plaza Santa Teresa, 6am-8pm daily), where the Lago family sells handmade guitars for US$70-115. Brightly painted metal crosses, candelabras, and masks can be bought from **Ignacio and Víctor Bautista,** a father-son team, at their store (Londres 235).

Especially beautiful are the brightly colored *retablos,* portable altars made of wood and plaster, which were once used by mule drivers to pray for a safe journey. The *retablos* usually have two opening doors that reveal a religious scene on top and a secular one on the bottom. Good places to buy these and other crafts are **Seminario San Cristóbal** (Plaza Mayor), **Galería Unión** (Portal Unión 25), **Galerías Artesanales Pascual** (Plazoleta San Agustín, Cusco and Asamblea), and **Mercado Artesanal Shosaku Nagase**

Brightly colored *retablos* are popular in Ayacucho.

before Easter, is Peru's best-known religious festival. Other important festivals in Ayacucho include **Carnaval** (usually the last day of Feb.), **Inti Raymi** (late June) at Lago Pumaqocha, the **Virgen de Cocharcas** (Sept. 8-11) in Quinua, the feast of **El Señor de Maynay** (mid-Sept.) in Huanta, and **Vilcas Raymi** (July 28 weekend) at Vilcashuamán.

TOP EXPERIENCE

SHOPPING
★ Barrio Santa Ana

A short walk above Ayacucho is the Barrio Santa Ana, a quirky neighborhood with cobblestone streets that is filled with an amazing variety of **crafts workshops.** At the center of it all is the Plazuela Santa Ana, which is graced with the colonial **Iglesia Santa Ana de los Indios** and lined with artisans' studios.

At **Galería Latina** (Plazuela de Santa Ana 107 and Plazoleta 605-A, tel. 066/31-1215, 8am-7pm daily), Alejandro and Alexander Gallardo are the third and fourth generation

(Plazoleta María Parado de Bellido, Bellido and 9 de Diciembre).

The best place to buy **ceramics** is the town of **Quinua,** which is famous for miniature clay chapels known as *iglesias de Quinua* that are placed on the roofs of homes for good luck. Ceramics workshops in Quinua include the **Sánchez** and **Lima families** and **Galerías Limaco,** all on Sucre, the main street.

FOOD

Ayacucho has an excellent range of restaurants. Do not miss the local specialty *qapchi,* a delicious sauce of *queso fresco* and chives over boiled yellow potatoes.

Peruvian and International

Past its humble door, **Wallpa Sua** (Garcilaso de las Vega 240, tel. 066/40-3987 or 066/31-3905, 6pm-11pm daily, US$7-9) is a warmly lit republican house with great food, ranging from spit-roasted chicken to tender steaks smothered in basil and garlic. On Friday and Saturday nights there is a bit of regional music.

The best place for *comida típica* is **Restaurant La Casona** (Bellido 463, tel. 066/31-2733, 11:30am-10pm daily, US$5-8). Locals fill the tables for the daily lunch *menú* of *qapchi* or *puca picante.* Portions are huge and prices reasonable. **Los Álamos** (Cuzco 215, tel. 066/31-2782, 7am-10pm daily, US$4) has a good US$3 *menú,* tasty grilled trout, and a pleasant colonial courtyard.

The top option in Ayacucho is **Via Via Café** (Portal Constitución 4, Plaza de Armas, tel. 066/31-2834, 8am-10:30pm daily, US$8-10) with a large menu and great view on the second-floor balcony overlooking the Plaza de Armas. For breakfast, there are pancakes, fruit salad, and omelets. For lunch, try the alpaca stir fry with a quinoa salad; for dinner, pastas, trout, or chicken.

Pizza

Pizzeria Italiana (Bellido 486, tel. 066/31-7574, 5:30pm-11:30pm daily, US$7) serves pizzas from a wood-fired oven in a cozy atmosphere. Another option is **Mamma Mia** (28 de Julio 262, tel. 066/31-4612, 4pm-midnight daily, US$6-9).

Cafés, Bakeries, and Ice Cream

For breakfast or a light snack, **Cafe-Bar New York** (28 de Julio 178, tel. 066/31-3079, 9am-11:30pm Mon.-Sat., US$2) has a peaceful, sun-filled colonial patio. The busy **Café La Miel** (Portal Constitución 11-12, Plaza de Armas, tel. 066/81-7183, 10am-10pm daily) has good service, excellent coffee, empanadas, and desserts; or get a cone to go. Another good spot for ice cream, including *chicha morada* flavor, is **Creamz** (Proceres 114, cell tel. 996-346-111, 9am-8pm Mon.-Sat.). **Lalo's Cafe** (28 de Julio 178, tel. 066/31-1331, 7am-1pm and 4pm-10pm Mon.-Sat.) is a warm café, good for an evening espresso with a slice of cake or pie. Try the cherimoya mousse, *pie de lúcuma,* and empanadas.

Markets

Maxi Market (28 de Julio 100) and its neighbor **Maxi's** (28 de Julio 236) have a reasonable selection of cold cuts, yogurts, and dry goods. There has been talk about opening an American-style mall in Ayacucho, which would likely have all the typical services, including a grocery market. This is probably a few years off, but ask around to see if there has been progress.

ACCOMMODATIONS

There are great hotel options in Ayacucho, for both the budget and the upscale traveler—even the best hotels are relatively inexpensive. Rates triple for Semana Santa (the week before Easter), and rooms are booked months in advance.

US$10-25

An excellent option is **Hostal El Mesón** (Arequipa 273, tel. 066/31-2938, www.hotelelmesonayacucho.com, US$18 s, US$20 d). Clean rooms with tile floors front a sunny courtyard and include cable TV. Some rooms have private baths, and there is 24-hour hot water.

The best deal in town is **Hotel Tres Máscaras** (Tres Máscaras 194, tel. 066/31-2921, www.hoteltresmascaras.galeon.com, hoteltresmascaras@yahoo.com, US$19 s, US$26 d, with bath). The gardens and cool sitting areas have great views of the surrounding hills. Large carpeted rooms have good beds, cable TV, and lots of hot water. The hotel has single rooms with shared bath for about US$13.

Another great deal is the quiet, comfortable **Hostal Florida** (Cuzco 310, tel. 066/31-2565, US$15 s, US$20 d), with comfortable beds, hot water, cable TV, and even heating. The sunny second-floor terrace has great views over the city. A lesser option, but only half a block from the Plaza de Armas, is **Hostal Marcos** (9 de Diciembre 143, tel. 066/31-6867, US$14 s, US$21 d, with breakfast), with large and clean though plain rooms and parquet floors, Wi-Fi, and hot water. Another central option is **Hotel Yañez** (Mariscal Cáceres 1210, tel. 066/31-4918, US$18 s, US$25 d, with breakfast), which stands out for its spacious rooms.

US$25-50

Location can't get better than **Via Via** (Portal Constitución 4, tel. 066/31-2834, www.via-via.world, US$35 s, US$46 d, with breakfast). Located in a restored colonial building right on the Plaza de Armas, Via Via has uniquely designed rooms with hardwood floors and tiled baths. Hot water and Wi-Fi are available, as well as a book exchange. Service is available in English and Dutch. It has an excellent restaurant where you can sit down with a *lomo saltado* and a Belgian beer after a long day of activities.

Close to the center, **Hotel Sevilla** (Libertad 635, tel. 066/31-4388, www.hotelsevillaperu.com, US$25 s, US$40 d), has large comfortable rooms with hot water, Internet access, and cable TV. The **Santa María** (Arequipa 320, tel. 066/31-4988, US$34 s, US$45 d) stands out for its modern architecture, interesting art, and luxurious furniture. The huge rooms

are decorated with dark wood armoires and comfortable beds. Downstairs is a bar with leather couches for sipping cocktails. The elegant courtyard of **Hotel Santa Rosa** (Lima 166, tel. 066/31-4614, www.hotelsantarosa.com.pe, US$30 s, US$45 d, with breakfast) is a beautifully restored colonial building, but the rooms don't match up.

A good option away from the main plaza is **Hotel Sierra Dorada** (Mariscal Cáceres Mz. I, Lote 21, tel. 066/31-9639, www.sierradorada.com.pe, US$28 s, US$47, with breakfast). Located on a quiet park, the carpeted rooms have hot water, cable TV, and Wi-Fi. It also has a restaurant with a good selection of regional dishes like *puca picante* and *cuy chactado*.

US$50-100

From the outside, Ayacucho's most luxurious hotel is **Hotel Plaza** (9 de Diciembre 184, tel. 066/31-2202, www.dmhoteles.pe, US$50 s or d, with breakfast), which was recently acquired by the DM Hoteles chain; the rooms need an update. Spend a bit more—US$110 a night—on one of the six suites overlooking the Plaza de Armas.

One block from the Plaza de Armas, **Hotel Universo** (Grau 105, www.hoteluniversoayacucho.com, US$36 s, US$60 d, with breakfast) is another good option with phones, cable TV, and Internet access. Its blue walls and beds with crisp white sheets make for easy sleeping.

INFORMATION AND SERVICES

Visitor information is available at the helpful **Iperú office** (Portal Municipal, Plaza de Armas, tel. 066/31-8305, www.peru.info, 9am-6pm Mon.-Sat., 9am-1pm Sun.) on the Plaza de Armas and also at the airport. The **tourist police office** (2 de Mayo 103, tel. 066/31-5845) is near the intersection with Arequipa.

Health care is available at **Centro de Salud Hospital Regional de Ayacucho** (Independencia 355, tel. 066/31-7436, emergency tel. 066/31-2180, 8am-8pm daily)

The Saywite Stone

On the road to Cusco, 47 kilometers outside Abancay, is the **Saywite Stone** (7am-sunset daily, US$2.50), an immensely interesting half-egg-shaped boulder that was dragged down from the fields above and carved with what appears to be the Inca empire in miniature. Among other things, there are obvious architectural models of Machu Picchu, Choquequirao, Ollantaytambo, Pisac, and Tipón, all roughly geographically oriented. The four corners (*suyos*) of the Inca empire (Tawantinsuyo) are represented by four square indentations, or windows, on the blank side of the rock. Animals represent the three realms of Inca cosmology: a monkey and a condor represent the heavens; a puma and a deer represent the earth; and a frog and a snake are the area beneath the ground.

Perhaps most interesting, the different climates of the Inca empire are spread around the rock and conjured by their corresponding animals—octopus and lobster for the coast, llama for the mountains, and jaguar, wild pig, and tapir for the rainforest. Finger-width channels lead from above to all these areas before draining off the rock through miniature tunnels. One theory is that priests poured llama blood or *chicha* on the rock in order to control or predict rainfall. Crops would be good in whatever region of the rock was reached by the liquid. Unfortunately, some of the figures have been chipped away—by the Spanish, locals say—and are hard to distinguish. Ask the person collecting tickets for some of the harder-to-see details.

The rock was the center of a religious complex. A labyrinth of stone walls next to the rock was probably once a granary and home for the priests. A staircase leads down a ridge past a series of restored pools. At the bottom of the hill, a huge boulder has been split in half and is carved with steps leading nowhere, another set of four square windows, carved circles, and other mysterious geometric figures. In the fields above and on the other side of the Abancay-Cusco road, there is a boulder field with another half-carved stone that is similar in appearance. The Saywite Stone is about an hour from Abancay and three hours from Cusco. Bus drivers between the two cities can drop travelers at the site, which is well-known and marked with signs. From Cusco, the trip to the Saywite Stone leads through the spectacular Apurímac Canyon.

or **Clínica el Nazareno** (Quinoa 428, tel. 066/31-4517, 7am-10pm Mon.-Sat.). For pharmacies, **Inkafarma** (28 de Julio 262, tel. 066/31-8240, www.inkafarma.com.pe, 7am-10:30pm daily) has the widest selection. It has two other locations in the city, at Mariscal Cáceres 609 and Independencia Mz. A.

The **Banco de Crédito** (Portal Union 28, on the Plaza de Armas) and **Interbank** (Jr. 9 de Diciembre 183) both have ATMs and are typically open 9am-6pm Monday-Friday and Saturday morning. The **post office** (tel. 066/31-2224, 8am-7pm Mon.-Fri., 8am-6pm Sat.) is at Asamblea 293.

Fast **Internet cafés** are at Cusco 136 (US$0.50 per hour) and Bellido 532. There are private **telephone booths** for international calling at Bellido 364 and also on the Plaza de Armas.

GETTING THERE AND AROUND

One-hour flights from Lima are available daily through **StarPerú** (Portal Constitución 17, Plaza de Armas, tel. 066/31-6660 or 066/31-6676, www.starperu.com, 8:30am-7pm Mon.-Sat., 9am-noon Sun.) or **LC Perú** (9 de Diciembre 160, tel. 066/31-6012, www.lcperu. pe, 8:30am-6:30pm daily). The airport is four kilometers out of town, a US$2.50 taxi ride.

With a paved highway connecting Ayacucho to Pisco on the coast, bus times to Lima have shortened to as little as nine hours. The bus route from the coast crosses a 4,480-meter-elevation pass along the Ruta de los Libertadores, which José de San Martín traveled before proclaiming the independence of Peru in 1821 (the battles, and official independence, came over the next three years). Except for Cruz del Sur, all of the companies have buses leaving from the new **Terminal Terrestre Plaza Wari** (last block of Javier Pérez de Cuéllar, tel. 066/31-1610). Tickets can be bought here, but some companies also have offices near the Plaza de Armas. The best company for the Ayacucho-Lima route are **Cruz del Sur** (Mariscal Cáceres 1264, tel. 066/31-2813, www.cruzdelsur.com.pe), which has three night buses. Other options are **Tepsa** (cell tel. 989-015-357, www.tepsa.com.pe), with buses leaving in the morning and night, and **Civa** (tel. 066/31-9948, www.civa.com.pe).

Before the terrorism of the 1980s, many travelers went from Lima to Huancayo and then on to Ayacucho and Cusco. This route is once again becoming popular. The best company for the Huancayo-Ayacucho route is **Expreso Union Molina** (tel. 066/31-9989), with both day and night buses (US$8-10). As usual, we recommend traveling during the day—the views are incredible. There are actually two routes: The faster one goes low through the towns of Huacrapuquio, Imperial, Acostambo, Izcuchaca, and Mayocc, where it meets up with the high route before continuing to Huanta and Ayacucho. The higher route is 12 hours of dusty, bumpy driving, and unfortunately, it is used more frequently because it goes through more populated areas.

The best company for traveling south to Andahuaylas (10 hours), Abancay (15 hours), and Cusco (22 hours) is **Los Chancas** (Terminal Terrestre Plaza Wari). A private car and driver can be rented from Ayacucho to Andahuaylas (US$115), or for the one-way trip to Cusco (US$330).

The rough dirt roads between Ayacucho and Andahuaylas are the most spectacular part of the journey to Cusco. The route first heads up and over the frigid puna before descending to the Pampa Valley, a cobalt-blue river meandering through subtropical desert. On the other side lies the Apurímac department and the Quechua town of Chinchero.

The road then climbs to a series of stunning views and switchbacks along precipices that drop hundreds of meters before arriving in the pleasant Andahuaylas valley.

After the dark years of terrorism, all the highways in and out of Ayacucho are now safe. By no means should travelers continue on the road past Quinua into the Apurímac Valley, which is Peru's top cocaine-producing region and the last remaining holdout of the Shining Path terrorist group.

Ayacucho is teeming with three-wheeled *mototaxis* (US$1).

ANDAHUAYLAS AND ABANCAY

Tourism has not yet reached Andahuaylas, a city of steep, narrow alleys that has some of the poorest demographics of the Peruvian sierra. The city sits on the banks of the Río Chumbau and is sandwiched between the smaller towns of San Jerónimo and Talavera. Most travelers stop here for the night only because Andahuaylas is midway in the Ayacucho-Cusco odyssey—it's roughly 10 hours by bus to either place. This is a good place to stretch your legs and walk through pleasant countryside and friendly villages. Besides buses, the other way to travel to and from Andahuaylas is with **LC Perú** (Teófilo Menacho 115, tel. 083/42-1591, www.lcperu.pe), which has direct daily flights to Lima. The town is best known for its annual **Yawar festival** ("blood festival"), where condors are tied, one by one, onto the back of a bull, representing a symbolic confrontation between the Inca (condor) and the Spanish (bull).

Along with Andahuaylas, Abancay is mostly a resting stop for travelers along the Ayacucho-Cusco route. Abancay is at the center of one of the purest Quechua-speaking zones in Peru, and even urbanites speak a Quechua-Spanish hodgepodge. The road between Abancay and Cusco was paved in 2002, cutting travel time between the two cities to four hours.

Food

The best restaurant in Andahuaylas is **Pico Rico** (Constitución and Andahuaylas, 5pm-midnight daily, US$4), which serves one thing and does it well: *pollo a la brasa,* with soup, french fries, and salad.

In Abancay, the formerly state-owned **Hoteles Turistas** (Díaz Bárcenas 500, tel. 083/32-1017, 7am-10pm daily, US$3-5) serves good salads and grilled meats in its dining room. There is also **Wachi** (Lima 862, cell tel. 984-726-976, 8am-3pm daily), which has the best *comida típica* in town.

Accommodations

In Andahuaylas, there is **Sol de Oro Hotel** (Juan Antonio Trelles 164, tel. 083/42-1152, US$25 s, US$35 d), with large comfortable rooms with cable TV and parquet floors.

In Abancay, the best place for a comfortable night's sleep is the quiet **Hostal El Imperial** (Díaz Bárcenas 517, tel. 083/32-1578, www.hotelimperialabancay.com, US$18 s, US$28 d), with great beds, cable TV, hot water, parking, and good service. Rooms without private baths are about half the price.

Huaraz and Vicinity

Under Huaraz's facade of sprawling cement-and-rebar buildings, muddy rivers, and haphazard produce markets, there is a thriving tourist town full of quaint hostels, coffeehouses, and delicious French restaurants. The city, at 3,028 meters elevation, is the heart of the **adventure sports** scene in the **Cordillera Blanca**—and all of Peru. It has the best range of guides, agencies, and equipment shops. With a bit of common sense, hustle, and money, it is possible to arrive in Huaraz with no equipment and, within a few days, leave for a trek, climb, or bike trip. But beware of hustlers, con artists, and phony guides; their services also abound.

People in Huaraz are friendly, gregarious, and especially festive. The Plaza de Armas is often blocked off by a stream of children's parades, *marinera* contests, and military formations. In the evenings, people stroll up and down **Luzuriaga,** the town's eyesore of a main drag, passing a variety of restaurants, gear shops, and travel agencies. To the north, the market stretches along the **Río Quilcay.**

Some advice: Keep an eye on your backpack, don't leave the bus station with an unknown guide, be careful where you eat, and take at least two days to acclimatize before heading up into the mountains.

SIGHTS

The sights described are easy day trips in or around Huaraz. Often Huaraz agencies include Chavín de Huántar and Lagunas Llanganuco in this day-trip category, but we recommend giving these sights at least a day and overnight, respectively, as described in their own sections later in this chapter.

City Tour

Huaraz's chief attraction is the **Museo Arqueológico de Áncash** (Luzuriaga 762, on the Plaza de Armas, tel. 043/42-1551, 8:30am-5pm Tues.-Sun., US$3.50). It contains a well-organized collection of stone sculptures from the local Chavín (2000-200 BC) and Recuay (AD 200-700) cultures. Upstairs are displays of pottery, textiles, and metal objects from the later Wari, Chimú, and Inca cultures, which also occupied this valley.

The Plaza de Armas, which was once a sprawl of concrete and tile, has been refurbished with pleasant green spaces and benches. Directly uphill from the Plaza de Armas is the **Iglesia Soledad,** rebuilt after the 1970 earthquake and surrounded by a pleasant plaza. There are a few good hotels in the neighborhood and some of the best views of both the Cordillera Blanca and sunsets over the Cordillera Negra.

Huaraz

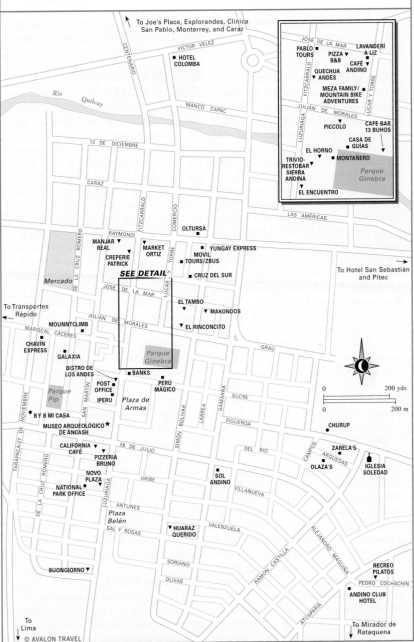

To Joe's Place, Explorandes, Clínica San Pablo, Monterrey, and Caraz

VICTOR VELEZ

● HOTEL COLOMBA

CENTENARIO

Río Quilcay

MANCO CAPAC

13 DE DICIEMBRE

CARAZ

RAYMONDI

MANJAR ▼ REAL

CREPERIE ▼ PATRICK

Mercado

To Transportes Rápido

JOSÉ DE LA MAR

MOUNNTCLIMB ■

MARISCAL CÁCERES

CHAVIN EXPRESS ■

GALAXIA ■

BISTRO DE LOS ANDES ■

POST OFFICE ■

IPERU

Parque Pip

B Y B MI CASA ●

MUSEO ARQUEOLÓGICO ★ DE ÁNCASH

CALIFORNIA ▼ CAFÉ

PIZZERIA BRUNO

NOVO PLAZA

NATIONAL ■ PARK OFFICE

BUONGIORNO ▼

To Lima

© AVALON TRAVEL

Detail inset

JOSÉ DE LA MAR

PABLO TOURS ■

FITZCARRALD

PIZZA ▼ B&B

QUECHUA ▼ ANDES

LAVANDERÍA LIZ

CAFÉ ▼ ANDINO

MEZA FAMILY/ MOUNTAIN BIKE ● ADVENTURES

JULIÁN DE MORALES

LUZURIAGA

LUCAR Y TORRE

PICCOLO ▼

CAFE BAR 13 BUHOS ■

CASA DE GUÍAS ■

EL HORNO ■

TRIVIO- RESTOBAR ▼ SIERRA ANDINA

▼ MONTAÑERO ■

Parque Ginebra

EL ENCUENTRO ■

LAS AMÉRICAS

OLTURSA ■

FITZCARRALD

COMERCIO

MARKET ORTIZ ■

TORRE

LUCAR

■ YUNGAY EXPRESS

MOVIL ▼ TOURS/ZBUS

■ CRUZ DEL SUR

SEE DETAIL

JOSÉ DE LA MAR

EL TAMBO ▼

▼ MAKONDOS

JULIÁN DE MORALES

▼ EL RINCONCITO

Parque Ginebra

GRAU

To Hotel San Sebastián and Pitec

SAN MARTIN

■ BANKS

PERÚ ▼ MÁGICO

Plaza de Armas

SIMÓN BOLÍVAR

LARREA

GAMARRA

SUCRE

FIGUEROA

28 DE JULIO

DEL RIO

CHURUP ●

CAMPOS

ARGUEDAS

ZARELA'S ▼

OLAZA'S ▼

IGLESIA SOLEDAD ■

DE LA CRUZ ROMERO

TARAPACA 27

27 DE NOVIEMBRE

LUZURIAGA

URIBE

SOL ANDINO ■

VILLANUEVA

ANTUNES

Plaza Belén

SAL Y ROSAS

▼ HUARAZ QUERIDO

VALENZUELA

RAMÓN CASTILLA

ALEJANDRO MAGUINA

RECREO PILATOS ▼

PEDRO COCHACHIN

ANDINO CLUB HOTEL ●

SORIANO

OLIVAS

ATUSPARIA

To Mirador de Rataquena

0   200 yds
0   200 m

For a view of the city, head up to the **Mirador Rataquenua,** a lookout marked with a giant cross. The safest way to get here is by taxi (US$5 round-trip). We don't recommend walking, even in groups, as there have been several assaults in this area.

Wilcahuaín

Monumento Arqueológico de Wilca-huaín (7 kilometers north of Huaraz, 9am-4pm Tues.-Sat., 9am-2pm Sun., US$2) consists of two imposing stone buildings constructed around AD 600-900, when the Wari empire expanded north from the Ayacucho area and took over the local Recuay civilization. The main building has a gravity-defying roof of thick stone slabs and three floors of finely wrought, spooky stone chambers. These rooms once held the mummified bodies of prominent leaders, kept dry by ventilation ducts running throughout the complex. The outer walls were decorated with sculpted heads, one of which remains today in the shape of a mountain lion.

Combis (US$1) are marked "Wilcahuaín"; ask your hotel for directions to the bus stop, or take a taxi (US$3). The two ruins are a few hundred meters apart along a dirt road. Ask your hotel or the local police about walking back through the countryside and villages. There have been recent reports of assaults on travelers in this area.

Cooperativa Artesanal Don Bosco

Catholic priest Ugo de Censi began the non-profit **Cooperativa Artesanal Don Bosco** (Catholic Parish, Jangas, just north of Huaraz, tel. 043/83-7105, www.artesanosdonbosco.com, 9am-noon and 2pm-4pm Mon.-Fri.) in 1970 as a way to give people working skills and an escape poverty. The organization has blossomed from its roots in Chacas, a small town on the other side of the Cordillera Blanca, into a large workshop in Jangas, just north of Huaraz. Teenagers learn how to make contemporary furniture, ceramics, blown glass, weavings, and stone sculptures, which are then shipped around the world. The organization has stores in Lima's Barranco neighborhood (San Martín 135, tel. 01/713-1344, 10:30am-7pm Tues.-Sat.) and Cusco (Tomasa Tito Condemayta 500A, tel. 084/23-2736) where you can buy their work.

ENTERTAINMENT AND EVENTS

Trivio-Restobar Sierra Andina (Parque Periodista, cell tel. 943-919-850, 8am-11pm daily) is the in-town taproom for Sierra Andina, the city's rapidly growing microbrewery. All of Sierra Andina's craft ales are on tap, plus a good selection of cocktails and locally grown organic food for lunch or dinner. It also has its own line of organic coffee.

The hot spot for dancing is the **El Tambo** (José de la Mar 776, tel. 043/42-3417, 8pm-dawn daily, cover US$5 on weekends), with Top 40 pop, salsa, and techno spun by a DJ. It also has rooms for live music and mingling over cocktails. Several other nightlife options are nearby, including the popular **Makondos** (José de la Mar 812, from 8pm Fri.-Sun., cover varies), which blasts disco and Latin pop until the wee hours of the morning. For a mellow beer, try **Cafe Bar 13 Buhos** (Parque Ginebra, tel. 043/42-9881, 11am-midnight daily), well-known among locals and travelers for its homemade "Lucho Beers."

Huaraz's biggest celebration is **Semana Santa,** the week before Easter, when Huaraz natives and their friends return home from Lima. There are important religious processions on Good Friday and Easter Sunday, along with a lot of partying and a carnival-like spirit (think water balloons). During the **Fiesta de Mayo** (May 2-9), there are processions and dance festivals for Huaraz's earthquake-controlling patron saint, El Señor de la Soledad (Our Lord of Solitude).

RECREATION

From trekking to biking to community tourism, the options for activity in Huaraz are diverse, and there are a number of ways to organize each activity. You can arrange details from abroad, which is preferable if you plan to do popular treks during peak season. Or you can arrive in Huaraz and make arrangements then. This option is more complicated during peak season.

Either way, an invaluable resource, once you're in Huaraz, is the Casa de Guías (Parque Ginebra s/n, tel. 043/42-7545, www. agmp.pe, 8:30am-1pm and 4pm-7pm Mon.-Sat.). As the Mountain Guide Association of Peru, the Casa de Guías trains and certifies guides according to international standards, provides contact with Huaraz's certified mountain guides, and helps with trip planning. In its office, you can find maps, route information, weather forecasts, and snow condition reports. Here you can also make contact with certified guides who can lead almost any trip imaginable; less expensive guides-in-training (*aspirantes*), a good choice for nontechnical routes; and porters, *arrieros* (muleteers), and cooks.

For safety, and because of the technical demands of many of Huaraz's climbs, it is essential to work with a certified mountain guide and to give yourself a couple of days to acclimatize. Remember that Huaraz is at 3,050 meters elevation and the mountains above are much higher; altitude sickness is a common problem. All the companies listed work with certified guides and can recommend acclimatization hikes. For trips during high season (May-Aug.), these companies should be contacted a month or two in advance. If you are planning your trip independently, you can verify your guide's legitimacy by asking to see his official Mountain Guide Association identification card. Beware, because there are many fly-by-night agencies.

Trekking and Climbing

Surrounded by three distinct and impressive mountain ranges, Huaraz offers access to a variety of multiple-day to multiple-week treks and climbs. The majority of trekking and climbing trips use porters and muleteers to carry food and equipment. This leaves trekkers with a lighter load and better prepared to confront the area's high altitudes. Treks, because they usually do not reach elevations over 5,000 meters, do not require previous training. Climbs, by contrast, summit high glacier-covered peaks and demand the use of ice axes, crampons, and technical climbing knowledge. Some prior experience is often essential.

A Huaraz classic, Montañero (Parque Ginebra 30-B, tel. 043/42-6386, www.trekkingperu.com) is the agency and shop of Selio, who founded the Casa de Guías, and his wife, Ana. The Peruvian couple coordinates trips to the traditional circuits and is now offering multiday alternative trips around Alpamayo and to deep valleys near Huaraz. Out of their office, the couple also runs an excellent gear rental shop, where you can find everything from crampons to parkas. Between them, they speak English, French, and German.

MountClimb (Gabino Uribe 732, Belén, tel. 043/42-4322 www.mountclimb.com.pe) is an equally good place to buy maps and rent cutting-edge gear. It recently relocated to a bigger location a block away from the main square. The owner, Alfredo Quintana, and his brother Jaime are fully certified mountain guides who lead climbs, treks, ice-climbing courses, and guided ski descents. Alfredo, who also directs rescue operations at the Mountain Guide Association of Peru, speaks English and manages guides that speak French and Italian.

Sol Andino (Gamarra 815, tel. 043/42-2205, www.solandino.com), run by the Angeles family, and Explorandes (Gamarra 835, tel. 043/42-8071, www.explorandes.com) both operate well-organized, high-quality trips. Sol Andino is known primarily for its climbing expertise. Explorandes has operated trekking trips for almost 40 years and has been awarded for its environmental stewardship (the company uses biogas, composts, and packs out all inorganic trash). A popular trek is the seven-day Best of the Cordillera Huayhuash trip.

A solid budget agency is Galaxia Expedition (Parque del Periodista, Mz. Unica, Block 36, Marsical Cáceres 428, tel.

043/42-5355, www.galaxia-expeditions.com). The agency offers basic trekking trips (US$60 pp per day) as well as mountain-biking adventures, including a 10-day trip, and rock and ice climbing tours. It also rents brand-name equipment. Other agencies that get good reviews include **Quechua Andes** (Luzuriaga 522, 2nd Fl., cell tel. 943-562-339, www.quechuandes.com) and **Infinite Adventures** (Parque Ginebra 118, tel. 043/42-7304, www.infiniteadventuresperu.com), both of which offer several multiday treks or day hikes.

Fully certified mountain and trekking guide **Val Pitkethly** (133 Rundle Crescent, Canmore, Alberta, Canada, T1W 2L6, tel. 403/678-6834, valpitk@gmail.com) treks and climbs in the Cordillera Huayhuash and Cordillera Blanca each year from May to September. Val is also the founder of **Light Education Development** (www.lighteducationdevelopment.org), a charity that provides solar lighting and health care to remote mountain villages. There are volunteer opportunities for those that have medical training, speak some Spanish, and who don't mind working in isolated areas.

Richard Hidalgo (richard_hidalgo@yahoo.com) is a certified guide who speaks excellent English and is one of Peru's best-known mountaineers. Richard is now on a crusade to solo-climb without oxygen the world's 14 peaks over 8,000 meters. At the time of writing, he has successfully climbed four of the peaks. A knowledgeable trekking resource who has spent a lot of time in the Cordillera Huayhuash and runs logistical support for expeditions is **Chris Benway,** owner of **Café Andino** (Lúcar y Torre 530, 3rd Fl., tel. 043/42-1203, www.cafeandino.com). Chris is available at the café or through his company **La Cima Logistics** (cafeandino@hotmail.com).

WHEN TO GO

The traditional climbing season is May to August, but the best snow conditions are usually found in June and July. The rainy season ends in March, but heavy snows can still strike in April and May. By August, snow cover over the glaciers is relatively thin and route-finding is more difficult.

GUIDES

To guarantee your safety, work only with a guide who is certified by the Huaraz's Casa de Guías, which represents the Mountain Guide Association of Peru. Accidents, and sometimes fatalities, happen each year in the Cordillera Blanca because trip leaders with insufficient training and experience try to guide trips. By law, all agencies are required to use certified guides.

Even if you are an experienced climber, you have a much better chance to summit with a certified guide who has already climbed a route a few times *that season*. He or she will know the latest routes, the condition of the snow pack, and the right acclimatization schedules. The going day rates are US$80-100 for a mountain guide for moderate peaks like Pisco, Urus, and Ishinca, and US$100-140 for technical peaks such as Tocllaraju, Huascarán, Chopicalqui, Artesonraju, and Alpamayo.

Before you pay, make sure that your agency or guide understands and abides by **Leave No Trace** (www.lnt.org) principles. Huaraz is filled with informal agencies and gear shops that can sell stolen gear; avoid them.

ENTRY FEES

By Peruvian standards, visiting Parque Nacional Huascarán is not cheap. Climbers and trekkers must pay US$1.50 directly to the community of Chasapampa and then US$20 for a park pass that lasts one month. Day-trippers ante up US$2 for the same pass. The national park fee can be paid at the park's headquarters in Huaraz or at ticket booths at Laguna Llanganuco, Pastoruri Glacier, the village of Musho on the way to Huascarán, and in Quebrada Ishinca. This park, like most in Peru, is badly underfunded and needs all the money it can get for trail maintenance, trash removal, park rangers, rescue infrastructure, endangered species protection, and community-based programs.

Local communities throughout the Huaraz area have recently begun charging informal fees in an attempt to get their fair share from the local trekking traffic. Collón, for instance, charges US$5 to groups that enter the Quebrada Ishinca. In other areas, such as Quebrada Quilcayhuanca, there is a gate where climbers need to pay in order to pass through the territory (although trekkers without pack animals can just climb over). In the Cordillera Huayhuash, these village fees total about US$30.

MAPS, GUIDEBOOKS, AND INFORMATION

Agencies and cafés in Huaraz sell maps, which are also available at the South American Explorers Club in Lima. For the Cordillera Blanca, the 1:100,000 map published by Carhuaz resident Felipe Díaz gives a good overview of basic trekking routes but does not give enough detail for climbers. The Austrian Alpine Club and Alcides Ames, the owner of B y B My House, have published a 1:100,000 topo map for the north and south ends of the Cordillera Blanca. For the Cordillera Huayhuash, the Alpine Mapping Guild has a 1:50,000 scale map (US$15), which is on sale in Huaraz.

The best climbing guide for the Cordillera Blanca is Brad Johnson's *Classic Climbs of the Cordillera Blanca,* which has up-to-date information on the area's rapidly changing snow and ice routes. Another good guide for the Huaraz area is Globetrotter's *Trekking and Climbing in the Andes,* coauthored by Val Pitkethly. It has a good description of the 12- to 14-day Huayhuash circuit, the Llanganuco-Santa Cruz trek, a two-week loop around Alpamayo's remote north side, and an exploratory circuit through the less-crowded valleys near Huaraz.

The best sources of up-to-date information are climbers and guides returning from the areas where you are headed. Casa de Guías in Huaraz is the area's number-one information center.

GEAR

High-quality equipment can be rented for affordable prices in Huaraz. You can request prices and make reservations ahead of time by emailing the agencies, which also sell gear, but at a significant markup.

Most U.S. airlines no longer allow passengers to fly with used camping stoves, even in checked luggage. Your alternatives are to rent a stove in Huaraz (MSR Whisperlites and similar models are available) or to bring a new stove (in the box) and then sell it in Huaraz. Selling used gear, either to a shop or other climbers, is easy.

Pretty much all supplies, with the exception of freeze-dried food, are available in markets in Huaraz and Caraz. You'll find pasta, powdered soup, cheese, powdered milk, beef jerky, dried fruit, and more. White gas (*bencina blanca*) is sold at hardware stores and along Avenida Luzuriaga. Get a recommendation from an agency or gear store to ensure you find the highest-quality gas, and fire up your stove before you go to make sure everything works.

ACCLIMATIZATION

Acclimatization in Peru is key. Even the first camps of many of the major climbs and trekking routes are high enough to make people seriously ill. As an example, if you are going to climb in the popular Quebrada Ishinca—launching pad for Ishinca, Urus, and Tocllaraju—the first day's walk to the lodge leads to 4,350 meters elevation. The other major climbs are even worse: Pisco's refuge is at 4,665 meters, and Huascarán's is at 4,700 meters. Most of the passes in the Cordillera Huayhuash are between 4,500 and 5,000 meters, and the second day of the popular Santa Cruz trek is at 4,700 meters.

Instead of falling ill and ruining your trip, spend your first day in Huaraz walking slowly up, through mountain villages, toward the Lazy Dog Inn or the Urbanización El Pinar. Another option from Huaraz is to hop aboard a *combi* heading east up over the Cordillera Negra and get off at **Callán Pass** (4,225 meters). If you have a group, a taxi will only cost around US$30. From here you can walk or mountain bike back to town on a network of dirt trails. That night, sleep in Huaraz.

For the second night, many trekkers camp at their trailhead. Climbers, however, take advantage of the other good acclimatization possibilities near Huaraz. A good second-day walk is **Laguna Churup** (4,485 meters), and a flat nearby option is **Quebrada Quilcayhuanca.** There is a place to camp at Pitec, the village near the Churup trailhead, at 3,850 meters.

Another second-day option, if you have your own transportation, is a slightly longer drive up to the refuge in **Quebrada Llaca** (lodging US$15 pp, area admission US$5 pp). There is a lodge here and excellent camping spots. A knife-edge moraine trail has mind-blowing views of **Ranrapalca** (6,162 meters) and the near-vertical south face of the **Ocshapalca glacier** (5,888 meters). The lodges on the outskirts of Huaraz make good starting points.

HAZARDS AND PRECAUTIONS

While the vast majority of trekkers to the Huaraz area never encounter any threats to their personal safety, certain touristy areas have a history of thefts or assaults. Use caution in these areas. Robberies, sometimes at gunpoint or knifepoint, have been reported at Mirador Rataquena, the bouldering area at Huanchac, and Laguna Churup. When visiting these areas, you should not go alone and should avoid nightfall.

Base-camp theft has decreased in recent years. If you are organizing your own trek, hire a camp guardian (US$20 per day), or strike a deal with your *arriero* so that there is someone in camp during the day to watch over your equipment and supplies.

The Cordillera Huayhuash route passes through several larger villages, such as Llamac, Pocpa, and Huayllapa. Here, trekkers can supplement their supplies with common items like cheese, potatoes, and beer. It is not a good idea, however, to rely on the availability of these products, as supplies are limited and expensive. The long Huayhuash route also slows medical evacuation, delaying it as much as several days.

Accident risk in Peru's tropical glaciers has been increased by their rapid retreat. Huascarán's ice fall has become notably less stable in recent years. In 2003 a huge blocks of ice fell down the 350-meter face of Alpamayo, killing eight climbers and leading the U.S. climbing magazine *Rock and Ice* to question whether accidents caused by unstable ice conditions are linked to human-induced climate change. Huascarán and Alpamayo are the two most popular and well-known peaks in the Cordillera Blanca, but plenty of other mountains of similar difficulty exist that do not involve such a level of objective danger.

In case of an accident, climbers should contact the **Casa de Guías** or Caraz's **High Mountain Rescue Unit** (Unidad de Salvamento de Alta Montaña, in Spanish). Any rescue will cost hundreds of dollars, and if a helicopter is involved, it will be thousands. Consider buying an international insurance policy that covers high-risk sports.

ROCK AND ICE CLIMBING

If you're coming to Huaraz to mountaineer, don't forget your quick-draws and rock shoes. Local crags fill the valley and stretch 20 to 200 meters. The best crag near Huaraz is Chancos, which offers eight bolted routes on sedimentary rock with big, chunky holds ranging 5.6 to 5.9. To reach Chancos from Huaraz, head to the bridge area near Centenario and take a Carhuaz *combi* north for 11 kilometers to Marcará. From here, the crags are about a 30-minute walk up the road, on the left side. There is a nice river for bathing, and the Chancos hot springs are nearby.

A closer spot, though less developed, is Monterrey, seven kilometers north of Huaraz, which has a handful of sport routes about 12 meters long. Other spots for all levels of climbing are Antacocha, one hour by bus from Huaraz, and Balcón de Judas, 20 minutes away. Huanchac, near Huaraz, is not recommended for bouldering.

For bouldering and rock climbing, a must is Hatun Machay, a 200-hectare rock forest about 1.5 hours from Huaraz in the Cordillera Negra near the town of Pampas Chico. Climbers can spend a few days exploring its massive rock towers, boulders, and caves. A short distance away is a lookout point where you can catch a glimpse of the Pacific Ocean on a clear day. **Andean Kingdom** (Parque Ginebra 120, next to Casa de Guías, tel. 043/42-5555) and **Quechua Andes** (Luzuriaga 522, 2nd Fl., cell tel. 943-562-339, www.quechuaandes.com) offer trips to Hatun Machay.

Advanced climbers will have plenty to keep them busy in the polished granite walls that line many of the Cordillera Blanca valleys. Over the past several years, teams of climbers have put up both free and aid routes on the cliffs of Quebrada Llaca and Ishinca. The best-known hard-core areas are in the Rurec Valley and the Torre de Parón, also known as the Sphinx.

Mountain Biking

In Huaraz, there is at least one agency that has well-maintained mountain bikes, Trek or better, with front suspension. Julio Olaza at **Mountain Bike Adventures** (Lúcar y Torre 530, tel. 043/42-4259, www.chakinaniperu.com) offers a range of guided mountain-bike trips and bike repairs. Julio is a longtime Huaraz resident who speaks perfect English. Rental rates, which include a guide, start at US$30 per day. The other agencies, mostly along Luzuriaga, have cheaper bikes and often do not supply helmets.

The best day trips and views are to be had in the Cordillera Negra, which has single-tracks with 1,000 meters elevation change that lead back to Huaraz. Longer trips can take you up and over the Cordillera Negra to the Pacific Ocean or through the Cordillera Blanca, on valley single-track, and over 4,500-meter passes. The longer trips require support vehicles to carry gear.

Day Hikes

In the dry hills of the Cordillera Negra and the steep valleys of the Cordillera Blanca there are plenty of options for good day hikes. A 40-minute taxi drive will drop you at the start of the trail, and hikes can range two to nine hours in length. In both ranges, the trails fade in and out of grasses and can be a challenge to follow, but with a guide or an adventurous spirit and an early start, you can easily make it to your destination and back in one day. The Casa de Guías can provide good maps and trail information; Michel Burger, the French owner of **Pérou Voyages** (Luzuriaga 702, 2nd Fl., Plaza de Armas, tel. 043/42-9556, www.perouvoyages.com), has spent many weekend mornings scoping out trails. If he is in town, Michel, who speaks French, Spanish, and German, is happy to give information about hikes. His son-in-law, Martín la Puente, who manages the Huaraz office, can also provide good advice.

Horseback Riding

The Lazy Dog Inn (Marian Cachipampa Rd., Km 3.1, cell tel. 943-789-330, www.thelazydoginn.com) has horses for guided rides on community trails that pass by farms and quiet rural roads with an awesome view of the Cordillera Blanca. Call or email ahead of time as rides need to be booked in advance.

Rafting and Kayaking

Low water levels in Río Santa have made rafting and kayaking less accessible in recent years. Water levels continue to be the highest between November and May, but year-round the water is murky. Consequently, Huaraz is a good option for beginning kayakers or rafters.

Dario Alva at **Peruvian Classic Adventures** (Parque del Periodista, Huaraz, cell tel. 943-632-671, www.peruvianclassic.com) offers a variety of kayaking and rafting tours depending on your level of experience. Prices vary depending on group size and trip length. His agency also does trekking, mountaineering, and horseback riding.

Fishing

While you may not catch a fish large enough to inspire a tale, there are decent opportunities for fishing around Huaraz. Stocked lakes, such as Lago Querococha in the Cordillera Blanca, are the best option. According to the regulations of Parque Nacional Huascarán, it is illegal to keep fish less than 25 centimeters in length. There are few places that rent fishing gear on its own, but some agencies, like **Pérou Voyages** (Luzuriaga 702, tel. 043/42-9556, www.perouvoyages.com), will provide gear as part of a trekking tour.

Community Tourism

As you head up to the hillsides around Huaraz, you pass through several traditional Andean communities. Here, life revolves around family, agricultural work, and the Sunday soccer game. Many houses still do not have electricity, educational resources are limited, and poverty discourages people from investing many resources in their daily lives. To experience how people live in these local communities and to help them through volunteer work or by participating in their daily activities, you can contact two locally based organizations.

Responsible Travel Peru (Eulogio del Rio 1364, below the La Soledad school, tel. 043/42-7949, www.responsibletravelperu.com) has an excellent selection of experiences in rural indigenous communities throughout Peru. Near Huaraz, it offers homestays in Vicos or Humacchuco, which normally involve a Pachamanca feast, as well as trips to Huaripampa to learn about Andean weaving. Respons also has treks to lakes like Llanganuco.

Andean Alliance (Marian Cachipampa Rd., Km 3.1, cell tel. 943-789-330, www.andeaalliance.org), a nonprofit run by the Lazy Dog Inn's Canadian owners, tries to match your skills and availability with community projects based at the community center Yurac Yacu. Focus is on education, leadership, outdoor education, and microbusiness:

a seasonal café, a women's group, and local walking guides.

Tour Agencies and Guides

The conventional day tour leaves Huaraz at 9am, returns at 7pm or 8pm, costs US$12-15pp, and includes transportation and a guide. Bring plenty of warm clothes, a bag lunch, and sun protection, and make sure your guide speaks English well.

The most reliable tour operator is **Pablo Tours** (Luzuriaga 501, tel. 043/42-1145, www.pablotours.com). Other options are **Chavín Tours** (La Mar 590, tel. 043/22-2310 or cell tel. 943-788-093, www.chavintours.com.pe) and **Quechua Andes** (Luzuriaga 522, 2nd Fl., tel. 943/56-2339, www.quechuaandes.com).

FOOD

Huaraz is filled with a variety of high-quality restaurants, comparable only to Cusco or Arequipa.

Peruvian

Café Restaurant Rinconcito Minero (Julián de Morales 757, tel. 043/42-2875, 7am-11pm daily, US$3-10) may be known for its *tacu tacu* (a fried rice and bean patty), but the menu is extensive, including breakfast and fish.

For country-style Peruvian fare in a garden setting, head to one of the many *recreos* along the Huaraz-Caraz Highway. One we especially like is **La Colina** (100 meters from Essalud, no phone, 11am-6pm daily, US$7-10) just outside Huaraz near the EsSalud Hospital. Lunch is flavorful and full of roasted guinea pig, rabbit, pisco sours, and *chicha de jora*. In Huaraz there is also **Recreo Pilatos** (Pedro Cochachín 146, tel. 043/42-2444, noon-5pm daily, US$2). It serves steaming white-corn tamales and huge plates of *chicharrón*.

Peruvian Fusion and Fine Dining

The centrally located and French-owned **Bistro de los Andes** (Plaza de Armas, tel. 043/42-9556, noon-10pm Mon.-Sat.,

5pm-10pm Sun., US$6-10) is considered one of the more elegant choices in Huaraz. It has a good menu that includes grilled trout and pesto pasta, along with an extensive wine list.

Creperie Patrick (Luzuriaga 422, tel. 043/42-6037, 11am-11pm Mon.-Sat., 5pm-10:30pm Sun., US$4-8), also French owned, invites a long and leisurely meal. The service is unhurried, and the flavorfully prepared crepes, fish, meat, and chicken dishes deserve to be enjoyed. The textured restaurant walls and dark wooden tables create an intimate setting, and the espresso and wine list are both good.

International

You won't find any other eatery in the country with so many varieties of chili sauces as ★ **Chilli Heaven** (Parque Ginebra, next to Casa de Guías, tel. 043/22-1313, chilliheaven@hotmail.com, 8am-10pm Mon.-Sat., 4pm-10pm Sun., US$5-10). All are good and spicy enough to go along with the Indian and Thai curries (with rice or noodles), Mexican food, or the pizzas. For another option, check out ★ **Trivio-Restobar Sierra Andina** (Parque Periodista, cell tel. 943-919-850, noon-11pm Tues.-Sun., US$6-10), which has good steaks, pastas, hamburgers, and its own organic coffee. Grab one of the Sierra Andina craft ales with your meal.

Pizza

Pizza B&B (José de la Mar 674, tel. 043/42-1719, 5pm-11pm daily, US$5) is not simply an excellent pizza place. The French owners have a menu that offers fresh salads, very good pastas, their famed wood-fired pizzas, and the real and genuine *flambée flammenkuche,* the house specialty. Additionally, this is the place to find an interesting and high-alcohol-content variety of Belgian, British, French, and German beers (US$8-12).

A good family option, **Pizza Bruno** (Luzuriaga 834, tel. 043/42-5689, 3pm-11pm Mon.-Sat., 5pm-11pm Sun., US$5) has games for the kids and white tablecloths for the parents. Try the pizza caprese; the French chef

also serves salads, crepes, pastas, and steaks. The busy **El Horno** (in front of Parque Ginebra, tel. 043/42-1004, www.elhornopizzeria.com, 4:30pm-11pm daily, US$5) serves thin-crust pizzas, large salads, grilled meats, and sandwiches.

Cafés, Bakeries, and Ice Cream

Café Andino (Lúcar y Torre 530, 3rd Fl., tel. 043/42-1203, www.cafeandino.com, 9am-10pm daily, US$3-8) is a great meeting spot for travelers, coffee lovers, and avid readers. The Peruvian-U.S. owners, Ysabel Meza and Chris Benway, are warm hosts and an endless gold mine of information about mountain climbing and trekking in the Cordillera Blanca and Huayhuash. Their café is filled with maps, books, and big tables, perfect for trip planning. As you while away the day over books, magazines, Wi-Fi, and board games, order up a strong cup of joe (Chris roasts his own beans), a salad, sandwich, or even *lomo saltado*. The menu is inventive and diverse.

California Café (28 de Julio 562, tel. 043/42-8354, www.huaylas.com, 7am-7pm Mon.-Sat., 7am-2pm Sun., US$3-5) feels as if it was lifted out of laid-back Berkeley, California. The strong espressos, tempting desserts, board games, Wi-Fi, magazines, a big book exchange, and couches will keep you seated for hours. Breakfast and light meals are served.

Restaurant Encuentro Grill and Coffee (Luzuriaga block 6, Parque del Periodista, tel. 043/42-7971, 8am-11pm daily, US$4-7) has tables set in a sunny square and is a good place to sit and have a beer, lemonade, or coffee. It serves Peruvian food such as tamales, *trucha,* and roasted guinea pig as well as sandwiches, pastas, and grilled meats.

Markets

Huaraz's market runs along Raimondi from Luzuriaga down to Cruz Romero and is generally open from dawn to dusk daily. The best selection is in a market building at the corner of San Martín and Raimondi. Inside are a few booths that supply a wide range of food for trekkers, including some imported products (although no freeze-dried food). Surrounding the market are stalls of fruits, vegetables, mountain cheese, and freshly slaughtered chickens. Anything you cannot find here, like fresh bread, will be in the minimarkets on San Martín.

The best grocery stores, which do not have a good section of produce, are **Market Ortiz** (Luzuriaga 401, tel. 043/42-1653, 8am-11pm daily) or, on the opposite side of town, **Novoplaza** (Luzuriaga 882, tel. 043/42-2945, 7am-11pm Mon.-Fri., 7am-midnight Sat., 8am-11pm Sun.).

ACCOMMODATIONS

A top destination for international trekkers and climbers, Huaraz is full of high-quality hostels. Prices for lodging and transportation double or even triple during high season (May-Aug.) and the July 25-August 5 national holidays. To get a room at some hotels, you'll need to make reservations three months in advance.

Under US$10

Alpes Huaraz (Ladislao Meza 112, tel. 043/42-8896, www.hostalalpeshuaraz.com, US$8 dorm, US$18 s, US$24 d with private bath) is a charming bed-and-breakfast spot at great value. Close to the Plaza de Armas, it has hot water, free Wi-Fi, a kitchen, and a bar.

US$10-25

Jo's Place (Daniel Villazón 276, tel. 043/42-5505, josplacehuaraz@hotmail.com, US$16 s, US$20 d, with private bath) is north of the Río Quilcay and about a 15-minute walk from city center. Here, Joe Parsons, a British expat, and his Peruvian wife have created a friendly and relaxed collection of rooms that ring a hammock-filled garden. All guests have access to a simple shared kitchen, Wi-Fi, a TV and DVD room with books, laundry service, and long-term storage space.

B y B Mi Casa (27 de Noviembre 773,

tel. 043/42-3375, www.micasahuaraz.jimdo. com, US$18 s, US$27 d, with breakfast) is a charming home tucked away in a central but tranquil neighborhood. The six rooms spiral around a sunny courtyard. Beds are comfortable, and rooms have a writing desk and private baths. The hostel is in the home of Francisca Ames, the wife of the late Alcides Ames, who was one of the area's foremost glaciologists.

US$25-50

A solid favorite among climbers is ★ **La Casa de Zarela** (Julio Arguedas 1263, tel. 043/42-1694, www.lacasadezarela.hostel.com, US$25 s or US$30 d). Spiral stairs lead up from a sunny courtyard to rooms and terraces with spectacular Cordillera Blanca views. The 17 rooms are simple but a good value, with Wi-Fi. Breakfast is served in the homey downstairs area, with very good coffee and the best burritos in town. There is also a bar, and a rooftop kitchen is available for guest use. It also has four-bed dorm rooms (US$14 pp).

The popular family-run ★ **Churup Bed and Breakfast** (Amadeo Figueroa 1257, La Soledad, tel. 043/42-4200, www.churup. com, US$27 s, US$36 d, with breakfast) has 15 simple rooms intermixed with nicely furnished sitting areas, a top-floor lounge, and even a foosball table. The book exchange, laundry area, shared kitchen, equipment rental, and Spanish classes are likely to tempt you out of your room and into conversations with other travelers. Owners Nelly and Juan Quiros and their son Juan Manuel, a trekking guide, serve a fortifying breakfast and offer cheaper downstairs bunk rooms (US$10 pp) without breakfast.

Huaraz native Tito Olaza has anticipated the traveler's every need and answered it in his intimate nine-room guesthouse **Olaza's Bed & Breakfast** (Julio Arguedas 1242, tel. 043/42-2529, www.olazas.com, US$29 s, US$36 d, with breakfast during May-Aug.). The water is hot, the shared kitchen is sparkling, and the fourth-floor lounge has a DVD player, a fireplace, and a fridge full of cold beer. Breakfast is served on the sunny rooftop patio, and views of the mountains are explained on a notecard that accompanies your hot coffee.

US$50-100

Hotel Colomba (Francisco de Zela 210, tel. 043/42-1241, www.huarazhotel.com, US$54 s, US$72 d), once a hacienda, has been converted into a series of large rooms spread out through a labyrinth of gardens and grassy lawns. Lucho and Sylvana Maguiña, the Peruvian-Argentine owners, are extremely generous and kind. And with all the birds, peace, and quiet, you might think you were in the countryside. This hotel is north of the Río Quilcay and a few minutes' taxi ride to the center.

A bit out of the town center, **San Sebastián Hotel** (Italia 1124, tel. 043/42-6960, www.sansebastianhuaraz.com, US$42-54 s, US$56-70 d, with breakfast) is a very relaxed, safe option. All rooms have recently been built or remodeled, so baths are new and beds are plushly covered with duvets. The main lobby has Internet access, Wi-Fi, big sofas, and a TV with a DVD player. Its adjoining restaurant serves national and international dishes.

US$100-150

The **Andino Club Hotel** (Pedro Cochachín 357, tel. 043/42-1662, www.hotelandino.com, US$100 s, US$115 d) is the luxury hotel of Huaraz, with an elegant lobby, great views, and a very good international restaurant. Room styles vary according to location within the hotel, and it is worth asking in advance which services your room will have. More expensive rooms include bathtubs and terraces with views, and there are also accessible rooms and mini apartments with kitchens, DVD players, and whirlpool tubs. Many international climbing and trekking agencies stay here with their groups, so make reservations well ahead of time.

Outside Huaraz

Snowcapped peaks tower above **The Lazy Dog Inn** (Marian Cachipampa Rd., Km 3.1, cell tel. 943-789-330, www.thelazydoginn.com, US$75-125 for 2 people, depending on room type, with breakfast and dinner), which rests at the foot of the Cordillera Blanca. This unique bed-and-breakfast, 20 minutes outside Huaraz, is the home of Diana Morris and Wayne Lamphier, a Canadian couple who open their stylish adobe lodge and two adobe cabins to guests. All the rooms are tastefully decorated and painted in warm colors. Amenities include Wi-Fi access, on-site horses, and an outdoor sauna. You can also camp for US$22 pp. If you coordinate your visit in advance, Diana will help you plan treks, day hikes, and horseback rides from the inn.

INFORMATION AND SERVICES

The best spot for trekking and climbing info is **Casa de Guías** (Parque Ginebra s/n, tel. 043/42-7545, rescue line 941-946-818, www.agmp.pe, 8:30am-1pm and 4pm-7pm Mon.-Sat.), but all the trekking and climbing agencies, along with **Café Andino** (Lúcar y Torre 530, 3rd Fl., tel. 043/42-1203, www.cafeandino.com) sell maps and books.

On the Plaza de Armas, the government's **iPerú** (Luzuriaga 734, 2nd Fl., Pasaje Atuspáría, tel. 043/42-8812, www.peru.travel, 9am-6pm Mon.-Sat., 9am-1pm Sun.) gives limited advice but can provide lists of official trekking agencies. **Parque Nacional Huascarán** (Sal y Rosas 555, tel. 043/42-2086, 8:30am-1pm and 2:30pm-6pm Mon.-Fri., 8:30-noon Sat.) sells entry tickets to the park (climbing and trekking US$23, day visits US$2).

Good websites on Huaraz are www.huaraz.com and www.andeanexplorer.com. The outfits that maintain these websites also put out helpful brochures with good area maps. Another good source of information is the English-language newspaper *The Huaraz Telegraph* (www.thehuaraztelegraph.com). Weather information can be found at www.senamhi.gob.pe.

Police and Emergency

The 24-hour **tourist police office** (Luzuriaga 724, beside the town hall, tel. 043/42-1351) is in a small passageway on the west side of the Plaza de Armas. There is also a 24-hour **national police office** (Sucre 250, tel. 043/42-1330). For mountain emergencies, call the **Casa de Guías** (tel. 043/42-7545) or the Caraz-based 24-hour **Departamento de Salvamento de Alta Montaña (DEPSAM)** (High Mountain Rescue Department, tel. 043/39-1163, 043/39-1669, or 966-831-514).

Health Care

The best clinic in town is **Clínica San Pablo** (Huaylas 172, tel. 043/42-8811, 24 hours daily). For nonemergencies, the public hospitals are much cheaper. The best is **Hospital Víctor Ramoz Guardia** (Luzuriaga, block 13, tel. 043/42-4146 or 043/42-1861, 24 hours daily).

On Luzuriaga, there are several big well-stocked chain **pharmacies** like Boticas Fasa, Inkafarma, and Boticas Arcángel. Most are open 7am-11pm daily.

Banks and Money Exchange

Clustered around the Plaza de Armas are several banks with ATMs: **Banco de Crédito, Scotiabank, Banco Continental,** and **Interbank.** Banks are generally open 9am-6pm Monday-Friday and 9am-1pm Saturday.

Communications

The post office, **Serpost** (Luzuriaga 714, tel. 043/42-1030, 8am-10pm Mon.-Fri., 8am-6pm Sat.), is on the Plaza de Armas.

There are many fast **Internet cafés** around town, and several are on Sucre, east of the Plaza de Armas. These cafés are open approximately 7am-11pm daily. At the corner of Sucre and Simón Bolívar, a handful of **call centers** sell phone cards and have phone booths where you can make local, national, and international calls 7am-10pm daily.

Volunteering

The best volunteering option in the Cordillera Blanca is undoubtedly **The Center for Social Well Being** (cell tel. 974-673-095, www.socialwellbeing.org). The goal of this nonprofit organization, founded in 2000 by veteran anthropologist Patricia Hammer, is to improve the lives of Andean people.

Laundry

The best laundries are the **Lavandería Liz** (José de la Mar 674, tel. 043/42-1719, 5pm-11pm daily, US$1 per kilogram) and **Lavandería Denny's** (José de la Mar 561, tel. 043/42-9232, 8am-9pm Mon.-Sat., US$1 per kilogram). There is also a *lavandería* on the corner of Lucar and Torre.

GETTING THERE AND AROUND

LC Perú (tel. 043/42-4734, Lima tel. 01/204-1313, www.lcperu.pe) has daily flights to and from Lima to the area's airport, which is 32 kilometers north of Huaraz in Anta.

Huaraz is a comfortable eight-hour bus ride from Lima. The highway runs up to Lago Conococha at 4,000 meters elevation before dropping into the Callejón de Huaylas and Huaraz. Buses going back and forth to Lima often start and end in Caraz, passing Huaraz en route. In recent years, bus companies have begun to pay particular attention to safety, and it is common for all passengers to be videotaped before departure. These extra measures have made night travel safer.

The best option for Lima-Huaraz travel is **Móvil Tours** (Confraternidad Oeste 451., tel. 043/42-9541, www.moviltours.com.pe, 7am-11pm daily), which has six daily buses to Lima with a late-night, 180-degree reclining seat service, just like first class on a flight. Móvil also goes to Chimbote and Trujillo. **Oltursa** (Antonio Raimondi 825, tel. 043/42-3717, www.oltursa.pe) has three daily buses between Lima and Huaraz. A similar service, but not as comfortable, is provided by **Cruz del Sur** (Simón Bolívar 491, tel. 043/72-0444, www.cruzdelsur.com.pe). The company has a morning and a night bus to Lima.

To reach Chavín de Huántar and the cities east of the Cordillera Blanca in the Callejón

Chavín de Huántar

de Conchucos, **Empresa de Transportes Sandoval** (Mariscal Cáceres 330) has buses leaving every four hours and charges about US$4.50. There are also *colectivos* (US$9) that leave from Cáceres.

For making the interesting journey across the high plains east of Huaraz to Huánuco, **Transportes El Rápido** (28 de Julio, behind the Iglesia San Antonio, tel. 043/42-2887) will get you as far as the midway point of La Unión (5 hours) for US$6. Buses leave at 6am and 1pm daily. The company also travels to Huallanca (4 hours), a starting point for treks in the Cordillera Huayhuash.

For heading north to **Monterrey,** catch the Línea 1 *combi* (30 minutes, US$0.30) that leaves from the corner of Luzuriaga and 28 de Julio. The departure point can change, so ask your hotel or the Iperú office before heading out. Another option is to take a taxi (US$4). To reach **Recuay** and points along the highway south of Huaraz, head to the Transportes Zona Sur terminal (Gridilla and Tarapacá).

Taxis are cheap in Huaraz and cost US$1-1.50 for in-town travel.

★ CHAVÍN DE HUÁNTAR

Chavín de Huántar (9am-4pm Tues.-Sat., 9am-2pm Sun., US$4), three hours east of Huaraz, was the capital of the Chavín culture, which spread across Peru's northern highlands 2000-200 BC. The site includes a sunken plaza ringed with stylized carvings of pumas and priests holding the hallucinogenic San Pedro cactus. A broad stairway leads to a U-shaped stone temple, called the **Castillo,** which rises 13 meters off the ground in three levels of stone.

This site was visited by Italian explorer Antonio Raymondi in the 19th century and later excavated in the early 20th century by Julio Tello. Both men brought back elaborately carved pillars, which are now on display in Lima's museums. Tello developed an elaborate theory that Chavín de Huántar was the launching pad for all of Peru's advanced cultures. Recent excavations have revealed that the city was preceded by Caral and other important centers on the coast, but Chavín's importance is still irrefutable. During its peak in 400-200 BC, the Chavín culture spread across Peru as far as Ayacucho in the south and Cajamarca in the north. Its exotic deities, which included the puma and a mythical deity with a staff in its hand, became central icons throughout Peru's ancient art and iconography.

The highlight of Chavín de Huántar is the series of underground chambers beneath the main temple. Illuminated by electric light, three of these passages converge underground at an extraordinary stone carving, known as the **Lanzón.** This granite pillar is carved with a frightening mythical being, which has thick snarling lips and a pair of menacing, upward-arching canines. Heavy earrings hang from the ears and snakes appear to grow from the head. The notched top of the pillar extends upward into an upper gallery, where priests may once have performed rituals.

Its underground architecture gives Chavín de Huántar an entirely different feel than the other cultural ruins of northern Peru. The impression is partly playful and partly terrifying. As you wind your way through impressive ventilated tunnels that once led to dressing and ceremonial rooms, you can't help imagine the terrible existence of the prisoners who were also kept in the tight underground passageways.

Many of Huaraz's agencies offer a day tour to Chavín de Huántar, which leaves Huaraz at 9:30am and returns about 10 hours later. Although this is an efficient way to see the ruins, with a tour group you are unlikely to perceive the true magnitude of the sight, because all agencies hit the ruins at the same hour (right after lunch). There's a bit of herding as people try to move in and out of tight spaces. It is advisable to go on your own, spend the night in Chavín, and head to the ruins early in the day. At the entrance, you can contract a Spanish-speaking guide (US$8). This way, you'll also have time to check out the **museum** (9am-4pm Tues.-Sat., 9am-2pm Sun., free) on the other side of town, about a 20-minute walk from the Chavín de Huántar ruins.

Food

Café Renato (Huayna Cápac 285, Plaza de Armas, tel. 043/45-9007, 7am-9pm daily, US$4) makes its own yogurt, cheese, and *manjar,* which it serves up in a small corridor of a patio. The café can also arrange horseback riding trips. Next door to the ruins, **Buongiorno** (17 de Enero 520, tel. 043/45-4112, lunch daily, US$5) has a flavorful and interesting menu, which features local foods

like trout, guinea pig, and *pachamanca.* Service can be slow. **Mama Raywana** (Plaza de Armas, cell tel. 943-530-292, 8am-9pm daily, US$4) has filling sandwiches and hot drinks.

Accommodations

Hotel Inca (Wiracocha 170, Plaza de Armas, tel. 043/45-4021, US$15 s, US$25 d) is located right on the Plaza de Armas. In business more than 20 years, this place is a solid choice for a night's sleep in order to see the ruins. The family-run hotel is friendly, but it doesn't have much of a menu, and any meals need to be ordered in advance. On the north side of the Plaza de Armas there is **Hostal Gantu,** which has refurnished rooms with private baths and a hot shower.

Information and Services

The Plaza de Armas has both call centers and Internet cafés. For health matters, the **Centro de Salud** (24 hours daily) is on the main road, heading toward San Marcos.

Getting There and Around

There is a spectacular three-day trek that crosses the southern end of the Cordillera Blanca from **Olleros,** a village just south of Huaraz, to Chavín de Huántar. The trek, which is not crowded, heads along an ancient trade route up and over **Yanashallash Pass** at 4,700 meters elevation.

From Huaraz, buses by **Empresa de Transportes Sandoval** (Mariscal Cáceres 330, tel. 043/42-8069) head to the town of Chavín (US$4.50), about one kilometer north of the ruins. *Colectivos* also leave when full from Cáceres for Chavín (US$9 pp).

Callejón de Huaylas

Huaraz lies at the top of the Callejón de Huaylas, a river valley that cuts between the Cordilleras Blanca and Negra. As you descend into the valley, there are a handful of pleasant towns. Among them, Carhuaz, Yungay, and Caraz are reasonable base-town alternatives to Huaraz.

MONTERREY

Easygoing Monterrey is seven kilometers north of Huaraz. Known for its hot springs and saunas, the town also has a few worthwhile hotels and restaurants. The **Baños Termales** (hot springs, 7am-5pm daily, US$1.50) include two large pools, of varying temperatures, along with private bathing rooms. Don't be put off by the appearance of the water, which is stained brown by minerals. Slightly past Monterrey, **La Reserva** (Huaraz-Caraz Hwy., Km 8, tel. 043/42-4865, 8am-6pm Tues.-Sun.) offers Turkish baths as well as steam and dry saunas. The facilities are clean and well-kept.

Food and Accommodations

There are several small *recreos,* or country restaurants, near Monterrey. The best is **El Ollón de Barro** (Huaraz-Caraz Hwy., Km 7, tel. 043/42-3364, 11am-5pm Tues.-Sun., US$3-8), which serves up huge portions of *chicharrón,* huge red *rocoto* peppers stuffed with spiced meat, local trout, and grilled meats. Tables are spread around a grassy lawn, and there is a playground for kids. Owners Patrick and Adela also run Creperie Patrick in Huaraz. Another good option is **El Cortijo** (Huaraz-Caraz Hwy. s/n, tel. 043/42-3813, 8am-7pm daily, US$5-12), where tables spill out onto a grassy bougainvillea-lined garden, and lunch is often a pisco sour, *papa a la huancaína, pachamanca,* and *humitas.*

There are no good budget options in Monterrey, and prices rise during high season. The best lodging choice is the peaceful El

Patio de Monterrey (Huaraz-Caraz Hwy., Km 206, tel. 043/42-4965, www.elpatio.com. pe, US$85 s, US$100 d, with breakfast). The colonial-style hotel, with tile roofs, a stone terrace, and a water fountain, has rooms with nice furniture and all the modern amenities, but not cable TV. Many of the rooms look out over gardens, and meals are served in a dining area with a fireplace.

Getting There and Around

From the corner of Luzuriaga and 28 de Julio in Huaraz, catch the Línea 1 *combis* to Monterrey (30 minutes, US$0.30). You can also take a taxi (US$3) from Huaraz to Carhuaz.

On the Huaraz-Caraz Highway in Monterrey, you can catch a *combi* back to Huaraz or on to the other towns in the Callejón de Huaylas.

CARHUAZ

Carhuaz is a quiet town with spectacular views of **Hualcán.** At 2,650 meters above sea level, the town is about 400 meters lower than Huaraz and about 32 kilometers farther down the valley. Carhuaz has just the right amount of tourism infrastructure to make it a comfortable place to stay without being a go-go tourist destination. It is a pleasant relief from Huaraz. The relaxing Plaza de Armas is full of fragrant rose gardens and palm trees. The town's **Wednesday market** and especially the **Sunday market** are busy and diverse. Colorfully dressed vendors hawk local fruits and vegetables, dried herbs, crafts, and even livestock.

The outskirts of Carhuaz stretch into the Cordilleras Negra and Blanca, which means the town has some great options for day trips. For US$3, you can hire a taxi to take you to **Mirador Ataquero** in the Cordillera Negra. Walk back following a trail that drops you on the edge of town. There are rustic hot baths above town at the **Baños de la Merced** (US$0.30). *Combis* heading that direction leave the Plaza de Armas once an hour, or hire a round-trip taxi (US$6). The **Cueva de Guitarreros,** a cave that was inhabited 12,000 years ago, is an hour's walk west of Tingua, the town north of Carhuaz.

Another great day excursion is hiking in the Cordillera Blanca. Take an early-morning *combi* heading east up the **Quebrada Ulta** to Chacas. Before the *combis* wind the final switchbacks to the high pass of **Punta Olímpica** (4,890 meters), there are starting points for two excellent day hikes. The first leads to **Laguna Auquiscocha** (4,320 meters), where there is a granite waterfall reminiscent of Yosemite Falls. The second leads to the stunning alpine cirque around **Lago Yanayacu** (4,600 meters). The last Carhuaz-bound *combi* leaves Chacas around 4pm.

Food and Accommodations

There are some good restaurants serving regional dishes for lunch just outside Carhuaz. Try **La Cabana** (noon-5pm daily, US$5), located a few kilometers from Carhuaz in Acopampa, or **Mama Mechi** (noon-5pm daily, US$5-8) on the main road to Carhuaz from Acopampa. For ice cream, check out **Helados Provenir,** on the Plaza de Armas.

For a modern and centrally located option, the immaculate **El Abuelo Hostal** (9 de Diciembre 257, tel. 043/39-4456, www. elabuelohostal.com, US$45 s, US$60 d, with breakfast) has a first-floor lobby opens onto a lovely garden full of local trees and plants. Upstairs the rooms have Andean rugs, comfortable beds, and modern baths. There is also a terrace with great views of the Cordillera Negra. Textiles, ceramics, and maps are sold. It also serves international food and coffee. A clean and safe budget option is Carhuaz is **Hotel La Merced** (Ucayali 724, tel. 043/39-4280, US$15 s, US$20 d), with cable TV and nice views of the mountains.

Five minutes from Carhuaz is the relatively new ★ **Montaña Jazz** (Carretera Chunchun s/n, Barrio Eccana, cell tel. 986-778-898 or tel. 043/63-0023, www.montanajazzperu.com, bungalows US$100-150). It has four cozy bungalows for couples or families that want to be out in the country but still close enough to town. The bungalows have a fireplace, and three of them have fully-equipped kitchens. The hotel now has a restaurant serving pizzas, trout, and other homemade dishes. There is also an area for barbeques and bonfires.

Information and Services

An extraordinary source of information, and an all-around nice guy, is local resident **Felipe Díaz,** who authored the Cordillera Blanca's most used trekking map. If you speak Spanish, he will talk your ears off about all the exciting trekking options in the area. Ask for him at El Abuelo hostel (9 de Diciembre 257, tel. 043/39-4456, www.elabuelohostal.com). Carhuaz also has a small **tourist office** (Comercio 530, tel. 043/39-4249, ext. 202, 7:30am-12:30pm and 1:30pm-4pm Mon.-Fri.).

Several **pharmacies** ring the Plaza de Armas. Hours are typically 8am-1pm and 3pm-10pm daily. **Banco de la Nación** has a branch on the Plaza de Armas, but there is no ATM in town. The **post office** (8am-noon and 2pm-5pm Mon.-Sat.) is also on the Plaza de Armas.

Getting There and Around

Carhuaz is 30 minutes north of Huaraz. For long-distance trips to Lima and Chimbote (both 8 hours), **Móvil Tours** (Progreso 757, tel. 043/39-4141) and **Yungay Express** (Progreso 672, tel. 043/39-4352, 7am-8pm daily) are good options. The latter also has buses to Huallanca.

To get to Carhuaz from Huaraz, hop a Caraz-bound *combi* and get off in Carhuaz. From Carhuaz's Plaza de Armas, *combis* leave every 15 minutes heading south to Huaraz, north to Caraz, and, on market days, west toward the Mirador Ataquero and the Cordillera Negra. You can also take a taxi (about US$22).

YUNGAY

Yungay, 54 kilometers north of Huaraz, is a quiet town with minimal services, but it is the closest launching point for Lagunas Llanganuco and classic peaks such as Pisco and Huascarán.

The original village was the site of a horrific tragedy in 1970, when an earthquake dislodged an immense chunk of mud and ice from Huascarán. The resulting *aluvión* destroyed the town and killed 18,000 people, nearly the entire village. The few hundred survivors of the tragedy built a new settlement on a nearby, more protected site. New Yungay is a mix of modern buildings and 100 or so prefab wooden cabins that were donated by the former Soviet Union. The silt plain above the old village has been converted into the **Campo Santo Cemetery** (8am-6pm daily, US$0.60) and remains a solemn place. The only evidence of the original village is the tops of a few palm trees that once ringed the town's square and now just barely stick out of the hardened mud, and the church's old facade.

In the floodplains nearby, huge boulders and a crumpled bus attest to the power of the mudslide. Miraculously, a huge white statue of Christ, which stands above the town's hilltop cemetery, survived the flooding. It was there that a few hundred people clambered to safety during the mudslide. From this statue, there are views over the entire valley up to the flanks of Huascarán, where the path of the mudslide can still be seen. There are two festivals here in October, including **Virgen del Rosario** (first week of Oct.) and the town's anniversary, October 25-28.

Lagunas Llanganuco

These two pristine lakes, surrounded by rare *Polylepis* trees, are perched high in the glacial valley above Yungay at 3,850 meters elevation. Between the tumbling glaciers of Huascarán's north summit (6,655 meters) and Huandoy (6,160 meters), the lake and its turquoise waters, a result of glacial silt, glow in the midday sun. The first lake is Chinacocha. Rowboats can be rented (8am-3:30pm daily) here. The second lake is Orcon Cocha, and the best mountain views are a bit farther on.

The highway from Yungay passes these lakes en route to Portachuelo Llanganuco, a high pass at 4,767 meters, and leads to the towns of Vaquería, Colcabamba, and Yanama in the Callejón de Conchucos. Shortly before the lakes, there is a control booth of the Parque Nacional Huascarán, which charges day visitors US$2.50 and overnighters US$23.

Lagunas Llanganuco

These lakes are one of the starting points for the popular Santa Cruz trek. The base camp for climbing Pisco and the newly built Refugio Peru are a four-hour hike from the Lagunas Llanganuco. The best time to visit the Lagunas Llanganuco is at midday, when the sun is brightest. In the afternoon, the lakes fall into shade and winds whip their waters.

Food and Accommodations

While it's nothing fancy, **Chicken Progreso** (Areas Graziani s/n, tel. 043/39-3184, 7am-10pm daily, US$2.50-5) serves up large portions of spit-roasted chicken with fries and salad, or *lomo saltado*. **Restaurant Alpamayo** (Km 255 on the highway, tel. 043/39-3090, 8am-10pm daily, US$2-4) serves fortifying breakfasts of *chicharrón* and *tamal* and a range of Peruvian food throughout the day.

There aren't a lot of options for spending the night in Yungay, but one place is **Hotel Rima Rima** (Miguel Grau 275, tel. 043/39-3257, www.hotelrimarima.com, US$18 s, US$29 d, with breakfast). Another option is **Hostal Gledel** (Areas Graziani s/n, US$5 pp). This very simple but clean hostel has solar-powered electricity and rooms with shared baths. The nicest rooms are upstairs. About five minutes from Yungay is the family-owned **La Casita de Mi Abuela** (Barrio Huascarán s/n, Mancos, tel. 043/44-2010, US$12.50 s, US$25 d), which offers impressive views of Huascarán.

Getting There and Around

During high season (June-Aug.), mini-buses take tourists from Yungay to Lagunas Llanganuco (26 kilometers). Early-morning buses for Yanama, on the other side of the Callejón de Huaylas, also leave from Yungay. The bus stop is at the intersection of Graziani and 28 de Julio. You can ask to be dropped off at the lakes. *Combis* run frequently heading north to Caraz or south to Huaraz.

CARAZ

Caraz, at the north end of the Callejón de Huaylas, is the valley's best option for those who are looking for a peaceful, less touristy alternative to Huaraz. It is a pretty town with a graceful plaza and a colonial air. A market comes alive each day with fresh food, colorful basketry, gourd bowls, votive candles, and woven hats. Around the town are the brilliant glaciers of Huandoy, where the Río Santa begins to tumble toward the Pacific.

Despite its small size, Caraz offers good hotels and well-equipped, knowledgeable climbing and trekking agencies. At 2,285 meters, Caraz is 800 meters lower than Huaraz and enjoys much warmer weather. Its nickname, Caraz Dulzura (Sweet Caraz), denotes its reputation as a land of *manjar blanco*, a rich caramel spread.

Caraz is well positioned for the valley's major climbing and trekking endeavors. It is near a trailhead for the popular Santa Cruz trek and is close to Alpamayo. It is also the starting point for explorations into the rugged northern regions of the Cordillera Blanca. Carry cash, since credit cards are not generally accepted in town.

Sights

There are a few excellent day excursions from Caraz. Just north of town, a road leads 32 kilometers up past towering granite walls to the spectacular **Laguna Parón,** the largest lake in the Cordillera Blanca. A dozen snow pyramids hem the lake in on all sides, including the perfect towers of Artesonraju (6,025 meters), Pirámide Garcilaso (5,885 meters), and Chacraraju (6,185 meters). This is a good spot for camping. Avoid walking around the south shore of Laguna Parón, as there are some very dangerous impassable sections. There have been fatalities in this area.

Just a few kilometers north of Caraz is **Tumshukaiko,** a huge archaeological site that looks like a fort and may have been built by the Chavín people. To walk here from

Caraz

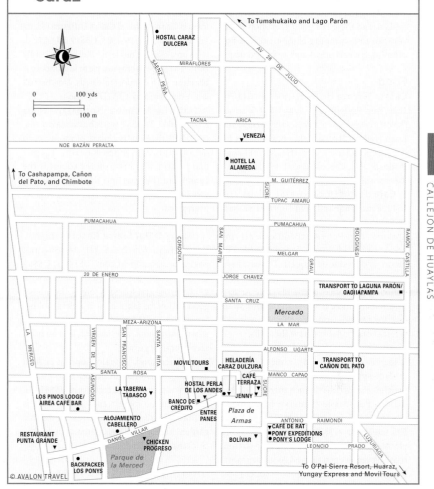

To Tumshukaiko and Lago Parón

HOSTAL CARAZ DULCERA

MIRAFLORES

SÁENZ PEÑA

AV. 28 DE JULIO

0   100 yds
0   100 m

TACNA   ARICA

NOE BAZÁN PERALTA

VENEZIA

To Cashapampa, Cañon del Pato, and Chimbote

HOTEL LA ALAMEDA

M. GUITÉRREZ

SUCRE

TÚPAC AMARU

PUMACAHUA

PUMACAHUA

CORDOVA

SAN MARTÍN

MELGAR

GRAU

BOLOGNESI

RAMÓN CASTILLA

20 DE ENERO

JORGE CHAVEZ

SANTA CRUZ

TRANSPORT TO LAGUNA PARÓN/ OAÒ∥AГAMPA

Mercado

MEZA-ARIZONA

LA MAR

LA MERCED

VIRGEN DE LA ASUNCIÓN

SAN FRANCISCO

SANTA RITA

ALFONSO UGARTE

SANTA   ROSA

MOVIL TOURS

HELADERÍA CARAZ DULZURA

SUCRE

TRANSPORT TO CAÑON DEL PATO

MANCO CAPAC

CAFÉ TERRAZA

LOS PINOS LODGE/ AIREA CAFÉ BAR

LA TABERNA TABASCO

HOSTAL PERLA DE LOS ANDES

JENNY

BANCO DE CRÉDITO

ENTRE PANES

Plaza de Armas

ANTONIO   RAIMONDI

ALOJAMIENTO CABELLERO

CAFÉ DE RAT

PONY EXPEDITIONS

PONY'S LODGE

DANIEL   VILLAR

RESTAURANT PUNTA GRANDE

CHICKEN PROGRESO

BOLÍVAR

LEONCIO   PRADO

LUZURIAGA

Parque de la Merced

BACKPACKER LOS PONYS

To O'Pal Sierra Resort, Huaraz, Yungay Express and Movil Tours

© AVALON TRAVEL

AYACUCHO AND THE CORDILLERA BLANCA
CALLEJÓN DE HUAYLAS

Caraz's main Plaza de Armas, follow San Martín uphill, take a left on 28 de Julio, and continue to the bridge over the Río Llullan. The ruins are another 300 meters from here and before the road for Laguna Parón.

A fully paved road heads west over the Cordillera Negra toward a gigantic stand of *Puya raimondii* plants at **Abra Huinchus** (4,300 meters). This road leads to the coast and, in the dry season, makes for a spectacular and fast mountain-bike descent.

Recreation

Pony Expeditions (Jr. Sucre 1266, tel. 043/39-1642 or cell tel. 944-941-214, www.ponyexpeditions.com) was founded in 1993 by Peruvian couple Aidé and Alberto Cafferata and is the most solid adventure outfit in Caraz. It has top-rate equipment and offers a range of climbing, trekking, mountain biking, and fishing trips. Treks offered include the famous Santa Cruz loop (4 days, 3 nights), Alpamayo (12 days, 11 nights), bike rentals to Cañón del Pato (US$20 pp), and guided climbs on nearly all of the technical peaks around Laguna Parón. English and French are spoken, and there is a good gear shop where you can rent camping equipment and buy camping-gas cartridges and very good maps.

Food

Café la Terraza (Jr. Sucre 1106, tel. 043/30-1226, 8am-9:30pm Tues.-Sun., US$3-5) serves flavorful espresso, omelets, sandwiches, and main courses. It also makes box lunches for day hikers and has a great selection of homemade *lúcuma,* chocolate, and *manjar blanco* ice creams.

Café de Rat (Jr. Sucre 1266, tel. 043/39-1642, 8am-10am and 6pm-10pm Mon.-Sat., US$5) is the most charming spot in Caraz, upstairs from Pony's Expeditions, serving breakfast, salads, pasta, wood-fired baked pizzas, and fondue on request. The café has a cozy atmosphere, with a balcony from which there is a great view of the Plaza de Armas. Additionally there is Wi-Fi and a book swap. Ask for crayons and sign the wall with an original drawing if you have the skills.

Another good spot near the Plaza de Armas is the new **Entre Panes** (Daniel Villar 211, 7:30am-8pm daily, US$3), which serves up delicious sandwiches, lunch menus, and hot drinks. For classic Peruvian food there's **Restaurant Punta Grande** (Daniel Villar 595, tel. 043/39-1131, 8am-7pm daily, US$3), a pleasant garden restaurant serving fresh trout roasted over an open fire and good corn tamales. Stop at **Chicken Progreso** (Daniel Villar 326, US$3) for juicy *pollo a la brasa* and french fries. For pastas, head over to **Restaurant Venezia** (Noe Bazan Peralta 231, US$4).

Accommodations

The most tasteful option in town is **Los Pinos Lodge** (Parque San Martín 103, tel. 043/39-1130, US$40 s, US$54 d, with breakfast). The lobby and 12 spacious rooms are filled with antiques, which give the house a colonial feel. Grassy gardens enclose the house and are perfect for post-trek sunbathing. Travel information, bike rental, book exchange, and a DVD library are available to all guests.

Tucked away in a neighborhood above town is **Grand Hostal Caraz Dulzura** (Sáenz Peña 212, tel. 043/39-1523, US$19 s, US$27 d, with breakfast), a modern hotel with friendly staff. The large rooms are plain but impeccably clean with comfortable beds. Downstairs is a restaurant and a TV/DVD room.

Hotel La Alameda (Noe Bazán Peralta 262, tel. 043/39-1587, www.hostallaalameda.com, US$10-15 pp) is a maze of rooms, each one of surprisingly different quality. The primary distinction between the rooms is the comfort of the beds and shared versus private baths. Regardless, all rooms are slightly overpriced.

Just one kilometer outside town is the sprawling **O'Pal Sierra Resort** (Huaraz-Caraz Hwy., Km 265.5, tel. 043/39-1015, www.opalsierraresort.com, US$48 s, US$60 d). A series of rustic bungalows (some with kitchenettes) and spacious rooms, the inn is a good option for families or travelers looking for privacy. On the grounds are a playground, a swimming pool, a restaurant, and 60 hectares of orange groves.

Another good bungalow option is **Apu Ecolodge** (Jabón Rumi s/n, cell tel. 995-194-288, www.apuecolodge.com, from US$45). In addition to the comfortable rooms, there is a climbing wall, a barbeque area, an organic garden, and several pet animals, including chickens and guinea pigs.

Information and Services

Caraz is headquarters of the national police's **Departamento de Salvamento de Alta Montaña (DEPSAM)** (High Mountain Rescue Department, tel. 043/39-1163, 043/39-1669, or 966-831-514, www.pnp.gob.pe, 24 hours daily). The **tourist office** (San Martín, tel. 043/39-1029, 7:45am-1pm and 2:30pm-5pm Mon.-Fri.) has city maps, though the best information is available from the agencies on the Plaza de Armas.

Pharmacies, many of which are near the Plaza de Armas, are usually open 8am-1pm

Peru's tallest peak, Huascarán

and 2pm daily. From Ramón Castilla and Santa Cruz, cars also leave for Cashapampa trailhead for the Santa Cruz trek, every hour starting at 6am daily. Trekkers can use these cars to get to and from Caraz.

Several bus companies travel to Lima from Caraz, with a stop in Huaraz along the way. **Móvil Tours** (José Olaya 104, tel. 043/39-1922) is the best among the Lima-bound bus companies; it has four buses a day. **Yungay Express** (Luzuriaga 327, tel. 043/39-1492, 8am-7pm daily) has a daily bus down the Cañón del Pato (9 hours, US$6) to Chimbote; from there, same-day buses can be taken to Trujillo. A taxi between Caraz and Huaraz will cost about US$36.

TOP EXPERIENCE

★ CORDILLERA BLANCA

The spectacular wilderness of the **Parque Nacional Huascarán** includes Peru's tallest peak, **Huascarán,** and every bit of the Cordillera Blanca above 4,000 meters elevation, except for Nevado Champará at the extreme northern end. The land drops away on all sides of this long but narrow range, creating an interesting island habitat for several endangered species. Among the park's 340,000 hectares are *Puya raimondii,* the largest bromeliad in the world, and forests of endangered *Polylepis,* the highest-altitude trees in the world. Andean condors can be seen here, as can populations of vicuñas, white-tailed deer, Andean dwarf deer, Andean lynx, foxes, pumas, and more than 100 species of birds.

The Cordillera Blanca, when seen from afar, looks like a huge wall of glaciated peaks rising from the Río Santa Valley. Nevertheless, the range dips low enough in places to allow trekking routes, and a few roads, to cross it. The road to Chavín de Huántar, one of Peru's most enigmatic ancient ruins, tunnels through the lowest pass at 4,450 meters. The valley on the far side of the range, the western end of the Callejón de Conchucos, is an isolated and remote area of small towns linked only by rough dirt roads. Glaciers spread over

and 4pm-10pm daily. **Banco de Crédito** (Daniel Villar 217, 9am-6pm Mon.-Fri., 9am-1pm Sat.) and **Banco de la Nación** are near the Plaza de Armas on Raimondi, both with ATMs. **Pony Expeditions** (Jr. Sucre 1266, tel. 043/39-1642 or cell tel. 944-941-214, www.ponyexpeditions.com) will change U.S. dollars and euros.

Fast **Internet cafés,** some with telephone booths, can be found on just about every corner. Most locations are open 7am-10pm daily. Caraz is the only city in the valley which offers free municipal Wi-Fi in and around the Plaza de Armas. Connect to MuniCaraz 24 hours daily.

Getting There and Around

Combis leave frequently along the highway south toward Yungay and Huaraz. When full, cars leave from the corner of Ramón Castilla and Santa Cruz at 5am and 1pm daily for the one-hour drive to Pueblo Parón, a village nine kilometers from Lago Parón. Cars from Pueblo Parón return to Caraz at 7am, noon,

much of the terrain, along with more than 300 lakes. Inside the Parque Nacional Huascarán, thousands of people continue their traditional ways of life. For the most part, the range's inhabitants live below the poverty line, subsisting on maize, quinoa, and *kiwicha* grains and a variety of potatoes and other tubers. Their latest source of income is providing burros for the foreigners who pass through this world-class trekking and climbing paradise.

The roads that lead up and over the Cordillera Blanca provide good access for day hikes. To hike here, stay in any of the villages along the Callejón de Huaylas, including Huaraz, Carhuaz, and Caraz. Then contract a taxi or horse or hop aboard a *combi*—but make sure to plan for your return ride in the afternoon. Many agencies in Huaraz offer cheap day excursions to Lagunas Llanganuco or Pastoruri Glacier for US$8-10 and can pick you up at any of the towns along the way. Another option is to hike in to one of the refuges and use them as launching pads for day hikes.

Routes

LAGUNA 69

A good day hike is the three-hour trek up to Laguna 69, a stunning turquoise glacial lake located at 4,600 meters elevation. From Caraz, it is a two-hour drive to reach the trailhead at Cebollapampa, located at Km 31 on the route between Yungay and Yanama. From there, it is a 7.5-kilometer hike up 750 meters to the lake, which is nestled at the base of **Chacraraju.** There are spectacular views of Huascarán, Huandoy, Chopicalqui, and Pisco. Public transportation and taxis can take you to the trailhead, and agencies also organize treks. Pony Expeditions organizes a trip to the lake (US$18 pp).

SANTA CRUZ TREK

The most spectacular, and crowded, trekking route in the park is the four- to five-day, 40-kilometer Santa Cruz trek, which traditionally begins from the small settlements of **Vaquería** or **Colcabamba** and ends at **Cashapampa** near Caraz. The high point of the pass is **Punta Unión,** at 4,760 meters, and the rest of the trek is all downhill along the Quebrada Santa Cruz, which offers a series of emerald lakes and mesmerizing views of Taulliraju, Alpamayo, Quitaraju, Artesonraju, and other snow peaks. Two days can be added to the beginning of the trek by starting at Lagunas Llanganuco and heading over the **Portachuelo Llanganuco** pass at 4,767 meters. Acclimatized and fit trekkers can hike this route with a light backpack, and burros can be contracted at Vaquería or Colcabamba. This route can also be approached in the opposite direction, starting in Caraz and finishing near Huaraz.

NORTHERN CIRCUIT AROUND ALPAMAYO

A two-week, 150-kilometer option starts in **Cashapampa** and involves a huge northern circuit around **Alpamayo.** The trek takes in pristine mountain scenery and a rollercoaster ride of high passes on Alpamayo's remote northern side, including **Paso los Cedros** at 4,900 meters elevation. If you start from Cashapampa, the final days of the trek lead down the **Quebrada Santa Cruz** along the traditional route. This trek is operated by Pony Expeditions in Caraz and is almost always done with burros.

QUEBRADA QUILCAYHUANCA

Just above Huaraz, we recommend a two- or three-day hike up the Quebrada Quilcayhuanca, with a longer option to climb over a high pass and descend **Quebrada Cojup** on the return. Another option is a hike into **Quebrada Rajucolta,** two valleys over. All of these are pleasant two- or three-day hikes up into the valleys to lakes. Because few travelers walk these routes, they are safe to do alone or with another person. No burros are required.

OLLEROS-CHAVÍN TREK

There are at least two highly recommend routes that cross the Cordillera Blanca south

Classic Peaks of the Cordillera Blanca

Peak	Altitude (meters)	Altitude (feet)	Time	Alpine Grade
Huascarán	6,768	22,204	6-8 days	PD-AD
Chopicalqui	6,354	20,847	4-6 days	AD
Tocllaraju	6,034	19,792	4-5 days	AD
Artesonraju	6,025	19,762	4-5 days	AD+
Alpamayo	5,947	19,511	6-8 days	AD+ or D
Pisco	5,752	18,872	3-4 days	PD
Ishinca	5,534	18,151	3 days	PD
Urus	5,495	18,028	3 days	PD

Note: The alpine grading system is a French method for rating climbs according to their technical difficulty, number of belays, quality of rock, exposure to heights, objective dangers, etc. F = easy (*facile*), PD = moderately difficult (*peu difficile*), AD = fairly difficult (*assez difficile*), D = difficult (*difficile*), TD = very difficult (*très difficile*), ED = extremely difficult (*extrêmement difficile*), ABO = horrible (*abominable*).

of Huaraz and end at the ruins of **Chavín de Huántar.** The best-known version starts from **Olleros,** a village just south of Huaraz, and heads up and over **Punta Yanashallash** at 4,700 meters elevation along an ancient trade route. If you get a ride up the dirt road above Olleros, this 35-kilometer route should take three to four days and can be done with or without a burro.

QUEBRADA CAYESH CLIMB

The other route that takes you to Chavín is a 40-kilometer, four- or five-day route. It requires a bit of mountaineering and starts above the village of Pitec (above Huaraz) and climbs the Quebrada Quilcayhuanca and then forks south into the Quebrada Cayesh. At the end of the valley, a rough trail leads up and over a snowy pass next to **Nevado Maparaju** (5,326 meters). This peak can be climbed from the saddle before continuing down the pass on the other side to the village of **San Marcos,** eight kilometers from Chavín de Huántar. Because of the technical demands of this route, it is best done with a guide. Regardless, ask around about conditions before you try

this route, as we have received reports that the far side of the pass is badly melted out and difficult to descend. You should bring all your own technical equipment, like crampons and ice axes, and inquire beforehand if there are snow-covered crevasses or other conditions that might merit a rope.

Accommodations

Three lodges have been built inside the park to accommodate visitors in the three most popular climbing areas. Built by **Operazióne Mato Grosso** (tel. 043/44-3061) and operated by **Refugios Andinos,** the lodges are similar to what you might find in the European Alps. Each one has rooms of 60 bunks, and there is a large downstairs dining area with an amiable kitchen staff. Rates are reasonable: US$30 includes lodging, breakfast, and dinner. Hot teas and other drinks average US$1.50-3. All profits go to aid projects.

The **Refugio Ishinca** (4,390 meters) is in the Quebrada Ishinca, a four-hour walk from the village of Collón and the launching point for Urus, Ishinca, and Tocllaraju. **Refugio Peru** (4,765 meters) is a three-hour walk from

Llanganuco and at the base of Pisco. **Vivaque Giordano Longoni** (5,000 meters) is a four-hour walk from the village of Collón and at the base of Ranrapalca. **Refugio Don Bosco Huascarán** (4,675 meters) is a four-hour walk from Musho at the base of Huascarán. **Refugio Contrayerba** (4,140 meters) is a one-hour walk from Yanama. All these peaks, except for Huascarán and Tocllaraju, could be climbed directly from these *refugios*, eliminating the need for a tent, though climbers usually bring one in which to bivouac.

There's also a refuge in **Quebrada Llaca** (lodging US$32 pp, admission to the area US$20 pp) owned by the Mountain Guide Association of Peru, and managed with the Casa de Guías.

Getting There

Transportation options for accessing different areas of the park range from public *combis* to private cars from Huaraz, Carhuaz, Yungay, and Caraz.

★ CORDILLERA HUAYHUASH

Though only 30 kilometers long, the Cordillera Huayhuash packs in some incredibly dramatic mountain scenery. It is one continuous serrated ridge that falls away into fluted snow faces and glaciers. Seven peaks here top 6,000 meters, and another seven are over 5,500 meters. The highest peak, Yerupajá (6,634 meters), is the second-highest peak in Peru and is followed by Siulá Grande (6,356 meters). Here, Joe Simpson fell into a crevasse and lived to tell the story in *Touching the Void.*

The Huayhuash is 50 kilometers southeast of the Cordillera Blanca yet utterly different. First, there are no broad U-shaped valleys in the Huayhuash that lead over high passes to the other side. Instead, trekkers must walk around the outer edges of the range, climbing up and over passes between 4,500 and 5,000 meters. To manage these heights, nearly all trekkers use *arrieros* and burros, which can be contracted easily at the range's trailheads. The peaks here tend to be extremely technical,

with the exception of Nevado Diablo Mudo, and require guided expertise as well as previous experience. Because of Huayhuash's altitude, we recommend three days of acclimatization in Huaraz before a trip.

The other main attraction to the Cordillera Huayhuash is its raw wilderness feel. Although daily *colectivos* and buses have made the area easily accessible, the rocky ridges ceding to turquoise lakes and wide, open rolling grasslands draining into the Amazon basin give the area a pristine feel. Condors are seen here frequently, along with a range of migratory birds, and small herds of vicuñas live up in the narrow valleys. A great website is www.huayhuash.com.

Routes

The time-honored trek in the Cordillera Huayhuash is a 12-day loop around the entire range that begins and ends in the village of Llamac. These days, this route is somewhat shorter because new roads have been built onward from Chiquián, creating different trailheads. From Chiquián, *combis* now travel to Llamac via a new mining road, which shortens the route by a day. This trek continues clockwise around the entire range and crosses eight passes between 4,600 and 5,000 meters elevation before completing the circle at Pacllón, where a new road returns to Chiquián.

A few groups are now entering through **Huallanca,** a village at 3,400 meters that lies along the dirt road between Huaraz and Huánuco. Huallanca was rarely used as an entry point in the past because it was a long one- or two-day slog to get to the Huayhuash. But *combis* now travel along a new road that goes as far as the village of Matacancha. Trekkers usually get off beforehand at the tiny village of **Ishpac** and head over the 4,700-meter Cacanpunta Pass en route to their first campsite at **Lago Mitacocha.** This trek essentially does half of the full circuit and skirts the range's eastern side. After a campsite at **Lago Carhuacocha,** the trail diverges, and trekkers have to decide between a 4,600-meter pass or a pass 200 meters higher with better views of the glaciers. The next camps are at the village of Huayhuash and then on to Laguna Viconga, where hot springs are 1.5 kilometers to the southwest. The final day is a long walk over rolling hills out to Cajatambo, where a good road leads to Pativilca on the coast.

Because of the new Huallanca access, trekkers can now see a good bit of the Cordillera Huayhuash in five days. But there is a downside. Huallanca, at 3,400 meters, is the same altitude as Cusco and takes some getting used to. Those who come from the coast usually have to spend a day or two in Huaraz before trekking. Another issue is that each day of this five-day route includes a pass over 4,600 meters, which is a feat even for the acclimatized. The full circuit, on the other hand, has three days of acclimatization on rolling hills before hitting this string of knockout passes. Another problem is luggage: Five-day trekkers come in from the Huaraz side of the range and exit at the coast, so they have to carry everything with them. And, of course, this route misses the mountain views on the west side of the range. Val Pitkethly guides trekkers in the Huayhuash each year and has written the Globetrotter guide *Trekking and Climbing in the Andes.* She highly recommends the full circuit for all the above reasons, but also because "it's just too beautiful a place to rush through."

Accommodations

There are hostels and restaurants in all the main access towns of the Cordillera Huayhuash, but if you choose to trek with an organized agency, you will probably never visit them. In Chiquián, try the Hotel Nogales (Comercio 1301, 3 blocks from the Plaza de Armas, tel. 043/44-7121, www. hotelnogaleschiquian.com, US$6 s, US$12 d, cheaper rooms have shared bath). In Cajatambo, Hostal Huayhuash (Plaza de Armas, tel. 01/244-2016, US$10 s, US$15 d) is a decent budget place with hot water and a restaurant. There are a few basic hostels in

Huallanca, from where public transportation leaves to Matacancha and Ishpac (90 minutes).

Getting There

Transportes El Rápido (28 de Julio, behind Iglesia San Antonio, tel. 043/42-2887) in Huaraz has a bus at 5am and 2pm daily to Chiquián (3 hours, US$3) and at 6am and 3pm daily to Huallanca (4 hours, US$4), continuing on to La Unión (10 hours). Empresa Andia (Lima tel. 01/427-9176), on the main plaza of Cajatambo, has buses at 6am Monday, Wednesday, and Friday to Lima (9 hours, US$12.50).

★ CORDILLERA NEGRA

Though overshadowed by the snowy summits of the Cordillera Blanca, the brown mountains of the Cordillera Negra on the other side of the valley offer some great day hiking and biking. Routes often begin up in high-altitude grasslands and follow trails that have been used for centuries, passing Andean villages, old bridges, creeks, and fields along the way. There is a range of difficulty for bikers, from broad traverses to dodgy downslope single-track, and the views of the glaciers and snowy peaks are like something out of a fairy tale. Caraz has the best accessibility to the Cordillera Negra, and Alberto Cafferata at Pony Expeditions (Jr. Sucre 1266, tel. 043/39-1642 or cell tel. 944-941-214, www.ponyexpeditions.com) in Caraz and Julio Olaza at Mountain Bike Adventures (Lúcar y Torre 530, tel. 043/42-4259, www.chakinaniperu.com) in Huaraz can give good up-to-date suggestions.

Getting There

There are dirt roads leading into the Cordillera Negra from Huaraz and throughout the Río Santa Valley from Yungay, Carhuaz, Caraz, and Huallanca. Private transportation can always be hired to ascend these roads and, because most trails lead downhill, it is almost impossible to get lost. You might consider arranging your transportation through an agency.

The North Coast and Highlands

Depending on your perspective, it is either a terrible injustice or happy circumstance that most visitors never see northern Peru, which holds many of Peru's best ruins, untrammeled wilderness, and world-class surf breaks. Because 9 out of 10 foreign tourists begin in Machu Picchu in the south, the average visitor simply runs out of time.

On the north coast, however, you'll find one of the richest and most diverse archaeological zones in all of the Americas. An ocean teeming with fish and desert coastline punctuated by verdant river valleys formed a cradle of civilization comparable to Egypt or Babylon. The most important cultures were the Moche, Chimú, and Sicán empires, who built elaborate adobe cities over a millennium and a half before being conquered by the Inca around 1470.

Little was known about these cultures because the Inca carefully erased memory of them in order to consolidate their own power. But in the late 1980s, the world glimpsed the splendor of these forgotten civilizations when archaeologists unearthed royal tombs from the Moche and Sicán cultures. The tombs, somehow overlooked by 500 years of diligent grave robbers, were filled with exquisite works in gold and silver, including gigantic earrings, breastplates, and delicately worked spiders perched on webs of gold. The tombs gave archaeologists their first clear understanding of the complex social and religious structure of these northern empires. The objects found in the tombs are now on display in two fabulous new museums outside Chiclayo: Museo Tumbas Reales de Sipán and Museo Sicán.

After exploring the ancient coastal civilizations, head east into the Andes and you'll find the mighty Marañón Canyon, which slices through the mountain range, offering subtropical climates at its riverbed and high-altitude altiplano at its rim. Here, explorers continue to find lost cities and tombs built

---

Previous: surfing in northern Peru; the adventurous journey to Huancabamba. **Above:** countryside outside of Cumbemayo.

The North Coast and Highlands

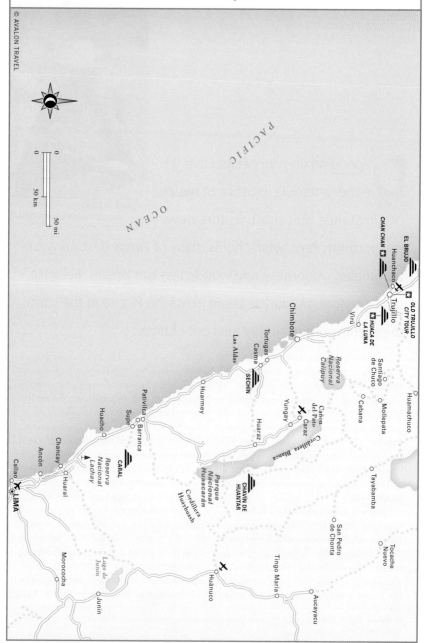

© AVALON TRAVEL

PACIFIC OCEAN

0 50 km
0 50 mi

EL BRUJO

CHAN CHAN

Huanchaco

OLD TRUJILLO CITY TOUR

Trujillo

HUACA DE LA LUNA

Virú

Chimbote

Reserva Nacional Calipuy

Santiago de Chuco

Huamachuco

Tortugas

Casma

Las Aldas

SECHÍN

Cañon del Pato

Cabana

Mollepata

Yungay

Caraz

Tayabamba

Huaraz

Cordillera Blanca

Huarmey

Pat?vilca

CHAVÍN DE HUANTAR

San Pedro de Chonta

Supe

Barranca

CARAL

Parque Nacional Huascarán

Tocache Nuevo

Huacho

Reserva Nacional Lachay

Cordillera Huayhuash

Chancay

Ancón

Huaral

Morococha

Lago de Junín

Junín

Huánuco

Tingo María

Aucayacu

Callao

LIMA

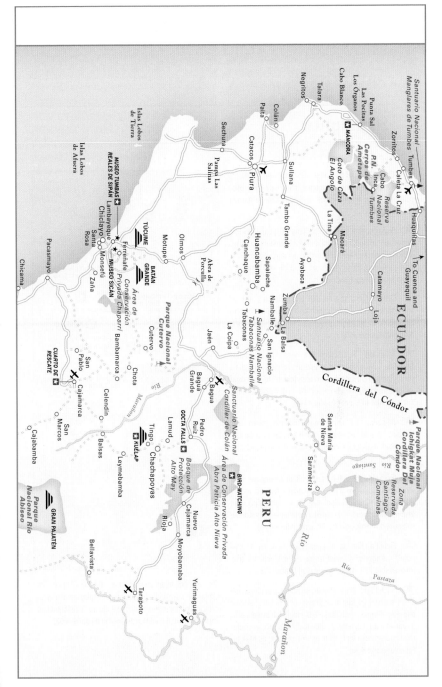

Look for ★ to find recommended
sights, activities, dining, and lodging.

Highlights

★ **Old Trujillo City Tour:** See Trujillo's Spanish homes and churches, then soak in colonial elegance with a drink on the Plaza de Armas (page 399).

★ **Huaca de la Luna:** This 10-story adobe pyramid is an impressive monument to the Moche culture, with recently uncovered murals and commanding views of Trujillo and the surrounding valley (page 401).

★ **Chan Chan:** Wander the adobe ruins of the elaborately sculptured former capital of the Chimú, the biggest pre-Inca empire in South America (page 403).

★ **Museo Tumbas Reales de Sipán:** Outside Chiclayo, this museum is dedicated to the dazzling objects found inside a series of royal Moche tombs, which recall the splendor of King Tut's tombs in Egypt (page 414).

★ **Máncora:** This small fishing town has become a surfing mecca, with a stunning coastline that attracts wave-riders from around the world (page 432).

★ **Cuarto de Rescate:** Contemplate this single stone room with perfect blocks and water channels. Historians believe Inca Atahualpa was imprisoned here for eight months—only to be executed in the end by Pizarro (page 444).

★ **Gocta Falls:** A two-hour trek from the small village of Cocachimba brings you to this impressive 771-meter waterfall (page 453).

★ **Kuélap:** This stone citadel, perched on a limestone ridge hundreds of meters above the Río Tingo, includes 420 round houses and a variety of bizarre buildings—it's no wonder that many visitors find it as impressive as Machu Picchu (page 458).

★ **Bird-Watching at Abra Patricia:** Observe some of the most spectacular bird species in this pristine montane cloud forest, including the spatuletail hummingbird (page 462).

by the Chachapoya people, which fiercely resisted the Inca as they expanded north. The first stop when traveling from the coast is Cajamarca, a hidden gem of Peru's Andes, where Francisco Pizarro's men captured Inca Atahualpa in 1532, marking the beginning of the end of the Inca empire. Outside the city, roads that are still in use by local farmers have been adapted in recent years into trekking routes. Exploring the remote villages and sprawling countryside through these ancient trails is one of the best ways to experience Peru's highland culture.

PLANNING YOUR TIME

It's a common dilemma: How can I see Machu Picchu, Cusco, *and* the wonders of Peru's north? Even though Peru's two richest archaeological regions are at opposite ends of the country, it is possible to see both within two weeks. The logical start is to fly to colonial Trujillo and see Chan Chan and the Moche *huacas*. From there, you can either stay on the coast and take a bus to Chiclayo for the Lords of Sipán treasures, Túcume, and the Museo Sicán, or head into the mountains to Cajamarca, to take in the sculptured stone canals of Cumbemayo and Cuarto de Rescate. After this, travelers can fly from Chiclayo or Cajamarca to Lima, and then Lima to Cusco, to continue on with Inca and Spanish history.

For those with more time, the principal attractions of the north can be thought of as a sideways U, starting in Trujillo. The first leg of the journey is to Cajamarca, which serves as a launching point for the journey through the Marañón Valley to Chachapoyas. Whereas Cajamarca, Trujillo, and Chiclayo can be visited in as little as two days each, the remote and spread-out ruins of Chachapoyas require several days at minimum—especially considering the effort it takes to get there. InkaNatura in Lima and Vilaya Tours in Chachapoyas offer well-organized tours that follow this basic sequence.

For most, Peru's northern beaches are an inessential side trip. But surfers and beach-lovers jet from Lima to Peru's northernmost city of Tumbes, then take public transportation an hour or two south to Máncora. After just a morning's travels, they are walking on white sand and eating ceviche, having left the ruins to the archaeologists.

Still another option is to head east after visiting Chachapoyas and travel the dramatic route into the Amazon basin to Tarapoto and Yurimaguas, from where cargo boats leave daily for a three-day journey to Iquitos. Getting from Chachapoyas to Iquitos is a stunning journey of a week or more, taking in nearly all of Peru's climates, with an easy escape flight back to Lima.

Caral and Sechín

Most visitors to Peru's northern coast make the trip from Lima to Trujillo in a straight eight hours, a journey that begins in the dusty sprawl of the capital's shantytowns and cuts through a string of grimy towns best known for stinky fishmeal factories and a bustling trade with mountain towns of the Ancash province. But if you have the time, there are a few overlooked ruins and beaches that warrant a visit.

CARAL

Six pyramids arranged around a central courtyard form what archaeologists have recently hailed as the oldest city of the Americas. Caral is in fact the largest of a series of 18 city sites that stretches up into the Río Supe Valley, beginning with the Aspero pyramid, near the town of **Supe** on the coast. Although Caral's pyramids were discovered in the 1950s, excavations did not begin until 1996, when a puzzling lack of ceramics tipped archaeologists off to the site's antiquity. Subsequent digs atop one of the oldest pyramids unearthed a 10-year-old boy wrapped in a cane mat, which scientists carbon-dated to 2900 BC. Visitors are few, as the site is well off the highway and few people know about it. For the moment, the elaborate courtyards, amphitheater, and 12-meter-high pyramids with views over the valley must be explored with a guide. These guides, who are often students, can be contracted at the entrance and charge about US$6. The site serves as an excellent introduction to later, but related, cities such as Sechín, Chan Chan, and Sipán farther up the coast.

Recreation

To arrange a guide in advance, contact the Lima- and Huaraz-based **Miguel Chiri Valle** (tel. 01/423-2515, www.angelfire.com/mi2/ tebac). Miguel, a fluent English speaker, will arrange transportation and accommodations to and from Lima or another northern city.

Food and Accommodations

With an early start from Lima, it should be possible to visit Caral and continue northward to Casma or even Trujillo. If you decide to overnight in the area, there are a few options in **Barranca,** which is within taxi distance of Caral. On the main drag, **Hostel Emilio** (Gálvez 651, tel. 01/235-5224, US$12.50 s, US$25 d) offers huge, comfortable rooms with TVs. The best option is **Hotel El Chavín** (Gálvez 222, tel. 01/235-2358, www. hotelchavin.com.pe, US$31 s, US$57 d), which has rooms with cable TV, a pool, and a restaurant with a good selection of dishes.

Recommended restaurants include **Restaurant Gitana** (near the intersection of Bolognesi and the Panamericana, 10am-8pm Mon.-Sat., US$4-6), known for its *ceviche mixto.* **Pollería Roky's** (Alfonso Ugarte 119, 11am-10pm daily, US$4) is a good, clean option for rotisserie chicken.

Getting There and Around

Caral is most easily reached via a dirt road that begins on the Panamericana about three kilometers north of Huacho. There is another bumpier, though more scenic, road up the Río Supe Valley that begins about three kilometers south of Supe. This road crosses the Río Supe at one point and becomes impassable during the mountain rainy season, October to May.

The best way to reach Caral is to contract a round-trip taxi (US$14) in Huacho or Supe, though cheaper *colectivos* also run from Huacho. It is about 45 minutes on either route. Allow one or two hours to see the ruins.

FORTALEZA DE PARAMONGA

Traveling north through Barranca and the nearby town of **Pativilca,** you'll find the Fortaleza de Paramonga (Panamericana, Km 210, 9am-1pm and 2pm-5pm daily, US$1.50) a fascinating introduction to the Chimú empire. The massive adobe fortress, which may have had both religious and military functions, comprises seven defensive walls constructed on a hill next to the highway. It is still possible to see remnants of the murals admired by Hernando Pizarro when he passed by the fortress in 1533, less than half a century after an invading Inca army overran the fort in its conquest of the Chimú empire. If traveling from Barranca, go to the north end of town and take a *colectivo* or *combi* to travel four kilometers north to the village of Pativilca, where you can either walk the remaining three kilometers or take a taxi (US$2).

SECHÍN

While some of Peru's adobe ruins require a little imagination to understand, no such effort is required for Sechín (5 kilometers southeast of Casma, 8am-1pm and 2pm-5pm daily, US$1.50), a temple complex built around 1500 BC. Along the temple's base, hundreds of warriors with their mutilated prisoners are carved into the granite with startling and gruesome detail. Soldiers carved into stone columns march on both sides toward the temple entrance with decapitated heads of the defeated hanging from their bodies. The range of human cruelty exhibited at Sechín is a prelude to the rituals of human sacrifice during the Moche and Chimú empires. The adjacent **Museo Max Uhle** contains reconstructed murals along with models of Sechín and other nearby ruins. Bilingual guides are available for the museum and the temple (US$4).

For archaeology buffs, Sechín is only one of several sites in the **Casma** area that can be visited in a daylong circuit. Nearby lies **Sechín Alto,** a deteriorated U-shaped complex. Farther south, at Km 361 on the Panamericana, but only accessible with a 4WD vehicle, is the fortress of **Chanquillo,** a watchtower surrounded by three concentric walls.

Food and Accommodations

The best lodging option around Casma is at **Tortugas,** a beach town 22 kilometers north of Casma that is marked by a huge blue arch at Km 391 on the Panamericana. **El Farol** (tel. 043/41-1064, www.elfarolinn.com, US$25 s, US$29 d) is perched on the hills at the southern end of Tortugas's stone-and-sand beach and offers breathtaking views of the surrounding desert hills and the clear blue waters. There is good snorkeling, safe swimming, a fine assortment of seafood restaurants, and a secluded beach that is a short walk over the hills to the south. Make reservations during summer and holidays. The hotel's restaurant (11am-10pm Mon.-Sat., US$5-9) also has the best food in Tortugas. The chefs prepare fresh *lenguado* (sole) with a mouthwatering garlic-tomato sauce.

Getting There and Around

Several bus companies stop at Casma, which is a five- or six-hour drive from Lima. A recommended bus company is **Flores,** which heads to Trujillo and beyond. Casma, along with Chimbote farther north, is also the starting point for the dramatic, though bumpy, ride over the 2,800-meter Callán Pass to Huaraz, which offers excellent views of snow-covered mountains. Taxis charge about US$10 for the 15-minute drive north to Tortugas. The cheaper three-wheeled canopied motorcycles are not recommended for the exposed highway drive.

Trujillo and Vicinity

Modern-day Trujillo has one of Peru's greatest collections of colonial homes, but it is only the latest city over the last few millennia in the Moche Valley. A few kilometers on the other side of town is the **Huaca de la Luna,** where archaeologists continue to unearth pristine murals from the Moche civilization (AD 1-850). Then there is **Chan Chan,** a vast city of elaborately sculpted walls that served as the capital of the Chimú, the largest pre-Inca empire in Peru (AD 900-1470). When Inca Pachacútec and his son Túpac Yupanqui conquered the city in the 1470s, they were dazzled by the grandeur of the largest adobe city in the world. At the coastal village of **Huanchaco,** 14 kilometers west of Trujillo, fisherfolk launch their reed rafts into the surf as they have for thousands of years.

Trujillo thrived after the arrival of the Spaniards, who, like the Moche and Chimú before them, reaped tremendous wealth from the fertile Moche Valley and the nearby ocean. Shortly after conquering Peru, Pizarro came to Trujillo in 1534 and helped found the city named after his hometown in Spain, Trujillo de Extremadura. Large sugarcane haciendas flourished here and financed large homes, churches, and a way of life that included two icons of *criollo* culture, the Peruvian *paso* horse and the *marinera* dance.

Trujillo became a center of Peru's war of independence from Spain. It was the first Peruvian city to declare itself independent of Spain, in December 1820. Liberator Simón Bolívar later established himself here after moving his way down the coast from Ecuador.

Trujillo

To Casa Andina Private Collection
To Lima

0
0
200 yds
200 m

RESIDENCIAL VANINI

UNIVERSIDAD NACIONAL DE TRUJILLO

JUAN PABLO II
JESÚS DE NAZARETH
LARCO
ESPAÑA
UGARTE
BOLOGNESI
ALMAGRO
ORBEGOSO
HUAYNA CAPAC
ESPAÑA
MIGUEL GRAU
AYACUCHO
GAMARRA
JUNIN
COLÓN
ESTETE
BOLIVAR
TRIBUTO ▼
COSTA RICA
BOLIVAR
ALMAGRO

PIZZERIA PIZZANINO
SAN ANDRÉS

SALON DE TE 'SANTA DOMINGO'

'POST OFFICE
LAN PERU ▼
IPERU ■
CASA URQUIAGA ★

JUGERIA SAN AGUSTIN ▼
Mercado
CASA DEL MARISCAL DE ORBEGOSA ★
MUSEO DE ARQUEOLOGI A E HISTORIA ★

OLD TRUJILLO CITY TOUR ✚
HOTEL LIBERTADOR

Plaza de Armas

CATEDRAL ✚
IGLESIA DE LA MERCED ▼
CASA DE LA EMANCIPACIÓN ★
PALACIO ITURREGUI ★

EL CELLER DE CLER ▼

CAFÉ AMARETTO ▼

HOTEL COLONIAL ▼
RESTAURANT VEGETARIANO EL SOL ▼
METRO
ASTURIAS ▼

CASONA DEZA CAFÉ ▼

MUSEO DEL JUGUETE/CAFÉ ▼

IGLESIA Y MONASTERIO EL CARMEN

A RAYMONDI
MANSICHE
ZEPITA
ESPANA
INDEPENDENCIA
SAN MARTIN
PIZARRO
JUNIN
LA CONSTANCIA

ESTADIO MANSICHE

MUNAY WASI HOSTEL

Plazuela el Recreo

OLD TOWN WALL ★

BUS TERMINALS

MIRAFLORES

NINON
NINUN
ESPAÑA
AVALON TRAVEL
Mercado Mayorista

PACIFIC OCEAN
Río Moche
TRUJILLO BYPASS
To Huanchaco
✈ AIRPORT
COMBI'S
AMAZONAS
PANAMERICANA

CHAN CHAN ✚
HUACA ESMERALDA ✚
HUACA DE LA LUNA ✚
HUACA DEL SOL

AMERICA SUR
COSTA RICA
ESPAÑA
ORBEGOSO
PIZARRO
LOS INCAS
INDUSTRIAL

Plaza de Armas

IGLESIA MANSICHE ▼
HUACA ARCO IRIS ✚

MAP AREA

From the Casa Urquiaga on the Plaza de Armas, Bolívar planned the campaign that culminated in the battle of Ayacucho, where Spanish forces were turned back for good on December 9, 1824.

A century later, a bohemian movement flourished in Trujillo that produced Peru's best poet, César Vallejo; painter and musician Macedonio de la Torre; and one of Peru's most controversial political leaders, Víctor Raúl Haya de la Torre. Vallejo eventually emigrated to France, but Haya de la Torre launched what would become one of Peru's most influential political parties: APRA, the Alianza Popular Revolucionaria Americana. With its call for worker rights, APRA was banned by the military governments of the time. As repression against the party continued, a crowd of angry Apristas attacked an army outpost in 1932 and killed 10 soldiers. In retaliation, the government rounded up nearly 1,000 Apristas, trucked them out to the sands near Chan Chan, and executed them by firing squad. Haya de la Torre was exiled to Mexico but returned and was elected president in 1962—only to have the victory voided as a fraud by the military government.

Great effort has been made to preserve Trujillo's colonial feel, including the burial of electrical and power lines. But at least one well-intentioned effort has backfired. The city government banned buses and *micros* from entering the city center in 1990, causing an explosion in the taxi pool. These days the air pollution and constant honking of *taxistas* as they troll for passengers is unbearable. If you prefer quiet and clean air, we suggest that you consider staying in nearby Huanchaco. Remember, in Trujillo and much of the north, people take their siesta seriously and most sights are closed 1pm-4pm.

SIGHTS
★ Old Trujillo City Tour
Allow at least half a day on foot to see Trujillo's colonial core, which offers a dense cluster of well-preserved homes and churches to the north of Plaza de Armas. Start at the northern edge of town at **Avenida España,** the congested beltway that was once a six-meter wall built 1680-1685 to ward off pirate attacks. The crumbling military wall was knocked down in 1942, but a section has been preserved at the intersection of España and Estete. The waterworks for colonial Trujillo can be seen a few blocks away at **Plazuela El Recreo** (Estete and Pizarro), where the Spaniards extended Moche and Chimú irrigation channels in order to deliver river water to the aristocratic households of the city. The *plazuela* is graced with an elegant fountain, carved from local marble in 1750 and then relocated from the Plaza de Armas in 1828.

The **Iglesia y Monasterio El Carmen** (Bolívar 826, tel. 044/23-3091, 7am-8am daily), a Carmelite monastery founded in 1724, is home to Trujillo's best collection of colonial art. The monastery has somehow withstood the earthquakes that have rocked Trujillo and houses the city's best-preserved gilded baroque altar. Its *pinacoteca,* or **painting gallery** (4pm-5:15pm Mon.-Fri.), contains 150 colonial works, including *The Last Supper* by Otto Van Veen, who was Peter Paul Rubens's mentor.

If you have extra time, the University of Trujillo's **Museo de Arqueología e Historia** (Junín 682, tel. 044/47-4850, 9am-4:30pm Mon.-Sat., US$2) is nearby and traces Peruvian history from 12,000 BC to the arrival of the Spaniards. Because the university is directing the excavations at the Huaca de la Luna, the museum contains excellent artifacts from that site. Just a peek inside the courtyard will give you a sense of the grandeur of the **Palacio Itúrregui** (Pizarro 688, tel. 044/23-4212, 8:30am-10am Mon.-Fri., US$1.75), which now houses the Club Central. The house was built in 1855 in the Italian neo-Renaissance style by General Juan Manuel Itúrregui and has three plazas ringed with ornate columns. If you stop by between 10am and 8pm you will have access to just the patio.

Nearby is the headquarters of the APRA political party (Pizarro 672). Close by is the **Casa de la Emancipación** (Pizarro 610, tel.

The Peruvian Hairless Dog

When at the ruins in Chiclayo and Trujillo, don't be alarmed if you see mud-brown, bald dogs lying prostrate in the afternoon sun. They are neither diseased nor street mutts, but rather fine specimens of the Peruvian Hairless, declared a distinct breed by Kennel Club International in 1986 and a national treasure by the Peruvian government in 2001. These declarations capped a modern-day struggle of legitimacy for an ancient dog known commonly in Peru as *perro calato* (naked dog) or *perro chino* (Chinese dog).

Archaeologists know that the Peruvian Hairless has been around Peru for at least 4,000 years because the dogs are pictured in Vicus and Chavín ceramics and their skeletons have been found in the tombs of the Moche, who considered them both guardians and guides of the dead. They were also favored by Inca nobles, who kept them as pets.

Peruvian Hairless dogs

044/48-1145, 9am-1pm and 4pm-8pm Mon.-Sat., free), a beautifully restored republican home where Marquis Torre Tagle signed a document declaring Trujillo's independence from Spain in 1820—long before the *libertadores* arrived. The house hosts cultural events and contains a small exhibit on César Vallejo, Peru's most famed poet, who was born in the nearby mountain town of Santiago de Chuco. Another block south on Pizarro is the **Iglesia de La Merced** (Pizarro 550). This 17th-century church was built by Portuguese artist Alonso de las Nieves and has an impressive rococo organ and cupola. When the order lacked the money for a traditional wood and gold-plated altar, they instead opted to paint one onto the wall in 1755—the only painted altar in the city. Near the altar is an interesting juxtaposition of the virgins that most embody the Old and New Worlds: Mexico's brown-skinned and dark-haired Virgen de Guadalupe and Spain's blue-eyed and blond Virgen Fátima.

Around the corner is the 17th-century **Casa del Mariscal de Orbegoso** (Orbegoso 505, 9:30am-1pm and 4pm-7pm Mon.-Sat.). The house is a showcase for the features of

colonial homes: a plaza of *canto rodado* (river stones), brick and lime floors, simple ceilings, and enormous, sparsely decorated rooms. The house was originally the home of José Luis Orbegoso, who led troops during the War of Independence and served as president of Peru 1833-1838.

The **Plaza de Armas** is where Martín de Estete began to lay out the city grid in December 1534, in preparation for Francisco Pizarro's arrival the next year. At the center of the plaza is the Monumento de La Libertad, and the face of the winged figure holding a torch closely resembles that of Simón Bolívar. On the other side of the plaza is the **Casa Bracamonte,** occupied by the Ministerio de Salud and not open to visitors. Its most famous features are a *balcón de celosia* (a wooden balcony from which women could see but not be seen) and finely wrought iron windows, an art form that flourished in 18th-century Trujillo.

Compare the colonial style of Casa Orbegoso with the more elegant republican design of **La Casa Urquiaga** (Pizarro 446, 9:30am-3pm Mon.-Fri., 10am-1:30pm Sat., free). This house is one of the best-preserved and most elegant republican houses in Trujillo. The original house was destroyed in the 1619 earthquake and was remodeled at least twice, most recently in the mid-19th century. Simón Bolívar lived here during his military campaign against Spain, and many of his personal possessions remain in the house, including his mahogany writing desk and personal china.

Construction of Trujillo's **Catedral** (Plaza de Armas, 7am-noon and 4pm-9pm daily, free) began in 1610 but had to begin anew after the devastating earthquake on February 14, 1619, which destroyed the city and prompted townspeople to adopt Saint Valentine as their patron. A more recent earthquake, in 1970, partially destroyed the main altar, which contains an image of Saint Valentine, among other saints. The cathedral's **museum** (9am-1pm and 4pm-7pm Mon.-Fri., 9am-1pm Sat., US$1.50) contains the shadowy paintings of the baroque Quito school as well as access to the catacombs.

Museo del Juguete

Opened in 2001 by Trujillo-born artist and painter Gerardo Chávez, the **Museo del Juguete** (Independencia 705, tel. 044/20-8181, 10am-6pm Mon.-Sat., 10am-1pm Sun., US$1.75) exhibits an unusual collection of 1,000 pieces that include toys as old as a 2,500-year-old Vicus whistle, Chanca raddolls, 18th-century French biscuit dolls, metal toy cars, and battalions of tin soldiers. Chávez aims to build the largest private toy collection in Latin America. He most likely will succeed.

★ Huaca de la Luna

To see the latest discoveries of Peruvian archaeology, head eight kilometers south of Trujillo toward two massive, crumbling adobe mounds that rise from the desert. These were built during the Moche empire (AD 100-800). The farther one, Huaca del Sol (Temple of the Sun), was an administrative center, and the other, **Huaca de la Luna** (Temple of the Moon, www.huacasdemoche.pe, 9am-4pm daily, US$3.50, includes an English- or Spanish-speaking guide

and museum entry), was a religious complex. This *huaca* has been the focus of a well-funded archaeological campaign since 1991 and has produced some of the most dazzling and best-preserved murals in Peru.

The shape of the *huaca* mirrors that of **Cerro Blanco,** an adjacent mountain that has a curious arching dike of black rock near its summit. The Moche probably believed this arch represented the rainbow serpent, a fertility symbol that appears alongside Ai-Apaec, the deity that decorates the walls of Huaca de la Luna. Archaeologists believe the first single, compact platform of the *huaca* was built around AD 100. But every century, the Moche apparently sealed the bodies of deceased rulers into the *huaca* and then completely covered the platform with a new, stepped platform above it. In this way, over 700 years, the L-shaped temple evolved into a 100-meter-long stepped pyramid with as many as eight stepped levels. The overall shape is oddly similar to temples of the Maya, a culture that some say influenced the Moche.

Because of the gold buried here, the temple has been the target of relentless plundering by *huaqueros* since at least colonial times. A dozen caves penetrate the base of the *huaca,* and a massive house-size hole is found up top, with an alley cut through the sides of the pyramid where the grave robbers cleared debris. Although much treasure and many murals have been lost, the *huaquero* holes have helped archaeologists examine cross sections of the temple's various platforms. On the north face, archaeologists have discovered a stairwell and a horizontal mural of soldiers performing a victory dance. Elaborate designs of Ai-Apaec in the form of a snake, crab, octopus, spider, and even a potato and a corn cob have also been found. In 1997, just a few inches from a *huaquero* hole, archaeologists discovered a cane basket filled with gold disks, textiles, and characteristic feline images, an indication that tombs remain hidden nearby and below, hidden in hundreds of feet of adobe bricks.

The top of Huaca de la Luna, nearly 10 stories high, offers an impressive view of Huaca

Human Sacrifice at Huaca de la Luna

Archaeologists believe Huaca de la Luna was a center for human sacrifice because murals often show Ai-Apaec, the fearsome Moche deity, with a crescent-shaped ceremonial knife (called a *tumi*) in one hand and a severed human head in the other. Additional proof came in 1996, when archaeologists discovered the skeletons of more than 40 men, age 15-32, buried in thick sediment near the back of the *huaca*. The men—many with their throats, hands, and legs cut or pelvic bones ripped out—were apparently sacrificed to stop the El Niño rains that partially destroyed the temple and forced the Moche to relocate farther north. Above the skeletons is the pyramid's upper throne, which appears in Moche ceramics depicting human sacrifice, and a sacred rock from which the victims were apparently thrown into the mud below. In a famous scene known as the Presentation, often painted on ceramic copies around Trujillo, a priest appears to cut open a prisoner's chest to either remove his heart or drain out blood. A cup of blood is then presented to the ruler, possibly to be drunk. High levels of uric acid found in the bones of Moche rulers in the Sipán tombs could, scientists say, indicate they drank blood—or that they ate a lot of shellfish.

del Sol, which was built with an estimated 100 million adobe bricks and is considered one of the largest adobe structures in the world. Few excavations have been done at **Huaca del Sol,** however, and there is little for visitors to see. Much of the *huaca* was eroded in the 17th century when the Spaniards diverted the Río Moche in a failed attempt to uncover hidden treasure.

A museum featuring excavated objects, the **Museo Huacas de Moche,** has been added to the visitors center complex.

The Huaca de la Luna can be reached via taxi (US$6) from central Trujillo or via the *combis* at Suárez and Los Incas near the Mercado Mayorista that say "Campiña de Moche." Make sure the *combi* lets you off at the visitors center entrance. There have been reports of tourist muggings on the outskirts of the ruins site.

Huaca Arco Iris and Esmeralda

As a warm-up for Chan Chan, head first to the restored **Huaca Arco Iris** (Rainbow Temple, 9am-4:30pm daily, US$3.50, includes Huaca Esmerelda and Museo Chan Chan), which was built by the Chimú around AD 1200 before being covered, and partially preserved, by desert sands. The temple is guarded by six-meter-thick clay walls, and there are two

main platforms inside connected by a ramp. The first platform contains seven restored adobe panels that are carved with the namesake motif of the *huaca*, two lizard-like beings with an arching rainbow or serpent overhead. The exact meaning of the mural has been lost, but many archaeologists believe it represents a kind of rain dance or fertility ritual.

The second platform contains 14 niches that were probably used to store ritual objects such as textiles, shells, seed necklaces, and gold objects. Local legend has it that Huaca Arco Iris was also the home of Takaynamo, the mythical bearded man who arrived by raft to found the city of Chan Chan. At the top of the *huaca*, there was probably a small temple where priests communicated with the gods.

To get to Huaca Arco Iris, take a taxi (US$2) one-way and have it drop you off; there are plenty of taxis in the area for your return.

Another *huaca* that is often mentioned in tourist literature but only worth visiting if you have extra time is **Huaca Esmeralda** (9am-4:30pm daily, US$3.50, includes Huaca Arco Iris and Chan Chan). This partially restored *huaca* consists of two superimposed platforms with areas for storing foods and stylized carvings of nets with birds and fish. The best options to get here are to go with a guided tour from Trujillo or take a taxi (US$3) round-trip, as the neighborhood is not safe.

★ Chan Chan

The highly evolved Chimú civilization emerged in AD 900 after the decline of the Moche culture and stretched 1,300 kilometers from Chancay, near present-day Lima, to Tumbes. It was Peru's largest pre-Inca empire, and its capital was **Chan Chan** (9am-4pm daily, www.chanchan.gob.pe, US$3.50, includes Huaca Arco Iris, Huaca Esmerelda, and Museo Chan Chan), now reduced to 20 square kilometers of eroded adobe. The city was abandoned in the 1470s, when Chan Chan was overrun by the army of Inca general Túpac Yupanqui.

In its heyday, Chan Chan was an elaborately sculpted and painted adobe city with nine-meter-high walls and an intricate complex of ramps, courtyards, passages, terraces, towers, gardens, palaces, and homes for an estimated 30,000-60,000 people. One of the most important archaeological sites in Peru, it was declared a UNESCO World Heritage Site in 1986, which has helped protect it somewhat from looting.

At the center of the ruined city are 10 royal compounds, or *ciudadelas,* built by successive Chimú dynasties, that cover six square kilometers. Only the upper strata of Chimú society was allowed to enter these palaces, through a single north entrance that breached massive walls. The palaces were used during the life of the king and then sealed and converted into a mausoleum upon his death, a custom also followed by the Inca in Cusco. The most often visited of these is Ciudadela Tschudi, which some say has been restored too much, but the signed pathway helps visitors make sense of it all.

From the entrance, the pathway leads into a vast walled plaza where religious ceremonies were once held. The king sat on a throne near a ramp at the front of the square and was flanked by hundreds of priests and other court attendants, while human sacrifices were made on an altar in the center of the square. The walls are decorated with reliefs of sea otter-squirrels—a fertility symbol passed down from Moche times—and cormorants. The acoustics of the plaza are stunning: the ocean, more than a kilometer away, roars on a windless day. From the plaza, the circuit continues down a corridor decorated with pelicans and zigzagging fish designs that probably represented the ocean tide and currents. On the opposite wall are diamond-shaped designs of fishing nets, a motif seen throughout Chan Chan. This passageway leads to a more intimate square with a ceremonial altar

ceremonial Chan Chan figure, with stylized sea otters in the background

(now covered in adobe to preserve it) and a U-shaped audience chamber.

One of the more surprising sights of Tschudi, given the desert surroundings, is a pool with a marsh reed at one end that was probably once a pleasure garden for Chimú royalty and a place for worshiping the moon. Unlike the Inca, the Chimú apparently valued the moon over the sun because it comes out during both day and night and controls the oceans. It was here that El Niño rains in 1983 uncovered two adolescent sacrifice victims, one with a mask of gold and another with a collar of rainforest seeds used in shamanic rituals. At the back of the palace complex is the royal tomb surrounded by niches where human sacrifices were probably placed. Most of Chan Chan's tombs, once laden with gold and silver objects, were ransacked as early as Inca times, according to colonial documents. Near the end of the circuit, there are warehouses and a ceremonial hall with 24 niches that were probably used for idols. The nearby **Museo Chan Chan** (9am-4pm daily) does not have much of interest except for a collection of *tumi* knives and a display showing the evolution of Chimú pottery.

For US$10, a taxi will make the round-trip from Trujillo and wait while you are in the ruins. Wandering through the endless maze of ruins outside Chan Chan's Tschudi Palace is not advised, as assaults on tourists have been reported. The neighborhood around Huaca Arco Iris and especially Huaca Esmeralda can also be dangerous. We recommend a guided tour that includes all of these sites plus the museum—you'll learn more, and will be relaxed and safe.

ENTERTAINMENT AND EVENTS

Trujillo has a well-hidden but interesting nightlife, which gets going around 10:30pm. The best pub in town is **Chelsea Pub Restaurant** (Estete 675, tel. 044/25-7032, 12:30pm-5pm and 7pm-1am daily), which has a restaurant that serves lunch and different kinds of live music depending on the night. Another good spot for live music, especially jazz, is **Museo Café Bar Trujillo** (Independencia 701, tel. 044/34-6741, 9am-12:30am Mon.-Sat.). The top discotheque in Trujillo is **AMA** (tel. 044/42-2941, www.amadisco.pe, 11pm-5am daily), located in the Real Plaza shopping mall. Another option for dancing is the disco-pub **Tributo** (Almagro and Pizarro, cell tel. 949-711-045, 9pm-close Thurs.-Sat.), just off the Plaza de Arms, or **Nuestro Bar** (Bolognesi and Pizarro, tel. 044/22-1620, www.nuestrobar.pe, 9pm-close daily). On the edge of town, there's **Hop's** (Av. Húsares de Junín and Venezuela, tel. 044/47-1013, www.hops.com.pe, from 6pm daily, US$5.50), a microbrewery that brings wheat, Pilsen, or Munich beer to the table in special dispensers. For late-night munchies, head to **Jano's Pub** (Pizarro, 24 hours daily), Trujillo's well-frequented 24-hour hamburger shop a few blocks west of the Plaza de Armas.

Marinera dancers from up and down Peru's coast flock to Trujillo in the last weeks of January and the first week of February for the **National Marinera Contest.** In between rounds of judged dancing, the city comes to life with cockfights, horse-riding championships, a multitude of parties, and even surfing contests at Huanchaco. The partying is especially intense during the last weekend when the dancing finals take place.

Trujillo has a similar fiesta called **Festival de la Primavera,** a celebration of the beginning of spring during the last week of September or the first weeks of October. The event is best known as a showcase for Trujillo's other icon of Peruvian *criolla* (coastal) culture, the *caballo de paso.* These graceful horses with tripping gait allow riders to float even during a full trot and are highly prized around the world. Because the best *caballos de paso* are bred in ranches around Trujillo, buyers flock to this event. Year-round horse shows are given at **Fundo Palo Marino** (Via de Evitamiento, Km 569, tel. 044/60-3355, www.palomarino.com, 10am-5pm Tues.-Sun.).

RECREATION
Tour Agencies and Guides

Several tour companies in Trujillo cover the city, Huaca de la Luna y Sol, Chan Chan, and even El Brujo. The best is **Colonial Tours** (Independencia 616, tel. 044/29-1034, www.colonialtoursnorteperu.com, daily, US$12.50), based at Hotel Colonial. It has guides that speak English and French.

If you prefer a personal tour, **Karmen Linares Santos** (cell tel. 948-883-626 or 985-588-460, karmelinsa@hotmail.com) is fluent in English; and **Michael White** (Cahuide 495, tel. 044/29-9997 or cell tel. 949-662-710, casadeclara@yahoo.com) tackles both English and Spanish, plus French, Italian, and German.

FOOD
Peruvian

Asturias (Pizarro 739, tel. 044/25-8100, www.asturiascafeteria.com, 8am-midnight daily, US$3-9) is a Trujillo classic. There are US$3 lunch menus and an à la carte menu with meat and fish dishes, pastas (including vegetarian options), and salads, as well as sandwiches, fruit juices, and desserts. Open only at lunch, **Restaurant Romano Rincón Criollo** (Estados Unidos 162, Urb. El Recreo, tel. 044/24-4207, noon-4pm, US$8-12) is a great place to enjoy regional food such as ceviche, fried fish, and stewed duck. A good spot for fish and seafood is **Squalo's** (Calle Cienfuegos 250, Urb. La Merced, tel. 044/29-5134, 11am-5pm daily, US$5-12). There are also chicken, beef, and duck dishes.

Two blocks from the Plaza de Armas, **El Mochica** (Bolívar 462, tel. 044/22-4401, www.elmochica.com.pe, 9am-11pm daily, US$5-12) is the eatery to explore the spicy and intense flavors of Trujillo's regional food, whether it is seafood, stewed goat, or duck. Highlights include *sopa shambar* (a tasty, thick soup of wheat, vegetables, and pork) and *tallarines con pichón* (spicy spaghetti served with stewed baby pigeons)—a delicacy hardly found elsewhere.

Peruvian Fusion and Fine Dining

Chef and founder Héctor Solís's ★ **Fiesta** (Av. Larco 954, Vista Alegre, tel. 044/42-1572, www.restaurantfiestagourmet.com, noon-10pm Mon.-Sat., noon-6pm Sun. and holidays, US$15-25 without wine) is one of the best restaurants in northern Peru, and perhaps the entire country. Specialties include *tiradito de mero en salsa de ají mochero* (grouper carpaccio with *mochero* chili sauce) and *pechuga de pato al grill con cama de puré de loche* (grilled duck breast served over a *loche* pumpkin puree), among 50 other dishes. A favorite is the *ceviche de mero a la brasa,* a warm ceviche. If you want to indulge yourself, this is the place to go.

Las BóVedas (Independencia 485, Plaza de Armas, tel. 044/23-2741, www.libertador.com.pe, 6am-10:30am, noon-3pm, and 5pm-11pm Mon.-Sat., US$10-30 without wine) is the refined gourmet restaurant of the Libertador Trujillo Hotel, serving dishes like mushroom and shrimp risotto with grilled loin. There is a good selection of Chilean, Argentine, and Spanish wines. Located on the second floor of a colonial building with a wrap-around balcony, **El Celler de Cler** (Independencia 588, tel. 044/31-7191, 6:30pm-12:30am daily, US$10-15) has a charming ambiance, nice wine selection, and juicy steaks, along with Peruvian classics.

Chifa

Chifa Ah Chau (Gamarra 769, tel. 044/24-3351, 12:45pm-2:45pm and 6pm-11pm daily, US$5-10) has the best Chinese food in the city. A plain doorway will lead you to a long corridor with curtained eating booths. The portions are generous and the food is tasty.

Pizza

A good option for pizzas with local flavor is **Pizzanino** (Juan Pablo II 183, tel. 044/26-3104, 6pm-10pm daily, US$8). For delivery, the best option is the excellent **Pizzeria Pizza Roma** (cell tel. 949-704-575 or tel.

044/65-1824, 5pm-11pm daily, US$8), which also serves delicious lasagna and other pasta dishes.

Vegetarian

Restaurant Vegetariano El Sol (Zepita 704, 8am-11pm daily, US$3-6) doesn't offer much in the way of atmosphere, but the vegetarian plates are yummy and reasonably priced.

Cafés, Bakeries, and Ice Cream

Try Café Amaretto (Gamarra 368, tel. 044/22-1451, 8am-11pm Mon.-Sat., US$2-6) for tasty salads, sandwiches, and fruit drinks. The tuna salad is superb. Stop back in the evening for a cappuccino and homemade *lúcuma* cake.

Owned by Trujillo-born artist Gerardo Chávez, Café Bar del Museo del Juguete (Independencia 701, at Junín, tel. 044/34-6741, 5-midnight Mon.-Sat.) is Trujillo's classiest café. The ambience has a touch of Old World Paris with an antique cash register, a wooden bar, and a piano in the back room. Specialties include *mistela* (the house drink), a *sánguche de pavo* (turkey sandwich), and tamales. Part of the proceeds go to the Museo del Juguete, right above the café. The café often has jazz and other live music in the evenings.

Perhaps the best café in Trujillo is Casona Deza Café (Independencia 630, tel. 044/47-4756, noon-11pm Tues.-Sun.), which provides delicious coffee in a colonial house decorated with beautiful artwork and antiques; you can also enjoy your meal in its quiet patio. But Juguería San Agustín (Bolívar 522, tel. 044/24-5712, 8:30am-8:30pm Mon.-Sat., 9am-1pm Sun.) gets the top mark for its large, delectable chicken and pork sandwiches. You can't go wrong for about US$3.

For traditional breakfasts with tamales or *humitas de queso,* stop by Salón de Té Santo Domingo (Pizarro 268, tel. 044/47-4789, 8am-1pm and 5pm-9pm daily, US$2-4).

Markets

Most of Peru's biggest grocery stores are in Trujillo, well-stocked with produce and other goods. The closest option to the main plaza is Metro (Pizarro and Junín, 9am-10pm daily). Other options are the Plaza Vea (tel. 044/42-1793, 8:30am-10pm daily) in the Real Plaza shopping center, a Tottus (tel. 044/60-4614, 9am-10pm daily) in Mall Aventura Plaza.

ACCOMMODATIONS
US$10-25

The family-run Munay Wasi Hostel (Colón 250, tel. 044/23-1462, www.munaywasihostel. com, US$10 dorm, US$15 s with breakfast) is one of the better budget options in town. A few blocks from the central plaza, the place feels more like staying at a friend's home, with a shared kitchen, free Wi-Fi, and a small book exchange. There are nice reading areas downstairs and a restaurant with room service.

US$25-50

The charming Hotel Colonial (Independencia 618, tel. 044/25-8261, www. hostalcolonial.com.pe, US$30 s, US$40 d, breakfast not included) has simple and tasteful rooms, with cable TV and Wi-Fi, arranged above a courtyard adorned with Huanchaco's *tótora*-reed boats. Hotel San Andrés (Juan Pablo II 157, tel. 044/25-8236, www.hotel-sanandres.com, US$45 s, US$59 d, with breakfast) is a clean and comfortable modern hotel that is walking distance to Trujillo's center. It has a restaurant, a rooftop pool, and all the amenities. Rooms have phones, Wi-Fi, cable TV, and room service.

US$50-100

Southwest of central Trujillo is El Brujo Hotel (Santa Teresa de Jesús 170, La Merced, tel. 044/22-3322, www.elbrujohotel.com, US$70 s, US$90, with buffet breakfast), a modern, three-star hotel located in the quiet and safe neighborhood of La Merced. Rooms are nice, with comfortable beds and impeccable baths. Amenities include 24-hour room service, Wi-Fi, a business center, an auditorium, transportation service, a bar-restaurant, and laundry. It has a second location downtown on Independencia.

US$100-150

The Wyndham-owned **Hotel Costa del Sol Trujillo** (Los Cocoteros 505, Urb. El Golf, tel. 044/48-4150, www.costadelsolperu.com, US$100 s or d) has a colonial feel, with 120 spacious and comfortable rooms arranged around gardens and a central pool. It is a 10-minute drive outside town, but the relaxed setting and clean air are worth it. The facilities include two saunas, an indoor pool, and an excellent restaurant.

Hotel Gran Marqués (Díaz de Cienfuegos 145-151, Urb. La Merced, tel. 044/48-1710, www.elgranmarques.com, US$100 s, US$125 d, US$150 junior suite, with buffet breakfast) is on a quiet side street about a five-minute drive from the city center. The hotel offers a modern spa, well-equipped rooms with Wi-Fi and air-conditioning, excellent service, and a good breakfast buffet. Transportation to and from the airport is included.

With its colonial facade and a sun-filled atrium, ★ **Libertador Trujillo Hotel** (Independencia 485, Plaza de Armas, tel. 044/23-2741, www.libertador.com.pe, US$140, US$240 junior suite) is *the* four-star hotel in town. Part of the Peruvian luxury hotel chain Libertador, it is located on the north side of the Plaza de Armas. The rooms are large and modern, with touches of colonial decor, and are sheltered from outside noise. Services include Wi-Fi, a sauna, buffet breakfast, a gym, and a jewelry shop. Las Bóvedas Restaurant, off the lobby, serves very good *comida criolla*, northern Peruvian specialties, and international cuisine. Another top option is the new **Casa Andina Private Collection** (El Golf 591, Urb. Las Flores del Golf III, tel. 044/48-0760, www.casa-andina.com, US$100 s or d), with comfortable, quiet rooms, buffet breakfast, a gym, and a pool.

INFORMATION AND SERVICES

The very helpful visitor information office **Iperú** (Independencia 467, tel. 044/29-4561, 9am-6pm Mon.-Sat., 9am-1pm Sun.) is on the Plaza de Armas. The **tourist police** (Federico Geldres, Mz. L, Lote 2, tel. 044/29-1705, 8am-8pm daily) are located in the Mochica neighborhood.

The best medical service in town is at **Clínica Peruano-Americana** (Mansiche

the Libertador Trujillo Hotel

810, tel. 044/24-2400 or 044/22-1773, 24 hours daily).

Banks are scattered around the center of town. **Banco de Crédito** (Gamarra 562) and **Banco Continental** (Pizzarro 620, 2nd Fl.) both have locations close to the Plaza de Armas. Both have 24-hour ATMs and are open approximately 9am-6pm Monday-Friday. Banco de Crédito is also open Saturday morning.

The post office, **Serpost,** is at Independencia 286. **Internet** access is widely available in the streets surrounding the Plaza de Armas, and most cafés are open 9am-11pm daily.

Lavanderías Unidas is at Pizarro 683 (tel. 044/20-0505). You can also try **American Dry Cleaners** (Bolognesi 782, tel. 044/29-2045). **Librería SBS** (Mall Aventura Plaza, Av. América Oeste 750, tel. 044/60-7344) has a few titles in English and a good selection of books in Spanish.

GETTING THERE AND AROUND

LATAM (Diego de Almagro 490, Lima tel. 01/213-8200, www.latam.com, 9am-7pm Mon.-Fri., 9am-1pm Sat.) has one-hour daily flights between Trujillo and Lima. **Avianca** (www.aviancaa.com) flies the same route.

All of these bus companies are recommended and have daily service, usually in the evenings, for the eight-hour haul to Lima: **Oltursa** (Ejército 342, tel. 044/26-3055, www.oltursa.pe), **Cruz del Sur** (Amazonas 437, tel. 044/72-0444, www.cruzdelsur.com.pe), **Ormeño** (Ejército 233, tel. 044/25-9782), and **Línea** (America Sur 2857, cell tel. 949-030-703, www.linea.pe).

The recommended **Móvil Tours** (Panamericana Norte 558, tel. 044/28-6538) has comfortable daily buses to Huaraz and Chachapoyas, and **Línea** has frequent buses to Chiclayo (3 hours) and Cajamarca (6 hours). Most of the bus companies head north as well, and Ormeño offers service to Ecuador.

Taxis within the city center cost US$1.25; *combis* and *colectivos* are US$0.30 but only operate outside the center. Rental cars are available at **Global Car** (Martinez de Compagnon 428, Of. 101, Urb. San Andrés, tel. 044/29-5548, www.gpt.pe).

HUANCHACO

A considerably more laid-back base from which to independently visit the ruins around Trujillo is Huanchaco, an ancient fishing village that has exploded over the last few decades into a favorite resort for Peruvians and a well-worn destination on the Gringo Trail. Even as new adobe homes fill the 14-kilometer gap between Huanchaco and Trujillo, this beach town still maintains a good bit of its village charm. Huanchaco has an excellent assortment of inexpensive and well-run hostels and restaurants for a range of travelers.

Huanchaco is the mythical landing spot of Takaynamo, the bearded founder of the Chimú empire who reputedly ordered the construction of Chan Chan around AD 1200. Even before Takaynamo's arrival, however, Huanchaco's fisherfolk were using their exquisitely crafted *caballitos de tórtora,* reed rafts with gracefully curved bows that are depicted on 2,000-year-old Mochica ceramics. About 80 full-time fisherfolk straddle their *caballitos* each morning, legs dangling into the water on each side as they fish with line and hook or drop weighted gill nets. The anglers surf in on the waves in the afternoon and then stand their boats upright to dry. Called *patacho* in the indigenous language spoken first by the Moche and later by Chimú, the boats are made of tied bundles of reeds, which are cut from the marsh (*wachaque*) at the north end of town. A few residents still speak the nearly extinct language, including one elderly woman who is known for singing Moche ballads.

Most visitors to Huanchaco come for a rest from the rigors of travel and enjoy the relaxed nightlife that includes occasional bonfires on the beach, roving musicians, and a few pubs. Brazilians cram into the hostels along the beach, sure proof of good surfing. This is a great place to learn how to surf, with gentle waves, surfboards for rent, and quality instructors.

There is an important historical site on the hill above the town: **Santuario de la Virgen del Socorro,** reputed to be the second-oldest church in Peru. The yellow church with a colonial facade and a large bell tower has served as a landmark for sailors ever since the Spaniards built it atop a Chimú temple in 1540. After a Spanish caravel sunk one late night in a storm off the coast, legend has it that a box floated to shore containing the Virgen del Socorro (Virgin of Rescue). It sparked the conversion of Huanchaco's natives, so the story goes, and has been venerated ever since.

A word of caution: Any beach spot popular with foreigners will have its share of *bricheros,* delinquents who specialize in ripping off tourists. They will often befriend travelers by offering free surfing lessons, only to end up in a bar later that night where the gringo is left with the bill. Travelers who wander the streets of Huanchaco—or most other cities in Peru, for that matter—late at night either drunk or on drugs are asking to be robbed.

Entertainment and Events

There are occasional beach bonfires, but for more of a party head to **El Kero Restobar** (La Ribera 612, tel. 044/46-1184, 8am-1am daily, US$4). During the day it serves breakfast and lunch, while in the evening its upper floors open into a lounge with a good list of cocktails and dancing.

One of Huanchaco's more famous celebrations happens in the last days of June when a flotilla of *caballitos de tótora,* including a gigantic one made especially for carrying the religious image of San Pedro, arrives on the beach in Huanchaco atop breaking waves. The two-day festival of **San Pedro,** patron saint of fisherfolk, also includes a religious procession and celebrations.

Recreation

The Muchik Surf School (Víctor Larco 650, tel. 044/63-4603, www.escueladetablamuchik. com), run by brothers Omar and Chicho, is right on the main drag, and offers beginner to advanced surfing lessons. **Onechako Surf** (Victor Larco 640, cell tel. 949-202-361) also provides lessons in Huanchaco.

Food

Huanchaco offers many great budget eateries.

PERUVIAN

Located on the ground floor of the **Hotel Club Colonial** (De la Rivera 514, tel. 044/46-1015, 8am-11pm daily, US$9-12) is a restaurant by the same name serving a variety of dishes. Grab a ceviche or a plate of fettuccine on the terrace overlooking the Pacific, or move inside to the comfortable dining room. For fresh seafood prepared on a barbecue there is **La Equina** (Unión 120, tel. 044/46-1081, 9am-10pm daily, US$6-8). Grab a seat on the small sidewalk patio and enjoy the evening.

PERUVIAN FUSION AND FINE DINING

★ **Big Ben** (Av. Larco 1184, El Boquerón, tel. 044/46-1378, www.bigbenhuanchaco.com, 11am-5:30pm daily, US$4-16) has delicious seafood and fish dishes, including ceviches, *tiraditos,* crab, deep-fried calamari, chicken, and beef plates. Enjoy your meal sitting at a table on the terrace overlooking the beach.

VEGETARIAN

★ **Otra Cosa** (Av. Larco 312, El Boquerón, tel. 044/46-1346, 8am-10pm daily, US$5-8) has outstanding veggie food at very good prices, including fruit salads, healthy breakfasts and lunches, and the best coffee in Huanchaco. The restaurant is part of Otra Cosa Network, a Peruvian NGO, and the restaurant is managed by locals with the support of European and North American volunteers.

CAFÉS, BAKERIES, AND ICE CREAM

Laid-back **Chocolate Café** (La Rivera 752, tel. 044/46-2420, 8:30am-6pm Wed.-Mon., US$5) is one of the best restaurants in town. In addition to yummy desserts like lemon pie, it serves pancakes and eggs for breakfast, and soft tacos with a salad for lunch. Don't forget the chocolate milk shake!

Accommodations

Huanchaco hotels and lodges might offer discounts outside holidays and the summer months (late December to March).

Hostal Naylamp (Víctor Larco 123, tel. 044/46-1022, www.hostalnaylamp.com, US$5 dorm, US$12-18 s, US$18-25 d) is an ocean-front hostel offering a safe, clean, friendly, and relaxed atmosphere, a garden full of hammocks, and an open kitchen. Its upstairs rooms have an ocean view, and camping (US$5 pp), along with tent rental, is available.

La Casa Suiza (Los Pinos 308, tel. 044/63-9713, www.casasuiza.com, US$7 pp dorm, US$20 s) is a few blocks from the beach. Started in the 1980s by a Swiss woman, Heidi Stacher, the small hostel is now managed by Frenchman Philippe Faucon. The place has small but neat rooms (there are cheaper rooms with shared baths; check the website for rates) that are integrated into a hip decor. Services are plentiful and include laundry, kitchen, surfboard rentals, book exchange, and Wi-Fi. It also serves breakfasts and small lunches. Reserve in advance.

Las Palmeras de Huanchaco (Av. Larco 1624, Sector Los Tumbos, tel. 044/46-1199, www.laspalmerasdehuanchaco.com, US$47 s, US$47-72 d) is a good option with a wide variety of rooms, including doubles at three different levels facing the ocean or the pool. It's on the northern end of Huanchaco, and there are family rooms with kitchenettes (US$89) and semi-suites (US$72). Amenities include a café-restaurant, laundry service, and Internet access. Rooms are very nice, with cable TV and impeccably clean baths.

Located on the promenade is the six-room **Hotel Club Colonial** (De la Rivera 514, tel. 044/46-1015, US$35-50, with breakfast). It's a great choice, especially if you get one of the three rooms with a view of the Pacific. A fantastic restaurant is located on the ground floor of the same building.

One of the best options in Huanchaco, ★ **Bracamonte Hotel** (Los Olivos 160, tel. 044/46-1162, www.hotelbracamonte. com.pe, US$65 s, US$80 d) is owned by the Bracamonte family, which started renting small rooms in the early 1980s. Decades years later, they have built a three-star hotel with comfortable bungalows and a dazzlingly clear pool, a restaurant and bar, a game room, and Internet service.

Getting There

From Trujillo, US$0.75 *colectivos* run along Avenida España before heading to Huanchaco. You can also catch a *combi* on España at the corners with Independencia or Pizarro. The *combis* are white with dark-blue stripes and they are marked "Huanchaco." A taxi for the 10-minute drive will cost US$4-5.

NORTH TO PACASMAYO

The Chicama Valley, just north of Trujillo and the Moche Valley, is a worthwhile location for those in search of the world's longest left-breaking wave, or who want to further explore Moche archaeology.

El Brujo

About 60 kilometers north of Trujillo, reachable only via unmarked dirt roads, is **El Brujo** (9am-5pm daily, US$3.50). Out-of-the-way and unexplored, El Brujo is difficult to tour without a guide but is considered one of the more important ceremonial centers of the north coast, used from 3000 BC through colonial times. If you enjoyed seeing Chan Chan and the *huacas* outside Trujillo, El Brujo is the logical next step: a complex blend of the ancient cultures of the Chicama Valley, but above all, the Moche. The site is essentially three *huacas*.

Huaca Cortada contains reliefs of Moche warriors, a *tumi* in one hand and a decapitated head in the other. There is also Huaca Prieta, but the most excavated is the Huaca Cao, a huge platform with murals on five levels depicting figures of priests, sacrificial victims, and dancing warriors—similar to those recently unearthed at Huaca de la Luna. In 2005, on the northern side of the Huaca Cao, archaeologists unearthed the tomb of the mummy Señora del Cao. The second-oldest female mummy to be discovered in Peru, the Señora del Cao is covered in tattoos that suggest that she was a political dignitary, not a religious leader. Directly west of the Huaca Cao stand the remains of a Jesuit cathedral that the Spaniards built to emphasize their dominance over the Moche culture. And to the east, 1,000-year-old bits of fabric pop out of the unexplored Lambaque cemetery from AD 800.

Although you can technically visit El Brujo without a guide, it is easier to navigate both the unmarked roads and the ruins with a personal guide (US$50) or with a Trujillo tour company (minimum 2 people, US$70). The nearest public transportation goes only to Magdalena de Cao, which is five kilometers from El Brujo, and because there are only a few *mototaxis* in Magdalena de Cao, you will probably end up walking to the site. To get to Magdalena de Cao, take a bus from Trujillo's Santa Cruz terminal (3rd block of Calle Santa Cruz, Chicago neighborhood) to Chocope. From Chocope, take a *colectivo* or *combi* to Magdalena de Cao.

Chicama

Puerto Chicama is a plain beach near an ugly town with only a few run-down places to stay and eat. As Chicho, the Huanchaco surfing pro, explains, "the only good thing Chicama has is waves," which, March-June, form the longest-breaking surf in the world. The wave ranges 1-2.5 meters in height and runs a reputed 2.5 kilometers. Four separate waves that link together, the megawave is the result of a flat, sandy beach, steady crosswinds, and southern and western ocean currents. Locals joke that surfers need a spare set of legs to surf it and a *combi* ride to make it back up the beach afterward.

From Trujillo, take a bus from the Santa Cruz terminal (3rd block of Calle Santa Cruz, Chicago neighborhood) that says "Puerto Chicama." You can try catching the bus from Óvalo Grau near the Museo Cassinelli, however these are often full.

Chiclayo and Vicinity

Among Peru's large cities, Chiclayo stands out as an underdog with a humble beginning. The city began as a mule-watering spot amid the opulent cities of Ferreñafe, Lambayeque, and Zaña, which were founded by the Spanish between 1550 and 1565. But in a twist of history, these once-proud Spanish towns have withered while mestizo Chiclayo has boomed in recent years as the commercial hub of northern Peru. There is not much colonial architecture in Chiclayo, but there are a few things you will not find elsewhere: a crooked street layout based on winding farmers' lanes and a witches market that sells potions and amulets.

Chiclayo is northern Peru's number-one travel destination because of the **Moche** and **Sicán** cultures, which built elaborate cities and tombs in the surrounding desert from AD 100 until the arrival of the Inca in 1470. The Moche tombs of the royal lord and priest of Sipán were unearthed in 1987 and 1991, respectively, stunning archaeologists with their complexity and beauty. These were finds as important in Latin American history as the unearthing of Tutankhamen's tomb in Egypt. After several world tours, the gold objects from these tombs and three other royal tombs are on display at the state-of-the-art **Museo Tumbas Reales de Sipán** in Lambayeque.

The Moche empire declined around AD 750 and a new culture known as the Sicán (or Lambayeque) emerged to build **Batán Grande,** a complex of pyramids 57 kilometers outside Chiclayo. In 1991, Japanese archaeologist Izumi Shimada discovered two royal Sicán tombs, filled with beautiful gold masks, jewelry, and solid-gold disk earrings that rival those of the Lords of Sipán. The objects are now on display at **Museo Sicán** in Ferreñafe, another fascinating, well-designed museum that is a must-see. Around AD 1050, the Sicán, frustrated by an El Niño-spurred drought, set fire to Batán Grande and built the even more elaborate city of **Túcume,** which is 33 kilometers north of present-day Chiclayo. Túcume's 26 adobe pyramids, reduced by time to dirt mountains, are spread through a dramatic desert at the base of Cerro Purgatorio.

Other sites of interest around Chiclayo include **Zaña,** an affluent colonial city that is now a ghost town of stone arches, columns, and church facades; **Huaca Rajada** (Cracked Pyramid), the twin adobe pyramids where the Lords of Sipán were found; **Monsefú,** a market town known for its woven straw and cotton goods; and **Santa Rosa,** a beach and fishing village with *caballitos de tótora* and a few good *cebicherías.*

It is possible, but not recommended, to see both the Sipán and Sicán museums in a single exhausting day. A better option is to follow the cultures and visit the Sicán sites—Gran Batán, Museo Sicán, and possibly Túcume—in one day; the Sipán sites—Huaca Rajada, Museo Tumbas Reales, and finally Museo Bruning—another day; and on a third day visit the optional sites of Zaña, Monsefú, and Santa Rosa.

SIGHTS
City Tour

The first inhabitants of present-day Chiclayo were indigenous people forced to settle here as part of a Spanish *reducción.* Religious conversion began here in 1559 when Franciscan friars from Trujillo founded **El Convenio San María.** The remains of this convent, all but ruined by El Niño rains, can be seen on Calle San José at the Parque Principal. Most of Chiclayo's streets were once dirt lanes that led to the convent and are named after saints.

Chiclayo does not have a Plaza de Armas but rather a **Parque Principal,** which was inaugurated in 1916. Historians believe this park once served as a goat corral for José

Domingo Chiclayo, the town's namesake, who came here after Zaña was destroyed in a 1720 flood. (The city may have been named for him, although the word also means "place where there are green branches" in the all-but-lost Mochica language.) Near the Parque Principal is the historic municipal building and **La Catedral,** built in 1869 by José Balta, Chiclayo's most famous citizen, who launched a coup in the 1830s and briefly served as president of Peru. The other main churches in town

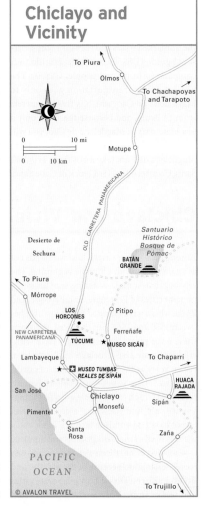

Chiclayo and Vicinity

© AVALON TRAVEL

Chiclayo

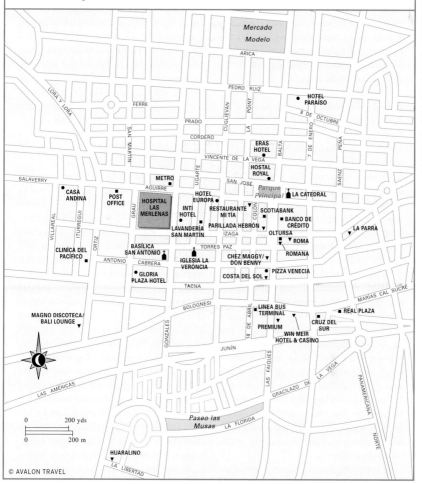

are even more recent: **Iglesia La Verónica** (Torres Paz and Alfonso Ugarte) was built in the late 19th century, and **Basílica San Antonio** (Luis Gonzáles and Torres Paz) was built in 1946.

Chiclayo has a highly interesting **Mercado de Brujos** (Arica, inside the Mercado Modelo, 7am-5pm daily). Here are piles of all the materials used by Peru's *curanderos*—shark jaws, deer legs, snakeskins, potions, scents, amulets, and *huayruro* (rainforest beads for warding off a hex). There are heaps of dried mountain herbs and San Pedro cacti, which, when sliced and reduced in boiling water, form a hallucinogenic drink used by shamans—and an increasing number of travelers. Shamans can be contracted here for fortune-telling or healing sessions. But beware of sham artists or shamans who dabble in the dark side—they are everywhere and can pose a real threat to your psychic health. It is always best to make *curandero* contacts through a trusted source.

If you have spare time in the evening, head to **Paseo Las Musas** (José Balta and Garcilazo de la Vega), an odd promenade with Greco-Roman statues and a triumphal arch sustained by armless Egyptian beauties. It is a charming Chiclayan invention, often filled with wedding parties emerging from the cathedral, five blocks away.

Huaca Rajada

About 28 kilometers east of Chiclayo, **Huaca Rajada** (Cracked Pyramid, cell tel. 979-644-542, 9am-5pm daily, US$3) is the original tomb site where the remains of the Señor de Sipán were discovered. The tombs have been decorated with replicas of the original findings and offer a comprehensive understanding of what archaeologist Walter Alva discovered when he excavated these 12 Moche tombs. Close by is a small museum with photos from the 1987-1989 excavations.

South of the tombs are two pyramids, built by the Moche around AD 300, that today look like clay mountains, along with a lower platform, about 120 meters long, where *huaqueros* plundered before they were caught. The pyramids are composed of *argamasa,* an adobe mixture that includes water, earth, seashells, ceramic fragments, llama dung, small stones, and algaroba branches. This mixture sat for 20 days before being put in cane molds and baked in the sun. The pyramid itself was built in huge, separate blocks of bricks in order to allow shifting, and prevent cracking, during an earthquake.

It is possible to climb to the top of the largest pyramid for a good view of the surrounding fields and the village of Sipán, a community of sugarcane workers who protested Alva's excavations and continue to feel resentful that their town has received so little financial benefit from all of Sipán's riches. The town received electricity only in 2001, and there is a long-delayed proposal to install running water and sewerage. Five police officers and an archaeologist are stationed full-time to protect the pyramids, which have not yet been excavated, along with the platform, which, according to archaeologist Julio Chero, is 75 percent excavated.

To efficiently include Huaca Rajada in a full day of sightseeing, it is best to take a guided tour from Chiclayo. If you take public transportation, start early in the day, as there are no places to stay in Sipán. Buses to Sipán leave from the Terminal de Epsel at the corner of Avenida Oriente and Nicolás de Piérola in Chiclayo. From there it is a short walk to the ruins, where Spanish-speaking guides can be hired.

★ Museo Tumbas Reales de Sipán

Give yourself at least two hours to see the extraordinary **Museo Tumbas Reales de Sipán** (Juan P. Vizcardo y Guzmán s/n, tel. 074/28-3977, 9am-5pm Tues.-Sun., US$3.50), 11 kilometers north of Chiclayo in Lambayeque. The museum, shaped like a Moche pyramid, contains the gold masks, scepters, jewelry, and other objects of the royal Moche tomb discovered by archaeologist Walter Alva in 1987. This museum succeeds in evoking the full grandeur and sophistication of the ancient Moche civilization (AD 100-850) in a way that adobe pyramids, now reduced to mud mountains, often do not. After nearly 500 years of continuous tomb looting up and down the coast of Peru, it is nothing short of a miracle that these tombs remained undisturbed. Their meticulous excavation has unlocked many of the mysteries of Moche society, built around a hierarchy of kings, priests, and military leaders. Come with a guide (or hire a Spanish-speaking one at the museum for US$5) who can explain Moche cosmography and point out things a first-timer would miss. For example, the king and priest discovered in these tombs are depicted on the ceramics and murals found throughout the 600-kilometer-long Moche empire.

To reach Museo Tumbas Reales, hire a taxi in Chiclayo for US$5 or take a US$0.50 *combi* ride from Vicente de la Vega and Leonardo Ortiz, in front of the Otursa bus terminal. You can also take a *colectivo* (US$0.75) from the third block of Calle San José. Slightly cheaper

King Tut's Got Nothing on the Lords of Sipán

Peruvian archaeologist Walter Alva knew he had found something big at Huaca Rajada in 1987 when he unearthed more than 1,000 ceramic pots—with the food, apparently, for an afterlife journey. A bit deeper Alva found the skeleton of a sentry with the feet cut off—symbolizing eternal vigil—and the remains of wood beams that once supported a tomb. Below was a disintegrated sarcophagus with heavy copper fastenings, an array of gold covers and decorations, and, at the bottom, a Moche king in all his splendor. Around and on top of him were huge earrings of turquoise and gold, breastplates of delicately threaded shell beads, a necklace of gold spheres and another of huge peanut shells—10 of which were in silver, 10 in gold. By his hand lay a scepter with an inverted gold pyramid decorated with scenes of human sacrifice. Gold balls were found in the king's mouth, abdomen, and right hand, and a silver ball was found in his left. There were seven sacrificial victims buried along with the king—the sentry, a general, a standard bearer, three young women, and a child—along with two llamas and a spotted dog.

After carbon-dating the tomb at AD 300, Alva's team found an earlier tomb nearby that may have belonged to the grandfather, referred to as El Viejo Señor de Sipán (The Old Lord of Sipán). This ruler was buried along with a woman and a decapitated llama, and although the tomb is smaller, the 53 gold objects found here show the highest level of craftsmanship. There are exquisite gold balls of spiders straddling their webs, necklaces with minute gold and silver filigree, and jewelry with the same octopus and crab motifs found in the recently uncovered murals at the Huaca de la Luna near Trujillo.

Alva's team discovered 10 other tombs, including that of a Moche priest—the mythical "bird man" who appears alongside the king in the human sacrifice ceremonies depicted on Moche ceramics and murals. The priest was found with a gold scepter capped with an *ulluchu*—this sacred fruit, now extinct, is believed to have prevented blood from coagulating during ceremonies of human sacrifice. It may also have had hallucinogenic properties as well, judging by the dazed looks on the faces of several flying priests.

The excavation of these tombs began with a midnight call that local police made to Alva's home in 1987. Grave robbers digging at midnight near Huaca Rajada, the Moche Pyramid near the village of Sipán, had found a royal tomb and begun lugging rice sacks filled with gold objects. At one point, the robbers quarreled and one of them was killed in the ensuing fight. When police found out they called Alva and launched an international search for objects that had already been smuggled overseas. Police recovered a few objects, including a gold mask and a gold plate, called a *taparabos,* which the Moche elite hung behind their bodies. This last piece was recovered by the U.S. FBI, which arrested a Panamanian diplomat in Philadelphia in 1997 trying to sell the piece for US$1.5 million. For a fascinating account of the Sipán heist and the worldwide network of antiquities smugglers, read American novelist Sidney Kirkpatrick's *Lords of Sipán.*

combination tickets are available at the Museo Tumbas Reales for those who plan on also visiting Huaca Rajada and Túcume.

Museo Arqueológico Nacional Bruning

Lambayeque is also home to the **Museo Arqueológico Nacional Bruning** (Huamachuco, block 7, tel. 074/28-2110, 9am-5pm daily, US$3), an interesting museum founded in 1925 and remodeled in 2006. Museo Bruning has an eclectic collection: Sicán gold masks with the famous winged eyes and red patina of mercury ore found at Batán Grande; a variety of weapons and musical instruments found at Túcume; and a Moche ceramics collection that includes marine animals, an enigmatic vase of a man straddling what appears to be a torpedo, and other Moche vases depicting a range of human disease and sexual practices. This ceramics collection alone is worth the visit.

After the colonial center of Zaña was destroyed in a flood in 1720, Lambayeque flourished and several important colonial homes and churches were built. Now Lambayeque is a sleepy town with one new hotel and a handful of restaurants. Worth seeing if you have the time is **Iglesia San Pedro,** a large yellow-and-white church on the main square that was completed by 1739. Inside are large murals and 10 altars, the oldest being the baroque Virgen de las Mercedes. One block away is the **La Casa Montjoy** (Dos de Mayo and San Martín), with the largest balcony in Peru—over 65 meters long! It was from here that liberator José de San Martín gave the first shout of independence in 1820.

Batán Grande

This sprawling pyramid complex, set amid a dry-forest nature reserve, was the first Sicán capital and the source for the majority of the plundered gold that was either sold to private collections or—before collecting became popular in the 1940s—simply melted down. **Batán Grande** (57 kilometers northeast of Chiclayo, tel. 074/28-6182, 8am-6pm daily, free) is about 30 minutes' drive farther along the same road that leads to Museo Sicán. The royal tombs were discovered in front of Huaca de Oro (Gold Pyramid), one of 34 adobe pyramids in the 300-hectare Reserva Bosque Pómac. The excavated tombs have been covered up to deter grave robbers, and there is little to see except the pyramids, which look like huge dirt hills. They were badly eroded by the El Niño rains of 1982 and 1998, which did, however, boost the surrounding dry forest of algaroba, ficus, *zapote,* and *vichayo* trees (one algaroba tree, forced to the ground by its own weight, is reputed to be 800 years old and is the center of shamanic rituals). There is interesting wildlife in the reserve: 41 species of birds, numerous reptiles (iguanas, snakes, lizards), as well as foxes, deer, anteaters, and ferrets—though the spectacled bear and puma long ago disappeared from this forest.

More than anything, the reserve is a depressing case study of how Peruvians, driven by necessity, continue to plunder their cultural and natural treasures. Villagers frequently venture into the park at night to cut down trees for lumber or dig around the pyramids, though *huaqueros* are no longer finding the treasures they used to find here. The punishments for these crimes are ridiculously light, and there are few guards patrolling the 5,800-hectare nature reserve. Because of the difficult conditions, local groups have taken it on themselves to develop a volunteer ranger program to protect the trees in the forest as well as general ecotourism infrastructure. Locals have been trained to give tours of the cultural and natural resources in the park, and park rangers give tours too. Both appreciate tips. Because the site is large and hard to find, it is best to see it on an organized tour.

Túcume

Túcume, the final capital of the Sicán culture, is 35 kilometers along the old Panamericana from Chiclayo. Archaeologists believe that Túcume was built after the Sicán burned and abandoned their former capital of Batán Grande around AD 1050. The most stunning thing about Túcume is the landscape, which can best be seen from a lookout on **Cerro Purgatorio**—a huge desert mountain rising in the midst of 26 eroded adobe pyramids scattered throughout 200 hectares of surrounding *bosque seco.* There is a powerful energy to the place, especially at dawn and dusk, which is probably why the Sicán people chose it in the first place and why many shamanic rituals continue here today (notice all the makeshift hearths for ceremonies).

Walking around these huge pyramids can make for interesting viewing—the Huaca Larga is an astonishing 700 meters long, 280 meters wide, and 30 meters tall. The area is commonly referred to as the **Valle de las Pirámides,** which is easy to understand from the lookout on Cerro Purgatorio, which offers a view over the entire complex.

Archaeologists believe the pyramids, like the Huaca de la Luna and Huaca del Sol outside Trujillo, are superimposed structures built in

The Myth of Naymlap

The deepest mystery of the Sicán culture is the identity of a man with a beak-shaped nose and *ojos alados* ("winged" or almond-shaped eyes), who is depicted everywhere on Sicán masks, ceramics, and images. Like the Chimú's mythical Takaynamo, who landed at Huanchaco, the Sicán culture has a well-recorded legend of a mythical king who arrived by sea around AD 750 with a wife and full royal court. This king, named Naymlap, founded a temple and installed an idol known as Yampallec—the origin of the name Lambayeque. Upon his death, the relatives of Naymlap spread the rumor that the king grew wings and flew away, leaving his son to rule. The dynasty founded by Naymlap included 12 kings, according to historical evidence. According to legend, the last Naymlap king, Fempellec, committed a series of sins that caused a devastating flood and a period of crisis for the Sicán people. This is certainly possible: Nearly 1.5 meters of water coursed through Batán Grande during the El Niño floods of 1982 and a similar event might have caused the Sicán to abandon and burn the city in AD 1050. The Sicán then moved their capital to Túcume, where even larger pyramids were built.

phases. These pyramids were probably inhabited by priests and rulers even after waves of conquest (and new construction) by the Chimú in 1375 and the Inca in 1470. Atop Huaca Larga, for instance, archaeologists have uncovered a Chimú **Temple of the Mythical Bird** from around 1375 with an even newer Inca tomb, built of stone from Cerro Purgatorio, on top. The heavily adorned and scarred body inside the tomb was apparently a warrior who was buried with two other males and 19 females between the ages of 10 and 30.

To get local transportation to Túcume, you have to get to Lambayeque first by taking a *combi* at Vicente de la Vega and Leonardo Ortiz, in front of the Otursa bus terminal in Chiclayo. Frequent *combis* run to Túcume from in front of Lambayeque's market, 2.5 blocks from Museo Tumbas Reales. From the town of Túcume, it is another 3.5 kilometers to the ruins, either a 15-minute walk or a US$0.75 *motocar* ride.

Museo Sicán

The **Museo Sicán** (Av. Batán Grande s/n, tel. 074/28-6469, 9am-5:30pm Tues.-Sun., US$6) is 18 kilometers outside Chiclayo in Ferreñafe. Though overshadowed by the Museo Tumbas Reales, this modern museum has a fabulous collection of gold objects of the Sicán culture, which succeeded the Moche in AD 850 and

succumbed to the Chimú in 1375. The Sicán people, also called the Lambayeque, were the first culture in Peru's north to discover bronze, which they made by mixing arsenic with copper—a technique learned from the Tiahuanaco and Huari cultures in southern Peru. The Sicán were at the hub of a great commercial network that moved emeralds and shells from Ecuador, gold nuggets from the Amazon, and mercury ore for their metallurgy from Peru's southern sierra.

As lifestyle dioramas in the museum show, the Sicán buried their kings in a unique way: deep within vertical shafts, sometimes accompanied by more than 20 sacrificed attendants and more than a ton of metal and other objects. Archaeologists believe that up to 90 percent of all gold plundered from tombs in Peru comes from Sicán sites in the Lambayeque Valley. Indeed, Sicán masks, with their characteristic *ojos alados* (winged eyes), are found in private collections all over the world. In 1936, renowned Peruvian archaeologist Julio Tello managed to track down a huge collection of gold artifacts looted from Huaca La Ventana in Batán Grande. Fortunately, Tello was able to save many of these objects for Lima's Museo de Oro.

Yet little was known about the Sicán civilization until 1991, when Japanese archaeologist Izumi Shimada excavated two royal

Sicán tombs at the first Sicán capital of Batán Grande. In the east tomb, the king was surrounded by sacrificed women and buried upside down, his decapitated head placed in front of him. The mass of objects in the tomb included two huge golden arms, a square copper-gold mask stained red with mercury ore, and several *cuentas* (massive heaps of shell beads). The west tomb is even larger, with similar gold masks and *cuentas* surrounding the king, along with niches containing women, sacrificed in pairs. DNA and dental tests have revealed that the two kings, and many of the women in both tombs, were close relatives. Spanish-speaking guides (US$8) are available outside the museum. *Colectivos* to Ferreñafe can be taken from the Terminal de Epsel at the corner of Avenida Oriente and Nicolás de Piérola in Chiclayo.

Chaparrí

Peru's first private nature reserve, founded in 2001, **Area de Conservación Privada Chaparrí** (cell tel. 978-896-377 or tel. 072/84-2557, www.chaparri.org) is an extraordinary option for those interested in exploring a unique ecosystem. The 34,000-hectare reserve of dry forest is administered by the local campesino community and funded by Peruvian photographer Heinz Plenge with the support of several Peruvian corporations and large environmental organizations. The park's goal is to reintroduce and preserve endangered species such as the *pava aliblanca* (white-winged turkey), *el oso de anteojos* (the spectacled bear), the guanaco (a camelid), and the Andean condor, the world's largest flying bird. You can see Chaparrí during a day trip or spend the night at its eco-lodge. In either case, be sure to contact them before you arrive.

ENTERTAINMENT AND EVENTS

Chiclayo hot spots include the sleek and modern **Magno Discoteca** (José Leonardo Ortiz 490, tel. 074/23-6266, www.mango.pe, 10:30pm-close Thurs.-Sat.) with three different areas that vary in price and VIP status.

spectacled bear at the Area de Conservación Privada Chaparrí

Spanning nearly an entire block near the bus stations, **Premium** (Balta 94-98, cell tel. 956-129-818, 7pm-4am Mon.-Sat., 7pm-close Sun., US$4-11) is part classic pub, part flashy karaoke stage, and part bright modern café.

Monsefú, a town known for embroidered cotton and woven straw goods sold at a daily market, is also famous for the procession of **El Señor Nazareno Cautivo de Monsefú.** According to legend, this effigy of Christ floated ashore one day and is chained inside the church because it has escaped before to perform miracles in other towns. The festival begins August 31 and involves fireworks, dances, and music, until the final and biggest party day, September 14. Other important festivals include the **Purísima Concepción** in Túcume in February and the **Señor de la Justicia** on April 25 in Ferreñafe.

RECREATION
Tour Agencies and Guides

Guided tours are a good option for getting to Chiclayo's far-flung sites and having them explained by an informed guide. One of the most comprehensive operators in Peru's north is **InkaNatura Travel,** which has a Chiclayo office (Manuel María Izaga 730, Of. 203, tel. 074/23-4496, www.inkanatura.com). InkaNatura runs a range of local cultural tours that can be linked to longer excursions in Trujillo and Chachapoyas. InkaNatura also has an office in Lima (Manuel Bañon 461, San Isidro, tel. 01/440-2022, www.inkanatura.com).

Another recommended local agency is **Tumi Tours** (Colón 599, tel. 074/22-5371, www.tumitours.com, US$80 for 2 people, or US$22 pp in larger groups), which has organized tours to the major museums, Túcume, and even the southern beach towns like Santa Rosa.

For a private guide, call **Sysy Moreno** (tel. 074/20-6387 or 979/67-0775, sysysilva@hotmail.com), a detail-oriented, Spanish-speaking guide. The friendly, English-speaking guide **José Jimenez** (tel. 074/22-1403 or 976/29-3860, jjpeko@hotmail.com) will go to any site you want for about US$15 pp, two-person minimum.

FOOD

There is a wide variety of restaurants in Chiclayo nowadays, from top-end gourmet places to bustling little eateries. Local specialties include *seco de cabrito* (goat marinated in *chicha de jora* and vinegar) and *arroz con pato a la chiclayana* (duck cooked in dark beer, mint, and cilantro).

Peruvian

Romana (Balta 512, tel. 074/22-3598, 7am-1am daily, US$5-8) is the best mid-range restaurant in town. *Palta rellena* (stuffed avocado), spicy plates of *ají de gallina, arroz con pato, lomo saltado,* and flaky apple pie are served up on white-and-blue tables. The *chicha morada* here is excellent. Midday *menús* are US$5.

Around the corner is **Roma** (Manuel María Ízaga 710, tel. 074/20-4556, 6:30am-10pm daily, US$3-4), which has a less expensive and varied menu but is a locals' favorite in business for 60 years. Apart from their restaurant menus, both Romana and Roma have a good selection of hot drinks, breakfasts, sandwiches, desserts, and milk shakes.

Meat lovers should head to **Restaurant La Parra** (Manuel María Ízaga 752, tel. 074/22-7471, 12:30pm-12:30am daily, US$5), one of Chiclayo's best restaurants. The restaurant serves huge portions of grilled meats, roasted chicken, and ceviche. Have *brochetas de lomo* (beef skewers) washed down with a pitcher of sangria.

Peruvian Fusion and Fine Dining

The front door of ★ **Restaurant Fiesta Gourmet** (Salaverry 1820, tel. 074/20-1970, 10am-10pm Mon.-Sat., 10am-5pm Sun., US$8-20 without wine) is always closed, but if you ring the bell, a suited gentleman will lead you through the converted house, past white tablecloths and stately wine glasses to a quiet patio. Peruvian couple Bertha and Alberto Solís opened this restaurant in 1983 and, with the help of their son and chef Héctor Solís, have since expanded with locations in Trujillo, Lima, and Tacna. Try the *seco de cabrito* (roast goat) or *tiradito de lenguado* (flounder carpaccio).

Páprika (Av. Balta 399, tel. 074/22-7272, 6am-midnight Mon.-Sun., US$15), inside Costa de Sol Hotel, is highly recommended. Dishes include ostrich *paupiette* with champagne-sauce fettuccini, and the more Peruvian *loche* pumpkin mousse with tuna sauce.

Restaurant El Huaralino (La Libertad 155, Urb. Santa Victoria, tel. 074/27-0330, noon-5pm and 7pm-10:30pm Mon.-Sat., noon-5pm Sun., US$10) used to be a four-fork restaurant. Now, while the food is still up to par, the restaurant's lacy tablecloths and chair covers give it a dated feel. The restaurant's famed dish is *pato en ají a lo huaralino* (slow-cooked duck in a three-pepper sauce).

Pizza

At **Chez Maggy** (Av. Balta 413, tel. 074/20-9453, 6:30pm-midnight daily, US$4-8), you'll first have to slip past the warm wood-fired oven before you can slide into your table and order up a large pizza and sangria. Delivery is also available. **Pizzeria Venecia** (Av. Balta 365, tel. 074/23-3384, 6pm-midnight daily, US$4-7) has friendly staff and excellent variety of pizzas.

Cafés, Bakeries, and Ice Cream

Don Benny (Balta 465, tel. 074/20-6452, 6am-1am daily, US$1-5) scoops up *manjar* ice cream cones and towering *lúcuma* sundaes. But should you need something more filling, there is also a large selection of breads, cheeses, cold cuts, and empanadas.

Markets

The **Mercado Modelo** (Av. Balta 961, 6am-6pm daily) is a huge and friendly produce market. Modern supermarkets are increasingly common. There is a **Metro** supermarket (Gonzáles and Aguirre, 9am-10pm daily) only a few blocks from the Parque Principal.

Outside Chiclayo

★ **El Cantaro** (Dos de Mayo 180, tel. 074/28-2196, 9am-5pm daily, US$6.50) in **Lambayeque** is your best bet for delicious regional favorites such as *pepián de pavo* (turkey breast with a ground peanut and corn sauce) or the unusual but tasty *tortilla de raya* (ray omelet). At lunch the restaurant often fills up with tour groups. A second option in Lambeyeque and just as good is **El Rincón del Pato** (Av. Augusto B. Leguía 270, tel. 074/28-2751, 10am-6pm daily, US$4-7). The restaurant serves duck in every imaginable way, as well as fish and other seafood.

ACCOMMODATIONS

Chiclayo's lack of colonial history has resulted in a glut of modern concrete hotels that are efficient but drab. A notable exception is Los Horcones, located outside the city.

US$10-25

Palmira Hotel (Belaúnde 978, Urb. La Primavera, tel. 074/22-4115, www. palmirahotelchiclayo.com, US$15 s, US$20 d) is a low-budget hotel that is a five-minute taxi ride from Chiclayo's busy and noisy downtown. Rooms are clean and have wall-to-wall mirrors and nice baths. There is Wi-Fi, cable TV, 24-hour room service, laundry, parking, and a café-bar. Definitely a good value.

US$25-50

Hotel Paraíso (Pedro Ruiz 1064, tel. 074/22-8161, www.hotelesparaiso.com.pe, US$35 s, US$40 d) is on Parque Obrero, a few blocks away from Plaza de Armas. Rooms have modern baths, cable TV, and ceiling fans. Executive rooms include breakfast and Wi-Fi. Amenities include a workout room, Internet stations, a 24-hour restaurant, parking, lockers, and a boutique.

Eras Hotel (Vincent de la Vega 851, tel. 074/23-6333, www.erashotel.com, US$38 s, US$45 d, with breakfast and airport transfer) has clean rooms painted in light colors. They have cable TV, mini fridges, and phones. The hotel has laundry service, Internet access, and a restaurant. There are executive rooms for US$45.

US$50-100

Casa Andina (Federico Villarreal 115, tel. 074/23-4911, www.casa-andina.com, US$65-81 s or d) is a favorite for businesspeople. The large rooms in this seven-story hotel come with flat-screen TVs, mini fridges, and desks. The hotel has a pool and an Internet center, and its restaurant, La Plaza, serves a good breakfast buffet as well as lunch and dinner. There is a steep fee of about US$10 per day to get Wi-Fi in the room.

Inti Hotel (Luis Gonzáles 622, tel. 074/23-5931, www.intiotel.com, US$69 s, US$90 d, with buffet breakfast) is a three-star lodging six blocks west of Chiclayo's Plaza de Armas. Rooms are carpeted and have soundproof windows, cable TV, and Wi-Fi. There is a good restaurant-bar-café called El Kero.

The Win Meier Hotel & Casino (Bolognesi 756, tel. 074/22-8172, www.win-meier.pe, US$90 s, US$113 d, US$189 suite), formerly the Garza Hotel, is halfway between the airport and the Plaza de Armas. There are 94 rooms with air-conditioning, Wi-Fi, cable TV, and good baths. Amenities include a swimming pool, a restaurant, a casino, and karaoke.

US$100-150

Costa del Sol (Balta 399, tel. 074/22-7272, www.costadelsolperu.com, US$99 s, US$110 d, US$140 suite, with buffet breakfast) is a couple of blocks from the Plaza de Armas. The intimate rooms are decorated in red and tan and have fridges, phones, cable TV, Wi-Fi, and big baths. Up on the roof, the whirlpool tub, dry sauna, and clear-paneled pool make for a relaxed afternoon. Facilities include a small gym, a good bar, and a restaurant.

Outside Chiclayo

If you enjoy natural beauty, stay at ★ **Los Horcones de Túcume** (cell tel. 951-831 705, www.loshorconesdetucume.com, US$100 s, or US$120 d, with breakfast) in Túcume. This rural lodge, built according to the building techniques of the ancient Moche culture, is in the backyard of the 26 massive pyramids of Túcume. Twelve airy rooms, made of adobe and algaroba beams, open up to covered terraces and views of the surrounding fields. Bamboo trellises drip with purple poinciana flowers that shade outdoor spaces from the hot sun. The hotel has a pleasant harmony that appeals to people from around the world who come here to be close to Túcume and enjoy starry nights.

INFORMATION AND SERVICES

Chiclayo has an **Iperú tourism office** (San Jose 823, tel. 074/20-5730, 9am-6pm Mon.-Fri., 9am-1pm Sun.). The **tourist police office** (Sáenz Peña 830, cell tel. 978-951-330) is open 24 hours daily.

A recommended health clinic for travelers is the **Clínica del Pacífico** (Ortiz 420, tel. 074/22-8585, www.clinicadelpacifico.com. pe, 24 hours daily). Off the Parque Principal,

at Balta and Aguirre, are two reliable chain pharmacies, **Boticas Arcángel** (tel. 074/20-5999) and **Inkafarma** (tel. 074/20-8648).

Banco Continental, Scotiabank, and **Banco de Crédito,** all on Balta between Izaga and Aguirre, all have offices and ATMs. They are typically open 9am-6pm Monday-Friday and Saturday morning. A handful of currency exchange houses are on the same block. If you're cashing travelers checks, rates vary, so shop around.

The Chiclayo post office, **Serpost** (Elias Aguirre 140, at Miguel Grau, tel. 074/23-7031, 8am-8pm Mon.-Sat.), is about six blocks from the Parque Principal. **Internet access** and **laundry** are widely available around town, and providers are open from early in the morning to late in the evening.

GETTING THERE AND AROUND

Flights arrive at **Aeropuerto José Abelardo Quiñones Gonzáles** (Bolognesi s/n, tel. 074/23-3192, 7am-11pm daily), which is two kilometers east of downtown. Taxis should cost US$3 from inside the airport.

Many buses to Chiclayo travel only at night. Bus terminals are spread out along Bolognesi, five blocks or more from the main park. For traveling to and from Lima, we recommend three companies: **Oltursa** (Balta 598, tel. 074/23-7789, www.oltursa.pe), whose terminal (Av. Vicente de la Vega 101, tel. 074/22-5611) is outside the center; **Cruz del Sur** (Bolognesi 888, tel. 074/72-0444, 3am-11:45pm daily), which has one morning bus and five evening buses; and **Línea** (Bolognesi 638, tel. 074/23-3497, www.transporteslinea. com.pe, 4:30am-11pm daily). Línea also has regular buses to Chimbote, Piura, Cajamarca, Huaraz, and Jaén. **Móvil Tours** (Bolognesi 199, tel. 074/27-1944) has daily buses to and from Chachapoyas (10 hours, US$12.50) or Tarapoto (15 hours, US$23).

Chiclayo is a nice city to walk around, but if you're in a hurry, in-town taxis cost US$1.25. Even longer trips, as far as Túcume, can be negotiated for surprisingly cheap.

Piura

Piura was magically described in *Casa Verde,* Mario Vargas Llosa's masterful novel that divides this city into two main barrios: the Mangachería, a sprawling den north of the city center, known for beautiful women, gambling, and the novel's namesake brothel; and Gallinacera, south of present-day Calle Sánchez Cerro, the respectable side of the city known for singers, *guitaristas,* and players of the *cajón.* The north-south boundary remains today. The farther south you walk toward Piura's laid-back and pleasant Plaza de Armas, the gentler the town becomes. Narrow colonial streets and classic old homes conjure up what life was like in the 19th century when this town's population was only 5,000.

Historically, Piura had a tough time establishing its roots. The first Piura city, named San Miguel de Piura, was founded by Francisco Pizarro in 1532 before the conquest of the Inca. But every attempt to build up a city was frustrated by the vagaries of torrential flooding and pirate attacks. The city changed location several times until 1588, when it moved to its present-day location and the cathedral was established. Piura is safe, but being so far inland, it is the hottest of Peru's northern cities. Unfortunately, even its new location hasn't completely protected Piura. El Niño floods hit the city hard in 1983, 1992, and 1998.

Outside the city is the town of Catacaos, one of Peru's major arts and crafts markets, and the pleasant beach of Colán. Among Peruvians, Piura is famous as a center for *brujería,* or witchcraft. The heart and soul of this tradition is centered on the lakes region near the mountainous Huancabamba, seven hours from Piura.

SIGHTS

Inside the **Catedral** (tel. 073/32-7112, 7am-noon and 5pm-8:30pm daily, free) is a gold-covered altar and paintings by Ignacio Merino (1817-1876), one of Peru's leading painters, who was born in Piura but spent most of his life in France. One of the cathedral's more venerated images is a replica of baby Jesus (usually buried under teddy bears). The original Jesus figure was made in Spain by a Carmelite nun who prayed nightly to see baby Jesus. One night, during her dreams, her wish was fulfilled. She awoke, molded the statue, and died shortly afterward. Over time, the image has become renowned for producing miracles.

The relaxing **Plaza de Armas** is ringed with tamarind trees and is reigned over by a marble liberty statue given to the city in 1870 by then-president José Balta. A half block from the Plaza de Armas is the home of **Admiral Miguel Grau** (Tacna 662, erratic daytime hours, free), Peru's foremost naval hero. Grau's brilliant military maneuverings during Peru's disastrous War of the Pacific (1879-1883) continue to be a source of consolation for Peruvians.

Follow Tacna past the cathedral on your right before coming to Miguel Grau, the city's main commercial street. Farther north along Tacna—and the parallel streets of Arequipa, Libertad, and Lima—there are narrow streets with **colonial buildings** made of cane and adobe and fringed with fine woodworking.

Where Tacna meets Sánchez Cerro, you will find the 18th-century **Iglesia de Carmen,** which has evening Mass at 7pm daily. The religious museum has a golden baroque altar and Cusco school-style paintings, but its pulpit was robbed of its carved angels and four evangelists. In the 1980s, crimes like this closed down the neighboring Benedictine convent.

Other lesser sites in Piura include **Iglesia San Francisco** (near Lima and Ica), where Piurans announced their independence from Spain in 1821; and the **Museo Municipal Vicús y Sala de Oro** (Huánuco and Sullana,

Piura

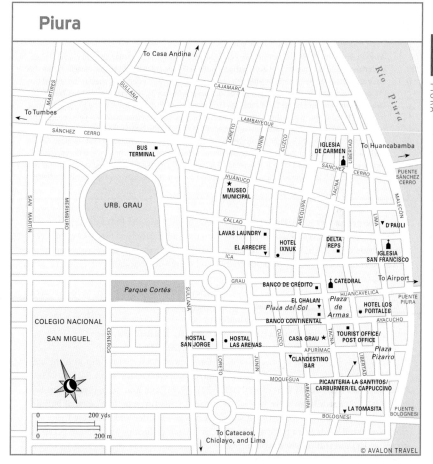

To Casa Andina

MARTINEZ

SULLANA

CAJAMARCA

To Tumbes

SÁNCHEZ CERRO

LAMBAYEQUE

LORETO

JUNÍN

CUZCO

Rio Piura

BUS TERMINAL

IGLESIA DE CARMEN

SÁNCHEZ CERRO

LIBERTAD

To Huancabamba

PUENTE SÁNCHEZ CERRO

HUÁNUCO

★ MUSEO MUNICIPAL

TACNA

AREQUIPA

LIMA

MALECÓN

D'PAULI

SAN MARTIN

MERIMBURO

URB. GRAU

CALLAO

LAVAS LAUNDRY ■

EL ARRECIFE ▼

ICA

HOTEL IXNUK ▼

DELTA REPS ■

IGLESIA SAN FRANCISCO

Parque Cortés

SULLANA

GRAU

BANCO DE CRÉDITO ■

CATEDRAL

HUANCAVELICA

To Airport

PUENTE PIURA

COLEGIO NACIONAL

SAN MIGUEL

CISNEROS

EL CHALAN ▼
Plaza del Sol ▼

BANCO CONTINENTAL

Plaza de Armas

HOTEL LOS ■ PORTALES

AYACUCHO

HOSTAL SAN JORGE ●

● HOSTAL LAS ARENAS

CUZCO

CASA GRAU ★

APURIMAC

TOURIST OFFICE/ POST OFFICE ■

Plaza Pizarro

LORETO

JUNÍN

▼ CLANDESTINO BAR

LIBERTAD

MOQUEGUA

AREQUIPA

PICANTERIA LA SANTITOS/ CARBURMER/EL CAPPUCCINO

▼ LA TOMASITA

BOLOGNESI

PUENTE BOLOGNESI

0 — 200 yds
0 — 200 m

To Catacaos, Chiclayo, and Lima

© AVALON TRAVEL

tel. 073/30-2803, 9am-5pm Mon.-Fri., 9am-1pm Sat., 9am-noon Sun., US$2.50), with a variety of ceramics and gold objects from the Vicus culture, which thrived nearly 2,000 years ago on Cerro Vicus, 27 kilometers east of Piura. Objects found on Vicus, and now on display at the museum, include a gold feline head with sharp teeth and extended tongue.

ENTERTAINMENT AND EVENTS

Piura is a peaceful town where nightlife is mellow and sometimes nothing more than a stroll through the plaza with an ice cream.

Two blocks from the Plaza de Armas is **ClanDestino Bar** (Apurimac 535, tel. 073/33-1367, 8pm-close daily), which has a good selection of cocktails that you can enjoy while checking out the photo exhibits it puts on or paintings from local artists that hang from its walls. It also shows movies during the week, and sometimes has live music.

The **Semana Santa** (Easter Week) celebration of Catacaos is famous around Peru—especially its Palm Sunday procession, a re-creation of Jesus's entry into Jerusalem that features a locally famous white burro. One of North Peru's most sacred shrines is that of **El Señor Cautivo** in the small mountain town of Ayabaca, where pilgrims from Ecuador and

The War of the Pacific

With his British-built destroyer *Huascar*, Peruvian admiral Miguel Grau managed to elude a larger, and more modern, Chilean fleet during the War of the Pacific (1879-1883). He repeatedly broke the Chilean blockade, disrupted the enemy's communications, and even managed to bombard the Chilean city of Antofagasta. In the battle of Iquique, on March 21, 1879, Grau sunk the Chilean destroyer *Esmeralda* and killed Chile's top naval officer, Arturo Prat. In a show of magnanimity—not returned by Chileans when they later sacked and burned most of the country—Grau picked the surviving sailors out of the water and returned them to a Chilean beach. He even sent the objects he found alongside Prat's body, along with a consolatory letter he penned, to Prat's widow. Grau's end came in October of that year when the entire Chilean fleet chased the *Huascar* down, exploding its control tower and killing Grau instantly. That battle marked a critical turning point in the war, allowing Chile to invade Peru and seize the port of Arica and nearby valuable nitrate fields.

Peru converge October 12-13. During the first week of October there is a festival of *tondero*, a livelier version of the *marinera*, at the **Club Grau** (Av. Los Cocos 120, tel. 073/30-9930) in Piura.

FOOD

Given the dry, hot climate of Piura, many budget restaurants close during siesta (1pm-4pm daily), and others open only in the afternoon.

Peruvian

Picantería La Santitos (Libertad 1001, tel. 073/30-9475, 10am-6:30pm daily, US$5-7) is extraordinary. Start with an *algarrobina* (a creamy cocktail made from pisco and carob syrup) and a powerful *cebiche de conchas negras* (black scallop ceviche). For really hot days, grab a table in its air-conditioned room.

Another recommended option for local dishes is **La Tomasita** (Tacna 853, tel. 073/32-1957, www.latomasitarestaurant.com, 9am-5pm daily, US$5-7), three blocks from the Plaza de Armas. The *tacu tacu* dishes and *mero con arroz negrito* are excellent.

Río Grande (Malecón Eguiguren 680, tel. 073/30-3886, 11am-5pm daily, US$10-18) is a good option for fish and seafood. Recommended ceviches include *de lenguado* (flounder) and *mixto* (fish, octopus, squid, and scallops).

Don Parce (Tacna 642, tel. 073/30-0842, www.donparce.com, 7am-midnight daily), one block from the Plaza de Armas, offers an incredible variety of food—ceviche, deep-fried dishes, fish, soups, rice, regional dishes, and more—in abundant portions and good prices, in a relaxed atmosphere with Wi-Fi. They also set up a station in the food court of the Plaza del Sol.

Cafés, Bakeries, and Ice Cream

For a quiet dessert stop, slip into the cozy green-walled **D'Pauli** (Lima 541, tel. 073/32-2210, 9am-2pm and 4pm-10pm Mon.-Sat., US$4). This tiny café in a colonial building serves good coffee and tempting treats such as *crocante de lúcuma* and apple or pecan pie.

El Cappuccino (1014 Libertad, tel. 073/30-1111, 11:30am-11pm Mon.-Sat., US$4-10), with its enclosed patio, has a simultaneously classic and modern feel. Start with a pisco sour, then follow it up with a Thai chicken salad or spinach ravioli.

The local favorite for ice cream and *cremoladas* (like a fruit slushy) is **El Chalán** (Tacna 520, on Plaza de Armas, tel. 073/30-6483, 7:30am-11pm daily). A cold *cremolada* is your best bet to beat Piura's scorching afternoon heat. El Chalán is also known for its generous sundaes and megaburgers.

Markets

The big supermarkets in town are **Plaza Vea** (tel. 080/10-0020, 9am-10pm daily), which has a location on Óvalo Grau and at Sanchez Cerro with Valle Vise, and **Tottus** (tel. 073/60-5800, 9am-10pm daily), located in the new Open Plaza mall, which is a short taxi ride from the plaza and across the Río Piura.

ACCOMMODATIONS

Lodging in Piura falls into two categories: basic or luxury. There's not a lot in between to recommend. So we suggest you either go big or tuck your money away for another time.

US$10-25

Hostal Santa Lucía (Ayacucho 773, tel. 073/30-9464, www.hostalsantaluciapiura. com, US$18 s, US$22 d) is a good low-budget choice offering clean rooms with private baths, cable TV, and Wi-Fi.

US$25-50

Hostal las Arenas (Av. Loreto 945, tel. 073/30-5554, US$40 s, US$50 d) is three blocks away from Óvalo Grau and a short walk to the Plaza de Armas. The rooms are simple, clean, and comfy, with cable TV, fans or air-conditioning, and Wi-Fi. The hotel also has a small swimming pool, a café that serves a simple breakfast, and private parking. Rooms in the front of the hotel get a lot of the street noise.

US$50-100

In a residential neighborhood a few minutes out of the city center is **Mango Verde** (Country 248, tel. 073/32-1768, www.mangoverde.com.pe, US$50 s, US$65 d). This small hotel, decorated with plants and brightly colored art, offers simple but comfortable rooms. The hotel's best feature may be its third-floor terrace, with comfy sofas that are great for relaxing in the evening.

Hotel Los Portales (Libertad 875, tel. 073/32-1161, www.losportaleshoteles.com.pe, US$65-75 s, US$85d, with breakfast) is on the Plaza de Armas. Several of the hotel's rooms wrap around an elegant, sun-filled courtyard. The colonial house has large rooms with high ceilings, and modern remodeling has ensured that all rooms have air-conditioning, a fridge, cable TV, dial-out phones, Wi-Fi, room service, and well-equipped marble baths. The bar offers a complimentary welcome cocktail, and there's a restaurant by the pool.

Hotel Ixnuk (Ica 553, tel. 073/61-9693, www.ixnuk.com, US$60 s, US$100 d, with breakfast) is located two blocks from the Plaza de Armas. There is Wi-Fi, and each room has a flat-screen TV and a minibar. It has another location a few blocks away on Calle Lima with more spacious rooms at a higher cost. A new addition, the **Casa Andina Private Collection** (Ramón Mujica, Urb. San Eduardo el Chipe, tel. 073/28-5000, www.casa-andina.com, US$90 s or d) has comfortable rooms, cable TV, Wi-Fi, and air-conditioning, which travelers have come to expect from other hotels in the chain.

US$100-150

Costa del Sol (Av. Loreto 649, tel. 073/30-2864, www.costadelsolperu.com, US$105 s, US$129 d, US$205 suite, with buffet breakfast) is two blocks from Óvalo Grau in a less noisy neighborhood than central Piura. Rooms are big and tastefully decorated, with mini fridges, phones, cable TV, Wi-Fi, and big baths. Facilities include a swimming pool and a gym. A good bar and restaurant are available.

INFORMATION AND SERVICES

The **tourist office** (Ayacucho, on the Plaza de Armas, tel. 073/32-0249, 9am-6pm Mon.-Sat., 9am-1pm Sun.) is helpful with maps and city brochures. Driving maps may be available at **Touring y Automóvil Club de Peru** (Sánchez Cerro 1237). The **tourist police** (Av. Los Cocos 250) and can be contacted at cell tel. 997-559-685. In an emergency you can call **Piura Police** (Sánchez Cerro block 13, tel. 073/30-7641, 24 hours daily).

Find health care at **Hospital Reátegui** (Grau 1150, tel. 073/32-3181 or 073/30-3364, 24 hours daily) or **Hospital Cayetano**

Heredia (Independencia and Castilla, tel. 073/28-4760 or 073/34-2327, 24 hours daily). There are many banks near the Plaza de Armas, including **Banco Continental** (Ayacucho and Tacna) and **Banco de Crédito** (Miguel Grau 133). Both have 24-hour ATMs and are open 9am-6pm Monday-Friday and Saturday morning. There are also banks in the Plaza del Sol and Open Plaza shopping centers. *Cambistas* (money changers) cluster around Miguel Grau and Arequipa.

The post office, **Serpost** (tel. 073/30-9393, 8am-8pm Mon.-Sat.), is at Libertad and Ayacucho. There are several **Internet cafés** and call centers throughout town. Take your dirty clothes to **Lavas** (Cusco and Callao, tel. 073/58-4135, 9am-1pm and 4pm-7:30pm Mon.-Sat.). In the airport, **Zeta Bookstore** has English editions of international bestsellers, Peruvian novels, and guidebooks.

GETTING THERE AND AROUND

Most major carriers have daily flights into **Piura airport** (PIU, tel. 073/32-7733), which is two kilometers out of town. A taxi costs US$4-5. **LATAM** (Avelino Cáceres 147, Miraflores-Castilla neighborhood) has an office in the Open Plaza mall.

Most bus companies have offices on Sánchez Cerro, blocks 11-13. The best bus lines for getting back and forth to Lima are **Oltursa** (Bolognesi 801, tel. 073/33-5303, www.oltursa.pe) and **Cruz del Sur** (Circunvalación 160, tel. 073/33-7094, www.cruzdelsur.com.pe). **El Dorado** (Sánchez Cerro 1119, tel. 073/32-5875) has nine daily buses to Tumbes (US$5), with stops in Máncora. Next door is **ETTI** (Sánchez Cerro 1123), which also has daily buses to Tumbes and Máncora. **Sertur** (cell tel. 968-963-940 or 969-976-501) drives upscale minivans directly to Máncora and Tumbes (US$11), but these vans are only worth their high price if they aren't crowded. Secure buses depart daily from the **Línea station** (Sánchez Cerro 1215, tel. 073/30-3894, www.linea.pe) to Cajamarca,

Lima, Jaén, Huaraz, Chimbote, Chiclayo, and Trujillo.

Unless you are going to a bus station or one of the outlying luxury hotels, Piura's colonial center is compact and best done on foot. Local *motocars,* however, cost US$1. Should you need a reliable taxi company, call **Piura Taxi** (tel. 073/30-3999).

SIDE TRIPS
Catacaos

The village of Catacaos, a friendly, dusty little town 12 kilometers southwest of Piura, has the best arts and crafts market in northern Peru. The town is famous for a variety of **handicrafts** sold along four blocks of the old Calle Comercio, including panama hats, place mats, and other finely woven goods made of *toquilla* straw imported from Ecuador. Also watch for earrings and other jewelry wrought in gold and silver filigree, an art form that has flourished here since colonial times, when gold was imported from the Amazon and Cajamarca. There are also painted ceramics in the shape of rotund campesinos, wood carvings and kitchen utensils made of *zapote* wood, colorful hammocks, wicker lampshades and baskets, and some leather goods.

As a bonus, this bustling town has some excellent restaurants, or *picanterías,* for northern cuisine: Here you can find *seco de chabelo, tamalitos verdes, majafo de yuca,* and other dishes that combine local foods like plantain and cassava with beef and pork. The market is biggest on the weekends, and stalls are set up around 10am and taken down as late as 7pm.

To reach Catacaos, hire a taxi (US$5) or take a *colectivo* (US$1.25) from the 12th block of Avenida Loreto.

Colán

At 65 kilometers from Piura, this is the favorite local beach destination, a pleasant stretch of white sand with gentle waves perfect for swimming. The beach is fringed with stilted beach homes built during the 1950s, classic old wooden structures with long balconies facing west. There are few services such as restaurants and Internet access except at several resorts, which are all but dead in the off-season (late Mar.-early Dec.). The beach is presided over by **Iglesia San Lucás de Colán,** the first church the Spanish built in Peru, near the small town of Esmeralda. This magnificent and unique stone church, recently restored to its original thatch-and-mud roof, has ancient wood columns and, with typical Spanish shrewdness, is built atop a Chimú *huaca*. Inside you will find the coats of arms for the royal Spanish Hapsburg line.

Another 10 kilometers south along the coast is the picturesque fishing town of **Paita,** founded in the 16th century by the Spanish and the place where Manuela Sáenz, Simón Bolívar's mistress, spent her final days, ostracized from Lima society.

Transportes Dora (3rd block of Sánchez Cerro) in Piura has frequent taxis (US$0.75) to Paita, where you can take a *combi* (US$0.50) farther north to Colán.

Huancabamba

A truly adventurous journey that requires a minimum of four days and a lot of stamina leads to Huancabamba, a picturesque mountain town and the center of *brujería* (witchcraft and healing) for coastal Peru. The powers of the area's shamans and *curanderos* (healers) are legendary and are part of an ancient tradition in Peru that mixes natural medicine with spiritual beliefs. These healers play a major medical role in the countryside, where people sometimes lack even rudimentary health services. People seek cures for a variety of problems such as infertility or psychological ailments. Shamans attribute those

problems to *susto* (fear), whose symptoms resemble depression or post-traumatic stress syndrome because patients suffer from loss of appetite and insomnia. But probably the single largest group of seekers come for affairs of the heart: Jilted lovers place hexes on a competing suitor or bring a piece of clothing to lure back a departed lover. Others come to have a hex removed or to see into the future.

The physical center of all this work is **Huaringas,** a collection of 14 lakes at elevations over 3,900 meters, where healing ceremonies (*mesas*) typically include dunkings in icy-cold lake water and the use of herbs and hallucinogenic substances such as the San Pedro cactus. The most famous of these lakes is Shimbe, which can be reached after a day-long mule ride. But there are also closer lakes.

Huancabamba is also known as Resbalabamba, or "the city that walks," because the town's stratified, water-soaked foundation is causing the town to take an inexorable stroll downhill. In the area, there are excellent mountain-bike circuits and walks to Inca ruins. Guides are available in town.

The trip from Piura is a 215-kilometer, five- to seven-hour bus ride that passes through the scenic town of Chanchaque and over a bumpy mountain road before arriving at Huancabamba, around 1,950 meters elevation. In the town, there are several hostels and cheap restaurants. **Civa** (Centenario 110) has a bus that leaves Piura at 3pm daily for Huancabamba (US$14). From Huancabamba, Civa buses leave for Piura at 5pm daily. Once in Huancabamba, you still have a few hours of travel, first by *combi,* and finally on foot or mule.

The Northern Beaches

There is a secret about Peru that is jealously guarded by surfers around the world: The country has fabulous beaches, especially in the north, where the frigid Humboldt Current veers off into the Pacific and leaves behind a subtropical coastline bathed in balmy waters. Picture desert hills that ease into a winding, varied coastline of white sand and palm trees. There are many half-moon bays and beaches where odd volcanic formations break up the surf. These are safe for swimming; there are no currents and no sharks. But there are also many thundering point breaks and some of the best lefts in the world. Surfers flock here when waves are highest between January and March.

There is a lot of new development on these beaches, but the result, so far at least, is a pleasingly eclectic blend of mom-and-pop options—especially in the 25-kilometer stretch of spectacular coastline that includes the beaches of Órganos, Vichayito, Máncora, and Punta Sal. You can find excellent value for food and lodging, ranging from US$8 party hostels (mostly in Máncora) to exquisite bed-and-breakfasts for honeymooners and bungalows for families. Unless you love huge parties, do not come here during the major Peruvian holidays (New Year's, Easter Week, and July 28 Independence Day weekend), when rates double and beaches overflow with Limeños. If you value empty beaches and deep discounts on lodging, try the off-season between April and mid-December. In October, whales pass here on their way to southern Chile. The sun still shines, even on the occasional overcast day, and the temperatures are plenty hot (27-32°C). For surfers, there is always a wave, and for other adventures, there are local tour operators who tackle any trip, from fishing off the Máncora coast to rafting the Río Tumbes.

RECREATION

Surfing along the northern beaches ranges from gentle beginner waves in Máncora and Órganos to a monstrous pipeline wave in Cabo Blanco. For surf lessons, you can try the **Máncora Surf Shop** (Piura 352, Máncora, US$20 per hour). To rent surfboards or, if you are experienced, kiteboarding equipment, stop by **Hostal Las Olas** (Av. Pura s/n, Máncora, tel. 073/25-8099, www.lasolasmancora.com).

Run by an ecotourism specialist and her marine biologist husband, **Pacífico Adventures** (Los Órganos, tel. 073/25-7686, www.pacificoadventures.com) offers a range of professional nature-based trips. Spend the day **snorkeling** near Órganos or push off into deeper water and go **fishing.**

Don't travel to Tumbes to arrange trips to the **northern nature reserves;** either coordinate a trip with **Tumbes Tours** (Tumbes, tel. 072/52-4837, www.tumbestours.com), a longtime operator in the Tumbes area, or check out **Iguana's Trips** (Piura 245, Máncora, tel. 073/63-2762, www.iguanastrips.com, 9am-close daily). Before starting Iguana's Trips, the energetic Ursula Behr was a Class V raft guide in the Cusco area. Now she leads trips down the Río Tumbes (Class III) as well as hikes, horseback rides, and mountain bike rides through the Parque Nacional Cerros de Amotape.

CABO BLANCO

Cabo Blanco is the point where the frigid Humboldt Current collides with the lukewarm El Niño Current from the equator. The result is a dazzling fishing ground and, for surfers, a welcome break from wet suits and chilly coastal waters. There are some beautiful, lonely beaches around Cabo Blanco, but the hillsides are unfortunately marred by

An El Niño Warning

El Niño rains and floods along Peru's coast have been severe enough to spark the downfall of the Moche and Sicán empires, archaeologists say. But the El Niño cycles have become even more intense over the last half century, according to a United Nations report, because of global warming.

The warm, equatorial current is named after El Niño Jesús, or baby Jesus, because it arrives on the coast of Ecuador and Peru every year around Christmas. Some years, however, it extends far into the south Pacific and disrupts the Humboldt Current. The warm waters prevent the upwelling of deep, nutrient-rich waters, which causes anchovies to go elsewhere and ruins what is usually a world-class fishery. Winds across South America generally blow west to Asia, but during El Niño years they reverse and blow toward the continent, pushing up sea levels and sending huge systems of humid air toward Peru's desert coast.

One of the worst El Niño cycles of the century was 1983, when torrential rains began in Peru's north on January 4 and did not stop until the middle of July—the flooding alone destroyed 36 bridges and 1,685 kilometers of roads. Nine years later, in 1992, there was a similar El Niño. But both of these were dwarfed by the El Niño of 1998, which destroyed as much as 90 percent of the banana, rice, and cotton crops grown along Peru's northern coast. The floods killed several people in Piura when a bridge was swept away and created a huge, temporary lake in the middle of the Sechura desert between Chiclayo and Piura. The lake, known as Lago La Niña, forms after most El Niño years but had never been this big—300 kilometers, stretching as far as the eye could see. While it lasted, anglers even began working on the lake and charter boats offered tourist excursions.

Travel becomes difficult and dangerous, or even impossible, during El Niño years. In early 1998, the 20-hour trip from Lima to the Ecuadorian border took over four days. Buses would drive until they reached a washed-out bridge, where passengers would then wade through water, slog through mud, or board a boat toward buses waiting on the other side. Many people became trapped for days on end, waiting for waters in both the south and north to subside before continuing their journey.

pumping iron horses. It was once known internationally for the **Cabo Blanco Fishing Club,** which hosted a range of celebrities through the 1950s and 1960s, including Ernest Hemingway and Nelson Rockefeller. Now it's a world-renowned surfing destination. In June, and again October-January, Cabo Blanco has a monstrous, and dangerous, pipeline wave that reaches up to 3.5 meters and travels nearly 70 meters before closing out in a giant spray. The Cabo Blanco wave forms over sand but crashes in front of large rocks, which have left many surfers badly scraped and broken.

Getting There

Cabo Blanco is a 31-kilometer drive (about 30 minutes) south of Máncora. To get to the Cabo Blanco Fishing Club, pass the dirt turnoff for the town of Cabo Blanco and look for a run-down whitewashed building on the left.

LOS ÓRGANOS

Los Órganos, known locally as just Órganos, is a lower-key beach spot. Named after the wind, which makes an organ-like sound against the eroded rock walls of **Punta Veleros** (Sailboat Point), Órganos has a more remote feel than its neighboring towns. The town's accommodations are on the beach, slightly away from the center of town, and are good options for families and surfers wanting peace and quiet. A three- to eight-meter pipeline forms off Punta Veleros, slightly south of the main beach, November-March, and a beginner's wave forms a bit farther north July-February.

Hard-core surfers congregate around **Bungalows Playa Blanca** (Playa Punta

The Truth Behind Hemingway's Cabo Blanco

The rocky, dusty coastline around Cabo Blanco was rarely visited until the 1940s, when the English-owned International Petroleum Corp. (IPC) established itself in Talara and started setting up oil wells along the coast. That was the beginning of Peru's oil industry, which spread from here into the Amazon.

As far as Cabo Blanco is concerned, the story begins to get interesting around 1945 when foreign oil executives founded the Cabo Blanco Fishing Club, a simple building with a pool and a dozen rooms built atop a spectacular remote white-sand beach at Cabo Blanco. The club was not built to take advantage of the beach, however, but rather the world's richest marlin fishing ground, which lies off the coast here.

The size of the marlin caught here quickly attracted worldwide attention, beginning with a 465-kilogram black marlin caught by oil executive Alfred Glassell Jr. in 1952—Glassell still holds the world record for a 709-kilogram marlin he caught here. Over the next two decades, American companies took over IPC, and sport fishers from around the world flocked to the humble digs of the Cabo Blanco Fishing Club. Among these were a range of luminaries and movie stars who arrived in Talara via direct flights from the United States. The list includes Ernest Hemingway, Bob Hope, Nelson Rockefeller, and Britain's Prince Philip.

But the golden age of what became known as Marlin Boulevard ended in 1968 when the military government of Juan Velasco expropriated the oil wells. The hotel shut down soon after and is now a spectacularly sordid and peeling building that serves as home to a few hard-drinking local workers, along with a collection of chickens and dead seagulls. The beach in front of the club would still be spectacular were it not crisscrossed by pipes from nearby oil wells.

The stories from the fishing club are nonetheless still spectacular and fondly recounted by Pablo Córdoba, who owns Restaurant Cabo Blanco in town. John Wayne came here and met a woman from Paita whom he married and lived with until the end of his life. Many believe that Ernest Hemingway was inspired to write his *Old Man and the Sea* here, but the truth is he got the idea in Cuba. He did, however, spend 45 days here in 1956, drinking whisky and pisco sours, as he and director John Sturges filmed the movie with the same name.

The best-known story perhaps is that of the "million-dollar marlin." A wealthy New York City businessman arrived at the club in 1954 with his secretary. After a week of fishing, however, the fish weren't biting and, on the final day, the man had such a bad hangover that he decided to stay in bed. The secretary, however, ended up catching a 702-kilogram marlin, the women's world record, which still stands. The catch was front-page news in the United States, which was unfortunate for the married man because his wife met him at the airport with divorce papers. The settlement, of course, was US$1 million. "That was an expensive trip for that gentleman," chuckled one of the current residents of the fishing club.

Velero, tel. 073/25-7487, www.bungalows-playablanca.com, US$50 s, US$70 d, with breakfast). Here, stone bungalows surround a central patio restaurant. The hammocks, wicker furniture, and beachfront view are charming, but the faded furniture and sometimes loud restaurant music make this a less formal option.

Next door is a good option, especially for families: **La Perla** (Playa Punta Velero, tel. 073/25-7753, www.elaperla.com.pe, US$54 s,

US$62 d). The hotel, constructed by a Russian family, has Slavic touches—bright-red Baltic coast paint, paintings of windswept Russian landscapes, and a patio full of lacy hammocks. The rooms are immaculately clean, with sparkling tile floors, cable TV, and perfectly made beds in fair-size rooms. The owners are very affable, but they speak more Spanish and German than English.

For lunch, try **Bambú** (Ribera del Mar, no phone, 8am-7pm daily, US$5-7), where ceviche is the logical option. Customer favorites are striped marlin and *espada*. Vegetarians can get pasta dishes, and adventurous eaters should try the *timbal de mariscos*, a seafood casserole. Another place that gets good reviews for its seafood is El Manglar (no phone, lunch daily, US$6), located a block from the Plaza de Armas.

Getting There

To get to Órganos from Tumbes, either take an airport taxi (1.5 hours, US$40-50) or catch one of the frequent *colectivos* from Transportes Carrucho (corner of Tumbes and Piura, Tumbes). The ride costs around US$3 and takes two hours with stops along the way. Once you are dropped off in town, take a *motocar* (US$0.75) to the beaches on the south end of town.

LATAM has flights from Lima to Talara, about 60 kilometers south of Órganos. A taxi from the Talara airport to Órganos takes about 50-60 minutes (US$6-8 pp).

VICHAYITO

South of Máncora, the exposed beaches of Vichayito can be accessed from either the Panamericana near Órganos or via a dirt road from Máncora. The sprawling bungalow complexes that populate Vichayito's beaches offer a quiet and remote beach vacation. Should you want access to the city life of Máncora, stay at one of Vichayito's northern resorts.

Built in 1995, the Vichayito Bungalows (tel. 01/207-0440, www.vichayito.com, bungalows from US$200 for 2 people) continues to feel well designed and modern. The spectacular bungalows have five-meter-high thatched roofs, wood floors, and windows with soft muslin drapes. All bungalows face the ocean. Also take a look at the beautiful tents, which have all the amenities: flat-screen TVs, minibars, a wooden deck, and elegant baths with large tubs. There's also a large pool, a bar, and a restaurant.

Located in south Vichayito and best accessed from a point on the Panamericana near Órganos, Villa Sirena (tel. 01/442-9882 or 998/14-6222, www.villasirenaperu.

com, US$80 s or US$100 d, with breakfast) is both chic and eco-conscious. Bed frames are made of recycled wood but covered with crisp white duvets; roofs don't quite meet the walls, allowing the passing of a constant ocean breeze; and showers are circled off by native tree trunks. Both the pool and the open-air restaurant are protected by grassy sand dunes, which makes for pleasant afternoons of reading or dining on delicious classic Peruvian dishes (US$10-15).

The Lima-born chef Santiago Solari now lives in Vichayito, where he has opened up Naylamp Restaurant (Vivero Palo Santo, cell tel. 998-107-598, ssolaripe@yahoo.com, US$15-20 without wine), serving anything from a flounder ceviche to jumbo shrimp with curry sauce and pizzas, among other delicious options. Just stop by the restaurant during the high season.

Getting There

Without a private car, getting to Vichayito is a 15-30-minute *mototaxi* trip from Órganos (US$8). The ride follows the Panamericana until Vichayito Sur, where it picks up the bumpy, El Niño-destroyed Ex-Panamericana. From Máncora (US$8), the route is pure dirt road.

LAS POCITAS

Continuing north from Vichayito, there are very good accommodations in Las Pocitas. Accessing the area requires going down a rutted dirt road near the bridge leading into Máncora. Named after the sand pools that form around the beach rocks when the tide goes out, Las Pocitas has a string of compact hotel resorts with beachfront property and restaurants. There is a wider range of options here. The area is also closer to Máncora (10 minutes) than Órganos and Vichayito, but still far enough away to avoid the rowdy noise from Máncora's nightlife.

Near the southern tip of Las Pocitas is Máncora Beach Bungalows (tel. 073/25-8125, www.mancora-beach.com, US$55 s, US$68 d). American-owned, the hotel offers large comfortable rooms in a pleasant two-story building. Each room has solar-heated water, a large modern tiled bath, a phone, and a private porch with a hammock and sweeping ocean views. There are two pools and a game room with a Ping-Pong table. The staff here is a friendly and fun-loving family.

Honeymooners and couples looking for a romantic break should try **Sunset** (tel. 073/25-8111, www.sunsetmancora.com, US$72 s, US$86 d). The self-described "seafront boutique hotel" has only five rooms, which are intensely private and have spectacular second-story balconies. Inside, the large rooms are elegantly decorated with framed tapestries, elegant lighting, brush-painted walls, and vaulted bamboo ceilings. This hotel also has an excellent, if expensive, Italian restaurant, where an Italian chef rolls out authentic gnocchi and ravioli and then serves them with flavorful homemade sauces.

Hotel Las Arenas de Máncora (Lima tel. 01/611-9001, www.lasarenasdemancora. com, US$160 suite, with breakfast) is one of the better options in Las Pocitas. Nineteen spacious bungalows spread across a grassy palm-lined property. Each bungalow has a flat-screen TV and a DVD player, a private patio, air-conditioning, and a fridge. The

hotel management provides a video library, evening bonfires, and helpful service. The open-air restaurant serves up fresh seafood and is a good place to watch semitropical birds flit among the palm trees.

At the top of the lodging options is **DCO Hotel** (tel. 073/25-8171, www.hoteldco.com, US$223 suite, US$344 master suite), the area's ultra-hip boutique hotel. Attention to detail is everything here, from the pillow menu in its six ocean-view suites to the 2.5-hour spa session and the restaurant that serves classic Peruvian dishes as well as Italian, Thai, and sushi.

Getting There

During the day, *mototaxis* constantly pass between Máncora and Las Pocitas (US$2.50). At night, however, the *mototaxis* concentrate in Máncora, making it easy to find transportation back to Las Pocitas but more difficult to find a *mototaxi* into town.

★ MÁNCORA

Once a small fishing town with a few beach hotels, Máncora has become Peru's surfing mecca. There's always a wave here, ranging from beginner waves to six-footers when the swell is up.

Máncora is Peru's surfing mecca.

If you're on a smaller budget, or just want to party with other backpackers, Máncora is the place to be. During the summer (mid-Dec.-Mar.) and during vacations such as Easter Week and July 28, the town of Máncora overflows with surfers, hippies, Rastafarians, and young sun-worshippers from Lima and around the world. Máncora has become such a summer scene that it is hard to say which is its biggest attraction: the daytime waves or the parties at night. In response to the crowds, quite a few low-budget hostels, along with surf schools, restaurants, and bars, some of which are only open during the summer, have sprung up at the south end of town. During the off-season, Máncora is one of the few Peruvian beach towns that still receives a good flow of visitors and has a variety of restaurants to choose from. To get a better sense of the area, check out the fantastic website **VivaMáncora** (www.vivamancora.com).

For a party hotel, your best bets are **The Point** (tel. 073/25-8290, www.thepointhostels.com, US$8 dorm, with breakfast), which organizes a full moon beach party, and **Loki Máncora Hostel** (Piura 262, tel. 073/25-8484, www.lokihostel.com, US$9 dorm).

Hostal Las Olas (tel. 073/25-8099, www.lasolasmancora.com, US$43 pp, with breakfast) is a beachside spot popular with surfers. Painted in cream and green, the hotel has 16 rooms, each with a private balcony. The hotel can help set up surfing and kitesurfing lessons for guests. Another inexpensive beachfront option that gets good reviews is **Hotel Del Wawa** (tel. 073/25-8427, www.delwawa.com, US$31 s, US$50 d). The hotel has 14 basic rooms, six of which face the Pacific. It also has a restaurant with a good selection of seafood dishes, and staff can provide advice for surfing.

One of the benefits of staying in Máncora is the bigger selection of restaurants, including some cozy cafés, pizzerias, and fine dining. In the evening, the quiet patio of **Café Restaurante La Bajadita** (Piura 424, tel. 073/25-8385, 11am-10pm Tues.-Sun., US$6) is full of travelers and locals sipping sweetened

Máncora and Vicinity

Stingray Warning

Swimmers are not the only ones who love the warm, shallow waters of Peru's northern beaches. Stingrays occasionally bury themselves under a thin layer of sand and, when stepped on, will sting with a vengeance. Freshwater stingrays are also surprisingly common in many rainforest areas in Peru, especially in areas with sandy or silty bottoms. Like their saltwater relatives, they have a poison-producing organ and a painful tail stinger. They can grow up to 70 centimeters in length and weigh up to 15 kilograms. Peru's stingray is not nearly as painful as those in Baja Mexico or other parts of Latin America, but still a few words of caution are in order.

When arriving at the beach, ask the locals if stingrays are around. They come and go for a variety of reasons and do not appear at all in certain places. If you suspect there are stingrays, shuffle and bang your feet against the sandy bottom as you enter in order to scare them away. Even surer bets are to wear running shoes—water shoes or sandals are not sufficient protection—or tap the sand in front of you with a stick. If you get stung, a bite extractor kit (Sawyer makes a good one) can remove much of the venom and reduce pain. The best treatment, however, is to place your foot in a pot of hot water for 10-20 minutes. Like boiling an egg, hot water coagulates the protein in the stingray poison, reducing the swelling and the fierce, radiating pain that can make even the most stoic rainforest explorer burst into tears. If you are nowhere near hot water, you can always ask a friend to pee on your foot! As unappealing as this particular pain reliever may sound, it really works.

passion fruit juice and snacking on sandwiches. Looking to escape the standard continental breakfast? Head to **Green Eggs and Ham** (BirdHouse Commercial Center, tel. 073/25-8004, 7am-5pm daily, US$4) for waffles, french toast, pancakes, or omelets. Breakfast is served all day, along with lunch items in the afternoon.

For good ceviche, **El Espada** (5th block of Piura, tel. 073/25-8338, 8am-11pm daily, US$9) is a large place with a dining-hall feel; it also has lobster dishes, and a second location nearby. **Cesars** (Micaela Bastidas 164, tel. 073/25-8699, 8am-10pm daily, US$9) also has fresh ceviche as well as *parihuela* and *picante de mariscos*. The kitchen of **El Encuentro** (Pasaje Piura, across from BirdHouse, tel. 073/25-8048, 7am-10pm daily, US$1.50-7), or "The Find," whips up everything from natural juices to tuna steaks and *lomo saltado*.

For fine cuisine, you can't go wrong with chef Juan Seminario's **Sirena** (Piura 316, tel. 073/25-8173, noon-4pm and 7pm-11pm Wed.-Mon., US$10-13), which serves delicious Novoandino dishes, fusing local products with international ingredients and techniques. While the menu changes, you

are likely to find Peruvian tamales with an Asian curry sauce and a fresh tuna steak with Argentine *chimichurri* sauce. Set in a small boutique clothing shop, the atmosphere is chic but intimate, and during peak season, reservations are recommended. Sirena has a less formal option a few doors away at **Sirena Café Bar** (Piura 336, tel. 073/41-1625), which serves up lunches for about US$6 and has live music at night.

In the evening, light ocean breezes and classical music fill the Italian restaurant **Chan Chan** (Piura 384, tel. 073/25-8146, 5:30pm-midnight daily, US$4-12). Best known for its pizzas, Chan Chan also offers mushroom pasta, rich lasagna, and classic antipasto plates. Another popular choice for dinner is **Tao** (Piura 240, tel. 073/25-8056, noon-5pm and 7pm-11pm Thurs.-Tues., US$4-8), with shrimp curry, tuna steaks, and shrimp and peach salad.

There are several pizzerias in Máncora, but the best is **Antica** (Piura 336, tel. 073/25-8659, www.anticapizzeria.com.pe, 1pm-11:30pm daily, US$8), with a good selection of wood-fired pizzas, fresh pastas, and salads. For vegetarian dishes, there is **Angela's Place**

(Piura 396, tel. 073/41-1396, 8am-11pm daily, US$2.50-3). The whole-grain breads are dry and the passion fruit juice unsweetened, but the quinoa, garbanzo, and lentil dishes promise to be filling.

Small minimarkets, with sufficient dry goods selections and minimal produce options, are concentrated on Piura near the BCP ATM. Because of its competitive prices, **Roviluz** (Piura, in the Oltursa bus stop, 8am-10:30pm daily) gets the most local business. Closing hours are extended during high season. For an upscale mini mall, there is the beachfront **BirdHouse** (Pasaje Piura, 9am-9pm daily), with Internet, clothing stores, and even a bar. But know that travelers frequently complain of slow and inattentive service. For athletic clothing and surf gear, check out **Máncora Surf Shop** (Piura 352, cell tel. 998-220-770, 9am-9pm daily).

Getting There

From Lima, **LATAM** has daily flights to Talara, an oil town about 85 kilometers south of Máncora. If your hotel doesn't coordinate airport pickup, a taxi at the airport will take you to Máncora and the other towns for US$30-50.

Daily flights from Lima also go to Tumbes, farther north. Taxis can then be rented for the 1.5-hour, 127-kilometer journey from Tumbes to Máncora (US$40-50). Once at the Tumbes airport, you can also take a taxi into Tumbes (US$2) to **Transportes Carrucho** (corner of Tumbes and Piura, Tumbes), where buses leave regularly for Máncora and nearby beaches (US$3).

High-quality overnight buses, with restrooms and food service, travel from Máncora to Lima in 18 hours. **Oltursa** (inside Roviluz market, Máncora, www.oltursa.pe, 8am-9pm daily) runs buses leaving at 5:30pm and 6pm daily; prices range US$42-63. **Cruz del Sur** (Grau 208, Máncora, tel. 073/72-0444, www. cruzdelsur.com, 3pm-11:45pm daily) has a bus leaving at 5pm daily for US$50, but deals are available online. **Cial** (Piura 624, Máncora) and **Tepsa** (Grau 113, Máncora) each have

one bus daily with seats costing about US$35. **ETTI** (Grau 111, Máncora, tel. 073/25-8582) has several daily departures to Tumbes (1.5 hours), Piura (2.5 hours), Chiclayo (6 hours, with connection), and Trujillo (8 hours, with connection).

PUNTA SAL

Like Cabo Blanco, Punta Sal was once a beach favored by the foreign execs at the International Petroleum Company. This long half-moon beach of pure sand and lapping waves is better for bathing than for surfing. The laid-back atmosphere and remote setting tend to attract more Peruvians than foreigners. There are few services of any kind.

The pleasant backpacker hostel **Hospedaje Hua Punta Sal** (tel. 072/54-0403, www.hua-puntasal.com, US$45 d) has only seven rooms, so make reservations ahead of time—especially if you want an ocean view. There is no pool or hot water, but this hostel does offer two kayaks, body boards, a restaurant, and a bar that serves Cuba libres year-round. Across the street and off the beach is **El Bucanero** (tel. 073/54-0118, www. elbucaneropuntasal.com, US$34 s, US$43 d, with breakfast). The cactus-lined walkways of this hotel lead to a 24-hour restaurant, a TV pavilion, and various rooms. All have good mattresses, but only some have patios with hammocks.

Punta Sal Bungalows (tel. 072/54-0044, www.puntasalbungalows.com, US$62 s, US$170 bungalow) is a good family stop. The apartment-like bungalows accommodate up to six people and come with a fully equipped kitchen, DVDs, and even bicycles.

Club Hotel Punta Sal (Km 1192 Panamericana, Lima tel. 072/59-6700, www. puntasal.com.pe, US$125 s, US$215 d, with all meals) is four kilometers farther north along the beach. While this resort offers a full array of activities, including waterskiing, kayaking, tennis, and swimming, its most memorable feature is its replica pirate ship complete with an authentic masthead left by English pirates in Paita. The food is reputed to be excellent and plentiful, although the bungalows are a bit cramped.

Getting There

Punta Sal is several kilometers off a lonely stretch of the Panamericana between Máncora and Tumbes. Frequent Máncora-Tumbes *combis* can drop you off at the main turnoff to Punta Sal, at Km 1187, which is well marked with signs. Several *motocars* are usually waiting to bring you down to the beach. Do not do this at night. Club Hotel Punta Sal has a separate entrance farther north at Km 1192. From the Tumbes airport, you can also take a taxi into Tumbes (US$2) to **Transportes Carrucho** (corner of Tumbes and Piura, Tumbes), where buses leave regularly for the beaches (US$3). Have them drop you at Punta Sal and take a *motocar* to the beach.

TUMBES AND VICINITY

Tumbes is the main gateway for the cluster of excellent beaches near Máncora and also the closest city to the astounding north-south ecological corridor of nature reserves that includes ecosystems unique to Peru and a good variety of both mammals and birds. There are interesting mangrove swamps to

visit, with the only crocodiles in Peru, from the small fishing town of Puerto Pizarro.

That said, all of these reserves are serviced primarily by Máncora-based companies, and you shouldn't stay long (or at all) in Tumbes, a rough-and-tumble coastal town that has a history of hassling foreigners ever since Pizarro arrived here for the third and final time in 1532. Up until then, the resident Tumpis people, with their knowledge of the surrounding mangrove swamps, managed to turn back the Spanish army that later defeated the Inca. Pizarro left only a cross on the beach, at present-day Caleta La Cruz (Cross Bay), before moving his troops farther south, where he founded the city of San Miguel de Piura. Little has changed for foreigners in Tumbes, who continually complain of scamming money changers with rigged calculators, young pickpockets, and lousy service at local restaurants.

Sights

Tumbes's out-of-the-way location has kept visitors away from the country's only **mangrove swamps** and a fascinating chain of inland nature reserves that form the **Reserva de Biósfera del Noroeste** (Northwestern Biosphere Reserve). The mangrove swamps can be seen during an easy three-hour boat

crocodiles at Puerto Pizarro

Tumbes City

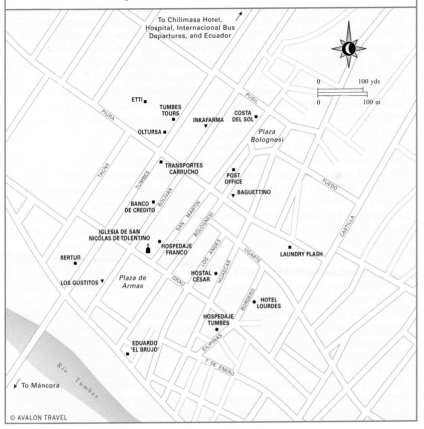

To Chilimasa Hotel, Hospital, Internacional Bus Departures, and Ecuador

ETTI

TUMBES TOURS

INKAFARMA

COSTA DEL SOL

OLTURSA

Plaza Bolognesi

PIURA

PUSIL

TRANSPORTES CARRUCHO

POST OFFICE

BAGUETTINO

FUEDO

TACNA

TUMBES

BOLIVAR

BANCO DE CREDITO

SAN MARTIN

BOLOGNESI

CASTILLA

IGLESIA DE SAN NICOLAS DE TOLENTINO

HOSPEDAJE FRANCO

LOS ANDES

UGARTE

LAUNDRY FLASH

SERTUR

HOSTAL CÉSAR

HUASCAR

LOS GUSTITOS

Plaza de Armas

GRAU

BORDEÑO

HOTEL LOURDES

HOSPEDAJE TUMBES

EDUARDO "EL BRUJO"

FILIPINAS

7 DE ENERO

Río Tumbes

To Máncora

0   100 yds
0   100 m

© AVALON TRAVEL

tour from **Puerto Pizarro,** a fishing port 13 kilometers north of Tumbes. Things to see include Peru's only crocodiles, endangered because of hunting but now slowly reproducing in a nearby nursery. There are also interesting sediment islands in the area, including Isla de los Pájaros, a good birding ground; Isla Hueso de Ballena; and Isla de Amor, which has a good swimming beach. All the agencies in town arrange visits to this area and the pristine mangroves at the **Santuario Nacional Manglares de Tumbes,** a nearly 3,000-hectare reserve that is an hour's drive from Tumbes and includes canoe, not motorboat, tours. There is no crocodile nursery at the Santuario, but you are likely to see a greater variety of birds. Puerto Pizarro can be visited without an agency tour by taking a *colectivo* that leaves from the fifth block of Calle Huascar in Tumbes, near Plaza Bolognesi, to Puerto Pizarro (US$0.75). From there you can walk 15 kilometers northeast along the coast on a dirt road to reach the small town of El Bendito, where fisherfolk sometimes take visitors out in canoes. To see the sanctuary, however, you will need a guide, and most of the guided trips include stops at Puerto Pizarro and El Bendito.

Tumbes is also the starting point for three inland reserves that form a north-south biological corridor critical for the conservation of the area's endangered species. Because roads into these parks are poor, government permission is required to visit, and there is no visitor infrastructure whatsoever. The easiest way to visit is with Tumbes Tours or with a Máncora agency. Make sure to bring bug repellent, and don't plan to go during the rainy season, January-mid-April, because often the roads are closed or impassable. If you have a 4WD vehicle, camping equipment, and a sense of adventure, you could also explore these parks on your own. Permits and updated information can be arranged through SERNANP, which administers the area and is located at new offices on the Panamericana north of the soccer stadium.

Your best bet for seeing a range of wild animals, and the area we most recommend, is the eastern **El Caucho** sector of the **Parque Nacional Cerros de Amotape.** This 75,000-hectare section of the national park butts up against Ecuador and encompasses one of Peru's only chunks of Pacific tropical forest. Here you will find endangered species such as the Tumbes crocodile, a local howler monkey called the *mono coto,* and a local sea otter, *nutria del noroeste.* El Caucho is filled with orchids and gigantic trees such as the *ceibo*—a tree with bright-green bark and umbrella-shaped crown—and *pretino,* a related tree with gray bark that drops seed pods the size of soccer balls. Anteaters, cats (well, just their prints), and a wide variety of birds can be seen in the reserve.

The heart of the sector is the **El Caucho** guard point, from which the area gets its name. It is 45 minutes from Tumbes on a rough dirt road, and the journey presently takes 2.5 hours in a 4WD vehicle, plus one hour of walking. Most agencies that visit this park offer overnight trips with camping near El Caucho, which is a good idea so that you can get up early in the morning to see wildlife. The hikes include swimming in rivers and spectacular scenery.

To the south and divided by the Río Tumbes lies the drier, hilly section of the national park. Sprawling across 91,300 hectares of equatorial dry forest, this sector has more sun exposure. Resident animals include pumas, gray and red deer, anteaters, and the Andean condor. A royal Inca highway ran along the ridge of the Amotape hills, and a few interesting ruins can be visited along the way into the park.

Farther south is a hunting reserve called the **Coto de Caza El Angolo,** a 65,000-hectare chunk to the southwest of the Amotape Mountains.

Recreation

The best, and sometimes only, way to visit the natural attractions around Tumbes is with a travel agency. Prices are per person based on groups of two or more. The main tours are the mangrove swamps (US$25-35 pp), day trips to Amotape or the Zona Reservada (US$50-60 pp), and a day tour that includes nearby mud baths, beaches, and archaeological sites (US$25-35 pp). The well-informed **Tumbes Tours** (Tumbes 334, tel. 072/52-4837, www.tumbestours.com, 8:30am-5:30pm Mon.-Sat.) is the only Tumbes-based agency.

Food

When in need of an empanada, swing by **Baguettino** (Piura 400, tel. 072/52-5148, 6am-9:30pm daily, US$1), where you can enjoy the flaky meat-and-raisin-stuffed pastry while peering onto the activity of Calle Piura. **Los Gustitos** (Bolívar 149, no phone, 7am-11pm daily, US$3.50) is recommended for *conchas negras*—black clams with an aphrodisiac kick that local fisherfolk harvest from among the roots in the mangrove swamps. Other options for good seafood during lunch or dinner are **Eduardo "El Brujo"** (Bolognesi and Malecón Benavides, cell tel. 972-893-918, 11am-11pm daily, US$9-12), which sometimes has live music in the evenings, and **Las Terrazas** (Andrés Araujo 549, tel. 072/52-1575, 11am-11pm daily, US$6-8).

For a finer dining experience and an international menu, try **El Manglar** (San Martín 275, tel. 072/52-3991, 6:30am-11:30pm daily,

US$6) inside the Hotel Costa del Sol. Among its 200 dishes, the restaurant offers ceviche, fajitas, pizzas, and grilled meats. At the moment Tumbes doesn't have a large supermarket, but there are a few small shops close to Plaza Bolognesi, including **Mini Market Juan Pablo** (10am-6pm Mon.-Sat.).

Accommodations

There are loads of cheap hotels in Tumbes to accommodate the border traffic to and from Ecuador. The very cheapest options, while clean, are unlikely to have hot water or toilet seats, and the mid- to higher-priced hotels have the amenities but not much charm.

Hospedaje Franco (Concordia 105, tel. 072/52-5295, US$16 s, US$23 d) is your best bet for a reasonably clean, quiet room with a private bath.

The plant-lined hallways of **Hotel Lourdes** (Bodero 118, tel. 072/52-2966, US$12 s, US$18 d) filter into a second-floor sitting room, which looks over the street. Rooms have firm mattresses and are quieter farther away from the street. Near the Plaza de Armas, the mid-range **Hotel B'liam** (Ugarte 309, tel. 072/52-5488, www.b-liam.com, US$40 s, US$55 d) has crisp sheets on the beds, air-conditioning in the rooms, and Wi-Fi.

The more expensive option is **Hotel Costa del Sol** (San Martín 275, tel. 072/52-3991, www.costadelsolperu.com, US$72 s, US$100 d, with breakfast), on the pleasant and quiet Plaza Bolognesi. The hotel itself is an oasis in this hot dusty city, with a nice pool, an excellent restaurant, and fully equipped rooms with air-conditioning.

Information and Services

The **visitor information office** (Carretera Panamericana Norte 1254, tel. 072/52-3699, tumbes@mitinci.gob.pe, 7:30am-1pm and 2pm-4:30pm Mon.-Fri.), located inside the Instituto Superior Pedagógico José Antonio Encinas, is friendly and helpful. The **Ecuadorian Consulate** (Bolívar 129, tel. 072/52-1739, 8am-2pm Mon.-Fri.) is on the plaza next to Restaurant Gustitos. Reach the local police at **San José District Police** (Novoa and Zarumilia, tel. 072/52-2525, 24 hours daily).

Jamo Hospital (24 de Julio 565, tel. 072/52-4775, 24 hours daily) or **Zorritos Medical Post** (Grau s/n, tel. 072/54-4158, 8am-8pm Mon.-Sat.) can be called in an emergency. For a pharmacy, try the **Inkafarma** (Bolívar 341, 8am-10pm daily), about two blocks from the Plaza de Armas.

Travelers can exchange money at **Banco de la Nación** (Grau and Bolívar) at the Plaza de Armas. There is also a **Banco de Crédito** (Los Libertadores 261) about half a block from the plaza. *Cambistas* (money changers) hang out on the corner of Bolívar and Piura, but many rip-offs and rigged calculators have been reported. **ATMs** are located at Bolívar 123 or Bolívar 209.

The Tumbes post office, **Serpost** (tel. 072/52-3866), is at San Martín 208. All **Internet** and **telephone** needs can be met on the pedestrian malls leading off the Plaza de Armas. For laundry, **Flash** (Piura 1012, 9am-1pm and 3:30pm-8pm Mon.-Sat.) offers same-day service and washes and dries clothes by the kilogram.

Getting There and Around

From Lima, **LATAM** (tel. 01/213-8200) has daily flights to and from Tumbes. Flights take almost two hours. **Cruz del Sur** (Tumbes 319, tel. 072/52-6200, www.cruzdelsur.com.pe, 3am-11:45pm daily, US$38-66) and **Oltursa** (Tumbes 948, tel. 072/52-6739, www.oltursa.pe, 8am-1pm and 2pm-6pm daily, US$43-61) have daily buses to Lima. The direct trip is about 20 hours.

To get from the Tumbes airport to Máncora, taxis can be rented at the airport (1.5 hours, US$40-50). Or take a taxi (US$2) into Tumbes to **Transportes Carrucho** (corner of Tumbes and Piura), where buses (US$3) and vans (US$3.50) leave for Máncora and nearby beaches when full.

ETTI (Tumbes 574, cell tel. 998-164-702) provides bus service to Máncora, Sullana, Piura, Chiclayo, and Trujillo.

To travel on to Ecuador, **Ormeño** (Tumbes Norte 1187, tel. 072/52-2894, www.grupo-ormeno.com.pe, 8am-6pm daily) has three buses a week to both Guayaquil and Quito. **Sertur** (Tumbes 253, cell tel. 968-963-940) shuttles modern 12-seat vans to and from Piura (US$11), but these expensive *combis* are only worth their fare if they aren't crammed full.

Tumbes is absolutely filled with *motocars,* which charge US$0.50 for an in-town trip, and *colectivos* that run north and south along the Panamericana.

Cajamarca

The first stop when traveling from the coast into the Andes, Cajamarca is probably the most charming city of Peru's **northern sierra,** where despite the economic boom fueled by gold mines, you can still see campesinos with straw hats, bright shawls, and wool spindles scuffle along the city's cobblestone streets. This laid-back city revolves around its Plaza de Armas, flanked by two spectacular colonial churches and brimming with strolling couples and screaming schoolchildren. Cajamarca's quaint countryside produces a cornucopia of products, including *manjar blanco* (a type of gooey caramel), wheels of edam and gouda, and fresh yogurt.

One of the pivotal moments of Latin American history happened in Cajamarca's Plaza de Armas on November 16, 1532, when a motley army of 160 Spanish conquistadores brought the entire Inca empire to its knees by capturing **Inca Atahualpa.** The Inca themselves had conquered the local **Caxamarca** people six decades earlier and used this area as a staging ground for invading the Chachapoya and Chimú. In Cajamarca's square, the Inca built large stone warehouses where tribute from the surrounding territories was stored. All these buildings were destroyed by the Spaniards.

The Caxamarca people probably built the mysterious and perfectly sculpted aqueducts at **Cumbemayo,** 20 kilometers southwest of Cajamarca. They were at the center of a busy commerce between the coast and the rainforest as well as between southern Peru and Ecuador. The Inca later improved these routes by constructing stone highways that crossed in the city's main square.

An exciting excursion for Cajamarca visitors is the possibility of trekking through the Cajamarca countryside via the **Qhapaq Ñan,** the old network of Inca trails that was mostly forgotten until an enterprising nonprofit organization known as **APREC** (Association for the Rescue of Cajamarca's Ecosystem) retraced and mapped them. While APREC is no longer operating in Cajamarca, travel agencies and a few hotels still offer treks on these routes, where guides can help visitors understand history, folklore, birding, and plants along the way. This is the best way to experience the culture and natural beauty of Cajamarca's countryside.

SIGHTS
City Tour

Cajamarca's Inca layout can best be appreciated from the top of **Cerro Santa Apolonia,** the hilltop shrine that towers over the city to the southwest. It can be reached either by taxi (US$2) or by a long walk up stone stairs. From the summit, you can see the Plaza de Armas, surrounded by the cathedral and the Iglesia de San Francisco. The plaza was at least twice as long during Inca times and surrounded by three stone warehouses filled with textiles made of cotton, llama, and vicuña wool, the last of which the Inca valued over gold. The clothing, a tribute paid by the surrounding northern empires, was woven by hundreds of women hand-picked by the Inca. These women lived in a convent-like building,

Cajamarca

© AVALON TRAVEL

To Porcón
and Posada
del Puruay

To Pena
Usha Usha

To Hacienda
San Vicente

To Cumbemayo

Cerro Santa
Apolonia

STAIRS

To Quinde,
Airport and
Ventanillas de
Otuzco

HOSPITAL
REGIONAL

COLEGIO
SANTA TERESITA

Río

San Lucas

Mercado
Central

Plaza de
Armas

SEE DETAIL

To Taberna El Diablo, Bus
Terminals, Baños del Inca,
and Hotel Laguna Seca

Streets:
PISAGUA, AMALIA, TARAPACÁ, PUGA, AMAZONAS, LA MAR, APURIMAC, CONTUMAZA, BAMBAMARCA, CHANCHAMAYO, SABOGAL, BATAN, COMERCIO, JUNIN, ANCON, UNION, HUANUCO, ATAHUALPA, CRUZ DE PIEDRA, SAN MARTIN, DOS DE MAYO, PRIMAVERA, GUADALUPE, URTEAGA, JIRON INCA, PERU, ANTISUYO, STA. APOLONIA, BELEN, PETATEROS, SAN, PABLO, URRELO, BELLAVISTA, SANTISTEBAN, ESQUINAS, AMALIA PUGA, AMAZONAS, DESAMPARADOS, HUANUCO, SOLEDAD, AYACUCHO, EL MAESTRO, EL MAESTRO, PROGRESO, LOS HEROES

Labeled locations:
LOS PINOS INN
CARPA BRUJA CAFÉ
HOTEL PRADO
PORTAL DE MARQUÉS
BANCO DE CREDITO
RESTAURANT
CASCANUEZ
LAVANDERI
A DANDY
CASA DE LA ABUELA
EL CABILDO HOSTAL
COSTA DEL SOL
INTERNET
DE BUENA LAVA
OM GRI/
PIZZERIA VACA LOCO
EL MARENGO LOCO
VILLANUEVA
COMPLEJO BELEN
HOSPEDAJE POSADA BELEN
CUARTO DE RESCATE
EL CAJAMARQUÉS
HOSPEDAJE LOS JAZMINES
GRAN HOTEL CONTINENTAL
MUSEO ARQUEOLOGICO
COLORS & CREATIONS
LA IDEAL PANADERIA
LOS BALCONES DE LA RECOLETA
D'LUKA
IGLESIA LA RECOLETA

Detail inset (Plaza de Armas):
CATEDRAL
PHARMACIES
QUERUBINO/
MINIMARKET
LA MERCED
CHIFA CENTRAL
DONDE OCTAVIO
CUMBE MAYO TOURS
RESTAURANT SALAS/
HELADERIA HOLANDA
LAS AMERICAS HOTEL
MEGA TOURS
EL SOL MINIMARKET
CAJAMARCA TRAVEL
INTER-BANK
DOS DE MAYO
POST OFFICE
IGLESIA DE SAN FRANCISCO
HOSTAL CASONA DEL INCA
Plaza de Armas
BATAN

0   200 yds
0   200 m

known in Quechua as *acllahuasi* or "house of the chosen ones."

Branching out diagonally, **Jirón Inca** leads from the Plaza de Armas to the east side of town and follows the route that Atahualpa traveled before his fateful meeting with Pizarro. The old Inca highway cuts through the fields to **Baños del Inca** and then switchbacks up between two hills on its way to Cusco. Following Jirón Inca west, the road leads up from the plaza, zigzags through the hills west of Cajamarca, and on to Quito. Ancient Inca highways also run northeast to the former Chachapoyas federation and southwest to the Chimú capital, Chan Chan.

The Caxamarca used Cerro Santa Apolonia as a shrine, the Inca carved their own altars at the lookout, and the Spanish worshipped at the hilltop Iglesia Santa Apolonia from 1571 until it was burned down by invading Chileans during the War of the Pacific (1879-1883). The Santa Apolonia image can now be found in the museum at the Iglesia de San Francisco. Scanning the horizon to the left of Cerro Santa Apolonia, there is a triangular, earth-colored summit poking up above the other hills. This is **Cerro San José,** also known as Cerro Carachugo, a sacred mountain exactly north of the city that, throughout history, has stood as a reference point.

In the Plaza de Armas, **La Catedral** (open during Mass, 6pm-7pm Mon.-Sat., 7:30am, 11am, and 6pm Sun., tel. 076/36-2599, free) contains the city's only original baroque altar, built in 1689. The construction of the cathedral dragged on for nearly a century (1682-1780) because the city's stonemasons constructed seven churches at once.

On the opposite side of the plaza, the **Iglesia de San Francisco** (7am-9am and 5pm-7pm daily, free) has a baroque facade that features two angels trumpeting the power of the pope, represented only by his papal hat or *mitra*. Inside are several interesting colonial religious images, including El Señor de la Caña, depicting Jesus in the hours before his Crucifixion. The church's **religious museum** (9am-noon Mon.-Sat.,

Cajamarca's cathedral, on the main plaza

tel. 076/36-2994, US$2) has a fabulous collection of 17th-century paintings that were made in serial fashion by indigenous painters in the Franciscan workshop. Because Cajamarca is situated between Cusco and Quito, these paintings show traits of both schools of painting.

Complejo Belén

The sprawling colonial religious monument **Complejo Belén** (9am-1pm and 3pm-6pm Tues.-Sat., 9am-1pm Sun., tel. 076/36-2601, US$2 includes Cuarto de Rescate) was built between 1627 and 1774. A Bethlemite religious order arrived from Nicaragua with the express purpose of building this hospital for the local indigenous people. The building, made of volcanic stone, is now a medical and archaeological museum.

Though the towers of the corresponding **Iglesia Belén** were never finished, the church has one of the most stunning baroque facades in all of Peru. Four angels float above swirling sculpted forms and guard a central

A Sovereign's Ransom

When Inca Atahualpa heard the news of a strange group of bearded white men traveling into his empire, his first thoughts were to breed their marvelous horses, sacrifice most of the Spaniards to the sun, and castrate the rest to guard his wives and do household chores. Atahualpa never dreamed of being captured by the Spanish—especially when surrounded by thousands of trained Inca soldiers.

It is hard to imagine Francisco Pizarro's audacity, leading his men in strict formation down into Cajamarca's valley as a sea of Inca soldier tents spread out before them. On November 16, 1532, Atahualpa was resting in hot baths outside town, celebrating his victory over his half-brother Huáscar and the end of a civil war that had killed thousands and badly damaged the empire's infrastructure. Pizarro had been traveling throughout the coast, rainforests, and mountains of South America for nearly two years in order to find the heart of the Inca empire. Atahualpa had 40,000 to 80,000 soldiers, fresh from battle. Pizarro had 170 men, and only 60 had horses.

Pizarro, nevertheless, invited Atahualpa to visit him on the main square of Cajamarca, which was flanked by three empty stone warehouses, each about 180 meters long. The Spaniards hid inside these buildings when the Inca arrived the next day, carried atop an elegant litter borne by 80 officials and accompanied by 5,000 elegantly dressed soldiers. Atahualpa was so confident of the encounter that he had come dressed for ceremony, not combat, and his men were armed only with light battle axes, slings, and rocks.

The first Spaniard to approach Atahualpa was Dominican friar Vicente de Valverde, who walked up to the Inca, explained his mission to spread the Catholic faith, and extended him a small breviary. After looking the book over, the Inca threw it on the ground and spat on it. Moments later, the Spaniards emerged in full force and created what must have been a terrifying spectacle for the Inca soldiers. Amid the cacophony of trumpets, cannon, and rattles, fully armored Spaniards on horseback charged into the crowd with lances and swords flying. As the Spaniards began their slaughter, the Inca panicked to such an extent that many suffocated in the rush. A wall nearly two meters thick was pushed over by the fleeing crowd.

But the Spaniards chased after them, lancing them down until well after dark, when an estimated 7,000 bodies lay littered across what is today central Cajamarca. Accounting for exaggeration and those killed by suffocation, English historian John Hemming estimates that each Spaniard killed an average of 15 Inca soldiers in those two gruesome hours. Pizarro, with a group of his soldiers, meanwhile had fought his way to Atahualpa's litter and dragged him inside one of the buildings. In just a few minutes, the New World's most powerful and best-organized empire had been brought to its knees.

Shortly thereafter, Atahualpa offered his infamous ransom: In exchange for his liberty, he would fill a large room—nearly 88 cubic meters—with gold and another two rooms with silver. Pizarro rapidly agreed and, as llama trains loaded with gold began to arrive in Cajamarca, he sent messengers back to the coast to call for reinforcements. Nine furnaces ran continuously between March 16 and July 9 to melt down nearly 10,000 kilograms of exquisite gold sculptures, chalices, and other priceless items into gold bars. The eventual result, according to Hemming, was 6,100 kilograms of 22-karat gold and 11,820 kilograms of good silver.

Though he met his ransom, Atahualpa was far from free. As rumors filtered to the Spaniards of a large army approaching, the Spaniards began to suspect that Atahualpa was plotting against them. Though Francisco Pizarro objected, and no trial was held, a majority of Spanish officers made the hasty decision to execute the Inca. As dusk fell on July 26, 1533, Atahualpa was led onto the main square. Atahualpa allowed himself to be baptized at the last minute, apparently to avoid being burned at the stake—and probably to allow his body to be mummified and venerated after his death, according to Inca custom. Instead he was hung from a rope. When Emperor Charles V learned of the execution some months later, he condemned the conquistadores for their audacity in killing a sovereign prince.

window. Through it, the souls of the dead entered before traveling down the nave onto the cupola, where more painted angels uphold the weight of heaven on their fingertips. The altar is neoclassical, from the late 19th century, and was replaced after the original was accidentally burned down.

A quick tour of the adjacent men's hospital—which operated until 1965!—shows how miserable conditions were: patients stretched out in dark niches, watching Mass so that the spirit of the devil would leave their bodies. They were bled nearly constantly, usually until they died, and families were not permitted to use either traditional medicines or burial rituals. After death, families paid dearly for masses that would elevate their loved one's status from hell to purgatory and finally to heaven.

Across the street is another hospital, built for women. The startling facade is a sculpted woman with four breasts, carved by indigenous artisans, that could be a fertility symbol. Inside is the **Museo Arqueológico** (8am-2:45pm Mon.-Fri., free), which displays an excellent collection of ceramics and implements of Andean life.

★ Cuarto de Rescate

The perfect Inca stonework at the **Cuarto de Rescate** (9am-1pm and 3pm-6pm Mon.-Fri., 8:30am-noon Sat.-Sun., US$2 includes Complejo Belén) was probably part of the sun temple, destroyed long ago by the Spaniards. It is believed that Atahualpa ordered this room to be filled entirely with gold objects for his ransom. The existing white line, which the Inca supposedly drew to mark the level, is certainly not genuine. One of the chroniclers, Cristóbal de Mena, wrote that the line was so tall that even the reach of the tallest of the Spaniards fell about a palm short, at about 204 centimeters. John Hemming and other historians contend that this room is probably where Atahualpa was held captive instead.

Baños del Inca

Six kilometers east of central Cajamarca,

Baños del Inca (5am-8pm daily) is supposed to be the original place where the Inca enjoyed his baths. The water is purest at 5am or 6am because the nighttime coolness naturally reduces the water temperatures. Later in the day, to keep from scalding visitors, the thermal water must be mixed with cool nonmineral water.

These thermal baths, known as the **Complejo Turístico Baños del Inca,** are managed by the local municipality and can receive more than 1,000 visitors a day. Avoid the crowds during weekends and Carnaval in February. There are different price schemes according to the quality of the tub, but the best is the restored *pabellón imperial* (royal pavilion, 5am-8pm daily), which offers 30-minute private baths (US$3 pp). The complex also includes a public pool, a sauna (US$3.50), and a spa with 30-minute massages (US$7).

Getting to the Baños del Inca is an easy 10-minute trip, either via taxi from central Cajamarca (US$3) or via cheaper *combis* that leave from Plazuela La Recoleta (US$0.30).

Ventanillas de Otuzco

About seven kilometers northeast of town, and often included in city tours, are the **Ventanillas de Otuzco** (highway to Otuzco, 9am-6pm daily, US$2). What appear to be 200 small windows carved into volcanic rock are actually 600-year-old burial sites from the Cajamarca culture. The original tombs were sacked and destroyed by the Spanish but, nonetheless, the structure maintains a sense of history and magnitude.

Cumbemayo

Located 20 kilometers southwest of Cajamarca up a dirt switchback that climbs to 3,510 meters, **Cumbemayo** (9am-6pm daily, US$2) is a shrine of pre-Hispanic carved water canals that still baffles archaeologists. The canals are at least 3,000 years old, but the exact date and the reason they were built are unknown.

The lines are so perfect and the rock ground so smooth that it is difficult to imagine these works of art being carved with

The Sackings of Cajamarca

Cajamarca has always been the center of gold production in Peru. Consequently, it has been the target of fierce sacking by different armies, first the Inca in 1470, then the Spaniards in 1532—the year that a ransom of 18,660 kilograms of gold was paid by **Inca Atahualpa** and promptly exported to Spain.

After nearly three centuries of once again accumulating gold, silver, and precious gems, Spanish priests had to hand them over in 1822 as **Simón Bolívar** demanded donations for the independence cause. Because the Spanish controlled southern Peru, Bolívar relied on churches and wealthy families in Trujillo, Cajamarca, and Lambayeque to finance the entire campaign.

But the worst sacking of Cajamarca happened during the **War of the Pacific** (1879-1883), when marauding Chilean soldiers demanded that the city pay a certain amount of gold and silver. When the town paid only a portion, the enraged Chileans burned the Santa Apolonia church and the altars of every church in town except for the cathedral, which was saved by the frantic begging of a priest. Soldiers stripped the cathedral's altar of its gold plating, however, and removed all the precious ornaments from the town's religious images—see the dense clustering of precious religious charms on the Virgin de Dolores in Iglesia San Francisco to get an idea of the wealth this must have represented.

obsidian hammers, the best technology of the time. If you arrive at this spot before 9am, and before the tour groups ascend, the religious explanation of Cumbemayo becomes more plausible. The area is covered in *ichu* grass and punctuated by bizarre volcanic formations (known as a *bosque de piedras*, or rock forest), and power and energy of the place is palpable.

A marked trail from the parking lot descends to a rocky formation and a cave with several mysterious petroglyphs. Follow the narrow path through the cave (a headlamp really helps) until you emerge on the other side. Then head up a hill and down a drainage to a trail junction. Follow the canals to the right until you reach a carved chair-like stone, which served a ceremonial purpose. Return the same way and follow the canals downhill, where the road leads back to the parking lot.

The road to Cumbemayo passes through villages where campesinos produce everything they need to live except for salt, matches, and kerosene. They live in *casas de tapial* or rammed earth homes. Their diet is mostly vegetarian, consisting of oca and *olluco* (two types of tubers), corn, supergrains such as *kiwicha* and quinoa, and lentils—or *chocho*, the bean-like seeds of a purple-flowered lupine

plant, which are cooked, mixed with tomato and cilantro, and sold on Cajamarca street corners.

To reach Cumbemayo, there is public transportation that leaves at 6am daily from behind Cerro Santa Apolonia on Avenida Peru. The *colectivos* will drop you within walking distance of Cumbemayo. A great walk can be returning down to Cajamarca by a clearly marked trail that dates back to pre-Inca times and is still used today. Ask around for directions and beware of dogs (having a stick and small rocks helps to keep them away). Other options to visit the site are a tour or a taxi.

Granja Porcón

This interesting, though somewhat controversial, tourism-oriented farming operation is 30 kilometers northeast of Cajamarca. **Granja Porcón** (www.granjaporcon.org.pe, cell tel. 976-682-209) has an 11,000-hectare plantation of coniferous forest situated between 3,200 and 3,800 meters elevation. In the middle of it, every aspect of local farm life, from milking cows to working with leather and wood, is on display. The farm is run like a well-oiled clock by an evangelical community under a co-op based system, with a rustic restaurant serving local trout and *cuy* (guinea pig). It also has a zoo with vicuñas, deer, lynxes, eagles, and even monkeys and jaguars.

Porcón's lodgings include **Casa Histórica** (US$18 per room), which has a living room and dining room, shared baths, and hot water 24 hours. The **Posada Granja Porcon** (US$25 s, US$36 d with breakfast) is a two-story building housing 10 rooms with private baths, carpeted floors, a huge fireplace, and an upstairs loft. To get here, contact the farm's Cajamarca office (Chanchamayo 1355, cell tel. 976-682-209) or a local travel agency. Porcón also offers private transportation for traveling groups in a 10-passenger van (US$57) or a 28-passenger mini-bus (US$137) to and from the airport or the bus station. The fare includes the entrance fee to the site.

Kunturwasi

The oldest gold forged in the Americas—2,800 years old, 1,000 years older than Sipán—was discovered in 1989 by a group of Japanese archaeologists. The place, on top of the hill La Conga, near a small village named San Pablo, about 130 kilometers west of Cajamarca, has been known for decades as **Kunturwasi** ("the house of the condor," US$1.60). Masks, crowns, chest plates, and other artifacts such as ceramics and stone jewelry with anthropomorphic designs—mainly incorporating jaguars, condors, and snakes—unearthed from a series of tombs confirmed that Kunturwasi was the most important ceremonial center in Peru's northern highlands during the Formative Period (2,500-50 BC).

Further explorations have uncovered ceremonial architecture that can be seen on a day visit from Cajamarca. But the main attraction is obviously the gold. A modern **museum** (cell tel. 976-679-484, 9am-6pm daily, US$2) built with Japanese financial aid exhibits around 200 artifacts, including an exquisitely made crown with 14 human faces, showing a highly developed technique used by these ancient Peruvians.

Tour agencies offer a full-day trip to Kunturwasi with transportation, lunch, a visit to both the museum and the ruins, and all tickets included. Independent travelers can also reach San Pablo on their own, taking a *colectivo* (2 hours, US$5.50) from Angamos 1125 in Cajamarca.

ENTERTAINMENT AND EVENTS

Cajamarca's nightlife normally gets going Thursday to Saturday. Bars and clubs come and go, but for the moment, some of the city's popular spots include the following. For a discotheque, try **El Diablo** (Av. Atahualpa, Km 2, no phone, 9pm-close Thurs.-Sat.), located on the road from central Cajamarca to Los Baños del Inca. A trendier spot with a good selection of cocktails is **Taita** (Plazuela Belén, no phone, 4pm-midnight Mon.-Wed., 4pm-1am Thurs.-Sat.), while **Full Skee** (Amazonas 709, no phone, 5pm-2am daily) is a decent option for a beer.

Peña Usha Usha (Amalia Pugia 142, cell tel. 976-461-433, 9pm-dawn Thurs.-Sun., US$6) is the best place for local live music, as musicians play *música criolla* until the early hours of the morning. The bar is liveliest on the weekends. Ask at your hotel for updated information about other places in the city.

Every February or March, serene Cajamarca explodes in a riot of water balloons, paint, elaborate parades, and roaming bands of tipsy youths singing *coplas*, the rhymed couplets of colonial *carnavales*. If you do not want to get drenched in water, paint, or worse, avoid Cajamarca at this time. If you do go, have fun! This is Peru's wildest **Carnaval**—actually, it's called a *carnavalón* (a huge carnival), and all hotels are booked.

Cajamarca also has a beautiful **Corpus Christi** celebration in May or June, which includes parades, live music, dancing, bullfights, and horse shows. The village of Porcón Bajo celebrates a colorful **Semana Santa** (Easter Week) with traditional songs and the carrying of a heavy wooden cross on Palm Sunday.

Greater Cajamarca

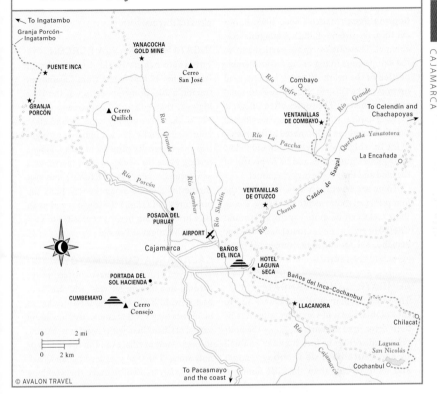

SHOPPING

A few handicraft shops above the Plaza de Armas on Dos de Mayo sell leather goods, ceramics, alpaca wool sweaters, jewelry, and handwoven hats. **Colors & Creations** (Belén 628, tel. 076/34-3875, www.cajamarcacyc.com, 9:30am-1:30pm and 3pm-7pm Mon.-Sat., 10am-6pm Sun.), across from El Complejo Belén, has a small but good-quality selection of unique and locally made jewelry, baskets, weavings, and ceramics.

A taxi ride (US$2) from the Plaza de Armas to the **El Quinde** shopping mall (10am-10pm daily) will allow you to find anything you might need: medicine (Boticas Fasa and Inkafarma), ice cream (Heladeria Holanda), groceries (Metro), and the cash to pay for it all (ATMs).

RECREATION
Qhapaq Ñan Treks

Cajamarca's countryside is stunning and ranges from the high-altitude puna, where only the hardy *ichu* grass grows, to lush pastures where farmers lug around metal jugs of milk. Although there are only a few pockets left where people speak Quechua, the mountain folk maintain their centuries-old lifestyle. They live in *casas de tapial,* weave their clothes, grow indigenous foods, and rely on herbs and natural medicines.

Interesting hiking routes around Cajamarca are offered by travel agencies listed below and the recommended **Hotel Laguna Seca** (Manco Cápac 1098, Baños del Inca, tel. 076/58-4300, www.lagunaseca. com.pe). These treks expose participants to the campesinos living along a considerable portion of the nearly 30,000-kilometer road network of the Qhapaq Ñan (Great Paths) that cross Cajamarca. The routes often integrate existing natural wonders and archaeological sites that have been rediscovered in the tracing of the Inca highways. Trekkers should follow their guide's guidelines and be respectful of the land and the people they encounter.

There are several options, including the four principal routes mentioned below. Doing these treks can be quite expensive (around US$100 or even more per route) due to the low demand. Ask around at recommended travel agencies as costs vary.

COMBAYO-CAÑÓN SANGAL

The most popular of all treks takes you to the colonial town of Combayo after a two-hour drive from Cajamarca. Along the best-preserved section of Inca highway you will see the **Ventanillas de Combayo,** larger and more remote than the cliff tombs at Otuzco. The 10-kilometer day hike includes the Cañón Sangal, a canyon formed by two thin rock ridges punctured by the Río Chonta. The countryside in this area has not been altered by European cows imported in the 1940s. Thus, a staggering abundance of native plants, trees, and birds can be seen, starring the **gray-bellied comet,** an endemic and endangered hummingbird species.

COCHAMBUL-BAÑOS DEL INCA

This 20-kilometer, two-day hike begins in the small hacienda of Cochambul and leads first to Laguna San Nicolás, full of *pejerrey* (kingfish), which are caught with handmade nets and reed rafts. You set up camp here and can visit the fort of Coyor, an unexcavated Inca-Caxamarca battle site. Next stop is the town of Chilacat, where everyone makes guitars.

Along the way there is an excellent section of paved Inca highway with knee-high walls on each side. End at the Baños del Inca for a pleasant thermal bath.

INGATAMBO-GRANJA PORCÓN

This route begins in the tiny hamlet of Ingatambo, 47 kilometers from Cajamarca, tracing a 20-kilometer section of the Inca highway that led from Cajamarca to Quito. The walk, which usually takes around eight hours, can also be divided into an overnight trip. Start near the ruins of an Inca *tambo,* a resting place for *chasquis* (foot messengers who formed a sort of Pony Express), and visit campesino families along the way. Enter the pine forests of Granja Porcón and end at an Inca bridge. From here, it is possible to visit or stay overnight at Porcón.

CAJAMARCA-CUMBEMAYO

When you visit Cumbemayo, instead of returning in a bumpy car ride, why not walk back downhill? The three-hour walk follows a bit of Inca highway that connected the Chimú capital of Chan Chan with Cajamarca, passing through Andean villages and an Inca *huaca* or holy stone. The trail was used by horseback riders as late as 1940 to make the weeklong ride to the coast.

Tour Agencies

Recommended sightseeing agencies include **Cumbe Mayo Tours** (Amalia Puga 635, tel. 076/36-2938, www.cumbemayotours. com, 8am-9pm daily) and **Destinos Viajes & Servicios** (Amalia Puga 633, tel. 076/34-1821, www.destinosviajes.pe, 8am-8pm daily), owned by Carlos Mantilla, who also is an excellent guide. These companies are on Plaza de Armas and offer half- and full-day tours to sights around Cajamarca for about US$8-12.

FOOD

Cajamarca is Peru's dairy center, and from its verdant countryside come fresh butter, yogurt, *manjar blanco* (a caramel spread made of milk, sugar, and egg whites) and rich, sharp-tasting cheeses. Other local specialties include *chicharrón con mote* (deep-fried chunks of pork with boiled corn) and *caldo verde* (a "green" broth prepared with herbs). Desserts include *quesillo con miel* (a nonfat fresh cheese served with cane syrup) and *dulce de higos* (fig preserves).

Peruvian

Probably one of the oldest restaurants in the city and hugely popular with old-time Cajamarquino diners, **Restaurant Salas** (Amalia Puga 637, tel. 076/36-2867, 7am-10pm daily, US$4-10) still catches the spirit of the 1940s in its longtime spot on the Plaza de Armas. The food is good and abundant on your plate, whether it's *humitas, chicharrones,* guinea pig, trout, or a pork chop with fries and salad.

Don Octavio (Amazonas and Batán, tel. 076/34-0023, 8am-10pm Mon.-Sat., US$6) is a good choice for *comida típica*. Stop by for its multicourse lunch menu, which sometimes includes guinea pig.

International

They serve fresh fish and seafood during the day. At night it is all about meat on the grill. In either case, **Restaurant El Pez Loco** (San Martín 333, cell tel. 976-825-633, 9:30am-10pm Mon.-Sat., 9:30am-4pm Sun., US$5-10), the "crazy fish," is surprisingly a good spot for either choice, with friendly personnel and generous portions.

The name **OM Gri** (Amazonas 858, tel. 076/36-7619, 5pm-11:30pm Mon.-Sat., 6:30pm-11:30pm Sun., US$4-7) is derived from the pronunciation of the French *homme gris*. It specializes in delicious pastas, including Cajamarca's best meat and veggie lasagna.

Pizza

The charming **Pizzeria Vaca Loca** (San Martín 330, tel. 076/36-8230, 5pm-11pm daily, US$2.50-10) celebrates the cows and cheeses of Cajamarca. It's decorated with cowhide seat covers, paintings, and ceramics. The comfy cow booths are perfect for sipping sangria and eating pizza, spaghetti, or calzone. Other good pizzeria options include **New York Pizza** (Amalia Puga 1045, tel. 076/50-6215, 4pm-11pm daily, US$2-4) and **El Marengo Pizzeria** (Junín 1201, 6:30pm-10:30pm daily, US$5-7).

Cafés, Bakeries, and Ice Cream

Cascanuez (Amalia Puga 554, tel. 076/36-6089, 7:30am-11pm daily, US$3-6) is Cajamarca's traditional café; it serves the best sweet corn *humitas* in town, homemade pastries and pies, and decent coffee. It is the ideal spot for a sweet tooth after lunch or dinner.

The modern and softly lit **Panadería La Ideal** (Amalia Puga 307, tel. 076/36-7269, 7am-9pm daily, US$3) is the ideal place to order fresh bread, good sandwiches, and freshly squeezed fruit juices. There is a second location near the Plaza de Armas.

The Dutch-Peruvian owned **Heladería Holanda** (Amalia Puga 657, Plaza de Armas, tel. 076/34-0113, 9am-7pm daily, US$1.50-6) serves up the best homemade ice cream and gelato in the city, with flavors harvested from the surrounding countryside's native fruits. Other locations exist in the Quinde Shopping Plaza and Baños del Inca.

Markets

Cajamarca's bustling **Mercado Central** stretches along Amazonas and sells everything from dairy products to guinea pig. For cheeses and other dairy products, stop by **Villanueva** (Dos de Mayo 615, tel. 076/34-0389, 8am-2:30pm and 3pm-9pm daily) or roam along the seventh and eighth blocks of Amazonas.

For general groceries, try **El Sol Multimarket** (Amazonas 679, 8am-11pm daily), or **Hipermercados Metro** (10am-10pm daily) at El Quinde Shopping Plaza.

ACCOMMODATIONS
US$10-25

The German-owned **Hospedaje Los Jazmines** (Amazonas 775, tel. 076/36-1812, www.hospedajelosjazmines.com.pe, US$20 s, US$33 d private bath) is a converted colonial house with six older and darker rooms around a front courtyard and seven lighter and bigger rooms in the back addition. It has Wi-Fi and a quite good restaurant at the side. A percentage of the profits go to helping children with Down syndrome.

US$25-50

Los Balcones de la Recoleta (Amalia Puga 1050, tel. 076/36-3302, www.hostalbalcones. jimdo.com, US$23 s, US$30 d) is a charming colonial house with vine-covered balconies and an overflowing garden. Nearby is the charming Iglesia La Recoleta, and the Plaza de Armas is only a five-minute walk. The rooms are quiet, with cable TV, Internet access, hot water, and phones.

Hostal Casona del Inca (2 de Mayo 458, tel. 076/36-7524, www.casonadelincaperu. com, US$36 s, US$50 d, with breakfast) is conveniently situated across the Plaza de Armas and decorated with painted plates and masks in the interior. The yellow-and-red rooms have a simultaneously homey and artistic touch. The beds have been improved and the baths are quite new.

The centrally located **Los Pinos Inn** (La Mar 521, tel. 076/35-5991, www.lospinosinn. com, US$45 s, US$60 d) has an Old World touch, with antiques and paintings decorating its pleasant halls. Rooms are comfortable enough, with cable TV, hot water, and Wi-Fi.

US$50-100

Las Americas Hotel (Amazonas 622, tel. 076/36-3951, www.lasamericashotel.com.pe, US$55 s, US$70 d, with breakfast buffet) caters either to business travelers or tourists. As a result, there is a fast Internet connection, Wi-Fi, a bar with a long drink menu, and a huge TV for watching soccer games. The rooms are comfortable, carpeted, and feature room service and cable TV.

Hotel El Portal de Marqués (Comercio 644, tel. 076/34-3339, www.portaldelmarques.

com, US$50 s, US$62 d, with breakfast) has a quiet garden with a sitting area and a fountain. The hotel's 33 rooms are small, but their facilities have been renovated, and the bedding is good.

Posada del Puruay (Carretera Porcón, Km 4.5, tel. 076/36-7028, www.posadapuruay. com.pe, US$72 s, US$86 d) is a restored 1822 hacienda, with elegant rooms spread around a stone courtyard, in the middle of a country paradise about 15 minutes from Cajamarca. The grounds include horse stables, eucalyptus and pine forests, and a botanical garden. You can take out Peruvian *paso* horses for circuits through the countryside, grab a mountain bike, or hike one of the area's many trails. The restaurant is excellent, with a wide variety of food, including vegetables from the organic garden, homemade apple pie, and a *calientito cajamarquino,* a hot rum drink ideal for cold mountain nights.

US$100-150

The best spa and thermal baths in Peru are at the **Hotel Laguna Seca** (Manco Cápac 1098, Baños del Inca, tel. 076/58-4300, www. lagunaseca.com.pe, US$125 s, US$150 d, with buffet breakfast). The hotel draws from the same hot springs that Atahualpa enjoyed in 1532, and which now run through the hotel grounds in steaming, open canals. Although the hotel's architectural style is true to the original 1930s hacienda, all the rooms are outfitted with modern amenities: Wi-Fi, cable TV, king beds, mini fridges, and bathrobes. Guests truly feel in the lap of luxury when they slip into their huge personal tubs filled with hot springs water.

Costa del Sol (Cruz de Piedra 707, tel. 076/36-2472, www.costadelsolperu.com, US$120 s, US$145 d, with buffet breakfast) has prime real estate next to the cathedral on the Plaza de Armas. The sofa-filled lobby, where tea and coffee are always available, and the spacious rooms match its location. Rates include access to a small pool, pickup from the airport, and rooms with cable TV, Wi-Fi, and safes. The restaurant, open 24 hours daily, is quite good, with excellent cappuccinos. It also has a gym and karaoke.

INFORMATION AND SERVICES

Located inside the Complejo Belén, the regional tourism office, Dircetur (Belén 631, tel. 076/36-2997, 7:30am-1pm and 2:30pm-5:30pm) provides written guides and maps. The police station (tel. 076/36-2944 or 076/36-2941) is on Plaza Amalia Puga. The tourist police (tel. 076/50-7826) are located at Comercio 1013.

The best health care is at Clínica Limatambo (Puno 265, tel. 076/36-4241 or 0800-20-900, www.limatambo.com.pe). Fill prescriptions or pick up medicine at Boticas Arcángel (Batán 155 or Amazonas 693, 7am-midnight daily) or Boticas Fasa (El Quinde Shopping Plaza, 7am-11pm daily). There is also an Inkafarma (Amazonas 688) a block from Plaza de Armas.

Near the Plaza de Armas are the large national banks with ATMs. Most are open 9am-6pm Monday-Friday (some close midday for lunch) and Saturday morning. You'll find Interbank (Dos de Mayo 546, Plaza de Armas), Banco de Crédito (Apurímac 717), and Scotiabank (Amazonas 750). Cajamarca's post office is Serpost

(Amazonas 443, tel. 076/36-4065, 8am-8:45pm Mon.-Sat.). Internet cafés are everywhere. Most are open from 8 or 9am to 10pm or 11pm and charge US$0.60 per hour.

Lavandería Dandy (Amalia Puga 545, tel. 076/36-8067, 8am-8pm Mon.-Sat., US$1.50 per kilogram) is good and reasonably priced.

GETTING THERE AND AROUND

LATAM and LC Perú have daily flights to Cajamarca's airport, three kilometers east of the Plaza de Armas. Taxis to town cost US$4.

Cruz del Sur and Tepsa have daily bus services direct and nonstop from Lima to Cajamarca (15 hours). Transportes Línea (Av. Atahualpa 318, tel. 076/36-6100, www.linea.pe, 7am-11pm daily) goes daily to Cajamarca from all major coastal cities, including Lima, Trujillo (7 hours), and Chiclayo (6 hours).

To reach Celendín (4 hours), Transportes Palacios and Transportes Rojas have buses leaving daily. To reach Leymebamba (10 hours) and Chachapoyas (12 hours), Transportes Virgen del Carmen (Atahualpa 333) leaves at 4:30am daily.

Taxis are ubiquitous and cheap (US$2-4) in Cajamarca, although traffic congestion can make walking faster.

Chachapoyas and Vicinity

The Chachapoya region (Chachapoyas is the name of the city; Chachapoya is the name of the civilization) is a huge swath of cloud forest in northern Peru that stretches between the Marañón and Huallaga Rivers, containing some of Peru's most rugged and least explored terrain. Every decade or so explorers in this region discover a major archaeological site from the Chachapoya, a mysterious civilization that disappeared from Peru shortly before the Spanish arrived in the 16th century.

Because of their geographical isolation from the rest of Peru, the Chachapoya

developed unique forms of architecture and urban living that continue to baffle archaeologists. They also had a reputation for being feisty and independent, and the Inca spent more than a century trying to subdue this well-defended confederation. The Inca finally prevailed and wiped out every trace of this once-great culture just decades before the Spaniards arrived. What remain are hundreds of stone-built cities, funerary sites, and other ruins that are often covered by thick cloud forest. This same wilderness hosts endangered species such as the

Chachapoyas and Vicinity

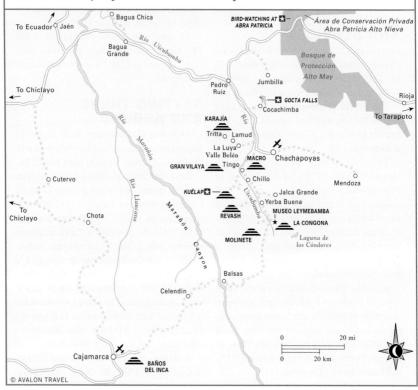

© AVALON TRAVEL

Andean bear and the marvelous spatuletail hummingbird.

Considering all there is to see and do, it is surprising how few travelers come to this area. The absence of visitors is largely due to difficult accessibility. Currently there are no commercial flights to Chachapoyas, so travelers arrive via road from Cajamarca (12 hours), Chiclayo (10 hours), or Tarapoto (6 hours). Apart from Kuélap, most ruins must be accessed by a day or multiday hike.

Most visitors use the small city of Chachapoyas as their base for exploring the region. Although it is located hours from the ruins, it has the best services and transportation options in the area. Chachapoyas, at 2,335 meters elevation, is geographically closer to

the Andes than to the Amazon, so its nights are chilly and its sunny days are hot.

Besides Chachapoyas, a growing number of travelers are now staying at smaller villages along the Río Utcubamba road leading to Choctamal and Leymebamba. These options are increasingly popular because of their comfortable lodges, shorter travel times to the ruins, the promise of peaceful evenings, and the beautiful surroundings.

SIGHTS
City Tour

Chachapoyas was founded in 1545 by conquistador Alonso de Alvarado. The location of the city was moved several times, but the present-day capital of the Amazonas region contains

Gocta Falls

quite a few colonial homes with wooden balconies and large courtyards. Two of the best colonial homes, **Casona Monsante** (now a hotel) and **Casa de las Dos Rosas,** are on Calle Amazonas and can be visited.

On the **Plaza de Armas** is a small exhibit at the **Museo Amazonas Arqueológico** (Ayacucho 908, 8am-1pm and 3pm-5:45pm daily, free), which contains a range of Chachapoya artifacts, including mummies, ceramics, and utensils.

Catch a cab (US$2) and head to the **Mirador de Luya Urco** viewpoint, where on a clear day you get a good panoramic view of the city and the surrounding mountains.

★ Gocta Falls

With a height of 771 meters, the existence of **Gocta Falls** was made public in 2006 by a German engineer, Stefan Ziemendorff, and a group of Peruvian explorers. Initially it was stated that Gocta was the third-highest freefalling waterfall in the world, after Angel Falls in Venezuela and Tugela Falls in South Africa.

Months later, after much global debate about whether this was accurate or not, the World Waterfall Database ranked Gocta as the 14th highest.

The trip is two hours by car to Cocachimba, a small town where you can already see the waterfall in the distance. At Cocachimba you register (US$3.50) and then you or your group get assigned local guides (US$11) who carry plastic ponchos for guests in the event of rain. The hike is pretty straightforward and perhaps more strenuous on the way back to the village. Horses are available (US$13) for those who want to ride.

Either way, the trek is great and the view of the waterfall is quite spectacular once you reach the last leg of the trail. Gocta can appear either as a thin stream of water or a monstrous fall of roaring water, depending on the season. It falls from an impressive steep semicircular escarpment covered with clouds and vegetation. Travel agencies around the Plaza de Armas offer this full-day tour with private transportation (usually a van), all tickets, and lunch for US$20, but rates can be negotiated depending on the number of people in the group.

If you have the time, **Gocta Lodge** (www.goctalodge.com, tel. 042/52-6694, US$90 s, US$110 d) is a great place to stay overnight. Located a few meters from Cocachimba, the lodge has 10 rooms and suites, all with magnificent views of the waterfall in the distance, very comfortable beds, and amenities.

SHOPPING

Rusti-k (Ortiz Arrieta 672) sells textiles, ceramics, and other crafts made by community co-ops. **La Casa del Sarcófago** (Ortiz Arrieta 680) sells wood sculptures, textiles, ceramics, and leather.

Café Fusiones (Ayacucho 952, Plaza Mayor, tel. 041/47-9170, 7am-10:30pm Mon.-Sat., 8am-1pm and 5:30pm-10:30pm Sun.) sells not only the best organic coffee in town but also textiles and other crafts made by people in local communities.

RECREATION

The area surrounding Chachapoyas has breathtaking geography and is a paradise for trekking in the wild mountains and montane cloud forest. Archaeological sites such as **Laguna de los Cóndores** and the vast area of **Gran Vilaya** can only be reached and explored by multiday treks, most often made with horses and mules. Trekking, camping, or homestays in villages are the best ways to understand the life of the modern-day Chachapoya, whose fair skin and light eyes have fueled much speculation as to their ancestry. The scenery includes plunging waterfalls, squawking parrots, and ridge tops blanketed in dense fog.

Unlike some other parts of Peru, contracting a guide or going with a guided tour is definitely the best approach in Chachapoyas. Travelers who forge out on their own can spend hours, even days, looking for ruins that blend perfectly into the lush landscape or, even worse, suffer an accident in a remote place. That said, be careful when hiring trekking guides. Either use the agencies listed here or get recommendations from reputable traveler reports.

Tour Agencies and Guides

Vilaya Tours (Amazonas 261, cell tel. 941-708-798, www.vilayatours.com) is managed by Rob Dover, a friendly and knowledgeable Englishman who has lived in Chachapoyas since 1997. Vilaya Tours offers an extraordinary series of treks to out-of-the-way places. A two-week trek through the roadless mountains south of Leymebamba, along an old Inca Trail, includes a visit to the ruins of Cochabamba, a remote imperial Inca site with double-jambed doorways, fountains, and *kancha* enclosures. The agency also leads the best treks to Laguna de los Cóndores, regular trips to the Gocta waterfall, and excellent multiday hotel-based tours.

InkaNatura Travel (Manuel Bañon 461, San Isidro, Lima tel. 01/440-2022, www.inkanatura.com) offers high-end and recommended multiday culturally oriented trips.

Nights are spent in cozy lodges and dining on generous meals, and days are filled with visits to the major ruins and museums. Transportation is generally by car, although some trips include short hikes and horseback rides.

Cloudforest Expeditions (Puno 368, www.kuelapnordperu.com, tel. 041/47-7610) is an English- and German-speaking agency offering tours in the Chachapoya region and the rest of northern Peru. The owner, Oscar von Bischoffhausen, a Peruvian of German descent, is knowledgeable and friendly and personally guides his tours.

Nuevos Caminos Travel (Ayacucho 952, tel. 041/47-9170, www.nuevoscaminostravel.com) offers an alternative way to explore the region. Trips are tailored to your interests, visiting Kuélap and other major sites, but keeping in mind a sustainable and responsible way to travel. Tours can last up to 15 days, including a period of time volunteering in Huanchaco, near Trujillo, and working with farmers near Chachapoyas. For details and costs, contact owner Marilyn Velásquez, an inspiring woman who sometimes leads the groups herself.

FOOD
Peruvian

Restaurant El Tejado (Santo Domingo 426, tel. 041/47-7592, noon-4pm and 7pm-9pm daily, US$3-7) is by far the best eatery in Chachapoyas. Great *menús* (US$3) on weekdays and specialties such as *tacu tacu* (a fried bean and rice patty topped with beef or fried egg), as well as chicken, pork, and beef dishes, make this place a favorite.

Sabores del Perú (Dos de Mayo 321, tel. 041/47-9181 or 954/44-9180, 8am-10pm Mon.-Fri., 8am-11pm Sat.-Sun., US$6-8) has a wide variety of Peruvian meals, from a steamy *sopa criolla* to *pollo a la brasa*. Food is tasty and abundant.

Despite a cold, nondescript atmosphere, **La Tushpa** (Ortiz Arrieta 753, tel. 041/47-7471, 1pm-11pm daily, US$1-3) serves mouthwatering *brochetas, parrillas* (grilled meats), and *anticuchos* (grilled beef-heart skewers). The prices are dirt cheap and the kitchen immaculate.

Pizza

The wood-fired pizza at **Candela** (2 de Mayo 728, Santo Domingo, 5pm-11pm Mon.-Sat., US$4-6) is the best in Chachapoyas. Try the chorizo or margherita pizzas.

Vegetarian

Restaurant Vegetariano El Eden (Grau 448, tel. 041/47-8664, 7am-9pm Sun.-Fri., US$1-2) has the best and cheapest *menú* in town. It serves excellent yogurts, salads, soups, and large helpings of rice and soy-based dishes. Vegetarian or not, don't miss this place.

Cafés, Bakeries, and Ice Cream

Café Fusiones (Ayacucho 952, tel. 041/47-9170, 7am-10:30pm Mon.-Sat., 8am-1pm and 5:30pm-10:30pm Sun., US$2-5) serves excellent organic coffee from Rodríguez de Mendoza province, east of Chachapoyas, supporting fair trade in the region. Biscuits, homemade desserts, and delicious sandwiches are also available in the cozy coffee shop. Volunteers help out and offer information. This café also has a book exchange, board games, and Wi-Fi.

Another favorite, **Terra Mía Café** (Chincha Alta 557, tel. 041/47-7127, 7am-10:30pm daily, US$3), is the only place in town—and likely in all of Amazonas—that serves waffles for breakfast. Stop by in the evening for dessert. **Mass Burguer** (Triunfo 1051, tel. 041/47-7225, 9am-1pm and 4pm-10pm daily, US$3-5) is a warmly lit café with wooden tables and a nice garden. It is a good option for an evening snack.

The front room of **Panadería San José** (Ayacucho 816, tel. 041/47-7339, 6:30am-10pm Mon.-Sat., 8:30am-noon and 4:30pm-9pm Sun., US$1-3) bustles with bread-buyers, but the back room is full of quiet conversation and locals sipping coffee as they eat

tamales. The café will specially prepare early-departure breakfasts.

Markets

For the best selection of groceries, try **Mini-Market** (Ortiz Arrieta 528, Plaza Mayor, 7am-11pm daily), where there is also a restaurant serving spit-roasted chicken. The **Mercado Central,** full of local fruits and vegetables, is on Libertad between Grau and Ortiz Arrieta, behind the Plaza de Armas.

ACCOMMODATIONS

US$10-25

A good budget option near the Plaza de Armas is the **Chachapoyas Backpackers** (2 de Mayo 639, tel. 041/47-8879, www. chachapoyasbackpackers.com, US$13 s, US$17 d). There is the option of shared or private baths. Amenities include Wi-Fi, an open kitchen, laundry, and a book exchange. It also offers Spanish classes and can help organize tours to Kuélap and other sites.

Hotel Puma Urco (Amazonas 833, tel. 041/47-7871, www.hotelpumaurco.com, US$21 s, US$32 d, with breakfast), conveniently half a block from the Plaza de Armas, offers comfy rooms, hot water, cable TV, Wi-Fi, a garage, and laundry service. **Kuélap Hotel** (Amazonas 1057, tel. 041/47-7136, www.kuelaphotel.com, US$15-35 s, US$30-50 d) has a wide variety of rates, depending on room amenities.

US$25-50

The most charming budget option in town is the family-run **Hostal Revash** (Grau 517, tel. 041/47-7391, US$25 s, US$32 d, with breakfast), a rambling colonial house with 14 huge rooms surrounding a plant-filled courtyard. The house has wood floors, very comfy beds, cable TV, Wi-Fi, and modern baths with very hot water. It's amazingly quiet despite being right on the plaza. On the first floor is the office of **Andes Tours,** managed by the same family.

La Casona Monsante (Amazonas 746, tel. 041/47-7702, www.lacasonamonsante. com, US$25 s, US$47 d) is the best-preserved colonial house in Chachapoyas. The rooms are huge and sparsely decorated to show off the ancient doors, high ceilings, and tile floors. Beds are comfortable, and all rooms have cable TV and Wi-Fi. Breakfast is available (US$2-3) as well has heaters (US$4 per day).

Hotel Vilaya (Ayacucho 734, tel. 041/47-7664, www.hotelvilayachachapoyas.com, US$30 s, US$38 d, with breakfast) is a modern four-story hotel with 20 large, very corporate, carpeted rooms with comfortable beds, phones, cable TV, Wi-Fi, and hot water. There is a café-bar downstairs.

Just out of town, **Villa de Paris** (entrance to Chachapoyas, Jr. Dos de Mayo, Block 15, tel. 041/79-7944, www.hotelvilladeparis.com, US$30 s, US$48 d) has a beautiful setting overlooking the Utcubamba valley. Comfortable bungalows for five people (US$100) are also available.

US$50-100

The highly recommended **Casa Andina** (Carretera Pedro Ruiz, Km 39, cell tel. 969-335-840, US$63-80 s or d) is located 20 minutes from Chachapoyas in a refurbished colonial hacienda. The rooms here come with flat-screen TVs and Wi-Fi, but in the evenings you may want to disconnect and enjoy the quiet, star-filled night. The hotel has a pool, beautiful gardens, and a great restaurant that serves a breakfast buffet and barbecue on Sunday.

INFORMATION AND SERVICES

For health care, the two options are **Hospital Regional Virgen de Fatima-Chachapoyas** (Daniel Alcides Carrion 035, tel. 041/47-7792 or 041/47-7016, 24 hours daily) and **Hospital Higos Urco-EsSalud** (Ortiz Arrieta 604, tel. 041/57-9516, 24 hours daily). There are several pharmacies in town. **Inkafarma** (Grau 533, 8am-10pm daily) is located a block from the Plaza de Armas.

Banks with ATMs include **Banco de la Nación** (Ayacucho, block 8) and **Banco de Crédito** (Ortiz Arrieta 576, on the plaza).

Both banks are open 9am-6pm Monday-Friday and Saturday morning.

The post office, **Serpost** (tel. 041/47-7017, 8am-8pm Mon.-Sat.), is at Amazonas 1220. Chachapoyas has speedy **Internet,** and normal Internet café hours are 8am-10pm daily. On the Plaza de Armas, there are several *locutorios* that post their rates for local, national, or international phone calls.

The best place for laundry is **Lavandería Clean** (Amazonas 813, tel. 041/47-9020, 8am-1pm and 3pm-9pm Mon.-Sat., 9am-1pm and 3pm-9pm Sun., US$1.50 per kilogram), one block from the plaza and offering same-day service.

GETTING THERE AND AROUND

Most visitors arrive to Chachapoyas via either the bus from Chiclayo (10 hours) or from Tarapoto (6 hours). Intrepid and adventurous spirits who aren't afraid of heights continue south toward Leymebamba, and then up and out of the Utcubamba Valley to drop into the awe-inspiring Marañón Valley.

A private company owns the city airport, but flights have not been reestablished since a plane crashed here in 2003. Check with a local travel agency to learn more about the possibility of flights to Chachapoyas, as Peruvian media has reported recently that flights could soon resume.

Colectivos and taxis run the one-hour route on an excellent paved highway from Chachapoyas to **Pedro Ruiz,** a town on the Chiclayo-Tarapoto Marginal Highway where buses headed in either direction can be caught.

Etcaosa serves Bagua Grande, Pomacochas, and Nueva Cajamarca in modern sedan or station wagon cars from Pedro Ruiz (Av. Marginal 231). From Nueva Cajamarca, **Transportes Cajamarca** (Av. Cajamarca Sur 650) goes to Moyobamba, Tarapoto, and Yurimaguas daily.

Combis serve the Chachapoyas-Leymebamba route (US$4), and all points in between, leaving from Grau 302.

ROAD TO KUÉLAP

Choctamal is one of the villages along the bumpy road to Kuélap. Very close by is **Choctamal Marvelous Spatuletail Lodge** (cell tel. 995-237-268, U.S. tel. 407/963-9876, www.marvelousspatuletail.com, US$45 s, US$55 d), which is named after a local endemic hummingbird. The lodge sits high on a hilltop and has a direct view of Kuélap from its bedroom balconies. The rooms with wooden floors are elegant, though Spartan, and there are plenty of blankets for the area's chilly nights. The outdoor hot tub, sunset over the valley, and delicious breakfast are not to be missed.

LEYMEBAMBA

Leymebamba, near the head of the Utcubamba Valley at 2,200 meters elevation, is a quiet town with cobblestone streets and a stone church. Situated 80 kilometers south of Chachapoyas, the road between towns is not paved but it is in surprisingly good condition. En route to Celendín and Cajamarca, the road from Leymebamba climbs out of the Utcubamba watershed and plunges into the Marañón Canyon.

Leymebamba was one of the first Chachapoya towns that **Inca Túpac Yupanqui** encountered in 1472. Here, the sovereign celebrated the Inti-Raymi festival, a celebration of the summer solstice from which Leymebamba derives its name. The town celebrates its patron saint **Virgen del Carmen** in mid-July.

The ruins of **La Congona** are a three-hour walk above the city. Ask at the Museo Leymebamba or at one of the lodgings about how to get there.

Museo Leymebamba

The **Museo Leymebamba** (Av. Austria s/n, San Miguel, cell tel. 971-104-907, Lima tel. 01/261-4422, http://museoleymebamba.org, 9:30am-4:30pm Tues.-Sun., US$5), two kilometers southwest of Leymebamba on the highway leading to Cajamarca, is an extraordinary introduction to the Chachapoya culture.

The museum was opened in 2000 after the 1997 discovery of approximately 200 mummies and 2,000 artifacts at **Laguna de los Cóndores**, which can only be reached via a 10-hour mule ride on muddy trails heading south from Leymebamba. A team led by bioarchaeologist Sonia Guillén carefully excavated the site and, in the process, revealed much of what is known about the Chachapoya.

The mummies are housed and exhibited in a temperature-controlled chamber. They were found in cliff tombs above the lake, which perfectly preserved the mummies despite the high humidity of the montane cloud forest. DNA from these mummies helped scientists decipher the migration patterns, diseases, and genetic origins of the Chachapoya. Other artifacts include collections of colorful shawls, feathered headdresses, baskets, sandals, flutes, and artistic renderings found at Kuélap and other sites.

The museum was built using old Chachapoya construction techniques and local building traditions. Apart from the artifacts, the museum also contains scale models of Chachapoya cities and tombs and an ethnographic exhibition on the modern-day descendants of the Chachapoya.

The museum has a small shop with interesting books written by Guillén and Adriana von Hagen about the Chachapoya and the archaeological digs. The artisan Miguel Huamán Revilla sells his crafts here. Across the road from the museum is **Kentikafé**, "the hummingbird café," where you can observe at a very short distance these small creatures, including the marvelous spatuletail hummingbird. Coffee, sandwiches, and especially the hot chocolate are as marvelous as the hummingbirds.

Food and Accommodations

La Tushpa (16 de Julio 612, Plaza de Armas, 7am-10pm daily, US$2-4) is a good place to have lunch or dinner. Sitting on the back patio, you can watch as your trout is fried over an open wood-burning stove. The best eatery in town is **Cely** (La Verdad 530, 6am-10pm daily, US$3-5), which offers a daily *menú* for US$1.50 and other dishes such as *lomo saltado,* soup, beans, and pizzas. Early breakfasts are also available.

La Casona de Leymebamba (Amazonas 223, tel. 041/83-0106, www.casonadeleymebamba.com, US$38 s, US$50 d, with breakfast) is by far the best place to stay in town. Features include large rooms with private baths and delicious breakfasts. The owner, Nelly Zumaeta, is welcoming and extremely helpful.

Getting There

All buses from Cajamarca to Chachapoyas stop in Leymebamba. *Combis* leave on a paved road to Leymebamba from Grau 302 in Chachapoyas.

Chachapoya Archaeological Sites

This section covers the most-visited archaeological sites in the Chachapoyas area, in order of traveler popularity, with rough instructions on how to get there. Remember that finding many of the lesser-known ruins is difficult and you run the risk of getting lost if you do not get a guide. The best place to get guides is Chachapoyas.

★ KUÉLAP

Perched on a limestone ridge above the Utcubamba Valley and rediscovered by a local judge in 1843, **Kuélap** (8am-4:30pm daily, US$5) must have been a nearly impenetrable fortress. This imposing stone citadel, 700 meters long and 110 meters at its widest, is surrounded by a huge wall reaching heights of 11 meters over sheer cliffs. Visitors enter from the east, via one of three funnel-shaped defensive entrances that penetrate the massive and remarkably intact walls.

Situated above are the remains of more than 400 circular stone houses, grain silo-like homes. Peaked, conical thatch roofs top these two-story homes, and their midsection is marked by protruding stones, which probably served as gutters to keep rain away from the foundations. Friezes with zigzag, rhomboid, or serpentine designs wrap many of the buildings. Cloud forest trees, like *nogal,* encircle the moss and bromeliad-covered ruins. Cool mountain breezes and buzzing hummingbirds sweep through the complex.

From the east entrance, there is a network of marked paths leading right to what was once the most fortified part of the citadel. At the top of a stone D-shaped lookout tower, archaeologists found a cache of 2,500 shaped rocks—sling ammunition.

Square buildings, which may have been built by the Inca, lie near the center of the platform. Nearby, Canadian anthropologist Morgan Davis and a team from Levanto have reconstructed a round house, complete with its thatched roof.

Kuélap's most famous building, however, is a stone tower whose walls widen as they go up as if it were an upside-down inkwell or *tintero*—its name in Spanish. Animal sacrifices were found inside, so archaeologists believe this building had a religious purpose. Others, though, say it was a solar observatory or cemetery.

Most visitors arrive to Kuélap via a day tour or three-hour *combi* ride from Chachapoyas. Backpackers can opt for a five-hour, 10-kilometer hike from the village of **Tingo.** The trail follows a path of stone slabs laid by the Chachapoya. The trail, best hiked in the cool of the morning, rises 1,210 vertical meters from Tingo and is marked with red arrows. For those that don't want to hike, there is now an easier, faster alternative to see Kuelap from Tingo. At the end of 2016, a gondola project was completed in the town, which transfers visitors to the site in one of 26 cable cars over a distance of 4 kilometers and 1,000 vertical meters in 20 minutes. The gondola, a public-private partnership, was launched in order to attract tourists to the region. Tickets cost about US$5.

There are a few basic lodging options near the ruins, including the **El Imperio Kuelapino** (cell tel. 941-735-833, US$5 pp) and **Luna de Kuélap** (no phone, US$5 pp). Ask about lodging options and meals when you sign in for the ruins. There are also a few *hospedajes* in Pueblo María with basic accommodations and meals.

From Chachapoyas, *colectivos* (US$7) leave from the corner of Grau and Salamanca at 4:30am daily. If you book your place on the morning bus the night before, it will pick you up at your hotel. Often the afternoon bus is full, so arrive ahead of time. The bus passes Tingo, Choctamal, Longuita, and María en route to Malcapampa, a 15-minute walk from Kuélap. There are no fixed return *colectivos*. One option to return is to hike four hours to Tingo, where *colectivos* leave for Chachapoyas until 5pm. In the case of Kuélap, it seems most sensible to go with a local Kuélap agency. If you have a group, a private *combi* can be rented in Chachapoyas for the round-trip journey to Kuélap (about US$60).

KARAJÍA

At Karajía, clay sarcophagi with human forms and eerie, oblong faces stand over dramatic cliff ledges. Made by the **Chipuric** subculture, the tombs were sacked and shattered long ago. But at least one group of six figures remains. Binoculars are a must to see the sculptural details and the skulls perched on top of them.

There are two ways to reach Karajía, which is a 70-kilometer drive northwest of Chachapoyas. The shorter route is a half-hour walk from **Cruzpata,** a village at the end of a dirt road. Villagers charge a US$2 entrance fee. To reach Cruzpata from Chachapoyas, take a *combi* (US$2) for the 1.5-hour trip to Luya. Luya *combis* depart a block from the Chachapoyas market at Ortiz Arrieta 364. From Luya, take a *colectivo* (US$7) in the main square to Cohechan. After the driver drops the other passengers, pay a bit more to be taken to Cruzpata. Guides can be hired at Cruzpata for US$5, although there are signs indicating the way.

The other route also starts in Luya, but it branches off to Lamud and Trita, the starting point for a 1.5-hour walk that crosses the valley and should be avoided in rainy season (Dec.-Mar.). For this walk, it is best to hire a guide in Trita, Lamud, or Luya for about

Karajía

US$12 per day. Consider a visit to Pueblo de los Muertos later in the same day. Public transportation to Lamud and Trita leaves from Luya's main square.

REVASH

Revash is a collection of house-like tombs perched on cliff ledges. The hundreds of mummies were looted long ago, but what remains are several tombs in good condition, and red-and-white paintings of people, animals, and other abstract designs. Out of respect for the site and its preservation, visitors should not scramble onto the ledges but use binoculars to view them from a distance. Apart from the main site, there are 18 lesser sites spread through this Santo Tomás Valley.

To reach Revash, *combis* leave from Salamanca 957 in Chachapoyas for Leymebamba. Get off at Yerba Buena, which is south of Ubilón and Tingo. At this point, a taxi can take you another 30 minutes west on a dirt road that crosses the bridge. Proceed until you see a house built of sheet metal, where the trail begins. The walk up to the tombs takes three hours, and they are difficult to find without a guide. Guides can be contracted along the way at Estancia Chillo or in the nearby village of Yerba Buena. *Combis* leave regularly from the second block of Grau in Chachapoyas to Yerba Buena. Most days, *combis* from Leymebamba to Chachapoyas pass Yerba Buena after 3pm.

LEVANTO, YALAPE, AND COLLA CRUZ

The picturesque village of Levanto (2,600 meters) and the Inca and Chachapoya ruins around it make for a pleasant day trip. Levanto is part of the popular three-day trek that begins in Chachapoyas, passes through Magdalena and Tingo, and ends at Kuélap. Accommodations and food can be obtained along the way. This trail follows the Inca highways that ran from Cusco to Quito, crossing the coast and the rainforest.

Chachapoyas Tours (Grau 534, 2nd Fl., Plaza de Armas, cell tel. 941-963-327, U.S. tel. 866/396-9582, www.kuelapperu.com) has the best directions for this trek. It operates a **backpacker lodge** (US$8 pp) in Levanto whose construction mimics a thatched Chachapoyas home but which has flush toilets, electricity, and hot water. The lodge donated a ceramic kiln to the surrounding community to help generate new income.

The hiking from Chachapoyas to Levanto is approximately five hours. The same is true from Levanto to Tingo, but it is six hours from Tingo to Kuélap. To shorten the hike, take a *colectivo* from Chachapoyas to Levanto. Departures are supposedly at 5:30am daily from the corner of Sosiego and Cuarto Centenario, but it is best to confirm beforehand. The return car leaves Levanto at 2pm. A private car charges US$15-20 one-way.

On the road between Chachapoyas and Levanto are the ruins of Yalape, a residential complex made of white limestone that sprawls on a hill overlooking Levanto. There are fine defensive walls with diamond-shaped frieze patterns and numerous vine-covered walls and buildings. Nearby is an ancient Inca aqueduct.

U.S. archaeologist Morgan Davis restored an Inca garrison at the crossroads Colla Cruz, a 20-minute walk from Levanto. The round Chachapoya-style building, built atop a flawless Inca stone foundation, has a reconstructed three-story thatch roof. Ask for directions in Levanto.

GRAN VILAYA

Gran Vilaya is a vast area of a once-populated cloud forest that was "discovered" and publicized in 1985 by U.S. swashbuckler Gene Savoy. Starting from the Belén Valley, Savoy walked to the village of Vista Hermosa, clearing a trail along the ridge above the town. In 10 days of constant work, he found the ruins of several large urban settlements, which he somewhat absurdly called Chacha Picchu. Locals now call the ruins Pueblo Viejo and accuse Savoy of stealing gold and smuggling other objects from the sites.

There are about 150 sites in this area, of which 15 are considered exceptional. Visitors should plan a few days for exploring them and an additional three days of travel. Getting a guide in Chachapoyas is strongly recommended. Impressive sites include the Inca steps of **La Escalera,** which have amazingly survived centuries of mule hooves. Nearby is **La Pirquilla,** an area with dozens of well-made round buildings partially covered in the cloud forest. **Cacahuasha** is a large village perched on top of a mountain. The site is divided into two sections, separated by a saddle, and includes 10-meter walls similar to those found at Kuélap. This was probably a ceremonial center and has extraordinary views over the valley. Other recommended sites are the large ruins of Tulupe and Lanche, as well as Machu Llagata and Paxamarca. **Machu Llagata** was an important ceremonial center that has a ridge-top lookout tower and a large plaza with circular houses extending in all directions. **Paxamarca** covers about 20 hectares atop a ridge and includes ceremonial terraces, numerous circular buildings, and rectangular buildings with trapezoidal doorways, proof of Inca occupation following their invasion circa 1480.

LA CONGONA

If you get to Leymebamba, take the three-hour hike up into the hills northwest of the town. There lies **La Congona,** a small site with some of the most beautiful ruins in the region. This five-hectare hilltop contains a few circular homes that are in excellent condition. A few of these homes were built on unusual square platforms. Inside the homes are elaborate stone niches, probably ceremonial, and outside are wide walking balconies and highly elaborate stone friezes. A lookout tower boasts an extraordinary flight of curved switchback steps, from which it is possible to look across the Utcubamba Valley to the ruins of Cerro Olán. A guide is recommended for this trek; ask at the Museo Leymebamba. Visitors should register in the Leymebamba tourist office on the plaza and pay a US$1.75 archaeological tax before venturing into the hills or trek to La Congona.

OTHER ARCHAEOLOGICAL SITES

The region has a nearly limitless number of ruins to explore for those with the time and physical stamina—and there are plenty to be discovered as well. Here are more recommended ruins in the Utcubamba Valley, listed from north to south.

Pueblo de los Muertos

The **Pueblo de los Muertos** site, which translates to Village of the Dead, groups funeral houses that were built onto a cliff ledge and plastered with mud. The round houses are decorated with serpents and other abstract anthropomorphic symbols. Hire a guide in Lamud for this hike, which is a strenuous one-hour walk. It is important to view the tombs from a distance only. By crossing to the main ledge, tourists put the buildings and themselves in jeopardy. To reach Lamud, see the directions for Karajía.

Jalca Grande and Ollape

Jalca Grande is a Quechua village with cobblestone streets and thatched roofs. The older generation still speaks Quechua and lives as it has for centuries. But sheet-metal roofs, cement roads, and Spanish are cropping up. This town has kept the area's anthropologists busy over the years. One block west of the main square is a Chachapoyas home, known as **La Choza Redonda,** which was continuously occupied for centuries until 1964. The house, with a double zigzag frieze at the top, remains in nearly perfect condition and served as the model for Morgan Davis's reconstruction of Inca and Chachapoyas homes in Levanto and Kuélap.

A 30-minute walk to the west of the city is **Ollape,** a town that once had 150 buildings. It is now possible to see a number of platforms with rhomboidal and zigzag friezes that are different from the friezes at other sites. To reach Jalca, take a minibus (US$3.50) from Chachapoyas at Ortiz Arrieta 372. The minibuses leave at 8am and 4pm daily.

Laguna de los Cóndores

Laguna de los Cóndores competes with Gran Vilaya as Chachapoyas's most popular trek. You reach this stunning lake after a one- or two-day hike from Leymebamba. The trail traces through remote cloud forest filled with Chachapoyas ruins, bromeliads, and birds before arriving at a spectacular lakeside tomb site. Contact Chachapoyas's **Vilaya Tours** (Amazonas 261, tel. 041/47-7506, www.vilayatours.com) for treks in this area.

CHACHAPOYAS TO AND FROM CHICLAYO

The trip, by ground, from Chachapoyas to Chiclayo or vice versa is a bumpy 10-hour bus ride. **Móvil** (Libertad 464, Chachapoyas, tel. 041/47-8545; Bolognesi 199, Chiclayo, tel. 074/27-1940) has daily buses (US$18 one-way).

CHACHAPOYAS TO AND FROM TARAPOTO

Lago Pomacochas

A good stop on the way to Tarapoto is Lago Pomacochas (2,200 meters), a miniature lake 31 kilometers east of Pedro Ruiz. The lake's blue-green waters and extensive *tótoras* (marshlands) are the last of the highlands before the highway follows the Cordillera Oriental and descends, along the Río Mayo watershed, toward the Amazon. Pomacochas is an excellent spot for bird-watchers.

★ Bird-Watching at Abra Patricia

Abra Patricia is a high pass (2,270 meters) on the highway between Pedro Ruiz and Tarapoto and is part of a great bicycle route. It is also the short name for the **Área de Conservación Privada Abra Patricia-Alto Nieva,** a private protected area created in 2007 and located within the buffer zone of the **Bosque de Protección Alto Mayo.** Both are protected areas with some of the highest bird counts on earth. The area's bird list includes 317 species, of which 23 are considered globally threatened. These include the endangered long-whiskered owlet, the ocher-fronted antpitta, the royal sunangel, Johnson's tody-tyrant, and, of course, the marvelous spatule-tail hummingbird.

The Owlet Lodge and **Estación Biológica Lechucita Bigotona** (tel. 041/81-6814, Chachapoyas, www.ecoanperu.org) is a lodge and biological station located around Km 364.5 on the highway between Pedro Ruiz and Moyobamba, owned by ECOAN (Asociación de Ecosistemas Andinos), which is funded and sponsored by a series of international nature and conservation organizations, including Bird Life International, IUCN, Conservation International, and 10 other institutions.

The lodge has three spacious and comfortable bungalows: Fenwick, Conoco, and Jeniam, each with two rooms, a double and a single, and a shared bath. There is hot water and electricity in the evenings. Internet access via satellite is available in the dining-lounge area. The lodge kitchen offers three meals per day, served in the spacious dining room.

CHACHAPOYAS TO AND FROM CAJAMARCA

Celendín

If you are making the Chachapoyas-Cajamarca overland journey in a 4WD vehicle, Celendín (2,648 meters) is a friendly place to stay for the night and will give you a flavor of northern rural living. There is an interesting market on Sunday.

There is good food in **La Reserva** (Dos de Mayo 549, tel. 076/55-5415, 8am-11pm daily, US$2-4). To cure a sweet tooth, visit **Heladería El Rosario** (Pardo 426, tel. 076/55-5109, 10am-11pm daily, US$1-3) on the Plaza de Armas.

A few new hotels have popped up in Celendín in the last few years. A new option is the **Hotel Villa Madrid** (3rd block of Pardo, tel. 076/55-5123, US$14 s, US$22 d). Rooms have private baths, hot water, Wi-Fi, and cable TV. It is still fairly basic but a nice change.

Banco de la Nación (Dos de Mayo 518) is the only bank in town and has an ATM, which works exclusively with Visa debit cards.

Background

The Landscape

Peru's foreboding terrain belies its extraordinary fertility. The country's arid coastal climate is caused by the frigid Humboldt Current, which sucks moisture away from the land. But these Antarctic waters also cause a rich upwelling of plankton, which in turn nourishes one of the world's richest fishing grounds. Peru's earliest societies took root near the ocean and depended on mollusks and fish for their survival.

The snow-covered mountains and high passes of the **Cordillera de los Andes** would appear to be an impediment to the spread of advanced cultures. But the slow melting of the snowpack provides the desert coast with a vital source of year-round water. Once ancient Peruvians developed irrigation technologies, Peru's early inhabitants began converting Peru's desert valleys into rich farming areas. The ingenious aqueducts at Nasca, which carry mountain water for miles underneath the desert floor, are still in use today.

In the more moderate topography of North America and Europe, temperature differences and climate zones are largely a question of latitude. But in Peru, climate zones are caused not by latitude but by altitude. Peru's coast can rise from sea level to over 4,000 meters in less than 100 kilometers, creating a variety of climates for fruits, vegetables, grains, and potatoes. The same phenomenon occurs to an even greater extent where the Andes plunge into the Amazon, a dizzying range of ecosystems that nourish a huge variety of fruits and medicinal plants such as the coca leaf.

Peru's cultural diversity has always been determined by its geography. Trade routes from the Amazon over the Andes to the desert coast were key to the flourishing of Peru's ancient cultures. The Chavín people, based in the Andes south of the Cordillera Blanca, deified jaguars, snakes, caimans, and other Amazon animals in their enigmatic carvings. They traded their high-altitude grains and potatoes for fruits from the Amazon and dried fish and vegetables from the coast.

GEOGRAPHY

Peru's total land area is 1.29 million square kilometers, about three times the size of California. Peru's narrow strip of arid desert coast runs 2,400 kilometers between the borders of Ecuador and Chile. Some 50 rivers cascade from the Andes to the coast, though only about one-third of these carry water year-round. In Peru's extreme south, the coast forms part of the **Atacama Desert,** one of the driest places on earth.

The Andes rise so abruptly from the coast that they can be seen from the ocean on a clear day. They represent the highest mountain chain on earth next to the Himalayas. **Huascarán,** Peru's highest peak at 6,768 meters, is the world's highest tropical mountain. The Andes are divided into different ranges (called *cordilleras* in Spanish), which often run parallel to each other.

Between these mountain ranges lie fertile inter-Andean valleys and grasslands between 2,300 and 4,000 meters elevation—the so-called breadbasket of Peru, where the majority of its indigenous highlanders live and produce about half the country's food supply. The Inca and other cultures terraced and irrigated this landscape to grow a range of crops, including maize, hardy grains, and indigenous tubers.

On the journey between Cusco and Lake Titicaca, travelers can appreciate the most extreme of Peru's mountain climates, the **puna** or **altiplano.** These rolling grasslands

---

Previous: vicuñas in the Peruvian highlands; a flower carpet prepared in Ayacucho during Semana Santa celebrations.

between 4,000 and 4,800 meters look bleak but form rich pasturelands for Peru's variety of camelids, including wild guanacos, domesticated llamas and alpacas, and highly prized vicuñas. These animals continue to provide wool, meat, and transportation for Andean highlanders.

On the eastern side of Peru, the Andes mountains peter out into a series of ecosystems that cascade into the Amazon basin. Near the top of the eastern edge of the Andes is the **montane cloud forest,** a mist-drenched, inhospitable place that is one of Peru's most biodiverse habitats. Here live 90 varieties of hummingbirds and over 2,000 types of orchids and butterflies. Mountain streams cascade down these slopes, eventually merging to form the broad winding rivers of the lowland rainforest. This carpet of green is the largest rainforest on the planet, making up almost 60 percent of Peru's territory and stretching thousands of kilometers through Brazil to the Atlantic Ocean.

CLIMATE

Peru's weather is a complex set of patterns caused by the Humboldt Current, the Andes, and the jet stream, which blows northwest and picks up the Amazon's moisture as it travels.

On the coast, the southwesterly trade winds that blow toward Peru are chilled as they pass over the frigid waters of the Humboldt Current. When these cold winds hit Peru's sunbaked coast, they gradually warm and rarely release rain because their ability to hold water increases. Clouds form only when the air begins to rise over the Andes, dropping rain over Peru's mountain valleys and high grasslands.

During much of the year, however, a curious temperature inversion occurs along much of Peru's coast. The rising air from the coast is trapped beneath the warm air over 1,000 meters, which is never cooled by ocean breezes. Fog blankets sections of the coast, and light drizzle falls—mainly, but not only between April and September.

The jet stream heads west over the Amazon basin toward the Andes, picking up transpiration from the Amazon basin. As this warm, humid air rises over the Andes it also condenses into a fine mist that nourishes the cloud forest. As it rises even higher over the puna, it falls as rain.

The heaviest periods of rain in the Peruvian Amazon and Andes occur between December and April, a time that Peruvians refer to as the *época de lluvia* (the rainy season). The first rains, however, begin in October, which is the beginning of the highland planting season. Soon after, rain from the Andes begins to cascade down on the coast, where desert farmers use it for irrigation, and into the Amazon, where rivers become swollen and muddy.

EARTHQUAKES AND EL NIÑO

Peru is prone to a series of natural disasters caused by both its young geological formation and its peculiar climate. On the western edge of South America, the Nasca Plate is slowly sliding beneath the continent, and the resulting friction causes periodic earthquakes and volcanic eruptions. The area most affected by this is southern Peru, especially **Arequipa.** The city averages roughly one major earthquake per century, most recently in 2001.

The hardest-hit region, however, has been the **Callejón de Huaylas,** a river valley situated between the Cordillera Negra and Cordillera Blanca ranges, where earthquakes cause glacial lakes to burst their dams and send huge mudslides (*aluviones*) to the valley below. In 1970, an earthquake measuring 7.8 on the Richter scale destroyed 90 percent of Huaraz and triggered an *aluvión* that buried the nearby town of **Yungay** within minutes, killing thousands. The town has been rebuilt, and the only traces of old Yungay are the tops of a few palm trees poking out above the silt plain. These trees once graced the town's square.

El Niño, the periodic fluctuation in the water temperature of the Pacific Ocean, wreaks havoc across Peru and appears to be having increasingly dramatic highs and lows.

In 1982 and 1998, El Niño events dumped torrential rains onto Peru's northern desert, causing floods that washed out bridges and stranded highway motorists for weeks. These natural phenomena also caused droughts in the southern Andes and a collapse in Peru's coastal fishery.

ENVIRONMENTAL ISSUES

Peru suffers from a range of environmental problems that are caused in large part by mines, fishmeal factories, oil and natural gas wells and pipelines and processing centers, illegal lumber operations, and other extractive industries. These industries have operated with little oversight in Peru for decades as a result of a weak political system that is cash-starved and corrupt. Legislation governing extractive industries, along with regulatory agencies, is improving in Peru but there is still a large informal industry that doesn't abide by the regulations.

Unregulated gold mining is a major source of mercury pollution and deforestation in the Peruvian Amazon. Formal mining companies take environmental measures, but contamination from zinc, copper, silver and gold mines still occurs. Social conflicts are a result of community opposition to mining, often over environmental concerns. Protests can quickly turn violent and result in road closures due to blockades. In 2016, there were large protests over a Chinese-owned copper mine, Las Bambas, in Apurimac.

Over the last three decades, gas and oil exploration in the Amazon has caused water pollution and deforestation and has had a huge impact on indigenous communities. The biggest gas project is the Camisea Gas Field, which is exporting 13 trillion cubic feet of natural gas from the lower Urubamba basin, one of the most remote and pristine areas of the Peruvian Amazon. In northern Peru, indigenous people held weeks of protests in 2016 over oil spills from a state-owned pipeline built in the 1980s.

Sewerage treatment is also seldom implemented in Peru, and water pollution and algae blooms in rivers are a serious problem. The situation is especially acute around Lima, where certain local beaches are often declared unsafe for swimming. Across the country, trash is dumped in landfills and burned. Because there is very little recycling in Peru, much of the plastic garbage ends up blowing across the land and floating down rivers.

Population growth is also exerting tremendous pressure on Peru's resources, especially in the highlands. Overgrazing and deforestation for firewood have caused the area's thin soils to wash away in many areas. The loss of vegetation combines with heavy rains to cause mudslides, known locally as *huaycos*. A series of floods and mudslides in the Cusco area in January 2010 swept away bridges, roads, and the railroad that leads to Machu Picchu. The weeks of continuous rains also flooded large areas of fields of the Sacred Valley. As a result, 3,000 tourists were stranded for almost a week in Aguas Calientes, the town near Machu Picchu, and were finally evacuated with helicopters. Worse, thousands of farmers lost their crops and homes.

In the Amazon, conflict between the Peruvian government and the Amazon's indigenous peoples reached a boiling point in 2009. Tensions had already been simmering, and occasionally flaring, because of government efforts over the last decade to regulate smalltime gold panning, timber poaching, and illegal hunting in various parts of the Amazon. But a violent protest erupted in Bagua, northeastern Peru, in June 2009 when the Peruvian government suddenly opened up new areas of the Peruvian Amazon to oil and gas developers. The legislative move was made without the input of indigenous communities who reside in the area and was seen as a clumsy effort to comply with a recent free trade agreement with the United States. In the resulting protest, 33 people—both police officers and civilians—were killed and 200 were injured. Shortly

Ecotourism: Leave No Trace

Travelers to Peru can either help or hurt the country's long-term survival depending on how they plan their trip and how they behave. A good ecotourism reference in the United States is **The International Ecotourism Society** (TIES, U.S. tel. 202/789-7279, www.ecotourism.org), which defines ecotourism as "responsible travel to natural areas that conserves the environment and improves the well-being of local people." A handful of Peru's rainforest operators belong to this association. Find out whether the lodge or agency you have chosen lives up to these basic principles set forth by TIES:

· Minimize impact.

· Build environmental and cultural awareness and respect.

· Provide positive experiences for both visitors and hosts.

· Provide direct financial benefits for conservation.

· Provide financial benefits and empowerment for local people.

· Raise sensitivity to host countries' political, environmental, and social climate.

· Support international human rights and labor agreements.

A huge concern in Peru's main trekking areas, such as the Inca Trail and the Cordillera Blanca, is environmental degradation as a result of sloppy camping. A wonderful resource for traveling lightly through wilderness is **Leave No Trace** (www.lnt.org), which has pioneered a set of principles that are slowly being adopted by protected areas around the world. More information on these principles can be found on the LNT web page:

· Plan ahead and prepare.

· Travel and camp on durable surfaces.

· Dispose of waste properly.

· Leave what you find.

· Minimize campfire impacts.

· Respect wildlife.

· Be considerate of others.

Great pains have been made throughout this book to recommend only agencies and lodges that have a solid ethic of ecotourism. But the only way to truly evaluate a company's environmental and cultural practices is by experiencing them firsthand. Your feedback is tremendously valuable to us as we consider which businesses to recommend in the future.

Please send your experiences—both positive and negative—to us at feedback@moon.com (www.moon.com).

after the protests, the Peruvian congress reversed the legislative change. The 2016 documentary *When Two Worlds Collide* tells the story of that conflict.

Natural Protected Areas

As of 2017, there were 77 natural areas protected by the Peruvian government, under the administration of **SERNANP** (Servicio Nacional de Áreas Naturales Protegidas por el Estado), which total almost 17 percent of the country's territory. There are 14 national parks, 3 of which have been classified internationally as Natural World Heritage Sites. These are Huascarán, Manu, and Río Abiseo, a huge swath of remote cloud forest in northern Peru that includes the Chachapoya archaeological site of Gran Pajatén.

Only tourism and scientific research are allowed inside national parks, which are meagerly funded by the government but luckily can count on private donations from international organizations. The other strict categories of protection in Peru are the historic sanctuaries—Machu Picchu and the Inca Trail are classified and protected under this designation—and the natural sanctuaries, such as the mangrove areas in Tumbes.

Other designations include national reserves or *reservas nacionales,* such as Paracas, Titicaca, and Pacaya Samiria, and reserved zones or *zonas reservadas* like the area surrounding the Cordillera Huayhuash or Sierra del Divisor on the Peru-Brazil border. Additionally, there are communal reserves or *reservas comunales* protecting large portions of land where the main Amazon indigenous communities are, and protected forests or *bosques de protección,* among other lesser classifications.

Since 2001, Peru's government has allowed protected areas that are administered privately or through regional, municipal, or community organizations. Currently there are 17 regional conservation areas or *áreas de conservación regional,* such as Tamshiyacu Tahuayo in the rainforest, and 114 private conservation areas or *áreas de conservación privada,* with Chaparrí the first to be created on the northern coast. These areas have proved to be managed more effectively than the state-administered parks and reserves. There is a current tendency of protecting more and more forests and other ecosystems under this new system.

Plants and Animals

Peru is located in the heart of the richest and most diverse region in the world. Few countries can rival Peru's biodiversity, which holds world records for highest diversity of birds (more than 1,800 species), butterflies (more than 3,500), and orchids (3,500). There are at least 6,300 species of endemic plants and animals, along with an estimated 30 million insects.

PLANTS
Desert

Few plants can grow in the bone-dry conditions of Peru's southern and central coast, which is dominated by shifting sand dunes and arid desert. The irrigated valleys, however, are covered in cash crops, including olives, grapes, nuts, and a range of fruits and vegetables. In Peru's northern valleys, the hotter temperatures are ideal for the cultivation of cotton, rice, mangos, limes, and sugarcane.

The coast northeast of Chiclayo is covered by vast tracts of *bosque seco,* a scraggly low-lying forest composed mainly of algaroba (carob), a mesquite-like tree whose sweet pods are the base of the *algarrobina* cocktail. Other trees in these forest include ficus, *zapote,* and *vichayo.*

Even farther north, the climate turns subtropical and occasional patches of palm trees line up near the beaches along with the large **mangrove swamps** north of Tumbes. The swamps are protected as part of the Santuario Nacional Manglares de Tumbes, which includes Peru's only chunk of Pacific tropical forest. There are orchids and gigantic trees such as the ceiba, with its umbrella-shaped crown, and the *pretino,* which drops seed pods the size of basketballs.

Andes

The high grasslands region or **puna** is home to a collection of bizarre plants with endless adaptations for coping with the harsh climate. Many of them have thick, waxy leaves for surviving high levels of ultraviolet radiation and fine insulating hairs in order to cope with frequent frosts. They grow close to the ground for protection from wind and temperature variations. In Peru's north, wet grasslands known as *páramo* stretch along the northwestern edge of the Andes into Ecuador. The *páramo* has a soggy, springy feeling underfoot and serves as a sponge to absorb, and slowly release, the tremendous amounts of rain that fall in the area.

Peru's most famous highland plant, the *Puya raimondii* grows in the puna, from Huaraz all the way south to Bolivia. The rosette of spiky, waxy leaves grows to three meters in diameter and looks like a giant agave, even though the plant is in the bromeliad family along with the pineapple. The *Puya* lives for a century and, before it dies, sends a giant spike three stories into the air that eventually erupts into 20,000 blooms. Once pollinated, the plant's towering spike allows it to broadcast its seeds widely in the wind.

The spiky tussocks of grass known as *ichu* are the most ubiquitous feature of Peru's high plains. Highlanders use this hardy grass to thatch their roofs, start their fires, and feed their llamas and alpacas. Cattle, which were imported from Europe in the 16th century by the Spanish, are unable to digest it. Cows can only eat the *ichu* when it sprouts anew as a tender green shoot. Hence, highlanders burn large tracts of hillside every year to make *ichu* palatable for cows.

The high deserts of southern Peru, such as those on the way to the Colca Canyon, are so dry that not even *ichu* can survive. Instead, green blob-like plants called *yareta* spread along the rocky, lunar surface. This plant's waxy surface and tightly bunched leaves allow it to trap condensation and survive freezing temperatures. It is currently considered an endangered species.

A few trees can be found in Peru's montane valleys. **Eucalyptus,** which was imported to Peru from New Zealand, is used widely by highlanders for firewood and ceiling beams. Eucalyptus is useful but also highly invasive; its rapid spread has greatly reduced the numbers of Peru's most famous highland tree, **queñual,** currently also endangered. This scraggly, high-altitude, onion skin-like tree can still be seen in abundance, however, in the Parque Nacional Huascarán.

Amazon

The cloud forests that blanket the eastern escarpments of the Andes are a remarkable tumble of gnarled trees that cling to the steep, rocky soil. These trees have evolved to trap the thick blankets of mist that form when humid rainforest air cools as it rises over the Andes. Aerial plants, such as ferns, mosses, orchids, cacti, and bromeliads, cover the trees and are collectively known as **epiphytes.** Because they have no roots to the soil, they must gather all of their water and nutrients from the passing mist. This forest has a dark, primeval feel and is seen in the surrounding areas of Moyobamba and Tarapoto, Machu Picchu, throughout the Chachapoya region, and on the road to Parque Nacional Manu. The Peruvians somewhat poetically call cloud forest the *ceja de selva* or the "eyebrow of the rainforest."

The forest takes on a whole different feel farther downhill in the lowland tropical rainforest, where steep slopes give way to swampy soil and the rivers become slow and muddy. The trees are huge, often over 60 meters tall, and the understory is dark and curiously free of plants. Huge gray vines, as thick as the human body, descend from the highest branches into the ground. These are the **strangler figs** called *matapalo,* which begin life high in the canopy where birds and bats drop their seeds after gorging on the fig fruit. After dropping their vines to the forest floor, these vines merge together and form a sheath that envelops the tree, slowly choking off its nutrients. When the host tree dies, the parasite strangler fig remains in its place. They are often the largest, noblest trees in the forest, and it is hard to believe they began life as assassins.

Life in the rainforest is a battle for sunlight. This becomes readily apparent to those who climb up to the tree platforms or canopy walkways that have been built in the jungle lodges.

Medicinal Plants of the Amazon

There are very few modern health clinics in Peru's Amazon. Local people are not concerned, since they have relied for centuries on village *curanderos* (healers) and the abundant pharmacy of plants in the rainforest. Most of the medicines are based on the complex chemical defenses that plants produce to defend themselves from insects and other predators. North American and European pharmaceutical companies spend a lot of time and money to meet with *curanderos* and investigate the efficacy of various plants and herbs.

Here are the top 10 medicinal plants you are likely to see in the rainforest.

- *Uña de gato,* or cat's claw, is a hairy vine named for its catlike tentacles. The bark is boiled for tea or soaked in alcohol and then consumed to treat prostate and lung cancer, rheumatism, and arthritis.

- *Jergón sacha,* or fer-de-lance plant, is an understory herb with bark patterns identical to those of the Amazon's poisonous fer-de-lance snake. The plant's root is made into a tea as an effective remedy against this snake's bite. The root can also be applied directly to the wound.

- *Hierba luisa,* or lemongrass, smells like citron and is a prime ingredient in both Inca Kola, the national soft drink, and citronella, the natural insect repellent. When boiled, it makes a stress-reducing tea.

- *Bellaco caspi,* scientific name *Himatanthus sucuuba,* exudes a white latex when its bark is cut. The gooey substance can be used to heal cuts, set broken bones, and even suffocate the botfly larvae that burrow beneath human skin.

- *Ojé* grows 25 meters high at up to 1,000 meters elevation. This tree also exudes white latex, which is used in a variety of medical treatments: toothache, cleaning the digestive system, rheumatism, and snakebites.

- *Pan de árbol,* or breadfruit, is a staple food on Pacific islands and in Southeast Asia. It was imported to Peru in the 19th century. In the Amazon, its leaves are used for cleaning and sterilizing after a woman gives birth.

- *Clavo huasca* is a pungent, clove-scented vine. It is a powerful aphrodisiac and is one of the ingredients used in Siete Raices, a tonic that serves as an energizer, reduces fever, and boosts the immune system.

- *Achiote* is a shrub-like tree with a red, spiky fruit from which the Yagua people extract a crimson dye for painting their bodies and palm-fiber skirts. It is also used to treat dysentery, venereal diseases, hepatitis, and skin rashes.

- *Sangre de grado,* or dragon's blood, is a medium-size tree that exudes a reddish latex used to stop vaginal hemorrhaging during childbirth. It is also used to decrease scarring and wrinkles.

- *Cocona* is a tree that yields a tomato-like fruit that is high in vitamin C and often served as a juice. It is also taken to control nausea and to treat snake or insect bites.

(Information taken from James L. Castner, S. Lee Timme, and James A. Duke, *A Field Guide to Medicinal and Useful Plants of the Upper Amazon,* Gainesville, Florida: Feline Press, 1998.)

Perched high in the canopy are an astounding number of epiphytes, far greater than in the cloud forest. Each of these plants has made adaptations to deal with the intense sunlight and evaporative breezes of the upper canopy. **Tank bromeliads** have long leaves that work as troughs to collect rain, while the orchids store water in their bulbous stems. All the plants, especially the cacti, have tough, waxy skins to retain moisture. These epiphytes are here not only for the sunlight, but also for the breezes that help disperse seeds and the vast

The Sustainable Brazil Nut

Despite the severe depredation generated by the informal gold mining and the unorganized timber industry, the Amazon still has a hopeful model for rainforest development.

Although it's useful as lumber, the **Brazil nut tree,** locally known as *castaña,* is often the largest tree left standing in the forest because its nuts are more valuable than its wood. The tree's round seedpods look like the pod inside a coconut and fall to the ground in December and January. Each pod contains between 12 and 24 Brazil nuts, and a single tree can produce as many as 500 kilograms in a year. The nuts are sold as food or for a burgeoning overseas organic products industry that uses its oil in lip balms and skin lotions.

The tough shells prevent birds from eating the seeds before they ripen and are used by local people as candle holders. Only one species of insect—the bee—is physiologically able to pollinate the Brazil nut tree's flowers. Once pollinated, the tree relies on only one animal for the dispersal of its seeds: the brown agouti, a rabbit-size rainforest rodent who collects the seeds and buries them in the ground for later eating. Luckily for the tree, the agouti either forgets where the hole is or returns after the seeds have already germinated. People have often tried to bury and germinate Brazil nut seeds, without success. Apparently the mild-mannered agouti has a few well-kept gardening secrets.

The base of a Brazil nut tree is also a good place to find the deadly bushmaster snake, which is perfectly camouflaged among the leaves as it waits for the agouti. For this reason, Brazil nut workers use a forked pole to pick up Brazil nut seeds off the ground. Otherwise, just imagine.

number of bats, birds, and insects that forage in the canopy and serve as pollinators.

The fight for sunlight is evident on the forest floor when a large tree falls over, dragging its vines and smaller trees along with it. The sun-filled clearings created by falling trees are called "light gaps" and form fascinating mini ecosystems for fast-growing pioneer trees, such as the *cecropia.* Its thin gray trunk, often marked with white rings, twists in odd shapes to catch the sunlight with its huge palm-shaped leaves. These clearings are wonderful places to examine the epiphytes, insect nests, and other forms of canopy life.

Large rainforest trees include mahogany (*caoba*), cedar (*cedro*), and *tornillo,* a highly valuable wood for making furniture that can now be found only in Peru's stands of primary forest. You might also see the **Brazil nut tree,** which drops round pods containing seeds used to make organic oils and lip balms. There is also the **kapok,** also known as ceiba, which is readily identifiable by its huge red seed pods hanging from branches. When these pods open, they release seeds that are borne by the wind on cotton-like tufts, which

Amazon residents use for making hunting darts. At the ground level, the kapok stands out for its huge buttress roots, which fan out and are often wider than the tree itself.

If you scuff the ground with your foot you will understand the reason for the roots. Rainforest soil is amazingly poor because all the minerals are either sucked up by the voracious competition of plantlife or leached away by the constant rains. As a result, even the roots of the largest trees run along the surface in a desperate search for minerals. Because rainforest trees lack the deep taproots of temperate-forest trees, they need buttress roots to help stay upright, especially during the violent windstorms that snap the tops of many trees right off.

Another surprising difference between temperate forests and rainforests is the age of the trees. In the United States, old-growth forests take centuries to develop. But rainforests are much more dynamic—the average life of a tree here is a mere 80 to 135 years.

For people used to the pines and oaks of temperate forests, the sheer variety of trees in the rainforest can be overwhelming. There are more than 1,000 different tree species in Peru's Amazon, and even finding the same tree twice can be a challenge. There is no complete guide to rainforest trees; even if one existed, it would be the size of a telephone book.

Instead of trying to keep a mental catalog of the trees you see, it makes more sense to try to understand how different trees use common defenses to survive. The thorns and spikes on many rainforest trees serve as a protection against animals, while peeling bark prevents vines from climbing the trunk. Many leaves have thin hairs or contain a complex array of toxins that serve as protection from the predation of caterpillars and insects. Other trees have developed symbiotic relationships to survive. The *palo santo* (holy tree), for instance, has hollow chambers and a gooey nectar that provide food and lodging to fire ants. These ants are totally dependent on the tree for survival and will chase off any predator that would otherwise feast on the tree.

ANIMALS
The Coast
The rich oceans off Peru's coast support a wide variety of marine mammals and seabirds. Sea lions, seals, and the endangered **Humboldt penguin** can be observed at the **Reserva Nacional de Paracas** and the new **Reserva Nacional de las Islas, Islotes y Puntas Guaneras** (this reserve, created in 2010, protects all islands and guano points along the Peruvian coast). Hundreds of thousands of birds also roost on these protected islands, which are covered in thick layers of guano. There are more than 200 bird species at Paracas, including a variety of gulls, pelicans, boobies, cormorants, frigate birds, hawks, ospreys, and vultures. You are likely to see a pink Chilean flamingo or even an Andean condor.

The dry forests farther north begin to support a variety of mammals, such as gray and red deer, anteaters, foxes, pumas, and the endangered *oso de anteojos* (spectacled bear or Andean bear). A few dozen unique forest birds also live here, along with a range of iguanas, snakes, and lizards. Peru's small chunk of Pacific coastal forest near the border with Ecuador is home to the only crocodile in Latin America, the endangered **Tumbes crocodile.**

Andes
The most ubiquitous animals of Peru's Andes are the four species of native **camelids** that eat the high-altitude *ichu* grasses and produce wooly coats as protection from the rain and cold. Two of these, the llama and alpaca, were domesticated thousands of years ago by Peru's highlanders, who tie bright tassels of yarn onto the animals' ears. Herds of the much smaller and finely haired vicuña can be seen in the sparse grasslands above Ayacucho, Arequipa, and Cusco. The fourth camelid, the guanaco, is harder to spot because its main range lies south in Chile and Argentina.

Other animals in the Peruvian Andes include white-tailed deer, foxes, and the puma. The only animal you are likely to see, however, is the viscacha, which looks like a strange mix between a rabbit and a squirrel.

There is a huge range of **birds** in the Andes, the most famous of which is the **Andean condor,** the world's largest flying bird. Its range extends from the high rainforest, including Machu Picchu, all the way to the coast. It can easily be seen in Colca Canyon, along with a variety of other raptors, including the impressive mountain caracara, which has a black body, red face, and brilliant yellow feet. There are also falcons, which have a russet belly and can often be seen hovering over grasslands in search of mice or birds.

A variety of water birds can be seen at Lake Titicaca and in the cold, black lakes of the Andean puna. The Andean grasslands are one of the habitats for the Andean goose, a huge, rotund bird with a white belly and black back, and a variety of shimmering ducks, including the puna teal and crested duck. There are even flamingos and a few wading birds, such as the red-billed puna ibis. One of the most interesting birds, which can be seen in the river near Machu Picchu and in Colca Canyon, is

The Amazing Leaf-Cutter Ant

They crawl, fly, hop, and sting. There is no way to avoid contact with tens of thousands of insect species in the Amazon, which are, so to speak, the real dominators of the rainforest.

The most visible of these is the leaf-cutter ant, which clears neat paths from its colony to the areas where it collects its leaves. These paths are often littered with discarded leaf fragments and can surprisingly stretch a kilometer or more. There are many species of leaf cutters, but all make underground colonies that can reach the size of a living room. The red-colored colonies are made from earth, while black ones are made from partially chewed twig fragments.

Anywhere from 1 million to 2.5 million workers live inside a leaf-cutter colony, divided into five castes:

· The queen, or egg-layer

· Male reproducers, who fertilize the queen

· Leaf-cutters, who chew and transport the leaves

· Leaf travelers, who remove the waxy cuticle from the leaf and protect the treasure from parasitic Phoridae flies

· Cultivators, who tend and fertilize a fungus that grows on the leaves

Biologists believe these leaf-cutters are responsible for nearly half of all herbivore consumption in the neotropical region, but the ants do not actually eat the leaves. Instead they pile them up inside their colony to cultivate a fungus, which occurs only in leaf-cutting colonies and is the ants' only food source. The ant and fungus rely on each other for survival, an example of how specific and complex rainforest symbiosis can be.

BACKGROUND
PLANTS AND ANIMALS

the **torrent duck.** This amazing swimmer floats freely down white water that stymies even experienced rafters.

Amazon

The Amazon is a zoo without bars. Exotic birds flit through the air, turtles line up on riverside logs to sunbathe, and pig-size aquatic rodents called capybaras submerge like submarines under the water's surface. Sloths clamber slowly through the trees along with noisy troops of monkeys. Just in the low rainforest around Puerto Maldonado and Parque Nacional Manu, there are more than 600 bird species, 1,300 species of butterflies, an estimated 30 million insect species, and a range of animals including tapirs, armadillos, anteaters, caimans, otters, anaconda snakes, and the sovereign of all, the jaguar. Farther north in the Iquitos basin is a slightly different range of birds and animals, including the pink river dolphin and the manatee.

The Amazon's lush greenery can make these animals hard to spot. To see much of anything, you need a good pair of binoculars and an experienced guide to spot them for you. As a result, the longer you stay in the rainforest and the farther you are from the cities, the more you will see.

A walk in the rainforest, however, will nearly always produce sightings of **monkeys.** Among the most common are troops of large playful squirrel monkeys, which shake the branches in search of sugary fruit. Accompanying them are black-fronted nunbirds, which eat the katydids that jump away from the commotion. You will also hear (and hopefully see) red howler monkeys and observe the pygmy marmoset, the smallest monkey on earth.

There are various snakes, which is the reason rainforest guides usually walk in front of visitors to inspect or "clean" the path. There are also plenty of iridescent **frogs,** some of which have elaborate chemical defenses on their skin that Amazon residents use for their poison blow-darts. Colorful **butterflies** flit through the forest, and if you're sweating, one might land on your shirt to eat your salt. Most of all you will see **insects,** including long lines of leaf-cutter ants carrying bits of everything on their backs toward their huge ground nests. You may not see them but you will hear thousands of cicadas, which make a deafening chorus by vibrating a plate under their wings.

All Amazon jungle lodges offer an early-morning boat cruise to see **birds.** The ringed kingfisher darts above the river with its light blue body, russet belly, and white-ringed neck. Mealy, orange-winged, and festive parrots squawk noisily through the air. You may see the Cuvier's toucan, which sometimes uses its huge tricolored beak for eating eggs and baby chicks from the nests of other birds. Smaller, colorful birds such as flycatchers, cotingas, and tanagers can often be observed perched on branches. Raptors, such as the slate-colored hawk and yellow-headed caracara, perch

on dead branches above the river. Rustling through lakeside bushes is the hoatzin, a stinky chicken-like bird with a spiky crest and a grunting call. If you're lucky, you might see an Amazonian umbrella bird, nicknamed "the Elvis bird" for a crown of feathers that flops over its head, resembling the King himself.

Macaw clay licks are one of the rainforest's more extraordinary sights. They are found throughout the Amazon basin, generally on riverbanks where minerals are highly concentrated. Assorted parrots, parakeets, and macaws congregate at them every morning to eat the mineral-rich mud. The largest (and smartest) birds are the **macaws,** with the more common species being the chestnut-fronted, the scarlet, and the blue-and-green. Dozens of these birds can be seen at the world's largest clay lick, near the Tambopata Research Center. There are also salt licks that attract mammals, including one at the Manu Wildlife Center that attracts reliable nighttime views of tapirs and brocket deer.

History

Apart from natural diversity, Peru also is the cradle of human civilization in the ancient Americas. Its cultural groups were far more diverse, for example, than the Mesoamerican cultures that spread through present-day Central America and Mexico.

The first Peruvian states were worshipping at stepped adobe platforms on the coast 5,000 years ago, before the Egyptians were building their pyramids at Giza. And as the Roman empire spread across modern-day Europe, Peru's first empire states were moving like wildfire across the Andes. The **Chavín** and **Tiahuanaco** cultures established patterns of religion, commerce, and architecture that remain alive today among Peru's Quechua-speaking highlanders.

Western notions of conquest and military-backed empires do not fit easily over Peruvian history. Peru's three large empires—the

Chavín, the Huari, and the Inca—spread across Peru in three stages that historians call "horizons." Like the Aztec empire in Mesoamerica, these cultures spread more through commerce and cultural exchange than through military force. Even the Inca, who were capable of raising vast armies, preferred to subdue neighbors through gifts and offers of public works projects. The Inca used military force only when peaceful solutions had been exhausted.

Following the arrival of Europeans in the New World, Peru's history follows the same basic stages as other areas of North and South America. There was first a colonial period, which lasted longer and ended later than in the United States; a war of independence; and then a period of rapid nation building and industrialization in the 19th and 20th centuries.

ORIGINS OF HUMAN CIVILIZATION

Human life in Peru, indeed all over the Americas, is a relatively recent event made possible when the last ice age allowed human settlers to cross the Bering land bridge that connected present-day Russia to Alaska between 20,000 and 40,000 years ago. Another theory suggests that early migration may also have been possible from the Polynesian Islands in the South Pacific. Either way, the first evidence of human civilization in Peru has been dated to as early as 20,000 BC at Pikimachay Cave outside Ayacucho, where arrowheads, animal skeletons, and other remains were found.

These first human residents began domesticating Andean camelids and *cuys* (guinea pigs) as early as 7000 BC, establishing small hunter-gatherer villages 1,000 years later. Nomadic people followed animal migration patterns, exchanging mountain winter for the warmer coastal summers. Potatoes were first cultivated around 6000 BC in the Lake Titicaca region. Around 2900 BC, humans began to plant crops such as manioc, quinoa, lima beans, and cotton at Caral, establishing Peru's long-standing agricultural tradition. Caral, some 200 kilometers north of Lima, had an estimated population of about 3,000. It is Peru's oldest known city and lays claim to the title of oldest city in the Americas.

CHAVÍN, THE UNIFIER

Considered the South American counterpart of China's Shang or Mesopotamia's Sumerian civilizations, Chavín flourished around 900 BC during the First or Early Horizon era (1000 BC-AD 200). Chavín managed to unite coastal, highland, and eastern lowland societies with its powerful religious ideology.

The Chavín built an elaborate stone temple at Chavín de Huántar, southeast of Huaraz, decorating it with finely carved stone sculptures and elaborate iconography. These figures depict their worship of a supreme feline deity—the jaguar—as well as other creatures such as snakes, caimans, and natural spirits.

Despite being known for its brilliant and innovative metallurgists, builders, and strategists, Chavín began to fade around 300 BC. Its influence, however, would resonate through Peru's civilizations for the next 1,000 years.

THE REGIONAL DEVELOPMENT

A variety of cultural groups sprang up to take the place of the Chavín. On the north coast, the Moche (220 BC-AD 600) began building the Huaca de la Luna, a stepped adobe pyramid south of present-day Trujillo. Highly militaristic and religious, the Moche spread throughout Peru's northern coast. They are best known for finely crafted metallurgy and ceramics.

On the south coast, the Nasca (100 BC-AD 700) began making elegant weavings from cotton and camelid fiber that are considered today the most advanced textiles produced in pre-Columbian America. Their complex cosmography is evident in the Nasca Lines, giant etchings in the desert floor. Around AD 100 the Nasca also built Cahuachi, a large temple complex that was probably a pilgrimage site.

In the southern Andean region, the Tiahuanaco (AD 200-1000) built an elaborate stone urban and ceremonial center on the southern shores of Lake Titicaca. They also developed a system of raised-bed farming that allowed them to cultivate crops despite the area's freezing temperatures.

The Huari culture (AD 600-1100) was the first in South America to establish a true empire. They also built the first well-populated cities, like their capital, Huari, north of Ayacucho. Archaeologists believe 70,000 people lived here comfortably.

Around AD 650 the Huari spread south toward the Tihuanaco culture near Lake Titicaca and Cusco, where they built the huge walled city of Pikillacta. The city spreads across 47 hectares of rolling grasslands and contains a maze of walled stone enclosures and elaborate stone aqueducts.

By the time the empire faded around AD 900, the Huari had left an indelible pattern of organization over Peru that would be repeated in larger scale by the Inca.

THE KINGDOMS OF THE LATE HORIZON

Once again, as happened after the Chavín culture, Peru splintered into various independent kingdoms after the fall of the Huari. The most important of these were spread along the coast and included the Chimú, Sicán, and Ica-Chincha cultures.

The **Chimú** built their mud city, Chan Chan, north of Trujillo and a short distance from the adobe stepped platforms built earlier by the Moche. Chan Chan is the largest city ever built by Peru's pre-Hispanic cultures, and its walled plazas, passageways, temples, and gardens spread over nearly 20 square kilometers. Over time, the kingdom would spread along the coast of Peru from Chancay, a valley north of Lima, to the present-day border with Ecuador.

As the Chimú were flourishing, other descendants of the Moche culture known as the **Sicán** were building adobe pyramids at Batán Grande, farther north near Chiclayo. Discoveries of royal Sicán tombs there in 1991 revealed a wealth of gold masks, scepters, and ceremonial knives. After a devastating El Niño flood destroyed the center, the Sicán began building even larger pyramids a bit farther north at Túcume. By 1350, the Sicán culture was conquered by the Chimú.

Peru's south coast was dominated by the **Ica-Chincha** kingdom, which spread along Peru's southern desert valleys. This culture developed elaborate aqueducts for bringing water from the mountains under the desert floor.

During this time, other cultures flourished throughout the highlands. The largest of these was the **Chachapoya,** a mysterious federation of city-states that spread across the cloud forests of northeastern Peru. The Chachapoya's most celebrated city is Kuélap, a stone citadel perched atop a sheer limestone bluff.

Other cultures included the **Caxamarca** near present-day Cajamarca, the **Huanca** and **Chancas** in the central highlands, and the **Colla** and **Lupaca** near Lake Titicaca. One of these groups, almost too small to mention, was a diminutive tribe of highlanders in the Cusco area known as the **Inca.**

THE INCA EMPIRE

The Inca empire (referred to in Quechua as the Tahuantinsuyo, or "Four Corners") and its origins are obscured by myth. Historians believe that Manco Cápac, the first Inca leader, began his rule around AD 1200. For more than two centuries the Inca developed slowly in the Cusco area, until 1438, when the neighboring Chancas people threatened to overrun their city. Though Inca Viracocha fled the city, his son Inca Yupanqui beat back the Chancas, took over from his disgraced father, and changed his name to Pachacútec, the "Shaker of the Earth." He launched the meteoric rise of the Inca empire, which within a century would stretch for more than 4,000 kilometers from southern Chile to northern Ecuador and include huge chunks of what is now Bolivia and Argentina as well. Pachacútec was also responsible for much of the Inca's monumental architecture, including the fortress of Sacsayhuamán and, in the Sacred Valley, Pisac and Ollantaytambo. Historians also believe he built Machu Picchu, which may have been a *llacta* (administrative center).

Though the Inca are known for their fine stonework, their greatest accomplishment was the organization of their empire. Cusco was actually smaller than other capitals of pre-Hispanic Peru, but the Inca imperial city was at the center of a paved road network that led throughout the empire.

The Inca offered rich economic and cultural benefits to neighboring cultures that submitted peacefully to their rule. When the Ica and Chincha lordships were integrated into the empire, the Inca helped build a vast aqueduct near present-day Chincha that is still used. Though the Inca changed the names of places they conquered and encouraged the spread of their religion and language, they accepted a wide degree of cultural diversity. Spanish chroniclers such as Pedro Cieza de León were impressed with the tremendous variety of languages and native dress in Cusco at the time of the conquest. The Inca also behaved brutally to those who opposed them. After waging a long war against the Chachapoya, the Inca deported half the population to other parts of the empire as part of the forced-labor scheme.

Pachacútec's son and grandson, Túpac Yupanqui and Huayna Cápac, spent most of their lives abroad, extending the Inca empire to its farthest limits. Huayna Cápac, born in Tumipampa (present-day Cuenca, Ecuador) died in 1527 during a smallpox epidemic that devastated Peru's population and was probably introduced by the Spaniards, who had set foot on the northernmost fringe of the Inca empire during a preliminary trip in 1526. Huayna Cápac's sudden death led to a devastating civil war between his two sons, Huáscar and Atahualpa, which had just ended when the Spaniards began their march from Tumbes in 1532.

SPANISH CONQUEST

Francisco Pizarro and his men rode through desert and into the Andes and found Atahualpa and an army of 80,000 Inca soldiers at Cajamarca. Atahualpa had just crushed the forces of his half-brother Huáscar and was returning, jubilant and victorious, to his home city of Quito.

The Spaniards invited Atahualpa to a meeting the next day in Cajamarca's square and planned a bold ambush. Firing their harquebuses and charging with their horses and lances, the Spaniards sparked a massive panic, killed at least 7,000 Inca soldiers, and took Atahualpa hostage. The Inca offered to pay a ransom that, when melted down six months later, amounted to an astounding 6,100 kilograms of 22-karat gold and 11,820 kilograms of good silver. The Spaniards executed Atahualpa anyway.

The Spaniards achieved their successes over far superior Inca forces not only because of their guns, dynamite, steel, and horses but also because Pizarro understood how to play Inca politics. After Atahualpa's death, the Spaniards befriended Manco Inca, another son of Huayna Cápac, and declared him the new leader of the Inca empire. Manco Inca did not remain a docile puppet for long, however, after the Spaniards sacked Cusco for all of its gold and raped the wives of Inca nobles. After the gold was gone, Francisco Pizarro left Cusco and headed for the coast to found Lima, which would soon become the capital of the newly declared Spanish Viceroyalty of Peru.

In 1536, Manco Inca launched a rebellion and laid siege to Cusco with an army of an estimated 100,000 soldiers. Against overwhelming odds, the Spaniards routed the Inca from their fortress of Sacsayhuamán during a week of constant fighting. Manco Inca repelled an army of Spaniards at Ollantaytambo in the Sacred Valley before retreating to the rainforest of Vilcabamba. For the next 35 years, the Inca would use this rainforest stronghold to continue their resistance against the Spaniards until the last Inca leader, Túpac Amaru, was captured and executed in 1572.

Just after the Inca rebellion, the Spaniards themselves erupted into civil war after differences arose between Francisco Pizarro and his junior partner, Diego de Almagro. After a series of bloody clashes, Pizarro's forces won out over the almagrista faction in 1538, and Pizarro shocked the king in Spain by executing Almagro. A few years later, Pizarro himself was murdered by a group of almagristas that included Almagro's son.

THREE CENTURIES OF VICEROYALTY

Cusco became a center of religious art during the viceroyalty but otherwise fell out of the spotlight after the conquest as the Spaniards turned their attention to mines. In a cynical use of Inca tradition for Spanish ends, Viceroy Francisco de Toledo in 1574 legalized the Inca's old labor scheme of mita in order to force huge numbers of the indigenous people to work at the Potosí silver mine, in present-day Bolivia, and the Santa Bárbara mercury mine near Huancavelica. Far from home, thousands of these workers perished while working in virtual slavery at these mines.

Indigenous people in other parts of Peru were not being treated much better. Some were forced to relocate to *reducciones* or new settlements that allowed the Spaniards to better tax them and convert them to Christianity. Rich farmland was divided into *encomiendas*, and all the indigenous people living on it became slaves to the Spanish owner, known as the *encomendero*. Other times they were herded into sweatshops (*obrajes*), where they made textiles and other objects for export under prisonlike conditions.

Given the abuse, it is not surprising that an uprising spread across Peru in the late 18th century. The leader of the 1780-1781 revolt was Túpac Amaru II, who claimed to be a direct descendant of the last Inca, Túpac Amaru. After a year-long rebellion, the Spaniards finished off Túpac Amaru II as they had his ancestor two centuries before: He was garroted in Cusco's main square, and then his body was ripped apart by teams of horses pulling in opposite directions.

INDEPENDENCE

After nearly three centuries of being administered from Spain, the locally born people of the Peruvian viceroyalty began to itch for independence. News of the American Revolution in 1776 and the French Revolution in 1789 filtered to Peru and encouraged a longing for freedom.

The descendants of Europeans born in Peru, known as *criollos*, were increasingly resentful of the privileges according to Spaniards, or *españoles*, who held all the powerful positions in the viceroyalty. Colonial society was classified into a hierarchy that attempted to make sense of, and control, the mixing among races in colonial Peru. The main categories included *mestizo* (European-indigenous), *mulato* (European-African), *negro* (African), *zambo* (indigenous-African), and *indio* (indigenous). Despite the apparent rigidity, recent scholarly work has revealed that racial lines in the viceroyalty were surprisingly fluid and had more to do with wealth than skin color. Wealthy *mestizos* were usually considered *criollos*, for instance.

When Napoleon forced Spain's King Charles IV to abdicate in 1808, independence movements erupted across South America. By 1820, the last bastion of Spanish control was Peru, which for centuries had served as the main Spanish port and administrative center for South America. After liberating Chile, Argentine general José de San Martín routed the royalist forces from Lima in 1821 and proclaimed the symbolic independence of Peru. But he ceded control over the independence struggle to Venezuelan general Simón Bolívar, whose troops won two separate battles in Peru's central highlands in 1824 against the last strongholds of Spanish forces.

Bolívar envisioned a grand union of South American states known as Gran Colombia, which was modeled on the United States. After serving as Peru's first president for two years, he returned to Bogotá, Colombia, in a last-ditch attempt to hold the federation together. Bolívar's scheme fell apart as the former colonies bickered among themselves, and Peru plunged into a half century of chaos. During the four decades following Bolívar's departure, more than 35 presidents came and went.

Despite the chaos, Peru's rising class of merchants found new opportunities for making money besides mining. The biggest business came from bird excrement, or guano, which covered the islands off Peru's coast and was used as an effective fertilizer.

Despite the abundance of natural resources, Peru was devastated by the War of the Pacific against Chile (1879-1883), when Chilean armies sacked most of Peru's major cities. Peru was forced to cede an entire southern province to Chile—Tarapacá—which contained valuable fields of nitrate, used to make fertilizer. After the war, Peru plunged into bankruptcy and had to negotiate with its British creditors, who agreed to forgive the debt in exchange for 200 million tons of guano and a 66-year concession over the country's railroads. The British-owned Peruvian Corporation was set up in Arequipa in 1890 and built the current railroads that lead to Arequipa and Cusco.

THE 20TH CENTURY

As foreign investors increased their grip over Peru's main industries, worker dissent began to simmer following the Russian Revolution. In 1924, exiled political leader Víctor Raúl Haya de la Torre founded the **Alianza Popular Revolucionaria Americana (APRA)**, a populist workers' party that still exerts tremendous influence over Peruvian politics. When Haya lost the 1931 elections, his supporters accused the government of fraud and attacked a military outpost in Trujillo, killing 10 soldiers. In response, the Peruvian military trucked an estimated 1,000 APRA supporters out to the sands of Chan Chan and executed them by mass firing squads.

Peru's economic development in the mid-20th century was hampered by the hacienda system of land ownership inherited from the viceroyalty. The independence movement had passed leadership to the *criollos*, but otherwise Peru's economic structure remained the same—a minority of Peruvians of direct European descent still controlled the bulk of Peru's land and wealth. As Peru moved from an agricultural economy to an industrial one, country folk flocked to Lima in search of a better life and built sprawling shantytowns, around the city. Pressure for land reform began to grow.

Fernando Belaúnde, architect and politician, was president of Peru during the 1960s and instituted a few moderate reforms, but he was overthrown in 1968 by General Juan Velasco, who, despite being a military man, launched a series of radical left-wing reforms that stunned Peru's white elite and transformed the Peruvian economy. He expropriated nearly all of Peru's haciendas and transferred the land to newly formed worker cooperatives. Velasco kicked out foreign investors and nationalized their fish-meal factories, banks, oil companies, and mines. He introduced food subsidies for urban slum dwellers and, in a gesture of recognition to Peru's indigenous population, made Quechua the official second language of Peru.

Velasco's restructuring was so rapid and ill-planned that nearly all of Peru's major industries plunged to new lows, and the country entered a severe economic crisis. Velasco was overthrown in 1975; some historians claim the CIA was behind the coup. His successor, pro-U.S. military leader Francisco Morales Bermúdez, attempted to control the economic chaos. Amid widespread strikes in the late 1970s, APRA politician Haya de la Torre headed a constituent assembly that finally secured full suffrage for all Peruvian citizens and the return to democracy.

TWENTY YEARS OF POLITICAL VIOLENCE

In 1980, Peru's first full democratic election in 12 years coincided with the first actions of **Sendero Luminoso** (Shining Path), a terrorist group based on Maoist ideology that rose out of the country's economic chaos and social inequity. Shining Path rose alongside the much smaller **Movimiento Revolucionario Túpac Amaru (MRTA)**. Both organizations terrorized Peru's countryside over the next two decades and began receiving significant financial support from the cocaine business, which had just begun to grow rapidly in the upper Huallaga Valley.

Between 1980 and 2000, Andean villagers were frequently caught in the crossfire between these terrorist organizations and the Peruvian army. The Shining Path would force the villagers to give them food or supply information, and the army in retaliation would massacre the whole village, or vice versa. The worst massacres of the conflict occurred between 1983 and 1984, the same years that Latin American economies collapsed under a debt crisis and that Peru's north was devastated by El Niño rains.

The APRA candidate, Alan García, won the 1985 elections at age 35 because he offered a hopeful future. He promptly shocked the international finance community by announcing that Peru would only be making a small portion of its international debt payments. García's announcement sparked a two-year spending spree followed by Peru's worst economic collapse ever, with hyperinflation so extreme that restaurants were forced to increase their menu prices three times each day. Peru's struggling middle class saw their savings disappear overnight.

The disastrous economic policies of García's administration only added fuel to the guerrillas' cause. The government unsuccessfully sought a military solution to the growing terrorism, allegedly committing widespread human rights violations. The most important cases include the Accomarca massacre (1985), where 47 peasants were executed by the Peruvian armed forces; the Cayara massacre (1988), in which some 30 were killed and dozens disappeared; and the summary execution of around 200 inmates during prison riots in 1986. An estimated 1,600 forced disappearances took place during García's presidency. In 2003 the Truth and Reconciliation Commission reported that more than 70,000 people were killed during the terrorism years, and 75 percent of them were Quechua highlanders. Half were killed by Shining Path, a third by government police and armed forces, and the rest by smaller rebel groups and militias or are so far unattributed.

In the late 1980s, Peruvian novelist Mario Vargas Llosa led a series of middle- and upper-class protests against García's plan to nationalize Peru's banking system. Vargas Llosa appeared likely to win the 1990 election but was defeated by Alberto Fujimori, a low-profile university rector of Japanese descent who appealed to Peru's mestizo and indigenous voters mainly because he was not part of Lima's elitist white society.

THE FUJIMORI REGIME

Soon after winning the elections, Fujimori reversed his campaign promises and implemented an economic austerity program. His plan aimed to stimulate foreign investment by slashing trade tariffs and simplifying taxes. Fujimori also began privatizing the state-owned companies that President Velasco had nationalized in the late 1960s and early 1970s. This program, nicknamed "Fuji-Shock," caused widespread misery among Peru's poor as food prices shot through the roof. Fortunately, the program also sparked an economic recovery. Inflation dropped from 7,650 percent in 1990 to 139 percent in 1991.

After struggling to convince Peru's congress to pass legislation in 1992, Fujimori strained international relations with the United States and other countries after he dissolved the congress in his famous *autogolpe* or "self-coup." That same year, Peru's level of terror reached a high point when Shining Path detonated two car bombs in the heart of Lima's middle-class Miraflores neighborhood, killing 25 people and injuring more than 250.

That same year, Fujimori's popularity shot through the roof when the Peruvian military captured both Shining Path leader Abimael Guzmán and the main leaders of the MRTA. The economy began to pick up and, by 1993, was one of the fastest-growing in the world. Fujimori launched a new constitution and recovered international support by reopening congress.

Having tackled Peru's twin nightmares of terrorism and inflation, Fujimori easily beat former UN secretary-general Javier Pérez de Cuéllar in the 1995 elections. The following year, 14 MRTA terrorists led by Néstor Cerpa took 800 prominent hostages after storming a cocktail party at Lima's Japanese ambassador's residence. After releasing most of the hostages, the terrorists held 72 prisoners and maintained a tense standoff with the military for four months, until April 1997. As the situation grew desperate, Fujimori authorized Peruvian commandos to tunnel under the embassy and take it by surprise. The operation was an amazing success. One hostage died during the operation—of a heart attack—and one military commando was killed under fire. Few Peruvians raised objections to the fact that all 14 MRTA members were shot to death—including the ones who had surrendered.

Fujimori ran for a controversial third term in 2000, even though he himself had changed the constitution to allow presidents to run for only one reelection. Once again, Fujimori fell out of favor with the international community when he strong-armed his way into the elections against economist Alejandro Toledo. After alleging vote fraud in the main election, Toledo refused to run in the runoff, and the international community threatened sanctions. Fujimori went ahead with the election anyway and was elected president.

A huge scandal broke in September 2000, when videos were leaked to the media showing Fujimori's head of intelligence, Vladimiro Montesinos, bribing generals, journalists, politicians, and business executives. The resulting investigation uncovered more than US$40 million in bribes.

Fujimori conveniently resigned from the presidency, via fax, while on a state visit to Japan. Back in Peru, an international warrant for his arrest was issued because of his involvement in paramilitary massacres of left-wing political activists in the early 1990s. In 2005, when Fujimori left Japan to return to Peru and launch a campaign for the presidency, he was arrested in his stopover city of Santiago, Chile. He was held for six months in jail on charges of corruption and human rights' violations and was extradited to Peru. At the end of a 15-month trial, in April 2009 Fujimori was sentenced to 25 years in prison for ordering security forces to kill and kidnap civilians.

Montesinos was also arrested in Venezuela after being on the run for eight months and is in a high-security prison near Lima—one he helped design to house Peru's most feared criminals. About US$250 million of his pilfered funds have been recovered from foreign bank accounts. Following Fujimori's departure, congressman Valentín Paniagua became interim president before Alejandro Toledo was elected in 2001.

RETURN TO DEMOCRACY

Toledo's political inexperience and lack of strong leadership caused his popularity to plunge. Toledo did, however, establish a stable and growing economy. In an amazing development that perhaps only South American politics could conjure, Alan García, who presided over disastrous security and economic crises in the 1980s, returned to Peru after years in exile, claimed he'd learned from his mistakes, and won the 2006 election against populist Ollanta Humala, who was inspired if not financially supported by Venezuelan president Hugo Chávez. García's return to the presidency was a result of voting against Ollanta, a turn of events not many Peruvians were happy with. Nevertheless, García's second presidency was quite successful. He forged trade agreements with Brazil and increased foreign investment. Peru's economy boomed, even in the face of the world economic crisis. However, many voters complained that García shifted from his center-left ideological position to a more neoliberal tack.

As García was finishing his second presidency in 2011, Peruvians were faced with another election dilemma between two highly polarizing figures: Humala and Keiko Fujimori, the daughter of Alberto Fujimori. On the one hand, many Peruvians were worried that a Humala administration would mean the nationalization of the economy, like in Venezuela, and an end to Peru's decade-long economic growth. Many others were also terrified that the election of the younger Fujimori would bring about a return to the elder Fujimori era, with rampant corruption, political intimidation, and human rights abuses.

Peruvians decided to go with Humala, who backed off from his original policy platform, called "The Great Transformation," and promised to respect democratic institutions and support economic growth. Over his five-year term, Humala continued the political and economic policies of his predecessors Alan García and Alejandro Toledo. And like Garcia and Toledo, Humala saw his popular support tumble by the end of his term, as Peru's economy slowed and concerns about crime grew.

Pedro Pablo Kuczynski, an Oxford-educated economist and former World Bank official, won Peru's presidential election in 2016, defeating Keiko Fujimori by a very narrow margin. Like Humala five years earlier, Kuczynski got a swell of support from those that opposed Fujimori. Opposition to his opponent, more than support for his candidacy, helped to push him over the edge by a slight margin of 40,000 votes, making it the tightest election in Peruvian history.

Government and Economy

GOVERNMENT

Elected in 2016, President Pedro Pablo Kuczynski has continued support for a market-friendly economy while stressing the need to improve the efficiency of the Peruvian state to expand basic services like running water and electricity to the poor. One of his biggest challenges will be to work with the opposition-controlled Congress to pass legislation. But like Humala, García, and Toledo, Kuczynski is expected to oversee a democratic government in a stable political atmosphere. This is quite a contrast to the authoritarian years of the 1990-2000 Fujimori regime.

Fujimori dissolved Peru's bicameral legislative system during his *autogolpe* in April 1992 and launched a new constitution with a single congress with 120 seats. Fujimori's new constitution allowed the president to run for two consecutive terms, a law that was changed after he resigned. In the current system, the president appoints a council of ministers, which is presided over by the prime minister. Apart from the president, Peruvian voters also elect two vice presidents. Voting is compulsory between the ages of 18 and 70, and those who do not vote can be fined. Members of the military were not allowed to vote in the past, but now they can.

One of the weak points of Peru's democracy is its judicial branch, which is rife with corruption. It is still common to read in the media about scandals involving judges who have been bribed to free prisoners or make a favorable ruling. The country's top courts include a 16-member supreme court and a constitutional tribunal. Each of Peru's regions also has a superior court that serves as a court of appeals for the lower courts. There is a huge backlog of cases in the Peruvian court system, and temporary courts have been set up.

During the Fujimori government, terrorist suspects were tried in secret military courts in order to protect judges from reprisals. Under such a system, many people were sent to jail with unfair trials. Under Toledo's government, some of these suspects received new trials in civilian courts. The judicial branch is also currently prosecuting those accused of corruption under the Fujimori government.

While the extent of corruption under Fujimori was exceptional, it is not unique to his government. High-level members of García's APRA party were caught in an oil-for-cash kickback scheme in 2008, leading to the resignation of the prime minister and the rest of the president's cabinet. A congressional committee uncovered that García's administration provided pardons to hundreds of jailed drug traffickers in exchange for payment. Humala's wife, Nadine Heredia, is being investigated over money laundering accusations. In 2016, Brazilian construction firm Odebrecht acknowledged that it paid at least $29 million in bribes to Peruvian officials to win contracts for infrastructure projects during the administrations of Toledo, García, and Humala. President Kuczynski, who was prime minister under Toledo, has promised to take a harder stance against corruption.

ECONOMY

The investment-oriented reforms of the Fujimori years caused Peru to be one of the fastest-growing economies in the world between 1994 and 1997. Much of this growth was easy, however, because in many cases Peru's factories were simply returning to the level of production they had achieved before the chaotic 1980s.

Peru's stock market plummeted in early 1995 because of the "Tequila Effect" caused by Mexico's Zapatista revolution and the collapse of that country's economy. Peru's economy stagnated between 1998 and 2001 because of a variety of other factors, including the El Niño floods of 1998, global financial turmoil, and the collapse of the Fujimori government in 2001. From 2001 to 2011, Peru's investment-friendly policies made it one of the fastest growing economies in the world.

But in June 2011, Peru's stock market fell 12 percent, its biggest one-day crash ever, after the election of left-winger Ollanta Humala as president. Initial concerns from the business community that Humala would reverse Peru's economic policies proved unfounded. Humala's sudden shift surprised even some of his closest allies, and by the end of 2011 many of those allies had left the administration, resulting in a president with little support by the end of his term five years later.

Kuczynski took over in 2016 as Peru's economy was recovering. With a gross domestic product of about US$200 billion, Peru's key sectors include manufacturing, agriculture, mining, retail services, and banking. Vital among those sectors is mining. Peru is a top global producer of copper, gold, silver, zinc, and lead, which account for about half of its exports. The recent decline in metal prices has hurt the economy. Peru has been able to withstand the slowdown better than other resource-rich countries in Latin America thanks to the start of new copper mines that are boosting production, which helps offset lower metal prices. Foreign investment in mining, oil and gas, and tourism are expected to play an important role in Peru's economy.

People and Culture

Peru's people are as diverse as the country's landscape. Prior to the Spanish conquest, it was only the Inca that united the Andean and coastal regions of Peru under their leadership, and only for a few decades. Before the Inca, Peru was covered by a patchwork of diverse cultures created by the country's extreme geography; coastal valleys were separated by long stretches of barren desert, and canyons and peaks in the high Andes led to a high degree of cultural isolation. The rainforest remained impenetrable, with indigenous communities living in isolation for centuries until Jesuit missionaries set up outposts in the 18th century. At least 65 different ethnic groups live in the Peruvian Amazon today.

Peru's cultural mix arguably began during the Inca empire, when the forced-labor scheme, *mita,* was used to move rebellious groups to other parts of the empire where they would cause less trouble. The Spaniards continued *mita* and moved indigenous peoples long distances to work in different mines. Spanish men quickly took up with local women, and a large mestizo population grew. Enslaved Africans were imported to Peru during the viceroyalty, and large numbers of Asian workers were brought to work in plantations and on the railroad lines from 1850 to 1920. There were also waves of Italian and Palestinian immigrants, and a pocket of German and Austrian colonists established themselves in the rainforest at Oxapampa, in the Chanchamayo area.

As well as immigration from outside Peru, there has been substantial migration within the country from rural to urban areas, especially during the height of

Sacred Leaf, White Gold

Peru is one of the world's biggest producers of cocaine, along with Colombia. Peru's cocaine industry rakes in about US$1 billion per year and employs an estimated 200,000 Peruvians, mainly in remote rainforest areas. In the Apurímac Valley, Peru's top cocaine-producing region, profits from trafficking have supported remnants of the Shining Path, the notorious terrorist group. But despite the unwanted title as a hub of cocaine production, recent UN data on Peru's cocaine industry offers a sliver of good news. In 2015, the area used to cultivate coca leaf—the raw ingredient for cocaine—fell for a fifth consecutive year after previously increasing steadily. Supporting that decline is an increase in eradication of the crop.

The truth is, coca has not always been a curse for Peruvians. The plant has been used for millennia in the Andean world, mainly for its medicinal properties and religious significance. Archaeologists have found supplies of coca leaves in 3,000-year-old mummies. The Moche might have been the first to chew the leaves, a custom spread widely afterward by the Inca, who decided that planting coca should be a state monopoly, limiting the use of it to nobles. During the colonial period, Phillip II of Spain recognized the drug as an essential product for the well-being of the Andean inhabitants but urged missionaries to end its religious use. Viewed as having a divine origin, coca has been an important part of the religious cosmogony in the Andean world since pre-Hispanic times. Coca leaves play a crucial part in shamanic offerings and are read in a form of divination by *curanderos*.

But coca is also used in everyday activities. Men chew leaves as they work in the fields, and women use it to ease the pain of childbirth. When a young man is about to ask a woman to marry him, he first must present a bag of leaves to his future father-in-law. Coca leaves have been used for millennia as a stimulant to overcome fatigue, hunger, and thirst. Once you arrive at Cusco's airport, you will likely be greeted with a hot cup of *mate de coca,* an infusion made from the leaf, to combat altitude sickness (*soroche*).

Shining Path terrorism during the 1980s. Lima has grown into one of South America's biggest cities, with a population of nearly nine million.

DEMOGRAPHICS

Peru's population today is around 30 million and growing about 1.6 percent each year. Nearly half the people, or 45 percent, are indigenous, 37 percent are mestizo, and 15 percent are of European descent. The remaining 3 percent are of African, Japanese, and Chinese descent and also include a tiny pocket of 250,000 Amazon indigenous people divided into 65 ethnic groups. There remains a cultural and economic divide, passed down from colonial times, between the upper class of European descent and the middle and lower classes of mestizos and indigenous people. But Peru's racial dividing lines have, even since colonial times, been based more on economics than on skin color. Marriage certificates from the 18th century, for instance, reveal that affluent mestizos were automatically considered *criollos* because of their wealth. In the same way, a full-blooded indigenous person in today's society goes from being an *indígeno* to a mestizo the moment he or she abandons indigenous dress and puts on Western clothing.

Peru is still a comparatively poor country but has made huge advances, both in the Fujimori years and during the economic boom of the past decade, with drops in illiteracy and infant mortality rates. Poverty remains stubbornly high in rural areas; the highest rates continue to be in the Andes, especially the regions of Apurímac, Ayacucho, and Huancavelica in the south and Cajamarca in the north. Nearly 40 percent of the people live in the informal economy—that is, in isolated country hamlets or disenfranchised city slums, eking out a living outside government taxes and services.

Making and taking cocaine, coca's most popular derived product, today remains a nasty business. Villagers in the impoverished Apurímac Valley and other areas of Peru grow the plant because they can get as much as US$3 per kilo for the leaves, many times more than they would receive for selling coffee, bananas, or other fruit. Cultivating coca takes a lot out of the soil, and fields therefore have to be changed constantly. The Huallaga Valley, once covered in cloud forest, is nearly denuded and covered with a patchwork of eroding fields.

The process of making cocaine is even worse. The leaves must first be crushed underfoot and soaked in water to remove their essence. This water is then mixed with kerosene and other toxic chemicals and stirred until a white substance floats to the top. This substance, known as *pasta básica*, is further refined to make pure cocaine. About 400 kilograms of coca leaves produces one kilo of cocaine. The villagers who help stir the *pasta básica* can readily be identified by their scarred arms, burned pink by the toxic chemicals.

The cocaine industry has also wreaked havoc on Peru's cities. Though cocaine is widely available in Peru, the real problem lies in the shantytowns on the outskirts of Lima. Because cocaine is too expensive, teenagers smoke cheap cigarettes made from *pasta básica*, which is different from crack cocaine but equally powerful, and become addicted immediately.

Experts say that the collapse of the Medellín and Cali cartels in the mid-1990s probably boosted Peru's cocaine business. Unlike Colombia, Peru hasn't received the same type of financial aid for its antidrug plans; while cocaine production has fallen steadily in Colombia thanks to billions of dollars in assistance from the United States, it has risen in Peru.

While the United States and Europe continue to funnel support to Andean countries, the newest player in fighting the global cocaine trade is Brazil, the second-biggest consumer of cocaine after the United States. Brazilian officials are now taking a more active approach with Peru to curb production. Brazilian and Peruvian police regularly cooperate in joint antidrug operations in Peru.

LANGUAGE

Peru's official language is Spanish, though about four million people in Peru's highland population speak Quechua, the language of the Inca, also known as *runa simi*. Among Quechua speakers, there is a huge range of language variations depending where they are located. These mini dialects have grown as a result of the isolating effects of Peru's extreme geography. In the Lake Titicaca area, there is a smaller group of Peruvians who speak Aymara, the language of an ethnic group that spreads into Bolivia. The Amazon is home to 11 percent of Peru's population, divided into 65 ethnic groups and about 14 linguistic families.

RELIGION

The Spanish conquest dotted Peru with magnificent cathedrals, a plethora of churches, and a long-lasting, combative relationship with **Roman Catholicism**. About 80 percent of the current population consider themselves Roman Catholic. Although that figure is far from the actual number of practicing parishioners, it does indicate the connection Peruvians feel toward the religion, more by tradition than by real practice. Festivals like Lima's day of Santa Rosa mean a citywide holiday, and the day of San Blas invites horns and processions in Cusco.

Roman Catholicism, though, is a relatively recent addition to Peru's long list of religions. Peru's first civilization began around 2000 BC, and it, along with the country's other major civilizations, was based on a set of unifying religious beliefs. These beliefs often incorporated **nature worship.** Deities like the sun, the ocean, the mountains, and mother earth appear in the imagery of several successive cultures. Representations of serpents, felines, and birds also make repeated appearances in pre-Hispanic religious iconography. Serpents symbolize the ground, felines the human life, and birds (often in the form of eagles) the air or gods. In these pre-Hispanic cultures, there was also a strong tie between religion and hallucinogenic experiences, which were usually performed for their curative properties.

As cultures rose and fell, and even when the Spanish conquered the Inca empire, Peru's religions tended to adapt, fluctuate, and blend. The Inca were known for allowing their conquered cultures to continue their own religious practices as long as they also followed Inca religion. When the Spanish arrived and imposed Roman Catholicism, the Inca quietly integrated their imagery. A grand Last Supper painting in Cusco's cathedral shows Jesus eating a guinea pig.

Nearly 500 years after the Spanish conquest, this fusion of religious beliefs continues to define Peru's spiritual and religious customs, and the subject is a draw for many tourists. In areas like Cusco and Lake Titicaca, the traditional mountain cultures continue to use **shamans** to bless their homes and purify their spirits. In turn, travelers contract with shamans to perform offering or cleansing ceremonies. The Sacred Valley is known for its **energy centers,** and people come from around the world to meditate there. In the rainforest, use of hallucinogenic ayahuasca is an essential part of sacred ceremonies.

Peru is also gaining followers of newer religions. **Protestant groups, Jehovah's Witnesses, Mormons,** and **Adventist groups** have started small but vigilant communities throughout the country. Above all, Peru is a profoundly religious country, and outright atheism is relatively rare and generally frowned upon.

FOOD

One thing Peruvians are undeniably proud of is their food. Peru's biodiversity provides the country with a generous and varied amount of fresh ingredients. These include a range of seafood, sweet corn, *ajíes* (peppers) and tubers—of the 3,000 varieties of potatoes documented in Peru, only 40 are eaten—exotic fruits, succulent river fish, palm hearts, and wild game.

The Spanish conquest of Peru brought together two great culinary cultures of the 16th century: Mediterranean cooking techniques and Andean ingredients. When Pizarro's men landed in Peru, they had their first taste of corn, tomatoes, avocados, potatoes, peanuts, alpaca meat, and blistering *ají* peppers. The Spaniards brought olive oil, lime, and garlic to the table and shortly thereafter created a local supply of lamb, beef, pork, wheat, rice, and sugar.

Things got even more complex with the arrival of Africans and North African Arabs during the viceroyalty, Chinese workers in the mid-19th century, and successive waves of Italian and Japanese immigrants. Such a succulent mix in the pot created a bewildering range of dishes and entire subsets of Peruvian cuisine, such as *chifa,* a mixture of Cantonese and local *criollo* cooking.

Peruvian cuisine is still evolving and is difficult to classify into pat categories. Because Peruvian cooks work only with ingredients at hand, there do tend to be styles of Peruvian cooking separated by geography. Here are some highlights you should not miss.

Peru's coast is known for *comida criolla,* creole cuisine, which is based mainly on a huge range of seafood, including *corvina* (sea bass), *lenguado* (sole), *cangrejo* (crab), *camarones* (freshwater shrimp), *calamar* (squid), *choros* (mussels), and *conchas negras* (black scallops).

One of the more famous dishes is ceviche (*cebiche*): chunks of raw fish marinated in lime juice, spiced with *ají,* and served with sliced red onions, slices of sweet potato, and *choclo* (boiled maize kernels) or *cancha* (roasted maize kernels). A delicious variation of ceviche is *tiradito,* which can be easily explained as a fish carpaccio topped with a *ají* and *rocoto* sauce over the cuts. Fish fillets can be served in a variety of ways, including *sudado* (steamed), *a la chorillana* (basted with onion, tomato, and white wine), or *a lo macho* (fried with yellow peppers or *ají amarillo*).

Other *comida criolla* favorites are *anticuchos,* grilled beef-heart brochettes served with a wonderful assortment of spicy sauces. *Papa rellena* is mashed potato stuffed with meat, vegetables, onions, olives, boiled eggs, and raisins and then fried. *Papa a la huancaína* is a cold appetizer of potatoes smothered in a spicy sauce made from Andean cheese, milk, crackers, and *ají amarillo.* Another popular dish of Asian influence (some say now that it actually has French influence) is the richly-flavored *lomo saltado,* made with strips of beef stir-fried with tomatoes, onions, *ají amarillo,* and fries made of (preferably but not only) yellow potato. This dish can be found, literally, in any corner of Peru.

Sopa a la criolla is a cream soup made up of a mildly spicy concoction of noodles, beef, milk, and peppers with a fried egg on top. If you are in the mood for *chifa,* which you can have anywhere in Peru, try *tallarín saltado,* which is noodles spiced with ginger, soy sauce, green onions, bok choy, and any kind of meat, including beef or chicken or shrimp, depending on what kind you order. To drink, try a pitcher of *chicha morada,* a delicious juice made from purple corn mixed with clove, cinnamon, and lime juice.

Arequipa is well known for its robust, generous, and spicy food. *Chupe de camarones* is a cream-based soup with potatoes, milk, eggs, and lima beans, and laden with succulent sea shrimp. *Rocoto relleno* is another emblematic dish consisting of a bell pepper-like chili, stuffed with meat, chopped onions, raisins, and black olives and then baked with a cheese topping. *Ocopa* is made of a spicy peanut sauce with *huacatay* (black mint) served over slices of boiled potatoes and garnished with eggs and black olives.

In the north, between Trujillo and Piura, some specialties are *seco de cabrito,* which is roasted goat marinated with *chicha de jora,* corn beer, and coriander, served with rice, and *arroz con pato,* which is duck stewed in black beer with spices and coriander, served with green rice.

Peru's Andean cuisine stands out for a range of meats, *choclos,* high-altitude grains such as *kiwicha* and quinoa, and a huge variety of more than 200 edible tubers, including potatoes, freeze-dried *chuño* (actually dehydrated potatoes), and tubers like *olluco* and oca. The high point of mountain cooking is *pachamanca,* which means "earth oven" in Quechua and consists of a variety of meats, tubers, corn, beans, and native herbs roasted underground with red-hot rocks. Andean restaurants often serve *trucha,* which is fried mountain trout, and *cuy* (guinea pig), either roasted (in Cusco), stewed (in Huaraz), or fried (in Arequipa).

Soups and broths are widely consumed in the highlands at any time of the day but especially during the early morning. Lamb, beef, hen, or certain parts of these animals are all good to make a tasty broth. For vegetarians a good option is *sopa de quinua,* made with potatoes and quinoa grains. Lastly, make sure to sample *choclo con queso,* which is an ear of steamed corn with a strip of Andean cheese. Gulp it all down with *chicha de jora,* corn beer that can be *fresco* (fresh) or fermented.

In the Amazon rainforest, you have a whole new type of cuisine to sample. At the top of the list are the roasted fillets of succulent rainforest fish, including *paiche, doncella,* and *dorado. Patarashca* is fish fillets wrapped in banana leaves and seasoned with spices before being baked over coals. There is also *paca* fish steamed inside a bamboo tube. Iquitos is famous for *juanes,* a rice tamale stuffed with spices, chicken, and rice. A common game meat is *majá,* also called *picuro,* which is a medium-size rodent that can be grilled, stewed, or fried.

If you tried *chicha* in the highlands, you have to try *masato* in the rainforest, which is an alcoholic drink made from fermented yuca. Most of the rainforest dishes are garnished with palm heart, which is often cut into piles of paper-thin ribbons, or *plátanos verdes* (green plantains).

Did we mention dessert? On the coast, you can try *suspiro a la limeña,* a sweet custard topped with meringue and vanilla, and *mazamorra morada*, a purple pudding made from corn and potato flour mixed with clove, cinnamon, and fresh fruit. Peru's exotic fruits make incredible desserts with flavors that can be shocking to a North American or European palate. *Lúcuma*, or eggfruit, is a small fruit with a dark peach color and a rich, smoky flavor, often made into pies or ice cream, as is *maracuyá* (passion fruit). *Chirimoya* (custard apple) is so exquisitely sweet that it is often served on its own as *chirimoya alegre*. Other delicious fruits such as granadilla (another type of passion fruit), *guayaba* (guava), tuna (prickly pear fruit from cacti), and *guanábana* are made into delicious juices—or try a few slices of papaya sprinkled with lime juice and powdered cinnamon.

MUSIC AND DANCE

Traditional Peruvian music can be easily divided between *música criolla*, music from the coast, and *música folklórica*, known as music from the mountains and the rainforest. The best-known example of the latter is Simon and Garfunkel's 1970s hit "El Cóndor Pasa (If I Could)," arranged from an original song composed by **Daniel Alomía Robles** in 1913.

The *huayno* is the most popular dance form in Andean music. It originated in Peru as a combination of traditional rural folk music and popular urban dance music. High-pitched vocals are usually accompanied by a variety of instruments, including the *quena* (Andean flute), *charango* (a small mandolin), harp, saxophone, and percussion. In the last few decades *huayno* has undergone a huge change with the introduction of electronic instruments, including synthesizers and electric guitars. Nevertheless, the dance form utilizes a distinctive rhythm in which the first beat is stressed, followed by two short beats. The *huayno* is pop music for an audience of millions of listeners across the Andes. You can also hear it in parts of Lima, a product of the Andean migration to the city. Despite constant evolution, its themes remain the pain of love lost and being far from home.

Andean music sounds different from Western music in part because it relies mainly on the pentatonic scale instead of the diatonic scale. The instruments include different types of *quenas, zampoñas* (double-row panpipes including the *sicus*, which can be as tall as the musician playing it), *tarkas* (squared flutes that produce an eerie sound), and *antaras* (single-row panpipes). There is also a huge range of rattles, bells, and drums, such as the *tambor* and *bombo,* which are made from stretched animal skins. Most of these instruments, as excavations prove, have been used at least 5,000 years.

In the last five centuries Peru's highlanders have incorporated a range of wind and brass instruments, including clarinets, saxophones, trumpets, euphoniums, and tubas. But the most important European contributions were stringed instruments like the violin, the guitar, and the harp, which was transformed into the Andean harp. This instrument looks like a Western harp with 36 strings but has a half-conical, boatlike base that gives it a rich, deep sound. The 10-stringed *charango* is about the size of a mandolin and is made from wood or the shell of an armadillo.

Music evolved in a whole new way on Peru's coast, where enslaved people were brought from western Africa over three centuries to work on sugarcane and cotton plantations. Nowadays the Afro-Peruvian population—though small compared to that of other South American countries such as Colombia or Brazil—continues to exert a huge influence on Peru's music, food, and sports. The slaves brought with them African rhythms and combined them with Spanish and Andean music to create *festejo* and the *landó.* Dance forms sprung up alongside the music, including *zapateo*—a form of tap dancing—and *zamacueca*. In one frenetic dance known as El Alcatraz, women shake their hips furiously to avoid having their skirts lit on fire by men holding candles behind them.

The area of Afro-Peruvian music expands from Lima all the way south to the small town of El Carmen, including Mala, Cañete and Chincha. But it was in El Carmen where a renaissance began in the 1970s, mainly due to the **Ballumbrosio** family, which made Afro-Peruvian music famous around the world. Outstanding performers of this genre include **Victoria Santa Cruz, Susana Baca, Eva Ayllón,** and more recently **Novalima** (www.novalima.net), a band from Lima that blends Afro-Peruvian rhythms with electronic sounds. Novalima's albums, including *Afro, Coba Coba,* and *Karimba* can be bought online from Amazon.com and iTunes.

There is a wide range of percussive instruments used in Afro-Peruvian music. These include several types of drums, the rattling jawbone of a burro (known as a *quijada*), and a wooden box that is drummed with the hands (known as a *cajón*), among others.

The term *música criolla* refers directly to music played and danced by the *criollos.* The *vals,* which was inspired by the Viennese waltz, and the *marinera,* a very elegant dance from the northern coast similar to the Chilean *cueca,* both have unmistakable influences from Afro-Peruvian music as well. Major artists in this field include **Eva Ayllón** and **Chabuca Granda,** author of the popular *La flor de la canela.*

In these last 40 years, Peruvian music has evolved rapidly. In the late 1960s and 1970s, the traditional *huayno* fused with the tropical *cumbia.* As a result, *chicha* was born, the iconic music of highland immigrants living in Lima, having in **Chacalón y la Nueva Crema** the maximum exponent of this genre. Around the same period of time, hundreds of rock-based bands in the rainforest were turning to *cumbia,* either *tropical* or *psicodélica.* Legendary bands such as **Juaneco y su Combo** and **Los Mirlos** have been revived in U.S. and European compilations and through local bands in Lima, such as **Bareto.**

HANDICRAFTS

A stroll through any of Miraflores's handicrafts markets will show you the depth and variety of handicrafts in Peru. Weavings, knitting, pottery, jewelry, and carved gourds have made the long haul from the provinces into Lima. Each piece is modern but carries with it a tradition that has existed for centuries.

World-renowned for its textiles, Peru's **weaving** tradition is over 4,000 years old. Using the wool of alpacas, llamas, and the precious vicuñas, the pre-Columbian cultures wove their stories into textiles. Abstract figures, deities, and colors described the lifestyles of these people, who had no written language. In turn, the quality of the textile and the wool reflected one's social status and power. When the Spanish arrived, they introduced sheep's wool and silk into the custom. Now contemporary weavers have the advantages of machine-spun yarn and even woven fabrics. While those are undeniably used, there are still plenty of traditional weavers who continue to use natural dyes, drop spindles, and handmade looms.

The weaving culture exists primarily in the mountainous regions of Cusco, Huancayo, and around Lake Titicaca. In these areas, you are likely to see women walking through the streets, toting a basket of wool that they aptly drop and spin into yarn. Guided by memory and years of experience, the women then dip the wool into dyes and thread it into a weaving. The start-to-finish process can take anywhere from a month to several months, and consequently the minimum going price for a cloth is about US$100.

Knitting is another important aspect of Peru's textile tradition. *Chullos* (hats), *mangas* (arm warmers), *polainas* (leggings), *medias* (socks), and *monederos* (change purses), are all typical products of the Quechua and Aymara cultures. As with weaving, the most prominent knitting cultures live in Lake Titicaca's Isla Taquile, Cusco, and Huancavelica. Although customs change among communities, knitting responsibilities are typically divided between men and women. Women spin the yarn and men knit it into clothing, most often hats.

Ceramics have also played an important historical role. Cultures as ancient as the Chavín left behind ceramic remains, and even later cultures like the Moche, Nasca, and

Chimú were renowned for their craftsmanship and unique styles. The **Moche** perfected the skill of capturing human features and emotion; the **Chimú** pottery is recognized for its black surface; and **Nasca** ceramics are particularly prized because of their intricate paintings. When the Spanish arrived, they introduced a European form of pottery, which has been particularly influential in the designs of Urubamba-based ceramicist **Pablo Seminario.** Ceramics are best seen in the areas of Piura, Cusco, and Ayacucho.

Other important handicrafts, like carved gourds, jewelry, and even instrument-making, are best seen in the mountain areas. Again, Cusco, Ayacucho, and Huancayo make excellent bases to begin your exploring.

LITERATURE

The ancient Peruvians had a rich tradition of oral **poetry,** which consisted of two main poetic forms: *harawis,* a form of lyrical poetry, and *hayllis,* a form of epic poetry. Both forms described the daily life and rituals of the time and were recited by a poet known as the *harawec.*

A variety of 16th-century Spanish chroniclers, most notably **Bernabé Cobo** and **Pedro Cieza de León,** attempted to describe the exotic conditions of the New World through the confining looking glass of the Spanish world-view and lexicon. An entirely different perspective was presented by indigenous writer **Felipe Guamán Poma de Ayala,** whose decision to write the king of Spain, Philip III, blossomed into a 1,179-page letter titled *Nueva Crónica y Buen Gobierno.* The letter was written between 1613 and 1615 but only discovered in the Royal Library of Copenhagen in 1908. Apart from a detailed view of Inca customs, what is most fascinating about this work is the blend of Spanish and Quechua juxtaposed with a series of 400 ink drawings that portray the bloodiest moments of the Spanish conquest, as well as Inca festivities and traditions.

Inca Garcilaso de la Vega (1539-1616), the son of a Spanish conquistador and an Inca princess, was educated in Cusco and emigrated as a young man to Spain, where he spent the rest of his life writing histories and chronicles of his Inca homeland. His major work, *Comentarios Reales,* written in 1609, is a highly anecdotal and personal view of the Inca empire. It is the first example of a mestizo author from the New World grappling with the complexities of a torn identity.

During the viceroyalty, **theaters** in Lima and Cusco were at the center of the social life of the Peruvian aristocracy. Most of the productions were imported and written by Spain's Golden Age authors, who had no problem being approved by Peru's Catholic censors. Local playwrights were occasionally approved and their works, though innocuous on the surface, often contain subtle critiques of the viceroyalty's racial and political power structure. Scathing **poetic satire** was circulated secretly throughout upper-class Peruvian society and reflected the growing tensions as Peru's creole elite strained against the straitjacket of Spanish rule.

Following the 1821 independence, literary romanticism took root in Peru, evolving in an entirely different direction from its European counterpart. Instead of a preoccupation with personal identity and freedom, Peru's romantic writers fell into the task of nation-building and describing what it meant to be Peruvian. Some renowned authors of the period were **Carlos Augusto Salaverry** and **José Arnaldo Márquez.** At the same time, *costumbrismo* developed as a literary or pictorial interpretation of local everyday life, mannerisms, and customs. Peru's best-known writer of this style is **Ricardo Palma** (1833-1919), whose most famous work is a descriptive collection of legends and personality sketches known as *Tradiciones peruanas.*

Peru's best-known female writer is **Clorinda Matto de Turner** (1852-1909), born in Cusco, who wrote both in Quechua and Spanish. She edited a series of acclaimed literary journals, including *Peru Ilustrado,* and wrote a trilogy of novels, the best known of which is *Aves sin nido (Torn from the*

Nest), translated into English in 1904 and republished recently by Oxford Press and the University of Texas Press. Matto de Turner was forced into exile in Argentina after being excommunicated by the Catholic Church and having her house burned down. Forgotten for decades, she is slowly gathering recognition as one of the pioneers of Latin American feminism.

César Vallejo (1892-1938), poet, writer and journalist, is considered one of the great poetic innovators of the 20th century. His main works include *Los Heraldos Negros* (1918), the revolutionary *Trilce* (1922), and *Poemas Humanos* (published posthumously in 1939). Always a step ahead of the literary currents, each of Vallejo's books was distinct from the others and, in its own sense, revolutionary. Born in Santiago de Chuco in Peru's northern highlands, he moved to Paris in the 1920s, where he spent the rest of his life immersed in the vanguard movement and the rise of international communism. His complete poetry has been published in English by the University of California Press.

The growing industrialization of Peru in the 20th century and the continued oppression of the indigenous population gave birth to a new genre of socially conscious literature known as *indigenismo*. **José María Arguedas** (1911-1969) was born to a white family but was raised by a Quechua-speaking family in Andahuaylas, in Peru's southern Andes. His works of social realism portray the oppression of indigenous communities and helped inspire the liberation theologies that continue to cause conflict in Peru's Catholic Church. Two of his most famous novels, *Yawar Fiesta* and *Los Ríos Profundos* (*Deep Rivers*), have been published in English by the University of Texas Press.

Ciro Alegría (1909-1967) was a mestizo born in the Marañón Valley of northern Peru whose lyrical novels, like those of Arguedas, portray the suffering of Peru's Andean peoples. His best-known works are *La Serpiente de Oro* (*The Golden Serpent*) and *El Mundo Es Ancho y Ajeno* (*Broad and Alien Is the World*),

which became widely known outside Peru in the mid-20th century and were translated into several languages.

Awarded the Nobel Prize in Literature in 2010, **Mario Vargas Llosa** (born 1936) is one of Latin America's most significant novelists and essayists and one of the leading authors of his generation. Some critics consider him to have had a larger international impact and worldwide audience than any other writer of the "Latin American boom" of the 1960s. Latin America's boom writers dropped the regionalist, folkloric themes of their predecessors and experimented wildly with form and content. Nearly all of Vargas Llosa's novels, including his world-acclaimed *Conversación en la Catedral* (*Conversation in the Cathedral*), *La Guerra del Fin del Mundo* (*The War of the End of the World*), and *La Fiesta del Chivo* (*The Feast of the Goat*), have been translated into English and make an excellent introduction for those wishing to explore Peruvian literature. Once a supporter of Castro and communism during his youth, Vargas Llosa led a middle- and upper-class revolt against President Alan García Pérez in the late 1980s and then ran for president in 1990. After being defeated by Alberto Fujimori, Vargas Llosa went to Spain. Nowadays he splits his time between Lima, Europe, and the United States and remains actively involved in Peruvian politics and social issues. A prolific writer and columnist in newspapers around the world, Vargas Llosa is a die-hard defender of neoliberalism and unquestionably a seeker of freedom through his writing.

Alfredo Bryce Echenique (born 1939) is Peru's other best-known novelist. He has produced a dozen novels and numerous collections of short stories. After spending much of his life in Europe, he now resides in Peru.

Several middle-aged and young Peruvians are making waves on the international literary scene. **Alonso Cueto** and **Santiago Roncagliolo** both won international prizes for their 2006 novels, *The Blue Hour* and *Red April*, respectively. The works deal with Peru's history of terrorism and war. More recently,

Daniel Alarcón (born 1977), a Peruvian-born writer raised in the United States, has published *War by Candlelight,* an excellent collection of short stories, and *Lost City Radio,* his debut novel. He is also the founder of *Radio Ambulante,* an online radio program of Latin American stories.

SPORTS AND RECREATION

Peruvians go wild about *fútbol,* or soccer, which is the main social activity in small towns across Peru. Matches, such as a *clásico* between Alianza Lima and Universitario de Deportes ("La U"), will fill stadiums throughout the year in major cities across Peru. Cienciano, an underfunded team from Cusco, made world news when it defeated huge, internationally acclaimed teams such as River Plate in Argentina and Santos of Brazil—Pele's old team. In 2003 Cienciano became the first Peruvian team ever to win the coveted Copa Sudamericana.

Despite the general lack of financial support from the Peruvian government to sports, surfing and, more recently, boxing have made headlines in recent years due to the world championships obtained. Kids in Lima and other parts of coastal Peru often grow up surfing, and it is no surprise that several Peruvians are among the world's top-ranked international surfers.

Volleyball is also a quite popular sport, especially among the female crowd. The Peruvian women's team was one of the dominant forces in the 1980s, culminating in the silver medal won at the Seoul 1988 Olympics.

Paragliding has always been popular in Lima, where thermals rise along the ocean cliffs and allow hours of aerial acrobatics. Other adventure sports such as **rafting, kayaking, mountain biking, trekking,** and especially **mountain climbing** have lured a generation of young Peruvians, who often make a living working as guides for foreigners.

Bullfighting is a long-running and nowadays controversial tradition that can be traced back to Peru's colonial days. Lima's bullfighting season begins with the Señor de los Milagros (Lord of the Miracles) religious festival in October. Limeños and fans in general pack the city's main bullring, the historic **Plaza de Acho,** to see the Sunday-afternoon contests featuring internationally acclaimed bullfighters from Peru and Spain. Bullfighting is a standard part of many festivals celebrated in Peru's highland towns, despite animal rights organizations increasingly questioning and opposing this centuries-old tradition.

Essentials

Transportation

GETTING THERE

The most common way to arrive to Peru is by plane. That means you fly into Lima and then, in all likelihood, wait for a plane to Cusco or another city. Because of flight schedules, most visitors end up spending at least half a day in Lima—so plan on spending some time here. It's a big and bustling city, and we recommend visiting at the end of a Peru trip once you have learned to navigate a smaller Peruvian city, such as Cusco. Though Lima takes some getting used to, Peru veterans linger in the city for its food, unique cultural mix, museums, art scene—did we mention food?

Air

Because Peru lies in the same time zone as the eastern time zone of the United States and Canada, North American travelers feel no jet lag after arriving in Peru. Depending on where you are flying from in North America, the flight can be anywhere from 6 to 10 hours, and many people fly in the evening in order to catch early-morning connecting flights to Cusco. The cheapest tickets to Lima in high season start around US$500 from Fort Lauderdale through Spirit Airlines and JetBlue.

Most Europeans find it cheaper to travel to Peru via flights with stopovers in the United States or the Caribbean, though there are direct flights from Madrid and Amsterdam. The cheapest flights from major European cities start around US$1,300. Travelers from Asia, Africa, New Zealand, and Australia will also need to make at least one layover en route to Lima.

The most expensive times to fly to Peru are Christmas vacation and the busy tourism high-season months from June to August.

Prices begin to drop around May and September and are at their lowest during the shoulder seasons from October to December and January to April.

LIMA AIRPORT

All overseas flights from Europe and North America arrive in Lima at **Jorge Chávez International Airport** (LIM, tel. 01/511-6055 24-hour flight info, www.lap.com.pe). From here flights continue on to Cusco and other cities. Most planes from overseas arrive in the middle of the night, and flights to Cusco begin from about 5am onward. Some travelers wait in the airport for connecting flights, while the majority head to Miraflores, San Isidro, Barranco, or even Lima's historic center, where there is a good selection of hotels.

If you'd rather stay in the airport area overnight, the **Costa del Sol-Ramada** (Av. Elmer Faucett s/n, Aeropuerto Internacional Jorge Chávez, tel. 01/711-2000, www.costadelsolperu.com, US$220 s, US$250 d with buffet breakfast included) has a good restaurant, a sushi bar, and all imaginable amenities. The hotel is literally right across the taxi lanes in the airport.

Jorge Chávez has come a long way and is actually a pretty modern airport that is regularly recognized as one of Latin America's best airports. It has a range of services, including banks, money exchange booths, ATMs, a post office, stores, a café, food courts, duty-free shops, a rent-a-cell-phone service, and a recommended Quattro D ice cream shop with a playground, among other services. There is even the **Sumaq VIP Lounge,** voted Lounge of the Year 2009 by Priority Pass. If you want to store your luggage, go to **Left Luggage** (Domestic Arrivals side, tel. 01/517-3217,

---

Previous: Parque Nacional Cerros de Amotape in northern Peru; traveling in the Amazon rainforest by boat.

US$1.50 per item per hour, US$9 per piece per 24 hours).

Pushy taxi drivers will be waiting for you outside the airport. The best thing to do is contract a taxi through **Taxi Green** (tel. 01/484-4001, www.taxigreen.com.pe), a private company that has stands just outside luggage claim. Have your destination address written down. Taxi fares from the airport to the center and Miraflores should be around US$25. It also has vans for larger groups. You may be able to get a cheaper taxi if you negotiate with a driver in the airport parking lot, but be sure to know where you are going. Hardcore budget travelers will walk outside the gate of the airport and save a few dollars by taking a taxi, *combi*, or *colectivo* on the street. Be very careful with your luggage if you do this.

You no longer have to pay the airport tax on domestic and international flights at the airport. The tax is now included in your ticket. On your way home, arrive at the airport two to three hours in advance for international flights and one to two hours for domestic flights. If you are traveling in the evening, give yourself lots of time to get to the airport as rush-hour traffic (6pm-8pm) in Lima can be treacherous.

Velasco Astete International Airport (CUZ) in Cusco has flights arriving from La Paz, Bolivia, by **Amaszonas** (www.amaszonas.com), and **Coronel FAP Francisco Secada Vignetta International Airport** (IQT) in Iquitos has flights from Panama City by **Copa** (www.copaair.com).

CHEAP FARES

The best way to get a cheap fare to Peru is to travel outside the high-season months of June-August. Within Peru's three-month high season, it will be difficult to find a discount fare to Peru and onward to Cusco and other main destinations.

The easiest way to start a search for airfare is to use an airfare price comparison website like **Kayak** (www.kayak.com), which compiles the best prices from hundreds of sources, including online travel engines like Travelocity, Expedia, CheapTickets, and Orbitz. Other options include **Mobissimo** (www.mobissimo.com) and **Bookingbuddy** (www.bookingbuddy.com).

A slightly more difficult option is to find an agency with consolidator fares. Consolidators commit to selling huge blocks of tickets for airlines in exchange for preferred bulk rates. Most consolidators do not deal with the public, so the best way to get your hands on consolidated tickets is to call an agency that works with a consolidator. You can find one of these agencies by typing "Peru consolidator" or similar keywords into a Web search engine.

Consolidators sell out their cheap tickets early, especially during Peru's high season, so purchase well in advance. Be careful of fraud with online airline consolidator agencies. Before you purchase, call and make sure the company is legitimate. Always use a credit card so that you can protest a charge, if necessary.

Students and teachers can buy discounted airfare from **STA Travel** (www.sta.com). The website links to STA representatives in nearly 75 countries and has a search engine for cheap fares. Students can purchase a US$25 student ISIC card that entitles them to trip insurance, student airfares, and a range of discounts for everything from bus fare to museum admission. Student discounts are very common in Peru—get this card if at all possible.

FROM NORTH AMERICA

Direct flights from Miami are available, on a daily basis, through **LATAM** (www.latam.com) and **American Airlines** (www.aa.com). Airlines with flights from Miami with one layover to Lima include **Avianca** (www.avianca.com), with a stop in Bogotá, Colombia; and **Copa** (www.copaair.com), with a stop in Panama City, Panama.

From Fort Lauderdale, direct flights are available on **Spirit Airlines** (www.spiritair.com), from Los Angeles on **LATAM** (www.latam.com), from Dallas-Fort Worth on **American,** from Houston and Newark on **United** (www.united.com), and from Atlanta

Hassle-Free Routes into Ecuador

Most travelers heading up the coast for Ecuador make the crossing on the coastal highway at **Aguas Verdes,** a dirty, loud town of vendors, border guards, and rip-off artists. This crossing has become easier as relations between Peru and Ecuador have simmered down thanks to the **Itamaraty Peace Treaty** signed in 1988 by both countries in Brazil. Passengers still have to disembark at least twice to get passports stamped on each side, but the process now takes less than one hour.

The easiest way to cross the border here and avoid the hassle of Aguas Verdes is to use a bus line, such as Ormeño or Cruz del Sur. These buses stop at the Peruvian immigration office (9am-noon and 2pm-5pm daily), located three kilometers before Aguas Verdes. Then the buses roll through Aguas Verdes and military checkpoints at the bridge before stopping at the Ecuadorian immigration office (8am-1pm and 2pm-6pm daily) in the border town of **Huaquillas.** The process is possible, but complicated, to do by a combination of taxis and walking. Watch your belongings.

But for a more scenic and a less hectic crossing, try the **La Tina-Macará** crossing. The as-phalted, though rough, road winds through carob, kapok, and mango trees, but the journey can be hot, so travel with water. Direct buses leave from Piura in the morning and arrive by evening in the Ecuadorian mountain town of Loja.

The best of these companies is **Transportes Loja.** It is also possible to catch *colectivos* to the border from Sullana, a town along the way. There is no good lodging in La Tina so, if you get stuck at the border, try to stay in Macará, Ecuador.

Finally, there is the **Jaén-Loja** crossing, the option for the truly adventurous cross-country traveler who is looking for a break from the Gringo Trail and a shortcut between Chachapoyas and Ecuador's Vilcabamba. This two- or three-day trip involves lots of mountain scenery, and travelers who have done it say it's not nearly as difficult as it looks. This crossing starts in Jaén, a pleasant town with great lodging and restaurants, where you take a US$5 *combi* for the three-hour, 104-kilometer trip to San Ignacio. From there, take another US$4 *combi* for 44 kilometers to Namballe, then cross Río Calvas.

Once in the Ecuadorian town of La Balsa on the other side, catch a *combi* to nearby Zumba, where lots of buses run to Loja. Travelers say the route is safe, with decent lodging options and very friendly, inquisitive people along the way. With an early start, travelers can go from Jaén to Zumba in one day, and then Zumba to Loja in another.

on **Delta** (www.delta.com). From Toronto, **Air Canada** (www.aircanada.com) offers direct flights to Lima.

Recommended U.S. agencies that deal with a number of consolidators include **World Class Travel** (U.S. tel. 800/771-3100, www.peruperu.com), **eXito Latin American Travel Specialists** (U.S. tel. 800/655-4053, www.exitotravel.com), and **Big Sky Travel** (U.S. tel. 800/284-9809, www.bigsky-travel.com).

There are also several courier companies from the United States from which travelers may be able to find even cheaper fares in exchange for carrying packages to and from Peru. These fares come with heavy restrictions on flying times and luggage limits.

FROM MEXICO, CENTRAL AMERICA, AND THE CARIBBEAN

Direct flights from Mexico City are available through **Aeroméxico** (www.aeromexico.com). Taca, Copa, Avianca, and other airlines operate a range of direct and layover Lima flights from Cancún, Mexico; Santo Domingo, Dominican Republic; Havana, Cuba; Panama City, Panama; San José, Costa Rica; and San Salvador, El Salvador.

FROM EUROPE

The only direct flights to Lima from Europe are from Amsterdam on **KLM** (www.klm.com), and from Madrid though LATAM, **Iberia** (www.iberia.com), and **Air Europa** (www.aireuropa.com). Carriers that make one stopover en route to Lima also include LATAM, American, Delta, and Continental.

In the United Kingdom, good consolidators include **North-South Travel** (UK tel. 01245/608-291, www.northsouthtravel.co.uk), which gives part of its proceeds to an international development trust it has set up. Others include **Travel Bag** (UK tel. 0871/703-4698, www.travelbag.co.uk). **Flight Centre International** (UK tel. 0844/800-8660, www.flightcentre.co.uk) is good for tickets from the United Kingdom only.

From France, good consolidators include **Last Minute** (France tel. 0892/68-6100, www.fr.lastminute.com), **Nouvelles Frontières** (France tel. 0825/95-7000, www.nouvelles-frontieres.fr), and **Voyageurs du Monde** (Paris tel. 0142/86-1600, www.voyageursdu-monde.fr).

From Germany, a good option is **Last Minute** (Germany tel. 089/1792-3040, www.de.lastminute.com) or **Just Travel** (Germany tel. 089/747-3330, www.justtravel.de). In the Netherlands, try **Airfair** (Netherlands tel. 0900/771-7717, www.airfair.nl), and in Spain, there is **Barcelo Viajes** (Spain tel. 902/200-400, www.barceloviajes.com).

FROM ASIA, AFRICA, AND THE PACIFIC

From Asia there are currently no direct flights to Lima. All flights from Hong Kong, Tokyo, and other Asian cities first stop in the United States. Good Asian consolidators include **Japan's No 1 Travel** (Japan tel. 03/6870-6418, www.no1-travel.com), Hong Kong's **Four Seas Tours** (Hong Kong tel. 2200-7777, www.fourseastravel.com), and India's **STIC Travels** (India tel. 91/124-459-5300, www.stictravel.com).

From New Zealand and Australia, flights usually have stopovers in Los Angeles or Miami, or in Santiago or Buenos Aires, before heading to Lima. A good agency for flights to the United States is **Flight Centre International** (Australia tel. 133-133, www.flightcentre.com.au).

From Africa, travelers to Lima head to Europe first, although **South African Airways** (South Africa tel. 0861/359-722, www.flysaa.com) has a flight from Johannesburg to São Paulo, Brazil. A good African agency is **Rennies Travel** (www.renniestravel.com).

WITHIN SOUTH AMERICA

More than a dozen South American cities have daily flights by **LATAM** and **Avianca** to and from Lima, the regional hub for both airlines. Avianca flies to and from Guayaquil and Quito in Ecuador; Bogotá, Cali, and Medellín in Colombia; La Paz and Santa Cruz in Bolivia; Montevideo in Uruguay; Santiago in Chile; Buenos Aires in Argentina; and São Paulo and Rio de Janeiro in Brazil. **Aerolíneas Argentinas** (www.aerolineas.com) flies from Buenos Aires.

Bus

It is possible to reach Peru by international bus service from the surrounding countries of Paraguay, Uruguay, Ecuador, Bolivia, Chile, Brazil, and Argentina. The major buses that run these routes can be quite comfortable, with reclining seats, movies, and meals. The longest international bus trips leave from Lima. Some major neighboring cities from which buses travel to Lima are: Santa Cruz in Bolivia, Asunción in Paraguay, Córdoba and Buenos Aires in Argentina, Montevideo in Uruguay, São Paulo and Rio de Janeiro in Brazil, and Santiago in Chile. Buses leave frequently to and from La Paz, Bolivia, for the five-hour direct journey to Puno and on to Cusco. The main international bus companies are **Cruz del Sur** (Lima tel. 01/311-5050, www.cruzdelsur.com.pe), **Ormeño** (Lima tel. 01/472-1710, www.grupo-ormeno.com.pe), **Caracol** (tel. 01/431-1400, www.perucaracol.com), and **El Rápido** (tel. 0810/122-8906, www.elrapidoint.com.ar).

Boat

Some shipping lines offer regular departures from the United States or Europe to Lima's port of Callao. Some cruises include Peru in their itineraries, arriving in Callao or Pisco. **Mediterranean Cruises** (www.royal-olympic-cruises.com), departing from San Francisco, and **Affordable Cruises** (www.affordablecruisesweb.com) are some reputable companies to check out.

A variety of vessels, ranging from banana boats to luxury cruisers, chug up the Amazon River. **Transporte Golfinho** (Raimondi 350, Iquitos, tel. 065/22-5118, www.transportegolfinho.com, US$70 one-way) goes to the Peruvian-Brazilian-Colombian border every other day.

GETTING AROUND

Peru's diverse landscape includes long stretches of desert, high Andean passes, and endless tracts of swampy rainforest. Not surprisingly, Peru can be a complicated country to navigate. Nearly all of Peru's major rainforest destinations require a flight unless you want to spend a few days on a cargo boat or one day, sometimes three, riding in a bumpy bus. Train service is limited, except in the Cusco area, but new highways have made traveling by bus much faster and more comfortable than it was a decade ago.

Air

If you are on a tight schedule and want to see a range of places, flying is the best way to go. In Peru, a round-trip airfare can be less expensive than one-way, but that depends on the season and the airline. The best way to buy tickets or reconfirm them is through the airline's local office or website, where you can buy tickets online for almost all domestic flights. Finding tickets around Christmas, Easter, and the national holiday of Fiestas Patrias on the last weekend of July is expensive and difficult.

The major Peruvian airlines are **LATAM** (www.latam.com), **Avianca** (www.avianca.com), **StarPerú** (www.starperu.com), **Peruvian Airlines** (www.peruvianairlines.pe), and **LC Perú** (www.lcperu.pe). For domestic flights, it is worth pointing out that

LATAM has a two-tier pricing system. If looking online, you can find inexpensive flights on the Peruvian page (in Spanish). The same flights are much more expensive on the pages for residents of all other countries. LATAM says that it offers cheaper flights for residents because it wants to promote domestic tourism. If you buy a cheaper flight online and don't have residency status, you'll likely be forced to pay the difference when you arrive at the airport.

Bus

Because most Peruvians travel by bus, the country has an incredible network of frequent high-quality buses—much better, in fact, than in the United States or Europe. You will be safer if you avoid the dirt-cheap bus companies that pick up passengers along the way. Some of these buses have been adapted (stretched) to the point where they are structurally unsound.

Bus companies in Peru have a confusing variety of labels for their deluxe services, which include Imperial, Royal Class, Cruzero, Ejecutivo, Especial, and Dorado. The absolute best services, comparable to traveling business class on an airplane, are Cruz del Sur's Cruzero or Cruzero Suite class and Móvil's better service, 180° Bus-Cama class, which unfortunately only serves Huaraz. Deluxe bus service means nonstop (only to change drivers), more legroom, reclining seats, onboard food and beverage service, videos, safe drivers, and clean restrooms.

Reputable bus companies in Lima are **Cruz del Sur** (Lima tel. 01/311-5050, www.cruzdelsur.com.pe), **Ormeño** (tel. 01/472-1710 or 01/472-5000, www.grupo-ormeno.com.pe), **Móvil Tours** (tel. 01/716-8000, www.moviltours.com.pe), and **Oltursa** (tel. 01/708-5000, www.oltursa.pe).

Bus travel is easier in cities like Arequipa, Puno, and Cusco, where all the bus companies are consolidated in a main bus station, which is usually known as the *terminal terrestre*. Travelers can arrive there, shop around, and usually be on a bus in an hour or two. In other cities, such as Lima, each bus company has its own bus terminal, some even with VIP lounges, and travelers can save time by buying a ticket through an agency or at a Wong or Metro supermarket through **Teleticket.**

Luggage theft can still be a problem for bus travelers, especially for those who travel on the cheap bus lines. Always keep your hand on your luggage at a bus station. Once on the bus, the luggage that is checked underneath is usually safe because passengers can only retrieve bags with a ticket. The big problem is carry-on luggage. Place it on a rack where you can see it. Some people bring oversize locks to chain their luggage to a rack, but thieves will just razor into your bag and take what they want.

Assaults on night buses are still a problem in Peru, especially on less expensive buses. Highway bandits either hold the bus up by force or sometimes board as normal passengers and hijack it en route. Passengers are not hurt but are shaken down for their money and passports. Some companies use a camcorder to film all passengers getting on board, but no company can eliminate the risk entirely.

Train

For train service from Cusco to Machu Picchu there are two options: The Orient Express-owned **PeruRail** (www.perurail.com), and the newer entrant into the market **Inca Rail** (www.incarail.com). During high season, it is best to reserve tickets online ahead of time to travel to Machu Picchu. Buying tickets once you arrive in Cusco is a hassle, but many of Cusco's nicer hotels will purchase them for their guests. PeruRail and Inca Rail have online ticket purchase. There are several classes of service to Machu Picchu, with a tremendous variation in fares; Inca Rail is a bit cheaper.

The world's second-highest railroad runs from Lima to Huancayo through the Central Andes at a high elevation point of 4,751 meters. The service is managed by **Ferrocarril Central Andino** (www.ferrocarrilcentral. com.pe) with two different types of service.

Tickets can be bought online. Departures are about once per month for this 12-hour ride with stunning views.

Because of a new highway between Arequipa and Puno, passenger trains run on a charter-only basis between these two cities. PeruRail also operates trains from Cusco to Puno.

Combi and Colectivo

The cheapest way to move around a major city like Lima, Cusco, Iquitos, Trujillo, Arequipa, or Chiclayo is on public transportation. In Lima, the best public transportation between the center and Miraflores and Barranco is the rapid transit Metropolitano bus system, which has fixed stops along the Paseo de la República freeway before reaching downtown. For other parts of Lima and the rest of the Peru there are buses, *combis* (imported Asian vans that dart along the roads), and *colectivos* (station wagons with room for five passengers). The buses are cheap but slow, *combis* are a bit faster but tend to be very cramped, and *colectivos* are the fastest of all.

Bus fares usually hover around US$0.40-0.60; *colectivos* are about twice that, but fares go up on weekends and evenings. You can tell where buses and *combis* are going by the sticker on the front windshield, *not* by what is painted on the side. Before you take public transportation, ask a local person for specific directions to where you are going. It can be a fun, inexpensive way to travel around. To get off a bus or *colectivo*, simply say *"baja"* ("getting off") or *"esquina"* ("at the corner"). Fares are collected during the ride or right before you get off, by the *cobrador* or the man (rarely a woman) who also shouts out the route or destination the bus or *combi* is leading to, practically hanging out the bus door.

Taxi

The fastest but still not too expensive way to get around Peru's cities is via taxi or *mototaxi,* the three-wheeled canopied bikes that buzz around cities in the rainforest and the coast (but only in parts of Lima).

The typical fare for in-city *mototaxi* travel is US$0.40-1.

Assaults on taxi passengers can be a problem in Cusco, Lima, and Peru's other tourism hot spots. The best way to avoid this is to have your hostel call for a taxi or to flag down only registered taxis on the street. Avoid young, suspicious-looking drivers and beat-up cars with tinted windows and broken door handles. When traveling, sit on the backseat diagonally opposite the driver's.

Bargaining is an essential skill for anyone taking a taxi, because taxis in Peru do not use meters. Know approximately what the fare should be and stand somewhere where your taxi driver can pull over without holding up traffic. Always negotiate the fare before getting in the car. A typical bargaining conversation would start with you asking *"¿Cuánto cuesta a Barranco?"* (or wherever you're going); the taxi driver replies, *"Ocho soles."* You bargain with, *"No, seis pues,"* and so on. You get the picture. If you can't get the fare you want, wave the driver on and wait for the next taxi. Have in mind that rates can rise during rush hours and the evenings.

Private drivers can also be hired for the hour or day, or for a long-distance trip. The fee can often start at US$10 per hour and go up to US$60-70 for a full day. Ask at your hotel for recommended drivers.

Metro

The only municipal metro system is in Lima, with one line that connects Villa El Salvador in the south to San Juan de Lurigancho in the east. Going downtown, you can take it from the station at Javier Prado and Aviación in San Borja (near the National Theater) and get off at the Grau and Nicolás Ayllón stop. Visit www.lineauno.pe for a map and more information.

Car
RENTING A CAR

Renting a car does not usually make sense cost-wise in Peru because taking taxis or hiring a private car can be cheaper. Also, gas is expensive (about US$4-5 per gallon, depending on the grade), and distances between cities are considerable. Your best bet is to get to your destination and then rent a car to get around.

The phone book of any major Peruvian city is filled with rental car options, which are usually around US$80 per day once you factor in extra mileage, insurance, and other hidden costs. Four-wheel-drive vehicles are usually US$110-130 per day. Major rental companies include **Hertz** (www.inkasrac.com), **Avis** (www.avis.com.pe), and **Budget** (www.budgetperu.com). All these companies have offices in Jorge Chávez International Airport, Lima, Arequipa, and Cusco. Smaller companies operate in many other cities. To rent a car, drivers usually need to be at least 18 years of age, have a driver's license from their country, and have a credit card.

BUYING A CAR

Secondhand cars can be purchased for low prices in **Tacna,** the duty-free port that supplies the country with Asian imports. If you are staying in Peru for more than a month and have a traveling companion or two, this may not be much more expensive than taking high-quality buses. Traveling along Peru's remote dirt roads with a 4WD vehicle is an exhilarating, wild experience.

DRIVING IN PERU

Peru's highway system is much better than it was a decade ago, although gasoline is expensive and the road hazards are extreme. They include open utility-hole covers, herds of sheep or llamas, and rocks that have either rolled from the cliffs or have been left by drivers after working on their cars. Night is even more dangerous, with speeding buses and slow-moving trucks. Gas stations are far apart, and the only option on dirt roads is low-quality fuel siphoned from a rusting steel drum. So fill up frequently and consider carrying spare gallons of gasoline. Drivers should also be prepared with spare tires, tools, food, water, and sleeping bags.

Speeding or running yellow lights is a bad idea, as police will certainly pull you over, especially in Lima and other big cities. Because you are a foreigner, some police officers will threaten jail time and thousands of dollars in fines and loads of paperwork right before hauling you off to the *comisaría* (police station). Many drivers pay just to move along, while others adamantly refuse. It's up to you if you pay or not, but if money is requested, we strongly recommend against bribing, and especially do not offer a bribe on your own initiative. You might not get away with it, being a foreigner. Women police officers have a reputation of being quite tough to deal with, being tagged as *las incorruptibles,* "the incorruptibles." In general terms, crooked police are still a problem, but it is less common now than in the past.

A Peru driver's worst nightmare is getting in an accident. The general rule is *quien pega, paga* (whoever hits, pays), but foreigners are going to be hard-pressed to get any money from a Peruvian taxi or truck driver. The best way to protect yourself is to buy **car insurance** (about US$15 per day or US$35-70 per month, depending on the car). Even now that many cars in Peru are insured, it's usually less of a hassle to resolve the situation by both drivers heading together to a mechanic to get a repair estimate. In the case of a serious accident, let the courts decide whose fault it was or you will end up paying for everyone's damage and medical bills.

U.S. and European driver's licenses are valid for one month in Peru, and thereafter an **International Driving Permit,** available in the United States from **AAA** (www.aaa.com), is required. Drivers should also have the car's registration and their passports with them at all times, or police will offer to *llevarle a la comisaría* (haul you down to the police station).

Boat

There is no better way to experience Peru's Amazon than sitting in a hammock and watching the rainforest go by. This experience is easy to have on an Amazon cargo boat, which offer restrooms, plenty of deck space to sling a hammock, and kitchens that serve palatable meals. You need to be flexible on time, however, because boats wait until they are filled with cargo and rarely depart on the day they say they will.

The most popular routes start from **Yurimaguas** or **Pucallpa** and float toward **Iquitos** on chocolate-colored, torpid rivers. An even longer and more adventurous option is the **Río Urubamba** from **Quillabamba** all the way to Pucallpa. This journey includes incredible stretches of rainforest and passes through the **Pongo de Mainique,** an infamous white-water gorge that cuts through the Vilcabamba mountain range.

It is much faster to head downstream, and some routes become dangerous during high-water months between January and June. Some rivers are unsafe due to drug trafficking or conflicts with indigenous groups. These include the **Río Huallaga** above Tarapoto, the **Río Marañón** from Bagua to where it joins with the Río Huallaga, and any of the small rivers around Chanchamayo that drain into the **Río Urubamba.** Because of its big rapids, the **Río Apurímac** can also be dangerous. Raft it only with a skilled guide.

A more upscale option in the Iquitos area is a deluxe river cruise. These comfortable journeys will take you down the Amazon River toward Brazil or into the Reserva Nacional Pacaya Samiria.

The preferred mode of local travel in the rainforest is by **dugout canoe** or *peke-peke,* a name that perfectly describes the sound of the boat's engine. These boats, also used in parts of Asia, have a long propeller shaft that can be lifted out of the water for maneuvering or avoiding obstacles.

Boats also ply the waters of **Lake Titicaca;** they are inspected and carry life jackets for everyone. The captain even carries a cell phone for emergencies. Other boat options in Peru include **deep-sea fishing boats** that can be contracted in places like

Órganos and Punta Sal on the north coast, although there is no transportation service along Peru's Pacific coast.

Bicycle

Cycling is a great way to explore Peru's back roads and get to know local people along the way. Many of Peru's adventure agencies, especially those that offer rafting trips, rent **mountain bikes** starting at US$20 per day and up, though quality varies tremendously and the bikes are generally meant for local use only. Adventure agencies in Lima, Arequipa, Huaraz, Cusco, and Puno offer multiday bike expeditions with tents, a support vehicle, and a cook. These trips follow fabulous single-track routes up and over the mountains with mind-boggling descents on the other side.

Dozens of cyclists pass through Peru each year, during their epic Alaska-Patagonia pilgrimage. Those who want to start their tour from Peru will have to box their bike up and fly it with them, as good bicycles are extremely expensive in Peru. Some airlines provide a box in which your bike will fit once you take the handlebars off. If your bike is or looks new, smear mud on it so you can get through customs without having to pay duty taxes. Most people use mountain bikes to travel on dirt roads, often with slicks for road and highway travel.

When planning your route, keep in mind that the Panamericana is a dangerous bike route because buses pass at high speeds and the shoulder is cluttered with debris. The same applies for major routes into the mountains, including the Cañón de Pato near Huaraz. The best trips are on remote back roads, which are invariably spectacular and much safer. Keep in mind altitude, weather extremes, drinking water, and the complete lack of repair parts outside major cities.

Good sources of information include the **Adventure Cycling Association** (www.adventurecycling.org) in the United States. One of Peru's best-known bikers, **Omar Zarzar Casis** (www.aventurarse.com), has written a book in Spanish, called *Por los camino de*

Perú en bicicleta, describing 10 of Peru's most beautiful mountain-bike circuits, available in many Peruvian bookstores.

Hitchhiking

People in Peru are not afraid to flag down whatever transportation happens to pass by, and drivers usually charge them a bit of money for gas. Instead of sticking a thumb up, Peruvians in the countryside swish a handkerchief up and down in front of them to attract drivers' attention. We think hitchhiking is fairly safe on country roads where there are no other options. When near cities or large highways, though, always take buses. If you hitchhike, do it with a companion, and make sure your driver is sober before getting in.

TOURS

Organized tour groups are a good idea for travelers leery of traveling on their own or who long for a hassle-free, action-packed tour. A range of excellent though often expensive agencies operate in Peru and offer anything from general tours with a bit of soft adventure to well-tailored adventures for trekkers, climbers, bird-watchers, spiritual seekers, or just about any other group.

With the right company, tours can be safe and enlightening, and a great way to make new friends. Common complaints include a lack of flexibility on meals and lodging options, a go-go schedule that allows no time for relaxation, and a large up-front payment.

Before booking, read the fine print and ask a lot of questions. Find out what hotels you are staying in and then check them with this book. Look for hidden expenses like airport transfers, meals, and single rooms if you are traveling alone. Find out who your guide will be and what his or her experience and language skills are. Ask about the size of the group, the average age of the other passengers, and the cancellation policy. Get everything in writing and add up what all the costs would be using this book. Peru is a relatively inexpensive place to travel in, and you may be able to do it cheaper on your own.

Day-Tour Operators

Because of all the public transportation in Peru, independent travelers can usually find their way even to the country's most remote sites, if they don't mind waiting around for an hour or two, walking, and sometimes hitchhiking.

No one likes to be in a group of obvious tourists, but taking a day tour is the fastest, easiest, and sometimes cheapest way to see a given area's sights, like taking a group taxi. In most cities, tour agencies are clustered together on the main square or along a principal street. Before paying, confirm how good your guide's English is, and get tour details confirmed in writing, including sights visited, how many people maximum will be in the group, and whether the cost includes lunch and admission fees. If your guide does a good job, make sure to give him or her a reasonable tip.

Package Tours

Package tours typically include airfare, hotels, and some meals—but you choose what to do and where to eat. Many Peru-bound airlines offer package tours, including **American Airlines Vacations** (U.S. tel. 800/321-2121, www.aavacations.com), **Delta Vacations** (U.S. tel. 800/800-1504, www.deltavacations.com), and **United Vacations** (U.S. tel. 888/854-3899, www.unitedvacations.com). The web page of the **U.S. Tour Operators Association** (www.ustoa.com) has a search engine to find package tours and specialty tour operators. Resort hotels including Ica, Tarapoto, Puno, Cusco, Máncora, and Cajamarca often promote specials for Lima weekenders on their websites. These all-inclusive packages can be an excellent value for foreign travelers.

Overland Journeys

Many companies in the United States and the United Kingdom offer overland backpacking trips for large groups. You and 39 others hop on a retrofitted Mercedes bus for a one- or two-month tour that could begin in Santiago, Chile, or São Paulo and end in Lima, visiting Cusco, Machu Picchu, and all the other sites along the way. These companies strike bargains with hotels ahead of time and take care of all food, lodging, and transportation.

These trips move like an army, camp on beaches, advance along the Inca Trail, and leave behind a litter of soap opera romances. With a two-month trip costing around US$3,000, these trips are about as good a value as you are likely to find. A pair of budget-minded travelers could, however, do the same trip for the same cost or less. Last-minute Web specials often offer 25 percent discounts on these trips.

The best agencies to look at are **Dragoman Overland** (www.dragoman.com) and a highly recommended option, Australia-based **Tucán Travel** (www.tucantravel.com), which offers a range of trips that include language schools and customized packages for independent travelers.

International Tour Agencies

Peru has a huge range of good tour operators with overseas agents who can work with you regardless of what country you are calling from. The operators in Peru will be the ones you meet when you arrive here. The local operators are listed throughout this book. Contacting these operators directly can sometimes be cheaper, although they are officially supposed to offer the same price to you as their agent overseas does. Many of the agencies listed will organize a tour for as few as two people, with options for trip extensions. In the Cusco area, for instance, tour operators generally offer trip extensions to Lake Titicaca or the rainforest.

Adventure tourism is growing fast in Peru, and new tour operators appear every year. To keep abreast of the latest operators, watch the classified ads sections of adventure magazines such as *Outside* and *National Geographic Adventure* or online resources such as **Andean Travel Web** (www.andeantravelweb.com).

World Class Travel Services (U.S. tel. 800/771-3100, www.peruperu.com) is a leading seller of consolidated tickets and arranges professional, organized tours. It works with recommended operators in Peru, such as **Amazonia Expeditions.** World Class offers tours all over Peru, including a US$720 four-day package that includes all but a few meals for visiting Cusco, Sacred Valley, and Machu Picchu. World Class owner Bob Todd personally inspects all the hotels to which he sends clients and is willing to work with groups as small as two people.

CULTURE AND SOFT ADVENTURE

Keteka (www.keteka.com) is the brainchild of two Peace Corps volunteers who are using their network of contacts to provide authentic off-the-beaten-path tours in Latin America. In Peru they offer tours in Lima, including its food and culinary scene, and in Cusco and Machu Picchu, including a homestay in the remote Pacchanta community.

The Seattle-based nonprofit travel organization **Crooked Trails** (U.S. tel. 206/383-9828, www.crookedtrails.org) offers excellent travel programs that are culturally sensitive and with exciting off-the-beaten-path destinations around Peru for families, schools, universities, and almost any type of group. There are some 10 different packages, such as the Andes and the Sacred Valley, a 15-day tour including Cusco and Machu Picchu, along with homestays with villagers and their families in Vicos in the Cordillera Blanca. It also has packages that combine the Andes of Cusco and Machu Picchu with the southern coastal desert, and a package that combines the highlands with a community stay in the Amazon rainforest.

Far Horizons Archaeological & Cultural Trips (U.S. tel. 800/552-4575, www.farhorizons.com), a California-based agency, is the right choice for those with a passion for archaeology. Tours hit all of Peru's major ruins and are guided by an U.S. university professor. Along the way, guests attend lectures by Peru's most noted archaeologists, including Walter Alva, who excavated the Lord of Sipán tombs. Their tours often include a complete tour of the north coast, Chavín ruins in the Cordillera Blanca, Cusco, Machu Picchu, and Lima's main museums.

Nature Expeditions International (U.S. tel. 800/869-0639, www.naturexp.com) has been in business for more than three decades and runs a range of upscale trips throughout Peru. Its 12-day Peru Discovery trip passes through Lima, Arequipa, and the whole Cusco area and includes stays in top-notch hotels like the Casa Andina in Lima and Arequipa and the Hotel Libertador in Cusco. It works with groups of just two people and can arrange lectures on a range of topics, from natural healing to Peruvian cuisine.

For a more luxurious trip, **Abercrombie & Kent** (U.S. tel. 800/554-7016, www.abercrombiekent.com) pampers its travelers with small groups, the top hotels of the country, and luxury train travel. The trips are expensive, but there are occasional discounts available on its website.

Seattle-based **Wildland Adventures** (U.S. tel. 800/345-4453, www.wildland.com) is renowned worldwide for its diverse international trips. In Peru alone, it offers 10 distinct trips that cover the mountains and the rainforest. In addition to the more traditional Inca Trail and Cordillera Blanca treks, the company also offers trips designed especially for families. On a trip to Machu Picchu and Lake Titicaca, kids and their parents meet Quechua families, work in their fields, and visit their markets.

ADVENTURE AND NATURE TOUR OPERATORS IN NORTH AMERICA

Our top choice for treks anywhere in Peru is **Andean Treks** (U.S. tel. 617/924-1974, www.andeantreks.com). It is affiliated with the highly recommended Peruvian Andean Treks in Cusco, and its treks range from a six-day, five-night Inca Trail trek to a Salcantay trip (US$1,215 pp, minimum 5 people) and an 18-day Vilcabamba expedition. It has been around since the 1970s and has been a leader in taking care of the environment and porters—it's probably the only agency in Peru that pays a retirement pension to its porters.

Adventure Specialists (U.S. tel. 719/783-2076, www.adventurespecialists. org) is based out of a spectacular ranch in Westcliffe, Colorado, and has operated quality educational and creative adventure programs in Peru since 1971. Founder and co-owner Gary Ziegler, a fellow of the Royal Geographical Society and Explorers Club, is a true adventurer, archaeologist, and noted Inca expert. His expeditions have rediscovered and surveyed the important Inca sites Corihuayrachina, Cota Coca, and Llaqtapata. The company specializes in archaeology-focused horse trips around Cusco, but Ziegler and his crew can custom-design nearly any adventure you are looking for.

Adventure Life International (U.S. tel. 406/541-2677 or 800/344-6118, www.adventure-life.com) is a company based in Missoula, Montana, that is a good bet for budget-minded trekkers. Its 10-day Machu Picchu Pilgrimage includes Cusco, Machu Picchu, and a well-run Inca Trail trek for US$2,625. It also offers affordable trips to the fabulous Refugio Amazonas and Tambopata Research Center. It uses three-star family-run hostels and local guides, and gives independent travelers flexibility on where they eat. Maximum group size is 12, though it often sends off groups as small as two people.

South Winds (U.S. tel. 800/377-9463, www.southwindadventures.com) is based in Littleton, Colorado, and offers a range of eco-adventures from the rainforest to the high Andes. It comes highly recommended from people who have done the trips and from *Condé Nast Traveler* magazine.

GAP Adventures (Canada tel. 888/800-4100, www.gapadventures.com) stands for Great Adventure People and is one of Canada's lead tour outfits. It is a good choice for independent-minded travelers who prefer small groups. Groups stay in locally owned hotels, and GAP is known for socially responsible

tourism that includes a good deal of interaction with communities.

Our vote for best international climbing agency in Peru goes to Seattle-based **Alpine Ascents** (U.S. tel. 206/378-1927, www.alpineascents.com). The company's Peru guide, José Luis Peralvo, splits his time between Everest, his home in Ecuador, and Peru and has been guiding the world's toughest peaks for about two decades. Alpine Ascents is extremely responsible about acclimatization and small rope teams.

Other Peru adventure options can be found through the **Adventure Center** (U.S. tel. 800/228-8747, www.adventurecenter.com), which sells the packages of various operators from its offices in Emeryville, California.

ADVENTURE AND NATURE TOUR OPERATORS IN THE UNITED KINGDOM

Amazonas Explorer (Cusco tel. 084/25-2846, www.amazonas-explorer.com) has tons of local experience in Peru and an unmatched array of adventure trips that integrate kayaking, rafting, mountain biking, and trekking. It is constantly innovating new trips, with a team full-time in Cusco.

KE Adventure Travel (UK tel. 01768/77-3966, www.keadventure.com) is based in the United Kingdom and offers a range of high-quality climbs and treks—at considerably lower prices than its competitor, Mountain Travel Sobek. It works with top international trekking guides and is best known for treks around the Cordillera Huayhuash and Nevado Ausangate near Cusco. It also guides peaks in the Cordillera Blanca and leads multiple-sport trips that combine rafting, trekking, and mountain biking. It also offers family tours.

Based in Edinburgh, **Andean Trails** (UK tel. 0131/467-7086, www.andean-trails.co.uk) was cofounded in 1999 by a former South American adventure guide. The company leads interesting small-group mountain-bike and trekking adventures throughout Peru.

Journey Latin America (UK tel. 020/3603-8956, www.journeylatinamerica. co.uk) is the United Kingdom's largest operator of specialty tours and has been in business since 1980. It does rafting, kayaking, trekking, and cultural tours that can either be escorted groups or tailored for two people. It also sets up homestays and language classes.

Exodus (UK tel. 800/843-4272, www.exodus.co.uk) is one of the United Kingdom's larger adventure tour operators, with more than 25 years of experience and trips in countless countries. It offers a 15-day trip that includes Machu Picchu and Ecuador's Galapagos Islands for US$5,160.

World Challenge Expeditions (UK tel. 01494/42-7600, www.world-challenge.co.uk) is a London-based adventure company for student groups in Peru. Its coordinator in Peru, Richard Cunyus, is a full-time resident, takes great care of the students, and tracks down excellent adventures such as trekking in the Cordillera Huayhuash or paddling a dugout in the Reserva Nacional Pacaya Samiria. The company also works with many students from the United States.

ADVENTURE AND NATURE TOUR OPERATORS IN AUSTRALIA

World Expeditions (Australia tel. 1300/720-000, www.worldexpeditions.com. au) is Australia's leader in adventure tours and treks to Peru. It works with Tambo Treks, a small and reputable trekking outfit in Cusco. In Peru, trips include treks through the Lake Titicaca grasslands, forays into Colca Canyon, and longer trips that take in Peru, Bolivia, and the Amazon rainforest. It has representatives in the United Kingdom (enquiries@worldexpeditions.co.uk), and in the United States and Canada (info@world-expeditions.ca).

Visas and Officialdom

VISAS AND PASSPORTS

Citizens of the United States, Canada, United Kingdom, South Africa, New Zealand, and Australia currently do not require visas to enter Peru as tourists; nor do residents of any other European or Latin American country. When you enter the country as a tourist, you can get anything from 30 to 180 days stamped into both your passport and your embarkation card or TAM (Tarjeta Andina de Migración) card, which travelers must keep until they exit the country. If you require more than 30 days, be ready to support your argument by explaining your travel plans and showing your return ticket.

Extensions can be arranged at Peru's immigration offices in Lima, Arequipa, Cusco, Iquitos, Puno, and Trujillo for US$21. There are also immigration offices on the border checkpoints with Chile, Bolivia (at Desaguadero and Yunguyo), and Ecuador, although if you're already at the border, it is easier just to leave the country, stay the night, and reenter on a fresh visa.

Always make a photocopy of your passport and your return ticket and store it in a separate place. Carry your passport in a money belt underneath your clothing, or leave it in a security box at your hotel. If your passport is lost or stolen, your only recourse is to head to your country's embassy in Lima. If you have lost or had your passport stolen before, it may take up to a week while your embassy runs an international check on your identity.

PERUVIAN EMBASSIES AND CONSULATES ABROAD

If you are applying for a work visa or other type of special visa for Peru in the **United States,** contact the consular section of the Peruvian embassy (tel. 202/833-9860, www. embassyofperu.org), located in Washington DC. Additionally, there are Peruvian consulates in Atlanta, Boston, Chicago, Dallas, Denver, Hartford (Connecticut), Houston, Los Angeles, Miami, New Orleans, New York City, Paterson (New Jersey), San Francisco, and, Seattle.

In **Canada** the Peruvian embassy (tel. 613/233-2721, www.embassyofperu.ca) is in Ottawa, with consulates in Calgary, Montreal, Toronto, Vancouver, and Winnipeg. In the **United Kingdom** the embassy and consular section are both in London (tel. 020/7235-1917, www.peruembassy-uk.com). In **South Africa** the Peruvian embassy and consulate are in Pretoria (tel. 012/440-1030, consular-sectionperu@telkomsa.net).

In **Australia** the embassy is in Barton, Canberra (tel. 612/6273-7351, www.embaperu. org.au), with consulate offices in Brisbane, Melbourne, Sydney, and Perth. There is a complete list of Peruvian embassies and consulates around the world on the Foreign Relations Ministry website (www.rree.gob. pe/elministerio/Paginas/Directorio_de_ Misiones_en_el_Exterior.aspx).

FOREIGN EMBASSIES IN PERU

Many foreign travelers are surprised by how little help their own embassy will provide during an emergency or a tight situation abroad. If you have been robbed and have no money, expect no help from your embassy, apart from replacing your passport. The same applies if you have broken Peruvian law, even by doing something that would be legal in your own country. Go ahead and contact your embassy in an emergency, but don't wait for them to call back.

These embassies are all in Lima: **United States** (Av. La Encalada, Block 17, Surco, tel. 01/618-2000, http://lima.usembassy. gov, 7:30am-5pm Mon.-Fri.), **Canada** (Bolognesi 228, Miraflores, tel. 01/319-3200, 8am-12:30pm and 1:15pm-5pm Mon.-Thurs., 8am-noon Fri.), **United Kingdom** (Av. Larco 1301, 22nd Fl., Miraflores, tel. 01/617-3000, http://ukinperu.fco.gov.uk), **Australia** (La Paz 1049, 10th Fl., Miraflores,

tel. 01/630-0500, www.peru.embassy.gov.au), and **South Africa** (Víctor Andrés Belaúnde 147, Ed. Real Torre 3, San Isidro, tel. 01/612-4848, www.dfa.gov.za).

TAXES

Since 2011, airport departure taxes have been included in the ticket price for both international and domestic flights.

Foreigners do not have to pay the 18 percent value-added tax, commonly known as **IGV** or *impuesto general a las ventas,* on rooms or meals purchased at hotels. When you check into a nice hotel, the receptionist will photocopy your passport and your Andean immigration card, known as TAM. You receive the TAM, which is a white piece of paper, when you enter the country. Check your bill on leaving. Foreigners still have to pay the 18 percent IGV at upscale restaurants that are not affiliated with hotels. These restaurants often tack on a 10 percent service charge as well.

CUSTOMS

Peru's customs office (*aduana*) is notorious for being strict with travelers coming back from Miami with loads of imported goodies. That is why you will see a line of Limeños nervously waiting to pass through the Peruvian customs checkpoint. Travelers are allowed to bring three liters of alcohol and 20 packs of cigarettes into Peru duty-free. You can also bring in one laptop and US$500 worth of gifts, but not to trade or sell.

On your way home, it is illegal to leave Peru with genuine archaeological artifacts, historic art, or animal products from endangered species. If you're caught you will surely be arrested and prosecuted. Your home country will not let you bring in coca leaves.

BORDER CROSSINGS

Peru has around 10 official border crossings with Chile, Ecuador, Brazil, and Colombia. They are open year-round and are not usually a hassle as long as your passport and TAM card are in order.

POLICE

Peruvian police officers are incredibly helpful and, for the most part, honest. Always carry your passport with you or a photocopy of it if you decide to leave your passport where you are staying. Other means of identification are pretty much worthless, unless you're renting a car and need to show your driver's license or International Driving Permit. If you are stopped on the street, the only thing police are allowed to do is check your passport and Peruvian visa. If police hassle you for a bribe for whatever reason, politely refuse and offer to go to the police station, or just act like you don't understand.

Police will usually just give up and let you go. Police corruption is still a problem in Peru, but it is less common than a decade ago. If you have an encounter with a crooked cop, get the officer's name and badge number and call Peru's English-speaking **tourist police** (tel. 01/460-1060).

Peru has set up tourist police offices in Arequipa, Ayacucho, Cajamarca, Chiclayo, Cusco, Huancayo, Huaraz, Ica, Iquitos, Lima, Puno, Tacna, and Trujillo. In Lima, the emergency number for the police is tel. 105, but English-speaking operators are usually not available. Your best bet is to call the tourist police.

Conduct and Customs

ETIQUETTE

Peruvians invariably exchange a *buenos días* (good morning), a *buenas tardes* (good afternoon), or a *buenas noches* (good evening). Women and men greet each other with a single kiss on the right cheek, though indigenous people in the highlands generally just offer a hand—sometimes just a wrist if they have been working.

The title *señora* is reserved for older or married women with children and can be quite insulting if addressed to a younger girl. *Señorita* is for younger, usually unmarried women. *Señor* is used to address men, and *don* or *doña* is used for elder men or women as a sign of respect.

Machismo is very much a part of Peruvian culture, especially in rural areas. Men will often direct dinner conversation only toward other men. Women can handle this situation by directing conversation at both the men and women alike at the table.

Peruvians typically dress nicely and conservatively, especially when dealing with official business or entering a church. Women in these cases should consider wearing pants or a skirt that is longer than knee length, and men should avoid shorts or casual T-shirts. Despite

that, fashion in Lima and Amazon towns is more relaxed. You are likely to see men in shorts and women in shorts or short skirts. You should feel comfortable doing the same. Away from Lima or the rainforest, shorts can be worn when participating in an athletic activity that requires them: trekking, beach volleyball, or even running. Foreigners will call less attention to themselves if they wear generally inconspicuous clothing.

CULTURE

Family is still the center of Peruvian society. Extended families often live in neighboring houses, and young cousins can be raised together as if they were brothers and sisters, especially in rural areas and small cities and towns. Women travelers over the age of 20 might be asked whether or not they are married or have children.

Many Peruvians seem not to be bothered with high noise levels, a cultural difference that most Western foreigners find grating. Shops will blare merengue, *tecnocumbia,* and other Latin pop music to the point where conversation becomes impossible, but commerce goes on as usual. Radios tend to be turned up at the first sign of morning light, and laborers start hammering at dawn, so sleeping in is often out of the question. Earplugs can be handy in these circumstances.

Most Peruvians are also used to crowded spaces and don't mind sitting close to one another on buses and *colectivos*. While at the bank, they will stand just inches away from one another even though there is plenty of space around. In the highlands, houses tend to be small, often with many family members sleeping in the same room. Women travelers often think that men are pressing in on them, when actually they just have a different sense of personal space.

Peruvians also have a very different relationship toward time, taking things relaxed and slow without the hectic attitude of Westerners. If you agree to meet somebody at noon, expect to wait at least 15 to 30 minutes. You will inevitably sit in a restaurant longer than anticipated, waiting for your food, waiting for your bill, and then waiting some more for your change. You are never going to change this, so just sit back, be patient, and smile.

PANHANDLING

Whether or not to give money to those asking for it on the street is a personal decision. The hardest to turn down are the street kids with rosy, dirt-covered cheeks and an outstretched hand. In the countryside, children will frequently ask for money in exchange for having their picture taken. Remember that when you give them money, you are encouraging the practice in the future. Also, know that parents often have their children working as teams to collect money in the street. Instead of money, the best-prepared travelers give pens, notebooks, or other useful items.

Travel Tips

WHAT TO TAKE

Travel light and have a carefree vacation—drop-off laundry is common in Peru, so bring five days' clothing and put it all in a medium-size backpack.

For Peru's hot rainforest and coastal climates, we recommend light, fast-drying clothing that protects your arms and legs from sun and mosquitoes. Protect yourself from the sun with a wide-brimmed hat, bandannas, sunscreen, and sunglasses. These same clothes can be worn in the Andes, though you will want to add a lightweight rain jacket, fleece jacket, and silk-weight long underwear.

Miscellaneous items include a Leatherman-style folding knife, a small roll of duct tape for repairs, a mending kit, hand sanitizer, a headlamp with extra batteries, a camera, a voltage adapter, a water bottle, a roll of toilet paper (Peru's public restrooms are always out), binoculars, a pocket English-Spanish dictionary, a book, a journal, and a tiny calculator for confirming money exchanges. Don't forget your medical kit with standard medicines, insect repellent, water purification tablets, and antimalaria drugs.

Paperwork should include a valid passport, your plane ticket, a student card if you have one, a yellow vaccination booklet, travelers checks, an ATM card and a credit card, and a copy of your travel insurance details. Email yourself numbers for your travelers checks, passport, and credit cards in case these things get stolen. Photocopies of the first few pages of your passport and your plane ticket are also a good idea.

ACCOMMODATIONS

Choosing the right place to stay is key to having a relaxed, enjoyable trip to Peru. The quality of lodging ranges dramatically in most Peruvian cities and often has no correlation whatsoever with price. If you plan well, you should usually be able to find a safe and quiet room, with a charming environment and helpful staff.

Because where you stay makes a huge difference in the quality of your experience, we recommend making advance reservations by email—especially in hot spots like Lima, Arequipa, Huaraz, Cusco, and Puno and especially in the busy months of May-September. Rates can increase as much as 50 percent during local festivals or national holidays such as the July 28 Fiestas Patrias weekend.

Walk-in travelers often get better rates than those who make reservations over email, but those with a reservation often get the corner room with a view, the quieter space off the street, or the room with a writing desk—especially if you ask for it in advance.

Lodging rates can be negotiated at budget hotels. That said, most hotels, except the top-end ones, will probably have a low-season rate posted October-April, considerably lower than the usual rate posted year-round. But this depends on the city and can actually vary month to month.

Before you pay for a room, ask to see one or two rooms to get a sense of the quality standard at the hotel. Look carefully at how safe a hotel is, especially what neighborhood it is in, and avoid lodging around discos, bars, bus stations, or other places nearby that might make your room noisy at night. Inspect the bathrooms carefully and turn on the hot water to make sure it exists. If you are in a cold area, like Puno or Cusco, ask if the hotel provides electric heaters. If you are in a rainforest city, ask if there are fans. If you are planning to make calls from your room, ask if there is direct-dial service that allows the use of phone cards—otherwise you will have to wait for the receptionist to make your call at a hefty rate that can be as much as US$0.50 per minute for local calls.

Budget Hotels

The cheaper establishments are called *hospedajes,* and the *hostales* are usually a bit fancier. There are government rules that define the difference between both and a hotel. Key things to look for with a budget place are the quality of the beds, nifty perks like a shared

kitchen, free Internet access, or nowadays even Wi-Fi, the cleanliness of the bathroom, and how the water is heated. A few hotels use water heaters with a limited supply of hot water. A few others use electric showerheads, which heat water with an electrical current like that of a toaster oven. Often the device needs to be turned on at the showerhead or via a circuit breaker in the bathroom. The whole concept is unnerving, but the devices are surprisingly safe. The problem is that they often only make the water lukewarm. Fortunately, the majority have switched to gas water heaters.

Mid-Range Hotels

This category of lodging tends to encompass modern, charmless buildings with a fancy reception area and average rooms with tacky decorations. But they are usually a sure bet for hot water, safe rooms, phones, Wi-Fi Internet access, and refrigerators.

High-End Hotels

Nearly all major Peruvian cities have high-end hotels with the full range of international creature comforts, including swimming pools, Wi-Fi Internet access, spring mattresses, alarm clocks, refrigerators, loads of hot water, bathtubs, and direct-dial phones. The fancier establishments often have kitchenettes, slippers, bathrobes, and complimentary toiletries. Often suites are just a bit more expensive but much more luxurious. These hotels invariably charge an 18 percent value-added tax, which by law must be refunded to travelers as long as you ask and the hotel makes a copy of your passport.

DINING

Nowadays, a traveler's experience of Peruvian food can be a unique experience, considering that Peru has the best, most interesting, and most varied food on offer in Latin America. It can also be a double-edged sword, especially if you have a sensitive stomach. Many travelers return with fond memories of the exquisite and surprising range of flavors, while others return with their stomachs crawling with bacteria or parasites. Choose where you eat carefully and work from the recommendations in this book or from fellow travelers. Peruvians often recommend *huariques*, or hole-in-the-wall restaurants that work well for their hardy stomachs but not necessarily for yours.

Service at Peruvian restaurants is broken down into various steps, which include receiving the menu, ordering, waiting for food, waiting for the bill, and then waiting for change. If you are eating lunch, you can order from the *menú*, the fixed menu of the day, usually a list of prepared entrées and main courses that can be served quickly. À la carte items are more expensive than the *menú*. Many travelers choose to make their own breakfasts by buying yogurt, cereal, and some fruit if they have the facilities at their accommodations. If you get good service, it is encouraged to leave around 10 percent of the bill as a gratuity.

VOLUNTEERING

There are hundreds of volunteer opportunities in Peru, involving art and culture, community development, disability and addiction services, ecotourism and the environment, education, health care, and services for children and women. Although these organizations do not pay salaries, they often provide food or lodging in exchange for your time.

The most common complaint with volunteer work is that the organization is disorganized, there is not enough meaningful work, or that organizations are exploiting eager beavers for their own bottom line. For that reason, do your research and try to speak with people who have worked with the organization in the past.

An organization in Lima that connects volunteers with organizations is **Trabajo Voluntario** (www.trabajovoluntario.org). A good global resource for finding volunteer organizations is **Idealist** (www.idealist.org).

There are many Spanish-language schools that combine teaching with volunteering. If you take morning language lessons, the school will often set you up with volunteer work for a minimal administration fee.

There are also many Peru-based volunteer organizations. Check out **Lucho Hurtado's** programs in Huancayo (www.incasdelperu.org), the organization **Center for Social Well Being** (www.socialwellbeing.org) in Carhuaz in the Cordillera Blanca, and **Awamaki** (www.awamaki.org) in Ollantaytambo.

Crooked Trails (U.S. tel. 206/383-9828, www.crookedtrails.org) is a nonprofit community-based travel organization with excellent three- to four-week volunteer travel programs in communities located in countries such as Peru, Ecuador, Guatemala, India, Nepal, Thailand, Bhutan, and Kenya, creating true cultural exchange bonds that make positive contributions to host countries and achieve lasting effects on their travelers.

Cross-Cultural Solutions Peru (U.S. tel. 800/380-4777, UK tel. 01237/66-6392, www.crossculturalsolutions.org) runs highly professional volunteer programs mainly for students from the United Kingdom and the United States in Lima. In Lima, the company works in Villa El Salvador, the former shantytown that was a Nobel Peace Prize nominee for its community organization.

World Leadership School (U.S. tel. 303/679-3412, www.worldleadershipschool. com) helps middle and high schools in the U.S. create global programs with schools in Peru. During the 10- to 21-day programs, volunteers focus on a single global issue, such as climate change, education, or public health. Volunteers understand and develop competence with each issue by working on solutions at the community level. The programs include a leadership curriculum and mentorship from local leaders, who share their perspective and wisdom.

World Youth International (www.worldyouth.org.au) organizes volunteer programs in Cusco and other areas. Past volunteers have developed a fair-trade income project for women in Chinchero, or rebuilt parts of Pisco that were damaged by the 2007 earthquake.

Kiya Survivors (UK tel. 01273/72-1092, www.kiyasurvivors.org) works with special-needs children, abandoned women, and young single mothers. It is run by Suzy Butler, a British woman, in Cusco and offers volunteer placements of two to six months. A standard six-month placement includes in-country tours, accommodations, and a tax-deductible donation to the organization.

The highly recommended nonprofit **Mundo Azul** (Lima tel. 01/447-5190, www.mundoazul.org) is dedicated to conserving natural biodiversity, and its volunteers play a firsthand role in helping that mission happen. The two-week to month-long volunteer programs take participants to the ocean to research dolphin populations or dive into open water to collect marine species (only experienced divers can apply for the latter option).

Ania (Lima tel. 01/628-7948, www.aniaorg.pe) is an innovative nonprofit founded by Peruvian Joaquín Leguía in 1995 that has focused mainly on helping children across Peru and the rest of the world connect with their love for nature through a creative grassroots effort that includes Ania, a cartoon character, and a series of Tierra de Niños natural areas. These "Children's Lands" are owned, designed, and maintained by children and range from only a few square meters to a giant nature reserve near Puerto Maldonado. Call their office to discuss volunteer opportunities.

OPPORTUNITIES FOR STUDY

Peru has a variety of great Spanish-language programs in Lima, Huaraz, Cusco, Urubamba, Arequipa, Huancayo, and Puerto Maldonado. These programs offer either private instruction for US$7-15 per hour or much cheaper group classes that last between a week and a month. Many of these programs will also set up homestays, hikes, classes, and other activities. The schools vary in quality, so we recommend asking the school for email addresses of former students in order to contact them.

Many of the schools also engage in volunteer projects, which is a great way to immerse into Spanish. When choosing a school, think carefully about what situation will provide the most immersion. We recommend a homestay where you will not be able to speak English and a city where there are few foreigners.

Council on International Educational Exchange (www.ciee.org) organizes study-abroad programs and has links to a variety of programs.

British Exploring Society (UK tel. 0207/591-3141, www.britishexploring.org) runs annual science expeditions for British teenagers, though Americans also sign up. The trips usually include science "base camps" in unusual areas of Peru, along with trekking, rafting, and other adventure activities.

WOMEN TRAVELING ALONE

Machismo is alive and well in Peru, so women traveling in Peru should know what to expect. Most Latin men assume that a woman traveling on her own, especially a blond, must be promiscuous. So you have to set the record straight. At some level, there is the larger issue that some men feel threatened by women who travel abroad, study, work, and are generally independent because it conflicts with their perceptions of how women should be.

How you interact with men makes a huge difference. Speak with men you do not know in public places only. Treat them neutrally and avoid intimate conversation and behaviors, like friendly touches that might be misinterpreted. Wear modest clothing. Some say a fake wedding ring or a reference to a nonexistent husband or boyfriend helps, but that can also result in the reply *"no soy celoso"* ("I'm not jealous").

Peruvian men, and often teenagers, will ingratiate themselves with a group of female gringas and tag along for hours, even if they are completely ignored. The best way to deal with this is by telling them early on that you want to be alone: *"quiero estar sola, por favor."* The next step would be a loud and clear request to be left alone: *"déjeme, por favor."* The final step would be to ask passersby for help" *"por favor, ayúdeme."* The bad side of machismo is harassment, but the flip side is protection.

Be especially careful at night. Choose a hotel in a safe, well-lit part of town. Take care when flagging down a taxi and do not walk around alone at night, especially in tourist towns like Cusco. Walk with confidence and purpose, even if you do not know where you are going. Women who look lost are inevitably approached by strangers. Peruvian women ignore catcalls, aggressive come-ons, and flirtatious lines called *piropos,* which are almost a form of poetry among men. You should do the same.

Do not walk alone in out-of-the-way places in the countryside. We have heard reports of women who have been assaulted while walking alone on popular travelers' routes. Trek or hike in the daylight and with at least one other person. If you are robbed, surrender your purse rather than risk physical harm. Mace, whistles, alarms, and self-defense skills are effective tools that are likely to catch most assailants off-guard.

GAY AND LESBIAN TRAVELERS

Peru is far from progressive for gay and lesbian travelers, and Lima's gay scene is considerably smaller than that in other major South American capitals. There are a variety of well-hidden and exclusively gay bars, restaurants, and clubs in cities like Lima, and a growing number in Iquitos and Cusco, though none cater exclusively to lesbians. Most gay men in Peru's *machista* society are still in the closet and maintain heterosexual relationships as well as homosexual ones.

The only way to find out about gay and lesbian establishments is online. The concept of gay rights is still relatively new in Peru, so gay and lesbian travelers are advised to be discreet and exercise caution. The best resource is the bilingual website **Gay Lima** (http://lima.gaycities.com), written by a U.S. citizen living in Lima. It gives a good overview of gay and lesbian life in Peru and is updated constantly with the latest bars, nightclubs, and hotels, and also includes chat rooms and links. Another good online resource is **Gay Peru** (www.gayperu.com), a great site on gay travel, including gay-oriented package tours. For gay-owned and operated tour agencies there is **Gay Peru Travel** (tel. 01/447-3367, www.gayperutravel.com) and **Rainbow Peruvian Tours** (Rio de Janeiro 216, Miraflores, tel. 01/215-6000, ext. 2407, www.perurainbow.com).

For those interested in learning about gay rights in Peru, check the website in Spanish of the **Movimiento Homosexual de Lima** (www.mhol.org.pe), one of the oldest gay movements in Peru.

The San Francisco-based **Now Voyager** (www.nowvoyager.com) is a worldwide gay-owned, gay-operated full-service travel agency, as is **Purple Roofs** (www.purpleroofs.com). The **International Gay and Lesbian Travel Association** (www.iglta.org) has an extensive directory of travel agents, tour operators, and accommodations that are gay and lesbian friendly.

ACCESSIBILITY

Facilities for people with disabilities are improving in Peru but are far from adequate. Most restrooms are impossible to enter in a wheelchair. Hotel stairways are usually narrow and steep, and ramps are few and far between. Peru's sidewalks are hard to navigate with a wheelchair because they are frequently narrow, potholed, and lack ramps. Cars usually do not respect pedestrians, so cross streets with extreme caution.

The exceptions to the above are airports and high-end hotels. Peruvian hotel chains such as **Libertador** (www.libertador.com.pe) and **Casa Andina** (www.casa-andina.com) stand out for providing accessible rooms in hotels in Trujillo, Lima, Cusco, the Sacred Valley, the Colca Canyon, Arequipa, and Nasca.

PromPeru (www.promperu.gob.pe),

the government tourism commission, has launched a major accessibility campaign and now claims that more than 100 tourist facilities in Aguas Calientes, Cusco, Iquitos, Lima, and Trujillo have been approved for travelers with disabilities. PromPeru lists these wheelchair-accessible places on its website. Other resources for disabled travelers include **Access-Able Travel Source** (www.access-able.com) and **Society for Accessible Travel and Hospitality** (U.S. tel. 212/447-7284, www.sath.org).

SENIORS

Many organized tours of Peru cater to senior travelers. The major airlines offer discounts for seniors, as do international chain hotels, but other than that, senior discounts in Peru are nonexistent. For visiting the rainforest, Amazon cruise boats are an excellent option for people with limited walking abilities.

Good senior agencies include **SAGA Holidays** (www.saga.co.uk), which offers all-inclusive tours and cruises for those age 50 and older. **Road Scholar** (U.S. tel. 800/454-5768, www.roadscholar.org), which was created by **Elderhostel,** arranges study programs for people age 55 and over in countries worldwide, including Peru.

TRAVELING WITH YOUNG CHILDREN

With the right planning, traveling with kids through Peru can be a blast. Kids tend to attract lots of attention from passersby and can cause interesting cultural interactions. By traveling through Peru, children can learn a great deal and gain an understanding of how different life can be for people across the world.

Experts suggest that children should be involved in the early stages of a trip in order to get the most out of it. Children's books and movies that deal with the history of the Inca and the Spaniards will help your kids better relate to the ruins they will see later on. Parents should explain to children what they will encounter, prep them for the day's activities, and then hear from them how it went afterward.

Keeping your children healthy means taking precautions. Make sure your children get the right vaccinations, and watch what they eat while they are in Peru, because the major threat to their health is dehydration caused by diarrhea. Bacterial infection can be prevented by washing children's hands frequently with soap or using hand sanitizer.

For very young children, don't bother bringing your own baby food, as it is cheaper in the country. You will have a hard time, however, finding specialty items like sugar-free foods, which should be brought from home. Outside Peru's major cities, there is not much selection in supermarkets, so stock up while you can. Always carry a good supply of snacks and bottled water with you, as there can be long stretches where nothing to eat or drink is available.

Pack your **medical kit** with everything you will need for basic first aid: bandages and gauze pads, antibacterial ointment, a thermometer, child mosquito repellent (vitamin B acts as a natural mosquito repellent), envelopes of hydrating salts, and strong sunscreen. Items like Tylenol (*paracetamol infantil*), can easily be found in the local pharmacies, although quality varies. Medical services are very good in Lima and often quite good in the countryside, where city-trained, English-speaking medical students perform residency. Medical care is so cheap in Peru that parents should never hesitate about seeing a doctor. Bring photocopies of your children's medical records.

Think carefully about your travel arrangements. Kids are likely to enjoy a sensory-rich environment like the Amazon rainforest much more than back-to-back tours of archaeological ruins. Buses generally allow children to travel for free until age 5 or if they sit on your lap, but choose flights over long bus rides that could make kids crabby. Choose family-oriented hotels, which offer playgrounds and lots of space for children to run around unsupervised. If you ask for a room with three beds, you generally won't have to pay extra. If you have toddlers, avoid hotels with pools, because they are rarely fenced off. Children's rates for anything from movies to museums are common and, even if they are not official, can often be negotiated.

Because parents are often distracted by their children, families can be prime targets for thieves in public spaces like bus stations and markets. Even if you have taught your children to be extra careful about traffic at home, you will have to teach them a whole new level of awareness in Peru. Time moves slower in Peru, and families spend a lot of time waiting for buses, tours, or meals. Be prepared with coloring books and other activities.

Health and Safety

It pays to think ahead about your health before traveling to Peru. With the right vaccinations, a little bit of education, and a lot of common sense, the worst that happens to most visitors is a bit of traveler's diarrhea.

Things get more complicated if you decide to visit the rainforest, because Peru, like parts of Africa and Asia, lies in the tropical zone. Travelers who visit the Amazon should be vaccinated against yellow fever, be taking malaria medicine, and take full precautions against mosquitoes.

VACCINATIONS

Vaccination recommendations can be obtained from the **Centers for Disease Control and Prevention** (CDC, U.S. tel. 800/232-4636, www.cdc.gov/travel), which recommends getting vaccinated for **hepatitis A** and **typhoid** before traveling to Peru. **Yellow fever** vaccination is recommended for people traveling into the rainforest below 2,300 meters elevation. Rabies vaccination is recommended if you are going to be trekking through areas where the disease is endemic. **Hepatitis B** is recommended if you might be exposed to blood (for instance, health-care workers), plan on staying for more than six months, or may have sex with a local. Travelers should also be vaccinated against **measles** and **chicken pox** (those who have had these diseases are already immune) and have had a **tetanus-diphtheria** shot within the last 10 years.

Unless you are coming from a region in the Americas or Africa where yellow fever is a problem, you are not required by Peruvian law to have any vaccinations before entering the country. The yellow immunizations booklet, which doctors tell you to guard ever so carefully, is rarely checked, but you should carry it with your passport. The shots can be quite expensive, in the United States at least, and many of the shots require second or even third visits. Hepatitis A, for instance, requires a booster shot 6 to 18 months after the initial shot, which most people get after returning from Peru. Hepatitis B is generally received in three doses, and there are new vaccines now that combine both hep A and hep B in a series of three shots. Rabies is also given in three shots, although both yellow fever and typhoid are single shots.

Most vaccinations do not take effect for at least two weeks, so schedule your shots well in advance. If you are taking multiple-shot vaccinations such as hep B, you will need to receive your first shot five weeks before departing, even under the most accelerated schedule. Getting shots in Peru is easy and a lot cheaper than in the United States, but you will not be protected for the first two to four weeks. Places to get shots includes **Suiza Lab** (Angamos Oeste 300, Miraflores, tel. 01/612-6666, www.suizalab.com, 7am-9pm Mon.-Fri., 7am-6pm Sat., 7am-1pm Sun.).

TRAVELER'S DIARRHEA

Traveler's diarrhea pulls down even the stoutest of Peru travelers eventually and can be very unpleasant. It can be caused by parasites or viruses, but most often it is caused by bacteria carried in food or water. Plenty of other diseases in Peru are spread this way, including cholera, hepatitis A, and typhoid. Nothing is more important health-wise than thinking carefully about everything you eat and drink.

Only drink bottled water or water that has been previously boiled. Instead of buying an endless succession of plastic bottles, which will end up in a landfill, travel with a few reusable hard plastic bottles and ask your hotel to fill them with boiling water every morning. Refilling bottles is especially easy at hotels that have water tanks, or *bidones,* of purified water. Order drinks without ice unless you can be assured it is bagged ice or previously boiled water in order to make ice. Wipe the edges of cans and bottles before drinking or carry straws.

Avoid street vendors and buffets served under the hot sun. Instead, choose restaurants that come well recommended for taking precautions for foreigners. If the kitchen looks clean and the restaurant is full, it is probably all right. Before and after you eat, wash your hands with soap where available. Carry an antibacterial hand sanitizer as a backup.

The safest foods in restaurants are those that are served piping hot. Soups, well-cooked vegetables, rice, and pastas are usually fine. Eat salads and raw vegetables with extreme caution and confirm beforehand that they have been previously soaked in a chlorine solution. Better yet, prepare your own salads with food disinfectants for sale in most Peruvian supermarkets if you have the facilities to cook your own meals.

An exception to the no-raw-foods rule is ceviche, which is raw fish marinated in bacteria-killing lime juice. As long as you are in a reputable restaurant, ceviche is a safe bet.

Market foods that are safe include all fruits and vegetables that can be peeled, like bananas, oranges, avocados, and apples. Many local fruits are okay as well, including *chirimoya,* tuna (the prickly cactus fruit), and *granadilla.* Dangerous items include everything that hangs close to the ground and could have become infected with feces in irrigation water. These include strawberries, mushrooms, lettuce, and tomatoes. There are plenty of safe things to buy in the market and, when combined with other safe items like bread and packaged cheese, make for a great lunch.

ALTITUDE SICKNESS

Cusco sits at 3,400 meters elevation, and your main health concern should be altitude sickness. You will know if you're suffering from this illness very soon after your arrival. Symptoms include shortness of breath, quickened heartbeats, fatigue, loss of appetite, headaches, and nausea. There is no way to prevent it, but you can minimize the effect by avoiding heavy exercise until you get acclimatized and drinking plenty of water and liquids in general.

Many travelers carry acetazolamide, commonly known as Diamox, usually prescribed by a doctor in doses of 125 to 250 milligrams, taken during the morning and evening with meals. In Cusco everybody will say that coca leaf tea or *mate de coca,* taken in plentiful amounts, is the best remedy for *soroche,* the Quechua word for altitude sickness. And it works. A 100-milligram dose of the Chinese herb ginkgo biloba, taken twice a day, seems to work efficiently, too.

If you feel sick, it's good to know that all hospitals and clinics in Cusco have bottled oxygen. If you happen to be in a five-star hotel like Monasterio, Libertador, or Casa Andina Private Collection, they will provide oxygen in the rooms upon request. Keep in mind that altitude sickness, if not taken care of appropriately, can develop into **high-altitude pulmonary edema,** with acute chest pain, coughs, and fluid buildup in the lungs, or **high-altitude cerebral edema,** involving severe headaches coupled with bizarre changes of personality. In both cases, these illnesses can lead to death if not treated immediately and adequately.

Hospital Regional (Av. de la Cultura,

tel. 084/23-1640) and the **Hospital Lorena** (Plazoleta Belén 1358, Santiago district, tel. 084/22-6511) are the main health centers in Cusco. A bit more expensive, but faster and more reliable, is **Clínica Pardo** (Av. de la Cultura 710, tel. 084/25-6976). In an emergency situation try going to the hospital with a local if you're not fluent in Spanish.

MALARIA

Malaria is a concern for travelers who venture where the Andes slope into the Amazon below about 1,500 meters. There is a much greater chance of getting malaria in the rainforest of northern Peru, such as in the surroundings of **Tarapoto,** the **Reserva Nacional Pacaya Samiria,** or **Iquitos,** than there is in the southern rainforest of **Parque Nacional Manu** and **Puerto Maldonado** area.

The four species of parasite that cause malaria are all transmitted by a female mosquito, which bites most frequently at dawn and dusk. Symptoms include chills, sweats, headaches, nausea, diarrhea, and especially spiking fevers. We recommend that travelers heading to the Amazon protect themselves from mosquito bites and take antimalarial medicines.

Peru's mosquitoes, affectionately known as the Bolivian air force, have developed a resistance to **chloroquine,** the traditional malaria medicine. So that leaves three medicines available to travelers: **Mefloquine** is taken weekly both before and after leaving the rainforest, but it has a host of side effects. **Malarone** is taken daily and has few side effects but is very expensive. And then there is **doxycycline,** which is also taken daily but is very cheap. Doxycycline's side effects can cause upset stomach and make your skin sensitive to sunlight.

Unfortunately, none of these medicines are completely effective, and many have contraindications. Consult your doctor about which is most appropriate for you. After returning from the rainforest, finish your malarial meds completely. Malaria symptoms can take months to appear, and you should see your doctor if you experience fevers after

your return from Peru. More information is available in the United States through the **CDC**'s hotline (tel. 800/232-4636).

ZIKA

In 2016, the first case of Zika was reported in Peru. The virus has not, however, been as prevalent here as in some parts of Brazil and other neighboring countries.

AVOIDING MOSQUITO BITES

Apart from malaria, mosquitoes in Peru also transmit **yellow fever** and **dengue,** a flu-like disease that is usually not life-threatening. Ticks and smaller insects can also transmit **Chagas' disease.** With a few simple precautions against insects, Amazon visitors greatly reduce their risk of exposure to these diseases.

Begin by wearing long pants, long-sleeved shirts, good shoes, and a hat with a bandanna covering the neck. Clothes should preferably be thick enough to prevent mosquitoes from biting through, but that is hard to do in the rainforest. Lighter colors, especially white, for some reason, seem to keep mosquitoes away.

Spray your clothes with a **permethrin**-based spray, especially cuffs and sleeves. When arriving at the lodge, spray the mosquito net over your bed with the spray as well and let it dry before sleeping. Studies show that permethrin lasts up to several weeks on clothes, even after having been washed five or six times.

Apply a **DEET**-based solution when mosquitoes are present. Studies have shown that 20 to 33 percent DEET lasts for 6 to 12 hours (less if you are perspiring) and that anything over that strength produces only marginal improvements in protection. DEET is a highly toxic substance, so wash it off the skin as soon as possible. Use only 10 percent DEET on kids and none at all on infants. DEET will melt any plastic bag you store it in and will also ruin jewelry.

Many lodges provide a coil that can be lit and then smokes throughout the night, releasing a mild insecticide. These seem to work quite well. Make sure your mosquito bed net is wide enough so that you don't lie against it as you sleep—otherwise the mosquitoes will bite you right through it.

Peruvian mosquitoes, unfortunately, seem to pay no attention to natural repellents such as citronella or oils made from soybean and eucalyptus. Bring DEET-based lotion at least as a backup.

DOGS AND RABIES

There are lots of wild (or at least surly) dogs in Peru, as trekkers in places like the Cordillera Huayhuash soon find out. If you are planning to spend a lot of time trekking in Peru, you should consult with your doctor about getting a rabies vaccination.

There are lots of things you can do to avoid being bitten by a dog. As cute or as hungry as a dog may look, be careful about petting a dog in Peru unless you know the owner. Many street dogs have been mistreated and have highly unpredictable behavior.

If you are walking into an area with dogs, collect a few stones. All Peruvian dogs are acutely aware of how much a well-aimed stone can hurt, and they will usually scatter even if you pretend to pick up a stone, or pretend to throw one. This is by far the best way to stop a dog, or a pack of them, from bothering you.

If you do get bitten, wash the wound with soap and water and rinse it with alcohol or iodine. If possible, test the animal for rabies. Rabies is a fatal disease. If there is any doubt about whether the animal was rabid, you should receive rabies shots immediately.

HYPOTHERMIA

Peru's snow-covered mountains, highlands, and even cloud forests have plenty of cold rainy days, conditions in which hypothermia is most likely to occur. Watch yourself and those around you for early signs of hypothermia, which include shivering, crankiness, exhaustion, clammy skin, and loss of fine coordination. In more advanced hypothermia the person stumbles, slurs his or her speech,

acts irrationally, and eventually becomes unconscious, a state doctors refer to as the "metabolic ice box."

The key to preventing hypothermia is being prepared for the elements, and that starts with clothing. When you go for a hike, pack plenty of different layers in a plastic bag. Remember that cotton is great for evaporating sweat and cooling down on a hot day, but actually works against you in wet, cold weather. Artificial fibers like fleece or polypropylene work when wet because they wick water away from your body. Wool is another good choice because it insulates even when wet. And a waterproof poncho or a Gore-Tex jacket will help keep you dry. Having a lot of food and water is also important, and in demanding conditions you and everyone you are with should be fueling up constantly.

The key to avoiding hypothermia is catching it early. If you or someone in your group is shivering or having a hard time zipping up a jacket, take action immediately. In mild hypothermia, the body is still trying to warm itself, and all you have to do is support that process. Feed the person water and a variety of foods, from fast-burning chocolate to bread and cheese. Have them do vigorous exercises like squatting and standing over and over, or swinging their arms around like a windmill. If the person remains cold, set up a tent and put him or her in a sleeping bag with hot-water bottles. Monitor the person carefully until body temperature returns to normal. A person who was on the edge of hypothermia one day is more susceptible the next, so allow for at least a day or two of rest and recuperation.

HEAT EXHAUSTION

Peru's tropical sun and its climate extremes, from searing desert to steamy rainforest, can be dangerous for those who are unaccustomed to them. Like hypothermia, heat exhaustion is caused by environmental conditions that knock the body temperature out of whack. And like hypothermia, heat-related illnesses can be deadly if not treated in time.

People suffering from heat exhaustion

usually have been sweating profusely and have become dehydrated, which causes the person to have a headache. The skin appears pale and the person may vomit or feel dizzy after standing. The heart rate is elevated and, at first glance, the person appears to have the flu.

It is vital to take care of the problem before it gets worse. Find a shady spot—or create one with clothing—and give the person plenty of water, preferably mixed with electrolytes or at least a pinch or two of salt. Place damp, cool cloths on the person's face and back. Allow them to sleep if they feel drowsy. Another side effect of dehydration is painful heat cramps, which can be relieved by hydration and massage.

People are more prone to heat exhaustion when they are dehydrated, overweight, unaccustomed to a sunny or humid climate, and either very young or old. Taking it easy and drinking plenty of water is the best way to avoid heat exhaustion. Wearing a wide-brimmed hat and loose cotton clothing that covers the body is also important, along with applying plenty of sunscreen. If you exert yourself on a hot day, remember that you should be drinking two to four liters of water per day.

Travelers to Peru are often surprised at how fast they can get a sunburn. The country's close location to the equator means that sunlight is more direct. Even when it doesn't feel that warm, if you aren't protected you can burn faster than you would in Canada, the United States, or Europe. The risk increases at higher elevations. Protect against this like you would back home with a hat and sunscreen, which you can pick up at any pharmacy or supermarket.

SEXUALLY TRANSMITTED DISEASES

HIV/AIDS is a worldwide health problem that is spreading in Peru along with **hepatitis B** and other sexually transmitted diseases. The United Nations officially classifies Peru's HIV epidemic as low-level and estimated in 2011 that there were some 74,000 people in Peru living with HIV/AIDS. About 72 percent of the adults were men, more than half of whom identified as heterosexual. The number of infected women and children is rising.

Despite state-promoted campaigns that have increased the concept of safe sex in the public mind in Peru, many men still refuse to use condoms. Travelers should take full precautions before engaging in sex, beginning with the use of condoms.

MEDICAL CARE IN PERU

Peru has a multitiered health-care system, and care is generally pretty good considering the country's high level of poverty. Even small villages usually have a medical post, or *posta médica*, which is often staffed with a university-trained medical student completing his or her residency. Midsize cities like Huaraz have a range of health options, including a few government hospitals and a few private clinics. In general, the private clinics provide more personalized, high-tech service. A country doctor in Peru is probably going to identify your particular stomach ailment faster than a specialist in the United States, simply because the Peruvian doctor has seen your condition many times before.

For serious medical problems or accidents, we recommend that people travel to Lima. The best hospitals are there, and insurance companies abroad are often able to handle payments directly with them (elsewhere the patient is expected to shell out the cash and hopefully be reimbursed later).

Nearly all international medical policies will cover a speedy evacuation to your country if necessary, which is one of the main reasons to get insurance in the first place.

MEDICAL TRAVEL INSURANCE

Most medical insurance will not cover you while traveling abroad, so most travelers to Peru buy overseas medical insurance. Go with a reputable insurance company, or you will

Packing a Medical Kit

Having a small medical kit will come in handy over and over again in Peru, especially in remote areas. Here's a checklist of what should be included:

- antacid tablets (Tums)
- antihistamine (Benadryl)
- diarrhea medication (Imodium)
- motion-sickness medication (Dramamine)
- lots of ibuprofen (Advil)
- lots of acetaminophen (Tylenol)
- Pepto-Bismol (liquid is better)
- insect repellent (12-35 percent DEET or stronger)
- insect clothing spray (permethrin)
- water-purification tablets
- bandages, gauze pads, and cloth tape
- butterfly bandages or Superglue (for sealing gashes)
- Ace bandage
- decongestant spray (Afrin)
- packages of rehydration salts
- antibacterial ointment (Neosporin)
- fungus cream (Tinactin)

have trouble collecting on a claim. Nearly all Peru hospitals will make you pay up front, and then it's up to you to submit your claim.

Some U.S.-based companies that have been recommended by travelers include **Medex Assistance** (U.S. tel. 800/732-5309, www.medexassist.com), **Travel Assistance International** (U.S. tel. 800/821-2828, www.travelassistance.com), **Health Care Global** by Wallach and Company Inc. (U.S. tel. 800/237-6615, www.wallach.com), and **International Medical Group** (U.S. tel. 800/628-4664, www.imglobal.com). Students can get insurance through the **STA** (U.S. tel. 800/781-4040, www.statravel.com).

Some companies sell additional riders to cover high-risk sports such as mountain climbing with a rope, paragliding, and bungee jumping. One good company is **Seven Corners** (U.S. tel. 800/335-0611, www. sevencorners.com). Membership with the **American Alpine Club** (U.S. tel. 303/384-0110, www.americanalpineclub.org) is open to anyone who has climbed in the last two years and includes rescue and evacuation for mountain climbers around the world.

PRESCRIPTION DRUGS

Generic medicines are easy to buy in Peru, much cheaper than in the U.S. or Europe, although quality might not always be the same. Travelers used to stock up their medical kit

- hydrocortisone cream for bug bites

- Moleskin, both thin and foam

- tweezers

- scissors or knife

- syringe and needles

- thermometer

- CPR shield (if you are CPR-certified)

- latex gloves

Your doctor might suggest the following: Advil for pain (no more than 2,000 milligrams per day), Tylenol for fevers over 38.6°C (101.5°F), and Pepto-Bismol for stomach upset and diarrhea (it apparently has a slight antibiotic effect too).

The following antibiotics can be prescribed by your doctor before traveling as well: Keflex (cephalexin) works for systemic infections, like when a cut causes your foot to swell; Zithromax or erythromycin for respiratory infections; and ciprofloxacin for gastrointestinal issues—though it is better to consult a local doctor before taking any of these medicines. Acetazaolamide, commonly known as Diamox, is effective for altitude sickness. If you want to be super-cautious, an Epi-Pen or Ana-Kit that contains epinephrine is the best safeguard against severe allergic reaction to insect stings.

Travelers should also put in their medical kit their brief medical history, including recent allergies and illness. If you take prescription drugs, include written instructions for how you take them and the doctor's prescription as well, just in case you get stopped at customs.

The medical kit only works at the level of the person who is using it. If you can't take a first-aid course, a backcountry wilderness guide like that published by **Wilderness Medicine Institute** (www.nols.edu/wmi) will come in handy. Nearly all these medicines, including the antibiotics, can be bought in a pharmacy in Peru without a prescription—either generic or high-quality brands.

in Peru, but nowadays there are more restrictions with prescribed medicine, especially if you want to purchase it in big pharmacies, hospitals, or clinics. Specific birth control or allergy pills can be hard to find in Peru, unless you go to a private clinic pharmacy.

Although it's tempting, avoid self-medicating. Visiting a Peruvian doctor is inexpensive compared to U.S. and European costs. Anyway, they are the world's leading experts on bacteria and parasite conditions specific to Peru, so it's worth it. You can waste a lot of time and money, and negatively affect your health, taking ciprofloxacin, for instance, when another medicine would have been better.

ILLEGAL DRUGS

According to the present Peruvian Criminal Code, the use and possession of drugs for personal consumption is not punished if the quantities are under the amounts stipulated by law (Article 299: 2 grams of cocaine, 7 grams of marijuana). The problem is that almost no travelers and even very few police know this, and the police will probably still take you to the *comisaría* and charge you until a judge defines the amounts you were carrying. So to keep it safe, it is strongly recommended not to take drugs while in Peru.

The penalties for smuggling out drugs are very strict for **cocaine,** which is common and of very high purity in Peru, and not cut as often with all kinds of dangerous chemicals as in the United States and Europe. There is no bail for drug trafficking cases, and the legal process can drag on for years. Your embassy will most likely decline to get involved.

Peru is well known for confidence scams that involve drugs. A typical one generally targets men and can start with a random meeting in the street with an attractive young woman. After conversation and moving to a bar or discotheque the woman will offer up some drugs. Suddenly and unexpectedly, police appear from nowhere and the attractive gal disappears.

What follows is extortion in exchange for not being arrested. The so-called "police" will explain that you could spend the next five years or more in jail unless you give them money. If you don't react, they will take you to the police station. If you decide to offer them money, the police will drive you to a series of ATMs in order to take as much money as possible from your accounts. Several hours later, and after having your bank account cleaned out, you will probably be dropped off in some remote area of Lima. The worst part is that the perpetrators probably are not even real police.

CRIME

Peru is generally a safe country, so travelers should not feel paranoid. But as in any other place in the world, follow common-sense rules and realize that thieves target travelers because they have cash and valuable electronics on them. You will be easy prey for thieves only if you are distracted.

Be alert and organized and watch your valuables at all times. Your money and passport should be carried under your clothes in a pouch or locked in a safety box at your hotel. Keep a constant eye on your luggage in bus stations. When in markets, place your backpack in front of you so that it cannot be slit open. When in restaurants or buses, keep your purse or bag close to you.

Make yourself less of a target. Do not wear jewelry or fancy watches, and keep your camera in a beat-up hip bag that is unlikely to draw attention. Be alert when in crowded places like markets or bus stations, where pickpockets abound. Go only to nightspots that have been recommended. Walk with a sense of purpose, like you belong exactly where you are. When withdrawing money from an ATM, be with a friend or have a taxi waiting.

Experienced travelers can sense a scam or theft right before it happens and, 9 times out of 10, it involves momentary distraction or misplaced trust. If someone spits on you, latch onto your camera instead of cleaning yourself. If someone falls in the street in front of you or drops something, move away quickly. If an old man asks for your help in reading a lottery ticket, say no. If a stranger motions you over or offers a piece of candy, keep going. Be distrusting of people you do not know.

At nightspots, do not accept alcohol from strangers, as it might be laced with a sleeping drug. Do not do drugs. If you have been drinking, take a taxi home instead of walking.

Be careful when taking taxis and when changing money. When riding to the Jorge Chávez International Airport in Lima, lock your luggage in the trunk and hold onto your valuables. When traffic becomes heavy on Avenida La Marina, teams of delinquents have been known to break windows and snatch bags before speeding away on a motorcycle.

Information and Services

MONEY

Thanks to ATMs, getting cash all over Peru is about as simple, easy, and cheap as it is in your own country. U.S. banks usually charge a US$3 fee per transaction, but the benefits of using bank cards outweigh the risk of carrying loads of cash. Banks usually charge hefty commissions for cashing travelers checks, but a modest supply is nice to have along in case your bank cards are stolen (check with your bank before you go to find out if it is even possible to replace your bank cards overseas). Credit cards are useful and it's increasingly common to use them to purchase almost everything in big cities. Throughout the country Visa and MasterCard are easiest to use in restaurants and hotels, but also ask if establishments accept American Express. If your bank cards get stolen and you spend all your travelers checks, you can always get a cash withdrawal from your credit card. Bottom line: Rely on your ATM card and bring some travelers checks and a credit card or two.

Peruvian Money

The official Peruvian currency is the *nuevo sol* (S.), which at the end of 2016 was at about 3.3 per US$1. Peruvian bills come in denominations of 10, 20, 50, 100, and 200 *soles*. The *sol* is divided into 100 smaller units, called *céntimos,* which come in coins of 1, 5, 10, 20, and 50 *céntimos.* There are also heavier coins for 1, 2, and 5 *soles.* Beware that 2- and 5-*sol* coins look very much alike, the only difference being the size; 5-*sol* coins are slightly bigger. Currency calculations with today's rate can be made with online currency converters such as **XE.com** (www.xe.com). Exchange rates are commonly listed on signs in front of banks and exchange houses and are also posted in daily newspapers. For the official exchange rate, updated daily, go to the Central Bank's website (www.bcrp.gob.pe). The daily exchange rate is listed on the right side, under *Tipo de Cambio Interbancario Venta.*

Changing Money

The U.S. dollar, despite being the most common foreign currency to exchange, is far from being the strongest. Nowadays, it is fairly easy to exchange euros in most Peruvian towns and other currencies only in big cities.

Inspect your dollar bills carefully before leaving your country and treat them with care. Even slight rips will cause them to be rejected everywhere you go. In the best case, you might be able to cash a tattered bill on the street for a lower rate, but regardless, US$50 and US$100 bills are difficult to exchange. There are a few banks and money exchange houses in almost all big airports in Peru. Generally speaking, most Peruvians exchange their dollars at exchange houses, called *casas de cambio,* because they give a slightly higher rate than banks. These are usually clustered around the Plaza de Armas or main commercial streets in every city and town. In major cities, representatives of these *casas de cambio* will even come to your hotel to exchange money, depending on the amount.

In major cities, there are also money changers on the street who wear colored vests and an ID card. These people are generally safe and honest, though they will sometimes take advantage of you if you don't know the daily exchange rate. Never change money with unlicensed money changers, who will sometimes have rigged calculators. Whenever you change money on the street, check the amount with your own calculator.

When you change money, check each bill carefully to see that it is not counterfeit. Hand back all bills that have slight rips, have been repaired with tape, or have other imperfections. Insist on cash in 20- and 50-*soles* bills. Unless you are at a supermarket or a restaurant, the 100-*soles* bills are hard to change

Avoiding Counterfeit Money

Peru is one of the world's top producers of counterfeit U.S. dollars, so you need to be on the lookout for phony money. It includes U.S. bills, Peruvian bills and coins, and euros. Peruvians can recognize counterfeit *nuevos soles* quite easily, either in bills—mostly 100 and 50 notes, but also the 2- and 5-*sol* coins, which are very similar in design but a bit different in diameter. Getting money from an ATM or a bank reduces the risk but not totally. You will know when you have been scammed with a fake note.

Here are a few tips for avoiding counterfeit bills:

· **Feel and scratch the paper.** Counterfeit bills are usually smooth and glossy, while real bills are crisp and coarse and have a low reflective surface. For U.S. dollar bills, many Peruvians scratch the neck area of the person pictured on the bill. The lapel should have a bumpy quality, unless it is an old bill. Hold both ends and snap the bill—it should have a strong feel.

· **Reject old bills.** This includes ones that are faded, tattered, ripped, or taped, especially if they are U.S. notes. You will never get rid of these bills unless you trade them on the street at a lesser rate. Banks will not change them, unless they are Peruvian notes. Counterfeit bills are made of inferior paper and often rip.

· **Hold the bill up to a light.** In both Peruvian and American bills there should be watermarks and thin ribbons that only show up when put against a light source. In the U.S. $10 and $20 bills, the watermark is a smaller, though fuzzy, replica of the person pictured on the bill. These bills also have thin lines that run across the bill and say "US TEN" or "US TWENTY."

· **With Peruvian bills, look for reflective ink.** When you tilt a Peruvian bill from side to side, the ink on the number denomination should change color, like a heliogram. So far, Peruvian counterfeiters have been unable to reproduce this ink.

and you will end up waiting as someone runs across the street to find change for you.

Money Machines

ATMs, known as *cajeros automáticos,* are now commonplace in tourist towns, even small ones. The most secure ATMs are in glass rooms that you unlock by swiping your card at the door or that have a lock on the inside of the door to prevent others from entering when withdrawing cash. Most ATMs accept cards with Visa/Plus or MasterCard/Cirrus logos. Banco de Crédito and Global Net are the only machines that accept American Express cards. Interbank (available in most big cities in Peru) is the only bank with special ATMs that deliver coins. Unlike in Europe or the United States, ATMs deliver the cash you requested first and then will give your card back. If you forget to pull it out, it will be eaten by the machine and be quite difficult to get back. A tactic sometimes

used by thieves is to wait for people to withdraw a large amount of cash at an ATM or from a bank teller and then follow and rob them. For this reason, withdraw cash during the day, avoid large withdraws if possible, and be aware of your surroundings.

Banks and Wire Transfers

Banks are generally open 9am-6pm Monday-Friday, 9am-1pm on Saturday, and are closed on Sunday. Banks are useful for cashing travelers checks, receiving wire transfers, and getting cash advances on credit cards (Visa works best, but MasterCard and American Express are also accepted). Bank commissions for all these transactions range US$20-30, so it is worth shopping around.

A cheaper option for wire transfers is often **Western Union,** which has offices in many Peruvian cities. Call the person you want to wire money to you and give them an address and phone number where Western Union can contact you. Once your money has arrived, you just go to the Western Union office with your passport to pick it up.

Travelers Checks

American Express is the most widely accepted travelers check and can easily be exchanged in banks. From the United States these checks can be ordered over the phone by calling toll-free 800/721-9768. The best place to change travelers checks in Peru is at **Banco de Crédito,** also known as BCP, which often charges no fee at all. The other banks charge a 2.5 percent commission or a flat fee that can be as much as US$10. *Casas de cambio* charge even higher fees.

Remember to record the numbers of your travelers checks and keep them in a separate place. Some travelers email these numbers to themselves so that they are always available when needed. If you end up not using your travelers checks, they can always be converted into cash back home for their face value.

If your American Express travelers checks get stolen, you can call the company collect either in Peru (Lima tel. 01/372-5808, other cities 0801/13-333) or in the United States (tel. 801/964-6665). You can also go online to www.americanexpress.com.

Credit Cards

In recent times the use of credit cards has expanded to almost all big cities in Peru for even the smallest purchases. Be sure you ask, though. Not all cards are accepted everywhere. By far, the best card to have in Peru is Visa or MasterCard, though Diners Club and to a lesser extent American Express are increasingly accepted. Apart from their in-country toll-free numbers, most credit cards list a number you can call collect from overseas. Carry this number in a safe place or email it to yourself so that you have it in an emergency.

For Visa cards, you can also look online (www.visa.com) or call collect in the United States (tel. 410/902-8022). For MasterCard, see www.mastercard.com or call its collect,

24-hour emergency number in the United States (tel. 636/722-7111). For American Express, see www.americanexpress.com or call the company (U.S. tel. 905/474-0870). To contact Diners Club (www.dinersclub.com) while in Peru, call 01/615-1111.

Bargaining

Bargaining is common practice in Peru, especially at markets and shops, and to a minor extent in mid-range hotels. Bargaining can be fun, but don't go overboard. Have a good sense of what an item should cost beforehand. Ask them how much it costs (*"¿Cuánto cuesta?"*) and then offer 20 percent less, depending on how outlandish the asking price is. Usually vendors and shoppers meet somewhere in the middle. Some people bargain ruthlessly and pretend to walk out the door to get the best deal. On the other hand, a smile, humor, and some friendly conversation works better.

If you have a reasonable price, accept it graciously. There is nothing worse than seeing a gringo bargaining a campesino into the ground over a pair of woven mittens. We might go and have a coffee with the money we save, while the vendor might use it to buy shoes for his daughter.

Discounts

Student discounts are ubiquitous in Peru, so get an **ISIC card** (International Student Identity Card) if you can, and flash it wherever you go.

Tipping

Tipping is a great way for foreign travelers to get money to the people who need it the most—the guides, waiters, hotel staff, drivers, porters, burro drivers, and other frontline workers of the tourism industry. Though not required, even the smallest tip is immensely appreciated. It's also a good way of letting people know they are doing a great job. Tipping is an ethic that varies from person to person.

In restaurants a tip of 10 percent is ideal but not enforced. Try to give the tip to the waiter personally, especially when the table is outdoors or you pay with a credit card. It is not necessary to tip taxi drivers in Peru, but you should give a few soles to anyone who helps you carry your bags, including hotel staff or an airport shuttle driver. Assuming you were pleased with their service, you should tip guides, porters, and mule drivers at least one day's wage for every week worked. If they did a great job, tip more. Tipping in U.S. dollars or other foreign currency is not necessarily a good deal for these people, especially if they live away from big cities where they can't exchange the money. Tip in local currency.

MAPS AND VISITOR INFORMATION
Maps
To find topographic maps for remote areas, you will have to make a trip to Lima's **Instituto Geográfico Nacional** (Aramburu 1190, tel. 01/475-9960, www.ign.gob.pe, 8:30am-4:45pm Mon.-Fri.).

Good bookstores generally sell the better national maps, and we especially liked the maps in the back of the *Inca Guide to Peru* and the *Lima 2000* series (scale 1:2,200,000, www.lima2000.com). Many hotels and Iperú offices give out free city maps. Online map store **Omnimap** (www.omnimap.com) has several Peru maps for sale if you'd like to purchase one before arriving in Peru.

Tourism Offices
The Peruvian government has set up tourism offices—known as **Iperú** (tel. 01/574-8000, www.peru.travel)—in most major cities, including Tumbes, Chiclayo, Trujillo, Chachapoyas, Iquitos, Huaraz, Lima, Ayacucho, Cusco, Arequipa, Puno, and Tacna. They receive questions and have a website in English, French, German, Portuguese, Italian, and Spanish. They can give you brochures, maps, and basic info.

The Iperú office is also the place to go if you want to file a complaint or need to solve a problem. These can include a bus company not taking responsibility for lost luggage, a tour company that did not deliver what it

promised, or an independent guide who is not honest. In an emergency, you should contact the police and also call Iperú's 24-hour hotline (tel. 01/574-8000).

FILM AND PHOTOGRAPHY
Peru is a very photogenic country, and don't be surprised if you shoot twice as much as you were expecting. In Peru, photographing soldiers or military installations is against the law.

Digital Cameras
Memory cards and other accessories are easily available in Lima and other large Peruvian cities. These same businesses will usually take a full memory card and burn it onto a compact disc for about US$5—but that requires the toggle cable that comes with your camera. Bring a few large-capacity memory cards and an extra battery. Unless you have your own laptop, there will be long stretches where you will not be able to download your photos.

Film Processing
When it comes to conventional cameras, nearly every Peruvian city has a photo-processing lab, which is usually affiliated with Kodak. Quality varies, however, and if you are looking for highly professional quality, wait until you return home or get to a big city like Lima, Trujillo, Cusco, Arequipa, or Puno. Developing black-and-white or slide film is limited to big cities too.

Photo Tips
The main issue for photography on the coast and in the highlands is the intense sunlight. The ideal times to photograph are in the warm-color hours of early morning or late afternoon. Use filters that knock down UV radiation and increase saturation of colors. In the rainforest, the main problem is lack of light, so a higher ASA is recommended whether using conventional or digital cameras. If you want to take pictures of wildlife, you will have to bring a hefty zoom and have

a lot of time to wait for the shots to materialize. A good source of information on travel photography is **Tribal Eye Images** (www.tribaleye.co.uk). The author offers free tips on choosing equipment and film, general techniques and composition, photographing people, and selling your work. Other sites include **Photo.net** (www.photo.net/travel) and the members-only **PhotographyTips.com** (www.photographytips.com).

Photographing Locals

Photographing locals poses a real dilemma. On one hand, their colorful clothing and expressions make the best travel photos. But many Peruvians feel uncomfortable having their picture taken, and foreigners need to respect that. They might even ask you, with all right, *¿Porqué me tomas una foto?* "Why are you shooting a photo of me?" Before you take a picture of people, take the time to meet them and establish a relationship. Then ask permission to take their photo.

The most compliant subjects are market vendors, especially those from whom you have just bought something. Children in the highlands will ask for money in order to have their picture taken. Adults will even ask if you will be doing business selling their portraits.

COMMUNICATIONS AND MEDIA
Mail

Peru's national post office service is **Serpost** (www.serpost.com.pe), and there is an office in nearly every village, or at the very least a *buzón,* or mailbox. Postal service in Peru is fairly reliable and surprisingly expensive. Postcards and letters cost US$2-4 to the United States and Europe, and more if you want them certified. Letters sent from Peru take around two weeks to arrive in the United States, but less time if sent from Lima. If you know Spanish, check for a complete list of post offices by region and provinces on Serpost's website under "Red de Oficinas." To ship packages out of Peru use **DHL, FedEx,** or another courier service.

You can also receive mail at your country's embassy in Lima.

Telephone Calls

International rates continue to drop both from overseas into Peru, and from Peru overseas. Our favorite option for calling Peru is **Skype** (www.skype.com), as most Peruvians have a Skype account. Even if they don't, you can charge your Skype account with money and, via a service called Skype Out, use Skype to call a Peruvian land line or cell phone. A number of calling cards, which can be purchased online, also make calling Peru incredibly cheap. **Whatsapp** is also popular in Peru, and a good way to call or text domestically or internationally. **Alosmart** (www.alosmart.com) has a search engine for finding the best calling card depending on the type of calls you are going to make.

If you would like someone from home to be able to reach you, you should consider renting or buying a **cell phone.** In the baggage claim area of the airport, there are cell phone agents who rent phones from Peru's major carriers: Telefónica, Claro, and Nextel. Claro has the widest service. Buying a cell phone will cost you a minimum of US$30. If you take your cell phone from home with you and it is unlocked, you can instead buy just the SIM card for about US$5-10 and have a local number. A new phone comes with a standard number of minutes. Once you expend these minutes, you will need to buy a recharge card, which comes in denominations of US$3.50, US$7, or US$11. You can also charge your phone online. These cards allow callers to call both nationally and internationally—receiving calls is free once you have the phone.

Most towns have public phones on the main square and usually an office of **Telefónica,** Peru's main phone company. The phones are coin-operated, but most people buy telephone cards.

The most popular prepaid card is called 147 and can be bought in denominations of US$3-30 at most pharmacies, supermarkets, and from the Telefónica offices themselves.

Also available are HolaPerú cards for international calls. In either case, dialing the United States is more or less about US$0.80 per minute, and a local call, with 147, is about US$0.15 per minute. Surcharges are applied to all calls made from pay phones, so use your hotel phone or walk into any small store in Peru with the green-and-blue phone symbol above it.

All major **international phone cards** can be used in Peru, as long as you know the access code: AT&T is 0800-5000, MCI is 0800-50010, TRT is 0800-50030, and Sprint is 0800-50020. Worldlink has no direct access in Peru.

The cheapest way to make long-distance calls from Peru, however, is via the **net-to-phone** systems available at many Internet places for as low as US$0.17 per minute calling to the United States or Europe. There can be a lag when calling with most of these services, although Internet cafés that have cable service are usually crystal clear—often even better than a phone.

All long-distance calls within Peru are preceded by a 0 and the area code of that particular region, or department, of Peru. For instance, for calling Cusco all numbers are preceded by 084—these preceding numbers are listed whenever a number is listed in this book. All home phones in Lima have seven-digit numbers, and numbers are six digits in other towns and cities in the rest of the country. All cell phones have nine-digit numbers in all of Peru.

To call Peru from overseas, Peru's country code is **51**, and each of the 23 regions in Peru has a different area code. Cusco, for instance, is 84. So dialing a Cusco number from the United States would be 011 (used for all international calls) + 51 (country code) + 84 (city code) and then the number. All cities in Peru have two-digit city codes when dialing from overseas, except Lima. When calling Lima from the United States dial 011-51-1 and then the number. When dialing Lima from within Peru, however, you must first dial 01. This is the rule for landlines, but it changes slightly when dialing cell phones. From within Peru,

Peru's Area Codes

Abancay	83
Aguas Calientes	84
Arequipa	54
Ayacucho	66
Cajamarca	76
Chachapoyas	41
Chiclayo	74
Chincha	56
Cusco	84
Huancayo	64
Huánuco	62
Huaraz	43
Ica	56
Iquitos	65
Lima	1
Máncora	73
Nasca	56
Piura	73
Pucallpa	61
Puerto Maldonado	82
Puno	51
Tacna	52
Tarapoto	42
Trujillo	44
Tumbes	72

you can call any cell phone by directly dialing the nine digits (you don't need to dial the regional area code). For calling Peruvian cell phones from abroad, you just need the country code followed by the number. So to call a Peruvian cell phone from the United States you would dial 011 + 51 (country code) and then the nine-digit number.

To place a direct international phone call from Peru, dial 00 + country code + city code + number. The country code for Australia is 61, Canada is 1, the United Kingdom is 44, and the United States is 1. So, for example, for calling the United Kingdom from Peru, callers should dial 0044 before any number, and for the United States 001.

Collect calls are possible from many Telefónica offices, or you can dial the international operator (108) for assistance. The correct way to ask for a collect call is: *"Quisiera hacer una llamada de cobro revertido, por favor."*

The following codes can be called for help: directory assistance 103, emergency assistance in Lima 105, international operator assistance 108, national operator assistance 109, fire 116, and urgent medical assistance 117. The chance of finding an English-speaking operator at these numbers is slim. However, Iperú maintains a 24-hour English-speaking operator at Jorge Chávez International Airport in Lima for emergencies (tel. 01/574-8000).

Fax

Sending a fax from Peru to the United States is expensive, ranging US$2-9 per page to the United States or Europe. Instead of a fax, scan your document and send it as an email attachment. Fax machines are available at most hotels, photocopy stores, and Telefónica offices.

Internet Access

Internet cafés are everywhere, even in tiny towns. Using the Internet is cheap (US$0.40-0.70 per hour), and often you can also make cheap net-to-phone overseas calls using Skype.

There is a lot that goes into choosing an Internet café, however. First off, make sure it is a high-speed connection, which in Peru is generally referred to as "speedy." Some speedy connections, however, are much faster than others. If your email takes more than a minute or two to open up, we suggest you head elsewhere. Another huge factor is noise, especially with Internet places that cater to school kids, who show up each afternoon and shout and scream and wrestle with each other over who gets to use what machine.

Besides speedy, which is a DSL line, Lima and the bigger cities now have faster connections with cable modems and—most important—crystal-clear, dirt-cheap international calls. Sometimes a remote rainforest town can have a satellite Internet center, which is also amazingly fast.

Better than going to an Internet café is to find Wi-Fi and use your own device. Nowadays most upscale and medium-range hotels will have Wi-Fi access included in the room rates for guests traveling with laptops. In Lima and other touristed cities like Cusco, Arequipa, Trujillo, Puno, or Huaraz, you will find most cafés and restaurants have free Wi-Fi access.

Printed and Online News

Publications in Spanish are headed by *El Comercio* (www.elcomercio.pe), the largest and oldest standard daily newspaper with major credibility in Peru. It has a variety of supplements and magazines with good information on cultural activities and performing arts, including *Somos,* a weekly magazine published every Saturday. Among a dozen tabloids, two are worth checking out: *Perú21* (www.peru21.pe), with a moderate center political standing, and *La República* (www.larepublica.pe), traditionally left-oriented.

Caretas (www.caretas.com.pe) is a weekly magazine that has been around for more than half a century, founded by the Gibson-Zileri family. It is published every Thursday and contains a good deal of local political content, as well as sections devoted to art, humorous essays, interesting letters to the editor, jokes, crossword puzzles, and great photographs.

Some of the best investigative work is done by Web-based publications like *Ojo Público* (http://ojo-publico.com), with the slogan "The stories that others don't want to tell," and *IDL-Reporters* (www.idl-reporteros.pe), led by veteran reporter Gustavo Gorriti. Excellent investigative journalism is often done in *Poder* (www.poder360.com), especially by another veteran reporter, Ricardo Uceda.

Some useful news websites in English include **Peru This Week** (www.peruthisweek. com), which also has classified ads and vast information on cultural activities, tourism, and gastronomy, among other subjects. One of the oldest English-written newspapers in South America, *The Andean Air Mail & Peruvian Times* (www.peruviantimes.com) resurfaced some years ago on the Internet, offering feature articles, op-ed columns, and good overall coverage of what is going on in Peru. It's sister website, **Expat Peru** (www. expatperu.com) focuses more on service information such as legal aspects, traveling to Peru, and several discussion forums by topic, including travel.

WEIGHTS AND MEASURES

Peru uses the metric system for everything except gallons of gasoline.

Electricity

The electrical system of Peru is 220 volts and 60 cycles. If you absent-mindedly plug in a 110-volt appliance from the United States into a 220-volt Peruvian outlet, you will start a small fire. All high-end hotels (such as Casa Andina or Libertador, for example) have additional 110-volt outlets.

You can use 110-volt appliances in Peru with a converter, which can be quite heavy. You can buy one in an electronics shop, though they are cheaper in Peru. Make sure you get the right type, as a hair dryer needs a more robust converter than, say, a digital camera battery charger.

Voltage surges are common in Peru, so it is also a good idea to bring a surge protector from home that can be plugged in between your appliance and the converter. Most laptops and digital cameras these days can take either 110 or 220 volts, so check on this before you buy a converter.

TIME ZONES

Peru is in the same time zone as New York, Miami, Bogotá, and Quito. Peru does not use daylight saving time, meaning that its time remains constant throughout the year. The entire country is in the same time zone (GMT -5).

Resources

Glossary

abra: high pass

aguaymanto: an Inca fruit, also known as *capulí,* from which delicious jams, desserts, and other delicacies are made

ají: any chili pepper; yellow peppers are *ají amarillo*

ají de gallina: creamy chicken stew with yellow chili served over boiled potatoes, garnished with hard-boiled eggs and black olives

algarrobina: a sweet cocktail made from pisco and carob syrup

aluvión: mudslide; also *huaico*

anticuchos: grilled beef heart brochettes served with an assortment of spicy sauces

arroz con pato: duck with rice, originally from the north coast but now found everywhere

biscocho: butter cookie

bodega: storehouse for maturing wine or small grocery store

brochetas: chunks of marinated chicken or beef skewered on wooden sticks and grilled

café (con leche): coffee (with milk)

camarones: freshwater prawns/crawfish

camote: sweet potato

cancha: roasted corn kernels, a popular snack to nibble with beer, usually served with ceviche

canela: cinnamon

cañón: canyon

causa: cold mashed potatoes mixed with yellow chili peppers and a dash of lime juice, layered with chicken, tuna fish, shrimp, or veggies mixed with mayonnaise, avocado, and diced onions

cebiche: ceviche, the trademark of Peruvian cuisine: fish, shrimp, scallops, or squid, or a mixture of all four, marinated in lime juice and chili peppers for five minutes, traditionally served with corn, sweet potatoes, and onions

cebiche mixto: ceviche with fish and shellfish

cerveza: beer; also *chela*

chacana: a sacred symbol, also known as the Andean Cross, with varied and complex links to Inca cosmology; a common motif at Inca temples and other sacred sites

chancho/cerdo: pig/pork

chela: slang word for beer

chicha or *chicha de jora:* drink made from different kinds of fermented corn or peanuts, quinoa, or fruit

chicha morada: sweet, refreshing drink made from boiled purple corn and fruit, mixed with clove and cinnamon, and served chilled with a dash of lime juice

chicharrón: deep-fried pork, chicken, or fish

chifa: Peruvian-Chinese food/Chinese restaurant

chilcano: a refreshing drink made with pisco, ginger ale, lime juice, and a dash of Angostura bitters

chilcano de pescado: a fish broth good for hangovers

chirimoya: a sweet and pulpy, juicy white fruit with a mushy texture and a bitter dark-green skin

choclo: fresh Andean corn

choclo con queso: steaming-hot corn on the cob with slices of cheese and *ají* sauce

chupe: Quechua word for a highly concentrated soup with beef, fish, or seafood with potatoes, corn, vegetables, and sometimes milk

cocha: Quechua word for lake

conchitas negras: black scallop delicacy common in northern Peru

cordillera: mountain range

crocante de lúcuma: a meringue dessert made with a fruit called *lúcuma*

culantro: cilantro/coriander

cuy: guinea pig; stewed, fried, or spit-roasted

granadilla: sweet, pulpy passion fruit with a hard shell

guanabana: indescribably delicious rainforest fruit

guayaba: guava

huaca: in Quechua, a sacred object that is revered, such as a rock

huacatay: black mint

humita: fresh corn tamale that can be either sweet or salty

Inca Kola: a unique and quite sweet Peruvian soda pop originally made out of lemongrass

juanes: tamale stuffed with chicken and rice

jugo: juice

kiwicha: purple-flowered grain high in protein, which is folded into breads, cookies, and soups

lago: lake

laguna: lagoon

langostino: river or sea shrimp

limón: key lime or just lime

lomo saltado: popular and inexpensive dish of stir-fried beef loin, with strips of *ají amarillo,* onions, tomatoes, and french fries, served with rice

lúcuma: a small fruit recognizable by its dark peach color and smoky flavor; a popular ice cream, yogurt, and milk shake flavor

malecón: waterfront promenade

manjar: caramel

manzanilla: chamomile or chamomile tea

maracuyá: passion fruit, served as a juice, in a pisco sour, or in cheesecake

masato: alcoholic drink made from fermented yuca or manioc

mate de coca: coca-leaf tea

mazamorra morada: pudding-like dessert made from purple corn

mirador: lookout point

nevado: mountain

ocopa: a spicy peanut-based sauce, served over boiled potatoes and garnished with hard-boiled eggs and black olives

pachamanca: the utmost Andean meal, made up of beef, pork, alpaca, *cuy,* and chicken cooked together with potatoes, sweet potatoes, and lima beans inside heated stones in a hole in the ground, covered with herbs

paiche: Amazon fish; the largest freshwater fish in the world

palmito: ribbons of palm heart that look like pasta when served

palta: avocado

Panamericana: Pan-American Highway

papa: potato; Andean tuber originally from Peru and generic name for more than 3,000 different types of potatoes

papa a la huancaína: cold appetizer of potatoes in a spicy light cheese sauce with *ají amarillo*

papa rellena: fried oblong of mashed potatoes stuffed with meat, onions, olives, boiled eggs, and raisins

peña: a bar with late-night, often folkloric, musical performances

pescado: fish

piqueos: finger food

pirañas: piranhas; small, vicious, sharp-fanged fish found in oxbow lakes and rivers

pisco: grape brandy; distilled spirit

pisco sour: cocktail made with three parts pisco, two parts lime juice, and one part simple syrup, mixed with ice, a bit of egg white, and a dash of Angostura bitters

plátano frito: fried bananas

playa: beach

pollo: chicken

pollo a la brasa: rotisserie chicken

pomelo: grapefruit; also *toronja*

pongo: river gorge that is often dangerous in high water

puna: high plains, often grasslands

quebrada: narrow valley, ravine

quinoa: a round golden-brown grain, rich in protein

quipu: a system of knotted, multicolored cords that the Inca used to keep records and transmit data, such as weather forecasts, crop production, and accounting

río: river

rocoto: a red, bell pepper-shaped chili consumed in Arequipa

rocoto relleno: red bell pepper stuffed with meat and spices

sachatomate: a red fruit, also known as a *tamarillo,* that has an egg shape, an inside like a tomato, and a sweet, tangy taste

seco de cabrito: roasted goat marinated with *chicha,* served with beans and rice

s/n: abbreviation for *sin numero* (without number); refers to addresses with no street number

tacu tacu: bean and rice patty, fried in a pan and topped with a fried egg, beef or fish stew, or any other kind of garnish

tiradito: sashimi-like fish cuts with a chili sauce on top

toronja: grapefruit; also *pomelo*

tumbo: banana passion fruit

tuna: prickly pear from desert cactus

valle: valley

volcán: volcano

wayrana: a three-sided Inca building with the fourth side left open for ventilation

yuca: cassava root

Spanish Phrasebook

Spanish commonly uses 30 letters—the familiar English 26, plus four straightforward additions: ch, ll, ñ, and rr, which are consonants.

PRONUNCIATION

Spanish pronunciation rules are straightforward and easy to learn because—in contrast to English—they don't change. Spanish vowels generally sound softer than in English. (*Note:* The capitalized syllables below receive stronger accents.)

Vowels

a   like ah, as in "hah": *agua* AH-gooah (water), *pan* PAHN (bread), and *casa* CAH-sah (house)

e   like ay, as in "may": *mesa* MAY-sah (table), *tela* TAY-lah (cloth), and *de* DAY (of, from)

i   like ee, as in "need": *diez* dee-AYZ (ten), *comida* ko-MEE-dah (meal), and *fin* FEEN (end)

o   like oh, as in "go": *peso* PAY-soh (weight), *ocho* OH-choh (eight), and *poco* POH-koh (a bit)

u   like oo, as in "cool": *uno* OO-noh (one), *cuarto* KOOAHR-toh (room), and *usted* oos-TAYD (you); when it follows a "q" the u is silent; when it follows an "h" or has an umlaut, it's pronounced like "w"

Consonants

b, d, f, k, l, m, n, p, q, s, t, v, w, x, y, z, ch   pronounced almost as in English; h occurs, but is silent

c   like k as in "keep": *cuarto* KOOAR-toh (room), Tepic tay-PEEK (capital of Nayarit state); when it precedes "e" or "i," pronounce c like s, as in "sit": *cerveza* sayr-VAY-sah (beer), *encima* ayn-SEE-mah (atop)

g   like g as in "gift" when it precedes "a," "o," "u," or a consonant: *gato* GAH-toh (cat), *hago* AH-goh (I do, make); otherwise, pronounce g like h as in "hat": *giro* HEE-roh (money order), *gente* HAYN-tay (people)

j   like h, as in "has": *Jueves* HOOAY-vays (Thursday), *mejor* may-HOR (better)

ll   like y, as in "yes": *toalla* toh-AH-yah (towel), *ellos* AY-yohs (they, them)

ñ   like ny, as in "canyon": *año* AH-nyo (year), *señor* SAY-nyor (Mr., sir)

r   is lightly trilled, with tongue at the roof of your mouth like a very light English d, as in "ready": *pero* PAY-doh (but), *tres* TDAYS (three), *cuatro* KOOAH-tdoh (four)

rr   like a Spanish r, but with much more emphasis and trill. Let your tongue flap. Practice with *burro* (donkey), *carretera* (highway), and Carrillo (a proper name), then really let go with *ferrocarril* (railroad)

Note: The single small but common exception to all of the above is the pronunciation of Spanish **y** when it's being used as the Spanish word for "and," as in *Ron y Kathy.* In such case, pronounce it like the English ee, as in "keep": Ron "ee" Kathy (Ron and Kathy).

Accent

The rule for accent, the relative stress given to syllables within a given word, is straightforward. If a word ends in a vowel, an n, or an s, accent the next-to-last syllable; if not, accent the last syllable.

Pronounce *gracias* GRAH-seeahs (thank you), *orden* OHR-dayn (order), and *carretera* kah-ray-TAY-rah (highway) with stress on the next-to-last syllable.

Otherwise, accent the last syllable: *venir* vay-NEER (to come), *ferrocarril* fay-roh-cah-REEL (railroad), and *edad* ay-DAHD (age).

Exceptions to the accent rule are always marked with an accent sign: (á, é, í, ó, or ú), such as *teléfono* tay-LAY-foh-noh (telephone), *jabón* hah-BON (soap), and *rápido* RAH-pee-doh (rapid).

BASIC AND COURTEOUS EXPRESSIONS

Most Spanish-speaking people consider formalities important. Whenever approaching anyone for information or some other reason, do not forget the appropriate salutation—good morning, good evening, etc. Standing alone, the greeting *hola* (hello) can sound brusque.

Hello. *Hola.*
Good morning. *Buenos días.*
Good afternoon. *Buenas tardes.*
Good evening. *Buenas noches.*
How are you? *¿Cómo está usted?*
Very well, thank you. *Muy bien, gracias.*
Okay; good. *Bien.*
Not okay; bad. *Mal or feo.*
So-so. *Más o menos.*
And you? *¿Y usted?*
Thank you. *Gracias.*
Thank you very much. *Muchas gracias.*
You're very kind. *Muy amable.*
You're welcome. *De nada.*

Goodbye. *Adios.*
See you later. *Hasta luego.*
please *por favor*
yes *sí*
no *no*
I don't know. *No sé.*
Just a moment, please. *Momentito, por favor.*
Excuse me, please (when you're trying to get attention). *Disculpe* or *Con permiso.*
Excuse me (when you've made a mistake). *Lo siento.*
Pleased to meet you. *Mucho gusto.*
How do you say . . . in Spanish? *¿Cómo se dice . . . en español?*
What is your name? *¿Cómo se llama usted?*
Do you speak English? *¿Habla usted inglés?*
Is English spoken here? (Does anyone here speak English?) *¿Se habla inglés?*
I don't speak Spanish well. *No hablo bien el español.*
I don't understand. *No entiendo.*
My name is . . . *Me llamo . . .*
Would you like . . . *¿Quisiera usted . . .*
Let's go to . . . *Vamos a . . .*

TERMS OF ADDRESS

When in doubt, use the formal *usted* (you) as a form of address.

I *yo*
you (formal) *usted*
you (familiar) *tu*
he/him *él*
she/her *ella*
we/us *nosotros*
you (plural) *ustedes*
they/them *ellos* (all males or mixed gender); *ellas* (all females)
Mr., sir *señor*
Mrs., madam *señora*
miss, young lady *señorita*
wife *esposa*
husband *esposo*
friend *amigo* (male); *amiga* (female)
sweetheart *novio* (male); *novia* (female)
son; daughter *hijo; hija*

brother; sister *hermano; hermana*
father; mother *padre; madre*
grandfather; grandmother *abuelo; abuela*

TRANSPORTATION

Where is . . . ? *¿Dónde está . . . ?*
How far is it to . . . ? *¿A cuánto está . . . ?*
from . . . to . . . *de . . . a . . .*
How many blocks? *¿Cuántas cuadras?*
Where (Which) is the way to . . . ? *¿Dónde está el camino a . . . ?*
the bus station *la terminal de autobuses*
the bus stop *la parada de autobuses*
Where is this bus going? *¿Adónde va este autobús?*
the taxi stand *la parada de taxis*
the train station *la estación de ferrocarril*
the boat *el barco*
the launch *lancha; tiburonera*
the dock *el muelle*
the airport *el aeropuerto*
I'd like a ticket to . . . *Quisiera un boleto a . . .*
first (second) class *primera (segunda) clase*
round-trip *ida y vuelta*
reservation *reservación*
baggage *equipaje*
Stop here, please. *Pare aquí, por favor.*
the entrance *la entrada*
the exit *la salida*
the ticket office *la oficina de boletos*
(very) near; far *(muy) cerca; lejos*
to; toward *a*
by; through *por*
from *de*
the right *la derecha*
the left *la izquierda*
straight ahead *derecho; directo*
in front *en frente*
beside *al lado*
behind *atrás*
the corner *la esquina*
the stoplight *la semáforo*
a turn *una vuelta*
right here *aquí*
somewhere around here *por acá*
right there *allí*

somewhere around there *por allá*
road *el camino*
street; boulevard *calle; bulevar*
block *la cuadra*
highway *carretera*
kilometer *kilómetro*
bridge; toll *puente; cuota*
address *dirección*
north; south *norte; sur*
east; west *oriente (este); poniente (oeste)*

ACCOMMODATIONS

hotel *hotel*
Is there a room? *¿Hay cuarto?*
May I (may we) see it? *¿Puedo (podemos) verlo?*
What is the rate? *¿Cuál es el precio?*
Is that your best rate? *¿Es su mejor precio?*
Is there something cheaper? *¿Hay algo más económico?*
a single room *un cuarto sencillo*
a double room *un cuarto doble*
double bed *cama matrimonial*
twin beds *camas gemelas*
with private bath *con baño*
hot water *agua caliente*
shower *ducha*
towels *toallas*
soap *jabón*
toilet paper *papel higiénico*
blanket *frazada; manta*
sheets *sábanas*
air-conditioned *aire acondicionado*
fan *abanico; ventilador*
key *llave*
manager *gerente*

FOOD

I'm hungry. *Tengo hambre.*
I'm thirsty. *Tengo sed.*
menu *carta; menú*
order *orden*
glass *vaso*
fork *tenedor*
knife *cuchillo*
spoon *cuchara*
napkin *servilleta*
soft drink *refresco*

coffee *café*
tea *té*
drinking water *agua pura; agua potable*
bottled carbonated water *agua mineral*
bottled uncarbonated water *agua sin gas*
beer *cerveza*
wine *vino*
milk *leche*
juice *jugo*
cream *crema*
sugar *azúcar*
cheese *queso*
snack *antojo; botana*
breakfast *desayuno*
lunch *almuerzo*
daily lunch special *el menú del día*
dinner *comida* (often eaten in late afternoon); *cena* (a late-night snack)
the check *la cuenta*
eggs *huevos*
bread *pan*
salad *ensalada*
fruit *fruta*
mango *mango*
watermelon *sandía*
papaya *papaya*
banana *plátano*
apple *manzana*
orange *naranja*
lime *limón*
fish *pescado*
shellfish *mariscos*
shrimp *camarones*
meat (without) *(sin) carne*
chicken *pollo*
pork *puerco*
beef; steak *res; bistec*
bacon; ham *tocino; jamón*
fried *frito*
roasted *asada*
barbecue; barbecued *barbacoa; al carbón*

SHOPPING

money *dinero*
money-exchange bureau *casa de cambio*
I would like to exchange travelers checks. *Quisiera cambiar cheques de viajero.*
What is the exchange rate? *¿Cuál es el tipo de cambio?*
How much is the commission? *¿Cuánto cuesta la comisión?*
Do you accept credit cards? *¿Aceptan tarjetas de crédito?*
money order *giro*
How much does it cost? *¿Cuánto cuesta?*
What is your final price? *¿Cuál es su último precio?*
expensive *caro*
cheap *barato; económico*
more *más*
less *menos*
a little *un poco*
too much *demasiado*

HEALTH

Help me please. *Ayúdeme por favor.*
I am ill. *Estoy enfermo.*
Call a doctor. *Llame un doctor.*
Take me to . . . *Lléveme a . . .*
hospital *hospital; sanatorio*
drugstore *farmacia*
pain *dolor*
fever *fiebre*
headache *dolor de cabeza*
stomachache *dolor de estómago*
burn *quemadura*
cramp *calambre*
nausea *náusea*
vomiting *vomitar*
medicine *medicina*
antibiotic *antibiótico*
pill; tablet *pastilla*
aspirin *aspirina*
ointment; cream *pomada; crema*
bandage *venda*
cotton *algodón*
sanitary napkins use brand name, e.g., Kotex
birth control pills *pastillas anticonceptivas*
contraceptive foam *espuma anticonceptiva*
condoms *preservativos; condones*

toothbrush *cepilla dental*
dental floss *hilo dental*
toothpaste *crema dental*
dentist *dentista*
toothache *dolor de muelas*

POST OFFICE AND COMMUNICATIONS

long-distance telephone *teléfono larga distancia*
I would like to call ... *Quisiera llamar a ...*
collect *por cobrar*
station to station *a quien contesta*
person to person *persona a persona*
credit card *tarjeta de crédito*
post office *correo*
general delivery *lista de correo*
letter *carta*
stamp *estampilla, timbre*
postcard *tarjeta*
aerogram *aerograma*
airmail *correo aereo*
registered *registrado*
money order *giro*
package; box *paquete; caja*
string; tape *cuerda; cinta*

AT THE BORDER

border *frontera*
customs *aduana*
immigration *migración*
tourist card *tarjeta de turista*
inspection *inspección; revisión*
passport *pasaporte*
profession *profesión*
marital status *estado civil*
single *soltero*
married; divorced *casado; divorciado*
widowed *viudado*
insurance *seguros*
title *título*
driver's license *licencia de manejar*

AT THE GAS STATION

gas station *gasolinera*
gasoline *gasolina*
unleaded *sin plomo*
full, please *lleno, por favor*

tire *llanta*
tire repair shop *vulcanizadora*
air *aire*
water *agua*
oil (change) *aceite (cambio)*
grease *grasa*
My ... doesn't work. *Mi ... no sirve.*
battery *batería*
radiator *radiador*
alternator *alternador*
generator *generador*
tow truck *grúa*
repair shop *taller mecánico*
tune-up *afinación*
auto parts store *refaccionería*

VERBS

Verbs are the key to getting along in Spanish. They employ mostly predictable forms and come in three classes, which end in *ar, er,* and *ir,* respectively:

to buy *comprar*
I buy, you (he, she, it) buys *compro, compra*
we buy, you (they) buy *compramos, compran*

to eat *comer*
I eat, you (he, she, it) eats *como, come*
we eat, you (they) eat *comemos, comen*

to climb *subir*
I climb, you (he, she, it) climbs *subo, sube*
we climb, you (they) climb *subimos, suben*

Here are more (with irregularities indicated):

to do or make *hacer* (regular except for *hago,* I do or make)
to go *ir* (very irregular: *voy, va, vamos, van*)
to go (walk) *andar*
to love *amar*
to work *trabajar*
to want *desear, querer*
to need *necesitar*

to read *leer*
to write *escribir*
to repair *reparar*
to stop *parar*
to get off (the bus) *bajar*
to arrive *llegar*
to stay (remain) *quedar*
to stay (lodge) *hospedar*
to leave *salir* (regular except for *salgo*, I leave)
to look at *mirar*
to look for *buscar*
to give *dar* (regular except for *doy*, I give)
to carry *llevar*
to have *tener* (irregular but important: *tengo, tiene, tenemos, tienen*)
to come *venir* (similarly irregular: *vengo, viene, venimos, vienen*)

Spanish has two forms of "to be":

to be *estar* (regular except for *estoy*, I am)
to be *ser* (very irregular: *soy, es, somos, son*)

Use *estar* when speaking of location or a temporary state of being: "I am at home." *"Estoy en casa."* "I'm sick." *"Estoy enfermo."* Use *ser* for a permanent state of being: "I am a doctor." *"Soy doctora."*

NUMBERS

zero *cero*
one *uno*
two *dos*
three *tres*
four *cuatro*
five *cinco*
six *seis*
seven *siete*
eight *ocho*
nine *nueve*
10 *diez*
11 *once*
12 *doce*
13 *trece*
14 *catorce*
15 *quince*
16 *dieciseis*

17 *diecisiete*
18 *dieciocho*
19 *diecinueve*
20 *veinte*
21 *veinte y uno* or *veintiuno*
30 *treinta*
40 *cuarenta*
50 *cincuenta*
60 *sesenta*
70 *setenta*
80 *ochenta*
90 *noventa*
100 *ciento*
101 *ciento y uno* or *cientiuno*
200 *doscientos*
500 *quinientos*
1,000 *mil*
10,000 *diez mil*
100,000 *cien mil*
1,000,000 *millón*
one-half *medio*
one-third *un tercio*
one-fourth *un cuarto*

TIME

What time is it? *¿Qué hora es?*
It's one o'clock. *Es la una.*
It's three in the afternoon. *Son las tres de la tarde.*
It's 4am. *Son las cuatro de la mañana.*
six-thirty *seis y media*
a quarter till eleven *un cuarto para las once*
a quarter past five *las cinco y cuarto*
an hour *una hora*

DAYS AND MONTHS

Monday *lunes*
Tuesday *martes*
Wednesday *miércoles*
Thursday *jueves*
Friday *viernes*
Saturday *sábado*
Sunday *domingo*
today *hoy*
tomorrow *mañana*
yesterday *ayer*
January *enero*
February *febrero*

March *marzo*	**October** *octubre*
April *abril*	**November** *noviembre*
May *mayo*	**December** *diciembre*
June *junio*	**a week** *una semana*
July *julio*	**a month** *un mes*
August *agosto*	**after** *después*
September *septiembre*	**before** *antes*

Suggested Reading

HISTORY

Burger, Richard. *Chavín and the Origins of Andean Civilization.* London: Thames and Hudson, 1995. A groundbreaking investigation of the Chavín culture, which spread across Peru's highlands 2,000 years before the Inca.

Hemming, John. *Conquest of the Incas.* New York: Harcourt Brace & Co., 1970. This is a masterpiece of both prose and history, in which famed Peru historian John Hemming lays out a gripping, blow-by-blow account of the Spanish conquest of Peru. Hemming, who was only 35 when *Conquest* was published, has written nearly a dozen books about Inca architecture and the native people of the Amazon.

Heyerdahl, Thor, and Daniel Sandweiss. *The Quest for Peru's Forgotten City.* London: Thames and Hudson, 1995. Norwegian explorer Thor Heyerdahl was most famous for piloting the *Kon-Tiki* balsa-wood raft from Callao, Peru, to the Polynesian Islands in 1947. From 1988 until he died in 2002, Heyerdahl's obsession with early ocean travel focused on the inhabitants of Túcume, a complex of 26 pyramids north of present-day Trujillo that was built by the Sicán culture around AD 1050. This remains the best work on Túcume.

Kirkpatrick, Sidney. *Lords of Sipán: A True Story of Pre-Inca Tombs, Archaeology, and Crime.* New York: William Morrow, 1992. Shortly after grave robbers unearthed a royal tomb of the Sipán culture near present-day Trujillo, Sidney Kirkpatrick documented the underworld of artifact smugglers and their Hollywood clients. At the center of this real-life drama is Peruvian archaeologist Walter Alva, who struggles against an entire town as he fights to preserve his country's heritage.

MacQuarrie, Kim. *The Last Days of the Incas.* New York: Simon & Schuster, 2007. Peru travelers with time to read just one book should read *The Last Days of the Incas*, written by an Emmy Award-winning author and filmmaker with years of life experience in Peru. MacQuarrie has produced what is, beyond a doubt, the most readable, fast-moving, and factual account of Peru's Spanish conquest. He describes the conquest and its aftermath in detail and integrates both 16th century Spanish chronicles and recent historical research. Unlike the more scholarly *Conquest of the Incas* by John Hemming, *The Last Days* does not end with the collapse of the Inca empire—the final chapters are devoted to 20th-century explorers such as Hiram Bingham, who identified Machu Picchu as the center of the Inca empire, and Gene Savoy, who discovered the real "lost city" of the Inca—Vilcabamba.

Mosley, Michael. *The Incas and Their Ancestors.* London: Thames and Hudson, 1993. This masterly work is still the best general introduction to the history of Peru's early cultures, including the Nasca, Moche, Huari, and Tiahuanaco.

Muscutt, Keith. *Warriors of the Clouds: A Lost Civilization in the Upper Amazon of Peru.* Albuquerque: University of New Mexico, 1998. This book provides a good overview of what archaeologists know of the Chachapoya, a cantankerous cloud-forest empire that was never dominated by the Inca. The book is replete with beautiful images of ruins in the remote cloud forest of northeastern Peru.

Protzen, Jean-Pierre. *Inka Architecture and Construction at Ollantaytambo.* Oxford: Oxford University Press, 1993. Jean-Pierre Protzen spent years at the Inca site of Ollantaytambo in order to understand its historical significance and construction. This hard-to-find book is the best single work on Ollantaytambo, the most important Inca ruin after Machu Picchu.

Savoy, Gene. *Antisuyo: The Search for the Lost Cities of the Amazon.* New York: Simon & Schuster, 1970. Gene Savoy, who is second only to Hiram Bingham in his knack for sniffing out lost cities, describes in somewhat stilted prose his search for Espíritu Pampa, the last stronghold of the Inca.

Starn, Orin, Carlos Iván Degregori, and Rob Kirk, eds. *The Peru Reader.* Durham, NC: Duke University Press, 1995. This is a great paperback to bring on the airplane or a long train ride; it's stuffed with an endlessly entertaining and eclectic collection of short stories, anthropological essays, translated chronicles, and a bit of poetry.

Von Hagen, Adriana, and Craig Morris. *The Cities of the Ancient Andes.* London: Thames and Hudson, 1998. Writer Adriana von Hagen, daughter of the renowned German-born Peruvianist Victor von Hagen, and a curator of New York's America Museum of Natural History teamed up for this highly recommended introduction to Peru's major archaeological sites. This is the most concise and accessible history of Peru's ancient cultures, written around the centers and cities they left behind.

CHRONICLES

Cieza de León, Pedro. *The Discovery and Conquest of Peru: The New World Encounter.* Durham, NC: Duke University Press, 1999. Pedro Cieza de León arrived in Peru in 1547 as a wide-eyed 27-year-old, and he proceeded to explore every nook and cranny, describing everything as he went. He is the first Spaniard to describe Spanish mistreatment of Peru's natives. His reliable voice paints the Spanish-Inca encounter in simple and clear language.

Garcilaso de la Vega, Inca, and Harold Livermore, translator. *Royal Commentaries of the Inca and General History of Peru.* Austin: University of Texas Press, 1966. Inca Garcilaso was the son of a conquistador and an Inca princess who moved to Spain in his youth and spent the rest of his life documenting the myths, culture, and history of the Inca. Though criticized for historical inaccuracies and exaggeration, Inca Garcilaso's 1,000-page *Royal Commentaries* contains subtitles that make this work easy to thumb through.

Poma de Ayala, Felipe Guamán. *Nueva Crónica y Buen Gobierno.* Madrid: Siglo XXI, 1992. This magnificent 16th-century manuscript has become the New World's best known indigenous chronicle since it was discovered in the Royal Library of Copenhagen in 1908. It is a 1,200-page history of the Spanish conquest, told from the Andean point of view in an eclectic mixture of Quechua and Spanish. Its harangues against Spanish injustice are complemented by 400 drawings made by Poma de Ayala. The text was intended as a letter to Spanish King Philip III.

LITERATURE

Alarcón, Daniel. *War by Candlelight: Stories*. New York: Harper Perennial, 2006. Born in Peru and raised in Birmingham, Alabama, Alarcón returned to Peru on a Fulbright scholarship. He wrote a series of short stories that evoke the sorrows and beauty of a ravaged land with a precision and steadiness that stand in inverse proportion to the magnitude of the losses he so powerfully dramatizes. Floods and earthquakes destroy what little equilibrium remains in a relentlessly violent world in which the authorities and the rebels are equally vicious and corrupt.

Alegría, Ciro. *Broad and Alien Is the World*. Chester Spring, PA: Dufour Editions. This award-winning lyric novel (*El Mundo Es Ancho y Ajeno*, 1941) was written by a celebrated Peruvian novelist who spent his career documenting the oppression of Peru's indigenous peoples. Look also for Alegría's other classic, *The Golden Serpent* (*La Serpiente de Oro*). The Spanish versions of these works are available in most bookstores in Peru.

Bryce Echenique, Alfredo. *A World for Julius*. Madison, WI: University of Wisconsin Press, 2004. Bryce Echenique explores Peruvian society while describing a world of illusion created for little Julius, who eventually will have to fit perfectly in this society. A true masterpiece from one of Peru's top novelists.

Vargas Llosa, Mario. *Aunt Julia and the Scriptwriter*. New York: Penguin, 1995. This autobiographical tale of taboo mixes radio scripts with the steamy romance that a young radio writer carries on with his aunt—this is Vargas Llosa with Julia Urquidi, who became his first wife. This was one of Vargas Llosa's first novels revealing a glimpse into highbrow Lima society.

Vargas Llosa, Mario. *Captain Pantoja and the Secret Service*. New York: Harper Collins, 1978. This is the funny and ludicrous story of a faithful soldier, Pantaleón Pantoja, and his mission to begin a top-secret prostitution service for Peru's military in Iquitos, Peru. His problem is that he is too successful.

Vargas Llosa, Mario. *Conversation in the Cathedral*. New York: Harper Perennial, 2005. This is one of Vargas Llosa's masterworks. *Conversation in the Cathedral* takes place in 1950s Peru during the dictatorship of Manuel A. Odría. Over beers and a sea of freely spoken words, the conversation flows between Santiago and Ambrosio, who talk of their tormented lives and of the overall degradation and frustration that has slowly taken over their city. Through a complicated web of secrets and historical references, Vargas Llosa analyzes the mental and moral mechanisms that govern power and the people behind it. It is a groundbreaking novel that tackles identity as well as the role of a citizen and how a lack of personal freedom can forever scar people and a nation.

Vargas Llosa, Mario. *A Discreet Hero*. Alfaguara, 2013. Vargas Llosa's latest novel, and the first one since he won the Nobel Prize in 2010, takes place in modern, booming Peru. It tells the story of small business owner Felicito Yanaque of Piura, who finds himself being extorted by a local gang, and Ismael Carrera, a successful businessman that plots revenge against his sons who want their father dead.

Vargas Llosa, Mario. *The Dream of the Celt*. Santillana, 2010. The Dream of the Celt tells the story of Irishman Roger Casement, who traveled in the Congo and Peruvian Amazon as a British consul investigating abuses on rubber plantations in the early 20th century. Clement, who became an Irish nationalist after witnessing the abuses of colonial England, was hanged by the British in 1916.

Vargas Llosa, Mario. *The Green House.* New York: Harper Perennial, 2005. Vargas Llosa's classic early novel takes place in a Peruvian town, between desert and rainforest, where Don Anselmo, a stranger in a black coat, builds a brothel, bringing together the innocent and the corrupt: Bonificia, a young indigenous girl saved by the nuns, who becomes a prostitute; Father García, struggling for the church; and four best friends drawn to both excitement and escape.

TRAVEL AND EXPLORATION

Bingham, Hiram. *Phoenix: Lost City of the Incas.* Edited by Hugh Thomson. London: Phoenix Press, 2003. Bingham's classic description of how he discovered Machu Picchu lends historical detail to Peru's standout attraction and also explains why Bingham went on to become the leading inspiration for movie character Indiana Jones.

Kane, Joe. *Running the Amazon.* New York: Vintage, 1990. Starting from a glacier at 5,180 meters, Joe Kane and a team of adventurers attempted the never-before-done feat of navigating the entire length of the Amazon River from source to mouth. The story begins as an accurate description of life in Peru's highlands and ends with the difficulties of managing personalities in a modern-day expedition.

Lee, Vincent. *Sixpac Manco: Travels Among the Incas.* 1985. This self-published book is a must-read for Vilcabamba explorers and is available at the South American Explorers Club in Lima. It is out of print, but used copies can be found at Amazon.com or other Internet sites that sell used books. The book comes with highly accurate maps of the area around Espíritu Pampa and has an amusing, shoot-from-the-hip adventurer's attitude.

Mathiessen, Peter. *At Play in the Fields of the Lord.* New York: Vintage, 1991. Set in a malarial rainforest outpost, this Mathiessen classic depicts the clash of development and indigenous peoples in the Amazon rainforest. It was made into a motion picture as well.

Muller, Karin. *Along the Inca Road: A Woman's Journey into an Ancient Empire.* Washington DC: National Geographic, 2000. The author traces her 5,000-kilometer journey along Inca roads in Ecuador, Peru, Bolivia, and Chile. Along the way she shares her insights about modern exploration and Inca history.

Schneebaum, Tobias. *Keep the River on Your Right.* New York: Grove Press, 1998. In 1955, New York intellectual Tobias Schneebaum spent eight years living with the Akarama people in the remote Madre de Dios rainforest. His book describes his participation in homosexual and cannibalistic rituals and became an immediate rainforest classic when it was published in 1969.

Shah, Tahir. *Trail of Feathers: In Search of the Birdmen of Peru.* London: Orion Publishing, 2002. A 16th-century mention of Inca who "flew like birds" over the rainforest leads one journalist on a quest to unlock the secret of Peru's so-called birdmen. His journey takes him to Machu Picchu, the Nasca Lines, and finally into the Amazon itself.

Simpson, Joe. *Touching the Void.* New York: Harper Perennial, 2004. In 1985, Joe Simpson and Simon Yates attempted a first ascent of Siulá Grande, a forbidding peak in Peru's Cordillera Huayhuash. Simpson's subsequent fall into a crevasse, and his struggle to survive, will grip even nonclimbers. This book was made into a motion picture of the same name.

Thomson, Hugh. *The White Rock: An Exploration of the Inca Heartland.* New York: Overlook Press, 2001. British documentary filmmaker Hugh Thomson returns to Vilcabamba, where he explored in his early

20s, to weave a recollection of his travels together with an alluring blend of Spanish chronicles and Inca history. It contains vivid, sometimes scathing, depictions of local personalities and makes for a fast, exciting way to read up for a Peru trip.

TRAVEL GUIDES

Frost, Peter. *Exploring Cusco,* 5th ed. Lima: Nuevas Imágenes, 1999. This book continues to be one of the best-written, most readable historical and archaeological approaches to the Cusco area, written by long-time Cusco resident Peter Frost.

Johnson, Brad. *Classic Climbs of the Cordillera Blanca.* Montrose, CO: Western Reflections, 2003. Johnson has been guiding in the Cordillera Blanca for nearly two decades and presents detailed descriptions of the area's major climbing routes, together with three-dimensional maps and vibrant color photos. This is an award-winning guide to one of the world's top mountaineering destinations.

Wagner, Steven, and Matias Guzman. *Peru Surfing Travel Guide.* Buenos Aires: Gráficas Boschi, 2002. The authors had a tremendous time searching out Peru's breaks and writing the first book in English to South America's surfing mecca. This book can be found in Lima bookstores and ordered online in the United States.

Wust, Walter, et al. *Inca Guide to Peru.* Lima: Peisa, 2003. This excellent highway guide, sponsored by Mitsubishi, contains the country's best road maps and detailed descriptions of all the driving routes. There is also some historical and cultural information on each of Peru's main destinations, though little information on hotels and restaurants. This company has also published *Guía Inca de Playas,* which runs down all the remote camping and surfing spots along Peru's coast from Tumbes to Tacna. These books are for sale in Ripley department stores and most Lima bookstores.

Zarzar, Omar. *Por los Caminos de Peru en Bicicleta.* Lima: Editor SA, 2001. This is a guide to Peru's best mountain-biking routes. Though written in Spanish, the maps and itineraries are useful even for non-Spanish speakers.

NATURE AND THE ENVIRONMENT

Beaver, Paul. *Diary of an Amazon Guide: Amazing Encounters with Tropical Nature and Culture.* New York: AE Publications, 2001. Paul Beaver, owner of the Tahuayo Lodge near Iquitos, holds a PhD from the University of Chicago and has spent two decades exploring the upper Amazon. He provides a fast-moving, insightful, and humorous glimpse into both the nature and people of the area.

Forsyth, Adrian, and Ken Miyata. *Tropical Nature: Life and Death in the Rain Forests of Central and South America.* New York: Simon & Schuster, 1987. This well-written and at times humorous book lays out the principles of rainforest ecology in easy-to-read, entertaining prose. First-time rainforest visitors will understand much more of what they see in the Amazon after reading this book.

Kricher, John. *A Neotropical Companion,* 2nd ed. Princeton, NJ: Princeton University Press, 1999. Compared to *Tropical Nature,* this book offers a more detailed, scientific look at rainforest ecology, though it is still designed for nonbiologists. This is the bible for the Amazon enthusiast, with a good listing of animals, plants, and ecosystems and theoretical discussions of evolutionary biology and other advanced topics.

MacQuarrie, Kim, and André Bärtschi, photographer. *Peru's Amazonian Eden: Manu National Park and Biosphere Reserve,* 2nd ed. Barcelona: Francis O. Patthe, 1998. This book of stunning photos is more than just a coffee-table book. Kim MacQuarrie spent six months living with a previously uncontacted indigenous community in the Manu and writes an eloquent evocation of the people and wildlife of Peru's most pristine patch of Amazon.

MacQuarrie, Kim, with Jorge Flores Ochoa and Javier Portós. Photos by Jaume and Jordi Blassi. *Gold of the Andes: The Llamas, Alpacas, Vicuñas, and Guanacos of South America.* Barcelona: Francis O. Patthe, 1994. Another well-written book with large-format pictures of Peru's highlanders and the animals on which they depend.

Stap, Don. *A Parrot without a Name.* Austin: University of Texas Press, 1991. Poet-naturalist Don Stap accompanied two of Latin America's more renowned ornithologists, Ted Parker and John O'Neil, on birding expeditions into unexplored corners of the Amazon. The book blends Amazon adventure with a close look at the odd, obsessive life of ornithologists.

BIRDING

Clements, James, and Noam Shany. *A Field Guide to the Birds of Peru.* Temecula, CA: Ibis Publishing, 2001. Though much criticized by bird-watchers for its faulty pictures of certain birds, this US$60 tome catalogs nearly 1,800 birds known to reside in, or migrate to, Peru. This is the best alternative for birders unable to afford *Birds of Peru.*

Krabbe, Nils, and John Fjeldsa. *Birds of the High Andes.* Copenhagen: Denmark Zoological Museum of the University of Copenhagen, 1990. Birders consider this a must-have masterpiece. It includes all the birds you are likely to encounter in the temperate and alpine zones of Peru.

Schulenberg, Thomas, Douglas Stotz, Daniel Lane, and John O'Neill. *Birds of Peru (Princeton Field Guides).* Sanibel Island, FL: Ralph Curtis Books, 2007. This long-awaited bible

of Peru birding is coveted by every professional bird guide in Peru. It represents a huge step forward and was a colossal undertaking, as reflected by its beautiful color renderings of birds and its high price tag.

Valqui, Thomas. *Where to Watch Birds in Peru,* 1st ed. Peru, 2004. This comprehensive self-published guide to birding in Peru explains not only what birds you'll see where, but how to get there and where you might stay along the way. This is an excellent resource, and there's nothing else like it on the market. The book is now out of print, but you may be able to find a used copy.

Walker, Barry, and Jon Fjeldsa, illustrations. *Field Guide to the Birds of Machu Picchu.* Lima: Peruvian National Trust for Parks and Protected Areas, 2005. This portable guide, written by Cusco's foremost bird expert and owner of Manu Expeditions, is available in Cusco. It has 31 superb color plates and descriptions of 420 species.

PHOTOGRAPHY

Milligan, Max. *Realm of the Incas.* New York: Universe Publishing, 2001. English photographer Max Milligan spent years trekking to the remote corners of Peru to capture images that range from the sacred snows of Nevado Ausangate to the torpid meanderings of the Río Manu.

Weintraub, Adam L. *Vista Andina: A Photographic Perspective on Contemporary Life in the Andes.* PhotoExperience.net, 2010. Seattle-based photographer Adam Weintraub explores Cusco and surroundings through his lens, attempting a journalistic and zealous look into the intimate world of the city's inhabitants.

Wust, Walter, and Marie Isabel Musselman, ed., *Land of a Thousand Colors.* Lima: Peisa, 2002. This coffee-table book sparkles with the prose of Peruvian writer Antonio

Cisneros and painter Fernando de Szyslo. It captures Peru's diversity in large-format color prints that are organized not by content but by their color.

FOOD

Acurio, Gastón. *Peru: Una Aventura Culinaria.* Lima: Quebecor World Peru, 2002. This large-format photo book written in Spanish profiles Peru's array of foods in chapters titled Water, Land, and Air. It includes a range of recipes and profiles of Peru's leading chefs and is available in Lima bookshops.

Custer, Tony. *The Art of Peruvian Cuisine.* Lima: Cimino Publishing Group, 2003. This book has high-quality photos and an excellent selection of Peruvian recipes in both Spanish and English.

Morales, Edmund. *The Guinea Pig: Healing, Food, and Ritual in the Andes.* Tucson: University of Arizona Press, 1995. This is the first major study, with good pictures, of how Andean highlanders not only eat guinea pig but also use it for medicinal and religious purposes.

PromPeru. *Perú Mucho Gusto.* Lima: Comisión de Promoción del Peru, 2006. This Spanish-English book is a glamorous large-format cookbook. Starting with the history of the country's cuisine, the book gives a general overview of Peru's traditional cooking. The last chapter is dedicated to the creative chefs who will lead Peru's cooking into the future. Available in Lima bookstores.

SPIRITUAL AND ESOTERIC

Milla, Carlos. *Genesis de la Cultura Andina,* 4th ed. Cusco: Amaru Wayra, 2006. If you can read Spanish, this book presents esoteric theories based on many of Peru's ancient ceremonial centers. Milla's 2003 book, *Ayni: Semiotica Andina de los Espacios Sagrados,* focuses on astrology.

Villoldo, Alberto, and Erik Jendresen. *The Four Winds: A Shaman's Odyssey into the Amazon.* New York: Harper Collins, 1991. Even Peru's shamans respect this work, which documents the author's spiritual initiation into Amazon rituals.

WEAVING

Heckman, Andrea. *Woven Stories: Andean Textiles and Rituals.* Albuquerque: University of New Mexico Press, 2003. A series of ethnographic essays on Andean life and weaving by a researcher with two decades in the field.

Pollard Rowe, Anne, and John Cohen. *Hidden Threads of Peru: Q'ero Textiles.* London: Merrell Publishers, 2002. In vibrant pictures and concise prose, this book documents the extraordinary weavings of Q'ero, a remote town in south Peru where the authors have been researching for nearly four decades.

CHILDREN

Hergé, *The Adventures of Tintin: Prisoners of the Sun.* 1949. In this Hergé classic, a sequel to *The Seven Crystal Balls,* Tintin, Captain Haddock, and Snowy catch a steamer to Peru to rescue a kidnapped professor. The adventure leads them through the Andes and the Amazon, which are depicted in fascinating detail and through the romanticized lens of the mid-20th century.

Internet Resources

TRAVEL INFORMATION

Andean Travel Web
www.andeantravelweb.com
This is the best of several websites in Peru that evaluate hotels, restaurants, and agencies.

The Latin American Network Information Center
http://lanic.utexas.edu/la/peru
The largest single list of links on Peru has been compiled by the University of Texas.

Peru This Week
www.peruthisweek.com
This, along with www.expatperu.com, is a directory of resources for foreigners living and traveling in Peru.

Peru Links
www.perulinks.com
This huge website of links lists tons of hard-to-find Peru websites, including gay and lesbian clubs, alternative medicine, chat rooms, and more.

The Peruvian Times
www.peruviantimes.com
Lima's oldest English-language publishing house, which until recently published the *Lima Times,* is a good source for English-language Peruvian news.

South American Explorers
www.saexplorers.org
This website for the South American Explorers Club has books and maps for sale, an online bulletin board that helps travelers connect, information on volunteering, and other interesting links.

FLIGHT INFORMATION

Lima Airport
www.lap.com.pe
This is the home page of the Jorge Chávez International Airport in Lima.

Tráfico
www.traficoperu.com
This agency newsletter is an updated list of all international and domestic flights in Peru.

ECOTOURISM

Gorp
www.gorp.com
This joint production of Away.com, Gorp, and Outside Online has hundreds of travel stories on Peru, a list of top-20 travel destinations, and links to tour operators.

Planeta
www.planeta.com/peru.html
This ecotourism site includes articles, essays, and links to responsible tour operators.

SURFING

Peru Azul
www.peruazul.com
Peru's most popular website for surfing and ocean conditions along the coast is for Spanish speakers only.

ANDEAN CULTURE

Culture of the Andes
www.andes.org
A labor of love from Peru fanatics Russ and Ada Gibbons, this site focusing on Andean culture includes short stories, jokes, music, songs in Quechua, poetry, and riddles.

Index

List of Maps

LIST OF MAPS

Photo Credits

Also Available

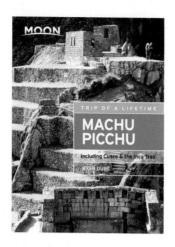

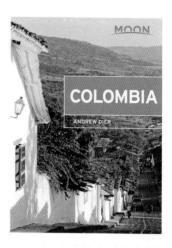

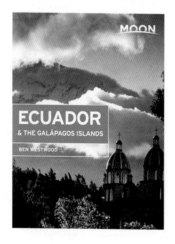

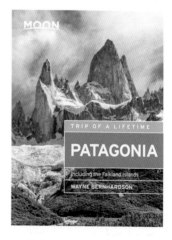

MAP SYMBOLS

≡≡≡	Expressway	○	City/Town	✈	Airport	⚓	Golf Course
───	Primary Road	◉	State Capital	✈	Airfield	P	Parking Area
⋯⋯	Secondary Road	⊛	National Capital	▲	Mountain	≜	Archaeological Site
- - - -	Unpaved Road	★	Point of Interest	✦	Unique Natural Feature	⛪	Church
────	Feature Trail	•	Accommodation				
- - - - -	Other Trail	▼	Restaurant/Bar	🌊	Waterfall	⛽	Gas Station
⋯⋯⋯	Ferry			▲	Park		Glacier
≡≡≡	Pedestrian Walkway	■	Other Location	🚩	Trailhead		Mangrove
⊞⊞⊞	Stairs	Λ	Campground	⛷	Skiing Area		Reef
							Swamp

CONVERSION TABLES

$°C = (°F - 32) / 1.8$
$°F = (°C \times 1.8) + 32$
1 inch = 2.54 centimeters (cm)
1 foot = 0.304 meters (m)
1 yard = 0.914 meters
1 mile = 1.6093 kilometers (km)
1 km = 0.6214 miles
1 fathom = 1.8288 m
1 chain = 20.1168 m
1 furlong = 201.168 m
1 acre = 0.4047 hectares
1 sq km = 100 hectares
1 sq mile = 2.59 square km
1 ounce = 28.35 grams
1 pound = 0.4536 kilograms
1 short ton = 0.90718 metric ton
1 short ton = 2,000 pounds
1 long ton = 1.016 metric tons
1 long ton = 2,240 pounds
1 metric ton = 1,000 kilograms
1 quart = 0.94635 liters
1 US gallon = 3.7854 liters
1 Imperial gallon = 4.5459 liters
1 nautical mile = 1.852 km

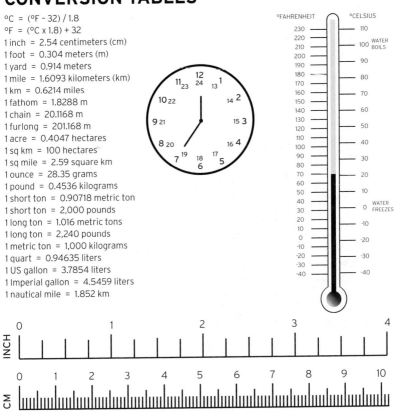

MOON PERU

Avalon Travel
Hachette Book Group
1700 Fourth Street
Berkeley, CA 94710, USA
www.moon.com

Editor and Series Manager: Kathryn Ettinger
Copy Editor: Christopher Church
Graphics Coordinator: Rue Flaherty
Production Coordinator: Rue Flaherty
Cover Design: Faceout Studios, Charles Brock
Interior Design: Domini Dragoone
Moon Logo: Tim McGrath
Map Editor: Mike Morgenfeld
Cartographers: Austin Ehrhardt, Larissa Gatt
Indexer: Greg Jewett

ISBN-13: 978-1-63121-637-4

Printing History
1st Edition — 2004
5th Edition — December 2017
5 4 3 2 1

Front cover photo: Machu Picchu © Michael S. Lewis / Getty Images
Back cover photo: Fiesta de la Virgen del Carmen parade at Pisac © Pixattitude | Dreamstime

Printed in China by RR Donnelley